LITIGATING INTERNATIONAL
LAW DISPUTES

Litigating International Law Disputes provides a fresh understanding of why states resort to international adjudication or arbitration to resolve international law disputes. A group of leading scholars and practitioners discern the reasons for the use of international litigation and other modes of dispute settlement by examining various substantive areas of international law (such as human rights, trade, environment, maritime boundaries, territorial sovereignty, and investment law), as well as considering case studies from particular countries and regions. The chapters also canvass the roles of international lawyers, non-governmental organizations, and private actors, as well as the political dynamics of disputes, and identify emergent trends in dispute settlement for different areas of international law.

NATALIE KLEIN is Dean of Macquarie Law School, Macquarie University, where she teaches and researches in various areas of international law, with a focus on the law of the sea and international dispute settlement.

LITIGATING INTERNATIONAL LAW DISPUTES

Weighing the Options

Edited by
NATALIE KLEIN

CAMBRIDGE
UNIVERSITY PRESS

University Printing House, Cambridge CB2 8BS, United Kingdom

Cambridge University Press is part of the University of Cambridge.

It furthers the University's mission by disseminating knowledge in the pursuit of education, learning and research at the highest international levels of excellence.

www.cambridge.org
Information on this title: www.cambridge.org/9781107017061

© Cambridge University Press 2014

This publication is in copyright. Subject to statutory exception and to the provisions of relevant collective licensing agreements, no reproduction of any part may take place without the written permission of Cambridge University Press.

First published 2014

A catalogue record for this publication is available from the British Library

Library of Congress Cataloguing in Publication data
Litigating international law disputes : weighing the options / edited by Natalie Klein.
pages   cm
Includes index.
ISBN 978-1-107-01706-1 (hardback)
1. Arbitration (International law)   I. Klein, Natalie (Natalie S.) editor of compilation
KZ6115.L58   2014
341.5'22 – dc23   2013040671

ISBN 978-1-107-01706-1 Hardback

Cambridge University Press has no responsibility for the persistence or accuracy of URLs for external or third-party internet websites referred to in this publication, and does not guarantee that any content on such websites is, or will remain, accurate or appropriate.

CONTENTS

Notes on contributors   *page* viii
Preface   xiv
Acknowledgements   xviii
Table of cases   xx
Table of treaties   xxxv

PART I

1   The place of international litigation in international law   3
    JOHN MERRILLS

2   Litigation versus dispute resolution through
    political processes   24
    SHIRLEY V. SCOTT

3   National and international litigation: partners or
    competitors?   42
    CHRISTOPHER WARD

PART II

4   Australia's experience in international litigation   61
    HENRY BURMESTER

5   Latin American states and the International Court
    of Justice   79
    XIMENA FUENTES

6   The United States as an international litigant   106
    MARK FELDMAN

7   European perspectives on inter-state litigation   130
    MICHAEL WOOD

v

CONTENTS

8 Asian perspectives on inter-state litigation   148

RODMAN R. BUNDY

9 African perspectives on inter-state litigation   166

MAKANE MOÏSE MBENGUE

PART III

10 Initiating territorial adjudication: the who, how, when, and why of litigating contested sovereignty   193

LEA BRILMAYER AND ADELE FAURE

11 Why litigate a maritime boundary? Some contributing factors   230

COALTER G. LATHROP

12 Litigating law of the sea disputes using the UNCLOS dispute settlement system   260

MD. SAIFUL KARIM

13 International environmental disputes: to sue or not to sue?   284

TIM STEPHENS

14 Why states resort to litigation in cases concerning the use of force   305

CHRISTINE GRAY

15 Adjudicating armed conflict   330

JOHN R. CROOK

16 Human rights as a subject of international litigation   353

IVAN SHEARER

17 The WTO dispute settlement system and underlying motivating factors for adjudication   375

M. RAFIQUL ISLAM

18 Resolving international investment disputes   401

CHESTER BROWN

19 Dispute settlement options for the protection of nationals abroad   436

NATALIE KLEIN

20 Litigating international law disputes: where to? 460
CESARE P. R. ROMANO

Index 472

NOTES ON CONTRIBUTORS

LEA BRILMAYER is the Howard M. Holtzmann Professor of International Law at Yale Law School. She has also taught as a visiting professor or full-time faculty at the law schools of the University of Chicago, the University of Texas, Harvard University, Columbia University, the University of Michigan, and New York University. During her first decade of teaching Professor Brilmayer's writing interests mainly concerned conflict of laws (in particular, personal jurisdiction and choice of law), federal jurisdiction and jurisprudence. Her interests have gradually turned to international law and international relations, which have led to two books: *Justifying International Acts* (1989) and *American Hegemony: Political Morality in a One-Superpower World* (1996). Professor Brilmayer has had extensive experience as a consultant in conflict of laws and private international law. She has also served as lead attorney in several important public international law arbitrations dealing with boundary issues (*Eritrea* v. *Yemen* and *Ethiopia* v. *Eritrea*), maritime delimitation (*Eritrea* v. *Yemen*) and civil compensation for violations of the laws of war (*Eritrea* v. *Ethiopia*).

CHESTER BROWN is Professor of International Law and International Arbitration at the Faculty of Law, University of Sydney, a barrister at 7 Selborne Chambers, Sydney, and a door tenant at Essex Court Chambers, London, and Maxwell Chambers, Singapore. He teaches, researches and practises in the fields of public international law, international dispute settlement, international arbitration, international investment law, and private international law. He previously served as Assistant Legal Adviser at the British Foreign and Commonwealth Office (2007–9), and prior to this he was a Senior Associate in the International Law and International Arbitration Group of Clifford Chance LLP, London (2004–7). He is the author of *A Common Law of International Adjudication* (2007), a major study on the applicable procedure and remedies before international courts and tribunals, which was awarded the American Society of International Law's Certificate of Merit.

NOTES ON CONTRIBUTORS

RODMAN R. BUNDY is a partner in Eversheds litigation practice group. Based in Singapore, he has over thirty years of experience as counsel and advocate in high-profile public international law litigations and international commercial arbitrations, including appearances before the International Court of Justice, the Iran–United States Claims Tribunal and various ad hoc investment and ICC arbitral tribunals. Rodman lectures on international boundary disputes at King's College, London, and is a frequent guest speaker at conferences and workshops on issues of public international law and upstream oil and gas operations. He is ranked by *Chambers* 2009 as 'a real talent' in the field of public international law and as 'an absolutely excellent advocate who has vast experience, especially in boundary cases'. *Legal 500* 2009 describes him as a 'star' partner and one of the leading experts in public international law.

HENRY BURMESTER AO, QC was Chief General Counsel in the Australian Government Solicitor (AGS) for over a decade and before that head of the Office of International Law in the Attorney-General's Department. In 2009 he became a Consultant Counsel to the AGS. He has appeared as counsel for the Commonwealth in leading constitutional cases before the Australian High Court.

JOHN R. CROOK is a judge on NATO's Administrative Tribunal. He is a former vice-president of the American Society of International Law and past editor of the *American Journal of International Law*'s section on Contemporary US Practice Relating to International Law. He served on the Eritrea–Ethiopia Claims Commission and is an arbitrator and consultant in international proceedings. During three decades in the US State Department's Office of the Legal Adviser he was US Agent at the Iran–United States Claims Tribunal, and was deeply involved in creating the UN Compensation Commission. He later was General Counsel of the Multinational Force and Observers, which operates peacekeepers in the Sinai Desert. He teaches international arbitration at George Washington University Law School.

ADELE FAURE is a joint degree student at Yale Law School and the Harvard Kennedy School. She is originally from Palo Alto, California, and received a BA in economics and international relations from Stanford University in 2007. She first became interested in international law while at Stanford, where she researched mechanisms compelling reimbursement of sovereign debt and the environmental implications of international trade agreements. Between college and law school she lived in San Francisco, Madagascar, South Africa, and France.

MARK FELDMAN is Assistant Professor of Law at the Peking University School of Transnational Law. He previously served as Chief of NAFTA/CAFTA-DR Arbitration in the Office of the Legal Adviser at the US Department of State. He holds a JD from Columbia Law School, where he was a James Kent Scholar and recipient of the Parker School Certificate in International and Comparative Law.

XIMENA FUENTES is Professor of Law at Universidad Adolfo Ibáñez and Associate Professor of Public International Law at Universidad de Chile. She holds a D.Phil. from Oxford University. She worked for the government of Chile in the *Peru* v. *Chile* maritime dispute before the International Court of Justice. She has represented the Republic of Chile and private investors before the International Centre for the Settlement of Investment Disputes (ICSID), and is a former co-rapporteur of the Committee on International Law on Sustainable Development of the International Law Association (2003–12).

CHRISTINE GRAY is Professor of International Law at the University of Cambridge and a Fellow of St John's College. She has written widely on the use of force, and she also works on reparation in international law. Her main publications are *International Law and the Use of Force* (3rd edn 2007) and *Judicial Remedies in International Law* (1987). She is a member of the editorial board of several journals, including the *British Yearbook of International Law*, the *Journal of Conflict and Security Law*, the *International and Comparative Law Quarterly*, and the *Cambridge Law Journal*.

M. RAFIQUL ISLAM is a professor of law at Macquarie Law School, Macquarie University. He obtained an MA in economics and an LLB (first class) from the University of Rajshahi, and an LLM and a Ph.D. from Monash University. His teaching and research interests are in public international law. He has published extensively in international law, human rights, international trade, and the constitutional law of Bangladesh. Professor Islam was the recipient of the Macquarie University Outstanding Teacher Award 2000. His recently published book is *International Law: Current Concepts and Future Directions* (2013).

MD. SAIFUL KARIM is a lecturer at the School of Law, Faculty of Law, Queensland University of Technology (QUT). Before joining QUT he was an associate lecturer at Southern Cross University. He also taught law at Macquarie University and at the University of the South Pacific. He has published extensively in the fields of public international law and environmental law and has presented research papers in a number of conferences and workshops organized by different academic and research organizations based in Asia, Australia, Europe, and North America.

NATALIE KLEIN is Dean of Macquarie Law School, Macquarie University, where she teaches and researches in different areas of international law, with a focus on law of the sea and international dispute settlement. Dr Klein is the author of *Dispute Settlement and the UN Convention on the Law of the Sea* (Cambridge University Press, 2005) and *Maritime Security and the Law of the Sea* (2011). Prior to joining Macquarie, she worked in the international litigation and arbitration area of practice of Debevoise & Plimpton LLP, served as counsel to the government of Eritrea and was a consultant in the Office of Legal Affairs at the United Nations.

COALTER G. LATHROP is principal and owner of Sovereign Geographic, an international boundary consultancy providing legal and cartographic services to clients throughout the world. He has acted as counsel before the International Court of Justice and the International Tribunal for the Law of the Sea. He holds a Master of Marine Affairs from the University of Washington, and a JD and an LLM in international and comparative law from Duke University. He is a member of the extended faculty at Duke Law and editor of *International Maritime Boundaries*. His research, writing, and speaking have focused on ocean law and the resolution of international disputes, including territorial sovereignty and maritime boundary disputes.

MAKANE MBENGUE is an associate professor at the University of Geneva Law School and a visiting professor at Sciences Po Paris (School of Law). He acts as a professor for regional courses in international law organized by the United Nations Office of Legal Affairs (OLA), and as counsel for states before the International Court of Justice, and has acted as a legal advisor for the World Bank and the Senegal River Organization, as well as a legal expert for the Secretariat of the Nile Basin Initiative, the International Labour Organization (ILO), the Swiss Federal Office of

Public Health, the World Health Organization (WHO) and Green Cross International.

JOHN MERRILLS has taught international law all over the world. He has held visiting posts at the Universities of Auckland and Toronto and has twice served as Dean of the Faculty of Law at Sheffield University, where he is now an Emeritus Professor. For eight years he was an Alternate Member of the UN Sub-Commission on Prevention of Discrimination and Protection of Minorities. He is the author of numerous books and articles on international law, and in 2007 was elected an Associate Member of the Institut de Droit International.

CESARE P. R. ROMANO is Professor of Law and W. Joseph Ford Fellow at Loyola Law School, Los Angeles. His expertise is in international law, but he also has substantial background in diplomatic history and economics. In 1997, he co-funded the Project on International Courts and Tribunals, which he continues to co-direct. In 2012, he became Senior Fellow of Pluricourts, the centre of excellence for the study of international courts of the Faculty of Law of the University of Oslo. He recently co-edited with Karen J. Alter and Yuval Shany *The Oxford Handbook of International Adjudication.*

SHIRLEY SCOTT is an associate professor and faculty co-ordinator of the programme for Master of International Law and International Relations at the University of New South Wales. She is co-chair of the Research and Planning Committee of the Asian Society of International Law, and vice-chair of the International Law Section of the International Studies Association. Her recent books include *International Law in World Politics: An Introduction* (2nd edn 2010), *International Law, US Power. The United States' Quest for Legal Security* (Cambridge University Press, 2012), and *International Law in the Era of Climate Change* (edited with Rosemary Rayfuse, 2012).

IVAN SHEARER is Emeritus Professor of Law of the University of Sydney, having retired from the Challis Chair of International Law in 2003, and is currently an adjunct professor of law at the University of South Australia. He has wide experience in teaching and practice and is presently involved as a member of arbitral panels convened under Annex VII of the International Convention on the Law of the Sea in two cases. From 2001 to 2008 he served as an elected member of the UN Human Rights Committee.

NOTES ON CONTRIBUTORS

TIM STEPHENS is an associate professor in the Faculty of Law at the University of Sydney and is co-director of the Sydney Centre for International Law. He holds a Ph.D. in law from the University of Sydney and an MPhil in geography from the University of Cambridge. He has published widely on issues of public international law, international environmental law, international climate law, and the law of the sea. He is the author of *International Courts and Environmental Protection* (Cambridge University Press, 2009) and *The International Law of the Sea* (with Donald R. Rothwell, 2010). In 2010 he was the recipient of the International Union for the Conservation of Nature Academy of Environmental Law Junior Scholarship Prize in recognition of his scholarship in the field of international environmental law.

CHRISTOPHER WARD is a recognized expert in the field of international law and practises extensively. He has particular expertise as an advocate in cases which involve the domestic and international law interface, and has worked regularly in areas as diverse as human rights, maritime boundaries, and diplomatic immunity. He also regularly accepts instructions in appellate and significant commercial and public law matters. He has appeared before all the major Australian courts and tribunals, including the High Court of Australia. He is president of the International Law Association (Australian Branch) and sits on a number of international law committees. He is a Visiting Fellow at the ANU Centre for International and Public Law, where he conducts research, teaching, and international advocacy.

MICHAEL WOOD, KCMG, is a member of the International Law Commission and a Senior Fellow of the Lauterpacht Centre for International Law, University of Cambridge. He is a barrister at 20 Essex Street, London, where he practises in the field of public international law, including before international courts and tribunals. He was Legal Adviser to the UK Foreign and Commonwealth Office between 1999 and 2006, having joined as an Assistant Legal Adviser in 1970.

PREFACE

This book is the result of research conducted for an Australian Research Council Discovery project entitled 'Choosing Litigation to Resolve International Law Disputes in the Protection of Australia's Offshore Assets, Its Citizens and Foreign Trade'. Australia has a rich experience in international adjudication and arbitration (referred to collectively as 'litigation'), and the case studies in the project focused on areas that have high political, social, and economic interest for both the Australian government and the Australian people. Issues related to Australia's marine resources (including whaling, fishing, and hydrocarbon exploitation) have been the primary subject areas litigated by Australia before international courts, as well as defending and asserting trade interests at the World Trade Organization (WTO). By contrast, the protection of Australian nationals abroad has not resulted in litigation, although it has been contemplated, despite the high media attention accorded to these issues on almost a daily basis. Through these case studies, a critical question posed was whether a comprehensive and integrated framework of legal and political factors could be devised to determine when international litigation should be pursued or rejected as a dispute settlement option. More simply, why do states litigate?

While the project had a focus on Australian practice, this book is intended to take some of the key lessons from those studies and consider them in a broader context, both substantively and geographically. From a substantive perspective, I have long been interested in the question of whether particular substantive areas of international law lend themselves more to litigation when disputes arise. Is there something about international trade law or the law of the sea that made states more amenable to the idea of including legal, binding, third-party dispute resolution in the key constitutive agreements in these areas? Or perhaps it is not the area of law per se, but the issues concerning international trade or maritime matters that make arbitration or adjudication a necessary regulatory component of these regimes?

PREFACE

From a geographic perspective, questions can be posed as to what extent one state's experience in litigation may be indicative of what another state's experience may be. Or, even if comparisons could not be drawn between different states, whether there may be regional trends one way or another in terms of state decision making vis-à-vis the use of litigation for the resolution of international law disputes. An immediate difficulty is the obvious fact that no one state is the same as another, but different histories, economic status, political power, government structures, and national interests will all inform decision making on how international disputes, and the legal dimensions of those disputes, should be resolved.

The intention behind this book has therefore been to provide a unique perspective on international adjudication and arbitration. Rather than just examining procedural requirements and the operation of different courts and tribunals, or exploring the legal principles as articulated by international courts and tribunals, this book seeks to link the very nature of different substantive areas of international law with the procedures that are typically preferred for resolving disputes over that particular subject area and to discern why such a preference may exist. The question is examined both in terms of the preferences and practice of particular states or regions, and in relation to different areas of substantive international law.

The book is therefore structured in three parts. The first part sets the scene, by considering the place of international litigation in international law, the political dynamics of inter-state litigation, and the increasing role of national courts resolving or contributing to international law disputes. The second part turns to case studies of particular country and regional experiences. Given the genesis of this book, the Australian experience is included, and the United States provides another individual case study. Regional perspectives are provided from Asia, Africa, Europe, and Latin America. The third part then turns to relatively discrete areas of international law in which each author addresses why particular dispute settlement procedures are available and which are most commonly utilized for that particular area of law. Each contributor was charged with the task of assessing the fundamental questions whether and why a certain dispute settlement procedure lends itself for use in relation to a particular substantive area of law.

The assignment was not an easy one. There is always an initial barrier to work through in terms of jurisdiction. Of course, some disputes cannot be resolved by an international court or tribunal because there is no court or tribunal available with jurisdiction over the subject matter of the dispute. Yet there is still much to consider around the decision making as to whether jurisdiction is or can be established. A starting point may be whether a state has accepted the jurisdiction of the International Court of Justice (ICJ), either under the optional clause of that Court's Statute or in a compromissory clause in a treaty. For international trade law and the law of the sea, states are compelled to accept the possibility of legal proceedings being instituted against them by dint of their participation in the overall regime. So the very fact that a state becomes party to a treaty that contains a compulsory dispute settlement regime indicates that a state has agreed, at least potentially, to international litigation. Whether a state follows through on a commitment to participate in international litigation provides another dimension to this question. The practice of states in deciding whether to refer a matter to ad hoc arbitration or to enter into a special agreement to consent to adjudication further provides ground for study as to why states select litigation to resolve international law disputes. States may also devolve the resolution of international law disputes to non-state actors, and so allow for the possibility of corporations pursuing investment treaty arbitrations or individuals presenting human rights claims directly to international courts or committees.

Even when the variety of jurisdictional avenues is identified, there is still a need to question why one procedure was selected over another, or why one was seemingly not contemplated at all. Resolving this issue may necessarily remain speculative. Government decision making may be opaque; even if reasons are provided publicly, there may be other factors that have been relevant but are not aired. Documents may only become available after the passage of a certain amount of time (or when released illegally), but a historical or documentary survey may not reveal what conversations occurred or the strength of personalities involved at the time. For the lawyers who worked on the cases and who may well have been privy to the thinking of primary government decision-makers as to how to resolve a particular dispute, they cannot reveal those discussions because of ethical constraints. There is still much analysis that can be undertaken based on the public record, but the limitations should be acknowledged. Moreover, generalizations cannot easily be made, and caveats and exceptions must frequently be noted.

There are also many ways that the question, 'why does a state litigate?', could be answered. The field is ripe for empirical research. Assessments of the number of cases in a particular area, the states presenting claims and how often, the number of treaties with compromissory clauses, the involvement as respondent or claimant can all be calculated and conclusions potentially drawn from these statistics. There is also scope for sociological research when attempting to drill down into the reasons for decisions of particular members of a government. Different theoretical paradigms (such as law and economics, realism, positivism, feminism) could each provide frames of reference for interpreting the decisions of states in relation to the different issue areas or national practice. The approach favoured in this book has been oriented towards international relations theory, without a wholesale adoption of any particular strand, inasmuch as the political dimensions have frequently been taken into account in assessing state decision making and the operation of the relevant courts and tribunals and legal principles in any given area.

Ultimately, we have provided many different answers to the core question of why states may choose adjudication or arbitration for the resolution of international law disputes. In doing so, we have hopefully contributed to the substantive areas under discussion, as well as to scholarship on international dispute settlement more generally, by giving readers something more to think about when considering the place of litigation in international dispute resolution.

Natalie Klein

ACKNOWLEDGEMENTS

This book, and the project from which it was drawn, was funded by the Australian Research Council through its Discovery Projects scheme. I am very grateful for the financial support provided in undertaking this research and facilitating the range of outputs from the investigations. This book is one such output. The funding was administered through Macquarie University and I thank the many staff members in the university and faculty research offices who provided assistance in obtaining the grant in the first place and then working through the administrative aspects of the project.

For the purposes of the project I benefited from the advice of an expert advisory group, which then expanded for a workshop dealing with core issues arising from the research. I am very grateful for the participation of Lea Brilmayer, Chester Brown, Henry Burmester, M. Rafiqul Islam, Md. Saiful Karim, Shirley Scott, Ivan Shearer, Tim Stephens, and Christopher Ward in this regard. The workshop was followed a year later by a conference, and my thanks to Cesare Romano for participating in the conference and for his support of the project.

Following the conference I was able to broaden the participants further for the purposes of this book. In doing so, I looked not only to academics in the field, but to those who are or had been involved in practice. I am extremely grateful to all the contributors for the time and effort they have taken in preparing their chapters, particularly those who were involved in cases at the same time. It has been a privilege for me to work with you all in seeing this book through to fruition.

My thanks to Finola O'Sullivan, the anonymous reviewers, and the editorial team at Cambridge University Press, who provided excellent advice on formulating this book at the outset. I also appreciate the patience and diligence afforded to me in bringing this book to its conclusion.

Throughout the life of the entire research project, I have benefited from research, editorial, and administrative assistance from a number of Macquarie Law School students. I have appreciated not only their intellect, but also their conscientiousness and good humour in undertaking the tasks set. In this regard, I would particularly like to thank Nicholas Lennings, Lauren Knapman, Danielle Selig, and, especially in the preparation of this book, Hiruni Alwishewa and Tejas Thete.

Finally, the forbearance, love and support of my family are what make all things possible for me, so special thanks to Matthew Kelly, Josh and Tessa, as well as to my mother, Sue Klein.

TABLE OF CASES

International

ADC Affiliate Ltd and ADC & ADMC Management Ltd v. Hungary, ICSID Arbitral Tribunal, Case No ARB/03/16, 2 October 2006 427n145

Administration of certain properties of the State in Libya (Italy v. United Kingdom and United Kingdom of Libya), [1952/1953] 12 RIAA 357 168n7

Aegean Sea Continental Shelf (Greece v. Turkey), [1978] ICJ Rep. 3 139

Aerial Herbicide Spraying (Ecuador v. Colombia), [2008] ICJ Rep. 174 85, 87, 293

Aerial Incident of 10 August 1999 (Pakistan v. India) (Jurisdiction), [2000] ICJ Rep. 12 143n49, 156, 312n34, 318n59

Aerial Incident of 27 July 1955 (Israel v. Bulgaria) (Preliminary Objections), [1959] ICJ Rep. 127 134n13, 312, 318n59

Aerial Incident of 3 July 1988 (Iran v. United States) (Order of 22 February 1996), [1996] ICJ Rep. 9 36n53, 153, 156, 312, 318

Aerial Incident of 4 September 1954 (United States v. USSR), Order, [1958] ICJ Rep. 158 465n14

Aerial Incident of 7 November 1954 (United States v. USSR), Order, [1959] ICJ Rep. 276 465n14

Aerial Incident of 7 October 1952 (United States v. USSR), [1956] ICJ Rep. 9 465n14

Affaire de l'attaque de la caravane du maharao de Cutch (Royaume-Uni contre Éthiopie), [1927] 2 RIAA 821 167n7

Affaire de la Société Radio-Orient (Etats du Levant sous mandat français contre Egypte), [1940] 3 RIAA 1871 167n7

Ahmadou Sadio Diallo (Republic of Guinea v. Democratic Republic of the Congo) (Preliminary Objections), [2007] ICJ Rep. 582 357n14, 401n5, 437n2

Ahmadou Sadio Diallo (Republic of Guinea v. Democratic Republic of the Congo) (Merits), [2010] ICJ Rep. 639 357, 357n16, 454

Ambatielos (Greece v. United Kingdom) (Merits), [1953] ICJ Rep. 10 10n23, 32, 139

Appeal Relating to the Jurisdiction of the ICAO Council, [1972] ICJ Rep. 46 153

Application for Revision of the Judgment of 11 September 1992 in the Case Concerning the Land, Island and Maritime Frontier Dispute, [2003] ICJ Rep. 392 100n67

xx

TABLE OF CASES

Application of the Convention on the Prevention and Punishment of the Crime of Genocide (Bosnia and Herzegovina v. Serbia and Montenegro) (Provisional Measures), [1993] ICJ Rep. 3   311n29, 319n62

Application of the Convention on the Prevention and Punishment of the Crime of Genocide (Bosnia and Herzegovina v. Serbia and Montenegro) (Judgment), [2007] ICJ Rep. 43   343n66, 356n9

Application of the Convention on the Prevention and Punishment of the Crime of Genocide (Croatia v. Serbia), [2008] ICJ Rep. 412   319n62

Arbitral Award Made by the King of Spain on 23 December 1906 (Honduras v. Nicaragua), [1960] ICJ Rep. 192   87n34, 98n57, 99n61, 211n19, 229

Arbitral award relating to Boundary Delimitation between South-African Republic (Transvaal) and Free State of Orange, [1870] 28 RIAA 125   167n7

Arbitration between Barbados and the Republic of Trinidad and Tobago, (2006) 45 ILM 800   271n69

Arbitration between Croatia and Slovenia (Croatia v. Slovenia), PCA, 13 April 2012   231n4

Arbitration between Croatia and Slovenia (Croatia/Slovenia), PCA, 4 November 2009   138n34

Arbitration between Netherlands and France (Netherlands/France), PCA, 12 March 2004   138n34

Argentine–Chile Frontier Case (Argentina/Chile), (1966) 16 RIAA 109   202n8, 207, 211n21, 219

Armed Activities on the Territory of the Congo (Democratic Republic of the Congo v. Rwanda) (Provisional Measures), [2002] ICJ Rep. 219   310n22

Armed Activities on the Territory of the Congo (Democratic Republic of the Congo v. Uganda), [2005] ICJ Rep. 168   314n41, 329n93, 342n64

Armed Activities on the Territory of the Congo (New Application: 2002) (Democratic Republic of the Congo v. Rwanda) (Jurisdiction and Admissibility), [2006] ICJ Rep. 6   318n59

Arrangement for the Settlement of Differences between the Sultan of Muscat and the Sultan of Zanzibar, and the Independence of their Respective States, [1861] 28 RIAA 107   167n7

Asian Agricultural Products Ltd v. Sri Lanka, (1997) 4 ICSID Rep. 246   402n8, 411n63, 433n164

Asylum Case (Colombia v. Peru), [1950] ICJ Rep. 266   87

Australia – Measures Affecting Importation of Salmon, Appellate Body Report, WT/DS18/AB/R (20 October 1998)   392n49

Australia – Measures Affecting Importation of Salmon, Panel Report, WT/DS18/R (6 November 1998)   392n49

Australia – Recourse to DSU Article 21.5 by US, WTO Doc. WT/DS126/RW (21 January 2000)   392n52

xxii   TABLE OF CASES

Australia – Subsidies Provided to Producers and Exporters of Automotive Leather, Panel Report, WT/DS126/R (16 June 1999)   392n51

Avena and Other Mexican Nationals (Mexico v. US), [2004] ICJ Rep. 12   17, 43, 82, 87, 120, 128, 356, 440n16, 456, 458

Award as to the boundary between the United Kingdom and the South African Republic (Transvaal), [1885] 28 RIAA 185   167n7

Azurix v. Argentina (Award), ICSID Arbitral Tribunal, Case No ARB/01/12, 14 July 2006   411n63

Bangladesh v. India, UNCLOS Arbitral Tribunal, 8 October 2009   231n4, 235, 242n39

Barbados v. Trinidad and Tobago (Award), [2006] 27 RIAA 147   231n4, 242n39, 271

Barcelona Traction, Light and Power Company Ltd (Belgium v. Spain) (Second Phase), [1970] ICJ Rep. 3   19n52, 139, 358, 401, 431n159, 454, 455n87

Bayindir v. Pakistan (Award), ICSID Arbitral Tribunal, Case No. ARB/03/29, 27 August 2009   433n163

Beagle Channel (Argentina/Chile) (Award), [1977] 21 RIAA 57   211n21, 223, 229, 230n4, 246

BG Group plc v. Argentine Republic (Final Award), UNCITRAL, 24 December 2007   429n151

BIVAC v. Paraguay, ICSID Case No ARB/07/9, 29 May 2009   413n78

Biwater Gauff (Tanzania) Ltd v. Tanzania (Award), ICSID Arbitral Tribunal, Case No. ARB/05/22, 24 July 2008   410n59

Border and Transborder Armed Actions (Nicaragua v. Costa Rica) (Order of 21 October 1986), [1986] ICJ Rep. 548   83n17, 84, 308n12

Border and Transborder Armed Activities (Nicaragua v. Honduras), [1986] ICJ Rep. 3; (Judgment)(Jurisdiction & Admissibility), [1988] ICJ Rep. 69   83–85, 306n4, 308n12, 313n39, 316n52

BP v. Libya, (1977) 53 ILR 297   411n65, 427n144

The Boundary Case between Honduras and Nicaragua (Honduras/Nicaragua), (1906) 11 RIAA 101   202n8

Case Concerning Application of the International Convention on the Elimination of All Forms of Racial Discrimination (Georgia v. Russian Federation) (Provisional Measures), [2008] ICJ Rep. 353   140, 318

Case Concerning Application of the International Convention on the Elimination of All Forms of Racial Discrimination (Georgia v. Russian Federation) (Preliminary Objections), [2011] ICJ Rep. 70   66n21, 140, 309, 318, 465n13

Case concerning Certain Property (Liechtenstein v. Germany) (Preliminary Objections), [2005] ICJ Rep. 6   136n20, 139

Case Concerning East Timor (Portugal v. Australia), [1995] ICJ Rep. 90   48, 62, 71–75, 76n51, 140

Case concerning Land Reclamation by Singapore in and around the Straits of Johor (Malaysia v. Singapore) (Award on Agreed Terms), PCA, 1 September 2005; (Decision of 1 September 2005) 27 RIAA 133   149n2

TABLE OF CASES

xxiii

Case concerning Rights of Nationals of the United States of America in Morocco (France v. United States), [1952] ICJ Rep. 176   139, 166

Case Concerning Trial of Pakistani Prisoners of War (Pakistan v. India), [1973] ICJ Rep. 328   36n52

Case Concerning United States Diplomatic and Consular Staff in Tehran (United States of America v. Iran), [1980] ICJ Rep. 3   107n10, 442n22

Certain Activities carried out by Nicaragua in the Border Area (Costa Rica v. Nicaragua), ICJ, General List No. 150, 18 November 2010   349n89

Certain German Interests in Polish Upper Silesia (Germany v. Poland) (Merits), [1926] (ser. A) No 7   401n2, 431n159, 453n75

Certain Phosphate Lands in Nauru (Nauru v. Australia) (Preliminary Objections), [1992] ICJ Rep. 240   62n4, 64n17, 71n34, 75n48

Certain Questions concerning Diplomatic Relations (Honduras v. Brazil) (Order of 12 May 2010), [2010] ICJ Rep. 303   85, 139

Chagos Archipelago (Mauritius v. United Kingdom), PCA, 20 December 2010 138n35

Chemtura Corporation v. Canada (Award), UNCITRAL, 2 August 2010   410n59

Chevron Corporation and Texaco Petroleum Company v. Ecuador (Interim Award), UNCITRAL, 1 December 2008   416n95

Chevron Corporation and Texaco Petroleum Company v. Ecuador (Partial Award on Merits), UNCITRAL, 30 March 2010   415n86

CME Czech Republic BV v. Czech Republic (Final Award), UNCITRAL, 14 March 2003   420n114

CME Czech Republic BV v. Czech Republic (Partial Award), UNCITRAL, 13 September 2001   420n114

CMS Gas Transmission Company v. Argentina (Award), ICSID Arbitral Tribunal, Case No. ARB/01/8, 12 May 2005   414n85, 419n111

Commission of the European Communities v. Ireland (Case C-459/03), [2006] ECR I-4635   271n66

Compañía de Aguas del Alconquija SA and Vivendi Universal SA v. Argentine Republic (Award), (2004) 25 ILR 1   427n145

Compañía de Aguas del Alconquija SA and Vivendi Universal SA v. Argentine Republic (Decision of Annulment), (2004) 6 ICSID Rep. 340   429n152

Conservation and Sustainable Exploitation of Swordfish Stocks (Chile/European Union), ITLOS, Case No 7, 20 December 2000   138n31

Construction of a Road in Costa Rica along the San Juan River (Nicaragua v. Costa Rica), ICJ, General List No. 152, 23 January 2012   85, 87, 97n54, 293

Continental Shelf (Libyan Arab Jamahiriya/Malta) (Merits), [1985] ICJ Rep. 13 230n4

Continental Shelf (Tunisia/Libyan Arab Jamahiriya) (Merits), [1982] ICJ Rep. 18 171n26, 184n75, 230n4

Continental Shelf (United Kingdom/France) (Award), [1977] 18 RIAA 3   230n4

xxiv TABLE OF CASES

Corfu Channel Case (United Kingdom v. Albania) (Preliminary Objections), [1948] ICJ Rep. 15   140, 314

Corfu Channel Case (United Kingdom v. Albania) (Merits), [1949] ICJ Rep. 4   140, 262, 314, 315

Corfu Channel Case (United Kingdom v. Albania) (Assessment of Compensation), [1949] ICJ Rep. 244   140, 141n37, 262, 304n1, 306n2, 324

Decision Regarding Delimitation of the Border Between the State of Eritrea and the Federal Democratic Republic of Ethiopia (Eritrea/Ethiopia) (Eritrea–Ethiopia Boundary Commission, 13 April 2002), (2002) 41 ILM 1057   183n75, 324n77

Délimitation de la frontière maritime entre la Guinée et la Guinée-Bissau (Guinée/Guinée-Bissau), [1985] 19 RIAA 149   230n4

Délimitation de la frontière maritime entre la Guinée-Bissau et le Sénégal (Guinée-Bissau/Sénégal) (Award), [1989] 20 RIAA 121   231n4

Délimitation des Espaces Maritimes entre le Canada et la République Française (Canada/France) (Award), [1992] 21 RIAA 267   231n4

Delimitation of the Maritime Boundary between Bangladesh and Myanmar in the Bay of Bengal (Bangladesh v. Myanmar) (Judgment), ITLOS, Case No. 16, 14 March 2012   247

Delimitation of the Maritime Boundary in the Gulf of Maine Area (Canada/United States), [1984] ICJ Rep. 246   37n58, 230n4

Deserters of Casablanca (France v. Germany), PCA, 22 May 1909   167n4

Dispute concerning Delimitation of the Maritime Boundary between Bangladesh and Myanmar in the Bay of Bengal (Bangladesh/Myanmar), ITLOS, Case No. 16, 14 March 2012   149n3, 231n4, 242n39, 244n49, 262n15, 277n88

Dispute regarding Navigational and Related Rights (Costa Rica v. Nicaragua) (Judgment), [2009] ICJ Rep. 213   85, 87n31

DRC v. Uganda (Provisional Measures), [2000] ICJ Rep. 111   311n27

Dubai–Sharjah Border (Dubai/Sharjah) (Award), (1993) 91 ILR 543   230n4

Elettronica Sicula SpA (ELSI) (United States v. Italy), [1987] ICJ Pleadings 3   115n59, 119n82

Elettronica Sicula SpA (United States v. Italy), [1989] ICJ Rep. 15   401, 431n159

Empresas Lucchetti SA and Lucchetti Peru SA v. Peru (Award), ICSID Case No. ARB/03/4, 7 February 2005   415–416

Eritrea's Damages Claims (Eritrea v. Ethiopia) (Final Award), (2009) 26 RIAA 505   351n94

Ethiopia's Damage Claims (Ethiopia v. Eritrea) (Final Award), (2009) 26 RIAA 631   324n81, 351n94

Ethiopia's Jus ad Bellum Claims 1–8 (Ethiopia v. Eritrea), (2006) 45 ILM 430   317, 324n78

European Communities – Export Subsidies on Sugar – Arbitration under DSU Article 21(3)(c), WTO Doc. WT/DS265/33, WT/DS266/33, WT/DS283/14 ARB (28 October 2005)   394n59

TABLE OF CASES

European Communities – Measures Affecting Asbestos and Asbestos-Containing Products, Appellate Body Report, WTO Doc. WT/DS135/9 (8 November 2000); WT/DS135/AB/R (12 March 2001)   383n22

European Communities – Regime for the Importation, Sale and Distribution of Bananas, Panel Report, WTO Doc. WT/DS27/R (22 May 1997)   388

European Communities – Regime for the Importation, Sale and Distribution of Bananas, Appellate Body Report, WTO Doc. WT/DS27/AB/R, AB-1997–3 (9 September 1997)   388

European Communities – Trade Description of Sardines, Appellate Body Report, WTO Doc. WT/DS231/AB/R (6 September 2002)   384

Factory at Chorzów (Germany v. Poland) (Indemnity), [1928] PCIJ (ser. A) No. 17 401, 431n159, 453n75

Fireman's Fund Insurance Company v. Mexico (Award), ICSID Arbitral Tribunal, Case No. ARB(AF)/02/1, 17 July 2006   411n66, 411n67

Fisheries Case (United Kingdom v. Norway), [1951] ICJ Rep. 116   262n13

Fisheries Jurisdiction (Federal Republic of Germany v. Iceland) (Merits), [1974] ICJ Rep. 175   29n16, 33n42, 140, 141n37, 245n52, 263n18

Fisheries Jurisdiction (United Kingdom v. Iceland) (Merits), [1974] ICJ Rep. 3 29n16, 33n42, 140, 141n37, 245n52, 263n18

Fisheries Jurisdiction Case (Spain v. Canada) (Jurisdiction of the Court, Judgment), [1998] ICJ Rep. 432   140

Frontier Dispute (Benin/Niger), [2005] ICJ Rep. 90   8n16, 183, 184n74, 211n19, 228

Frontier Dispute (Burkina Faso/Mali) (Provisional Measures), [1986] ICJ Rep. 3; (Judgment), [1986] ICJ Rep. 554   211n19, 229, 309n20, 311n26

Frontier Dispute (Burkina Faso/Niger), [2013] ICJ Rep. ___   186, 187n88, 188, 211n19, 228

Gabčíkovo-Nagymaros Project (Hungary/Slovakia) (Merits), [1997] ICJ Rep. 7   140, 287n17, 293n49, 297n67

Gas Natural SDG SA v. Argentina (Jurisdiction), ICSID Arbitral Tribunal, Case No. ARB/03/10, 17 June 2005   412n74

Glamis Gold Ltd v. United States (Award), UNCITRAL, 8 June 2009   410n59

Guinea-Bissau v. Senegal, [1989] 20 RIAA 121   234n12, 238, 242n37

Gulf of Fonseca Case (El Salvador/Nicaragua) (Central American Court of Justice, 9 March 1917)   262n13

Guyana v. Suriname (Award), UNCLOS Arbitral Tribunal, 17 September 2007; (2008) 47 ILM 164   231n4, 239, 242n39, 243n42, 245n50, 247, 257, 277, 317, 324–325

Haya de la Torre (Colombia v. Peru) (Judgment), [1951] ICJ Rep. 71   20n54

Hissène Habré v. Republic of Senegal, ECOWAS Court of Justice, Judgment No. ECW/CCJ/JUD/06/10 of 18 November 2010   180n63

Hoshinmaru (Japan v. Russian Federation) (Judgment), ITLOS, Case No. 14, 6 August 2007   279n95, 280n103

xxvi TABLE OF CASES

ICS Inspection and Control Services Ltd v. Argentine Republic (Jurisdiction), PCA, 10 February 2012   429n151

Impregilo SpA v. Pakistan (Jurisdiction), ICSID Arbitral Tribunal, Case No. ARB/03/3, 22 April 2005   428

In the matter of an arbitration before a tribunal constituted in accordance with Article 5 of the Arbitration Agreement between the Government of Sudan and the Sudan People's Liberation Movement/Army on delimiting Abyei Area and the Permanent Court of Arbitration Optional Rules for arbitrating disputes between two parties of which only one is a state, between the Government of Sudan and the Sudan People's Liberation Movement/Army, PCA, Final award, 22 July 2009 185n81

India – Antidumping Measures on Batteries from Bangladesh, WT/DS306/1, G/L/669, G/ADP/D52/1 (2004); WT/DS306/2, G/L/669/Add.1, G/ADP/D52/2 (2006) 394n61

India – Quantitative Restrictions on Imports of Agriculture, Textile and Industrial Products, Panel Report, WTO Doc. WT/DS90/R (1999)   394n59

Indonesia – Certain Measures Affecting the Automobile Industry – Arbitration under Article 21.3(c) of the DSU, WTO Doc. WT/DS54/15, WT/DS55/14, WT/DS59/13, WT/DS64/12 ARB (7 December 1998)   394n60

Indo-Pakistan Western Boundary (Rann of Kutch), (1968) 17 RIAA 1   160n54, 229

Indus Waters Kishenganga Arbitration (Pakistan v. India), PCA, 31 August 2012 149n6, 161

Interhandel Case (Switzerland v. United States) (Preliminary Objections), [1959] ICJ Rep. 6   139, 454

International Status of South West Africa (Advisory Opinion), [1950] ICJ Rep. 65 25n2, 167n5

Interpretation of Peace Treaties with Bulgaria, Hungary and Romania (First Phase), [1950] ICJ Rep. 65; (Second Phase), [1950] ICJ Rep. 221   5n7

Iron Rhine Arbitration (Belgium/Netherlands), PCA, 20 September 2005   138n34

Italy v. Cuba (Final Award), UNCITRAL, 1 January 2008   416n94

Japan – Measures Affecting Consumer Photographic Film and Paper (Fuji-Kodak), Panel Report, WTO Doc. WT/DS44/R (31 March 1998)   397n71

Joseph Charles Lemire v. Ukraine (Jurisdiction and Liability), ICSID Case No. ARB/06/18, 14 January 2010   410n61

Jurisdictional Immunities of the State (Germany v. Italy: Greece intervening) (Judgment), ICJ General List No. 143, 3 February 2012   137, 139, 296, 358n21

Kasikili/Sedudu Island (Botswana/Namibia), [1999] ICJ Rep. 1045   211n19, 228

LaGrand (Germany v. United States) (Merits), [2001] ICJ Rep. 466   120, 128, 356, 440n16

LaGrand (Germany v. United States) (Provisional Measures), [1999] ICJ Rep. 9   120, 128, 356, 456–457

TABLE OF CASES   xxvii

Lake Lanoux case (France/Spain), (1957) 12 RIAA 285   296
Land and Maritime Boundary between Cameroon and Nigeria (Cameroon v. Nigeria)
    (Preliminary Objections), [1998] ICJ Rep. 275   181n65, 181n67, 237n19
Land and Maritime Boundary between Cameroon and Nigeria (Cameroon v. Nigeria:
    Equatorial Guinea intervening) (Merits), [2002] ICJ Rep. 303   202n8, 211n20,
    228, 231n4
Land Reclamation by Singapore in and around the Straits of Johor (Malaysia v.
    Singapore) (Provisional Measures), [2003] ITLOS Rep. 10; [2005] 27 RIAA 133
    163n62, 270n60
Land, Island, and Maritime Frontier Dispute (El Salvador/Honduras: Nicaragua
    intervening), [1992] ICJ Rep. 351   87n35, 211n19, 225n50
Legal Consequences for States of the Continued Presence of South Africa in Namibia
    (South West Africa) notwithstanding Security Council Resolution 276 (1970)
    (Advisory Opinion), [1971] ICJ Rep. 16   171n25, 356n8
Legal Consequences of the Construction of a Wall in the Occupied Palestinian
    Territory (Advisory Opinion), [2004] ICJ Rep. 136   317n54, 325, 341n63
Legal Status of the South-Eastern Territory of Greenland (Denmark v. Norway), [1933]
    PCIJ (ser. A/B) No. 53   211n19
Legality of the Threat or Use of Nuclear Weapons (Advisory Opinion), [1996] ICJ Rep.
    226   317n53, 326n85 and n87
Legality of the Use by a State of Nuclear Weapons in Armed Conflict (Advisory
    Opinion), [1996] ICJ Rep. 66   326n86
Legality of Use of Force (Serbia and Montenegro v. Belgium) (Preliminary
    Objections), [2004] ICJ Rep. 279   308n17
Legality of Use of Force (Yugoslavia v. United States) (Provisional Measures), [1999]
    ICJ Rep. 761   33n37
LG&E et al. v. Argentina (Liability), ICSID Arbitral Tribunal, Case No. ARB/02/1,
    3 October 2006   419n111
Libyan American Oil Company (LIAMCO) v. Libya, (1977) 62 ILR 140   411n65,
    427n144
L'incident de Walwal (Italie contre Éthiopie), [1935] 3 RIAA 1657   167n7
Loewen Group, Inc. and Raymond Loewen v. United States (Award), ICSID Arbitral
    Tribunal, Case No. ARB(AF)/98/3, 26 June 2003   415n86
Maffezini v. Spain (Jurisdiction), ICSID Arbitral Tribunal, Case No. ARB/97/7,
    25 January 2000   412n74
Maritime Delimitation (Eritrea/Yemen) (Second Phase), [1999] 22 RIAA 335   231n4,
    236
Maritime Delimitation and Territorial Questions between Qatar and Bahrain
    (Jurisdiction), [1994] ICJ Rep. 112; (Admissibility), [1995] ICJ Rep. 6; (Merits),
    [2001] ICJ Rep. 40   9n18, 202n8, 228, 231n4, 262n15
Maritime Delimitation in the Area between Greenland and Jan Mayen (Denmark v.
    Norway), [1993] ICJ Rep. 38   202n8, 231n4, 232n8, 242n37

xxviii TABLE OF CASES

Maritime Delimitation in the Black Sea (Romania v. Ukraine) (Judgment), [2009] ICJ
Rep. 61   139, 231n4
Maritime Dispute (Peru v. Chile) (Order of 27 April 2010), [2010] ICJ Rep. 295   85,
100
Maritime Dispute (Peru v. Chile), ICJ, General List No. 137, 16 January 2008   80n7,
100, 231n4, 242n37
Mavrommatis Palestine Concessions Case (Greece v. United Kingdom) (Jurisdiction),
[1924] PCIJ (ser. A) No. 2   432n162, 437n2, 453n75
Measures Concerning Meat and Meat Products (beef hormones), Panel Report, WTO
Doc. WT/DS26/R/USA   390n45, 392
Measures Concerning Meat and Meat Products, Appellate Body Report,
WT/DS26/AB/R (13 February 1998)   390n45
Methanex Corporation v. United States (Final Award), UNCITRAL, August 2005
411n67, 415n89
Mexico – Measures Affecting Telecommunications Services, Panel Report, WTO Doc.
WT/DS204/R (2004)   394n60
Mexico – Taxes on Soft Drinks, WTO, Dispute Settlement Reports 2006, vol. 1, 261
394n60
Michelot Yogogombaye v. Republic of Senegal, African Court of Human and Peoples'
Rights, Application No. 001/2008, Judgment of 15 December 2009   179n62
Middle East Cement Shipping and Handling Co. v. Egypt (Award), ICSID Case No.
ARB/99/6, 12 April 2002   415n88
Military and Paramilitary Activities in and against Nicaragua (Nicaragua v. United
States) (Provisional Measures), [1984] ICJ Rep. 169   311n28
Military and Paramilitary Activities in and against Nicaragua (Nicaragua v. United
States) (Jurisdiction and Admissibility), [1984] ICJ Rep. 392   31n31, 87n32,
181n66, 237n19, 306n5, 320n63
Military and Paramilitary Activities in and against Nicaragua (Nicaragua v. United
States) (Merits), [1986] ICJ Rep. 14   82n11, 155n37, 305n1, 308n11, 316n51,
329n93, 341n60
Minquiers and Ecrehos (France/United Kingdom), [1953] ICJ Rep. 47   33, 139,
211n19, 216, 219, 229
Monetary Gold Removed from Italy in 1943 (Italy v. France, United Kingdom and
United States), (1954) ICJ Rep. 19   48n28, 139, 166n3
The MOX Plant Case (Ireland v. United Kingdom) (Order No. 6), PCA, 6 June 2008
138n34, 141n36, 147, 271n64 and n68
The MOX Plant Case (Provisional Measures), ITLOS, Case No. 10, 3 December 2001
263n20, 267, 270
The M/V Louisa Case (Saint Vincent and the Grenadines v. Spain), ITLOS, Case No.
18, 10 December 2010   138n32
The M/V *Saiga* Case (Saint Vincent and the Grenadines v. Guinea) (Judgment), ITLOS
Case No. 1, 4 December 1997   12n32

TABLE OF CASES

xxix

Nationality Decrees in Tunis and Morocco (Advisory Opinion), [1923] PCIJ (ser. B) No. 4   166n4

Noble Ventures Inc. v. Romania (Award), ICSID Arbitral Tribunal, Case No. ARB/01/11, 12 October 2005   413n78

North Sea Continental Shelf (Federal Republic of Germany v. Denmark; Federal Republic of Germany v. Netherlands), [1969] ICJ Rep. 3   10n22, 37n62, 139, 230n4

Northern Cameroons (Cameroon v. United Kingdom) (Preliminary Objections), [1963] ICJ Rep. 15   20n55, 169n16, 170n18, 188

Nottebohm Case (Liechtenstein v. Guatemala), [1955] ICJ Rep. 4   139, 356, 454

Nuclear Tests (Australia v. France) (Interim Measures), [1973] ICJ Rep. 99   140, 287n14

Nuclear Tests (Australia v. France) (Jurisdiction and Admissibility), [1974] ICJ Rep. 253   62n3, 66n22, 70n32, 140

Nuclear Tests Cases (New Zealand v. France) (Merits), [1974] ICJ Rep. 457   29n15, 141n37, 245n52

Nykomb Synergetics Technology Holdings AB v. Latvia (Award), UNCITRAL, December 2003   412

Oil Platforms (Iran v. United States) (Judgment), [2003] ICJ Rep. 161   40n76, 119–120, 155, 156n39, 312, 322n70 and n71, 341

Oil Platforms (Iran v. United States) (Preliminary Objections), [1996] ICJ Rep. 803   9n19, 155, 306, 321n69

Oscar Chinn (United Kingdom v. Belgium), [1934] PCIJ (ser. A/B) No. 63   166n4

OSPAR Arbitration (Ireland v. United Kingdom), PCA, 18 June 2001   138n34

Pac Rim Cayman LLC v. The Republic of El Salvador (Decision on the Respondent's Jurisdictional Objections), ICSID Arbitral Tribunal, Case No. ARB/09/12, 20 May 2011   127n133

Panevezys-Saldutiskis Railway (Estonia v. Lithuania), [1938] PCIJ (ser. A/B) No. 75   453n75

Payment of Various Serbian Loans Issued in France (France v. Yugoslavia), [1929] PCIJ (ser. A) No. 20   453n75

Phosphates in Morocco (Italy v. France), [1938] PCIJ (ser. A/B) No. 74   166n4, 453n75

Plama Consortium Ltd v. Bulgaria (Jurisdiction), ICSID Arbitral Tribunal, Case No. ARB/03/24, 8 February 2005   412n74

Prisoners of War – Eritrea's Claim 17 (Eritrea v. Ethiopia) (Partial Award), (2003) 26 RIAA 23   348n82 and n83

Prisoners of War – Ethiopia's Claim 4 (Ethiopia v. Eritrea) (Partial Award) (2003) 26 RIAA 73   348n82

Protection of French Nationals in Egypt, Order of March 29, 1950, [1950] ICJ Rep. 59   167n5

Pulp Mills on the River Uruguay (Argentina v. Uruguay), [2010] ICJ Rep. 28   102–103, 287n18, 293n50, 299–300, 302

XXX TABLE OF CASES

Questions of Interpretation and Application of the 1971 Montreal Convention arising from the Aerial Incident at Lockerbie (Libyan Arab Jamahiriya v. United Kingdom) (Preliminary Objections), [1998] ICJ Rep. 9   40n77, 140, 168n11

Questions of Interpretation and Application of the 1971 Montreal Convention arising from the Aerial Incident at Lockerbie (Libyan Arab Jamahiriya v. United States) (Preliminary Objections), [1998] ICJ Rep. 115   40n77, 140, 168n11

Questions relating to the Obligation to Prosecute or Extradite (Belgium v. Senegal), Judgment, 20 July 2012, [2012] ICJ Rep. ___   139, 180n64

Renta 4 SVSA v. Russian Federation (Preliminary Objections), UNCITRAL, 20 March 2009   413

Reparation for injuries suffered in the service of the United Nations (Advisory Opinion), [1949] ICJ Rep. 174   166n1, 168n8

Report of the French–Siamese Conciliation Commission, decision of 27 June 1947, (1947) 28 RIAA 433   221n37, 229

Request for an Examination of the Situation in Accordance with Paragraph 63 of the Court's Judgment of 20 December 1974 in Nuclear Tests (New Zealand v. France), [1995] ICJ Rep. 288   77n55, 287n14, 297n66

Request for Interpretation of the Judgment of 15 June 1962 in the Case concerning the Temple of Preah Vihear (Cambodia v. Thailand), ICJ, General List No. 151, 18 July 2011   149n4, 151n10 and n11, 293

Request for Interpretation of the Judgment of 15 June 1962 in the Case Concerning the Temple of Preah Vihear (Cambodia/Thailand) (Provisional Measures), [2011] ICJ Rep. 537   310

Responsibilities and Obligations of States Sponsoring Persons and Entities with respect to Activities in the Area (Seabed Mining Advisory Opinion), ITLOS Seabed Disputes Chamber, Case No. 17, 1 February 2011; (2011) 50 ILM 458   13n34, 301

Right to Information on Consular Assistance in the Framework of the Guarantees of the Due Process of Law, Inter-American Court of Human Rights, Advisory Opinion No. 16, 1 October 1999   457n100

Rights of Passage over Indian Territory (Preliminary Objections), [1957] ICJ Rep. 140   140, 152, 157

Ronald Lauder v. Czech Republic (Final Award), UNCITRAL, 3 September 2001   420n114

RSM Production Corporation v. Grenada (Award), ICSID Arbitral Tribunal, Case No. ARB/05/14, 13 March 2009   427n144

Salem case (Egypt, USA), [1932] 2 RIAA 1161   167n7

Salini Costruttori SpA and Italstrade SpA v. Jordan (Jurisdiction), ICSID Arbitral Tribunal, Case No. ARB/02/13, 9 November 2004   412n74

Saluka Investments BV v. Czech Republic (Partial Award), UNCITRAL, 17 March 2006   16n45, 410n59 and 61, 411n63, 412n71

Samoan Claims (Germany, Great Britain, United States), 9 RIAA 15   333n14 and n15

TABLE OF CASES

SD Myers v. Canada (Partial Award), UNCITRAL, 13 November 2000 412n69

SEDITEX v. Madagascar (No. 1), ICSID Arbitral Tribunal, Case No. CONC/82/1, 20 June 1983 426n143

SEDITEX v. Madagascar (No. 2), ICSID Arbitral Tribunal, Case No. CONC/94/1, 19 July 1996 426n143

SESAM v. Central African Republic, ICSID Arbitral Tribunal, Case No. CONC/07/1, 13 August 2008 426n143

SGS Société Générale de Surveillance SA v. Philippines (Jurisdiction), ICSID Arbitral Tribunal, Case No. ARB/02/6, 29 January 2004 413n78

SGS Societé Générale de Surveillance SA v. Paraguay, ICSID Arbitral Tribunal, Case No. ARB/07/29, Award of 10 February 2012 427n145

Siemens AG v. Argentina, ICSID Arbitral Tribunal, Case No. ARB/02/8, 6 February 2007 411n63

Société Commerciale de Belgique (Belgium v. Greece), [1939] PCIJ (ser. A/B) No. 78 453n75

South West Africa Cases (Ethiopia v. South Africa; Liberia v. South Africa) (Preliminary Objections), [1962] ICJ Rep. 319 169n12

South West Africa Cases (Ethiopia v. South Africa; Liberia v. South Africa) (Second Phase), [1966] ICJ Rep. 6 169n12

Southern Bluefin Tuna (New Zealand v. Japan; Australia v. Japan) (Provisional Measures) (1999) 117 ILR 148 62, 66, 67n26, 71, 74–77, 163, 263n18, 265, 267–268, 269n53, 270n59, 271, 290

Southern Bluefin Tuna (New Zealand v. Japan; Australia v. Japan) (Jurisdiction and Admissibility), (2000) 119 ILR 508 62, 66, 67n25, 71, 74–77, 163, 290

Sovereignty over Certain Frontier Land (Belgium/Netherlands), [1959] ICJ Rep. 209 139, 211n19, 229

Sovereignty over Pedra Branca/Pulau Batu Puteh, Middle Rocks and South Ledge (Malaysia/Singapore), [2008] ICJ Rep. 12 148n1, 157, 159n51, 211n19, 228, 262n16

Sovereignty over Pulau Ligitan and Pulau Sipadan (Indonesia/Malaysia) (Application for Permission to Intervene), [2001] ICJ Rep. 575 158n45

Sovereignty over Pulau Ligitan and Pulau Sipadan (Indonesia/Malaysia), [2002] ICJ Rep. 625 148n1, 157, 158n47, 211n19, 228

SS *Lotus* Case (France v. Turkey), [1927] PCIJ Ser. A No. 10 263n19, 453n75

SS *Wimbledon*, [1923] PCIJ (ser. A) No. 1 262

Tax Treatment for 'Foreign Sales Corporations' – Recourse to Arbitration by the United States under Article 22.6 of the DSU and Article 4.11 of the SCM Agreement, WT/DS108/ARB (30 August 2002) 390n45

Temple of Preah Vihear (Cambodia v. Thailand) (Merits), [1962] ICJ Rep. 6 149, 202n8, 211n18 and n20, 229

Temple of Preah Vihear (Cambodia v. Thailand) (Preliminary Objections), [1961] ICJ Rep. 24 149, 150n8

xxxii TABLE OF CASES

Territorial and Maritime Dispute (Nicaragua v. Colombia) (Judgment) ICJ, General List No. 124, 19 November 2012   80n7, 85, 87n31, 94, 97n54

Territorial and Maritime Dispute (Nicaragua v. Colombia) (Preliminary Objections), [2007] ICJ Rep. 832   202n8

Territorial and Maritime Dispute between Nicaragua and Honduras in the Caribbean Sea (Nicaragua v. Honduras), [2007] ICJ Rep. 659   80n7, 84, 85n28, 97n54, 202n8, 231n4

Territorial Dispute (Libya/Chad), [1994] ICJ Rep. 6   211n19, 228

Tesoro v. Trinidad and Tobago, ICSID Arbitral Tribunal, Case No. CONC/83/1, 27 November 1985   425n140, 426n143

Texaco/Calasiatic v. Libya, (1977) 53 ILR 389   411n65, 427n144

TG World Petroleum Ltd v. Niger, ICSID Arbitral Tribunal, Case No. CONC/03/1, 8 April 2005   426n143

Togo Eléctricité v. Togo, ICSID Arbitral Tribunal, Case No. CONC/05/1, 6 April 2005   426n143

Trail Smelter Arbitration (United States v. Canada), (1938 and 1941) 3 RIAA 1911   5n6, 288n22

Treatment in Hungary of Aircraft and Crew of United States of America (United States v. USSR), Order, [1954] ICJ Rep. 99   465n14

Trial of Pakistani Prisoners of War (Pakistan v. India), [1973] ICJ Rep. 328   153, 156, 246n52

United States – Definitive Safeguard Measures on Imports of Wheat Gluten from the European Communities, Appellate Body Report, WT/DS166/AB/R, AB-2000–10 (19 January 2001)   124n116, 390n45

United States – Import Prohibition of Certain Shrimp and Shrimp Products, Appellate Body Report, WTO Doc. WT/DS58/AB/R (6 November 1998)   383n20

United States – Imposition of Countervailing Duties on Certain Hot-Rolled Lead and Bismuth Carbon Steel Products Originating in the UK, Appellate Body Report, WTO Doc. WT/DS138/AB/R (7 June 2000)   383n21

United States – Measures Affecting the Cross-Border Supply of Gambling and Betting Services – Recourse by Antigua and Barbuda to DSU Art. 22:6 on the Understanding of Rules and Procedures Governing the Settlement of Disputes, Appellate Body Report, WTO Doc. WT/DS285/ARB (21 December 2007)   389n43

United States – Safeguard Measures on Imports of Fresh, Chilled or Frozen Lamb Meat from New Zealand and Australia, Appellate Body Report, WTO Doc. WT/DS177AB/R, WT/DS178/AB/R (1 May 2001)   386n32

United States – Subsidies on Upland Cotton, Appellate Body Report, WTO Doc. WT/DS267/AB/R (3 March 2005)   397

United States – Subsidies on Upland Cotton, Report of the Panel, WTO Doc. WT/DS267/R (8 September 2004)   397

TABLE OF CASES

United States – Sunset Reviews of Anti-Dumping Measures on Oil Country Tubular Goods from Argentina – Arbitration under Article 21.3(c) of the Understanding of Rules and Procedures Governing the Settlement of Disputes, WTO Doc. WT/DS268/12, ARB-2005–1/18 (7 June 2005)   394n60

United States – Tax Treatment for 'Foreign Sales Corporations', Appellate Body Report, WTO Doc. WT/DS108/AB/R, AB-1999–9 (24 February 2000)   390n45

United States – Tax Treatment for 'Foreign Sales Corporations', Panel Report, WTO Doc. WT/DS108/RW (20 August 2001)   390n45

United States Diplomatic and Consular Staff in Tehran (Judgment) (United States v. Iran), [1980] ICJ Rep. 3   33n41, 117n70, 154n30

United States Diplomatic and Consular Staff in Tehran (Order of 12 May 1981), [1981] ICJ Rep. 47   155n32

United States Diplomatic and Consular Staff in Tehran (United States v. Iran) (Order of 15 December 1979), [1979] ICJ Rep. 7   116n62, 154n29

Vienna Convention on Consular Relations (Paraguay v. United States) (Order of 9 April 1998), [1998] ICJ Rep. 248   35n48

Vienna Convention on Consular Relations (Paraguay v. United States) (Order of 10 November 1998), [1998] ICJ Rep. 426   456n94

Vienna Convention on Consular Relations (Paraguay v. United States) (Provisional Measures), [1998] ICJ Rep. 248   440n16

Volga Case (Russia v. Australia) (Prompt Release), (2003) 42 ILM 159   62, 77n54, 78n58, 262n17, 279–282

The Walfish Bay Boundary Case (Germany/Great Britain), (1911) 11 RIAA 267   207n13

Waste Management, Inc. v. Mexico (No. 2) (Award), ICSID Case No. ARB(AF)/00/3, 30 April 2004   410n60

Wena Hotels Ltd v. Egypt, (2004) 6 ICSID Rep. 89   411n63

Western Front, Aerial Bombardment and Related Claims – Eritrea's Claims 1, 3, 5, 9–13, 14, 21, 25 & 26 (Eritrea v. Ethiopia) (Partial Award), (2005) 26 RIAA 291   347n81, 348n84

Whaling in the Antarctic (Australia v. Japan), ICJ, General List No. 148, 31 May 2010   62n9, 74n46, 149n5, 156, 273n72, 289, 293, 304

White Industries Australia Ltd v. Republic of India (Final Award), UNCITRAL, 30 November 2011   415n86

Domestic courts

Alperin v. Vatican Bank 410 F 3d 532, 544 (9th Cir. 2005) (US)   56

Attorney General (United Kingdom) v. Heinemann Publishers Australia Pty Ltd [1988] HCA 25; (1988) 165 CLR 30 (Australia)   50

Baker v. Carr, 396 US 186 (1962) (US)   44, 46–47

xxxiv TABLE OF CASES

Banco Nacional de Cuba v. Sabbatino 376 US 398 (1964) (US)   45

Beanal et al. v. Freeport-McMoran, Inc. et al., [1999] USCA5 1266; 197 F 3d 161 (5th Cir. 1999) (US)   55

Buttes Gas and Oil Co. v. Hammer, [1981] QB 22 (HL); [1982] AC 888 (UK)   44, 45, 47, 50, 53

Decision Number 2–3/PUU-V/2007 (Petition by Scott Anthony Rush), [2007] Constitutional Court of the Republic of Indonesia, 93 (Indonesia)   439n8

Doe v. Unocal, [2003] USCA9 100; 395 F 3d 978 (9th Cir. 2003) (US)   55

Filártiga v. Peña-Irala, [1980] USCA2 576; 630 F 2d 876 (2nd Cir, 1980) (US)   54

Habib v. Commonwealth [2010] FCAFC 12 (Australia)   50n37, 53n49

Horta v. Commonwealth, (1994) 181 CLR 183 (Australia)   43, 48

Humane Society International v. Kyodo Senpaku Kaisha Ltd, [2005] FCA 664; [2006] FCAFC 116; [2008] FCA 3 (Australia)   43, 51, 52, 53

In re Austrian and German Bank Holocaust Litigation No. 98 Civ. 3938 (US)   55

In re Holocaust Victim Assets No. CV-96-4849, 2001 US App. LEXIS 30154 (2d Cir. 2001) (US)   55

Jose Francisco Sosa v. Humberto Alvarez-Machain et al., [2004] USSC 2852; 542 US 692 (2004) (US)   55

Kuwait Airways Corporation v. Iraqi Airways Co. (Nos. 4 and 5), [2002] UKHL 19; [2002] 2 WLR 1353 (UK)   45, 53

Occidental Exploration and Production Company v. Republic of Ecuador, [2005] EWCA Civ. 1116, [14]–[20] (UK)   402n6

Petrotimor v. Commonwealth [2003] FCAFC 83; (2003) 126 FCR 354 (Australia)   43, 48–52, 53, 56

Potter v. Broken Hill Proprietary Co Ltd (1906) 3 CLR 479 (Australia)   49n33

R v. Bow Street Metropolitan Stipendiary Magistrate; Ex parte Pinochet Ugarte [1998] UKHL 41; [2000] 1 AC 61 (UK)   45

Re Ditfort ex parte Deputy Commissioner of Taxation (NSW) (1988) 83 ALR 265; (1988) 19 FCR 347   46

Re Limbo Unreported G160 of 1989 (Australia)   50, 53

Sakata v. Japan, 13 Keishu 3225, Case No. 1959 (A) No. 710 (Japan)   46n23

Stewart v. Ronalds [2009] NSWCA 277 (Australia)   46n19

Thomas v. Mowbray, (2007) 233 CLR 307 (Australia)   50

Thorpe v. Commonwealth, (1997) 144 ALR 677 (Australia)   51

Underhill v. Hernandez 168 US 250 (1897) (US)   44, 45

Ungaro-Benages v. Dresden Bank AG, 379 F 3d 1227 (11th Cir. 2004) (US)   56n64

TABLE OF TREATIES

1794

Treaty of Amity, Commerce and Navigation, United States–Great Britain (signed 19 November 1794, entered into force 29 February 1796), 8 Stat. 116   108n12

1871

Treaty of Washington, United States–Great Britain (signed 8 May 1871, entered into force 17 June 1871), 17 Stat. 863   31, 110–111, 115, 331

1899

Convention for the Pacific Settlement of International Disputes (signed 29 July 1899, entered into force 4 September 1900), 32 Stat. 1799   174n41

1907

Convention for the Pacific Settlement of International Disputes (signed 18 October 1907, entered into force 26 January 1910), 36 Stat. 2199   174n42

1919

Treaty of Versailles (signed 28 June 1919, entered into force 10 January 1920), 225 Consol. TS 188   90, 335

1944

Convention on International Civil Aviation (opened for signature 1 December 1944, entered into force 5 March 1947), 15 UNTS 295   152n15

1945

Charter of the United Nations (opened for signature 26 June 1945, entered into force 24 October 1945), 59 Stat. 1031   131, 185, 422

1946

International Convention for the Regulation of Whaling (opened for signature 2 December 1946, entered into force 10 November 1948), 161 UNTS 72 441n17

1947

General Agreement on Tariffs and Trade (opened for signature 30 October 1947, entered into force 1 January 1948), 55 UNTS 194   375

xxxvi TABLE OF TREATIES

1948

American Treaty on Pacific Settlement (signed 30 April 1948, entered into force 6 May 1949), 30 UNTS 84   82n14, 175n46

1949

Geneva Convention (I) for the Amelioration of the Condition of the Wounded and Sick in Armed Forces in the Field (opened for signature 12 August 1949, entered into force 21 October 1950), 75 UNTS 31   336, 346, 347, 450

Geneva Convention (II) for the Amelioration of the Condition of Wounded, Sick and Shipwrecked Members of Armed Forces at Sea (opened for signature 12 August 1949, entered into force 21 October 1950), 75 UNTS 85   336, 346, 347, 450

Geneva Convention (III) relative to the Treatment of Prisoners of War (opened for signature 12 August 1949, entered into force 21 October 1950), 75 UNTS 135   336, 346, 347, 348, 450

Geneva Convention (IV) relative to the Protection of Civilian Persons in Time of War (opened for signature 12 August1949, entered into force 21 October 1950), 75 UNTS 287   336, 346, 347, 440n13, 450

1950

European Convention on Human Rights (opened for signature 4 November 1950, entered into force 3 September 1953), 213 UNTS 222   353, 360, 367, 442n26, 443n34

1951

Convention relating to the Status of Refugees (opened for signature 28 July 1951, entered into force 22 April 1954) 189 UNTS 150, as amended by the Protocol Relating to the Status of Refugees (opened for signature 31 January 1967, entered into force 4 October 1967), 606 UNTS 267   172

1955

Treaty of Amity, Economic Relations, and Consular Rights between the United States and Iran, Iran–United States (signed 15 August 1955, entered into force 16 June 1957), 284 UNTS 93   108n12, 119, 154–155, 321

1957

European Convention for the Pacific Settlement of Disputes (signed 29 April 1957, entered into force 30 April 1958), 320 UNTS 243   175n46

1958

Convention on the Continental Shelf (opened for signature 29 April 1958, entered into force 10 June 1964), 499 UNTS 311   49

1959

Antarctic Treaty (opened for signature 1 December 1959, entered into force 23 June 1961), 402 UNTS 71   26, 52, 269, 288

TABLE OF TREATIES

xxxvii

1960

Indus Waters Treaty, India–Pakistan (signed on 19 September 1960, entered into force 12 January 1961), 419 UNTS 125   161

1963

Act Regarding Navigation and Economic Co-operation between the States of the Niger Basin (signed 26 October 1963, entered into force 1 February 1966), 587 UNTS 9   176n49

Optional Protocol to that Convention concerning the Compulsory Settlement of Disputes (opened for signature 24 April 1963, entered into force 21 June 1985), 1400 UNTS 339   154, 456

Vienna Convention on Consular Relations (opened for signature 24 April 1963, entered into force 19 March 1967), 596 UNTS 261   35, 87, 154, 356, 440, 444–445, 454, 456

Treaty Banning Nuclear Weapon Tests in the Atmosphere, in Outer Space and Under Water (concluded 5 August 1963, entered into force 10 October 1963), 480 UNTS 43

1965

International Convention on the Elimination of All Forms of Racial Discrimination (opened for signature 21 December 1965, entered into force 4 January 1969), 660 UNTS 195   140, 309, 360

Convention on the Settlement of Investment Disputes between States and Nationals of other States (opened for signature 18 March 1965, entered into force 14 October 1966), 575 UNTS 159   172, 406, 407n35

1966

International Covenant on Economic, Social and Cultural Rights (opened for signature 16 December 1966, entered into force 3 November 1976), 993 UNTS 3   359

International Convention on Civil and Political Rights (opened for signature 16 December 1966, entered into force 23 March 1976, except for Art. 41, which entered into force on 28 March 1979), 999 UNTS 171   437

International Convention on Civil and Political Rights (Optional Protocol) (opened for signature 16 December 1966, entered into force 23 March 1976), 993 UNTS 3   365n46

First Optional Protocol to the International Covenant on Civil and Political Rights (opened for signature 16 December 1966, entered into force 23 March 1976), 999 UNTS 302   442

1968

African Convention on the Conservation of Nature and Natural Resources (signed 15 September 1968, entered into force 16 June 1969), 1001 UNTS 4   176n49

xxxviii   TABLE OF TREATIES

1969

Vienna Convention on the Law of Treaties (concluded 23 May 1969, entered into force 27 January 1980), 1155 UNTS 331   16

1971

Convention for the Suppression of Unlawful Acts Against the Safety of Civil Aviation (opened for signature 23 September 1971, entered into force 26 January 1973), 974 UNTS 178   153n17

1972

Agreement between the Government of Canada and the Government of the French Republic Concerning Their Mutual Fishing Relations off the Atlantic Coast of Canada (signed and entered into force 27 March 1972), 862 UNTS 209   238

Convention creating the Organization for the Development of the Senegal River (signed 11 May 1972), available at http://faolex.fao.org/docs/texts/mul16004.doc 176n49

1973

Convention on International Trade in Endangered Species of Wild Fauna and Flora (concluded 3 March 1973, entered into force 1 July 1975), 993 UNTS 243   273

Convention on the Prevention and Punishment of Crimes against Internationally Protected Persons, including Diplomatic Agents (opened for signature 14 December 1973, entered into force 20 February 1977), 1035 UNTS 167   154

1975

Statute of the River Uruguay (opened for signature 26 February 1975, entered into force 18 September 1976), 1295 UNTS 340   88, 102–103, 298

1977

Protocol Additional to the Geneva Conventions of 12 August 1949, and Relating to the Protection of Victims of International Armed Conflicts (Protocol I) (concluded 8 June 1977, entered into force 7 December 1978), 1125 UNTS 3   440n13

1978

Convention relating to the status of the River Gambia (signed 30 June 1978), available at www.fao.org/docrep/w7414b/w7414b0b.htm   176n49

Protocol of 1978 relating to the International Convention for the Prevention of Pollution from Ships (opened for signature 17 February 1978, entered into force 2 October 1983), 1340 UNTS 62   294n54

1980

Convention on the Elimination of All Forms of Discrimination against Women (opened for signature 1 March 1980, entered into force 3 September 1981), 1249 UNTS 13   361n29

TABLE OF TREATIES   xxxix

1981

Algiers Accords: Declaration of the Government of the Democratic and Popular
  Republic of Algeria, Iran–United States (signed and entered into force 20 January
  1981), 62 ILR 595   117, 154n31

1982

United Nations Convention on the Law of the Sea (opened for signature 10 December
  1982, entered into force 16 November 1994), 1833 UNTS 3   13n35, 62n6, 138,
  197, 235, 260

1984

Convention against Torture and Other Cruel, Inhuman or Degrading Treatment or
  Punishment (opened for signature 10 December 1984, entered into force 26 June
  1987), 1465 UNTS 85   180, 361n30

1987

Montreal Protocol on Substances that Deplete the Ozone Layer (opened for signature
  16 September 1987, entered into force 1 January 1989), 1522 UNTS 29
  292

1989

Convention on the Rights of the Child (opened for signature 20 November 1989,
  entered into force 2 September 1990), 1577 UNTS 3   361, 365
Treaty between Australia and the Republic of Indonesia on the Zone of Cooperation in
  an Area between the Indonesian Province of East Timor and Northern Australia
  [Timor Gap Treaty] (opened for signature 11 December 1989, entered into force
  9 February 1991), 1991 ATS, No. 9   48n26

1990

Agreement between the Federal Republic of Nigeria and the Republic of Niger
  concerning the equitable sharing in the development, conservation and use of their
  common water resources (signed 18 July 1990), available at www.fao.org/docrep/
  w7414b/w7414b10.htm   176n49
International Convention on the Protection of the Rights of All Migrant Workers
  and Members of their Families (opened for signature 18 December 1990, entered
  into force 1 July 2003), 2220 UNTS 3   361n32

1991

Convention on Environmental Impact Assessment in a Transboundary Context
  (opened for signature 25 February 1991, entered into force 10 September 1997),
  1989 UNTS 310   297

1992

United Nations Framework Convention on Climate Change (opened for signature
  9 May 1992, entered into force 21 March 1994), 1771 UNTS 165   303n95

xl   TABLE OF TREATIES

Convention on Biological Diversity (opened for signature 5 June 1992, entered into
    force 29 December 1993), 1760 UNTS 79   6n12, 273n76
Convention on Conciliation and Arbitration (opened for signature 15 December 1992,
    entered into force 5 December 1994), 1842 UNTS 121   6n11, 137n22
Convention on the Transboundary Effects of Industrial Accidents (opened for
    signature 18 March 1992, entered into force 19 April 2000), 2105 UNTS 457
    6n12
Convention on the Use of Transboundary Watercourses and Lakes (opened for
    signature 17 March 1992, entered into force 6 October 1996), 1936 UNTS 269
    6n12
North American Free Trade Agreement (signed 17 December 1992, entered into
    force 1 January 1994), 32 ILM 296   126n128

1993

Agreement between Australia and the Republic of Nauru for the Settlement of the Case
    in the International Court of Justice concerning Certain Phosphate Lands in
    Nauru, Australia–Nauru, (opened for signature 10 August 1993, entered into force
    20 August 1993), [1993] ATS 26, 32 ILM 1474   72n38

1994

Marrakesh Agreement Establishing the World Trade Organization (opened for
    signature 15 April 1994, entered into force 1 January 1995), 1867 UNTS 3   14n39,
    121n92, 376n5, 379n9
Energy Charter Treaty (opened for signature 17 December 1994, entered into force
    16 April 1998), 34 ILM 360   408, 418, 419n108
Agreement relating to the Implementation of Part XI of UNCLOS (opened for
    signature 28 July 1994, entered into force 28 July 1996), 1836 UNTS 42   302
Convention on the Safety of United Nations and Associated Personnel (signed
    9 December 1994, entered into force 15 January 1999), 2051 UNTS 363   441

1996

Comprehensive Nuclear Test-Ban Treaty (concluded 10 September 1996, not yet in
    force), 35 ILM 1439

1997

Kyoto Protocol to the United Nations Framework Convention on Climate Change
    (opened for signature 11 December 1997, entered into force 16 February 2005),
    1771 UNTS 107   287

2004

Dominican Republic–Central America–United States Free Trade Agreement (signed
    5 August 2004, entered into force 1 March 2006), 43 ILM 514   127

2006

Convention on the Rights of Persons with Disabilities (opened for signature 13 December 2006, entered into force 3 May 2008), 2515 UNTS 3   361

International Convention for the Protection of All Persons from Enforced Disappearance (opened for signature 20 December 2006, entered into force 23 December 2010), UN Doc. A/61/488   361

PART I

1

The place of international litigation in international law

JOHN MERRILLS

In 1982, the United Nations (UN) General Assembly passed a resolution known as the Manila Declaration on the Peaceful Settlement of International Disputes.[1] The Declaration confirms and elaborates certain provisions of the United Nations Charter and also of the Assembly's Declaration on Principles of International Law concerning Friendly Relations and Co-operation among States of 1970.[2] Thus paragraph 2 of Section I of the Manila Declaration, like Article 2(3) of the Charter, requires every state to 'settle its international disputes exclusively by peaceful means in such a manner that international peace and security and justice are not endangered'. The means available for settling disputes listed in these instruments are customarily divided into two groups. Negotiation, mediation, inquiry, and conciliation are termed diplomatic means, because the parties retain control over the disposition of their dispute and may accept or reject a proposed settlement as they see fit. Arbitration and judicial settlement, on the other hand, are employed when what is wanted is a binding decision, usually on the basis of international law, and these are therefore known as legal means of settlement.

Judicial settlement and arbitration provide states with ways of dealing with disputes through litigation, and as such provide the focus for this book, which will not be concerned with the various diplomatic methods, except incidentally.[3] This first chapter is intended to provide some general information on the significance of litigating disputes as a background for the more detailed treatments in later chapters. Historically, arbitration

---

[1] GA Res. 37/10, UN GAOR, 37th sess., 68th plen. mtg Supp. No. 51, UN Doc. A/RES/37/10 (15 November 1982).
[2] GA Res. 25/26, UN GAOR, 25th sess., Supp. No. 28, UN Doc. A/8028 (24 October 1970).
[3] For discussion of diplomatic methods of settlement see John G. Merrills, *International Dispute Settlement*, 5th edn (Cambridge University Press, 2011), chs. 1–4, 10, 11.

emerged before judicial settlement, and supplied the inspiration for the numerous courts and tribunals that now exist. The main features of arbitration are therefore a suitable place to begin.

Arbitration

Arbitration is the oldest of the legal methods of dispute settlement, and its origins for current international practice can be traced back more than two hundred years to the 1794 Jay Treaty. In that instrument, Great Britain and the United States agreed that various outstanding disputes should be resolved by panels of national commissioners appointed by the two states. These early Anglo-American commissions were not judicial tribunals in the modern sense, but were supposed to blend juridical with diplomatic considerations to produce what was in effect a negotiated settlement. The modern form of commission, however, is made up of arbitrators appointed by each side, together with one or more neutral members, who are required to follow a strictly juridical procedure and deliver a reasoned award. Variations on this basic pattern are possible, but the standard form of arbitration is now well established and employed in many kinds of international disputes.[4]

Traditionally, arbitration has been used for disputes in which the issues are legal and the desire to improve relations makes the idea of a binding settlement handed down by a third party attractive. Territorial and boundary disputes, for example, often fall into this category, as will be seen in later chapters.[5] For these and other types of dispute a further advantage of arbitration is that the parties define the question or questions they want the tribunal to answer and can also specify the basis of its decision. The definition of the issue is important because it establishes the scope of the arbitrators' jurisdiction. By defining the issue broadly, the parties can use arbitration to remove a major obstacle to good relations. Conversely (and more commonly), by defining the issue narrowly, they can prevent an investigation of wider questions. Such an investigation might cause more problems than it would resolve, or exclude from arbitration particular issues for which negotiation or some other means of settlement is considered more appropriate.

---

[4] On the development and use of arbitration see John L. Simpson and Hazel Fox, *International Arbitration: Law and Practice* (London: Praeger, 1959); Christine Gray and Benedict Kingsbury, 'Developments in Dispute Settlement: Inter-state Arbitration since 1945', (1992) 63 BYBIL 97; Merrills, above n. 3, ch. 5.

[5] See further Chapter 10, as well as Chapter 11, in this volume.

THE PLACE OF INTERNATIONAL LITIGATION 5

No less important than the definition of the issue is the parties' directive to the tribunal as to the criteria to be applied in making its decision. Often the tribunal's instructions are explicitly to decide the matter in accordance with international law. When there is no such directive, the parties' intentions must be inferred, and the usual practice is again to base the judgment on international law. Sometimes the parties want international law to provide the basis for the decision, but require particular aspects to be emphasized. This can be achieved by a suitably worded clause in the arbitration agreement (*compromis*). Similarly, if the parties are agreed that a solution in accordance with international law would not be appropriate for some reason, they can instruct the arbitrator to decide the case in accordance with equity, or on some other basis. The ability to specify the applicable law also enables the parties to require the arbitrator to apply national law, either alone, or in combination with some other system.[6]

Further control over the process of arbitration stems from the fact already mentioned that it is for the parties to choose their arbitrators. Although this, like other elements of an arbitration, requires agreement and so may cause delay, it means that the dispute will eventually be decided by a tribunal that has the parties' trust, a factor of fundamental importance in international litigation. As might be expected, difficulties can sometimes arise in appointing arbitral tribunals. If, for example, the parties cannot agree on the neutral members, a way of overcoming the problem is to allow the necessary appointments to be made by the president of the International Court of Justice (ICJ), or another disinterested third party. Similarly, in the rare case of a party attempting to sabotage an arbitration by refusing to appoint its own members,[7] a possible solution is a provision to the effect that, after three months, or some other suitable period, the necessary appointments may be made by an outside party.

The procedural arrangements are also a matter for the parties to determine. These govern the way in which the arbitration is to be conducted, where it is to be held, and how the proceedings will be paid for. It is usual to include in the arbitration agreement quite detailed provisions relating to such things as the number and order of the written pleadings, the oral stage of the proceedings, and the vital issue of time limits. Other matters which are normally covered in the *compromis* are how the tribunal

---

[6] See, e.g., *Trail Smelter Arbitration (United States v. Canada)* (1938 and 1941), 3 RIAA 1911.
[7] See *Interpretation of Peace Treaties with Bulgaria, Hungary and Romania (First Phase)*, [1950] ICJ Rep. 65; *(Second Phase)*, [1950] ICJ Rep. 221.

is to obtain evidence, whether it may appoint experts or conduct visits, whether it can order provisional measures, what languages will be used, how the decision will be taken, whether separate opinions are allowed and whether the award will be published. Although each of these matters can be negotiated separately, it is obviously convenient if the parties can agree on the use of standard provisions such as the model rules drawn up by the International Law Commission, the Permanent Court of Arbitration and other bodies.[8]

To encourage the use of arbitration, the 1899 Hague Convention established a list of qualified arbitrators, styled inaccurately 'the Permanent Court of Arbitration' (PCA), and created a bureau with premises, library, and staff that still exists and plays a major role in facilitating arbitration and other forms of peaceful settlement.[9] Like judicial settlement, arbitration is a method that can be employed ad hoc when a dispute arises, or provided for in advance by appropriate arrangements in a treaty. Consequently, it is to be found in the dispute settlement provisions of multilateral and bilateral conventions on a wide variety of subjects either as an optional or a compulsory procedure, and often in combination with other methods. The 1982 UN Convention on the Law of the Sea (UNCLOS), for example, gives a prominent role to arbitration,[10] as do the 1992 Stockholm Convention on Conciliation and Arbitration within the Commission on Security and Cooperation in Europe (CSCE)[11] and a number of recent conventions concerned with the environment.[12] In the dispute settlement system of the World Trade Organization (WTO),

---

[8] See the 'ILC Model Rules of Arbitral Procedure', (1958) II(12) *Yearbook of the International Law Commission*; text also in Simpson and Fox, above n. 4, 295; and the PCA's 'Optional Rules for Arbitrating Disputes between Two States' (1992), text in (1993) 32 ILM 572.

[9] Phyllis Hamilton, Hilmara C. Requena, Laurence de Blocq van Scheltinga, and Bette E. Shifman (eds.), *The Permanent Court of Arbitration and Dispute Resolution* (The Hague: Kluwer Law International, 1999); Belinda MacMahon and Fedelma Smith, *Permanent Court of Arbitration Summaries of Awards 1999–2009* (The Hague: TMC Asser Press, 2010).

[10] Merrills, above n. 3, 176–81.

[11] Convention on Conciliation and Arbitration (opened for signature 15 December 1992, entered into force 5 December 1994) 1842 UNTS 121; and see Merrills, above n. 3, 77–8 and 113.

[12] See, e.g., three conventions concluded in 1992: the Convention on Biological Diversity (opened for signature 5 June 1992, entered into force 29 December 1993) 1760 UNTS 79; the Convention on the Use of Transboundary Watercourses and Lakes (opened for signature 17 March 1992, entered into force 6 October 1996) 1936 UNTS 269; and the Convention on the Transboundary Effects of Industrial Accidents (opened for signature 18 March 1992, entered into force 19 April 2000) 2105 UNTS 457.

THE PLACE OF INTERNATIONAL LITIGATION

similarly, although the emphasis is on panel proceedings (described below), arbitration is also an option and for certain disputes is mandatory.

The use of arbitration in inter-state disputes must be distinguished from its use in a related context – to deal with disputes between a state on one side and an individual or corporation on the other. In cases of this type, known as mixed arbitrations, the tribunal's jurisdiction may derive from a contract, rather than a treaty, but in either event has international repercussions that are likely to be significant. The Iran–US Claims Tribunal,[13] for example, was set up in 1981 to handle a large number of disputes arising from the Iranian revolution, and exercised jurisdiction over both inter-state and private claims. Its decisions, running to more than thirty volumes, not only show the value of arbitration as a way of resolving serious and complex disputes of a commercial character, but, because the tribunal has had to address issues such as expropriation and state responsibility, have also made a telling contribution to international law.

Arbitration, then, is an important means of handling disputes, as its extensive use in international practice demonstrates. However, like every other method, it has certain limitations. Since everything is in the hands of the parties, both the decision to arbitrate and the conduct of the proceedings rest on their decisions. This means that many disputes are never arbitrated because the will to do so is lacking, while for those that are arbitrated, the arbitrators' powers are confined to those conferred in the *compromis*. A further limitation concerns enforcement. For although arbitration results in a binding decision, it can be difficult to ensure that an award is implemented in the absence of a procedure to compel the losing party to accept it. This does not mean that arbitral decisions are generally disregarded, for states have good reason to accept defeats gracefully. It is nonetheless a weakness. Ways of encouraging compliance are available, but the answer really lies with the protagonists. Arbitration, like other means of settling disputes in a world of sovereign states, relies for its effectiveness on responsible behaviour from the parties.

The International Court of Justice

Judicial settlement involves the reference of disputes to permanent tribunals for a binding decision. It is listed in the Manila Declaration

---

[13] See Charles Nelson Brower and Jason D. Brueschke, *The Iran–United States Claims Tribunal* (The Hague: Martinus Nijhoff Publishers, 1998).

immediately after 'arbitration', from which it developed, and is currently available through a number of courts with general or specialized jurisdiction. The only court of general jurisdiction is the ICJ at The Hague, which was founded in 1945 as the successor to the Permanent Court of International Justice (PCIJ), which was set up as part of the 1919 peace settlement. Courts with specialized jurisdiction include human rights courts and various other tribunals described in the next section. Any review of judicial settlement, however, must start with the ICJ.[14]

The Court is composed of fifteen judges who are elected for nine-year terms by the UN Security Council and UN General Assembly. The Court's Statute requires the judges to be broadly representative of 'the main forms of civilization and of the principal legal systems of the world', but they sit as independent judges, not as representatives of their national states. However, if a party to a dispute does not currently have a judge of its nationality on the bench, it is entitled to appoint an ad hoc judge who becomes a member of the Court for that case only. Cases are normally heard by the full Court, but if the parties wish, they can instead refer it to a smaller chamber.[15] Such chambers, which normally consist of five judges, have been used for several cases in recent years.[16] The composition of a chamber is in practice determined by the parties, making litigation before a chamber of the Court similar in this respect to arbitration.

The Court's authority to decide cases is conferred by the Statute and, as with arbitration, is based on the principle of consent. It is therefore open to states to agree to take future disputes, or any particular dispute, to the Court by concluding a treaty in appropriate terms, or to make a unilateral declaration under Article 36(2) of the Statute, known as the optional clause.[17] The latter, like a state's treaty commitment, can be unqualified – that is, covering all disputes – or, on the other hand, may be circumscribed by reservations or limitations, reflecting the types of dispute the state is prepared to litigate. In the event of a disagreement as

---

[14] For more detailed treatment of the International Court and its work see Arthur Eyffinger, *The International Court of Justice 1946–1996* (The Hague: Kluwer Law International, 1996); Merrills, above n. 3, chs. 6 and 7.

[15] See Rudolph Ostrinhansky, 'Chambers of the International Court of Justice', (1988) 37 ICLQ 30.

[16] See, e.g., *Frontier Dispute (Benin/Niger) (Judgment)* [2005] ICJ Rep. 90.

[17] For discussion of the optional clause with particular reference to recent practice see John G. Merrills, 'Does the Optional Clause Still Matter?', in Kaiyan Homi Kaikobad and Michael Bohlander (eds.), *International Law and Power Perspectives on Law, Order and Justice* (Leiden: Martinus Nijhoff Publishers, 2009) 431.

THE PLACE OF INTERNATIONAL LITIGATION 9

to whether jurisdiction has been accepted in a given case, the matter is decided by the Court, whose decision, according to Article 36(6), is final. Only states may be parties in cases before the Court, although Article 65 permits it to give advisory opinions on legal questions for the benefit of international organizations.

Disputes over jurisdiction must be dealt with at the outset and often form a separate stage of the proceedings. The legal issues that can arise when the Court's jurisdiction is challenged vary enormously, but centre on whether there is the necessary consent to the proceedings, as evidenced by a valid legal act. Thus the question may be, for example, whether the instrument alleged to be the basis for jurisdiction is a legally binding agreement[18] or, if that is not denied, whether the current dispute is covered by its terms.[19] Optional clause declarations have proved a particularly fruitful source of problems, a common cause of argument being whether the dispute falls within reservations in either party's declaration, although sometimes the validity of a reservation or of the declaration itself is at issue. Not all cases pose jurisdictional problems, but when they do the Court has to resolve the matter before it can proceed.

The Court's function is described in Article 38(1) of the Statute as 'to decide in accordance with international law such disputes as are submitted to it', and the list of materials which follows, beginning with 'international conventions' and ending with 'judicial decisions' and 'the teachings of . . . publicists', has come to be regarded as the core of modern international law. As well as interpreting and applying the law, the Court must, of course, also resolve any issues of fact that may be in dispute, and for this purpose it receives and assesses documentary and other evidence brought forward by the parties, the quantity of which can sometimes be very large. This may include the evidence of witnesses or experts, and the Court itself may decide to visit the scene, as happened in *Gabčíkovo-Nagymaros Project.*[20]

Under Article 38(2) of the Statute, the Court may at the request of the parties give a decision *ex aequo et bono* instead of on the basis of law. However, this provision, which blurs the distinction between adjudication and conciliation, has yet to be used in practice. A less radical alternative is to refer a case to the Court for a decision on an agreed basis. Like the

---

[18] See, e.g., *Maritime Delimitation and Territorial Questions between Qatar and Bahrain (Qatar v. Bahrain) (Jurisdiction)*, [1994] ICJ Rep. 112; and *(Admissibility)*, [1995] ICJ Rep. 6.

[19] See, e.g., *Oil Platforms (Iran v. United States) (Preliminary Objection)*, [1996] ICJ Rep. 803.

[20] *Gabčíkovo-Nagymaros Project (Hungary v. Slovakia) (Order of 5 February 1997)*, [1997] ICJ Rep. 3.

chambers procedure, this again brings adjudication close to arbitration, although the exercise of the Court's powers must always comply with the Statute. A further possibility is for the Court to extend its function on its own initiative by utilizing equitable considerations of various kinds.[21] While this is not a licence for freewheeling judicial legislation, it introduces a useful element of flexibility into the Court's decisions and may be seen in a number of contemporary cases.

In addition to its contentious and advisory jurisdiction, the Statute entitles the Court to exercise an incidental jurisdiction which includes the power to indicate provisional measures of protection, to allow third states to intervene in proceedings, and to interpret or revise a judgment. Because these powers are conferred by the Statute, they do not require any further expression of consent by the states concerned, and in appropriate circumstances the Court's exercise of its incidental powers can make a constructive contribution to resolving disputes. So, for example, provisional measures of protection can be used to preserve the parties' rights while litigation is in progress. Intervention takes account of the fact that disputes may involve more than two states. And interpretation and revision are designed to address problems that may arise after a decision is given.

When the ICJ decides a case, its judgment is binding on the parties and is final and without appeal. Whether it actually resolves the dispute, however, depends partly on whether the parties accept it – that is, whether they are prepared to treat it as binding – and partly on the precise question referred. States may, for example, prefer to use the Court only to obtain a decision on applicable rules and principles,[22] or to establish whether a dispute is subject to compulsory arbitration,[23] and in such cases further steps may be needed to achieve a final settlement. As regards the acceptance of decisions, difficulties can sometimes arise, especially when a party has tried unsuccessfully to challenge the Court's jurisdiction. On the other hand, disputes are often taken to the Court and resolved there without acrimony because the states concerned want a matter settled. In those cases, just as with arbitration, repudiation of the decision, as well as being unlawful, would merely return the dispute to the political arena and so be self-defeating.[24]

---

[21] Michael B. Akehurst, 'Equity and General Principles of Law', (1976) 25 ICLQ 801.
[22] As in the *North Sea Continental Shelf (Federal Republic of Germany v. Denmark; Federal Republic of Germany v. Netherlands)*, [1969] ICJ Rep. 3.
[23] As in the *Ambatielos (Greece v. United Kingdom) (Merits)*, [1953] ICJ Rep. 10.
[24] For discussion of the effectiveness of judgments see Constanze Schulte, *Compliance with Decisions of the International Court of Justice* (Oxford University Press, 2004).

THE PLACE OF INTERNATIONAL LITIGATION 11

Although the ICJ deals with a relatively small number of cases, it would be a mistake to underestimate its significance. Many treaties provide for the reference of disputes to the Court, and the number of states with optional clause declarations is steadily rising. As commitments of this kind tend to discourage disputes, this 'background' role of the Court is important. Likewise, it is not uncommon for litigation to begin and then for the matter to be settled without the need for a decision. More generally, the advantages of having the ICJ are that its existence relieves states of the need to set up a new tribunal whenever they wish to litigate; that, to the extent that the avoidance and settlement of disputes are assisted by the development of international law, a permanent body has the potential to contribute more to legal progress than intermittent arbitrations; and, finally, that the presence of the Court, together with a simple procedure for establishing its jurisdiction, gives adjudication a prominence in international affairs that it would not otherwise enjoy.

Other courts and tribunals

Among the various courts with specialized jurisdiction the most striking developments have unquestionably been those associated with human rights tribunals, notably the European Court of Human Rights in Strasbourg and the Inter-American Court in San José. Before 1970, the former was rarely employed and the American Court was only inaugurated in 1979. Today, however, the European Court, which was reconstructed in 1998, has an impressive jurisprudence[25] and although the American Court is less busy, it has made its mark with both contentious cases and advisory opinions.[26] In 2004, a third regional court was set up when the African Court of Human and Peoples' Rights in Arusha, Tanzania, was established by a protocol to the 1981 African Charter on Human and Peoples' Rights.[27] The work of the two older regional courts stems mainly from cases brought by individuals, and the African Court is likely to be similar. However, all three courts have jurisdiction over inter-state disputes,

---

[25] For an account of the Court and its work, including the changes made in 1998, see John G. Merrills and Arthur H. Robertson, *Human Rights in Europe*, 4th edn (Manchester: Juris Publishing, 2001).

[26] Jo M. Pasqualucci, *The Practice and Procedure of the Inter-American Court of Human Rights* (Cambridge University Press, 2003).

[27] Gino J. Naldi, 'Aspects of the African Court of Justice and Human Rights', in Duncan French, Matthew Saul and Nigel D. White (eds.), *International Law and Dispute Settlement: New Problems and Techniques* (Oxford: Hart Publishing, 2010) 321.

and both the European and the American courts have dealt with a small number of such cases.

Among other courts and tribunals concerned with cases involving individuals are the International Criminal Court (ICC)[28] and special criminal tribunals such as the International Criminal Tribunals for the former Yugoslavia (ICTY) and for Rwanda (ICTR). The special tribunals were set up by the UN Security Council exercising its powers under Chapter VII of the Charter.[29] As a result, their jurisdiction over war crimes, genocide, and crimes against humanity did not depend on consent from individual states. On the other hand, the ICC's jurisdiction derives from a treaty and in that respect is more limited. Unlike the special tribunals, its jurisdiction is also complementary to that of national courts, which means that it can only act after determining that a competent national court is unwilling or unable to prosecute.[30] Criminal courts are, of course, not designed to handle inter-state disputes, but as an increasingly important arena for international litigation merit at least a passing mention.

Courts with specialized jurisdiction of a quite different type are to be found in the 1982 UN Convention on the Law of the Sea (UNCLOS). For among several new institutions created by the Convention is a new court, the International Tribunal for the Law of the Sea (ITLOS), and a separate subsidiary organ, the Sea-Bed Disputes Chamber (SBDC).[31] ITLOS reflects the preference that many states had for a special court to handle disputes arising out of the new law contained in UNCLOS, and the Tribunal, which decided its first case in 1997,[32] has slowly begun to develop its own jurisprudence.[33] In the same way, the SBDC was set up because the complex arrangements in UNCLOS for exploiting the deep seabed were thought to be unsuitable for adjudication in the main

---

[28] William A. Schabas, *An Introduction to the International Criminal Court* (Cambridge University Press, 2001).

[29] SC Res. 827, UN SCOR, 48th sess., 3217th mtg, UN Doc. S/RES/827 (24 May 1993), as amended by SC Res. 1877, UN SCOR, 64th sess., 6155th mtg, UN Doc. S/RES/1877 (7 July 2009) (ICTY Statute); SC Res. 955, UN SCOR, 49th sess., 5453rd mtg, UN Doc. S/RES/955 (8 November 1994) annex (ICTR Statute).

[30] Rome Statute of the International Criminal Court (opened for signature 17 July 1998, entered into force 1 July 2002) 2187 UNTS 90.

[31] On the role of these organs in the dispute settlement system of the Convention see Natalie Klein, *Dispute Settlement in the UN Convention on the Law of the Sea* (Cambridge University Press, 2005); and Merrills, above n. 3, ch. 8.

[32] *M/V 'Saiga' Case (Saint Vincent and the Grenadines v. Guinea) (Judgment)* (ITLOS Case No. 1, 4 December 1997).

[33] See further Chapter 20 in this volume.

Tribunal. Until very recently, no cases had been decided by the SBDC, but in 2011 the Chamber handed down its first advisory opinion.[34]

The arrangements governing the organization and jurisdiction of ITLOS and the SBDC, together with the law to be applied, are set out in great detail in UNCLOS and show the thinking behind their creation. Among points particularly worth noting are that the jurisdiction of ITLOS is based on the principle of free choice of means, since it depends on states making a declaration nominating the Tribunal as their preferred option.[35] The SBDC, on the other hand, has a jurisdiction that is automatically accepted by all the parties to UNCLOS.[36] Both tribunals, unlike the ICJ, are open not just to states, but also to other entities, including organizations, and each is allowed to split into smaller chambers, in order to provide the parties, if they wish, with a process having some of the advantages of arbitration.

Functioning in a quite different sphere of operations is the WTO dispute settlement system.[37] Set up when the WTO was created in 1994, this complex system exists to deal with disputes relating to trade agreements, and involves a staged process featuring consultation between the parties and the possible use of mediation, conciliation, and arbitration in elaborate provisions that cannot be described in detail here.[38] At the centre of the system, however, is an arrangement for referring disputes to panels made up of independent experts whose role closely resembles that of arbitrators. Panel reports are then liable to review by the members of an organ called the Appellate Body. The latter functions as a kind of standing international trade court, which means that although the WTO procedures place considerable emphasis on negotiating a solution to disputes, the system as a whole is inflected with a strongly juridical character.

A feature of the WTO system is that the principle of free choice of means, normally so important in inter-state dispute settlement, is largely absent. While states are encouraged to settle disputes by agreement, if they fail to do so the complaining party is entitled to request a panel.

---

[34] *Responsibilities and Obligations of States Sponsoring Persons and Entities with respect to Activities in the Area (Advisory Opinion)*, ITLOS Seabed Disputes Chamber, Case No. 17, 1 February 2011.

[35] United Nations Convention on the Law of the Sea (opened for signature 10 December 1982, entered into force 16 November 1994) 1833 UNTS 3 (UNCLOS), Art. 287.

[36] UNCLOS, Art. 188.   [37] See further Chapter 17 in this volume.

[38] See Ernst-Ulrich Petersmann, *The GATT/WTO Dispute Settlement System* (Dordrecht: Kluwer Law International, 1997); Merrills, above n. 3, ch. 9.

When the panel has reported, recourse to the Appellate Body is again a matter of right and when the litigation stage is complete, a political organ, the Dispute Settlement Body, takes over to supervise implementation. Notable, too, is the fact that by subscribing to the WTO Agreement, states not only forgo the remedy of self-help, but also undertake to use its procedures exclusively. So, for example, if a dispute could be dealt with either through the WTO, or through a regional system, the former should receive priority.[39]

Although the WTO system is relatively new, it is now in constant use and regularly demonstrates its value. Trade disputes are complex, often involve crucial shifts in economic and political forces, and have the potential to arouse strong passions.[40] If this makes peaceful methods for resolving such disputes essential, it also means that methods that encourage accommodation are every bit as important as those that aim to enforce rules. That is why the WTO system features diplomatic as well as legal processes. Moreover, in international trade law, as elsewhere, adjudication works best when rules not only are applied impartially, but also enjoy general acceptance. Since the fairness of trade rules depends on the policies of the major players in the WTO, their ultimate responsibility as legislators underpins its system for dispute settlement.

Before leaving this topic it is worth recalling that from time to time tribunals are set up which, although not intended to be permanent, have more than a transient existence. The Iran–US Claims Tribunal, active over three decades, has already been mentioned and a rather similar body was the Eritrea–Ethiopia Claims Commission, which functioned between 2000 and 2009.[41] Established to hear claims alleging violations of international law arising out of the recent war between Eritrea and Ethiopia, the Commission issued a number of awards covering both the use of force and the *jus in bello*, including the treatment of prisoners of war, the selection of targets for aerial bombardment, and the destruction of cultural property.[42] Although tribunals such as these lack the longevity and prestige of their permanent counterparts, the fact that they deal with a series of cases on similar themes enables them to develop a jurisprudence

---

[39] Marrakesh Agreement Establishing the World Trade Organization (opened for signature 15 April 1994, entered into force 1 January 1995) 1967 UNTS 3 (DSU), Annex 2.

[40] See further Chapter 17 in this volume.

[41] John G. Merrills, 'Reflections on Dispute Settlement in the Light of Recent Arbitrations involving Eritrea', in Aristotle Constantinides and Nikos Zaikos (eds.), *The Diversity of International Law* (Leiden: Brill Academic Publishers, 2009), 109.

[42] See further Chapter 15 in this volume.

THE PLACE OF INTERNATIONAL LITIGATION 15

pertaining to their particular area of responsibility. They are thus in a position to contribute to the development of international law and in this respect exercise an influence comparable to that of permanent tribunals.

Judicial decisions and the development of international law

When states decide to have recourse to adjudication it is not because they wish to contribute to the development of international law. Indeed, that prospect may sometimes discourage litigation. But although going to court is normally motivated by a desire to resolve a specific dispute, not to swell international jurisprudence, the decisions of courts and tribunals often have just that effect. As already noted, Article 38(1)(d) of the ICJ's Statute requires the Court to apply 'judicial decisions' together with 'the teachings of ... publicists', although only as 'subsidiary means for the determination of rules of law'. The sources listed in Articles 38(1)(a), (b) and (c), namely 'international conventions', 'international custom', and 'the general principles of law recognized by civilized nations' are thus seen as having a clear priority. Moreover, the reference to judicial decisions in the Statute is preceded by the words 'subject to the provisions of Article 59', which provides for the Court's rulings to have binding force only between the parties and in respect of the particular case, so further limiting their impact. All this might suggest that the Court's decisions, along with those of other international courts and tribunals, have only a minor influence over the development of international law. That view, however, would be mistaken. While it would be wrong to exaggerate their significance, judicial decisions are rather more important in practice than Article 38(1)(d) seems to indicate.

There is no formal system of precedent in international law and no recognized hierarchy of courts. As a result, individual courts and tribunals are under no obligation to follow their own previous decisions, or those of other courts. In practice, however, neither of these features is of any great importance. International judges must justify their decisions and a good justification can be found in previous cases involving a similar point which will, of course, normally have featured prominently in counsel's argument. Other considerations, too, generally favour following precedent because, as a former ICJ judge put it,

> [S]uch decisions are a repository of legal experience to which it is convenient to adhere; because they embody what the Court has considered in the past to be good law; because respect for decisions given in the past makes

for certainty and stability, which are of the essence of the good administration of justice; and (a minor and not invariably accurate consideration)
because judges are naturally reluctant, in the absence of compelling reasons
to the contrary, to admit that they were previously in the wrong.[43]

There are, to be sure, cases that present a novel point where reliance
on precedent is not possible. Such cases obviously call for judicial inspiration emanating from elsewhere. On the other hand, any case of first
impression is likely, on account of its pioneering character, to be itself
a powerful precedent in future cases. Likewise, the fact that individual
arbitral tribunals do not possess a case law of their own prevents them
neither from utilizing the jurisprudence generated by others, nor from
handing down decisions that later tribunals can use in exactly the same
way. It is true that when considering the legal resources a given body
may employ it is vital to pay attention to the terms of its particular
mandate, which may, for example, require priority to be given to certain materials or exclude others. Nevertheless, as a general proposition
it is true to say that the decisions of international courts and tribunals
add to the culture's legal stock and as such increase its assets for the
future.

Particular examples of the role of judicial decisions may be seen by
considering the various sources to which the ICJ is directed in Article
38(1) of its Statute. International conventions, that is to say treaties and
specifically multilateral treaties, are the basic building blocks of modern
international law, and judicial decisions have a bearing on their operation
in several different ways. Although the framework of current treaty law is
to be found in the 1969 Vienna Convention on the Law of Treaties,[44] many
of its provisions derive from customary international law, as evidenced in
judicial decisions, while a number that do not so derive have been applied
in later cases, thereby defining their meaning more sharply and in some
instances confirming their standing as new customary law. As regards
the application of specific treaty obligations, too, judicial decisions have
been significant. So, for example, the key concept of 'fair and equitable'
treatment, which features in more than 2,000 bilateral investment treaties,
is regularly interpreted and applied.[45] And consideration of the meaning

---

[43] Hersch Lauterpacht, *The Development of International Law by the International Court*
(London: Stevens & Sons, 1958), 14.
[44] (Opened for signature 23 May 1969, entered into force 27 January 1980) 1155 UNTS 331.
[45] See, e.g., *Saluka Investments BV* v. *Czech Republic (Partial Award)*, UNCITRAL, 17 March
2006.

of 'an equitable solution' to maritime boundary disputes as required by Articles 74(1) and 83(1) of UNCLOS is a recurring feature of the case law.

Cases that turn on customary international law invariably raise one or both of two questions: has the alleged rule actually been proved to exist? And if it has, what is its content? Now courts and tribunals cannot make customary international law, which rests on the practice of states, supported by *opinio juris*, but in deciding whether there is adequate evidence of these requirements and the scope of any resulting obligation, judicial decisions may be highly significant. From the earliest days of the Permanent Court down to recent rulings of the ICJ, the record is replete with decisions that confirm or deny the existence of disputed customary rules.[46] Where the existence of the rule is not in doubt, the role of courts and tribunals is to give it concrete application, thereby clarifying its content in detail. Among the very many examples of judicial decisions performing this function are the law relating to boundaries and the acquisition of territory, to the use of force in international affairs, and to state responsibility.

Like customary international law, general principles of law are not invented by courts, but emanate from states and more specifically from national legal systems, where utilization of a given principle in a sufficient number of local cultures will merit its recognition as a general principle of international law. In this way a whole series of principles including estoppel, unjust enrichment, the lifting of the corporate veil, the principle *ex injuria jus non oritur*, and a number of others have now been identified.[47] Conversely, as with customary international law, not all such claims have been accepted and so from time to time rulings are given that a particular principle has insufficient acceptance to qualify.[48] Significantly, however, in both types of case it is the decisions of international courts and tribunals that are relied on as evidence of the legal position. Indeed, it may be asserted with some confidence that no general principle can properly be regarded as part of international law until it has received the imprimatur of endorsement in a judicial decision. This is therefore another way in which such decisions are important.

---

[46] For a review of the Court's latest practice see Alberto Alvarez-Jiménez, 'Methods for the Identification of Customary International Law in the International Court of Justice's New Millennium Jurisprudence 2000–2009', (2011) 60 ICLQ 681.

[47] Akehurst, above n. 21.

[48] For example, *Avena and Other Mexican Nationals (Mexico v. US)*, [2004] ICJ Rep. 12.

As well as their contribution to the substantive law, the decisions of courts and tribunals have a major part to play in developing the rules and principles concerned with the administration of international justice, including those relating to a range of procedural matters, from evidence to the review of awards, and to judicial remedies. Thus the early cases administered by the PCA include many decided when the framework for modern arbitration was being established and so contain numerous rulings on these matters that have been influential.[49] In more recent times, this trend has continued, with courts and tribunals of all types being required to address a variety of issues relating to the conduct of litigation. Some of these, such as remedies and the rules of evidence, were already the subject of a good deal of international practice, whereas others, such as the powers of a tribunal to interpret or correct an award, are of a more novel character. The outcome has been the emergence of what has aptly been termed 'a common law of international adjudication',[50] heavily influenced by judicial decisions.

So far in this survey the emphasis has been on the effect of judgments, where the binding part of any decision is to be found, and which therefore contain the most authoritative legal material. Not to be overlooked, however, are the separate opinions that individual judges may be authorized to deliver, if the judgment itself does not represent in whole or in part their unanimous view. Most international courts and tribunals allow such individual expression, and whether in the form of concurring or dissenting opinions they can contribute constructively to legal development. A dissenting opinion may throw the main judgment into sharp relief by indicating the argument that the court rejected. This leads to a better understanding of what was decided and of the wider implications of the case. Moreover, any separate opinion usually presents an alternative line of analysis, or contains a different emphasis, and as such may inspire or invite second thoughts about the point in the future. Thus, while the significance of separate opinions is relatively modest, their role in the application, interpretation, and development of the law should not be discounted.[51]

Writing in 1970, a prominent member of the ICJ observed that 'since specific legislative action with binding effect is not at present possible in

---

[49] For examples see the summaries of the work of the PCA above n. 8.

[50] Chester Brown, *A Common Law of International Adjudication* (Oxford University Press, 2007).

[51] See further Ijaz Hussain, *Dissenting and Separate Opinions at the World Court* (Dordrecht: Martinus Nijhoff Publishers, 1984).

the international field, judicial pronouncements of one kind or another constitute the principal method by which the law can find some concrete measure of clarification or development'.[52] Four decades later, many today would perhaps be more inclined to agree with another distinguished judge, who in 1995 cautioned against attaching too much significance to the words of judges and suggested that international law may now be 'getting beyond the stage when one hoped for more cases before the Court simply to get the law authoritatively stated and developed'.[53] But if there is now a great deal more international law than there used to be, there is, as a consequence, also more for international courts to interpret and apply and a greater demand for their services, owing to the increasing popularity of litigation. In this situation 'judicial pronouncements of one kind or another' have certainly not lost their value.

The wider significance of international litigation

The relevance of law and legal institutions to the settlement of international disputes is a subject which has generated an abundant and conspicuously varied literature. To some, the answer to all the world's problems is to be found in legal codes and international tribunals. To others, observing the disregard for legality which is often a feature of international crises, law at best has a marginal role in world affairs, and at worst is a well-meaning illusion. The strengths and limitations of legal methods bulk large in any review of peaceful methods of settlement and will be examined in some detail in the later chapters. As a background to that survey, and to conclude this introduction to the role of litigation, it may therefore be useful to identify a number of general considerations relating to how international courts and tribunals are currently used.

Two points are worth emphasizing at the outset. The first is that the significance of law in the world and the significance of adjudication are separate questions. While it is difficult to imagine adjudication without law, law without adjudication has long been normal in international affairs. The other point is that when courts and tribunals are utilized they do not operate in isolation, but regularly interact with political institutions and processes. So, for example, the referral of a dispute to the ICJ may be prompted by pressure from an intergovernmental organization, and

---

[52] *Barcelona Traction, Light and Power Company Ltd (Belgium v. Spain) (Second Phase)*, [1970] ICJ Rep. 3, separate opinion of Judge Sir Gerald Fitzmaurice, 65.

[53] Robert Y. Jennings, 'The International Court of Justice after Fifty Years', (1995) 89 AJIL 493, 498.

negotiations between the parties may be needed to establish the question to be asked, and may indeed continue on the substance of the dispute while litigation is in progress. At the post-adjudication stage, likewise technical assistance from the UN, or further negotiations, perhaps assisted by a mediator, may be needed to deal with boundary demarcation or similar issues concerning implementation.

As regards the kinds of dispute that litigation can handle, it is important to recognize that courts and tribunals have no all-embracing ability to solve international problems, but occupy a rather specialized place among the methods of dispute settlement. One reflection of this is that judicial organs, unlike political institutions, cannot be asked to deal with situations in which there is pervasive tension but no specific dispute to be resolved. Moreover, since the normal function of litigation is to end disputes by applying the law, many international problems are unsuited to adjudication because they do not present legal issues or the legal issues are subsumed into political or other considerations. Thus the ICJ has indicated that as a general rule it cannot take cases requiring, say, a political or economic appraisal, rather than a legal ruling,[54] and by the same token it must decline to answer questions that are moot or only of historical interest.[55]

What, then, is the special place of litigation? Because the decision of a court or tribunal is binding, it offers a good way of disposing of a troublesome problem when removing the stumbling block is regarded as more important than the actual result. Conversely, when the result is all-important, litigation is likely to be unattractive because it is simply too risky, a point that is reinforced by the knowledge that a legal ruling is not merely dispositive, but also tends to produce a winner-takes-all type of solution. Sometimes these limitations can be overcome by deliberately seeking only a partial solution or employing a choice of law clause that encourages compromise. However, that is not always possible. It is therefore not surprising that states are notoriously reluctant to make a general commitment to take their disputes to the ICJ, while being willing to do so in individual cases. It also explains the popularity of ITLOS and the WTO panels system, which are designed for a specific purpose, where the parties' commitments are defined and the judges have special expertise.

[54] See *Haya de la Torre (Colombia v. Peru) (Judgment)*, [1951] ICJ Rep. 71.
[55] See *Northern Cameroons (Cameroon v. United Kingdom) (Preliminary Objections)*, [1963] ICJ Rep. 15.

THE PLACE OF INTERNATIONAL LITIGATION 21

As well as finality, litigating a dispute has the benefit of an orderly and rational procedure and a legitimate outcome attributable to prior acceptance of the process by the parties.[56] Given these advantages, few would doubt that litigation is well suited to disputes of a technical character. Whether it is also feasible for inter-state disputes with a political dimension, however, is a more complex question.[57] In dealing with this issue, the ICJ has adopted a principle that is really quite basic to all international adjudication. It is that courts and tribunals exist to resolve legal problems, and so, provided a case presents a legal issue, they are not prevented from deciding it merely because it also has political elements.[58] It is easy to see that such a position is essential if adjudication is to function. Few disputes between states are devoid of political elements because states are political units. Therefore, to concede that a case could not be decided if it had political elements would enable almost any case to be blocked. Quite rightly, this absurd conclusion has been rejected.

Since most international disputes have both a legal and a political dimension, it should be no surprise to find that disputes are sometimes referred to legal and political institutions simultaneously. The Tehran hostages dispute, for example, between the United States and Iran was considered by both the ICJ and the UN Security Council, while in the Nicaragua dispute the Court, the Security Council and the Contadora process, a regional procedure, were all involved. Such cases clearly raise the question of the relationship between legal and diplomatic processes, on which the Court's view, as might be expected, is that each has its own sphere of operation and neither is entitled to priority over the other as a matter of principle.[59] This is useful as far as it goes, but leaves open such questions as whether the legality of the Security Council's actions may be challenged in legal proceedings, a problem to which as yet there is no clear answer.[60]

---

[56] See Richard B. Bilder, 'International Dispute Settlement and the Role of Adjudication', in Lori Fisler Damrosch (ed.), *The International Court of Justice at a Crossroads* (New York: Transnational Publishers, 1987), 155.

[57] See further Chapter 2 in this volume.

[58] For discussion of the cases in which this point has been made see Merrills, above n. 3, ch. 7.

[59] Ibid., ch. 10.

[60] Dapo Akande, 'The International Court of Justice and the Security Council: Is There Room for Judicial Control of Decisions of the Political Organs of the United Nations?', (1997) 46 ICLQ 309.

When the parties to a dispute opt for litigation by, for example, concluding an arbitration agreement, or jointly taking a case to the ICJ, they are, in effect, agreeing that the legal and the political dimensions of their dispute should be separated. When, on the other hand, a case is referred to a court or tribunal unilaterally, it may be a sign that the parties view the dispute differently, the applicant seeing the legal aspect as paramount, but the respondent stressing its political aspects and so regarding it as unsuitable for litigation. As already noted, a court is entitled to decide such a case provided it has jurisdiction, notwithstanding the parties' different perspectives, and will do so by isolating the legal element. In this way, the judges or arbitrators attempt to effect a 'depoliticization' of the dispute which the parties were unable to achieve consensually.

The point just made is critically important, because it means that although the courts and tribunals are formally competent to handle a dispute that presents legal issues, however sensitive its political background, the party whose main concern is with the non-legal elements of the dispute may not be willing to accept a legal decision. This plainly limits the contribution that litigation alone can make to the resolution of international disputes in practice. It is also why appreciating the interaction of legal and political processes is so vital and why, when describing the WTO system, attention was drawn to the role of consultation and the need for trade rules that all states can accept.[61] It is not enough to have courts and tribunals prepared to hand down legal decisions. Persuading states to use them and making their decisions effective are challenges rooted in their political context. These issues are considered further in the next chapter.

Conclusion

International law requires states to settle their disputes using only peaceful means. These include the legal means of arbitration and judicial settlement, both of which are designed to produce binding decisions, usually on the basis of international law. Arbitration employs a tribunal set up by the parties, whereas judicial settlement utilizes a standing court such as the ICJ. In either form the parties must have consented to the exercise of jurisdiction by the court or tribunal before a decision can be given. Although the main function of litigation is to resolve disputes, the fact that decisions must be justified by reference to legal principles means that they also assist the development of international law. Litigation, however,

[61] See further Chapter 17 in this volume.

is not suitable for all international disputes, and states sometimes disagree on whether it should be used in a particular case. Consequently, litigation is not a panacea, but when the necessary conditions are present, notably a dispute of the appropriate type and acceptance of the tribunal's jurisdiction, it can make a genuine contribution to international law and justice.

2

Litigation versus dispute resolution through political processes

SHIRLEY V. SCOTT

'Litigation', Shabtai Rosenne once observed, 'is but a phase in the unfolding of a political drama.'[1] While this is true, not every political drama includes a litigation phase. International law provides a range of methods of dispute resolution, including negotiation, mediation, and conciliation, and, despite the recent growth in the number of international courts and tribunals, it remains far more usual for states to settle differences through diplomacy and bilateral negotiations. The objective of this chapter is therefore to map some of the factors that national decision-makers could be expected to take into account when deciding whether or not to introduce a litigation phase into an unfolding political drama or the resolution of an international dispute. Examples will be drawn primarily from the International Court of Justice (ICJ or Court), as the 'classic' international court. The chapter begins, however, by establishing a distinction between a political and a legal perspective on third-party dispute resolution in international law.

Two competing paradigms within which to view international litigation

Let us begin by considering two competing world views or paradigms within which to consider the issue of litigation versus political resolution. First is the international law framework. Within this framework the starting point is the array of dispute resolution options listed in Article 33(1) of the UN Charter and the range of international courts and tribunals that states now have at their disposal. Questions may then be asked about the resolution of disputes via these methods. In this first framework, the

---

I should like to thank Orli Zahava for her valuable research assistance.

[1] Shabtai Rosenne, *The Law and Practice of the International Court, 1920–1996: The Court and the United Nations Vol. I*, 3rd edn (The Hague: Martinus Nijhoff, 1997), 3.

objective of using lawful methods to bring about the peaceful resolution of a dispute is a given and the main subjects of interest are the methods or institutions of dispute resolution. Our second framework is the political framework, and in this the real objective of those involved is far less clear and may not be known even to the international lawyers working on the case. Indeed, there are likely to be multiple objectives – per state – and it is conceivable that dispute resolution is not top of the list.

Why might a state not have the resolution of a dispute as its primary objective? It may be that no resolution appears possible, or simply that the state is in a better position with the matter in dispute than it will be under the terms of any likely resolution. Whereas the goal of resolving a dispute is centre stage in the international law paradigm, it may not even exist in the political framework. Indeed, although within the framework of international law a dispute is said to be a matter of objective determination,[2] in political terms one party may deny that any dispute exists. Similarly, even the resolution of the legal dispute may not mean that the parties accept that the dispute is ended and harmonious relations restored. Until that acceptance has been achieved, international lawyers may emphatically declare that it is resolved, but their declarations ring hollow. International law is ultimately a facilitator of dispute resolution, at the mercy of those it seeks to assist.

It is worth reviewing these points at the beginning of our investigation because it is all too easy to assume that states will want their disputes to be resolved, that there is something inherently noble about resolving a dispute.[3] Note that, even in international law terms, Article 33(1) of the Charter does not accord states a positive obligation to resolve all their disputes, but refers to the peaceful resolution of any dispute 'the

---

[2] As the ICJ said in the *International Status of South West Africa (Advisory Opinion)*, [1950] ICJ Rep. 65, 74,

> [I]t is not sufficient for one party to a contentious case to assert that a dispute exists with the other party. A mere assertion is not sufficient to prove the existence of a dispute any more than a mere denial of the existence of the dispute proves its non-existence. Nor is it adequate to show that the interests of the two parties to such a case are in conflict. It must be shown that the claim of one party is positively opposed by the other.

[3] In contrast, John Collier and Vaughan Lowe premise their textbook on the assumption that 'disputes – or, more strictly, the conflicts from which disputes emerge – are not wholly undesirable but have certain valuable characteristics, and that the proper function of law is to manage, rather than to suppress or resolve, conflict.' John Collier and Vaughan Lowe, *The Settlement of Disputes in International Law: Institutions and Procedures* (Oxford University Press, 2000), 1.

continuance of which is likely to endanger the maintenance of international peace and security'. What is sometimes held up as a model example of international co-operation – the Antarctic Treaty System – is premised on the non-resolution of the sovereignty dispute.

If our question is going to be that of the factors that would encourage a state to turn to international litigation, we are going to have to work within the political framework, albeit that nested within politics is the realm of international law. Several decades ago, Coplin wrote on the World Court when describing what he referred to as the 'international bargaining process',[4] and I think that that term – or perhaps the seemingly softer one of 'diplomacy' – remains useful when seeking to understand state behaviour in relation to the Court. It serves to underline the point that seeking a judgment from the ICJ is rarely an end in itself but a step in a broader political process. The Court may play a decisive role in international bargaining even where the case does not reach judgment on the merits.

Is the International Court of Justice an appropriate 'model' international court?

The ICJ is often treated as the classic international court, but one of the most striking developments in the international legal system since the end of the cold war has been the proliferation of international courts and tribunals.[5] The proliferation has been such that some 'envision a world where the international rule of law hinges on an integrated network of international courts that bring increased predictability and accountability to matters of economy and crime, war and peace'.[6] In this context, the ICJ could no longer be said to be typical of the courts and tribunals in operation – the number of bodies granting standing to non-state entities, for example, now far exceeds those whose jurisdiction is restricted to

---

[4] William D. Coplin, 'The World Court in the International Bargaining Process', in Robert W. Gregg and Michael Barkun (eds.), *The United Nations System and its Functions: Selected Readings* (Princeton: D. Van Nostrand, 1968), 317.

[5] Cesare P. R. Romano, 'The Proliferation of International Judicial Bodies: The Pieces of the Puzzle', (1999) 31 *New York University Journal of International Law and Politics* 709, 709.

[6] Daniel Terris, Cesare P. R. Romano, and Leigh Swigart, *The International Judge: An Introduction to the Men and Women Who Decide the World's Cases* (Hanover, NH: Brandeis University Press, 2007), 222.

states.[7] This raises the question whether conclusions drawn from state behaviour in relation to the ICJ are transferable to other courts and tribunals. There is a school of thought that the ICJ is not a particularly useful model for dispute resolution.[8] Findings from analysis of the ICJ may not be transferable to other contemporary international courts and tribunals.

Viewing all international courts and tribunals as functionally equivalent may be misleading. Romano has usefully divided international courts and tribunals into four types, only one of which he regards as classic international courts, or state-only courts, whose primary function is the resolution of inter-state disputes. In this category he places only the ICJ, the International Tribunal for the Law of the Sea (ITLOS) and the World Trade Organization (WTO) dispute settlement system. Second are human rights courts such as the European Court of Human Rights, the Inter-American Court of Human Rights and the African Court of Human and Peoples' Rights. Their purpose is to provide legal remedies to individuals whose human rights have been violated; according to Romano, viewing them as dispute settlers ignores their vital role as custodians and developers of the law. Third, and most numerous, are courts of regional economic and/or political integration, including the European Court of Justice, the Court of the European Free Trade Agreement and the Caribbean Court of Justice. These courts have many roles, including deciding disputes between organs of the community and member states, and between individuals or corporations and community organs or member states, on the content and implementation of community law. Fourth are international criminal courts, such as the International Criminal Court (ICC) and the International Criminal Tribunal for Rwanda (ICTR),[9] which do not really resolve disputes between states but function to rule on international crimes and, where appropriate, to mete out criminal punishment.

---

[7] Romano, above n. 5. Alvarez has cautioned us against assuming that this equates to 'real access'. José E. Alvarez, 'The New Dispute Settlers: (Half) Truths and Consequences', (2003) 38 *Texas International Law Journal* 405, 411–12.

[8] The view of Barry Carter, for example. See his remarks in 'Comparative Analysis of International Dispute Resolution Institutions', (1991) 85 *Proceedings of the Annual Meeting* (*American Society of International Law*) 64, 64.

[9] Cesare Romano, 'The United States and International Courts: Getting the Cost-Benefit Analysis Right', in Cesare Romano (ed.), *The Sword and the Scales: The United States and International Courts and Tribunals* (Cambridge University Press, 2009), 424.

It would therefore seem that, as the question we are addressing is that of the circumstances in which a state could be expected to choose to initiate litigation against another state, there are several reasons why it remains valid to begin by focusing on the ICJ. First, when a state is making such a choice, in many instances it does not have as great a choice of forum from which to choose as might seem to be the case from an initial glimpse at the spread of courts now in existence. Second, the World Court is the oldest of the courts and tribunals and, as their number has increased, it is still valid to analyse their emergence and development as institutions similar to, or with features contrasting those of, the ICJ. The United Nations is an atypical international organization insofar as it is both global and multi-issue, and yet few would suggest that the United Nations would be unimportant to a study of international organizations. And, third, the ICJ remains the only international court with general jurisdiction to hear a case on any question of public international law involving states, and is of systemic importance because of the possibility of its judgments being enforced by the UN Security Council. This chapter will therefore primarily draw on examples of state practice in relation to the ICJ, with some reference also to participation in dispute resolution processes of the WTO.

Factors that may influence a decision as to whether to initiate litigation

Recourse to the law in resolving disputes is usually chosen because it offers one or more of the parties certain short- or long-term benefits.[10] The central part of this chapter will therefore set out a series of questions that national decision-makers could usefully pose where the option of initiating litigation is on the table, in order to evaluate whether litigation would in the specific circumstances at hand be a good option. Of course, the question is more likely to have been placed on the table in a country whose legal culture involves plenty of litigation. By way of example here, the United States could be said to have a far more litigious legal culture than China. In traditional Chinese legal culture, litigation was something to be avoided.[11] The amount of litigation is changing, but both its domestic situation and its involvement with the ICJ remain

---

[10] Collier and Lowe, above n. 3, I.
[11] Esther Lam, *China and the WTO: A Long March towards the Rule of Law* (Austin, TX: Wolters Kluwer, 2009) 12.

in contrast to the United States, where, domestically, litigation has taken hold to such an extent that commentators have referred to a 'litigation crisis'.[12] There may not exactly be a litigation crisis in terms of the United States initiating a plethora of cases before the ICJ, but it is worth bearing in mind that the United States has, by international standards, been a very active participant in the life of the Court.[13]

States rarely turn to litigation as a first step in an emerging political drama. ICJ cases involving boundary disputes have, for example, usually followed resort to military conflict that has either resulted in stalemate or led the states involved to determine that further conflict would be too costly.[14] New Zealand spent a decade using bilateral negotiations and debate in the UN before resorting to the Court in the *Nuclear Tests* case;[15] the British and West German applications in the *Fisheries Jurisdiction* cases[16] followed more than ten years of intensive negotiations.[17]

States tend naturally to preserve their sovereign options,[18] and litigation imposes restraints on the range of arguments and moves a government can make.[19] Litigation is generally risky and time-consuming and its outcome unpredictable,[20] so the odds are weighted against a decision in favour of litigation. Where national decision-makers *do* decide to initiate litigation it can therefore be expected that they have determined their answer to one of the following questions in quite strong terms. But note that the results of the considerations below are in a complex relationship with each other, and so in most cases there is no simple correlation between

---

[12] G. Alan Tarr, *Judicial Process and Judicial Policymaking*, 5th edn (Boston: Wadsworth, 2010), 213.

[13] See further Chapter 5 in this volume.

[14] Robert O. Keohane, Andrew Moravcsik, and Anne-Marie Slaughter, 'Legalized Dispute Resolution: Interstate and Transnational', (2000) 54 *International Organization* 457, 480.

[15] *Nuclear Tests Cases (Australia v. France, New Zealand v. France) (Merits)*, [1974] ICJ Rep. 457.

[16] *Fisheries Jurisdiction (United Kingdom v. Iceland) (Merits)*, [1974] ICJ Rep. 3; *Fisheries Jurisdiction (Federal Republic of Germany v. Iceland) (Merits)*, [1974] ICJ Rep. 175.

[17] Dana D. Fischer, 'Decisions to Use the International Court of Justice: Four Recent Cases', (1982) 26 *International Studies Quarterly* 251, 255–6.

[18] Charles N. Brower, 'The Case for Cross-Border Litigation: The Continent that Sues Together Hews Together', (1974) 68 *American Society of International Law Proceedings* 239, 241.

[19] Max Sorensen, 'The International Court of Justice: Its Role in Contemporary International Relations', (1960) 14 *International Organization* 261, 275.

[20] Terry D. Gill, *Litigation Strategy at the International Court: A Case Study of the Nicaragua v. United States Dispute* (Dordrecht: Martinus Nijhoff, 1985), 52.

the answer to any one of the questions below and a decision to initiate litigation. There will be exceptions to every rule, and the variables differ depending on the government and issue in question. The list begins with those questions that are predominantly legal, veers into those with a good mixture of both the legal and political elements, and then moves to those that are predominantly political.

1 Would we be likely to win the case if there were a judgment on the merits?

Despite the fact that up to half of all cases taken to the ICJ do not result in a judgment on the merits,[21] a state contemplating litigation that perceives itself as having the upper hand in moral terms must also be confident that this advantage is mirrored in the relative strength of its legal case. Although by Article 38(2) of its Statute the ICJ is able to decide a case on the basis of equity and good conscience (*ex aequo et bono*) rather than in accordance with international law if the parties agree thereto, it has never done so. Australia did not want to go to the ICJ in the 1950s when in dispute with Japan over pearling, because officials in Canberra and London believed that Japan was in a stronger legal position.[22] Judgement is required to assess the legal strength of a government's position, and government lawyers play an important role in this determination.

Even if the answer were not in the affirmative, it is possible that participation in the development of the law may be considered an advantage. Indeed, it may on occasion be more useful to clarify the law than to 'win' the case. According to Rovine, the *North Sea Continental Shelf* cases demonstrated the possibilities of framing questions to give rise to legal advice rather than a final determination.[23] The very active participation of Europe and the United States in WTO dispute resolution means that these countries have played a role in shaping the relevant law, which is of great value when subsequent disputes are

---

[21] Erwin Müller and Patricia Schneider, 'The ICJ 1945–2001: Empirical Findings about its Performance and Recommendations for an Improvement of Its Efficiency', (2007) 3 *Review of International Law and Politics* 71, 80.

[22] Shirley V. Scott, 'The Inclusion of Sedentary Fisheries within the Continental Shelf Doctrine', (1992) 41 ICLQ 788.

[23] Arthur W. Rovine, 'The National Interest and the World Court', in Leo Gross (ed.), *The Future of the International Court of Justice Vol. I* (Dobbs Ferry, NY: Oceana, 1976) 324.

settled out of court, 'in the shadow of the law'.[24] It also means that one's own lawyers develop valuable expertise that non-participants do not develop.[25] On the other hand, there may be risk associated with clarifying that one's policy preferences or actions are not supported by law.

Assessments of one's likely success before an international court may take into account the make-up of the current bench and the record of the individual judges. The careers of some judges reflect more of a political inclination than those of others – having been an independent professor or lawyer, for example, may have been less politically infused than having worked for one's foreign service. Judicial writings of judges might indicate which way they would lean in a potential case.[26] It seems that in some cases states do make a thorough analysis of the individual judges on the bench but in others they do not.[27]

Middle powers – and, we might like to think, great powers – might weigh up not only their short-term gains but the longer-term benefit of referring a dispute to third party dispute resolution and being prepared to accept, and abide by, a potentially unfavourable outcome. The United Kingdom offered an important example of this as long ago as the 1870s, when it was not only prepared to submit disputes with the United States arising from the Civil War to arbitration, but accepted terms in the Treaty of Washington that would almost certainly ensure that it lost the *Alabama* arbitration.[28] Britain duly paid the $15,500,000 in gold awarded by the arbitral tribunal,[29] the approximate equivalent of £150 billion in today's terms.[30]

Although the United States decided no longer to accept the optional clause following the *Nicaragua* case,[31] it has been party to a number of cases before the ICJ since then,[32] and it is possible that the case encouraged

---

[24] See further Chapter 17 in this volume.

[25] See Shirley V. Scott, 'International Law and Developing Countries', in Robert Denemark (ed.), *The International Studies Encyclopedia Vol. 7* (Oxford: Wiley Blackwell, 2010) 4110.

[26] Fischer, above n. 17, 259.   [27] Ibid.

[28] Allan Nevins, *Hamilton Fish: The Inner History of the Grant Administration Vol. II*, rev. edn (New York: Frederick Ungar, 1957), 483.

[29] A. M. Stuyt, *Survey of International Arbitrations, 1794–1989*, 2nd edn (Dordrecht: Martinus Nijhoff, 1972), 96.

[30] Tom Bingham, 'The *Alabama* Claims Arbitration', (2005) 54 ICLQ 1, 1.

[31] *Military and Paramilitary Activities in and against Nicaragua (Nicaragua v. United States) (Jurisdiction and Admissibility)*, [1984] ICJ Rep. 392.

[32] See further Chapter 5 in this volume.

developing countries to think that the Court would not be biased against them. Incorporating a litigation phase into a political drama with a view to the long-term benefits of demonstrating support for the Court may, however, be a consideration that comes into play more often when a state is in the role of respondent than when deciding whether or not to initiate proceedings.

2 What is the attitude of the potential respondent state or states to the International Court of Justice and its jurisdiction?

The attitude of a state or group of states towards third-party dispute resolution in international law – and hence the prospects of their accepting the jurisdiction of the ICJ at all or in relation to a specific case – is shaped, very broadly, by the historical, political, and cultural experience and traditions of those states, their legal culture, and foreign policy traditions.[33] Although the geographical spread of the users of the Court has always been far-flung,[34] Asian and African states were notably underrepresented in the early years of the ICJ.[35] There has in recent years been a significant increase in the number of cases involving states from these regions.

If the potential respondent state has not accepted the jurisdiction of the ICJ and is unlikely to do so if invited, it may not be possible to bring a case before the ICJ, whether one wants to or not and whether or not one is in a strong position in relation to the merits. Sometimes the potential respondent state does not even accept that there is a dispute, as in the lead-up to the *Ambatielos* case involving Greece and the United Kingdom.[36] It is conceivable that a state may nevertheless move to initiate proceedings in such scenarios, perhaps for one of the reasons canvassed below, but this may not always bear fruit. When the Federal Republic of Yugoslavia in 1999 attempted to bring the United States before the ICJ in relation to NATO bombing during the Kosovo crisis, Yugoslavia tried to argue

---

[33] Gill, above n. 20, 50.

[34] Hugh Thirlway, 'The International Court of Justice 1989–2009: At the Heart of the Dispute Settlement System?', (2010) 57 *Netherlands International Law Review* 347, 349.

[35] R. P. Anand, 'Attitude of the "New" Asian-African Countries toward the International Court of Justice', in Frederick E. Snyder and Surakiart Sathirathai (eds.), *Third World Attitudes Toward International Law: An Introduction* (Dordrecht: Martinus Nijhoff Publishers, 1987) 163.

[36] *Ambatielos (Greece v. United Kingdom) (Merits)*, [1953] ICJ Rep. 10. See Shabtai Rosenne, *The World Court: What It Is and How It Works*, 4th edn (Dordrecht: Martinus Nijhoff, 1989), 174.

that the Court had jurisdiction on three grounds, one of which was the Genocide Convention, but the United States had entered a reservation to that provision and the Court found that it did not have jurisdiction in this case.[37] It is difficult to see that Yugoslavia gained much from this attempt.

Where the other state is likely to agree to submit the dispute to the Court by special agreement, then the chances are either that it thinks it is in the stronger legal position or that it is ready to compromise. It has often been with respect to cases specially submitted to it by ad hoc agreement that the ICJ has been truly effective.[38] Such arbitral-like cases, for example, the *Minquiers and Ecrehos* case,[39] tend to be characterized by decisive legal issues and low political cost.[40]

3 If there were a judgment in our favour, would the other party/ies accept it and comply with the ruling?

Here we reach the question of compliance. There is the possibility of winning, but also of the judgment not being satisfactorily implemented. This may be because the other party does not have the means or expertise to comply or because the state might come under intense domestic pressure not to comply or perhaps to comply in some nominal way. This is more likely where the respondent state has a low regard for the ICJ and its role. In respect of the *Diplomatic Staff in Tehran* case (1980),[41] the Court decided in favour of the United States, but the dispute was not resolved until the hostages had been released, and this was eventually brought about through mediation by Algeria. Other cases in which a decision against an unwilling state failed to settle a dispute include the *Fisheries Jurisdiction* cases (1974)[42] and the *Nicaragua* case.[43]

---

[37] *Legality of Use of Force (Yugoslavia* v. *United States) (Provisional Measures)*, [1999] ICJ Rep. 761.

[38] Mark W. Janis, *An Introduction to International Law*, 3rd edn (Gaithersburg: Aspen, 1999), 128.

[39] *Minquiers and Ecrehos (France/United Kingdom)*, [1953] ICJ Rep. 47.

[40] Janis, above n. 38, 130.

[41] *United States Diplomatic and Consular Staff in Tehran (United States* v. *Iran) (Judgment)*, [1980] ICJ Rep. 3.

[42] *Fisheries Jurisdiction (United Kingdom* v. *Iceland) (Merits)*, [1974] ICJ Rep. 3; *Fisheries Jurisdiction (Federal Republic of Germany* v. *Iceland) (Merits)*, [1974] ICJ Rep. 175.

[43] Above n. 31. See John G. Merrills, *International Dispute Settlement*, 4th edn (Cambridge: Grotius Publications, 2005), 175.

The evidence shows that states have complied with ICJ judgments in a majority of, though by no means all, contentious cases; compliance with provisional measures, however, has not been as good.[44] In deciding whether to initiate proceedings, national decision-makers need to consider what they would do if the other party or parties did not comply fully with the judgment, as well as to look in the mirror to consider whether they themselves would be happy falling into line with an unanticipated ruling. The fact that the other party might not accept a judgment and comply with the ruling does not necessarily rule out a decision to litigate if the objective is not resolution of the dispute per se.

4 How suitable is this issue for resolution through litigation?

This raises the question of the nature of the dispute itself and has both a legal and a political dimension. From a legal perspective, although the ICJ does not shy away from a case simply because it involves politics – if it did so, it might not be left with many cases to decide – the Court has operated on the principle that if the question referred to the Court is such that it cannot be resolved by applying legal criteria, then, unless its competence has been extended by the parties, it must decline to adjudicate.[45]

From a political perspective, international litigation may be more capable of resolving some matters than others. There is the possibility that even if the other parties were to comply, this might not resolve the dispute, or that virtually by definition the dispute is not amenable to any degree of compromise. This is most likely to be the case where the political salience of the issue is high – and if the objectives of the players are mutually incompatible. If, for example, the dispute centres on competing claims to sole use of a tract of territory and the nature of those claims is such that neither side could contemplate surrendering its claim, a judicial decision in favour of one party is by definition incapable of resolving the dispute.

5 Might recourse to the Court serve to level the playing field in our favour?

It is a fact of life that the more powerful more readily have their needs and wants satisfied than the less powerful. Recourse to the ICJ may serve to place a small or weak state on a more level bargaining field. Nauru initiated

[44] Constanze Schulte, *Compliance with Decisions of the International Court of Justice* (Oxford University Press, 2004).
[45] Merrills, above n. 43, 167.

proceedings against Australia in the ICJ in respect of a dispute over the rehabilitation of certain phosphate lands worked out before Nauru attained independence. The case was settled out of court by Australia agreeing to pay A$107 million in compensation over a number of years.[46]

On the other hand, a developing country is far less likely than a developed country to initiate litigation, for one or more of several reasons. First, while law can serve to level the playing field, it is also the case that the law at any point in time is more likely to reflect the interests of the great powers than the small states. In response to the refusal of the United States to extradite the Shah of Iran, the Ayatollah Khomeini pointed to the bias in international law when he asked,

> What kind of law is this? It permits the US Government to exploit and colonize peoples all over the world for decades. But it does not allow the extradition of an individual who has staged great massacres. Can you call it law?[47]

Second, if the developing or least-developed country is in dispute with one relatively more powerful it is quite possible that the more powerful state will link the subject of the litigation to another issue, such as military assistance, foreign aid, or trade. Paraguay filed an application with the ICJ in 1998 with respect to alleged violations by the United States of the Vienna Convention on Consular Relations. The ICJ found that, prima facie, it had jurisdiction,[48] and unanimously indicated provisional measures providing that Angel Breard, a Paraguayan national on death row in the United States, not be executed pending the final decision in the proceedings.[49] The US State of Virginia nevertheless went ahead with the execution. Although Paraguayan officials initially declared that they would pursue a binding Judgment against the United States, they withdrew the case following an apology from the US government.[50] A week later, in what to some observers appeared to be a related event, the United States and Paraguay signed a memorandum of understanding on the protection of intellectual property.[51]

---

[46] Nii Lante Wallace-Bruce, *The Settlement of International Disputes: The Contribution of Australia and New Zealand* (The Hague: Martinus Nijhoff, 1998), 200.

[47] Interview with Ayatollah Khomeini, *Time*, 7 January 1980, at 27, cited in Richard Falk, 'The Iran Hostage Crisis: Easy Answers and Hard Questions', (1980) 74 AJIL 413, 413.

[48] *Vienna Convention on Consular Relations (Paraguay v. United States of America) (Order of 9 April 1998)*, [1998] ICJ Rep. 248, [34].

[49] Ibid., [41].   [50] Ibid.

[51] South–North Development Monitor, 'Paraguay – A Trade-off with the United States', 16 November 1998, available at www.sunsonline.org/trade/process/followup/1998/11160798.htm.

Third is the enormous cost, legal expertise, and energy that goes into the preparation and presentation of a case before an international court. The Secretary-General's Trust Fund to Assist States in the Settlement of Disputes through the International Court of Justice was established in 1989, a voluntary ITLOS Trust Fund was established in 2001, and the Advisory Centre on WTO Law was established in 2001; all of these are designed to facilitate widespread participation. The issues surrounding the vast disparity in legal capacity are complex, however, and these initiatives may not be enough to entice a developing or least-developed state to choose litigation over other policy options.

6 Would our move to litigate likely serve as a catalyst to the other state/s being prepared to negotiate a settlement?

As we have already observed in the *Nauru* case, the introduction of a litigation phase into a dispute may be enough to bring a state – including those relatively more powerful – to the negotiating table. In instituting proceedings against India in 1973, Pakistan viewed the ICJ as a vehicle for breaking a stalemate in respect of the prisoners of war case, and after negotiations were resumed, Pakistan dropped the case.[52] Iran filed an application instituting proceedings against the United States in relation to the destruction of an Iranian civil aircraft by the United States warship USS *Vincennes* in 1988. The case was settled out of Court.[53]

7 Might referral of this dispute to the Court help the government to deal with domestic political pressure either from the public or from interest groups?

Domestic political manoeuvring may have very great bearing on determining a decision to pursue litigation, although the weight that domestic opinion brings to bear on the process likely varies among states. Executives presumably place a high priority on retaining office.[54] During the long months of the Iranian hostage crisis, public opinion in the United States

---

[52] *Case Concerning Trial of Pakistani Prisoners of War (Pakistan v. India)*, 1973 ICJ Rep. 328; see Fischer, above n. 17, 271–2.

[53] '*Aerial Incident of 3 July 1988 (Iran v. United States)*', (1996) 50 *ICJ Yearbook* 161.

[54] Todd L. Allee and Paul K. Huth, 'Legitimizing Dispute Settlement: International Legal Rulings as Domestic Political Cover', (2006) 100 *American Political Science Review* 219, 222.

no doubt influenced decisions of the Carter administration;[55] turning to the ICJ meant that it could at least show that it was doing something. In the case of the WTO, interested non-state actors tend to be wealthy firms or industry groups, often with substantial political constituencies, who have been quick to complain about allegedly unfair and discriminatory actions by their competitors abroad.[56] Although states retain formal gatekeeping authority in the GATT/WTO system, they thus often permit actors in civil society to set much of the agenda.[57] According to Collier and Lowe, in respect of the *Gulf of Maine* case,[58] it was local, as opposed to national, public concern that encouraged both governments to agree to litigate.[59]

Domestic populations tend to have relatively hawkish policy preferences.[60] It may not, therefore, be a desire to win on the legal merits that prompts a state to pursue litigation so much as a preparedness to offer concessions together with a perception that it would be unable to do so in direct bilateral negotiations.[61] A theme in the literature is that of the ICJ giving governments an excuse for compromising. In respect of the *North Sea Continental Shelf* case,[62] Danish authorities believed that the judicial process that preceded the resumption of negotiations enabled the government to make territorial concessions that would otherwise have been impossible because of strong domestic sentiments.[63] According to a study by Allee and Huth based on evidence taken from litigation over territorial disputes, leaders seek legal dispute settlement in situations in which they anticipate sizeable domestic political costs should they make concessions in bilateral negotiations.[64] International legal rulings thus provide 'political cover', enabling them to counter domestic political opposition to a controversial settlement.[65] In respect of trade, WTO dispute settlement processes have sometimes served as a means of getting round domestic

---

[55] David Patrick Houghton, *US Foreign Policy and the Iran Hostage Crisis* (Cambridge University Press, 2001), 2–4.

[56] Keohane et al., above n. 14.   [57] Ibid., 486.

[58] *Delimitation of the Maritime Boundary in the Gulf of Maine Area (Canada/United States)*, [1984] ICJ Rep. 246.

[59] Collier and Lowe, above n. 3, 9. It was then domestic public opinion that precluded either country from compromising. Andrea Kupfer Schneider, 'Not Quite a World without Trials: Why International Dispute Resolution Is Increasingly Judicialized', (2006) 1 *Journal of Dispute Resolution* 119, 126.

[60] Allee and Huth, above n. 54, 222.   [61] Ibid., 223.

[62] *North Sea Continental Shelf (Federal Republic of Germany* v. *Denmark; Federal Republic of Germany* v. *Netherlands)*, [1969] ICJ Rep. 3.

[63] Fischer, above n. 17, 271.

[64] Allee and Huth, above n. 54, 219. See further Chapter 10 in this volume.

[65] Ibid., 219.

political resistance to trade reform. Even decisions against the United States may have constituted means by which to catalyse decisive action by efficient, export-oriented US producers, and so are deemed useful by those elites that believe trade liberalization to be ultimately in the national interest.[66]

8 Could litigation be useful as a delaying tactic?

Although bargaining might continue while the case is before the ICJ, the intervention of the Court generally puts a temporary halt – potentially of several years – to the bargaining process.[67] Proceedings may be protracted, in part simply because of the procedures and working methods of the Court, a situation exacerbated by a full docket. The Court has not normally managed to dispose of more than three cases a year, so a situation in which there are, say, fifteen pending cases may mean a considerable wait.[68] Where delay is not sought, the likely length of proceedings may militate against a decision to refer a case to the ICJ or else an effort might be made to try to speed up the proceedings. When Burkina Faso and Niger referred their border dispute to the ICJ in 2010 the special agreement stipulated that the two states would submit their initial memorials within nine months of seizing the Court and counter-memorials nine months after the memorials; the two states would begin demarcation of the adjudicated boundary within eighteen months of the ICJ decision. Burkina Faso and Niger might well have sought to speed up the proceedings – the sixth boundary case from Africa – because the African Union Border Programme was encouraging African states to define their boundaries clearly by 2012.[69]

On the other hand, where delay is perceived as desirable, this delay can generally be extended through strategic planning on the part of either side. When Japan invited Australia to take a dispute over pearling to the ICJ in the 1950s, Australia agreed in principle, but then failed to accept the terms of the proposed *compromis*, permitting years of delay until the dispute was effectively superseded by developments in manufacturing in tandem with change to the relevant law.[70] Delay may take place at subsequent stages, even during the implementation of the ruling – as has

---

[66] Judith L. Goldstein and Richard H. Steinberg, 'Negotiate or Litigate? Effects of WTO Judicial Delegation on US Trade Politics', (2008) 71 *Law and Contemporary Problems* 257.

[67] Coplin, above n. 4, 327.   [68] Thirlway, above n. 34, 392.

[69] Julian Martin Thaler, 'Burkina Faso and Niger Refer Border Dispute to International Court of Justice', September 2010, available at http://web.worldbank.org/.

[70] Scott, above n. 22.

often been the case in respect of the WTO.[71] As with other considerations, the potential attraction of delay should not be viewed in isolation, since the judgment could impact the dispute in a way that outweighs the benefit of delay.[72]

9 Could resort to litigation damage relations with the other state/s or worsen the dispute?

Litigation may well be perceived as an unfriendly act,[73] although it is important to note that the bulk of a government's international legal business is likely to be generated by neighbours and allies, and where the general relationship is strong it may be quite possible to quarantine a dispute from the broader bilateral relationship. The significance of this factor probably depends to a considerable extent on the power disparity between the two parties. Where the disparity is great it may not ultimately be in the interests of the weaker state to win a legal dispute against a greater power if it stands to lose elsewhere in the relationship.

On the other hand, the dispute itself may already be causing considerable damage to the relationship. Tommy Koh has made the point that because of the tendency of Asian governments – particularly those of north-east Asia – to insist on resolving differences through bilateral negotiations rather than litigation, the disputes often remain unresolved even years later. The result is that the bilateral relationship as a whole is contaminated by what may ultimately be relatively minor issues.[74] In some instances, any constructive moves towards resolution of a dispute might represent a worthwhile step.

10 Would recourse to litigation help us to win the support of global public opinion and would that be helpful in this situation?

Some cases seem to represent the publicization of an issue as much as an attempt at resolution, insofar as it would seem predictable that the losing party would be unlikely to comply even with a decision in its favour or

---

[71] Krzysztof J. Pelc, 'Why Do Some Countries Get Better WTO Accession Terms than Others?', (2011) 65 *International Organization* 639, 658.

[72] Rovine, above n. 23, 323.

[73] See discussion in Philip C. Jessup, 'International Litigation as a Friendly Act', (1960) 60 *Columbia Law Review* 24.

[74] Tommy Koh, 'International Law and the Peaceful Resolution of Disputes: Asian Perspectives, Contributions, and Challenges', (2011) 1 *Asian Journal of International Law* 57.

to be able to do so in a way that settled the grievance.[75] Examples of very high-profile cases of this type would seem to include Iran's suit against the United States for the destruction of oil platforms in the Persian Gulf,[76] and the *Lockerbie* cases[77] brought by Libya against the United States and the United Kingdom.[78] Fischer considered that the United Kingdom and West Germany appeared to use the ICJ in the *Fisheries Jurisdiction* cases primarily as a means of communicating their bargaining position both to Iceland and to 'world public opinion'.[79] The initiation of litigation may focus critical attention on the opponent in the dispute.[80]

Conclusions: reaching a decision after reviewing the various factors

This chapter has suggested that a decision by national decision-makers to initiate the submission of a dispute to third-party dispute resolution is generally a pragmatic one, based on a calculation of potential costs and benefits. The discussion has posed ten questions, whose answers national decision-makers could usefully review before deciding to initiate international litigation. There are clear interconnections among these, which would seem to beg the question of how the decision-makers could reconcile answers with seemingly contradictory implications. Here it is suggested that a calculation of risk often is – or should be – made, premised on the foreign policy goals that are potentially to be addressed via litigation. Importantly, is success to be defined in terms of winning the legal dispute or of both 'winning' the litigation and resolving the conflict, or is it perhaps possible either that litigation could lead to a satisfactory outcome even without a 'win' or that a 'win' in court could worsen the dispute? Could the issuing of provisional measures in itself be regarded as a successful outcome? Second, how would an unfavourable outcome be defined and what would be the possible consequences of that? And, third, is the favourable or unfavourable outcome more likely in the current situation and what are the risks of getting it wrong?[81]

[75] Keohane et al., above n. 14, 481.
[76] *Oil Platforms (Iran v. United States) (Judgment)*, [2003] ICJ Rep. 161.
[77] *Questions of Interpretation and Application of the 1971 Montreal Convention arising from the Aerial Incident at Lockerbie (Libyan Arab Jamahiriya v. United Kingdom) (Preliminary Objections)*, [1998] ICJ Rep. 9; *Questions of Interpretation and Application of the 1971 Montreal Convention arising from the Aerial Incident at Lockerbie (Libyan Arab Jamahiriya v. United States) (Preliminary Objections)*, [1998] ICJ Rep. 115.
[78] Keohane et al., above n. 14, 481.   [79] Fischer, above n. 17, 266.   [80] Ibid., 266, 271.
[81] Terry Gill poses a similar list of questions. Gill, above n. 20, 51.

The difficulty for researchers in this field is, of course, how to know which of the various factors may have been decisive to the outcome in any particular decision to initiate litigation, since there may not be a publicly available written record of the deliberations. It is worth noting in conclusion that the questions canvassed in this chapter are essentially practical, empirical questions. Whether that *should* be the case, whether national decision-makers *should* make a pragmatic calculation of cost, benefit, and risks in each scenario, or whether they *should* want to avail themselves more often of the litigation option, is a normative question the answer to which I shall leave to others.

3

National and international litigation:
partners or competitors?

CHRISTOPHER WARD

> In fact the place of international law in municipal court cases today is a quiet and often unnoticed revolution in the nature and content of international law. It means that the strictly dualistic view of the relationship between international law and municipal law is becoming less serviceable and the old well defined boundaries between public international law, private international law and municipal law are no longer boundaries but grey areas.[1]

Robert Jennings identified the relationship between international law and domestic law in these terms in 1996. The intersection between public international law and domestic legal systems continues to challenge the accepted boundaries of each tradition.

One 'grey area' that has growing prominence is the use by private litigants of parallel international and domestic litigation strategies in issues that involve questions of public international law. This practice can arise because of the increasing intersections between public disputes concerning states and related private disputes between corporations and individuals. It can arise because the rights of individuals today have a sound base in international human rights law and may be vindicated before a domestic court. Finally, it can arise because of the existence and willingness of public interest litigants with interests in public international law outcomes to utilize domestic litigation strategies in the pursuit of those objectives.

The increasing intersection of public international law and domestic legal systems brings challenges both to the state in question and to the litigants involved. When a private litigant brings a public international law issue before a domestic court many obstacles are placed in the path of success. Disputes involving public international law remain one of the most difficult issues for domestic courts, and relatively unclear judicial

---

[1] Robert Y. Jennings, 'The Judiciary, International and National, and the Development of International Law', (1996) 45 ICLQ 1.

42

standards often provide uncertain and ambiguous outcomes for the litigants involved. Equally, the states involved are likely to find that underlying public international law issues are ventilated in an untraditional forum not of its choice. This chapter questions the motives that lead a litigant to choose domestic litigation over more traditional methods of agitating public international law issues.

The Australian experience is particularly pertinent because of the existence of domestic cases that have been pursued in relation to international incidents that have also formed the subject matter of cases before the International Court of Justice (ICJ). In *Horta* v. *Commonwealth*[2] and *Petrotimor* v. *Commonwealth*,[3] issues that related directly to the Timor Gap dispute between Australia, Indonesia, and East Timor were considered by the Australian High Court and the Full Court of the Federal Court. In *Humane Society International* v. *Kyodo Senpaku Kaisha Ltd*,[4] issues of Japanese whaling in Antarctic waters were considered by the Federal Court while the issue remained under diplomatic negotiation and subsequently became the subject of an application to the ICJ by Australia.

Formidable barriers are typically placed in the path of litigants who raise disputed issues of public international law before domestic courts. As this chapter will show, those barriers have historically proven to be almost insurmountable. However, it now seems that the first cracks have appeared, such that parallel domestic litigation may not be a lost cause and may be able to assist in the resolution of international disputes. The Australian experience is exemplary in this regard. It may therefore be expected that parties to disputes that raise questions of public international law will increasingly consider domestic litigation as a viable method of dispute resolution.

The chapter will first consider the traditional characterization of obstacles that confront private litigants who seek to raise questions of public international law before domestic (common law) courts. It will then consider the Australian experience of cases of that type, before finally considering the lessons to be drawn from the *Avena* litigation in the United States.

Barriers to domestic litigation

The barriers to domestic litigation relating to concurrent international litigation have traditionally been discussed by courts in terms of either 'justiciability' or the 'act of state' doctrine.

---

[2] (1994) 181 CLR 183. [3] [2003] FCAFC 83. [4] [2008] FCA 3.

44   CHRISTOPHER WARD

In *Underhill* v. *Hernandez*,[5] the US Supreme Court considered the ability of a US citizen to maintain proceedings against an officer of Venezuela who had refused to issue a passport. Chief Justice Fuller articulated what is now understood as the act of state doctrine as follows:

> Every sovereign State is bound to respect the independence of every other sovereign State, and the courts of one country will not sit in judgment on the acts of the government of another done within its own territory. Redress of grievances by reasons of such acts must be obtained through the means open to be availed of by sovereign powers as between themselves.

The act of state doctrine was confirmed by the US Supreme Court in *Banco Nacional de Cuba* v. *Sabbatino*.[6] However, in *Sabbatino* the Supreme Court retreated somewhat from an absolute rule, noting that international law did not itself require the application of a doctrine of act of state, thus suggesting a more flexible approach to the application of the act of state doctrine in the United States.

In 1962, in the US Supreme Court decision of *Baker* v. *Carr*,[7] Justice Brennan developed a related, but distinct, doctrine of justiciability. There, he characterized particular issues that were 'non-justiciable' before a domestic court: the conduct of foreign relations, the existence and duration of treaties, the existence of a state of war, and the recognition of foreign governments as holding valid political power over foreign territory.[8]

In *Buttes Gas and Oil Co* v. *Hammer*,[9] Lord Wilberforce in the United Kingdom's House of Lords was faced with a claim for defamation by Buttes, a Californian oil company. It alleged that it had been defamed in circumstances that could have required the judicial resolution of an underlying question of sovereign title to disputed territory. The defendant sought a permanent stay of proceedings because it was alleged that the issues involved the foreign relations between the United Kingdom and Iran.

Lord Wilberforce approached the matter on the basis that an absolute rule of non-justiciability was inappropriate, saying,

> The present case is more nearly within the category of boundary disputes between states. As to these it would be too broad a proposition to say that the mere emergence in an action here of a dispute as to the boundaries of states is sufficient to preclude the jurisdiction of the court.[10]

However, his Lordship went on to articulate a 'wider principle':

---

[5] 168 US 250 (1897).   [6] 376 US 398 (1964).   [7] 396 US 186 (1962).
[8] Ibid., 211–15.   [9] [1982] AC 888.   [10] Ibid., 926–7.

So I think that the essential question is whether... there exists in English law a more general principle that the courts will not adjudicate upon the transactions of foreign sovereign states. Though I would prefer to avoid argument on terminology, it seems desirable to consider this principle, if existing, not as a variety of 'act of state' but one for judicial restraint or abstention.[11]

Lord Wilberforce remarked that such a principle is 'not one of discretion, but is inherent in the very nature of the judicial process'.[12]

In the House of Lords, in *R* v. *Bow Street Metropolitan Stipendiary Magistrate, ex parte Pinochet Ugarte*,[13] Lord Nicholls said,

> The act of state doctrine is a common law principle of uncertain application which prevents the English court from examining the legality of certain acts performed in the exercise of sovereign authority within a foreign country or, occasionally, outside it. Nineteenth century dicta (for example, in *Duke of Brunswick* v. *King of Hanover*, 2 HLCas. 1 and *Underhill* v. *Hernandez*, 168 US 250) suggested that it reflected a rule of international law. The modern view is that the principle is one of domestic law which reflects a recognition by the courts that certain questions of foreign affairs are not justiciable (*Buttes Gas and Oil Co.* v. *Hammer* [1982] AC 888) and, particularly in the United States, that judicial intervention in foreign relations may trespass upon the province of the other two branches of government: *Banco Nacional de Cuba* v. *Sabbatino*, 376 US 398.[14]

Lord Nicholls further noted that

> More recently the courts in the United States have confined the scope of the doctrine to instances where the outcome of the case requires the court to decide the legality of the sovereign acts of foreign states: *Kirkpatrick & Co. Inc.* v. *Environmental Tectonics Corporation International*, 110 S.Ct. 701.[15]

More recently, in *Kuwait Airways Corporation* v. *Iraqi Airways Co.*,[16] the principle of non-justiciability was further criticized, Lord Nicholls apparently limiting the doctrine to cases in which there were no judicial or manageable standards by which to judge the issues.[17]

Thus it now appears that the apparently formidable barriers of non-justiciability and act of state may be more limited than was once understood. Shaw provides a useful taxonomy, describing 'act of state' as one,

---

[11] Ibid., 931.   [12] Ibid., 932.   [13] [1998] UKHL 41; [2000] 1 AC 61.
[14] Ibid., 106–7 (with whom Lord Hoffmann agreed).
[15] Ibid.   [16] (Nos. 4 and 5) [2002] UKHL 19; [2002] 2 WLR 1353.   [17] Ibid., [26].

narrow aspect of non-justiciability.[18] The different doctrines continue to influence the extent to which national courts can impact on international dispute settlement. Although there are some trends towards the recognition of international legal principles and matters of a necessarily international character being addressed within a domestic setting, a key difficulty has been ongoing confusion, both judicially and scholarly, regarding the differences and overlap between the various aspects of non-justiciability, as well as state immunity.

Within the Australian context, although it has been said that the categories described by Brennan J in *Baker* v. *Carr* ought not to be treated as absolute,[19] the cases discussed below make it clear that Australian courts have historically demonstrated a reluctance to determine disputes that relate to the nature of government actions in the field of foreign affairs. In *Re Ditfort ex parte Deputy Commissioner of Taxation (NSW)*,[20] Gummow J considered the applicability of the concept of justiciability to the conduct of Australia's foreign affairs. His Honour held that some matters fell outside the domain of judicial interpretation and resolution; these included statements by the government as to the existence of a state of war, the status of foreign territory, and the identity of a foreign government. However, His Honour did not conclude that all matters involving an element of public international law were not justiciable.[21]

While the 'political question' doctrine is a creation of common law, similar bars to litigation exist in civil law states, albeit through a multitude of considerations and different terms. The French *acte de gouvernement* remains the most widely recognized of these barriers internationally, largely due to the rather distinct French judicial system, although it is certainly not alone among civil law jurisdictions in its similarity to the more familiar 'act of state'. The Italian *atto politico* and *actos politicos* shared by several South American states are expressions of a similar judicial reticence towards consideration of matters with international legal consequences.[22] Greek and Japanese courts have also made reference to sovereign acts of state and the non-justiciability of matters that concern the exercise of foreign affairs powers by the executive.[23] Importantly, these civil law 'acts of state', while similar to justiciability principles outlined by

---

[18] Malcolm N. Shaw, *International Law* (Cambridge University Press, 2008), 186.

[19] See, e.g., *Stewart* v. *Ronalds*, [2009] NSWCA 277.

[20] (1988) 83 ALR 265; (1988) 19 FCR 347.   [21] (1988) 19 FCR 347, 368–9.

[22] Daniele Amoroso, 'A Fresh Look at the Issue of Non-justiciability of Defence and Foreign Affairs', (2010) 23 *Leiden Journal of International Law* 933, 934.

[23] Ibid.; *Sakata* v. *Japan*, 13 Keishu 3225, Case No. 1959 (A) No. 710.

Baker v. *Carr* and *Buttes Gas*, are not as broad in their application and, at least in the French experience, have an effect of uncertain extent regarding the acts of foreign governments.[24]

The difficulty is that doctrines of judicial restraint remain clothed in ambiguity and judicial discretion. As Lindell has said,

> Much remains to be done in identifying the proper use of justiciability in limiting judicial review and the precise factors that help to explain why some issues do not lend themselves to judicial adjudication ... [C]riteria suggested ... will not be sufficient by themselves if the concept of justiciability is to be much more than a discretionary and subjective tool by which a court may abstain from deciding difficult issues in cases where it is otherwise properly seised of jurisdiction at the instance of a competent litigant.[25]

As a consequence, the potential for national litigation to influence the outcome of international dispute settlement, and more specifically international litigation, is unpredictable.

Examples from the Australian experience

It may be acknowledged from the outset that the engagement of any national court with questions of international law, and particularly the contribution of a national court to the resolution of international disputes, will largely be determined by the constitutional and national law structures within which the particular court operates. The contribution of national courts may potentially form part of the domestic pressure experienced by a government as to what steps it should take in resolving an international dispute. Another contribution of national courts could be in the interpretation and application of international law within the national sphere, which could attract state responsibility if it entails a violation of the relevant legal principles or could provide further force to the position of the state in its interactions with other governments. It is, then, the very fear of taking on these proactive roles that may instead prompt a court to abstain from engaging with international disputes.

---

[24] See August Reinisch, *International Organizations before National Courts* (Cambridge University Press, 2004), 96; Ildikó Marosi and Lóránt Csink, 'Political Questions in the United States and in France', in Matthias Hoe (ed.), *Studia Iuridica Caroliensia*, Vol. 4 (Budapest: Kapa Mátyás, 2009) 121.

[25] Geoffrey Lindell, 'Justiciability', in Tony Blackshield et al. (eds.), *The Oxford Companion to the High Court of Australia* (Oxford University Press, 2001) 392.

48 CHRISTOPHER WARD

Two aspects of Australian judicial reticence in international matters were tested in the litigation that surrounded the Timor Sea dispute involving Australia, Indonesia, and East Timor. In 1989, Indonesia and Australia signed the Timor Gap Treaty.[26] By that treaty, jurisdiction to control oil and gas exploitation in an area of the Timor Sea between Australia and the territory of what is now Timor Leste was divided between Australia and Indonesia. The treaty was immediately condemned by many as illegitimate because it involved Australia dealing with a state that had occupied territory illegally by force.

That argument, together with arguments relating to the right of self determination, was put squarely to the ICJ by Portugal in the *Case Concerning East Timor* in proceedings instituted on 27 February 1991.[27] By its judgment of 30 June 1995, the ICJ declined to consider the substance of the dispute on the basis that to do so would involve it determining the rights and obligations of a third state (Indonesia), which was not before the Court.[28]

In *Horta* v. *Commonwealth*, the plaintiff (José Ramos Horta, subsequently to become the president of Timor Leste) alleged in the High Court that the Timor Gap Treaty was illegal, and was hence outside the executive power of the Commonwealth such that the treaty and its implementing legislation were invalid.[29] Five questions were posed to the full bench of the High Court, including questions of whether or not the allegations raised a justiciable controversy. However, the Court determined that even if the treaty was invalid for the purposes of international law, the domestic legislation under challenge remained a valid exercise of the external affairs power under the Constitution.[30] It was therefore unnecessary for the Court to consider the arguments relating to justiciability.

That was not the case in *Petrotimor* v. *Commonwealth*, where considerations of justiciability and the act of state doctrine were the primary basis on which the domestic litigation was resolved adversely to the plaintiff.[31]

---

[26] Treaty between Australia and the Republic of Indonesia on the Zone of Cooperation in an Area between the Indonesian Province of East Timor and Northern Australia [Timor Gap Treaty] (opened for signature 11 December 1989, entered into force 9 February 1991) 1991 ATS, No. 9.

[27] *Case Concerning East Timor (Portugal* v. *Australia)*, [1995] ICJ Rep. 90.

[28] Ibid., 105. Relying on the well-accepted principle of *Monetary Gold Removed from Italy in 1943 (Italy* v. *France, United Kingdom and United States)*, [1954] ICJ Rep. 19.

[29] (1994) 181 CLR 183.   [30] Australian Constitution, s. 51(xxix).

[31] (2003) 126 FCR 354.

Petrotimor Companhia de Petroleos SARL was a Portuguese company that held a petroleum exploration concession from Portugal dated 31 January 1974. At the time it granted the concession, Portugal was the colonial administering power of the territory that subsequently became Timor Leste. At that time, Portugal expressly claimed title to the seabed and resources of the so-called Timor Gap up to a point at least equal to the median line between Australia and the then Portuguese Timor.

Petrotimor brought its claim in the Australian Federal Court, primarily alleging that the concession amounted to property rights that had been acquired, other than on just terms, under the Petroleum (Australia–Indonesia Zone of Co-operation) Act 1990, which gave effect to the 1989 Timor Gap Treaty. Petrotimor argued that the Seas and Submerged Lands Act 1973 (Cth) defined the limits of Australia's maritime claims by reference to the 1958 Convention on the Continental Shelf (which in turn referenced the median line for delimitations of disputed continental shelves).[32] It was argued that the limits of Australia's continental shelf had been defined by legislation such that Petrotimor's concession must have been validly granted by Portugal and that the subsequent implementation of the Australia–Indonesia Zone of Co-operation Act effected an acquisition of the property rights created by the concession.

Petrotimor's status was of course inexorably linked to the territorial claims of Portuguese Timor, and subsequently Timor Leste, since it is clear that one of the primary reasons that the Petrotimor concession was granted was to demonstrate the legitimacy of the Portuguese territorial claims. Petrotimor's claim in the Australian Federal Court therefore raised directly considerations of justiciability, given that its resolution would inevitably require that court to consider questions relating to the competing claims of Australia and Timor Leste to the disputed seabed resources.

The matter was referred to a full court of the Federal Court. The court dismissed the claims, but was divided as to its reasons for that course.

Black CJ and Hill J suggested that because, in their view, it was an essential element of Petrotimor's claim that the validity of the Portuguese concession be tested, the claim failed because domestic courts are precluded from questioning rights granted by a foreign sovereign.[33] Black CJ

---

[32] Convention on the Continental Shelf (opened for signature 29 April 1958, entered into force 10 June 1964) 499 UNTS 311, Art. 6.

[33] *Petrotimor* v. *Cth*, (2003) 126 FCR 354, [42]–[43], applying the principle in *Potter* v. *Broken Hill Proprietary Co. Ltd* (1906) 3 CLR 479.

and Hill J also concluded that determination of the controversy by the court would create embarrassment to the executive in the conduct of its foreign relations and was therefore non-justiciable within the meaning of the doctrine of *Buttes Gas and Oil Co* v. *Hammer*.[34]

Beaumont J in a separate opinion considered that the matter was not a federal matter, such that the Federal Court lacked jurisdiction to entertain the claim at all. His Honour also held that the claims amounted to an attempt by Petrotimor to enforce a foreign governmental interest and thereby fell foul of the principle in *Attorney General (United Kingdom)* v. *Heinemann Publishers Australia Pty Ltd*.[35] Significantly though, His Honour did not join with the majority in relying on the 'act of state' or 'embarrassment' grounds.

The approach of three senior judges of the Federal Court to Petrotimor's claims demonstrates the reticence with which domestic courts often approach litigation that is directly related to parallel international disputes. On any view of it, the litigation in *Petrotimor* was complex, raising extremely complicated questions of substantive law as well as pushing the then-understood boundaries of judicial restraint. The decision of the court has been the subject of criticism,[36] including most recently by the Full Court of the Federal Court itself.[37] In the Australian High Court decision of *Thomas* v. *Mowbray*,[38] Gummow J and Crennan J described the principle of non-justiciability on which the decision of the Federal Court was based as a 'slippery term of indeterminate reference'.[39]

Some attempts to rely on domestic litigation to agitate matters of international concern will always clearly fall on the wrong side of the divide. Thus a case such as *Re Limbo*[40] in the Federal Court, in which Citizen Limbo (Mr Lindon) sought to restrain Prime Minister Bob Hawke and other parliamentarians from unlawfully allowing Australian land to be used at Pine Gap for the purposes of participating in the US missile defence arrangements because the use of nuclear weapons was illegal at

---

[34] [1982] AC 888. See the discussion in Cameron Sim, 'Non-justiciability in Australian Private International Law: A Lack of Judicial Restraint?', (2009) 10 *Melbourne Journal of International Law* 9.

[35] [1988] HCA 25; (1988) 165 CLR 30.

[36] E.g., Richard Garnett, 'Foreign States in Australian Courts', (2005) 29 *Melbourne University Law Review* 704.

[37] *Habib* v. *Commonwealth*, [2010] FCAFC 12. See particularly comments by Perram J at [30] and [40].

[38] (2007) 233 CLR 307.   [39] Ibid., 354.   [40] Unreported G160 of 1989.

international law, will be properly dismissed as an abuse of the process of the court, or as non-justiciable. Claims of a political character, claims that seek to compel the executive to take a particular stance in diplomacy, claims brought by a person who lacks standing, will all be legitimately dismissed.

A similar result would be reached in litigation of the type brought in *Thorpe* v. *Commonwealth*.[41] There, the plaintiff argued that the Commonwealth owed a fiduciary duty to Aboriginal people on the basis that their lands had been illegally invaded and that the Aboriginal people had been the subject of genocidal treatment. He sought an order in the nature of a positive injunction requiring the Commonwealth to move the UN General Assembly to obtain an advisory opinion from the ICJ as to the status of the rights of Aboriginal people in Australian land claims. The matter was determined by Kirby J sitting alone in the High Court, on the basis that there was no matter disclosed within the meaning of the Constitution. His Honour held, correctly, that the court had no power to control the manner in which the Commonwealth acted in foreign relations. It was not possible for a court to compel the Commonwealth to make diplomatic representations at the United Nations. The conduct of Australia's international relations was a matter solely within the power of the executive.

However, the decisions of the Federal Court in the *Humane Society International* litigation suggest that not every domestic case that is brought in parallel with an international dispute will be denied a hearing. Like *Petrotimor*, *Humane Society* involved an application made in domestic law closely related to an existing international dispute. Humane Society International commenced proceedings in the Federal Court seeking injunctions and declarations under the Environment Protection and Biodiversity Conservation Act 1999 (Cth) (the EPBC Act). The injunctions were sought to restrain whaling activities in the whaling sanctuary within Australia's claimed exclusive economic zone adjacent to Australia's claimed Antarctic Territory.

As in *Petrotimor*, the applicant was presented with formidable barriers to relief. The first substantial issue was the service of originating process on the foreign respondent. Allsop J initially refused leave to serve the statement of claim outside Australia.[42] His Honour noted that the Attorney-General had advised the court that

[41] (1997) 144 ALR 677.
[42] *Humane Society International Inc.* v. *Kyodo Senpaku Kaisha Ltd*, [2005] FCA 664.

an assertion of jurisdiction by an Australian court over claims concerning rights and obligations found in the EPBC Act, in the view of the Government, would or may provoke an international disagreement with Japan, undermine the status quo attending the *Antarctic Treaty*, and be contrary to Australia's long term national interests.[43]

His Honour went on to hold that those views were 'about considerations that are peculiarly within the field of the Executive Government, as involving political judgments (using that phrase in the broad sense) and lacking legal criteria permitting judicial assessment'.[44] His Honour held that because of those considerations, and the likely futility of any ultimate orders that the court could make, he should not exercise his discretion to authorize service of the originating process outside Australia.

That decision was overturned on appeal by the Full Court of the Federal Court.[45] Black CJ and Finklestein J held that:

> We take it to be settled law that provided the jurisdiction of the Federal Court is engaged by an action in respect of subject-matter with which the Court can deal, and the action is instituted by an applicant who has standing, and the action is not oppressive, vexatious or otherwise an abuse of process and, finally, the Court can assume jurisdiction over the defendant (by service or submission), the Court cannot refuse to adjudicate the dispute.[46]

Moore J dissented on the basis that the orders were ultimately unenforceable and therefore futile.

Following substituted service on the respondent, in *Humane Society International Inc. v. Kyodo Senpaku Kaisha Ltd*,[47] Allsop J granted the injunctive and declaratory relief sought. His Honour did so in the light of the views of the majority of the Full Court as to the irrelevance of the political context of the dispute and the fact that the respondent did not appear to resist the claim. His Honour was satisfied on the material provided by the applicant that the orders were soundly made.

As Klein and Hughes have noted,[48] it is curious and unfortunate that the court did not separately address the issues of embarrassment that were so central to the decision of the court in *Petrotimor*. The court decisions

---

[43] Ibid. [14].   [44] Ibid. [24].

[45] *Humane Society International Inc. v. Kyodo Senpaku Kaisha Ltd*, [2006] FCAFC 116.

[46] Ibid. [10].   [47] [2008] FCA 3.

[48] Natalie Klein and Nikolas Hughes, 'National Litigation and International Law: Repercussions for Australia's Protection of Marine Resources', (2009) 33 *Melbourne University Law Review* 163, 198–204.

are not easy to reconcile, and perhaps reflect the express conferral of public interest standing given by the EPBC Act. At the time of the decision, the legitimacy of Japan's so-called 'scientific' whaling programme was directly at issue in diplomatic bilateral and multilateral negotiations with Japan. Equally, as the Attorney-General had submitted to the court, Australia's Antarctic claim remains hotly disputed, and any attempt to enforce the injunctive orders of the court in the adjacent waters would have the potential severely to disrupt the diplomatic balance that surrounds the status of that claim.

Lessons learned from the Australian experience

Because the boundaries of the doctrine of judicial embarrassment remain uncertain, private litigants will be forced to continue to embark upon relatively risky litigation strategies that test the boundaries of the relationship between public and private international law. However, notwithstanding those caveats, it may be said that the decisions such as *Humane Society International*[49] reflect a more generous approach to questions of judicial restraint than was historically the case. They may lead to more frequent attempts by private litigants to utilize domestic court processes in the context of related public international law disputes.

It can be seen that there are two quite distinct rationales for the maintenance of domestic litigation that involves questions of public international law. One is public interest litigation of the type seen in the *Re Limbo* and *Humane Society International* cases. There, a plaintiff seeks to agitate the underlying issues of an international dispute by relying on such domestic common law and statutory rules as may be called in aid in the particular case.

The second basis for this type of domestic litigation is the private litigant who seeks to vindicate not public rights, but private rights, which are premised on a particular view of the underlying international dispute. Such cases include *Petrotimor*, *Buttes Gas*, and *Kuwait Airways Corporation*.

In both types of case, courts in Australia have historically been very reluctant to engage with the issues of public international law. In the case of litigation involving private rights, such judicial reluctance adds to the potential for serious injustice to be worked on an injured party.

---

[49] See also *Habib* v. *Commonwealth*, [2010] FCAFC 12.

54   CHRISTOPHER WARD

International law provides limited remedies to injured individuals. Compensation for injury is based on rules of state responsibility, which recognize the traditional primacy of the state and diplomatic considerations over individual rights. Yet domestic courts are often the only realistic forum in which serious wrongs may be righted. While it is clear that there are some disputes that are simply not amenable to judicial resolution, where disputes of private rights are clearly articulated those disputes ought not to be avoided by courts on the basis of uncertain and essentially discretionary doctrines.

Examples from the United States

The United States is in a somewhat unusual position, having developed a significant body of law based on the modern revival of the Alien Tort Claims Act (usually known as the 'Alien Tort Statute' (ATS)).[50] The ATS provides simply that

> [T]he district courts shall have original jurisdiction of any civil action by an alien for a tort only, committed in violation of the law of nations or a treaty of the United States.

Largely dormant for many years, as is now well documented the ATS provides a means by which the courts of the United States may consider directly allegations of breaches by aliens of the 'law of nations', wherever those breaches are alleged to have occurred. The role of US courts and the extent of limitations on the scope of the ATS have been the subject of significant judicial and academic consideration.[51]

The ATS was given modern life by the decision of the Second Circuit Court of Appeals in *Filártiga* v. *Peña-Irala*.[52] There the court considered allegations that the torture and murder in Paraguay of Joel Filártiga by the defendant (a Paraguayan official) amounted to a breach of the law of nations. The case was brought by the sister and father of the deceased.

In upholding the claim, the court relied strongly on the need for plaintiffs to demonstrate the existence of a clear breach of the law of nations, commenting that

---

[50] Originally part of the Judiciary Act 1789, 28 USC § 1350.
[51] E.g., Gerald P. McGinley, 'Of Pirates and Privateers – The Historical Background of the Alien Tort Claims Act with Some Suggestions for Its Future Use', (1992) 21 *Anglo-American Law Review* 138, 141.
[52] [1980] USCA2 576; 630 F 2d 876 (2nd Cir., 1980).

NATIONAL VS INTERNATIONAL LITIGATION

The requirement that a rule command the 'general assent of civilized nations' to become binding upon them all is a stringent one. Were this not so, the courts of one nation might feel free to impose idiosyncratic legal rules upon others, in the name of applying international law. Thus, in *Banco Nacional de Cuba* v. *Sabbatino*, 376 U.S. 398, 84 S.Ct. 923, 11 L.Ed.2d 804 (1964), the Court declined to pass on the validity of the Cuban government's expropriation of a foreign-owned corporation's assets, noting the sharply conflicting views on the issue propounded by the capital-exporting, capital-importing, socialist and capitalist nations. Id. at 428–30, 84 S.Ct. at 940–41.[53]

The Court went on to say in *Filártiga* v. *Peña-Irala*:

Here, the nations have made it their business, both through international accords and unilateral action, to be concerned with domestic human rights violations of this magnitude.[54]

Following the decision in *Filártiga*, the ATS was used to found a series of claims, many of which settled without final trial.[55] These included the cases *In re Holocaust Victim Assets*,[56] *In re Austrian and German Bank Holocaust Litigation*,[57] *Beanal* et al. v. *Freeport-McMoran, Inc.* et al.,[58] and the *Unocal* cases, culminating in *Doe* v. *Unocal*.[59]

In *Jose Francisco Sosa* v. *Humberto Alvarez-Machain* et al.,[60] a full attack on the ATS was mounted by the US executive, which filed a lengthy amicus brief that opposed the *Filártiga* interpretation of the ATS.[61] The US Supreme Court clearly retreated from an expansive view of the ATS, but stated that

The jurisdictional grant is best read as having been enacted on the understanding that the common law would provide a cause of action for a modest number of international law violations with a potential for personal liability.[62]

---

[53] Ibid., [18].   [54] Ibid., [49].

[55] For a useful discussion of historical justice claims, including claims under the ATS, see Beth Stephens et al., *International Human Rights Litigation in US Courts*, 2nd edn (Leiden: Martinus Nijhoff, 2008), particularly 543–6.

[56] No. CV-96-4849, 2001 US App. LEXIS 30154 (2d Cir. 2001).   [57] No. 98 Civ. 3938.

[58] [1999] USCA5 1266; 197 F 3d 161 (5th Cir. 1999).

[59] [2003] USCA9 100; 395 F 3d 978 (9th Cir. 2003).

[60] [2004] USSC 2852; 542 US 692 (2004).

[61] The arguments are considered in detail in Anne O'Rourke and Chris Nyland, 'The Recent History of the Alien Tort Claims Act: Australia's Role in its (Attempted) Downfall', (2006) 25 *Australian Year Book of International Law* 139.

[62] 542 US 692 at 30.

Although the court did not directly address the issues of justiciability, it was clearly aware of the potential for tension. It deliberately limited actions to those based on 'laws of nations' that were uniformly and strictly recognized by all, or at least an overwhelming majority of, nations. It expressly acknowledged the collateral consequences of making actionable a private wrong based on a breach of the law of nations. Those collateral consequences included the need to be wary of impinging on the primary responsibility of the executive and the legislature for the conduct of the foreign relations of the United States. The court said:

> Since many attempts by federal courts to craft remedies for the violation of new norms of international law would raise risks of adverse foreign policy consequences, they should be undertaken, if at all, with great caution.[63]

Similarly restrictive views of comity have caused the failure of other attempts to litigate human rights issues before US courts.[64] However, the case of *Alperin* v. *Vatican Bank*[65] is suggestive of a more flexible approach to questions of comity and restraint under the political question doctrine. There, the Court of Appeals for the Ninth Circuit was faced with an application by the plaintiffs against the defendant alleging the wrongful retention of wealth looted by the Nazi regime during the Second World War. The Court of Appeals for the Ninth Circuit held that resolution of the property claims, despite arising from a clearly political context, was not barred by the political question doctrine. The court noted that

> Although the political question doctrine often lurks in the shadows of cases involving foreign relations, it is infrequently addressed head on.[66]

In language reminiscent of the views of Beaumont J in *Petrotimor*, the Court said,

> Indeed, in our system of separation of powers, we should not abdicate the court's Article III responsibility – the resolution of 'cases' and 'controversies' – in favor of the Executive Branch, particularly where, as here, the Executive has declined a long-standing invitation to involve itself in the dispute.[67]

The Court then proceeded directly to address the political question doctrine, concluding that it did not bar the resolution of the property claims, although noting that the claim faced other formidable difficulties.

---

[63] Ibid., at 33.

[64] E.g., *Ungaro-Benages* v. *Dresden Bank AG*, 379 F 3d 1227 (11th Cir. 2004).

[65] 410 F 3d 532, 544 (9th Cir. 2005).   [66] Ibid.   [67] Ibid.

Indeed, the case against the Vatican Bank was ultimately dismissed on the basis that the Vatican Bank was an instrumentality of Vatican City and therefore protected by the doctrine of sovereign immunity.[68]

Concluding remarks

International courts and tribunals remain a primary avenue by which principles of international law are publicly articulated and developed. In particular, the existence in Europe of sophisticated international judicial machinery means that international, and not national, courts play a more significant role in the resolution of disputes with an international character.

However, outside the European court context, parties with grievances that raise questions of public international law have poor prospects of agitating the issue before an international tribunal. In those cases, national courts will play an increasingly important role. The role played by national courts in resolving international disputes will continue to be curtailed by judicial doctrines of abstention or non-justiciability. In the case of public interest litigation, judicial reticence not only limits the ability of public interest advocates to highlight their cause, it limits the role of domestic courts in the dialogue between domestic and international law. It has long been recognized that international tribunals can exert a normative pull on states despite the lack of any coherent doctrine of precedent in international law. Domestic tribunals are capable of exerting a similar, if not greater, normative pull. If that potential is to be realized it will be necessary for domestic courts to continue to develop much clearer standards by which the tensions inherent in litigation involving public international law disputes are managed. The experience of Australia and the United States suggests that some courts now recognize the artificial constraints of the doctrines of judicial restraint developed in the twentieth century. Incrementally, it appears that national courts may be moving towards a more flexible application of those doctrines, with a consequential increase in the likelihood that public international law issues will appear in domestic litigation.

[68] Decision of December 29, 2009, No. 08-16060, DC No. 99-cv-04941-MMC.

PART II

4

Australia's experience in international litigation

HENRY BURMESTER

This chapter examines Australia's experience in international litigation, particularly as an applicant but also as respondent, with a view to identifying the challenges and pitfalls that can arise. My consideration draws heavily on my personal involvement as a member of the government legal team in all of the contentious cases in which Australia has been a party before the International Court of Justice (ICJ) and the International Tribunal for the Law of the Sea (ITLOS). The views expressed are, of course, my own personal views and not necessarily those of the Australian government.

Australia, as a liberal democracy with a strong commitment to the rule of law, has had a long-standing policy of support for the peaceful settlement of international disputes through the use of bodies such as the ICJ. A middle-level power like Australia is a strong supporter of a rules-based system of multilateral co-operation and, as part of that, compulsory international dispute mechanisms.[1]

As part of this commitment, Australia has accepted the compulsory jurisdiction of the ICJ under the optional clause (albeit with certain reservations).[2] This has exposed it to cases as respondent. It has also, however, enabled Australia to pursue intractable environmental and resource disputes through use of the Court. As outlined below, Australia has seen international litigation as a useful way in which to seek to resolve disputes involving certain issues of national concern. This chapter seeks to explore the lessons learned from Australia's experience in this regard, with a view to shedding some useful light more generally on the benefits and pitfalls of international litigation. The lessons extend from the procedural

---

[1] See generally Henry Burmester, 'Australia and the International Court', (1996) 17 *Australian Year Book of International Law* 19, 20–5.

[2] ICJ, Declarations Recognizing the Jurisdiction of the Court as Compulsory, 22 March 2002, available at www.icj-cij.org/jurisdiction/index.php?p1=5&p2=1&p3=3&code=AU.

and tactical to more strategic aspects associated with the promotion and development of international law.

The experience of any state with international litigation is likely in many ways to be unique, in terms of both the cases that may arise and the domestic circumstances that may lead a state to commence proceedings. However, Australia's experience can, it is suggested, provide a useful case study. The cases on which this chapter will draw start with the *Nuclear Tests* case[3] against France where Australia was the applicant. Australia was a respondent in the *Nauru*[4] and *East Timor*[5] cases. Australia has also been a party in two cases under the UN Convention on the Law of the Sea (UNCLOS)[6] – as applicant in the *Southern Bluefin Tuna* case against Japan[7] and as respondent in the *Volga* case brought by the Russian Federation, seeking prompt release of a vessel.[8] Australia is currently an applicant at the ICJ in a case against Japan involving whaling in the Antarctic.[9]

This chapter does not analyse the individual cases in any detail.[10] Rather, it looks at common issues that arise in international litigation. Nor does the chapter consider other international disputes involving Australia such as those arising under the World Trade Organization Dispute Settlement procedures or arbitration under investment treaties.[11]

---

[3] *Nuclear Tests (Australia v. France) (Interim Measures)*, [1973] ICJ Rep. 99; *(Jurisdiction and Admissibility)*, [1974] ICJ Rep. 253 (*Nuclear Tests*).

[4] *Certain Phosphate Lands in Nauru (Nauru v. Australia) (Preliminary Objections)*, [1992] ICJ Rep. 240 (*Nauru*).

[5] *Case Concerning East Timor (Portugal v. Australia)*, [1995] ICJ Rep. 90 (*East Timor*).

[6] United Nations Convention on the Law of the Sea (opened for signature 10 December 1982, entered into force 16 November 1994), 1833 UNTS 3.

[7] *Southern Bluefin Tuna (New Zealand v. Japan; Australia v. Japan) (Provisional Measures)*, (1999) 117 ILR 148 (*Southern Bluefin Tuna*). See also *Southern Bluefin Tuna (New Zealand v. Japan; Australia v. Japan) (Jurisdiction and Admissibility)*, (2000) 119 ILR 508.

[8] *Volga Case (Russia v. Australia) (Prompt Release)*, (2003) 42 ILM 159 (*Volga*).

[9] 'Application Instituting Proceedings', *Whaling in the Antarctic (Australia v. Japan)*, ICJ, General List No. 148, 31 May 2010.

[10] For a brief analysis of the ICJ cases, other than the most recent one, see Nii Lante Wallace-Bruce, *The Settlement of International Disputes: The Contribution of Australia and New Zealand* (Dordrecht: Martinus Nijhoff, 1998). See also Natalie Klein, 'Litigation over Marine Resources: Lessons for Law of the Sea, International Dispute Settlement and International Environmental Law', (2009) 28 *Australian Year Book of International Law* 131.

[11] For a discussion of Australia's earlier engagement in WTO dispute settlement, see Gavan Goh, 'Australia's Participation in the WTO Dispute Settlement System', (2002) 30 *Federal Law Review* 203.

The cases in which Australia has been involved have concerned controversial issues, and none were begun by a special agreement between the parties to refer a discrete legal question for adjudication. Rather, the cases have all been begun unilaterally and, as a result, not unexpectedly, have raised jurisdictional issues. This is always an important consideration in international litigation. As well, while the cases have involved environmental and resource issues, the subject matter of a case provides little assistance in considering how a state can use international litigation. Rather, each case turns very much on its own circumstances, and that has largely determined the way the cases have been dealt with, procedurally and strategically.

This chapter will now turn to a consideration of some particular issues raised by international litigation. It will first look at jurisdictional issues, then turn to examine the decision to institute proceedings, the litigation process, and, finally, recurring procedural issues. It will use the cases involving Australia to illustrate these issues.

Jurisdictional issues – the need for consent

It is important to remember that international disputes can only be litigated with consent. This may be given in advance as part of a treaty regime, as is the case for certain matters under UNCLOS. Under that convention, parties can also choose different dispute settlement forums, with ad hoc arbitral tribunals the default mechanism.[12] For the ICJ, jurisdictional consent may be found in a treaty or optional clause declaration.[13] Jurisdiction is, however, often hotly contested and can often be a central issue for an applicant state in determining whether to use a particular dispute settlement body to resolve any dispute. Whether a respondent state decides to invoke a challenge to jurisdiction is an important strategic litigation decision.

Despite the considerable number of international disputes taken to litigation, there are many more where states take steps to prevent or avoid this occurring. Rarely is a state taken completely by surprise by the institution of proceedings against it. No state, including a state like Australia that generally supports peaceful international dispute mechanisms, exposes itself to a completely open-ended commitment in advance allowing it to be taken to an international tribunal in relation to all and any disputes. States weigh up their exposure to compulsory dispute settlement

---

[12] UNCLOS, Art. 287.   [13] Statute of the ICJ, Art. 36(1), (2).

mechanisms before ratifying treaties containing such provisions. As with UNCLOS, compulsory dispute settlement may be a necessary part of a particular treaty bargain. However, even then, choices may be possible as to preferred forum. States that accept the optional clause mechanism under the Statute of the ICJ[14] regularly review and alter their declarations having regard to their perception of their exposure to legal risks. Australia is no exception here.

Back in 1954 Australia ensured that its optional clause declaration would prevent Japan from unilaterally bringing a dispute over pearl fishing on the continental shelf before the ICJ.[15] This was done in recognition of the then uncertain state of international law and in the face of a real prospect of Japan responding to new regulatory measures adopted by Australia. In 1975, Australia made a wide-ranging optional clause declaration with few reservations. In 2002, Australia again altered its optional clause declaration, with a number of reservations including one to prevent unresolved maritime delimitation disputes with Australia being taken to the Court.[16] At the time Australia had a number of such situations, including with a newly independent Timor Leste. Australia did not act in advance to prevent Nauru commencing proceedings against it under the optional clause, although Australia then raised significant jurisdictional objections once the case was commenced.[17] Similarly, it did not act to prevent Portugal bringing proceedings in relation to the agreement Australia had reached with Indonesia over the exploitation of the maritime area between the then East Timor and Australia. In both cases, Australia decided to confront any case that might be brought head-on in the Court, including by raising jurisdictional and admissibility objections, rather than seeking in advance to prevent the cases from being instituted.

The decision of a state whether to take steps to avoid proceedings being instituted against it is an important strategic component in any consideration of the use of international litigation. The need for consent

---

[14] Statute of the ICJ, Art. 36(2).

[15] [1954] ATS 8; 186 UNTS 771. See also Shirley V. Scott, 'The Inclusion of Sedentary Fisheries within the Continental Shelf Doctrine', (1992) 41 *ICLQ* 788, 800.

[16] ICJ, above n. 2, [2002] ATS 5. The relevant reservation reads: 'This declaration does not apply to: ... (b) any dispute concerning or relating to the delimitation of maritime zones, including the territorial sea, the exclusive economic zone and the continental shelf, or arising out of, concerning, or relating to the exploitation of any disputed area of or adjacent to any such maritime zone pending its delimitation.'

[17] See *Certain Phosphate Lands in Nauru (Nauru v. Australia) (Preliminary Objections)*, [1992] ICJ Rep. 240.

can in certain situations be used to preclude any form of litigation or to influence the form of tribunal. Thus Australia, in a dispute with the United States over an alleged expropriation, indicated that it would only consent to the full bench of the ICJ determining the matter, while the United States was only prepared to have the matter determined by a carefully chosen chamber. In the event, no case was ever commenced.[18]

Even when states have taken steps to avoid cases being instituted against them, this will not ensure that proceedings are not commenced. Hence France had carefully drafted its optional clause declaration to exclude, inter alia, disputes concerning activities connected with national defence, a reservation clearly intended to cover its nuclear programme, including atmospheric nuclear tests. However, in *Nuclear Tests* Australia argued that the exception did not prevent any adjudication of Australia's case against atmospheric nuclear testing in the Pacific. Australia also, however, relied on jurisdiction conferred by the 1928 General Act for the Pacific Settlement of International Disputes.[19] This treaty had been largely forgotten and was viewed by many, including France, as no longer operative. The fact that Australia sought to base the mutual consent to jurisdiction on such an obscure treaty was seen by France as contributing to the illegitimacy of the whole proceedings. The case against nuclear testing was a matter that, through French eyes, went to the heart of its national security. It was not an environmental dispute as portrayed by Australia. Faced with these very unwelcome proceedings, France chose to stay away and not appear at all in the proceedings. It did, however, convey to the ICJ by letter in some detail its view that there was a manifest lack of jurisdiction for the Court to hear the matter.[20]

The more common response of states to unwelcome proceedings is to participate but to raise jurisdictional challenges. This will be further considered below. Jurisdictional challenges are not only directed to whether the particular subject matter of a dispute is covered by an appropriate submission to jurisdiction of the particular tribunal chosen by the applicant state. Not only must there be consent to subject matter jurisdiction but there must first be a 'dispute', and under certain treaties certain procedural prerequisites may need to be met. The importance of these issues was

[18] Burmester, above n. 1, 24.
[19] (Opened for signature 26 September 1928, entered into force 16 August 1929), 93 LNTS 343.
[20] *Nuclear Tests*, [1974] ICJ Rep. 253, 255 [4]. See also Joint Dissenting Opinion, at 328–58, which contains a detailed rebuttal of the French arguments concerning particularly the 1928 General Act, an issue which the court itself in its judgment did not address.

recently demonstrated in the *Case concerning the Racial Discrimination Convention.*[21]

The need for a dispute was a matter to which Australia gave careful consideration before instituting proceedings in the *Nuclear Tests* case. Often a dispute may simmer away for many years without the legal parameters of the dispute being carefully spelled out. Once Australia determined that the legality of atmospheric nuclear testing should be subject to adjudication it sent a carefully crafted diplomatic note outlining its view of the legal situation.[22] It also sought, before launching proceedings, to engage in a high-level dialogue on the scientific aspects of the harm resulting from such testing, in order to determine whether there was any common ground.

The subsequent finding of an absence of any continuing dispute following French unilateral undertakings was seen as reason by the Court to terminate the case at the jurisdiction phase.[23] The object of the dispute had, in the view of the majority, disappeared and there was, therefore, nothing on which to give a judgment. By contrast, the dissenting judges considered the jurisdiction arising under the 1928 General Act in some detail and the nature of Australia's claims, and reached the view that, jurisdiction having been established, the case should have proceeded to an adjudication on the merits of all or at least certain of the claims.[24]

In the *Southern Bluefin Tuna* case, Australia and New Zealand alleged a breach of Articles 64 and 116–119 of UNCLOS. Japan argued that no legal dispute existed, there being a dispute only over scientific data not suitable for judicial resolution. This argument did not succeed either at ITLOS or before the arbitral tribunal. At the jurisdictional phase, the arbitral tribunal found that while there was a dispute under UNCLOS, it did not have jurisdiction because of Article 281(1) of that Convention. Article 281(1) excludes disputes where the parties have agreed to seek settlement by means of their own choice and where that choice precludes

---

[21] *Case Concerning Application of the International Convention on the Elimination of All Forms of Racial Discrimination (Georgia v. Russian Federation) (Preliminary Objections)*, [2011] ICJ Rep. 70.

[22] See *Nuclear Tests (Australia v. France) (Jurisdiction and Admissibility)*, [1974] ICJ Rep. 253, 260 [24]–[26], 242–7, 279–80 (Judge Gros), 423–7 (ad hoc Judge Barwick).

[23] Ibid., 210 [24], 270–2 [55]–[59].

[24] Ibid., 372 (Judges Onyeama, Dillard, Jiménez de Aréchaga and Waldock), 388 (Judge de Castro), 454 (Judge Barwick).

any other procedure. The arbitral panel concluded that Article 16 of the 1993 Convention on the Conservation of Southern Bluefin Tuna 'excluded any further procedure' under UNCLOS.[25] This finding was different from a prima facie finding of jurisdiction made by ITLOS at the earlier provisional measures phase of the case.[26]

The need for jurisdiction is an essential first step if international litigation is to occur. The ability to demonstrate a reasonable possibility of jurisdiction is critical if provisional measures are to be sought. Australia's ability to do this was critical to its success in obtaining interim measures against France and Japan, even though both cases were later dismissed for a lack of jurisdiction. Even if it appears to an applicant state that a strong case for jurisdiction exists, this will not prevent possible robust challenges to the jurisdiction of the tribunal which may well succeed. This possibility is something that an applicant state needs to build into its litigation strategy. As will be discussed below, the best way for a respondent state to challenge jurisdiction is also an important matter of litigation tactics for that state.

The decision to institute proceedings

Determining whether jurisdiction is likely to exist is an essential first step, but the decision whether actually to institute proceedings is a significant step not taken lightly by any state. The two cases instituted by Australia against France and Japan respectively in the ICJ are almost forty years apart, but there are certain similarities in the lead-up to the decision to institute those proceedings.

Nuclear testing and whaling are both issues that in Australia attract wide public opposition. There was a groundswell of public demand in both instances for the government to take action. Diplomatic and similar action had made little impact. The possibility of international legal action was raised publicly, legal opinions from prominent international lawyers being provided to political leaders. In the case of French nuclear testing, Professor D. P. O'Connell provided an opinion.[27] In the case of whaling,

---

[25] *Southern Bluefin Tuna (New Zealand v. Japan; Australia v. Japan)* (Jurisdiction and Admissibility), (2000) 119 ILR 508, [50]–[59].

[26] *Southern Bluefin Tuna (New Zealand v. Japan; Australia v. Japan)* (Provisional Measures), (1999) 117 ILR 148, [33].

[27] Klein, above n. 10, 134.

there were a number of opinions provided that had been organized by environmental groups.[28] In both instances, the existence of opinions supporting the institution of proceedings was seized on by then opposition parties, and a commitment to legal action was taken up by them as part of election campaigns that saw those parties ultimately elected as new governments.[29]

Thus the contributions of members of the international law academy will in a democracy like Australia often be an important part of convincing a government to use litigation as a tool to resolve an international dispute. A government will no doubt seek its own advice, but, at least on controversial issues with public interest involved, the promptings of outside international lawyers appear to be important in raising litigation as a core strategy in seeking resolution of a particular dispute and forcing government to consider it carefully as an option.

Governments will not always act in response to pressure from international lawyers. For instance, the Australian government declined to commence proceedings against Singapore in relation to the carrying out of the death penalty against an Australian citizen, despite being provided with legal opinions strongly supporting such actions.[30]

Another significant consideration in relation to initiating proceedings is that litigation will never be the first option for any state. There will normally have been other attempts diplomatically or through international bodies to resolve the dispute. Thus, in the case of whaling, it was only after extended attempts within the International Whaling Commission to find a solution had failed, and after a Special Ambassador had failed to make any progress in direct talks with Japan, that proceedings were instituted. In the case of nuclear testing, there was a last-ditch ministerial visit to Paris before proceedings were commenced, following earlier bilateral scientific exchanges over the alleged harmful effects of atmospheric testing.

---

[28] See, e.g., Report of the International Panel of Independent Legal Experts on: Special Permit ('Scientific') Whaling under International Law, Paris, 12 May 2006, available at www.ifaw. org/ifaw/general/default.aspx?oid=167943, [83]. The panel comprised Laurence Boisson de Chazournes, Pierre-Marie Dupuy, Donald R. Rothwell, Philippe Sands, Alberto Székely, William H. Taft IV, and Kate Cook.

[29] See Australian Labor Party, *National Platform and Constitution* (2007) 145, [131].

[30] See Daniel Hoare, 'PM – UN official wants Van Nguyen case to face the International Court', 21 November 2005, ABC Online, available at www.abc.net.au/pm/content/2005/s1513049.htm. See also Julie Lewis, 'Explore International Legal Options for Bali Nine Now', says Professor', (2006) *Law Society Journal* 18, 18.

The reluctance of states to rush into international litigation is understandable. As with domestic litigation, any litigation carries risk and may incur considerable expense. The outcome is always unpredictable, as international tribunals seem to find unexpected ways in which to deal with cases before them. Any case is likely to produce some adverse consequences for the bilateral relationship with the respondent state, no matter how good the relationship may otherwise be. In many instances it can lead to considerable diplomatic and other repercussions.

In the *Nuclear Tests* case, France was outraged by the proceedings and launched a hostile public response in France and with the ICJ, despite not appearing before it. Relations between Australia and France were also adversely affected by the Australian public vitriol against France, manifested in boycotts of French goods and trade union bans on ships destined for France. Any government contemplating international litigation obviously needs to consider the likely impact on broader bilateral relations before instituting proceedings. Demonizing a state rarely assists the litigious process but may be an inevitable consequence if the litigation is not handled carefully. Fortunately, apart from the *Nuclear Tests* case, Australia's experience suggests that while instituting proceedings may not be welcomed by the other state, relations need not suffer unduly. This may be a reflection of the greater resort to international dispute settlement since the end of the cold war, but may also reflect the different nature of the particular disputes.

One reason, in my view, why proceedings against France were viewed so negatively by France itself was that the case attacked what at the time of the cold war was considered to be part of its essential national defence programme. In French eyes, the case did not raise second-order issues but went to the heart of France's national security. I consider that international litigation that raises such issues is far more likely to provoke a hostile response and is less likely to result in a positive outcome than litigation directed at important but nevertheless second-order issues.

This was reflected in the way in which France responded to the institution of proceedings. They considered them to be illegitimate and hence boycotted the hearings before the Court. As already mentioned, they sought to convince the Court by irregular means of the illegitimacy of Australia's case. Australia relied on an until then obscure 1928 treaty for jurisdiction. France's optional clause had expressly excluded matters of 'national defence' and the attempt by Australia to get round this by use of the old treaty was seen by France as improper. France ensured that the Court was provided by means of a letter with detailed arguments against any reliance on the 1928 treaty. The whole proceedings involved a bitterness not seen in any other proceedings with which I have been involved. This unpleasantness outside the Court was also evident in the strong division within the Court disclosed in its judgments at both the provisional measures phase and the subsequent jurisdiction and admissibility phase.[31]

The litigation process

Once a state decides to institute proceedings a number of important process issues arise. For a respondent state determining the best tactical response to the proceedings is also very important.

The experiences of Australia in its various cases highlight a number of important considerations. These include:

(a) any litigation is risky and the outcome unpredictable;
(b) success should not be defined solely as winning a case on its merits;
(c) the international politics of a case cannot be underestimated as an important factor in how a tribunal deals with the matter before it;
(d) tactical decisions in relation to the litigation process are critical.

I elaborate briefly on each of these issues.

First, as with any litigation, no matter how confident the legal advice may be as to a successful outcome, the result can never be guaranteed and surprises often emerge. In international litigation this is even more likely to be the case than in a more predictable domestic law setting. Hence procedural and jurisdictional objections can often serve as a convenient way for a court to avoid adjudication on politically difficult issues. This was certainly evident in the cold war era, but continues to be an issue today. Hence, in the *Nuclear Tests* case, the Court seized on the unilateral French undertaking not to conduct further atmospheric tests to bring the case to an end.[32] This was done over strong objections from significant members of the Court. No submissions on the issue were made by Australia, the most relevant undertakings having been made after the

---

[31] The voting in the provisional measures phase was 8 votes to 6, and at the jurisdiction and admissibility phase, 9 votes to 6.

[32] *Nuclear Tests (Australia v. France) (Jurisdiction and Admissibility)*, [1974] ICJ Rep. 253, 270.

AUSTRALIA'S EXPERIENCE IN INTERNATIONAL LITIGATION   71

oral hearing concluded.[33] This outcome was not predictable when the proceedings were instituted and even at the stage of oral argument.

In the *Nauru* case, the Court rejected Australia's jurisdictional objections involving the absence of third parties, being sympathetic to the Nauruan claims and considering that the presence of the other trusteeship parties was not essential.[34] In *East Timor*, by contrast, the Court found that the absence of an essential third party, Indonesia, prevented adjudication on the merits.[35] This was not entirely unexpected, but presumably Portugal considered after the *Nauru* case that the Court might be persuaded not to deal with the case in that way. However, the Court was able to distinguish the two situations.[36] In the *Southern Bluefin Tuna* case, the arbitral tribunal found that there was no jurisdiction to hear the merits, despite the prima facie finding of jurisdiction by ITLOS.

Dismissal of a case at the jurisdictional phase is thus a real possibility in many cases. However, this possibility does not mean that the institution of proceedings was unwise or that the proceedings may not still produce a beneficial result. Even if a case is dismissed on jurisdictional grounds, it may be possible to secure provisional measures before this occurs, and this alone may be a significant litigation outcome and have major consequences for the overall settlement of the dispute.

Thus, in the *Nuclear Tests* case, Australia's success at the provisional measures phase no doubt contributed to the public pressure on France to cease testing. The loss on jurisdiction following the unilateral French undertaking not to conduct more tests was, no matter that it may have been criticized legally, nevertheless a win for Australia in terms of bringing further testing to an end.

Australia's success before ITLOS in securing provisional measures against Japan increased the pressure on Japan to negotiate improvements in relation to conservation of bluefin tuna, even though Australia lost on jurisdiction before the Annex VII arbitral tribunal.[37] Similarly, the

---

[33] Ibid., 313 [6] (Judges Onyeama, Dillard, Jiménez de Aréchaga and Waldock).

[34] *Certain Phosphate Lands in Nauru (Nauru v. Australia) (Preliminary Objections)*, [1992] ICJ Rep. 240, 261–2 [55].

[35] *East Timor*, above n. 5, 102 [28]–[35].   [36] Ibid., 104–5 [34].

[37] For discussion on these negotiations see Tim Stephens, 'The Limits of International Adjudication in International Environmental Law: Another Perspective on the Southern Bluefin Tuna Case', (2004) 19 *International Journal of Marine Coastal Law* 177; Alastair Cameron, 'Is There Hope for the Fish? The Post-Arbitration Effectiveness of the Convention for the Conservation of Southern Bluefin Tuna', (2007) 15 *New York University Environmental Law Journal* 247.

rejection of jurisdictional objections may encourage a case to be resolved by negotiation, as happened between Australia and Nauru.[38]

The exposure of the issues in a case at a separate jurisdictional phase before reaching the merits can often serve as a valuable way to clarify underlying issues and facilitate ongoing negotiations. Whether to separate out jurisdictional issues for separate adjudication is an important factor of litigation strategy. Whether to seek provisional measures is also an important strategic decision that needs careful consideration when deciding to institute proceedings. These issues are further discussed below.

In the diverse international cases in which Australia has been a party, the international politics surrounding a case inevitably played an important if indirect part in the way in which the court or tribunal dealt with the matter. Since the end of the cold war, the ICJ is not as clearly divided on political grounds as it once was. However, in the *Nuclear Tests* case the divide between those judges who took a strong state sovereignty position and those more concerned with a focus on the proper legal analysis of the issues was very evident. At the provisional measures phase the dissenting judges were vehement in their assertion that nuclear testing was in effect a political and not legal issue. At the jurisdiction and admissibility phase the pragmatic and convenient result based on the unilateral French undertaking prevailed, but only over a strong dissent by a significant number of judges, including some of the most respected jurists on the ICJ, who appeared to eschew pragmatic political considerations and dealt with the jurisdiction and admissibility arguments in detail.

In *Nauru*, the sympathy of the majority of the ICJ for the applicant state in a case involving a 'colonial' situation was clearly relevant to the hesitation of the court to dismiss the case on jurisdictional grounds. In *East Timor*, while there was no doubt considerable sympathy on the ICJ for the Portuguese position, there was also no doubt a recognition that the 'absence of a necessary third party' objection if upheld would avoid difficult legal issues in relation to the principle of self-determination. Australian lawyers involved in the case certainly thought that the ability to point to comparable conduct to that of Australia by Portugal and other members of the European Union in dealing with the reality of

---

[38] The settlement is contained in Agreement between Australia and the Republic of Nauru for the Settlement of the Case in the International Court of Justice concerning Certain Phosphate Lands in Nauru, Australia – Nauru (opened for signature 10 August 1993, entered into force 20 August 1993), [1993] ATS 26, 32 ILM 1474. The agreement was not concluded until Australia had lodged its counter memorial on the merits, after the failure of its jurisdictional challenge.

Moroccan control of the Western Sahara was important material that may have helped to convince the ICJ to reject the admissibility of the case by reliance on the basis of the absence of an essential third party, Indonesia.[39]

The ability to point clearly to the direct impact of the politics of a case on its outcome will always be difficult, and is usually speculative. In some cases it will appear to be more likely to have played a part than in other situations. Nevertheless, the likely effect of the international political dimension on individual judges is a consideration that remains important in deciding if and where to litigate an international dispute, as well as in determining how best to frame any case.[40] The electoral systems used for international tribunals inevitably ensure that political dimensions intrude in the selection of judges,[41] and this may be relevant in predicting how some judges may react in individual cases. The nationality and background of the judges is not something that can be ignored when considering the likely response of an international court to a particular case.

This section has highlighted some of the many important tactical decisions and issues that arise from the start – whether to start the litigation and, if so, where. A state needs to have carefully worked out its objectives and strategy before it commences a case, while at the same time retaining the flexibility to adjust its position and tactics as the litigation unfolds. I turn now to some of the strategic and tactical issues that arise in relation to a case once it has been commenced.

The substantive case

Facts and evidence

One significant issue that Australia's experiences in international litigation demonstrates to be critical is the assembling and handling of the facts and evidence. At the same time, it is also clear that international tribunals are not well equipped to deal with complex factual or scientific matters.[42] The rules of evidence and concepts like burden of proof and use of

---

[39] *Case Concerning East Timor, Oral Proceedings*, CR1995/9, 61–65; CR1995/10, 1–10.

[40] Lyndel Prott, *The Latent Power of Culture and the International Judge* (Abingdon: Professional Books, 1979).

[41] Kenneth Keith, 'International Court of Justice: Reflections on the Electoral Process', (2010) 9 *Chinese Journal of International Law* 49.

[42] Carolyn Foster, *Science and the Precautionary Principle in International Courts and Tribunals* (Cambridge University Press, 2011).

74 HENRY BURMESTER

cross-examination of witnesses are relatively undeveloped. A state making a claim or defence must assume that it will need to prove all facts necessary for that purpose.[43] Some of the judges of the ICJ are beginning to recognize that the Court needs to handle better the way in which expert evidence is treated.[44] The way in which scientific evidence is dealt with in the *Whaling* case will be of interest in this regard.

In resource or environmental cases, scientific material will be critical, including at any interim measures phase. In the *Nuclear Tests* case, Australia went to considerable lengths to assemble relevant scientific information drawn from United Nations committees (e.g., UNSCEAR), independent scientific experts, and its own scientific bodies. In the *Southern Bluefin Tuna* case, Australia again produced an expert report from its own scientists and then backed that up with the views of an independent scientist.[45] In the *Whaling* case against Japan, scientific evidence will be an important component of the case.[46]

There is a temptation among some commentators who advocate litigation in a particular matter to downplay the importance of scientific evidence in seeking to make the legal case, including at any interim measures stage. But, as I learned as a very young government lawyer, and have seen demonstrated in all the international cases in which I have been involved, one's case is only as good as the facts. This is not only the case for environmental matters, but also for cases involving what appear to be essentially pure issues of law. Thus in the *East Timor* case I consider that Australia's success on jurisdictional grounds was assisted by being able to demonstrate that Australia's dealing with Indonesia as the state in fact in control of the relevant land territory of East Timor was in essence no different from the way in which the European Union, including Portugal, had dealt with the reality that Morocco controlled the area of Spanish Sahara.[47]

---

[43] Carolyn Foster, 'Burden of Proof in International Courts and Tribunals', (2010) 29 *Australian Year Book of International Law* 27.

[44] See, e.g., *Pulp Mills on the River Uruguay (Argentina v. Uruguay)*, [2010] ICJ Rep. 109, 117 (Judges Al-Khasawneh and Simma).

[45] 'Request for the Prescription of Provisional Measures Submitted by Australia', *Southern Bluefin Tuna Cases*, ITLOS, Case No. 3 & 4, 27 August 1999, Annex 4.

[46] Australia argued that 'having regard to the scale of the JARPA II program, to the lack of any demonstrated relevance for the conservation and management of whale stocks, and to the risks presented to targeted species and stocks, the JARPA II program cannot be justified under Article VIII of the [Whaling Convention].' 'Application Instituting Proceedings', *Whaling in the Antarctic (Australia v. Japan)*, ICJ, General List No. 148, 31 May 2010, 16 [37]. Art. VIII permits the issuance of special permits for scientific research.

[47] *Case Concerning East Timor, Oral Proceedings*, CR1995/9, 61–65, CR1995/10, 1–10.

Facts and evidence are inevitably important as to how a court reacts to the legal arguments and perceives the merits of a case. At the same time, one cannot fail to think that at times international courts are happy to find ways to deal with cases so as to avoid the need to confront highly contested scientific questions. If the parties had to produce and deal with the necessary complex evidence at the merits stage in both the *Nuclear Tests* and the *Southern Bluefin Tuna* cases to support the legal contentions, this would have been a considerable challenge not just for the parties but the court itself. This factual aspect should never be forgotten when a state considers the possibility of instituting proceedings and how best to conduct them procedurally, including whether to seek interim measures. The ability of Australia to marshal, at the interim measures stage, sufficient evidence to show prima facie 'irreparable harm' was critical to obtaining interim relief in the *Nuclear Tests* and *Southern Bluefin Tuna* cases. Prima facie jurisdiction is not all that needs be demonstrated.

Other procedural and logistical issues

There are a number of other procedural issues that should be mentioned as relevant to the way in which a state handles international litigation.

For a respondent state, the decision whether to institute preliminary objections based on jurisdiction or admissibility is a matter needing careful consideration. In *Nauru*, delay to any hearing on the merits was achieved by Australia raising preliminary objections.[48] The basis for these objections was largely discrete from the merits. By contrast, in the *East Timor* case, the aim of Australia was to resolve the matter as soon as possible, and the third-party issue was closely related to issues of substance. For this reason Australia chose not to raise separate preliminary objections but to have any jurisdictional issue dealt with at the same time as the merits.[49] This does not, however, ensure a quick hearing or result.[50] In the *Southern Bluefin Tuna* case, Japan raised jurisdictional issues separately and was successful at that stage. In the *Whaling* case, no preliminary objections were raised and the case has been set down for hearing after only one round of written proceedings. The decision of an applicant state

---

[48] *Certain Phosphate Lands in Nauru (Nauru v. Australia) (Preliminary Objections)*, [1992] ICJ Rep. 240, 243.

[49] 'Counter-Memorial of the Government of Australia', *East Timor*, [1995] ICJ Rep. 90, 9 [20]; *East Timor*, [1995] ICJ Rep. 90, [19].

[50] Proceedings were instituted in February 1991; the written pleadings (two rounds) were completed by July 1993. The hearing did not occur until January 1995 and judgment was on 30 June 1995.

whether to press for a second round carries considerable weight when the Court considers whether to agree to that and is an obvious important tactical decision for the applicant to consider.

Another issue that often confronts a state in international litigation is the possible appointment of an ad hoc judge. Except in *Nauru*, Australia has availed itself of this right in every case in which it has had the opportunity.[51] The presence of an ad hoc judge, in my estimation, has helped to ensure that Australia's argument and interests were properly and fully considered by the Court. The decision in *Nauru* not to appoint an ad hoc judge on the basis that *Nauru* also would not appoint one was, in hindsight, in my view, a mistake. It meant that Australia's arguments were perhaps not as directly represented to other members of the Court as they otherwise might have been.[52] Selection of arbitrators or members of ad hoc tribunals are also critical decisions for a state.

Another matter warranting careful consideration by a state is the selection of counsel to run the case. Australia has always chosen to run its cases with considerable involvement of its Solicitor-General and lawyers from the Attorney-General's Department. Much drafting and research has been done by its own government lawyers. Unlike some states, Australia does not use private law firms. At the same time, Australia has always considered it important to have the assistance of highly regarded international lawyers who regularly appear as counsel before the ICJ.

In cases before the ICJ other than the *Nuclear Tests* case, Australia has had a French-speaking counsel among its team. In certain of its ICJ cases, Australia has also drawn on the experience and stature of former judges or pre-eminent international lawyers. In the *Nuclear Tests* case, Australia received advice from Professor Roberto Ago (not yet a judge of the Court but already highly regarded) and also from Phillip Jessup, a former judge of the Court. Neither appeared as counsel, but their involvement in providing advice was known. In *Nauru*, Professor Eduardo Jiménez de Aréchaga, a former judge and president of the Court, was retained by Australia and appeared as one of Australia's counsel.

The failure to retain lawyers with the appropriate background can disadvantage a state. This was evident in the *Southern Bluefin Tuna* case

---

[51] Sir Garfield Barwick was appointed for *Nuclear Tests*, Sir Ninian Stephen for *East Timor*, Professor Hilary Charlesworth for the *Whaling* case, and Emeritus Professor Ivan Shearer for *Southern Bluefin Tuna* and *Volga* at ITLOS.

[52] Nauru also did not have an ad hoc judge. Judge Weeramantry was, however, a member of the Court. He had chaired the Nauru Commission of Inquiry into Rehabilitation and his book on the issue was available. He did not sit on the case (being obviously disqualified).

at the interim measures stage before ITLOS. Japan was represented at that stage principally by a US law firm with offices in Japan. They were unfamiliar with litigation in an international body like the Tribunal. When the case moved to the arbitral tribunal, Japan was represented by leading international lawyers familiar with international litigation.[53] Also, Russia in *Volga* had New Zealand lawyers who represented the owners of the vessel and it is suggested this was not an ideal arrangement.[54]

The final procedural matter I shall mention is the involvement of third states in any case. Such involvement can complicate a case and needs to be diplomatically handled. In the *Nuclear Tests* case, New Zealand brought its own case and made its own arguments. It appointed the same ad hoc judge as Australia and the cases were run separately but sequentially. The New Zealand arguments had their own nuance and were in some respects broader than those of Australia, as became important in 1995 when New Zealand sought to reopen the earlier case.[55] In the *Southern Bluefin Tuna* case, New Zealand commenced a similar case to that of Australia and the cases were joined. In the *Whaling* case, New Zealand successfully sought to intervene under Article 63 of the Statute in relation to the interpretation of Article VIII of the Whaling Convention.[56]

If an issue in litigation affects other states or has a regional impact, the involvement of other states in the case on the side of one of the parties may add to the impact of the argument of that party. However, in terms of case management, including the nature of the involvement of the third party, co-ordination of argument, and matters like the appointment of ad hoc judges, the involvement of third parties will need careful management if benefit rather than detriment is to result.

Conclusion

This consideration of some of the issues raised by international litigation involving Australia seeks to throw some light on when and how a

---

[53] Before the arbitral tribunal, Japan was represented, among others, by Professors Vaughan Lowe and Shabtai Rosenne.

[54] See remarks by ad hoc Judge Shearer in that case: *Volga Case (Russia* v. *Australia) (Prompt Release)*, (2003) 42 ILM 159, [19] (ad hoc Judge Shearer).

[55] *Request for an Examination of the Situation in Accordance with Paragraph 63 of the Court's Judgment of 20 December 1974 in Nuclear Tests (New Zealand* v. *France)*, [1995] ICJ Rep. 288.

[56] ICJ, 'Declaration of Intervention', 20 November 2012, ICJ Press Release 2012/34.

middle-power state like Australia uses and responds to international litigation to advance or protect its interests.

Assessing the effectiveness of international courts or tribunals is a difficult challenge.[57] It is suggested, however, that among the conclusions one can draw is that institution of proceedings in such bodies can be a useful circuit breaker in the case of some intractable disputes. It can in some situations assist in resolving a dispute, even if a substantive decision on the merits is never obtained, by clarifying the issues or forcing a respondent state to reassess its position.

The type of dispute where litigation may be useful will usually involve second-order issues. While Australia may have seen atmospheric nuclear testing as a second-order issue, to France it was certainly a first-order issue that should never have been a matter for third-party adjudication. Such disputes if taken to litigation are likely to be very vitriolic.

The other important consideration is that international litigation is not to be undertaken lightly. It is a matter that states need carefully to control. They should not allow private interests to distort the decision making process both in terms of instituting proceedings and more generally.[58] Even more than with domestic litigation, it is suggested that the unpredictability, resource intensity, and possible broader diplomatic ramifications suggest caution in relation to the use of litigation to resolve international disputes. It may also in some cases, particularly those related to maritime delimitation, deprive states of flexibility to craft their own solution. This said, for a state like Australia committed to a rules-based system, international dispute settlement is a valuable mechanism which in appropriate cases can assist in resolving otherwise intractable disputes. It should not be seen, however, as the first choice of means to resolve a dispute between states, and the risks and potential benefits need to be carefully weighed by a state before it decides to commence proceedings.

---

[57] Yuval Shany, 'Assessing the Effectiveness of International Courts: A Goal-Based Approach', (2012) 106 AJIL 225.

[58] See remarks by ad hoc Judge Shearer in the *Volga* case, above n. 54.

5

Latin American states and the International Court of Justice

XIMENA FUENTES

Latin American states have shown commitment to the principle of the peaceful settlement of disputes, in particular through international adjudication. This commitment can be traced back to 1876, when Argentina and Paraguay decided to submit their boundary dispute regarding the territory between the Pilcomayo and Verde rivers to the arbitration of the president of the United States.[1] One should also not forget to mention in this regard that the first international court in the history of international adjudication was the Central American Court of Justice, which was established by Nicaragua, El Salvador, Honduras, Guatemala, and Costa Rica in 1908. However, it was not a permanent court.[2] It was planned to last for ten years only, and in 1918 none of the parties agreed to an extension of the original term.

Of course, the main reason for preferring arbitration may be found in the degree of control that states maintain over the dispute.[3] From this perspective, judicial settlement certainly involves more risks for the litigating states because they do not control the appointment of the judges or the procedure. But judicial settlement may, precisely for these reasons, represent a preferable option when states want to insulate the final outcome from domestic criticism about how the procedure was handled or who was appointed arbitrator.

In this context, one may ask why Latin American countries, which have shown a certain inclination towards arbitration for the resolution of their

---

[1] Gordon Ireland, *Boundaries, Possessions and Conflicts in South America* (Cambridge, MA: Harvard University Press, 1938), 31–2.

[2] Text of the Convention for the Establishment of a Central American Court of Justice (20 December 1907), World Courts, Convention for the Establishment of a Central American Court of Justice, 2011, available at www.worldcourts.com/cacj/eng/documents/1907.12. 20_convention.htm.

[3] J. G. Merrills, *International Dispute Settlement*, 5th edn (Cambridge University Press, 2011), 189.

boundary disputes, in recent years have tended to prefer the International Court of Justice (ICJ). It is not the case that arbitration was not successful. On the contrary, arbitration in Latin America was extensively used, with good results, as a means of dispute resolution in the field of boundary disputes.[4] But it is undeniable that a decline in the use of arbitration in the Latin American context started in the early twentieth century.[5] The tendency to opt for the ICJ as a means of dispute resolution appeared later, at the beginning of the twenty-first century. As the ICJ is beginning to have an active role in the resolution of Latin American disputes and this new development raises many questions, this chapter focuses on the Court as a means of dispute settlement in the region.

The reasons for the active role that the ICJ is beginning to play in the resolution of Latin American disputes have not yet been explored in detail. However, various factors may have to be taken into account when attempting to elaborate an explanation. First, some authors have pointed out that new types of dispute have emerged.[6] Indeed, since the establishment of new maritime zones by international law, maritime disputes have appeared prominently in the workload of the Court. Four of the fourteen maritime delimitation disputes before the Court have involved Latin American countries.[7] Given the fact that the ICJ has created jurisprudence in the field of maritime delimitation, predictability and expertise might be factors that states take into account when deciding to submit this kind of dispute to the Court. Another factor that might be encouraging the use of the ICJ by Latin American countries is the existence of a treaty (the Pact of Bogotá) which contains the consent of the parties to the jurisdiction of the ICJ. The parties to the Pact may trigger a procedure before the Court without special agreement with the respondent. And a third criterion which must be taken into consideration is that, precisely because arbitration gives more control over the dispute to the parties, it is politically more risky for governments who might have to assume the whole

---

[4] L. D. M. Nelson, 'The Arbitration of Boundary Disputes in Latin America', (1973) 20 *Netherlands International Law Review* 267, 292.

[5] Ibid., 293.

[6] Jorge Domínguez, *Boundary Disputes in Latin America*, Peaceworks no. 50 (Washington, DC: United States Institute of Peace, 2003), 26.

[7] *Land, Island, and Maritime Frontier Dispute (El Salvador/Honduras: Nicaragua intervening)*, [1992] ICJ Rep. 350; *Territorial and Maritime Dispute between Nicaragua and Honduras in the Caribbean Sea (Nicaragua v. Honduras)*, [2007] ICJ Rep. 659; *Territorial and Maritime Dispute (Nicaragua v. Colombia) (Judgment)*, ICJ, General List No. 124, 19 November 2012; and *Maritime Dispute (Peru v. Chile)*, ICJ, General List No. 137, 16 January 2008 (pending).

responsibility for a bad outcome in the arbitration; recourse to the ICJ might contribute to mitigating the political criticism and recriminations that sometimes follow when a state loses a case.

Despite the fact that recourse to the ICJ is a more or less recent development in Latin America, Latin American countries have made important contributions to the functioning of the Court. For example, the optional clause as a mechanism to establish consent to the jurisdiction of the ICJ was an initiative of a Latin American diplomat. The optional clause formula, today incorporated into Article 36(2) of the ICJ Statute, was the original idea of a Brazilian diplomat, Raoul Fernandes, who put forward this proposal at the 1920 Committee of Jurists in charge of drafting the Statute of the Permanent Court of International Justice (PCIJ).[8]

Despite this general commitment to the peaceful settlement of disputes, it is clear that this does not suffice to eliminate the traditional problems affecting recourse by states to international adjudication. It comes as no surprise that states do not like to be taken to court and found to have breached international law. In the field of territorial boundaries, states do not like the prospect of a modification of the status quo. And it is clear that states will object to the jurisdiction of the court when they consider that their security interests may be affected by the proceedings.

With this in mind, the present chapter attempts to elucidate what Latin American cases have to tell us about the role of the Court in the resolution of international disputes in the region. It will be seen that there is a certain pattern in the Latin American cases before the Court: many have to do with past disputes in which treaties or decisions of international tribunals have already attempted to find a solution. This might indicate that Latin American states have shown a low level of commitment to standing by agreements that previous governments concluded in the past, and/or that those agreements were not successful in anticipating future problems in their application or interpretation. In addition, one could add that Latin American governments tend to show little desire to renegotiate and adapt old treaties or judgments to new situations.

Latin American states have been involved in twenty cases before the ICJ.[9] Ten Latin American states have deposited unilateral declarations

---

[8] Juan José Quintana, 'The Latin American Contribution to International Adjudication: The Case of the International Court of Justice', (1992) 39 *Netherlands International Law Review* 127, 136.

[9] Some of these cases were discontinued without further steps after the application. For example, in 1955, the United Kingdom submitted an application against Chile and Argentina on the question of sovereignty over Antarctica. In 1956, the Court ordered the removal of

82 XIMENA FUENTES

accepting the jurisdiction of the Court in accordance with Article 36(2) of the Court's Statute.[10] At least half of these declarations are not subject to conditions or are only subject to the general condition of reciprocity. In three of the contentious cases that involve Latin American states, the respondent has been the United States: the *Nicaragua* case,[11] the *Breard* case,[12] and the *Avena* case,[13] and most of the cases involve Nicaragua as either the applicant or the respondent state. While the subject matter of the Latin American cases before the ICJ varies, at least eight cases deal with territorial and maritime delimitation.

The bases of jurisdiction

In six cases involving Latin American states, a basis for the jurisdiction of the ICJ invoked by the applicant has been the Pact of Bogotá.[14] This is a multilateral treaty adopted at the Ninth Inter-American Conference in 1948, at the same time as the adoption of the Charter of the Organization of American States (OAS). The importance of the Pact of Bogotá in the context of the ICJ is that it establishes the compulsory jurisdiction of the Court as a means to resolve disputes. The original intention of the signatory states was to incorporate into the Pact the mechanism of the optional clause. Article XXXI states:

> In conformity with Article 36, paragraph 2, of the Statute of the International Court of Justice, the High Contracting Parties declare that they recognize, in relation to any other American State, the jurisdiction of the Court as compulsory ipso facto, without the necessity of any special

the case from the list of pending cases as there was no basis of jurisdiction and Chile and Argentina refused to grant *forum prorogatum*. The application submitted by Honduras on 28 October 2009 against Brazil for the diplomatic asylum provided to former Honduran president, Manuel Zelaya, was also discontinued after Honduras decided to withdraw the application.

[10] As of 2 November 2012, the Latin American states that have accepted the compulsory jurisdiction of the Court are Costa Rica, Dominican Republic, Haiti, Honduras, Mexico, Nicaragua, Panama, Paraguay, Peru, and Uruguay. See ICJ, Declarations Recognizing the Jurisdiction of the Court as Compulsory, 2012, available at www.icj-cij.org/jurisdiction/index.php?p1=5&p2=1&p3=3.

[11] *Military and Paramilitary Activities in and against Nicaragua (Nicaragua v. United States) (Merits)*, [1986] ICJ Rep. 14.

[12] *Vienna Convention on Consular Relations (Paraguay v. United States) (Order of 10 November 1998)*, [1998] ICJ Rep. 426 (*Vienna Convention*).

[13] *Avena and Other Mexican Nationals (Mexico v. US)*, [2004] ICJ Rep. 12.

[14] American Treaty on Pacific Settlement (signed 30 April 1948, entered into force 6 May 1949), 30 UNTS 84 (Pact of Bogotá).

LATIN AMERICAN STATES AND THE ICJ 83

agreement so long as the present Treaty is in force, in all disputes of a juridical nature that arise among them concerning:
a) The interpretation of a treaty;
b) Any question of international law;
c) The existence of any fact which, if established, would constitute the breach of an international obligation;
d) The nature or extent of the reparation to be made for the breach of an international obligation.

The Pact of Bogotá was adopted at the same conference that created the Organization of American States (OAS). However, only sixteen Latin American states have ratified it, and two states subsequently denounced it.[15] But the Pact of Bogotá has become increasingly important as a basis of jurisdiction for the ICJ from the late 1990s onwards. The first case in which the Pact of Bogotá served successfully as the basis of the jurisdiction of the Court was *Nicaragua* v. *Honduras*.[16] Prior to this case, commentators viewed the Pact as quite irrelevant in the context of the jurisdictional settlement of disputes.[17]

Despite the fact that the *Border and Transborder Armed Activities Case (Nicaragua* v. *Honduras)* was discontinued, the case is of the utmost importance for Latin American states, since the Court interpreted the optional clause method contemplated in Article XXXI of the Pact of Bogotá and concluded that it did not really operate as the optional clause method of Article 36(2) of the Statute of the Court. One of the arguments that Honduras put forward to object to the jurisdiction of the Court was that the reservations made by Honduras in relation to its unilateral declaration of acceptance of the jurisdiction of the Court of 20 February 1960 (amended on 21 May 1986) were to apply also to Article XXXI of the Pact of Bogotá. The Court was of a different opinion. The Court decided that,

---

[15] The states parties to the Pact of Bogotá are Bolivia, Brazil, Chile, Costa Rica, Dominican Republic, Ecuador, Haiti, Honduras, Mexico, Nicaragua, Panama, Paraguay, Peru, and Uruguay. The Pact entered into force on 5 June 1949.

[16] *Border and Transborder Armed Activities (Nicaragua* v. *Honduras) (Jurisdiction and Admissibility)*, [1988] ICJ Rep. 69.

[17] Even after this case, some commentators still had little confidence in the Pact of Bogotá as the basis of the jurisdiction of the Court. Writing in 1992, Quintana stated that 'none of the new members of the OAS have acceded to it, and, more importantly, the Pact has never been fully applied to an actual dispute between American States'. Quintana, above n. 8, 143. Indeed, by 1992, the only two cases in which the Pact of Bogotá was invoked as the basis of the jurisdiction of the Court had by that time been discontinued: *Border and Transborder Armed Activities (Nicaragua* v. *Honduras)*, above n. 16; and *Border and Transborder Armed Actions (Nicaragua* v. *Costa Rica) (Order of 19 August 1987)*, [1987] ICJ Rep. 182.

contrary to the views of Honduras, the reservations applicable to unilateral declarations deposited with the UN Secretary-General in accordance with Article 36(2) of the Court's Statute were not transmissible to the acceptance of the jurisdiction of the Court contained in Article XXXI of the Pact. In the Court's view, the acceptance of jurisdiction contained in this provision was not unilateral in nature. In other words, Article XXXI comprises the mutual agreement of the parties to the Pact to take their controversies to the ICJ.

An important consequence resulted from this approach: the Court concluded that the optional clause of Article XXXI was not amendable by unilateral action, but only through a modification of the Pact of Bogotá itself.[18] In other words, despite the fact that Article XXXI refers to the method of the optional clause of Article 36(2) of the Court's Statute, the Court's interpretation made it clear that this Article could be better described as establishing jurisdiction by agreement of the parties. This means that the only elements of unilateralism in the acceptance of the jurisdiction through Article XXXI of the Pact of Bogotá are (i) the decision by states to ratify the treaty, and (ii) the decision whether or not to make a reservation at the time of ratification of the Pact. One may wonder, then, why the drafters of the Pact of Bogotá decided to mention Article 36(2) of the Statute in Article XXXI of the Pact, when the result they achieved was that the jurisdiction of the Court was granted in accordance with Article 36(1) of the Statute of the Court.

In addition to the *Border and Transborder Armed Activities Case (Nicaragua* v. *Honduras)*, to date the Pact of Bogotá has been invoked in nine other cases before the Court:

Border and Transborder Armed Actions (Nicaragua v. *Costa Rica)*[19]
Territorial and Maritime Dispute between Nicaragua and Honduras in the Caribbean Sea (Nicaragua v. *Honduras)*[20]

---

[18] *Border and Transborder Armed Activities (Nicaragua* v. *Honduras)*, [1988] ICJ Rep. 69, [34]: 'Even if the Honduran reading of Article XXXI be adopted, and the Article be regarded as a collective declaration of acceptance of compulsory jurisdiction made in accordance with Article 36, paragraph 2, it should be observed that that declaration was incorporated in the Pact of Bogotá as Article XXXI. Accordingly, it can only be modified in accordance with the rules provided for in the Pact itself. Article XXXI nowhere envisages that the undertaking entered into by the parties to the Pact might be amended by means of a unilateral declaration made subsequently under the Statute, and the reference to Article 36, paragraph 2, of the Statute is insufficient in itself to have that effect.'

[19] *Border and Transborder Armed Actions (Nicaragua* v. *Costa Rica) (Order of 21 October 1986)*, [1986] ICJ Rep. 548.

[20] *Territorial and Maritime Dispute between Nicaragua and Honduras in the Caribbean Sea (Nicaragua* v. *Honduras)*, [2007] ICJ Rep. 659.

LATIN AMERICAN STATES AND THE ICJ

Aerial Herbicide Spraying (Ecuador v. Colombia)[21]

Dispute regarding Navigational and Related Rights (Costa Rica v. Nicaragua)[22]

Maritime Dispute (Peru v. Chile)[23]

Certain Questions concerning Diplomatic Relations (Honduras v. Brazil)[24]

Certain Activities carried out by Nicaragua in the Border Area (Costa Rica v. Nicaragua)[25]

Construction of a Road in Costa Rica along the San Juan River (Nicaragua v. Costa Rica)[26]

Territorial and Maritime Dispute (Nicaragua v. Colombia)[27]

After the submission of *Border and Transborder Armed Activities (Nicaragua v. Honduras)* in 1986, thirteen years passed before the Pact of Bogotá was again invoked as the basis of the jurisdiction of the ICJ in another case between the same parties: *Territorial and Maritime Dispute in the Caribbean Sea (Nicaragua v. Honduras).*[28] This time, Honduras did not object to the jurisdiction of the Court. It must be borne in mind that the unilateral declaration that Honduras deposited with the UN Secretary-General under Article 36(2) of the Court's Statute explicitly excluded territorial questions, including questions about the territorial sea and questions regarding rights of sovereignty, as well as jurisdiction concerning the legal status and limits of the exclusive economic zone and the continental shelf. Because the Pact of Bogotá serves as a separate basis for the jurisdiction of the Court, and taking into account the judgment of the Court of 1988, Honduras was prevented from invoking the reservations applicable to its unilateral declaration of acceptance of the jurisdiction of the Court.

---

[21] *Aerial Herbicide Spraying (Ecuador v. Colombia)*, [2008] ICJ Rep. 174.

[22] *Dispute regarding Navigational and Related Rights (Costa Rica v. Nicaragua) (Judgment)*, [2009] ICJ Rep. 213.

[23] *Maritime Dispute (Peru v. Chile) (Order of 27 April 2010)*, [2010] ICJ Rep. 295.

[24] *Certain Questions concerning Diplomatic Relations (Honduras v. Brazil) (Order of 12 May 2010)*, [2010] ICJ Rep. 303.

[25] *Certain Activities carried out by Nicaragua in the Border Area (Costa Rica v. Nicaragua)*, ICJ, General List No. 150, 18 November 2010.

[26] *Construction of a Road in Costa Rica along the San Juan River (Nicaragua v. Costa Rica)*, ICJ, General List No. 152, 23 January 2012.

[27] *Territorial and Maritime Dispute (Nicaragua v. Colombia) (Judgment)*, ICJ, General List No. 124, 19 November 2012.

[28] *Territorial and Maritime Dispute between Nicaragua and Honduras in the Caribbean Sea (Nicaragua v. Honduras)*, [2007] ICJ Rep. 659.

However, Honduras's presence before the Court in the *Territorial and Maritime* dispute with Nicaragua was not due to an inescapable obligation derived from the Pact of Bogotá and the Court's judgment of 1988. Indeed, it must be borne in mind that after the 1988 decision, Honduras had enough time to denounce the Pact of Bogotá. Therefore, if Honduras did not want questions of territorial sovereignty and maritime delimitation to be brought by Nicaragua to the Court, it should have contemplated such a denunciation. Moreover, it cannot be said that Honduras was taken by surprise by Nicaragua's application of 8 December 1999, because it should have guessed that its ratification of the 1986 Maritime Delimitation Treaty with Colombia in November 1999 would not be well received by Nicaragua.[29] The 1986 Treaty recognized implicitly that Colombia had sovereignty over certain islands, banks, and cays over which Nicaragua was preparing a claim of sovereignty. It is argued, therefore, that Honduras should have anticipated that Nicaragua would go to the Court to ask for a delimitation of their maritime zones. As Honduras made no attempt to avoid the jurisdiction of the ICJ, it is concluded that it probably considered that a decision by the ICJ might have a positive effect in its future relations with Nicaragua and other countries in the region.

To assess the role that the ICJ may play in Central America, it is necessary to consider that drawing maritime boundaries in the Caribbean Sea is a complex task, since it involves various states with overlapping claims. As such, the direct negotiation of bilateral treaties is not perhaps the best method of resolving these disputes, and the prospects of negotiating a multilateral treaty, given the historical differences between the various countries involved, are very low. Therefore recourse to the ICJ might be the best option to obtain the resolution of the many pieces into which disputes in the region are divided; it seems that Honduras shared this view, since it accepted the jurisdiction of the Court without complaint.

Since 1999, the Pact of Bogotá has experienced a revival. This treaty has been invoked as the basis of the jurisdiction of the Court in the *Nicaragua* v. *Colombia* case, in the three cases involving Nicaragua and

---

[29] For an overview of the complexity of the case and its relation to the *Nicaragua* v. *Colombia* maritime boundary issue, see Martin Pratt, 'The Maritime Boundary Dispute between Honduras and Nicaragua in the Caribbean Sea', IBRU Boundary and Security Bulletin, 2001, available at www.dur.ac.uk/resources/ibru/publications/full/bsb9-2 pratt.pdf.

LATIN AMERICAN STATES AND THE ICJ

Costa Rica, in the *Aerial Herbicide Spraying* case between Ecuador and Colombia, and in the *Maritime Dispute* between Peru and Chile.

With regard to other bases of jurisdiction, it should be mentioned that the optional clause[30] of Article 36(2) of the Statute of the Court has been one of the bases of the Court's jurisdiction in the three cases involving Costa Rica and Nicaragua: (i) *Navigational Rights on the River San Juan*, (ii) *Certain Activities carried out by Nicaragua in the Border Area*, and (iii) *Construction of a Road in Costa Rica along the San Juan River*.[31] Without doubt, the most important case in which the basis of the Court's jurisdiction was the optional clause mechanism of Article 36(2) of the Statute was the *Nicaragua* case against the United States.[32]

Recourse to the ICJ has also been based on special agreements in which the litigating parties have been able to agree on the questions to be resolved by the Court. Of the twenty cases that involve Latin American states before the ICJ, only three disputes have been referred to the ICJ on the basis of a special agreement in accordance with Article 36(1) of the Court's Statute: (i) The *Asylum Case*, between Colombia and Peru,[33] (ii) the *Arbitral Award Made by the King of Spain*, between Honduras and Nicaragua,[34] and (iii) the *Land, Island and Maritime Frontier Dispute*, between El Salvador and Honduras.[35]

Other disputes have been referred to the Court on the basis of compromissory clauses contained in a treaty, such as the disputes regarding compliance with the obligations contained in Article 36 of the Vienna Convention on Consular Relations: the *Breard* case (between Paraguay and the United States),[36] and *Avena and Other Mexican Nationals (Mexico* v. *United States)*.[37] Another case in point is the *Pulp Mills* case between

---

[30] For the purposes of this list of cases, the Pact of Bogotá should be considered under Art. 36(1) of the Court's Statute.

[31] *Dispute regarding Navigational and Related Rights (Costa Rica* v. *Nicaragua) (Judgment)*, [2009] ICJ Rep. 213; *Construction of a Road in Costa Rica along the San Juan River (Nicaragua* v. *Costa Rica)*, ICJ, General List No. 152, 23 January 2012; *Territorial and Maritime Dispute (Nicaragua* v. *Colombia) (Judgment)*, ICJ, General List No. 124, 19 November 2012.

[32] *Military and Paramilitary Activities in and against Nicaragua (Nicaragua* v. *United States) (Jurisdiction and Admissibility)*, [1984] ICJ Rep. 392.

[33] *Asylum Case (Colombia* v. *Peru)*, [1950] ICJ Rep. 266.

[34] *Arbitral Award Made by the King of Spain on 23 December 1906 (Honduras* v. *Nicaragua)*, [1960] ICJ Rep. 192.

[35] *Land, Island, and Maritime Frontier Dispute (El Salvador/Honduras; Nicaragua intervening)*, [1992] ICJ Rep. 350.

[36] 'Request for Provisional Measures', *Vienna Convention case (Order of 9 April 1998)*, [1998] ICJ Rep. 426.

[37] *Avena*, above n. 13.

88   XIMENA FUENTES

Argentina and Uruguay concerning the interpretation and application of the Statute of the River Uruguay.[38]

Objections to the jurisdiction of the Court

The only method that guarantees that the parties are really committed to the resolution of a dispute through adjudication is a special agreement (*compromis*) to refer the case to the ICJ. In all other cases, the time lapsed between the acceptance of the jurisdiction of the Court and the emergence of the controversy might mean that the states are no longer willing to appear before the Court. Only five of the twenty cases involving Latin American states before the ICJ have received objections to the jurisdiction of the Court, thus suggesting a limited degree of resistance to the Court's involvement in the resolution of disputes.

However, there is one limitation to the jurisdiction of the ICJ contained in the Pact of Bogotá that has proved to be problematic and, therefore, deserves a special comment in this chapter. In the case of the Pact, the negotiating states were not willing to accept the jurisdiction of the Court for all the disputes between them that might emerge. For this reason, Article VI of the Pact attempts to restrict the operation of the dispute settlement mechanisms established by the treaty. Article VI reads as follows:

> The aforesaid procedures, furthermore, may not be applied to matters already settled by arrangements between the Parties, or by arbitral award or by decision of an international court, or which are governed by agreements or treaties in force on the date of the conclusion of the present treaty.

The interpretation of this reference that Article VI makes to treaties that have settled a dispute or that govern a particular situation may give rise to some discrepancies. The fact that there is a treaty that governs a situation does not mean that a controversy has been resolved, given that most treaties are negotiated to govern the relations between the parties without need of a pre-existing controversy. Therefore it seems that there is a distinction to be made when reading Article VI which should be taken into account when trying to understand the rationale behind this limitation to the jurisdiction of the ICJ.

It is clear that Article VI of the Pact of Bogotá attempted to exclude from the jurisdiction of the ICJ those disputes already settled by arbitral award

---

[38] *Pulp Mills on the River Uruguay (Argentina v. Uruguay)*, [2010] ICJ Rep. 28.

or by a decision of an international court. Therefore the first objective of this provision was to avoid the reopening of disputes already settled by adjudication of an international tribunal. This interpretation is warranted by the *travaux préparatoires* of the Pact.[39]

It was Peru that proposed the inclusion of Article VI in the treaty. Peru's concern was not driven by worries about the reopening of already adjudicated cases, but by the potential for the reopening of matters already settled by the parties themselves through treaties concluded to resolve controversial situations. It seems that Peru was afraid that its neighbour Ecuador could attempt to challenge the Rio de Janeiro Protocol on Peace, Friendship and Boundaries of 1942, which put an end to an armed conflict between the two states. Indeed, the Rio de Janeiro Protocol settled a long-lasting boundary dispute between the parties. But it was clear that the Protocol did not satisfy everybody in Ecuador. Shortly after its conclusion, Ecuador indicated its disagreement with the demarcation process in the boundary sector between the source of the Quebrada de San Francisco and the mouth of the Yaupi river. The dispute was submitted to a single arbitrator, Captain Braz Dias de Aguiar, a Brazilian naval officer whose name was suggested by the neighbouring countries that acted as guarantors to the Rio de Janeiro Protocol. On 14 July 1945, the arbitrator handed down his decision. However, a small sector in the Cordillera del Cóndor remained unsettled as a result of new geographical facts discovered in 1947 regarding the fluvial system in the zone.[40] In September 1948, Ecuador stated that the fact that the Protocol of Rio de Janeiro could not be applied in this sector put into question the validity of the entire agreement.[41] Possibly this was the kind of reopening of settled disputes that Peru was anticipating and was trying to avoid when it proposed the incorporation of Article VI in the Pact of Bogotá.

Chile had concerns similar to those of Peru. Chile and Bolivia had signed a Peace Agreement in 1904 which delimited the boundary between the two states, but shortly after the conclusion of the agreement it became clear that Bolivia was not happy with it. Indeed, in 1920, Bolivia tried to obtain a revision of the agreement by the Assembly of the League of

---

[39] Ninth Conference of American States, *Acts of the Sessions of Committee III, Third Session* (1948), 134–36.

[40] Ronald St John, 'Conflict in the Cordillera del Cóndor: The Ecuador–Peru Disputes', *IBRU Boundary and Security Bulletin* (1996), available at www.dur.ac.uk/resources/ibru/publications/full/bsb4-1_john.pdf.

[41] Ibid.

Nations, invoking Article 19 of the Treaty of Versailles.[42] The Assembly appointed a commission of three jurists, who concluded that Article 19 did not allow the revision of treaties.[43]

This political context explains why Article VI excludes from the operation of the Pact of Bogotá matters that have been settled by arrangement between the parties. The use of the term 'settled' throws light on the fact that these are treaties that resolved ongoing disputes between the parties. It is for this reason that when Peru justified the inclusion of Article VI it made explicit reference to the principle of *res judicata*.[44]

However, Article VI also excludes from the application of the Pact all matters governed by agreements or treaties in force on the date of the conclusion of the Pact of Bogotá. These treaties, referred to in the second part of Article VI of the Pact, differ from treaties that have settled a dispute. This second type of treaty can be described as agreements that simply aim at governing the relations between the parties without need of a pre-existing dispute. Therefore the rationale for the inclusion of this second type of treaty is not necessarily connected to the principle of *res judicata*.

The argument could therefore be made that Article VI distinguishes between treaties that have settled a dispute between the parties, and treaties that simply govern the relationship between the parties with regard to certain matters. With this distinction in mind, Article VI could be read as requiring that treaties be in force at the date of the conclusion of the Pact of Bogotá only in relation to the second type of treaty (treaties that govern a certain matter). According to this interpretation the *ratione temporis* criterion contemplated in this provision should not be applied to the first part of Article VI, which relates to *res judicata*, because disputes that have been settled should never be allowed to be reopened irrespective of the date of their settlement.

The ICJ has had no opportunity to decide whether this interpretation, which distinguishes between two different rationales behind Article VI, is correct. It is true that the decision of the Court in the *Territorial and Maritime Dispute* case (Nicaragua v. Colombia) in the Preliminary

---

[42] Art. 19 of the Treaty of Versailles stated: 'The Assembly may from time to time advise the reconsideration by Members of the League of treaties which have become inapplicable and the consideration of international conditions whose continuance might endanger the peace of the world.'

[43] Hermann Mosler, *The International Society as a Legal Community* (Alphen aan den Rijn: Sijthoff & Noordhoff, 1980), 289–90.

[44] IX International Conference of American States, Acts and Documents, Acts of the Sessions of Committee III, Third Session, 27 April 1948, 136.

Objections phase could be read as disregarding any distinction between the *res judicata* and the *ratione temporis* aspects of Article VI. Indeed, in *Territorial and Maritime Dispute*, the ICJ interpreted that matters that are governed by treaties between the parties are the same as matters settled by arrangement between the parties for the purposes of the application of Article VI in the context of the case between Nicaragua and Colombia.[45] However, it is important to stress that the Court stated that the two situations had the same legal effects in the 'specific circumstances of the present case', which leaves open the possibility that in future controversies between parties to the Pact of Bogotá the distinction between treaties that settled a dispute and treaties that simply govern a particular situation can be made for the purposes of applying the critical date of the conclusion of the Pact of Bogotá (30 April 1948) only to the second type of treaty.

Article VI poses an additional practical problem to the operation of the Pact of Bogotá. The party that invokes Article VI as the basis of an objection to jurisdiction may find that the other litigant claims the nullity or termination of the treaty that allegedly has settled the dispute or that governs a certain matter. Or, in more general terms, it might be that the applicant argues that the matter brought before the Court does not fall within the scope of the treaty in question. This might only be a strategy to block the operation of Article VI, but it might well be a genuine question over which one of the parties would like to obtain a decision from the Court. From this perspective, Article VI certainly shows its weaknesses and defects as a limitation of jurisdiction clause. If the purpose was to limit the jurisdiction of the Court, avoiding the reopening of disputes, its drafting is definitely deficient for a very simple reason: in general terms, the use of the term 'settled' in Article VI means that this provision is making reference to the principle of *res judicata*, which in essence, is a defence on the merits of a case.

However, the purpose of the drafters of the Pact of Bogotá was to make Article VI work as a jurisdictional limitation that would stop the Court from looking at a case *in limine*. It was for this reason that the parties to the Pact of Bogotá included Article XXXIV, which provides:

> If the Court, for the reasons set forth in ... Article VI ... of this Treaty, declared itself without jurisdiction to hear the controversy, such controversy shall be declared ended.

---

[45] *Territorial and Maritime Dispute (Nicaragua v. Colombia) (Preliminary Objections)*, [2007] ICJ Rep. 832, [39].

The problems in the operation of Article VI were evidenced in the *Territorial and Maritime Dispute* case. Nicaragua contested sovereignty over certain islands. Colombia's position was that the question of sovereignty over those islands had been settled by the parties in the 1928 Bárcenas-Esguerra Treaty and, therefore, the question of sovereignty over the islands was beyond the jurisdiction of the Court by application of Article VI of the Pact of Bogotá. Furthermore, Colombia was clear in stating that Nicaragua's claim that the 1928 treaty had terminated due to Colombia's alleged breach of the treaty was instrumental to Nicaragua's attempt to avoid the effects of Article VI of the Pact of Bogotá:

> A purpose of so extraordinary a claim is to vitiate Colombia's valid objections to jurisdiction: to undermine its position that, under the Pact of Bogotá, the dispute is one settled by arrangement between the parties and governed by a treaty that was in force on the date of the conclusion of the Pact, and is still in force; and to undermine its position that the dispute arises out of facts antecedent to 1932. If the Court were to sustain such an argument, it would permit a State to evade limitations on the jurisdiction of the Court by means of a spurious claim, because the presentation of alleged violations before the Court would then of itself suffice to render those reservations – which are an expression of the will of states – ineffectual.[46]

Nicaragua was of the view that even if Article VI excluded the interpretation of treaties that settled a dispute between the parties, this provision could not be read as excluding a new dispute concerning the termination or nullity of that treaty. Furthermore, Nicaragua tried to persuade the Court not to decide the questions about the validity or effectiveness of the 1928 Treaty at the preliminary objections stage by claiming that the Court was prevented from deciding issues that implied looking at the merits of the case.[47] Irrespective of the real motivations of Nicaragua in claiming the nullity or termination of the 1928 Treaty, the argument that Article VI cannot prevent the examination of the validity and legal effects of a treaty is a sound one.

However, Nicaragua was not able to persuade the ICJ to dismiss the preliminary objections of Colombia. Nevertheless, it put the Court in the

---

[46] 'Preliminary Objections of the Government of Colombia, July 2003', *Territorial and Maritime Dispute (Nicaragua v. Colombia)*, available at www.icj-cij.org/docket/files/124/13868.pdf, Vol. 1, [48].

[47] 'Written Statement of Nicaragua, 26 January 2004', *Territorial and Maritime Dispute (Nicaragua v. Colombia) (Preliminary Objections)*, available at www.icj-cij.org/docket/files/124/13872.pdf, Vol. 1, [2.23].

difficult position of having to provide a good argument why the dispute, as presented by Nicaragua, should be dismissed *in limine*, despite the fact that it seemed to be linked to the merits of the case. According to Judge Abraham, the Court failed to provide a good answer.[48] In his view, 'this [was] ascribable primarily to the fact that the Court succumbed to the unfortunate influence of the unusual provisions it had to deal with'.[49] In the words of Judge Abraham, Article VI of the Pact of Bogotá, in combination with Article XXXIV, is an unusual provision. The problem is that the parties to the Pact of Bogotá aimed at achieving the legitimate purpose of excluding from the jurisdiction of the Court disputes that were already settled, but they also required that the Court should declare this lack of jurisdiction *in limine*. It seems that the drafters of the Pact of Bogotá were not aware that the application of Article VI necessarily requires the Court to go into the merits of a case because *res judicata* is a typical defence that attacks the merits of a case. As put by Judge Abraham,

> In other words, in the special system established by the Pact, what would be strictly a question on the merits under the general régime (for example, where the Court is seised solely on the basis of optional clause declarations), i.e., the question whether one State's claim against another accords or conflicts with treaty provisions in force in their relations, is transmuted into a question of *jurisdiction*.[50]

But Judge Abraham's view was not followed by the majority vote in the Court. Colombia was successful in convincing the Court to declare, at the preliminary objections stage, that sovereignty over the islands pertained to Colombia, as agreed in the 1928 Treaty. However, this need not be the case in future disputes before the Court, and then it might be that the parties to the Pact of Bogotá will realize that there were other possible formulas that might more easily have achieved their purpose of avoiding the reopening of already settled disputes. One of those other possibilities was to include in the Pact of Bogotá the so-called 'Belgian clause', which would have read, 'The dispute settlement mechanisms of the Pact cannot be invoked in relation to controversies that have emerged or that relate to facts that have occurred before the date of conclusion of this Pact.'

Is there any explanation for the particular and original drafting chosen for Article VI? Yes. Apart from the decision of the parties to prevent the reopening of already settled disputes, the negotiating parties agreed that

---

[48] *Territorial and Maritime Dispute (Nicaragua v. Colombia) (Preliminary Objections)*, [2007] ICJ Rep. 832, [7] (Judge Abraham).
[49] Ibid., [7] (Judge Abraham).   [50] Ibid., [8] (Judge Abraham).

the intention of the Pact of Bogotá was to provide a system that would resolve any disputes between the parties. Perhaps that was the reason why the Belgian clause was not even considered as an option; the Belgian clause is too explicit about the fact that certain disputes, those that precede a certain date, will have to remain open unless the parties agree on a case-by-case basis to refer them to a peaceful means of dispute resolution. Article VI also has the potential to leave certain genuine disputes unresolved, but it is certainly not explicit on this issue.

Some unforeseen effects of the poor drafting of the Pact of Bogotá: *Nicaragua* v. *Colombia*

On 19 November 2012, the ICJ handed down its decision in *Territorial and Maritime Dispute (Nicaragua* v. *Colombia)*. It must be recalled that Colombia objected to the jurisdiction of the Court. It was Colombia's contention that sovereignty over the islands in the Caribbean and the delimitation of their respective maritime zones were already settled by a 1928 Treaty and a 1930 Protocol between the parties. Therefore Colombia invoked Article VI of the Pact of Bogotá, which excludes from the jurisdiction of the Court disputes that have been settled by treaties concluded before the date of the Pact (1948). The Court accepted Colombia's argument only in part, and declared that the islands of San Andrés, Providencia, and Santa Catalina belonged to Colombia by application of the 1928 Treaty and, accordingly, that Article VI prevented the Court from entering into this issue. As to which other maritime features formed part of the archipelago of San Andrés and belonged to Colombia, the Court concluded that this issue had not been settled by the 1928 Treaty and that therefore this was a matter for the Court to decide. It also decided that the question of sovereignty over the islands of Roncador, Quitasueño, and Serrana was explicitly left out of the 1928 Treaty and therefore also fell within its jurisdiction. As regards the maritime delimitation, the fact that the 1930 Protocol stated that the San Andrés archipelago did not extend west of the 82nd meridian could not be interpreted, said the Court, as effecting a maritime delimitation between the parties.[51] Therefore the Court reached the conclusion that the maritime delimitation had not been settled by the 1930 Protocol.

Without a maritime delimitation agreement between the parties, the Court was called on to effect the delimitation in accordance with the rules

---

[51] Ibid., [115].

of general international law. These rules require the Court to take into account various factors in order to reach an equitable result. Normally the Court begins by drawing a median line that is later adjusted by application of the other equitable criteria. In this case, one of the most important considerations was the element of proportionality between the length of the relevant coasts of the parties, which played in favour of Nicaragua. In the result, the median line was moved closer to the coast of the archipelago of San Andrés, east of the 82° W meridian, and it was not drawn in its full north–south extension as had been requested by Colombia.

The judgment was received with great surprise in Colombia, which accused the ICJ of disregarding its security interests and the economic dependence of the population of San Andrés on the natural resources of the area. President Juan Manuel Santos, in a televised message broadcast to the country, stated that the judgment contained serious omissions, errors, excesses, and inconsistencies which were unacceptable to Colombia.[52] Therefore he promised to the country, and in particular the inhabitants of the archipelago of San Andrés, to give consideration to the use of all available mechanisms to protect Colombia's rights. In this context, the government of Colombia approached international lawyers to obtain an expert opinion on the legal options available to Colombia to 'face this judgment'.[53]

While Colombia waits for this legal report, it has already taken one step that shows its disagreement with the way in which the ICJ resolved the dispute. On 27 November 2012, Colombia withdrew from the Pact of Bogotá. President Santos has stated that territorial and maritime disputes should be resolved by agreement and not by international tribunals. The Court might be blamed for not having anticipated this reaction by Colombia and the negative effects that this might have for the future role of the Court in the peaceful settlement of disputes in the region. However, it is interesting to examine to what extent the operation of the Pact of Bogotá put Colombia and the ICJ itself in a position that made it extremely difficult to give weight to the fishing interests of the islanders, which now are ascribed an importance that had not transpired from the written pleadings submitted by Colombia.

---

[52] 'Message of President Santos to the country on 19 November 2012', available at www. youtube.com/watch?v=2Reyu0NrhoA%26;noredirect=1.

[53] Colombia has hired the services of Robert Volterra from Volterra & Fietta, and press information states that the expert opinion would be handed down in May 2013: www. colombia.com/actualidad/nacionales/sdi/56361/colombia-dara-a-conocer-estrategia-ante-fallo-de-la-haya-en-mayo.

During the preliminary objections phase, Colombia's position was that the 1928 Treaty and its Protocol of 1930 had established a maritime delimitation line along the 82° W meridian. It was clear that the 1928 and the 1930 instruments were treaties, and the question was one of interpreting whether or not the text of the documents could be read as effecting a maritime delimitation. For that reason, in Colombia's preliminary objections there is no mention of the present economic dependence of the population of the San Andrés archipelago on fishing in the waters under control of Colombia, because Colombia was concerned only with convincing the Court that the treaty established a maritime boundary.

Therefore, when the Court rejected this part of Colombia's preliminary objections and decided instead that there was no agreement regarding the maritime delimitation between the Colombian islands and the Nicaraguan coast, any alternative argument based on the use of the resources of the disputed area was bound to appear very weak. This is explained by the fact that once Colombia claimed that there was a maritime delimitation treaty in place, its control of those waters and the uses of the resources by the local population appeared as the necessary consequence of this mistaken belief. In other words, the preliminary objections contributed to building the idea that the economic dependence of the population of the islands on fishing in the disputed waters did not derive from an original economic and social link between the population and those waters, but from the fact that Colombia thought that it had the right under a treaty to exercise exclusive jurisdiction over those waters.

After the rejection of this preliminary objection by the Court, Colombia should have contemplated a different strategy regarding the role of the use of the natural resources of the area by the islanders under the delimitation. However, Colombia put little effort into elaborating a new strategy. It seems that Colombia was convinced that the Court would follow a median line which, after all, would be close to the 82° W meridian. That seems to explain why Colombia disregarded the possibility that the Court would apply the proportionality test and that Quitasueño would be denied a full maritime projection. These two possibilities certainly required from Colombia a greater elaboration of its arguments regarding the fishing interests of the population. It failed to do this. It might be the case that, having relied heavily on the existence of a maritime delimitation agreement at the preliminary objections stage, it was afterwards extremely difficult for Colombia to invoke the economic and social factors as equitable criteria in their own right.

Nicaragua

At this point, it is clear that Nicaragua deserves a section of its own in this chapter. Nicaragua has been the most active Latin American country before the ICJ. It has participated in nine cases before the Court either as applicant or respondent.[54] It was allowed to intervene in the *Land, Island and Maritime Frontier* case (El Salvador v. Honduras) (this was the first time that the ICJ allowed a third-party intervention under Article 62 of its Statute).[55] Moreover, the famous *Nicaragua* case against the United States is still a subject of debate, in particular, its effects regarding the resolution of disputes about the use of force before the ICJ.[56]

These developments raise the question why Nicaragua and its neighbours are so eager to utilize the ICJ. Of course, one could highlight the positive example that Central American states are giving to the international community by opting for the peaceful settlement of their disputes, allowing the Court to play a prominent role in the resolution of disputes in the region. However, one might also feel curious about their motives for opting for the Court and the unspoken reasons for such a course of action. Perhaps this frequency in the use of the Court is the manifestation of a lack of negotiating capacity in the Central American region and an inability to arrive at stable, sensible arrangements between the parties.

It is clear that Nicaragua has had and continues to have land and maritime boundary disputes with its neighbours. It is clear also that Nicaragua has not felt satisfied with the treaties that from time to time it has concluded for the resolution of these territorial and maritime disputes.

---

[54] At present, Nicaragua has two cases pending before the Court: *Certain Activities carried out by Nicaragua in the Border Area (Costa Rica v. Nicaragua)*, ICJ, General List No. 150, 18 November 2010; and *Construction of a Road in Costa Rica along the San Juan River (Nicaragua v. Costa Rica)*, ICJ, General List No. 152, 23 January 2012. The ICJ joined these proceedings on 23 April 2013. See ICJ press release, 'The Court Joins the Proceedings in the Two Cases', available at www.icj-cij.org/docket/files/150/17332.pdf. In the past, Nicaragua acted as an intervening state in *Land, Island and Maritime Frontier Dispute (El Salvador/Honduras)*. It also instituted proceedings against Honduras and Costa Rica for armed activities in the border (the two cases were later discontinued in 1992 and 1987 respectively). Another case, the *Territorial and Maritime Dispute between Nicaragua and Honduras in the Caribbean Sea (Nicaragua v. Honduras)* was decided by the Court on 8 October 2007. *Territorial and Maritime Dispute (Nicaragua v. Colombia)* was decided on 19 November 2012.

[55] 'Application to Intervene', *Land, Island and Maritime Frontier Dispute (El Salvador/Honduras) (Order of 28 February 1990)*, [1990] ICJ Rep. 3.

[56] Christine Gray, 'The Use and Abuse of the International Court of Justice: Cases concerning the Use of Force after Nicaragua', (2003) 14 *European Journal of International Law* 867.

98 XIMENA FUENTES

It must be recalled that Nicaragua put into question the validity of an arbitral award of 1906 by which the King of Spain had resolved a dispute between Nicaragua and Honduras.[57] More recently, in the *Territorial and Maritime Dispute* case (Nicaragua v. Colombia), Nicaragua questioned the validity of the 1928 Treaty with Colombia, claiming that at the time of its conclusion Nicaragua was occupied by the United States. It is also worth mentioning that the Nicaraguan application against Honduras in 1986 (*Territorial and Maritime Dispute in the Caribbean Sea*) was prompted by the fact that Honduras and Colombia had ratified a maritime delimitation agreement without taking into account Nicaragua's interests in the zone. And, in the still pending *Certain Activities in the Border* case (Costa Rica v. Nicaragua), Costa Rica claims that Nicaragua is not complying with the arbitral awards and the treaties that in the late nineteenth century settled the question of which state has sovereignty over the region.

Therefore it might be said that Nicaragua probably perceives that it has lacked sufficient negotiating power to obtain satisfactory arrangements with its Central American neighbours regarding boundary issues and the administration of the international boundary zone. This frustration with the treaties concluded by previous governments, which also applies to the awards of international arbitrators that have decided Nicaraguan boundary cases, is giving rise to attempts by Nicaragua to reopen old disputes.

For Nicaragua, the ICJ might be a better alternative for the resolution of disputes than direct negotiation. In the case of Costa Rica, it must be borne in mind that this country has no army and, therefore, it cannot demonstrate military power as against Nicaragua. In this context, Costa Rica also looks to the Court as the authority that might compel Nicaragua to abide by its international obligations. The question will be whether or not the parties will comply with future decisions of the ICJ. Already it seems that Nicaragua has not complied with the provisional measures that the Court ordered in the *Certain Activities in the Border Area* case.[58]

Boundary disputes and maritime delimitation cases: disregarding previous commitments

Eight of the twenty cases that involve Latin American countries before the ICJ relate to boundary disputes. With regard to land boundaries, it

---

[57] *Arbitral Award Made by the King of Spain on 23 December 1906 (Honduras v. Nicaragua)*, [1960] ICJ Rep. 192.
[58] 'Costa Rica protesta por incursión de nicaragüenses en territorio en litigio', *El País*, 31 October 2012, available at www.elpais.cr/frontend/noticia_detalle/1/74306.

is interesting to note that in each of the Latin American land boundary cases before the Court a treaty that allegedly settled the delimitation dispute was in place. Sometimes those treaties attempted to apply the *uti possidetis* principle. This was a pragmatic formula that was thought to avoid controversies between the newly born Latin American states concerning their international boundaries. The *uti possidetis* principle transformed the inherited administrative boundaries of the Spanish and Portuguese dominions into the international boundaries of the newly independent Latin American states. The principle also worked as a way of avoiding new claims by the European countries over territory that was not physically occupied, as it put all the territory lying within the new frontiers under the territorial sovereignty of the new states irrespective of effective occupation.[59]

It was obvious that the application of the *uti possidetis* principle would give rise to disputes, as it was not always clear where the old administrative boundary was. Latin American countries were more or less successful in resolving these disputes by arbitration. Indeed, Latin America can show a strong tradition of appointing arbitral tribunals for the resolution of boundary disputes. From the 1990s onwards, this practice changed and Latin American states began to refer boundary cases to the ICJ.

Cases regarding the determination of the *uti possidetis* line demonstrate that the parties were willing to refer genuine questions about the ambiguities of the *uti possidetis* line to international adjudication, and in this case it can certainly be said that Latin American states have contributed to the peaceful settlement of disputes. But there is a second type of boundary dispute between Latin American countries that shows precisely the opposite – an extraordinary resistance to definitive settlement.

In this regard, it is interesting to mention the *Honduras* v. *Nicaragua* case in which Nicaragua questioned the validity of the King of Spain Award of 23 December 1906.[60] According to the ICJ, the first time that Nicaragua questioned the legal effects of the Award was in 1912. The reasons invoked by Nicaragua to claim the nullity of the award were rejected by the Court on the basis that Nicaragua, in the period between 1906 and 1912, by 'express declaration and conduct, recognized the Award as valid'.[61]

---

[59] Malcolm N. Shaw, 'The Heritage of States: The Principle of *Uti Possidetis Iuris* Today', (1996) 77 BYBIL 98.

[60] The application was submitted to the ICJ by Nicaragua on 1 July 1958.

[61] *Arbitral Award Made by the King of Spain on 23 December 1906 (Honduras* v. *Nicaragua)*, [1960] ICJ Rep. 192.

Another case in point is the *Land, Island and Maritime Frontier* case between El Salvador and Honduras. These states were involved in a long-lasting dispute that escalated into a military conflict. On 1 December 1986, the parties, after failing to obtain the delimitation of the boundary by a mixed commission, submitted the controversy to a chamber of the ICJ. Nicaragua was granted permission to intervene with regard to the question of the legal status of the waters of the Gulf of Fonseca.[62] The Court handed down its decision on the merits on 11 September 1992, declaring that the Gulf was jointly owned by the three countries and deciding the land boundary dispute as well as the question of sovereignty over certain islands. Problems of implementation arose shortly after the judgment. The decision implied the displacement of some inhabitants in the area and therefore problems of implementation were easy to foresee.[63] There have been incursions by the Honduran police and the military into what El Salvador claims is its territory;[64] Honduras claims that El Salvador has issued logging permits for areas belonging to Honduras.[65] Moreover, it is said that Nicaragua has not complied with the judgment, but a problem lies in the fact that the ICJ itself decided that the decision was not binding on Nicaragua.[66]

In January 2002, Honduras took the matter to the UN Security Council, claiming that El Salvador failed to comply with the judgment. El Salvador responded with an application for the revision of the judgment before the Court, which was ultimately rejected.[67] According to Llamzon, after this final judgment, 'continuing border problems suggest that El Salvador may not be completely fulfilling its obligations to execute the judgment reasonably and in good faith', and that 'most of the problems of implementation stem from failures to negotiate'.[68]

At this point mention should be made of two cases pending before the Court, because they involve to a certain extent an attempt to challenge what was settled in the past by treaty or by international adjudication. In the *Maritime Dispute* case (Peru v. Chile), Chile's principal contention is

---

[62] 'Application to Intervene', *Land, Island and Maritime Frontier Dispute*, [1990] ICJ Rep. 3.

[63] See Aloysius Llamzon, 'Jurisdiction and Compliance in Recent Decisions of the International Court of Justice', (2008) 18 EJIL 815, 827.

[64] Ibid.   [65] Ibid.

[66] D. Arrese, 'Gulf of Fonseca', in Rüdiger Wolfrum (ed.), *Max Planck Encyclopedia of Public International Law* (Oxford University Press, 2012).

[67] *Application for Revision of the Judgment of 11 September 1992 in the Case Concerning the Land, Island and Maritime Frontier Dispute*, [2003] ICJ Rep. 392.

[68] Llamzon, above n. 62, 828.

that the maritime boundary has been established by agreement between the two parties. Peru, the applicant, denies that there has ever been an agreement on maritime delimitation and is therefore asking the Court to draw an equidistant line between the maritime zones of the two countries. If Chile is right that there is a maritime delimitation agreement in place, which the parties have signed and put into practice, then Peru's application should be considered as an attempt to reopen a matter that was already settled. Again, if Chile is right it would be paradoxical for Peru, the ideologist behind Article VI of the Pact of Bogotá, to attempt to reopen an issue that was already settled.

In *Certain Activities Carried out by Nicaragua in the Border Area* (Costa Rica v. Nicaragua), Costa Rica asserts that Nicaragua is occupying and using Costa Rican territory and that its activities not only imply illegal occupation but are causing harm to the environment. In this context, Costa Rica asks the ICJ to declare that Nicaragua has breached a number of obligations towards Costa Rica, among which Costa Rica includes the 1858 Treaty on Territorial Limits, the Arbitral Award by the President of the United States of 1888, and two Arbitral Awards by Edward Porter Alexander of 1897. In the view of Costa Rica, Nicaragua is attempting artificially to create a territorial dispute where there was none. In this regard, Costa Rica asserts that Nicaragua has always recognized that the territory now allegedly under dispute fell entirely under Costa Rican sovereignty.[69] In addition, Costa Rica requested provisional measures and the Court ordered the following: 'Each Party shall refrain from sending to, or maintaining in the disputed territory, including the *caño*, any personnel, whether civilian, police or security.' However, there have been accusations that Nicaragua is not complying with the provisional measures.[70]

The cases examined in this chapter show that Latin American states are willing from time to time to challenge treaties that were concluded by previous governments, some of them concluded in the nineteenth or the early twentieth century that today are no longer satisfactory to the states concerned. This lack of commitment to previous agreements, which is probably symptomatic of an institutional weakness affecting Latin American states, sometimes also affects compliance with decisions of international tribunals.

---

[69] 'Request for Provisional Measures', *Certain Activities carried out by Nicaragua in the Border Area (Costa Rica v. Nicaragua) (Orders of 8 March 2011)*, ICJ, General List No. 150, 18 November 2010, [34].
[70] 'Costa Rica protesta', above n. 57.

The ICJ as a replacement for other, more cost-effective mechanisms for the peaceful resolution of disputes

The previous sections of this chapter have demonstrated that some Latin American cases before the ICJ involve an attempt by one of the parties to reopen disputes that were settled in the past by treaties or judicial adjudication. This last section deals with a different but related problem: some disputes originate in the inability of the parties to establish mechanisms that might contribute to promote direct negotiations conducive to reaching satisfactory arrangements. This problem is yet another aspect of the lack of negotiating capacity that explains many of the Latin American cases before the Court. It is my contention that the *Pulp Mills* case between Argentina and Uruguay precisely serves to demonstrate this point.

Pulp Mills concerned the installation and operation of pulp mills on the banks of the River Uruguay, which forms the boundary between the two states. In 1975, Argentina and Uruguay concluded the Statute of the River Uruguay, the purpose of which was the establishment of joint mechanisms for the optimal and rational utilization of the river (Art. 1). The Statute established a commission for the management of the river, the Administrative Commission of the River Uruguay (CARU) (Art. 49). Argentina complained that the pulp mills that Uruguay authorized on the Uruguayan side of the river would cause environmental damage to the river and to Argentine territory. The ICJ decided that Uruguay breached procedural obligations contained in the 1975 Statute, namely, the obligation to inform CARU and Argentina of the activities that it planned to undertake in the river. The Court also decided that Argentina had failed to prove that significant environmental damage would occur. Therefore the operation of the Orion (Botnia) mill could continue.

Argentina asked the Court to find that Uruguay violated the procedural obligations established by the Statute of the River Uruguay and that a breach of the procedural obligations implied also a breach of the substantive obligations. The Court was not of the same view, and rejected this argument in its decision on provisional measures as well as in its final judgment. The Statute of the River Uruguay established a series of procedures to allow the CARU to take decisions regarding activities on the river. Apart from the fact that the composition of the CARU, as do many other commissions of this type, requires that half the members are appointed by each country, a further factor that made the decision process difficult was that non-compliance with the procedures did not result in a prohibition on undertaking activities on the river, unless those activities alone implied a breach of substantive obligations.

At this point it is useful to make a comparison between domestic and international law. Domestic law usually links procedural and substantive obligations in the field of environmental protection because this is a very cost-effective way of dealing with risk management. Thus, in many domestic legal systems, activities that pose a certain risk of environmental harm are subject to a regulatory system that requires prior notification, the provision of information, assessment of the risk of damage, and a system of prior authorization or issuing of permits by state institutions. Domestic legal systems adopt these regulatory systems for many reasons, including the fact that it can cost less to prevent environmental harm than to incur the expense of rectifying harm. Indeed, regulations and prior authorizations – that is, procedural obligations – reduce the chances of environmental harm.

Domestic legal systems can establish these regulatory regimes in a way that cannot be easily mirrored at the international level. Such systems are equipped with a central authority and are distributed among various state organs that have the power respectively to legislate and to implement and enforce the regulations. The international legal system lacks a central authority that could impose such public interest rules on states. In the context of the *Pulp Mills* case, this explains why the ICJ, in the absence of an agreement between the parties, did not have the power to establish a system of risk management that the parties had failed to include in the 1975 Statute of the River Uruguay. The Statute contains procedural and substantive obligations in relation to the protection of the river, but it was not agreed by the parties that the violation of the procedural obligations would entail *ipso facto* the prohibition from continuing with the planned activities. It is for this reason that the Court was clear that '[n]owhere does the 1975 Statute indicate that . . . a breach of procedural obligations automatically entails the breach of substantive ones.'[71]

Because the CARU was unable to resolve the dispute, Argentina activated Article 60 of the Statute of the River Uruguay and the case was brought before the ICJ. The Court concluded that Argentina and Uruguay had put in place a system of co-operation to prevent significant damage to the River Uruguay. This system included the creation of the CARU and the obligation to notify and inform it and the other party of activities that might cause significant damage to the other party. The ICJ decided

---

[71] *Pulp Mills on the River Uruguay (Argentina v. Uruguay)*, [2010] ICJ Rep. 28, [78].

that Uruguay had violated the obligation to inform and notify, but not that this violation meant it had also violated an obligation to protect the river. One may wonder whether it would have been more cost-effective for the parties to have established a system in which failure to comply with the procedural obligations would have resulted in a prohibition on undertaking activities in the river. Such an arrangement would have given the CARU and the central governments an opportunity to sit down with all the information necessary to discuss the alternatives before referring the case to the ICJ.

Conclusions

The practice of Latin American states in the field of the peaceful settlement of disputes is as diverse as in other parts of the world. Latin American countries have had occasion to apply all types of peaceful methods of dispute resolution. Each international dispute is different, and for that reason states try to opt for the most appropriate dispute resolution method in its particular context. Some people may regard international adjudication as a step towards a more evolved international legal system. However, given the present characteristics of this system, international adjudication is not always advisable and a number of factors have to be considered before taking the decision to submit a case to an international tribunal.

It is in this context that the trend of submitting cases to the ICJ by Latin American states has to be assessed. It is certainly difficult to second-guess the real motivations that lead states to initiate proceedings before the Court. It is of course the case that they do not always genuinely seek the resolution of an international dispute in accordance with international law or, at least, that this is not the main purpose of the initiation of judicial proceedings.

What the examination of some of the Latin American cases before the ICJ shows is that there are internal factors of a political and historical nature that sometimes make it difficult for Latin American governments to stand by the resolutions of disputes that previous governments have been able to agree. This means that in this part of the world from time to time certain states use the law and legal proceedings to keep international controversies open, when to do so is politically beneficial for a particular government.

This leads to the conclusion that Latin American countries have contributed immensely to the peaceful settlement of disputes, developing various ways in which to solve their differences. They invented the *uti possidetis* principle to avoid boundary disputes or to allow their resolution in accordance with international law. They have also contributed with a significant amount of experience to the establishment and operation of arbitral tribunals. It was a Latin American diplomat that devised the idea of the optional clause in the context of the PCIJ. And, today, Latin American countries continue to contribute to the peaceful settlement of disputes by submitting their differences to be resolved by the ICJ, showing with this that they have confidence in international law and in the capabilities and impartiality of the Court. However, these countries still face the challenge of ensuring that dispute resolution in the region aligns with the principle of finality.

6

The United States as an international litigant

MARK FELDMAN

In 1928, Manley O. Hudson, who would later serve as a judge at the Permanent Court of International Justice (PCIJ), observed that the United States 'seldom loses an opportunity to profess its loyalty to international arbitration in the abstract'.[1] Regarding the 'concrete application' of US arbitration policy,[2] however, Hudson found, with respect to a 1928 arbitration treaty between France and the United States, that 'the treaty realizes little of the purposes so expansively expressed in its preamble'.[3] When comparing the 1928 treaty with other arbitration treaties signed in the 1920s by countries other than the United States, Hudson concluded that the United States had 'lost her share of the leadership in the movement for international arbitration' and was 'lagging far behind other countries in the development of this means of peaceful settlement of disputes'.[4]

Similar arguments regarding US international adjudication practice continue to be made today.[5] Such arguments frequently highlight, with respect to the International Court of Justice (ICJ), the US withdrawal from

---

The author represented the United States as a non-disputing party in the *Pac Rim* v. *El Salvador* case, which is discussed below. The views expressed in this chapter do not necessarily reflect those of the US Department of State or the US government. The author thanks Jamie Briggs for substantial contributions to the chapter and Kim Yi-Seul, Liu Fangfang, and Ma Ji for excellent research assistance.

[1] Manley O. Hudson, 'The New Arbitration Treaty with France', (1928) 22 AJIL 368.

[2] Ibid., 369.   [3] Ibid., 372.   [4] Ibid., 373.

[5] See, e.g., José E. Alvarez, 'The Return of the State', (2011) 20 *Minnesota Journal of International Law* 223, 235: 'If the United States led the charge in favor of investor protections [under investment treaties], it now appears to be leading the drive in the opposite direction'; Sean D. Murphy, 'The United States and the International Court of Justice: Coping with Antinomies', in Cesare Romano (ed.), *The Sword and the Scales* (Cambridge University Press, 2009) 349: 'Arguably the United States has pursued an impossible position of both embracing the idea of the Court and yet distancing itself from the inevitable effects of that idea'; Andreas Paulus, 'From Neglect to Defiance? The United States and International Adjudication', (2004) 15 *European Journal of International Law* 783: 'The attitude of the United States towards international adjudication seems to have reached another low point.'

THE UNITED STATES AS AN INTERNATIONAL LITIGANT 107

compulsory jurisdiction[6] and jurisdiction under the Vienna Convention on Consular Relations (VCCR),[7] and, with respect to US investment treaties, the narrowing, according to many commentators, of available investment protections.[8]

This chapter will address the US experience as an international litigant as follows. First, the chapter will provide an overview of the period in which the United States served as a clear leader of the 'movement for international arbitration',[9] from the Jay Treaty to the Alabama Arbitration and the 1899 and 1907 Hague Peace Conferences. Second, the chapter will address arguments put forward by the United States in the *Hostages* case,[10] which represents a compelling instance of the 'concrete application' of US 'loyalty' to international arbitration.[11] Third, the ongoing US support for the permanent, supranational, and independent World Trade Organization (WTO) Appellate Body will be discussed. Finally, the chapter will address one structural challenge to sustaining support for US participation in investor–state disputes: the modest nature of US government victories in such cases, which is limited to obtaining the dismissal of claims brought by foreign investors.

The chapter reaches three conclusions. First, the *Hostages* case provides a compelling illustration of why states agree to third-party settlement of their disputes, and should continue to influence future US views on international adjudication. Second, the balanced and active nature of the US experience in WTO dispute settlement offers important insights that can inform future US practice before the ICJ. Third, the limited nature of

---

[6] See, e.g., Bruno Simma, 'International Adjudication and US Policy – Past, Present, and Future', in Norman Dorsen and Prosser Gilford (eds.), *Democracy and the Rule of Law* (Washington, DC: CQ Press, 2001) 54: 'US withdrawal from compulsory ICJ jurisdiction following the *Nicaragua* decision on jurisdiction sent a signal to the international community that states can avoid their international responsibilities by simply not appearing in court proceedings.'

[7] See, e.g., John B. Quigley, 'The United States' Withdrawal from International Court of Justice Jurisdiction in Consular Cases: Reasons and Consequences', (2009) 19 *Duke Journal of Comparative and International Law* 263, 264: 'The withdrawal from the VCCR Optional Protocol seemed to some as one more example of a go-it-alone approach by the United States.'

[8] See, e.g., Stephen M. Schwebel, 'The Influence of Bilateral Investment Treaties on Customary International Law', (2004) 98 *American Society of International Law Proceedings* 27, 30: Stating that the 2004 US Model BIT 'embodies regressive changes that are deplorable'.

[9] Hudson, above n. 1, 373.

[10] *Case Concerning United States Diplomatic and Consular Staff in Tehran (United States of America v. Iran)*, [1980] ICJ Rep. 3.

[11] Hudson, above n. 1, 368–9.

108 MARK FELDMAN

US government victories in investor–state arbitration places even greater importance on active engagement by the United States concerning key legal issues in order to maintain support for continued US participation in investor–state cases.

From the Jay Treaty to the 1907 Hague Peace Conference: The United States as leader of the international arbitration movement

There is general agreement that modern international arbitration began with the 1794 Jay Treaty between Great Britain and the United States,[12] which, following the War of Independence, settled unresolved issues between the two countries.[13] The Jay Treaty, under Article V, created a boundary commission (to precisely identify the St Croix river, which fixed the north-east boundary of the United States) and, under Articles VI and VII, created two commissions to address legal claims by British and US citizens (one concerning claims by British creditors of American debtors, the other concerning maritime claims of both British and US citizens).

The prospect of achieving peaceful dispute settlement was a key factor driving the US decision to consent to arbitration under the Jay Treaty.[14] However, at the same time, US interest in agreeing to arbitration with Great Britain in 1794 had been further strengthened by the particular factual circumstances facing the United States in the late eighteenth century.

As a 'young republic' established by a 'democratic revolution', the United States sought 'international recognition to deal with other states on an equal footing' and consenting to arbitration under the Jay Treaty 'according to international rules based on the equality of the parties'

---

[12] Treaty of Amity, Commerce and Navigation, United States–Great Britain, (signed 19 November 1794, entered into force 29 February 1796), 8 Stat. 116 (Jay Treaty).

[13] See, e.g., Bart Legum, 'Federalism, NAFTA Chapter Eleven, and the Jay Treaty of 1794', (2001) 95 *American Society of International Law Proceedings* 202: 'Today, the arbitral commissions established under the Jay Treaty are generally viewed as beginning the modern era of international arbitration'; R. Lillich, 'The Jay Treaty Commissions', (1962) 37 *St. Johns Law Review* 260: 'The modern era of Arbitration may be conveniently considered as commencing with the Jay Treaty of 1794', quoting William Evans Darby, *International Arbitration. International Tribunals*, 4th edn, (California: J. M. Dent, 1904), 769.

[14] See, e.g., M. E. O'Connell, 'Arbitration and Avoidance of War: The Nineteenth-Century American Vision', in Cesare Romano (ed.), *The Sword and the Scales* (Cambridge University Press, 2009), observing that 'President George Washington endorsed the Jay Treaty primarily because the commitment to arbitrate was likely to "prevent war and to bring about the peaceful settlement of misunderstandings and quarrels"' quoting M. Curti, *Peace or War: The American Struggle 1636–1936* (New York: W. W. Norton, 1936), 24.

THE UNITED STATES AS AN INTERNATIONAL LITIGANT   109

served such interests.[15] The United States at that time also experienced the shortcomings of the Articles of Confederation, which had proven inadequate for ensuring enforcement by the respective states of US commitments undertaken with respect to British creditors in the 1783 Treaty of Peace with Great Britain. The inadequate enforcement of Treaty of Peace commitments had increased tensions with Great Britain;[16] by agreeing to similar commitments in the Jay Treaty – signed after the 1787 US Constitution, under which treaties were made part of the 'supreme law of the land' – the United States could address issues concerning debts owed to British creditors 'with better chances of success'.[17]

Dispute settlement under the Jay Treaty ultimately was successful and legally significant. Although the debts commission created under Article VI 'deadlocked and failed',[18] the maritime claims commission created under Article VII issued more than five hundred awards,[19] totalling well over $11,000,000, most of which was recovered by US claimants.[20] For both commissions, the Jay Treaty text included detailed guidance on arbitrator selection,[21] the admission of evidence,[22] the timetable for considering complaints,[23] and governing law.[24]

The Jay Treaty also provided an opportunity for the United States to contribute significantly to the development of substantive international law with respect to the obligations of neutral states. Such contributions would later influence the Alabama Arbitration of 1872, which has been described as 'the high-water mark of international arbitration'.[25]

Article VII of the Jay Treaty authorized the maritime commission to hear claims against the United States arising from the capture of 'vessels and merchandise' belonging to British merchants that had been taken within US territory or taken by vessels that were originally armed in US ports. Correspondence from Secretary of State Thomas Jefferson, which is annexed to the Jay Treaty,[26] provided additional detail on the substance of the obligation that would apply to British neutrality claims against the

---

[15] Simma, above n. 6, 41.   [16] Legum, above n. 13, 203.   [17] Simma, above n. 6, 42.

[18] John R. Crook, 'The US and International Claims and Compensation Bodies', in Cesare Romano (ed.), *The Sword and the Scales* (Cambridge University Press, 2009) 297.

[19] Ibid.   [20] Lillich, above n. 13, 280.   [21] Jay Treaty, Arts. 6, 7.

[22] Ibid. Art. 6.   [23] Ibid.   [24] Ibid., Arts. 6, 7.

[25] O'Connell, above n. 14, 36. See also Tom Bingham, 'The Alabama Arbitration', (2005) 54 ICLQ 1, describing as a 'judicious assessment' the characterization of the Alabama Arbitration as 'the greatest the world had ever seen'.

[26] Letter from Secretary of State Thomas Jefferson to British Foreign Secretary George Hammond, 5 September 1793.

United States: as a neutral government,[27] the United States had to 'protect and defend' the 'vessels and effects' of British citizens located in US ports, waters, or 'seas near our shores,' and had to 'recover and restore' such vessels and effects 'to the right owners when taken from them.'[28] The US position set out in the Jefferson letter has been characterized as 'an epoch in the development of the usages of neutrality... [which] represented by far the most advanced existing opinion as to what those obligations were'.[29] Furthermore, the decisions of the maritime commission on the British neutrality claims ultimately served as 'fruitful precedent' for the Alabama Arbitration.[30]

The Alabama Arbitration arose from the 1871 Treaty of Washington, which referred to arbitration a set of claims known as the 'Alabama Claims'.[31] Those claims concerned certain acts committed by a number of ships, including the *Alabama*, which had been fitted in Great Britain and used by the Confederacy during the American Civil War.[32] The *Alabama* alone captured or destroyed dozens of Union ships.[33]

Notably, only two years before approving the Treaty of Washington, the US Senate in 1869 overwhelmingly rejected the Johnson–Clarendon Convention, which, like the Treaty of Washington, would have provided for third-party dispute settlement of claims against Great Britain arising from acts occurring during the American Civil War. The Johnson–Clarendon Convention had been negotiated by the Johnson administration but voted on by the Senate during the Grant administration. Andrew Johnson had been impeached in 1868 and his unpopularity in 1869 impacted the Senate's vote.[34] With respect to the substance of the document, the chairman of the Senate Committee on Foreign Relations, Charles Sumner,

---

[27] In 1793, President Washington had issued a Proclamation of Neutrality with respect to the 'state of war' that existed 'between Austria, Prussia, Sardinia, Great Britain, and the United Netherlands, on the one part, and France on the other'. J. B. Moore (ed.), *International Adjudications Ancient and Modern History and Documents*, 6 vols. (Oxford University Press, 1929–33), Vol. 4, 20. As one example of events that implicated US neutrality obligations, some British vessels, such as the *William*, were captured by French vessels that had been fitted in Charleston, South Carolina. Ibid., 22.

[28] Ibid., 6–7.

[29] Ibid., 24, quoting W. E. Hall, *A Treatise on International Law*, 2nd edn (Oxford: Clarendon Press, 1884), 550.

[30] Lillich, above n. 13, 280.

[31] Treaty of Washington, United States–Great Britain (signed 8 May 1871, entered into force 17 June 1871), 17 Stat. 863 (Treaty of Washington), Art. I.

[32] O'Connell, above n. 14, 35.   [33] Ibid.

[34] Charles E. Hill, *Leading American Treaties* (New York: Macmillan, 1922), 276, 291: 'The strained relations between President Johnson and Congress must be taken as one of the reasons of the decisiveness of the vote.'

noted that the Johnson–Clarendon Convention included 'not one word of regret'.[35] The Treaty of Washington, by contrast, opens with the expression of 'regret felt by Her Majesty's Government for the escape, under whatever circumstances, of the Alabama and other vessels from British ports, and for the depredations committed by those vessels'.[36]

The Treaty of Washington, like the Jay Treaty, included detailed provisions on dispute settlement. Article I provided that the Alabama Claims would be heard by a tribunal composed of five arbitrators, each one of whom would be appointed, respectively, by the United States, Great Britain, Italy, Switzerland, and Brazil. Article II provided for the appointment of an agent by each party to represent the party 'generally in all matters connected with the arbitration'. Article III required that each party deliver its 'written or printed case . . . in duplicate' to each of the arbitrators and to the agent of the other party within six months of the exchange of ratifications of the treaty.

Also like the Jay Treaty, the Treaty of Washington contributed significantly to the development of international law with respect to neutral state obligations. Article VI of the Treaty of Washington, which identified governing law,[37] included specific rules on neutral state obligations.[38] One such rule imposed on a 'neutral Government' was an obligation 'to exercise due diligence in its own ports and waters' to prevent the fitting of vessels within its jurisdiction that it had reason to believe would be used to 'carry on war' against states with which the neutral government was at peace, recalling the British right, under Article VII of the Jay Treaty, to bring claims for vessels 'taken by vessels originally armed' in US ports.[39]

Ultimately, the *Alabama* tribunal found Great Britain liable for the actions of certain ships built in Britain during the American Civil War, including the *Alabama*,[40] and issued a $15.5 million award in favour of

---

[35] Ibid., 291.   [36] Treaty of Washington, Art. I.

[37] Treaty of Washington, Art. VI: providing that claims would be governed by rules applicable to neutral governments set out in the treaty and 'principles of international law'.

[38] Great Britain had issued a Proclamation of Neutrality recognizing both the Union and the Confederacy as belligerents. O'Connell, above n. 14, 34.

[39] US leadership in the eighteenth and nineteenth centuries with respect to substantive international law on neutral state obligations is reflected in the text of the Treaty of Washington, which provided that Great Britain would not 'assent' to the neutrality rules set out in the treaty 'as a statement of principles of international law' that were in force at the time when the Alabama Claims arose. Rather, as stated in Art. VI of the treaty, Great Britain agreed to those neutrality rules to resolve the Alabama Arbitration claims out of a 'desire' to strengthen 'the friendly relations between the two countries and of making satisfactory provision for the future'.

[40] O'Connell, above n. 14, 36.

the United States, which was paid in full by Great Britain.[41] The British prime minister, William Gladstone, characterized the award as 'harsh' and 'punitive' but, at the same time, 'as dust in the balance compared with the moral example set' by two countries 'going in peace and concord before a judicial tribunal' rather than 'resorting to the arbitrament of the sword'.[42]

The success of the Alabama Arbitration 'rallied the peace movement to start lobbying for permanent machinery for the peaceful settlement of disputes'.[43] An important step towards the establishment of such 'permanent machinery' occurred with the formation of the Permanent Court of Arbitration (PCA), which was, according to Scott, the 'great and crowning glory' of the 1899 Hague Peace Conference.[44]

At both the 1899 and 1907 Hague Peace Conferences, the United States supported the establishment of a permanent international court.[45] That goal, however, was not fully achieved. Although Article 20 of the Hague Convention of 1899 provided for the creation of a Permanent Court of Arbitration, 'it is common knowledge that the court is not permanent, for it exists only for the special case and has to be created anew for each case submitted. There is indeed a permanent list from which the judges can be and indeed must be chosen for the particular case.'[46]

Responding to the ad hoc nature of the court that had been created in 1899, Joseph Hodges Choate, who led the US delegation to the 1907 Hague Peace Conference, expressed US interest in creating a genuinely permanent international court. The PCA's lack of permanence, Choate observed,

> has been an obvious source of weakness and want of prestige in the tribunal ... Let us, then, seek to develop ... a Permanent Court which shall

---

[41] Ibid.

[42] Bingham, above n. 25, 24, quoting H. C. G. Matthew, *Gladstone: 1809–1874* (Oxford: Clarendon Press, 1986), 186.

[43] O'Connell, above n. 14, 34. For a detailed discussion of the role of the nineteenth-century American peace movement in promoting the formation of a permanent international court, see Mark Janis, 'Americans and the Quest for an Ethical International Law', (2007) 109 *West Virginia Law Review* 571.

[44] James B. Scott (ed.), *The Hague Peace Conferences of 1899 and 1907*, Vol. I (Baltimore: Johns Hopkins Press, 1909), 254.

[45] See, e.g., James B. Scott, 'The Proposed Court of Arbitral Justice', (1908) 2 AJIL 772, 776: 'The United States ... have constantly declared that to them the tribunal established in 1899 was but the first step toward a permanent arbitral court of justice which they would have liked to have had established even in 1899.'

[46] Scott, above n. 44, 425.

THE UNITED STATES AS AN INTERNATIONAL LITIGANT   113

> hold regular and continuous sessions . . . consist of the same judges . . . pay
> due heed to its own decisions . . . and gradually build up a system of inter-
> national law . . . By such a step in advance, we shall . . . make the work of
> this Second Conference worthy of comparison with that of the Conference
> of 1899.[47]

As in 1899, however, the US position at the 1907 Hague Peace Conference in support of a permanent international court did not prevail.[48] The 1907 counterpart to Article 20 of the 1899 Hague Convention – Article 41 of the 1907 Hague Convention – did not add permanence to the Permanent Court of Arbitration: 'the contracting Powers undertake to maintain the Permanent Court of Arbitration, as established by the First Peace Conference'.[49]

Following over a century of leadership by the United States in support of peaceful dispute resolution between states through arbitration – from the Jay Treaty and the Alabama Arbitration to the 1899 and 1907 Hague Peace Conferences – the United States, as discussed below, ultimately failed to join the first genuinely permanent international court: the PCIJ.

From 1907 to 1946: two sharp turns in US sentiment towards a permanent international court

As discussed above, in 1907 the US delegation to the Hague Peace Confer-ence supported a permanent international court that could 'speak with the authority of the united voice of the nations' and 'command the approval and regulate the conduct of the nations'.[50] In 1935 the US Senate voted on whether the United States should join precisely such a court: the PCIJ, which had been formed in the aftermath of the First World War. The US Senate failed to approve the PCIJ protocol; thirty-six senators opposed the measure.[51] As a result, the United States did not participate in any matter before the PCIJ.

---

[47] Ibid., 427.
[48] The failure to establish a permanent court at the 1907 Hague Conference was largely due to disagreements over how judges would be selected. See David D. Caron, 'War and International Adjudication: Reflections on the 1899 Peace Conference', (2000) 94 AJIL 4, 21.
[49] James B. Scott (ed.), *The Hague Conventions and Declarations of 1899 and 1907* (Oxford University Press, 1915), 57.
[50] Scott, above n. 44, 427.
[51] Manley O. Hudson, 'The United States Senate and the World Court', (1935) 29 AJIL 303, 304.

114 MARK FELDMAN

Eleven years after the 1935 vote, the US Senate again considered whether the United States should join a permanent international court: the ICJ, which had been formed in the aftermath of the Second World War. Notably, the proposed ICJ commitment for the United States (compulsory jurisdiction) was more significant than the proposed PCIJ commitment for the United States (voluntary jurisdiction). Notwithstanding the greater commitment, only two senators opposed US acceptance of compulsory ICJ jurisdiction. As observed by one US State Department official in 1946,

> Truly the times had changed since 1936. A decade ago the resolution providing for United States membership in the Permanent Court of International Justice on a purely voluntary basis had met with a roar of protest in the Committee hearings, on the Senate floor, and in the country at large. Ten years later... not a single witness appeared before the subcommittee to oppose the acceptance by the United States of the compulsory jurisdiction of the new Court... Not a single voice of protest was raised against it.[52]

The divergent responses by the US Senate to US participation in a permanent international court can be explained, in part, by the divergent US sentiment towards, on the one hand, the League of Nations in 1935, and, on the other hand, the United Nations in 1946.

Hudson maintained that the US Senate's opposition to the PCIJ 'was based chiefly on its connection with the League of Nations, on a fear of ratification as a step toward joining the League, on apprehension of loss of independence by the United States and of loss by the Senate of its share of control of our foreign relations'.[53] US sentiment towards membership in the League of Nations, which initially had been mixed (largely due to sovereignty concerns),[54] did not improve following European government defaults on billions of dollars in war debts owed to the United States.[55]

---

[52] Francis O. Wilcox, 'The United States Accepts Compulsory Jurisdiction', (1946) 40 AJIL 699, 703.

[53] Hudson, above n. 51.

[54] See George A. Finch, 'The Treaty of Peace with Germany in the United States Senate', (1920) 14 AJIL 155, 168–9: amendments and reservations to the Treaty of Peace proposed by the Senate Committee on Foreign Relations were ' "governed by a single purpose and that is to guard American rights and American sovereignty" ', quoting Senate Report No. 176, 66th Cong., 1st sess., Part 1.

[55] See William O. Scroggs, 'Foreign Treatment of American Creditors', (1935) 14 *Foreign Affairs* 345: stating that war debts owed to the US government 'now amount to approximately twelve billions' and that '[a]ll the war debts, except the small amount owed by Finland, are now in default'; Hudson, above n. 51, 305: highlighting the war debts defaults as a key reason for the US Senate's failure to support the PCIJ protocol.

THE UNITED STATES AS AN INTERNATIONAL LITIGANT   115

In the aftermath of the Second World War, however, US views on joining a permanent international court changed dramatically. In 1945 and 1946 respectively, the US Senate voted 89–2 in favour of the United Nations Charter and 62–2 in favour of accepting compulsory ICJ jurisdiction.[56] Such actions reflected, according to Wilcox, 'the avowed policy of the United States to back to the hilt the United Nations'.[57]

The sharp turn in US sentiment, from 1935 to 1946, towards participation in a permanent international court recalled the earlier shift in US sentiment towards third-party dispute settlement of Civil War-related claims against Great Britain, from the Johnson–Clarendon Convention to the Treaty of Washington. As discussed below, US sentiment towards international dispute resolution, particularly with respect to participation in a permanent international court, would continue to fluctuate significantly in the second half of the twentieth century.

The *Hostages* case as a bridge to 1946

The 62–2 vote in 1946 by the US Senate in favour of accepting compulsory ICJ jurisdiction reflects a moment of exceptionally strong support for US participation in a permanent international court. That strong support continued to find expression over the following twelve years, when the United States, on eight occasions, initiated proceedings before the ICJ.[58] Over the past thirty years, however, the United States has withdrawn from compulsory ICJ jurisdiction, withdrawn from ICJ jurisdiction over disputes arising under the VCCR, and has initiated only one proceeding, more than twenty-five years ago, in the *ELSI* case.[59]

The most recent expression of sweeping US support for the ICJ occurred nearly thirty-five years ago, when the United States initiated proceedings in the *Hostages* case. On 29 November 1979, in response to the capture by Iranian students, earlier that month, of approximately one hundred hostages, including sixty-three Americans, at the US embassy in Tehran,[60] the United States initiated ICJ proceedings against Iran. The United States alleged 'multiple', 'serious', and 'profound' violations of Iran's international obligations, including Iranian obligations under the

---

[56] Wilcox, above n. 52, 699.   [57] Ibid.   [58] Murphy, above n. 5, 76–7.

[59] See 'United States – Application Instituting Proceedings', *Elettronica Sicula SpA (ELSI) (United States* v. *Italy)*, [1987] ICJ Pleadings 3.

[60] Warren Christopher and Richard M. Mosk, 'The Iranian Hostage Crisis and the Iran–US Claims Tribunal', (2007) 7 *Pepperdine Dispute Resolution Law Journal* 165, 167.

VCCR.[61] Among other forms of relief, the United States sought provisional measures of protection from the Court as well as the payment of reparations by Iran.

Throughout the proceedings in the *Hostages* case, the United States presented expansive arguments with respect to the role of the ICJ within the 'world community'. At the hearing on its request for provisional measures, the United States, represented by the US Attorney General and the Legal Adviser of the US Department of State, described the ICJ as reflecting 'the highest legal aspirations of civilized man', emphasized the 'expectation' of the 'world community' that the ICJ would act 'vigorously in the interests of international law and international peace' by affirming 'the rule of law among nations',[62] and recognized the power of the Court to bring Iran's conduct 'to an immediate end'[63] and to 'save lives and set human beings free'.[64]

The United States also addressed the legality of parallel action in the same matter by the UN Security Council and the ICJ, expressing support for a prominent ICJ role in safeguarding the rule of law. Shortly before the hearing on provisional measures, the UN Security Council had issued Resolution No. 457, which 'urgently call[ed]' on the government of Iran 'to release immediately' the individuals who had been taken hostage, and 'decide[d]' that the Security Council would 'remain actively seized of the matter'. At the hearing on provisional measures, the United States maintained not only that parallel action by the Security Council and the ICJ would be consistent with the UN Charter and the ICJ Statute, but also that the Court, if it should find that provisional measures were warranted under Article 41 of the ICJ Statute, would have a 'duty to indicate such measures, quite without regard to any parallel action which may have been taken by the Security Council'.[65]

In response to its request for provisional measures of protection, the United States promptly received relief. Five days after the hearing, and fewer than six weeks after Americans had been taken hostage in Tehran, the Court issued a unanimous order stating that Iran 'should immediately ensure' the return to the United States of control over the premises of the

---

[61] 'Application Instituting Proceedings', *United States Diplomatic and Consular Staff in Tehran* (*United States* v. *Iran*), ICJ, General List No. 64, 29 November 1979, 4–5.

[62] *United States Diplomatic and Consular Staff in Tehran (United States* v. *Iran) (Provisional Measures)*, [1979] ICJ Rep. 7, 21; ibid., 35–6.

[63] Ibid., 22.   [64] Ibid., 21.   [65] Ibid., 29.

THE UNITED STATES AS AN INTERNATIONAL LITIGANT   117

US embassy and 'should ensure the immediate release' of all American hostages in Iran.[66]

At the merits phase of the *Hostages* case, the United States continued to make expansive arguments with respect to the role of the ICJ within the world community. The United States identified the 'essential function' of the ICJ to be the 'maintenance of peaceful relations among states',[67] and recognized the power of the Court to create a 'maximum deterrent against' the repetition of Iran's conduct 'by any country in any part of the world'.[68] '[A]ny degree of tolerance' of Iran's conduct by the ICJ, the United States maintained, would lead to an 'unraveling of orderly international relations'.[69]

In its judgment on the merits, the ICJ again ruled in favour of the United States, finding that Iran's actions had violated treaty and customary international law obligations.[70] The Court ordered that Iran 'must immediately terminate the unlawful detention' of all American hostages in Iran and 'must immediately place in the hands of the protecting Power' (Switzerland) the premises and property of the US embassy and consulates in Iran.[71] The Court further ordered that Iran had to make reparation to the United States for injuries arising from the crisis, in an amount later to be determined.[72] Prior to such a determination, the United States withdrew its ICJ claim as part of its settlement with Iran in the Algiers Accords,[73] which in turn established the Iran–US Claims Tribunal, an

---

[66] Ibid., 21.

[67] *United States Diplomatic and Consular Staff in Tehran (United States* v. *Iran) (Oral Arguments)*, [1980] ICJ Rep. 249, 255.

[68] Ibid.   [69] Ibid.

[70] *United States Diplomatic and Consular Staff in Tehran (United States* v. *Iran) (Judgment)*, [1980] ICJ Rep. 3, 44.

[71] Ibid., 44–5.

[72] Ibid., 45. When ruling in favour of the United States, the Court noted that it could not 'fail to express its concern in regard to the United States' incursion into Iran' in April 1980 in a failed attempt by US military units to rescue the hostages: ibid., 44. The Court recalled that in its Order on provisional measures it had indicated that 'no action was to be taken by either party which might aggravate the tension between the two countries', and further observed that the US incursion into Iran was 'of a kind calculated to undermine respect for the judicial process in international relations'. The US operation did not, however, affect the outcome of the Court's decision because no question of responsibility flowing from the operation was before the Court: ibid.

[73] See Algiers Accords, [11] (requiring the United States to 'promptly withdraw all claims now pending against Iran before the International Court of Justice'), available at (1981) 81 *Department of State Bulletin* 1, 3.

118 MARK FELDMAN

international tribunal that would go on to resolve over 3,900 cases and that today, more than thirty years after its creation, continues to hear claims.[74]

The expansive arguments made by the United States in the *Hostages* case reflect the aspirations of an earlier era – the aftermath of the Second World War – when the US Senate, in 1946, overwhelmingly accepted compulsory ICJ jurisdiction. Such aspirations were also expressed in 1946 by Hudson in his vision for the Court:

> The conception of the judicial process as one of the methods of bringing about the peaceful settlement of disputes does not exaggerate the part which a court may play. Experience has shown that judges on the bench, operating within the severe limitations of the judicial process, can deal effectively with certain types of disputes between states.[75]

Since the *Hostages* decision, however, the United States has taken steps to limit its exposure to the ICJ, both in treaty negotiations (by declining to accept clauses providing for ICJ dispute settlement)[76] and in the withdrawal of prior acceptances of ICJ jurisdiction.

Indeed, only five years after making expansive arguments in the *Hostages* case with respect to the role of the ICJ within the world community, the United States withdrew from compulsory ICJ jurisdiction,[77] stating that '[o]ur experience with compulsory jurisdiction has been deeply

---

[74] See Iran–United States Claims Tribunal, available at www.iusct.net/.

[75] Manley O. Hudson, 'The New World Court', (1945) 24 *Foreign Affairs* 75.

[76] Murphy, above n. 5, 64.

[77] Following the *Hostages* decision and before the US withdrawal from compulsory jurisdiction, the United States jointly agreed with Canada to submit to a five-member chamber of the ICJ a maritime boundary dispute in the Gulf of Maine area. The chamber procedure, which is available under Art. 26 of the ICJ Statute, previously had not been used in an ICJ proceeding. Writing in a personal capacity, Davis Robinson, the former Legal Adviser at the US State Department who had worked on the *Gulf of Maine* case, observed that the United States, in jointly agreeing to submit the case to the ICJ, 'wanted to make good and appropriate use of the International Court of Justice as an institution and hoped that the first Chamber process would set a positive precedent for other nations in the peaceful resolution of their disputes': Davis R. Robinson, David A. Colson, and Bruce C. Rashkow, 'Some Perspectives on Adjudicating before the World Court: The Gulf of Maine Case', (1985) 79 AJIL 578, 581. As characterized by one member of the five-member chamber, Stephen Schwebel, the chamber 'rendered an important judgment determining a single, comprehensive maritime boundary, governing both the continental shelf and fishing above it, which Canada and the United States have accepted and implemented'. Stephen Schwebel, 'Reflections on the Role of the International Court of Justice', (1986) 61 *Washington Law Review* 1061, 1070. While the *Gulf of Maine* decision was not a complete victory for the United States, the positive US experience in the *Gulf of Maine* case

THE UNITED STATES AS AN INTERNATIONAL LITIGANT   119

disappointing' and that certain assumptions made by the United States when accepting compulsory jurisdiction in 1946 – in particular, that the Court would not be 'abused for political ends' – 'have now been proved wrong'.[78] The withdrawal was made less than one year after the issuance of the ICJ's decision on jurisdiction in the *Nicaragua* case, which found, over multiple US objections, that the ICJ had jurisdiction to hear claims by Nicaragua alleging that the United States had violated treaty and customary international law obligations by supporting and engaging in certain military activities in Nicaragua.[79] In the view of the United States, however, the laudable objective of 'peaceful adjudication of international disputes' by the ICJ had been, in the *Nicaragua* case, 'subverted by the effort of Nicaragua and its Cuban and Soviet sponsors to use the Court as a political weapon'.[80]

When withdrawing from compulsory ICJ jurisdiction in 1985, the United States stated that it would 'continue to make use of the Court to resolve disputes whenever appropriate', and announced that 'we have reached an agreement in principle with Italy to take a long-standing dispute to the Court'.[81] The United States ultimately did initiate ICJ proceedings in 1987 for the resolution of that dispute, which became the *ELSI* case.[82] Since the *ELSI* case, however, the United States has not initiated any proceedings before the ICJ – a span of more than twenty-five years.

The Legal Adviser of the US State Department expressed additional disappointment with the Court following the issuance of the ICJ's decision in the *Oil Platforms* case in 2003.[83] Although the ICJ had rejected Iran's claim that US military actions taken against Iranian offshore oil platforms breached US obligations under a 1955 Treaty of Amity between the two countries, the Court proceeded to address – in what the Legal Adviser characterized as 'non-binding dicta' – whether

---

 nevertheless contrasts sharply with the concurrent, but decidedly negative, US experience in the *Nicaragua* case, which led to the US withdrawal from compulsory ICJ jurisdiction.

[78] Department of State Letter Concerning Termination of Acceptance of ICJ Compulsory Jurisdiction, (1985) 24 ILM 1742, 1744.

[79] *Military and Paramilitary Actions in and against Nicaragua (Nicaragua v. United States) (Jurisdiction and Admissibility)*, [1984] ICJ Rep. 392, 442.

[80] Above n. 78, 1744.   [81] Ibid., 1745.

[82] 'United States – Application Instituting Proceedings', *Elettronica Sicula SpA (ELSI) (United States v. Italy)*, [1987] ICJ Pleadings 3.

[83] *Oil Platforms (Iran v. United States) (Judgment)*, [2003] ICJ Rep. 161.

the US actions 'qualified as self-defence under international law'.[84] The Legal Adviser observed that the Court's 'excursion' into the self-defence issue was 'regrettable as a matter of form'; 'even more regrettable' were statements in the Court's opinion that 'might be read to suggest new and unsupported limitations on the ability of states to defend themselves from armed attacks'.[85] The Legal Adviser further observed that the 'United States, for its part, will continue to follow what it understands to be a correct interpretation of international law on these points'.[86]

In addition to the US disappointment with the *Nicaragua* and *Oil Platforms* decisions, a string of ICJ cases brought against the United States in 1998, 1999, and 2003 – *Breard, LaGrand,* and *Avena* respectively – led to a second withdrawal of US consent to ICJ jurisdiction. Each of those cases concerned the failure by police in the United States to advise foreign nationals of their right to consular access under Article 36 of the VCCR. In 2005, the United States withdrew from the Optional Protocol to the VCCR, which provides for ICJ jurisdiction over VCCR disputes,[87] observing that the ICJ had interpreted the VCCR 'in ways we had not anticipated that involved state criminal prosecutions and the death penalty, effectively asking the court to supervise our domestic criminal system'.[88]

Finding that 'the United States is not happy with the decisions being rendered by the Court', Murphy recently concluded that 'In the near term, US policy makers will seek to avoid any involvement in matters before the ICJ.'[89] Such a US orientation towards the ICJ contrasts sharply with current US sentiment towards WTO dispute settlement, as discussed below.

---

[84] W. H. Taft IV, 'Self-Defense and the Oil Platforms Decision', (2004) 29 *Yale Journal of International Law* 295.

[85] Ibid., 306. [86] Ibid.

[87] See Quigley, above n. 7, 266: 'ICJ suits against the United States were the precipitating factor in its withdrawal from the [VCCR] Optional Protocol. The United States had been sued in 1998 [*Breard*], 1999 [*LaGrand*], and again in 2003 [*Avena*] by states party to the VCCR who alleged violations of VCCR Article 36, which relates to a consul's role in aiding nationals who are arrested. In each case, jurisdiction was based on the Optional Protocol.'

[88] Ibid., 272, quoting US State Department spokesperson Darla Jordan in Charles Lane, 'US Quits Pact Used in Capital Cases', *Washington Post*, 9 March 2005, available at www.washingtonpost.com/wp-dyn/articles/A21981-2005Mar9.html.

[89] Murphy, above n. 5, 98.

THE UNITED STATES AS AN INTERNATIONAL LITIGANT   121

Active US participation in World Trade Organization dispute settlement

While the United States has not initiated proceedings before the ICJ in more than twenty-five years, the United States has been, as stated in a recent report from the Office of the United States Trade Representative (USTR), 'one of the most active participants in the WTO dispute settlement process'.[90] According to USTR, as of December 2011, ninety-five complaints have been filed by the United States, and 138 against the United States, in the WTO.[91]

Such active engagement by the United States is particularly noteworthy given the supranational, independent, and permanent nature of the WTO Appellate Body, which is a 'standing' body composed of individuals serving fixed, renewable terms,[92] and supported by its own dedicated staff.[93] Although Appellate Body reports must be adopted by the WTO Dispute Settlement Body (DSB), such adoption is 'quasi-automatic',[94] given the operation of the 'reverse consensus' rule, under which Appellate Body reports are adopted unless all WTO members – including the winning party to the dispute – agree not to adopt the report.

The independence and permanence of the Appellate Body has been further enhanced by the decision to grant the Appellate Body control over its own working procedures,[95] which has been characterized by one commentator as demonstrating an 'extraordinary degree of confidence' in the institution.[96] Such control has enabled the Appellate Body to adopt its practice of 'collegiality', which, arguably, has 'transformed' a 'rotating

---

[90] Office of the United States Trade Representative, *2010 Trade Policy Agenda and 2009 Annual Report*, 2010, available at www.ustr.gov/2010-trade-policy-agenda.

[91] Office of the United States Trade Representative, *Snapshot of WTO Cases Involving the United States*, 2011, available at www.ustr.gov/trade-topics/enforcement/overview-dispute-settlement-matters.

[92] See Marrakesh Agreement Establishing the World Trade Organization (opened for signature 15 April 1994, entered into force 1 January 1995), 1867 UNTS 3 (DSU), Annex 2, Art. 17.

[93] See Claus-Dieter Ehlermann, 'Experiences from WTO Appellate Body', (2003) 38 *Texas International Law Journal* 469, 476: noting that the Appellate Body is supported by staff who are 'formally' part of the WTO Secretariat but who 'functionally' belong to the Appellate Body.

[94] Negotiations on Improvements and Clarifications of the Dispute Settlement Understanding, WTO Doc. TN/DS/W/82, 24 October 2005 (Communication from the United States), 1.

[95] DSU, Art. 17(9).   [96] Ehlermann, above n. 93, 478.

three-member appellate panel as envisioned by the DSU' into 'a seven-member fixed appellate bench',[97] by requiring each three-member panel[98] to 'exchange views'[99] with all Appellate Body members before finalizing a report. The Appellate Body also relied on its control over working procedures when finding that it had authority 'to accept and consider *amicus curiae* briefs in an appeal',[100] notwithstanding prior disagreement among WTO members over the admissibility of *amicus* briefs in WTO dispute settlement.[101]

Thus, a 'standing' Appellate Body composed of members serving fixed terms whose reports are adopted on a 'quasi-automatic' basis has, through control of its working procedures, further enhanced its permanence and independence. Notwithstanding those developments, US support for the Appellate Body remains strong.

One recent US proposal, entitled 'Improvements for the WTO Appellate Body', sought to further strengthen the permanent nature of the Appellate Body. In that proposal, the United States recognized the 'far-reaching consequences of many Appellate Body findings' and observed that 'there are certain institutional issues that may need to be addressed in order to strengthen the Appellate Body and thereby to enhance the dispute settlement system'.[102] In the proposal, the United States recommended that service as an Appellate Body member be converted from a part-time to a full-time position ('service on the Appellate Body is not a part-time job') as well as the addition of law clerks to support Appellate Body members on an individual basis, separate from and in addition to existing Secretariat staff.[103]

With respect to Appellate Body independence, however, the United States has sought, to some extent, an increase in WTO member supervision over legal analysis set out in panel and Appellate Body reports. In a

---

[97] Shoaib A. Ghais, 'International Judicial Lawmaking: A Theoretical and Political Analysis of the WTO Appellate Body', (2006) 24 *Berkeley Journal of International Law* 534, 543.

[98] DSU, Art. 17(1) requires 'any one case' to be heard by 'three' Appellate Body members.

[99] Appellate Review Working Procedures, WTO Doc. WT/AB/WP/6, 16 August 2010, Rule 4(3).

[100] Ibid., Rule 42.

[101] See, e.g., Richard H. Steinberg, 'Judicial Lawmaking at the WTO: Discursive, Constitutional, and Political Constraints', (2004) 98 AJIL 247, 251: the Appellate Body decision was made 'in the context of several years of North–South deadlock over whether to permit *amicus* briefs' in the WTO dispute settlement.

[102] Improvements for the WTO Appellate Body – Proposal by the United States, WTO Doc. WT/DSB/W/398, 16 January 2009, 1.

[103] Ibid., 2.

2005 submission, the United States observed that 'some limitations in the current procedures may have resulted, in some cases, in an interpretative approach or legal reasoning' by the Appellate Body and panels that 'could have benefitted from additional [WTO] Member review'.[104] One 'sensitive area' identified by the United States concerned instances in which the Appellate Body and/or panels 'might "fill the gap" ' when the relevant WTO text does not address an issue 'and consequently add to or diminish rights and obligations under the relevant agreement instead of clarifying those rights and obligations'.[105] Another 'sensitive area' identified by the United States concerned the application in WTO dispute settlement proceedings of 'legal concepts outside the WTO texts... including asserted principles of international law other than customary international law rules of interpretation'.[106]

Given those sensitive areas, the United States maintained that 'Members may wish to consider ways they can provide additional guidance to adjudicative bodies... including through procedures which strengthen Member control and flexibility'.[107] Such procedures, as proposed by the United States, could include the issuance by the Appellate Body of interim reports, 'thus allowing parties to comment to strengthen the final report', as well as the addition of a 'partial adoption' procedure, 'where the DSB would decline to adopt certain parts of reports while still allowing the parties to secure the DSB recommendations and rulings necessary to help resolve the dispute'.[108]

Thus the United States has sought to strengthen the permanence of the Appellate Body (by recommending a transition to full-time status for Appellate Body members with individualized law clerk support) while limiting, to some extent, its independence (by recommending use of interim reports and a partial adoption procedure). As recently stated by USTR, 'there is still room for improvement' in the WTO dispute settlement process.[109]

Such 'room for improvement', however, has not diminished US enthusiasm for pursuing relief in WTO dispute settlement: 'In 2009, the United States continued to be one of the most active participants in the WTO dispute settlement process.'[110] In the 111th Congress (2009–11), multiple bills reflected 'congressional concerns that the executive branch has not

---

[104] Communication from the United States, above n. 94, 1.   [105] Ibid.
[106] Ibid.   [107] Ibid., 2.   [108] Ibid.
[109] Office of the United States Trade Representative, above n. 90, 72.
[110] Ibid.

124 MARK FELDMAN

challenged restrictive foreign trade practices in the WTO to a sufficient degree'.[111]

The active US engagement in the WTO contrasts sharply with the lack of such US engagement in the ICJ. Murphy has outlined several explanations for the disparity. First, trade disputes are 'technical' in nature.[112] Second, the United States is in a 'relatively weaker position' vis-à-vis the EU and states such as China and Japan on trade matters as opposed to other matters.[113] Third, 'the outcome of WTO decision-making does not directly intrude into the US legal system' because a loss in the WTO requires the United States only to choose between making its law conform or facing 'WTO-authorized retaliation'.[114]

Notwithstanding those factors, many WTO disputes are high-profile and politically charged matters that, in the event of loss, can cause significant political harm. For example, concerning the *US Steel Safeguards* WTO dispute, Bhala and Gantz have observed, 'Seldom has protection of the domestic steel industry – a common practice for the United States and many other nations during the past thirty years – generated such legal and political disagreement both within the United States and between the United States and its major trading partners.'[115] Indeed, the Appellate Body's decision – which upheld a panel's findings that various steel safeguards applied by the United States violated international obligations under the WTO Agreement on Safeguards[116] – received considerable White House attention:

> The widely anticipated decision has been discussed for weeks at the White House. Mr. Bush is torn between continuing to help the steel industry and bolstering his electoral prospects in key industrial states with manufacturers and their unions or respecting international trade laws and increasing his chances to win new regional and global trade agreements.[117]

---

[111] J. Grimmett, 'Dispute Settlement in the World Trade Organization (WTO): An Overview', Congressional Research Service, 8 April 2010, 12 (discussing the Trade Enforcement Act of 2009 (H.R.496, Rangel), the Trade CLAIM Act (S.363, Snowe), and the Trade Enforcement and Priorities Act (S.1982, Brown)).

[112] Murphy, above n. 5, 96. [113] Ibid. [114] Ibid.

[115] Raj Bhala and David A. Gantz, 'WTO Case Review 2003', (2004) 21 *Arizona Journal of International & Comparative Law* 317, 394.

[116] *United States – Definitive Safeguard Measures on Imports of Certain Steel Products*, Appellate Body Report, WT/DS248/AB/R, AB-2003-3, 10 November 2003, [513].

[117] E. Becker, 'WTO Rules US Tariffs on Steel are Illegal', *New York Times*, 10 November 2003.

THE UNITED STATES AS AN INTERNATIONAL LITIGANT   125

There was, in addition, a third factor for the White House to consider: a threat by the EU of retaliation in excess of $2 billion in response to the Appellate Body report. When threatening retaliation, 'One strategy of the EU was to target states that were politically sensitive to the Bush administration.'[118] For example, a 'primary target' of EU retaliation was Harley-Davidson, which had 'significant operations' in the 'politically sensitive states' of Pennsylvania, Wisconsin, and Florida.[119] As discussed by Bhala and Gantz, the EU's threatened retaliation was designed to 'inflict the maximum political pain on the President's reelection'.[120] Six days before the DSB adopted the Appellate Body report, and ten days before retaliation by the EU,[121] the United States terminated the steel safeguards, citing 'changed economic circumstances'.[122]

Although WTO cases concern 'technical' issues and can expose a member only to retaliation (rather than an enforceable obligation to pay damages), a loss before the WTO, as illustrated by the *Steel Safeguards* case, can carry significant political costs. In the case of the United States, however, such losses must be balanced against the thirty-seven victories (as of December 2011) that the United States has obtained in WTO cases on 'core issue(s)'.[123] Consistent with that record, the United States maintains that 'the WTO dispute settlement process has proven to be an effective tool in combating barriers to US exports'.[124]

Unlike WTO dispute settlement, a loss for the United States in investor–state arbitration cannot be balanced against US government victories in investor–state cases; in investor–state arbitration, US claims are brought, and US victories are won, by individual US investors. The section below discusses the structural challenge arising from that dynamic.

Managing the structural challenge of investor–state arbitration

Unlike ICJ and WTO proceedings, US participation in investor–state arbitration is, by design, one-sided, in the sense that the US

---

[118] Benjamin von Liebman and Kasaundra Tomlin, 'Safeguards and Retaliatory Threats', (2008) 51 *Journal of Law & Economics* 351, 366.

[119] Ibid.

[120] Bhala and Gantz, above n. 115, 397, quoting the White House: Office of the Press Secretary (Press Briefing by Scott McClellan, 4 December 2003).

[121] Ibid., 395–6.

[122] Presidential Proclamation 7741 (4 December 2003) (68 Fed Reg. 68483–68484).

[123] Office of the United States Trade Representative, above n. 91.

[124] Office of the United States Trade Representative, above n. 90.

government appears as a respondent, while individual US investors appear as claimants. In the state-to-state setting of WTO dispute settlement, a headline such as 'United States Files WTO Case against China to Protect American Jobs'[125] is not uncommon. Such headlines, however, are not available to the United States in investor–state arbitration because US investors, rather than the US government, bring investor–state arbitration claims. Thus, the nature of a US government victory in WTO dispute settlement (for example, an Appellate Body decision on Chinese import restrictions is a 'Victory for America's Creative Industries'[126]) differs significantly from the nature of a US government victory in investor–state arbitration (for example, 'NAFTA Tribunal Dismisses Glamis Claim').[127]

The distinct nature of a US government 'victory' in investor–state arbitration presents a structural challenge to maintaining support for ongoing US participation in such disputes. Effective means, however, do exist for responding to that challenge. The United States cannot 'protect American jobs' by submitting claims to investor–state arbitration,[128] but the United States can, and does, highlight the importance of outbound investment for 'the US economy and American workers',[129] and the corresponding importance of securing treaty protections for US investors 'to ensure that US firms and workers can compete on a level playing field and are treated according to the rule of law in foreign markets'.[130] Those US policy interests are advanced by US participation in investor–state arbitration, which

---

[125] Office of United States Trade Representative, 'United States Files WTO Case Against China to Protect American Jobs', press release, 20 September 2011, available at www.ustr.gov/about-us/press-office/press-releases/2011/september/united-states-files-wto-case-against-china-prote.

[126] Office of United States Trade Representative, 'WTO Appellate Body Confirms Finding against China's Treatment of Certain Copyright-Intensive Products', press release, 21 December 2009, available at www.ustr.gov/about-us/press-office/press-releases/2009/december.

[127] United States Department of State, 'NAFTA Tribunal Dismisses Glamis Claim', 2009, available at www.state.gov/r/pa/prs/ps/2009/06a/124527.htm at 28 February 2012.

[128] It is possible that the United States could submit a claim to investor–state arbitration in its capacity as an 'investor', but such a claim would concern alleged losses sustained by the investor, not by other Americans. See, e.g., North American Free Trade Agreement (signed 17 December 1992, entered into force 1 January 1994), 32 ILM 296 (NAFTA), Art. 1139, where a 'party' to the NAFTA could be included within the definition of 'investor of a Party'.

[129] Office of United States Trade Representative Resource Center, available at www.ustr.gov/trade-topics/services-investment/investment.

[130] Ibid.

THE UNITED STATES AS AN INTERNATIONAL LITIGANT   127

enables US investors to bring their own claims against US investment treaty partners.

Importantly, however, investor–state arbitration serves 'US firms and workers' only if the 'US investors' bringing claims under US investment treaties are, in reality, US entities. In the context of one recent investor–state arbitration under Chapter Ten of the Dominican Republic–Central America–United States Free Trade Agreement (CAFTA-DR) – the *Pac Rim* v. *El Salvador* case – a petition signed by 244 international civil society organizations highlighted that very issue, maintaining that the claimant, in 'an abuse of process', had moved a subsidiary from the Cayman Islands to the state of Nevada in order to obtain access to the investor–state dispute settlement procedure under Chapter Ten of the CAFTA-DR.[131]

As in many US investment treaties, Chapter Ten of the CAFTA-DR includes a 'denial of benefits' provision, which is intended to allow host states to deny treaty benefits to claimants that have no genuine connection to their purported home state.[132] Thus denial of benefits provisions in US investment treaties help to ensure that a core policy goal driving US participation in investor–state arbitration – safeguarding the ability of US firms and workers to compete on a level playing field in foreign markets – is not undermined by non-US entities seeking to claim treaty benefits by incorporating shell companies in the United States.

Following the submission of the *Pac Rim* claim to arbitration under Chapter Ten of the CAFTA-DR, El Salvador invoked the CAFTA-DR denial of benefits provision. The United States, in the *Pac Rim* case, made a non-disputing party submission on a question of CAFTA-DR treaty interpretation, asserting that the CAFTA-DR denial of benefits provision could be invoked not only before, but also after, the submission of a claim to arbitration.[133] The tribunal ultimately agreed with that position.[134]

Sustaining support for US participation in investor–state arbitration will require ensuring that US investment treaties protect genuinely US

---

[131] See Manuel Perez-Rocha, 'Open Letter to World Bank Officials on Pacific Rim–El Salvador Case', 2011, Institute for Policy Studies, available at www.ips-dc.org/.

[132] Dominican Republic–Central America–United States Free Trade Agreement (signed 5 August 2004, entered into force 1 March 2006), 43 ILM 514, Art. 10(12)(2): providing that a party 'may deny the benefits' of Chapter Ten to an enterprise of another party that has 'no substantial business activity in the territory' of any other party and is owned or controlled by a person from the denying party or from a non-party.

[133] *Pac Rim Cayman LLC v. The Republic of El Salvador (Decision on the Respondent's Jurisdictional Objections)*, ICSID Arbitral Tribunal, Case No. ARB/09/12, 20 May 2011.

[134] Ibid., [4.85].

entities, which in turn will require the proper operation of denial of benefits provisions under those treaties. The United States has made a notable contribution to that effort in the *Pac Rim* case, and should remain actively engaged on the issue to ensure that the entities served by US investment treaties are in fact 'US firms and workers'.

Conclusion

The 'loyalty' of the United States to international adjudication in the 'abstract' has been consistent over time; the 'concrete application' of that policy, however, has fluctuated. The respective, and divergent, US views on the League of Nations in the 1930s and the United Nations in the 1940s significantly influenced the corresponding US sentiment towards participation in the PCIJ and the ICJ. Over fifty years earlier, divergent US sentiment towards the Johnson administration in 1869, on the one hand, and the Grant administration in 1871, on the other, affected US Senate views on whether to agree to arbitrate Civil War-related claims with Great Britain. More recently, the *Nicaragua* case had a significant impact on US sentiment towards the ICJ, resulting in the US withdrawal from compulsory ICJ jurisdiction only six years after the United States had characterized the Court, in the *Hostages* case, as reflecting 'the highest legal aspirations of civilized man'.

The subsequent US experiences in the *Oil Platforms, Breard, LaGrand,* and *Avena* cases further dampened US enthusiasm for participating in ICJ proceedings, to the point that, as Murphy concludes, the orientation of the United States in the short term will be to seek to avoid involvement with the Court.

Avoiding involvement in ICJ proceedings, however, may not be the best US response to the past few decades of ICJ jurisprudence, particularly given the US experience in WTO dispute settlement. The United States has lost many WTO cases, which, as illustrated by the *Steel Safeguards* dispute, can impose significant political costs. But the United States also has won many WTO cases, and both the executive and the legislative branches continue to look to WTO dispute settlement as an effective means for combating trade barriers. The WTO serves as an effective forum for the United States in significant part because the United States frequently initiates WTO proceedings; the ICJ cannot provide an effective forum for the United States if the United States seeks only to avoid engagement with the Court.

The *Hostages* case serves as an important reminder of how US participation in the ICJ can advance US interests. In that case, the United States emphasized the role of the ICJ in affirming the rule of law, maintaining peaceful and orderly international relations, and deterring the repetition of unlawful conduct by states. At both the provisional measures and merits phases of the *Hostages* case, the ICJ ruled in favour of the United States, confirming that the Court stands ready to award provisional relief promptly when warranted and that Iran's actions had violated both treaty and customary international law obligations.

On a larger scale, the *Hostages* case serves as a bridge to an earlier era – the aftermath of the Second World War – when US sentiment towards participation in a permanent international court was exceptionally high. Such strong US support for an international court itself recalls an age of over 100 years of US leadership – spanning the Jay Treaty, the Alabama Arbitration, and the 1899 and 1907 Hague Peace Conferences – in support of the use of international adjudication as a peaceful means for resolving international disputes.

To maintain US support for international arbitration under investment treaties, the United States must meet a structural challenge that does not arise in ICJ or WTO dispute settlement: the modest nature of US government 'victories' in investor–state cases, which is limited to obtaining the dismissal of claims. Responding effectively to that challenge will require continued emphasis on the importance of outbound investment for US firms and workers and the corresponding importance of securing treaty protections to provide a level playing field for those firms and workers. Ensuring that US investment treaty protections serve the interests of US firms and workers, rather than the interests of third-country nationals, will in turn require the proper application of denial of benefits provisions in those treaties. The United States should build on its work in the *Pac Rim* case and continue to demonstrate leadership on denial of benefits issues, which will help to ensure that the concrete application of US policy on international litigation includes strong support for ongoing US participation in investor–state arbitration.

7

European perspectives on inter-state litigation

MICHAEL WOOD

Until the cold war drew to a close, Europeans were divided into opposing camps. This was so as regards the peaceful settlement of disputes, as with much else. There were the states of 'Western Europe', an ideological rather than a geographical description, most of which were, in principle at least, favourably disposed to third-party international dispute settlement, within certain limits. And then there were the states of the Soviet bloc (the 'Eastern European Group', in UN terms), which were not. Among the first signs of change, in the 'perestroika' era, was a move by the Soviet Union and certain other 'Eastern European' states to accept third-party dispute settlement, *inter alia* by withdrawing reservations to dispute settlement clauses in some multilateral treaties, including in the human rights field.

The present chapter will look first at the general attitudes of the forty-nine European states[1] towards international dispute settlement, as demonstrated particularly by their actions within international organizations, and their acceptance of dispute settlement obligations, including, but not limited to, the optional clause under the Statute of the International Court of Justice (ICJ). It should be said at the outset that the picture is by no means uniform. It will then consider their actual practice and experience in inter-state dispute settlement. Finally, the position of the United Kingdom will be described in a little more detail. Its practice may serve as an example for the somewhat nuanced approach of many

---

[1] The term 'European' has various meanings, even in this context: see Michael Wood, 'A European Vision of International Law: For What Purpose?', in Hélène Ruiz-Fabri, Emmanuelle Jouannet, and Vincent Tomkiewicz (eds.), *Select Proceedings of the European Society of International Law: Volume 1, 2006* (Portland, OR: Hart Publishing, 2008) 151. It will be used here to include all forty-seven states of the Council of Europe (although some are geographically in Asia), together with Belarus and Kosovo. The Holy See/Vatican City is not covered, given its rather special position: see Gerd Westdickenberg, 'Holy See', in Rüdiger Wolfrum (ed.), *Max Planck Encyclopedia of Public International Law* (Oxford University Press, 2012), who among other things describes the papal role as mediator between states.

European states, an approach that seems to be suspended between idealism and realism.

Until recently, the attention of international lawyers has often focused almost exclusively on the ICJ. Of course, today it is a commonplace that there is a proliferation of 'international courts and tribunals'.[2] Some of these new international courts and tribunals do not deal, at least not principally, with inter-state disputes. But even if their jurisdiction concerns disputes between states and private persons (as in the field of human rights or foreign investment) they are an important part of the background.

Attitudes of European states towards international dispute settlement

The general attitudes of European states to international dispute settlement can be seen in their actions within the United Nations, their acceptance of the optional clause under the ICJ Statute, and their acceptance of regional instruments within Europe.

Not only have attitudes in Europe changed with the end of the cold war. So, too, have attitudes within the United Nations, which form an important part of the context within which to view the perspectives of individual states or the states of a particular region.

The peaceful settlement of disputes is one of the principles of international law set forth in the Charter of the United Nations. Article 2(3) of the Charter goes hand in hand with the prohibition on the use of force in Article 2(4). Article 33 imposes a general obligation to settle by peaceful means disputes that might lead to a breach of the peace. And under Article 36(3) the Security Council 'should take into consideration that legal disputes should as a general rule be referred by the parties to the International Court of Justice in accordance with the provisions of the Statute of the Court'.

The peaceful settlement of disputes goes much wider than litigation, which is the subject of this book. Thus the excellent, though now somewhat dated, *Handbook on the Peaceful Settlement of Disputes between States*,[3] has sections on the principle of the peaceful settlement of disputes; means of settlement (that is, negotiations and consultations, inquiry, good

---

[2] See Ruth Mackenzie, Cesare Romano, and Yuval Shany (eds.), *The Manual of International Courts and Tribunals*, 2nd edn (Oxford University Press, 2010).

[3] Office of Legal Affairs, United Nations, *Handbook on the Peaceful Settlement of Disputes between States* (1992), OLA/COD/2394.

132   MICHAEL WOOD

offices, mediation, conciliation, arbitration, judicial settlement, and resort
to regional agencies or arrangements); procedures envisaged in the Charter; and procedures envisaged in other international instruments.

Over the years there have been a number of initiatives at the UN inspired
by the Charter provisions, some more realistic than others, but generally
warmly supported by most European states. In *An Agenda for Peace*,
Secretary-General Boutros Boutros-Ghali called on all UN members to
accept the compulsory jurisdiction of the ICJ without any reservation.[4]
The General Assembly did not heed this call.[5] In *In Larger Freedom*,
Secretary-General Kofi Annan made the more realistic recommendation
that those states that had not done so should consider accepting the
Court's compulsory jurisdiction. In the 2005 Summit Outcome Document, the General Assembly adopted this recommendation as its own.[6]

More recently, a Security Council Presidential Statement of 29 June
2010 contained the following:

> The Security Council is committed to and actively supports the peaceful
> settlement of disputes and reiterates its call upon Member States to settle
> their disputes by peaceful means as set forth in Chapter VI of the Charter
> of the United Nations. The Council emphasizes the key role of the Interna-
> tional Court of Justice, the principal judicial organ of the United Nations,
> in adjudicating disputes among States and the value of its work and calls
> upon States that have not yet done so to consider accepting the jurisdiction
> of the Court in accordance with its Statute.
>
> The Security Council calls upon States to resort also to other dispute
> settlement mechanisms, including international and regional courts and
> tribunals which offer States the possibility of settling their disputes peace-
> fully, contributing thus to the prevention or settlement of conflict.[7]

The General Assembly, for its part, on 24 September 2012 adopted the
Declaration of the High-level Meeting of the General Assembly on the
Rule of Law at the National and International Levels, in which the heads
of state and government, and heads of delegation declared:

---

[4] An Agenda for Peace: Preventive Diplomacy and Related Matters, GA Res. 47/120 A, UN
   GAOR, 47th sess., 91st plen. mtg, Agenda Item 10, A/RES/47/120 A (18 December 1992).
[5] It was not reflected in GA Res. 47/120 A.
[6] 2005 World Summit Outcome, GA Res. 60/1, UN GAOR, 60th sess., 8th plen. mtg, Agenda
   Item 46 and 120, A/RES/60/1 (24 October 2005).
[7] Statement of the President of the Security Council, UN Doc. S/PRST/2010/11 (29 June
   2010). See also Statement of the President of the Security Council, UN Doc. S/PRST/2012/1
   (19 January 2012).

We recognize the positive contribution of the International Court of Justice, the principal judicial organ of the United Nations, including in adjudicating disputes among States, and the value of its work for the promotion of the rule of law; we reaffirm the obligation of all States to comply with the decisions of the International Court of Justice in cases to which they are parties; and we call upon States that have not yet done so to consider accepting the jurisdiction of the International Court of Justice in accordance with its Statute. We also recall the ability of the relevant organs of the United Nations to request advisory opinions from the International Court of Justice.[8]

All UN members (that is, forty-eight of the forty-nine European states) are *ipso facto* parties to the ICJ Statute,[9] all, that is, except Kosovo. Of the forty-nine states covered, forty are among the 115 members of the Permanent Court of Arbitration. The nine European states that are not yet members of the Permanent Court of Arbitration are Andorra, Armenia, Azerbaijan, Bosnia and Herzegovina, Georgia, Kosovo, Moldova, Monaco, and San Marino.

Acceptance of the compulsory jurisdiction of the ICJ through a declaration under the so-called 'optional clause'[10] is often, rightly or wrongly,

---

[8] Cooperation between the United Nations and the Eurasian Economic Community, UNGA Res. 67/10, UN GAOR, 67th sess., 40th plen. mtg, UN Doc. A/RES/67/10 (24 September 2012), [31]; Millennium Summit of the United Nations, GA Res. 54/254, UN GAOR, 54th sess., 93rd plen. mtg, Agenda Item 49(b), Supp. No. 49, UN Doc. A/RES/54/254 (23 March 2000, adopted 15 March 2000), 3.

[9] UN Charter, Art. 93(1).

[10] For accounts of the acceptances of the optional clause by individual European states, see Simone Dreyfus, 'Les déclarations souscrites par la France aux termes de l'article 36 du Statut de la Cour internationale de justice', (1959) 5 *Annuaire Français de Droit International* 258; Julien Feydy, 'La nouvelle déclaration française d'acceptation de la juridiction obligatoire de la Cour internationale de justice', (1966) 12 *Annuaire Français de Droit International* 155; Frans De Pauw, 'La Belgique et la compétence obligatoire de la Cour internationale de Justice', (1966) 2 *Revue Belge de Droit International* 49; Renata Szafarz, 'The Modification of the Scope of ICJ Jurisdiction in Respect of Poland', in Tasfir M. Ndiaye and Rüdiger Wolfrum (eds.), *Law of the Sea, Environmental Law and Settlement of Disputes: Liber Amicorum Judge Thomas A. Mensah* (The Hague: Martinus Nijhoff, 2007) 545; Michael Wood, 'The United Kingdom's Acceptance of the Compulsory Jurisdiction of the International Court of Justice', in Ole Fauchald, Henning Jakhelln, and Aslak Syse (eds.), *Festskrift til Carl August Fleischer* (Oslo: Universitetsforlaget, 2006) 621; Christian J. Tams and Andreas Zimmermann, 'The Federation Shall Accede to Agreements Providing for General, Comprehensive and Compulsory International Arbitration, The German Optional Clause Declaration of 1 May 2008', (2008) 51 *German Yearbook of International Law* 391; Christophe Eick, 'Die Anerkennung der obligatorischen Gerichtsbarkeit des Internationalen Gerichtshofs durch Deutschland', (2008) 68 ZaöRV 763. On the German approach more generally, see A. Zimmermann (ed.), *Deutschland und die internationale Gerichtsbarkeit* (Berlin: Duncker & Humblot, 2004); Stefan Oeter, 'Germany and the

seen as the touchstone of a state's commitment to the Charter principle of peaceful settlement of disputes.

European states were among the first to accept the optional clause of the Permanent Court of International Justice (PCIJ). They are still in the forefront of acceptance of the optional clause of the ICJ. Of the sixty-six states that have made such a declaration (fewer than one third of the UN membership), twenty-five are members of the Council of Europe.[11] It is a striking fact, however, that of the three Security Council permanent members from Europe only the United Kingdom has a declaration in force. As is explained further below, its declaration is subject to significant exceptions.

Luxembourg's declaration of 15 September 1930 remains in force by virtue of Article 36(5) of the Statute. Like a number made by European states, it contains no exceptions. Those with important exceptions, often in the military and security field, include Cyprus, Germany, Lithuania, Malta, Portugal, Slovakia, Spain, and the United Kingdom.

Recent acceptances of the optional clause include three from Europe: those of Germany on 30 April 2008/1 May 2008, Ireland on 15 December 2011, and Lithuania on 21 September 2012. Germany had previously accepted the optional clause under the Statute of the PCIJ for five years from 1927/1928. Its current declaration contains a sweeping military exception.[12] Ireland had also accepted the compulsory jurisdiction of the PCIJ, in 1929; as Ireland was not an original member of the United Nations, that declaration terminated with the demise of the PCIJ in 1946.[13] Ireland's declaration covers 'all legal disputes as specified in Article 36,

---

Recourse to International Courts and Tribunals', in Société Française pour le Droit International, *Comparative International Law Practice in France and Germany* (Paris: Editions A. Pedone, 2012), 141. For further on the French approach see Gilles Cottereau, 'La France et le recours aux juridictions internationales', in Société Française pour le Droit International, *Comparative International Law Practice in France and Germany* (Paris: Editions A. Pedone, 2012).

[11] Austria, Belgium, Bulgaria, Cyprus, Denmark, Estonia, Finland, Georgia, Germany, Greece, Hungary, Ireland, Liechtenstein, Lithuania, Luxembourg, Malta, Netherlands, Norway, Poland, Portugal, Slovakia, Spain, Sweden, Switzerland, United Kingdom.

[12] The German declaration excludes 'any dispute which (a) relates to, arises from or is connected with the deployment of armed forces abroad, involvement in such deployments or decisions thereon, or (b) relates to, arises from or is connected with the use for military purposes of the territory of the Federal Republic of Germany, including its airspace, as well as maritime areas subject to German sovereign rights and jurisdiction' (author's translation from German).

[13] Art. 36(5) of the Statute, as interpreted in *Aerial Incident of 27 July 1955 (Israel v. Bulgaria) (Preliminary Objections)*, [1959] ICJ Rep. 127, 136–42.

paragraph 2, with the exception of any legal dispute with the United Kingdom of Great Britain and Northern Ireland in regard to Northern Ireland.'[14] Lithuania did not make a declaration at the time of the League of Nations. Its 2012 declaration contains an unusual exception for

> any dispute which arises from or is connected with a military operation carried out in accordance with a decision taken by consensus or unanimity by international security and defence organisation or organisation implementing common security and defence policy, to which the Republic of Lithuania is a member.

In connection with the 2012 High-level Meeting of the General Assembly on the Rule of Law, certain European states, such as Italy, pledged to accept the Court's compulsory jurisdiction.

In 2008, the Committee of Ministers of the Council of Europe recommended to governments that they consider accepting the ICJ's jurisdiction in accordance with Article 36(2) of the Statute and that, when doing so, they give consideration as appropriate to the model clauses appended to the recommendation.[15] The model clauses covered such matters as the termination of acceptance of the ICJ's jurisdiction, the exclusion of disputes arising before a certain date, the exclusion of disputes which the parties agree to settle in some other way, the avoidance of 'surprise' applications, and the variation of the acceptance.

In connection with the High-level Meeting of the General Assembly on the Rule of Law at the National and International Levels, held on 24 September 2012, Switzerland, Netherlands, and the United Kingdom, apparently inspired in part by this activity within the Council of Europe, pledged to work together, and with the United Nations Secretariat, on

> the preparation by the end of 2014 of a publication to assist States wishing to recognize as compulsory the jurisdiction of the International Court of Justice (ICJ), including:
> – Examples of declarations recognizing as compulsory the jurisdiction of the ICJ (including possible reservations);
> – Examples of treaty provisions for the submission of classes of disputes to the ICJ; and

---

[14] All disputes between Ireland and the United Kingdom are excluded by the United Kingdom's own declaration, which excludes 'any dispute with the government of any other country which is *or has been* a Member of the Commonwealth' (emphasis added). Ireland ceased to be a member of the Commonwealth in 1949.

[15] Recommendation CM/Rec. (2008) 8 of 2 July 2008, adopted by the Committee of Ministers of the Council of Europe to member states on the acceptance of the jurisdiction of the ICJ.

136   MICHAEL WOOD

– Examples of special agreements for the submission of particular disputes
to the ICJ.

Another indication of a state's general interest in inter-state litigation is
whether or not it nominates persons to the lists of arbitrators provided
for in various international conventions. Here again an initiative was
undertaken within the Council of Europe to encourage member states to
make such nominations and to keep them up to date. In a recommendation adopted in July 2008, the Committee of Ministers of the Council of
Europe recommended

> that the governments of member states maintain, and keep under review,
> a list of treaties and other instruments which provide for the nomination
> of arbitrators and conciliators for inclusion in lists maintained for the
> purpose of implementing provisions concerning the peaceful settlement
> of disputes;

and

> that the governments of member states consider nominating arbitrators
> and conciliators in accordance with the instruments in question, and that
> they keep such nominations under review.[16]

Within Europe, inter-state cases may be brought unilaterally before
the European Court of Human Rights, although this has been rare, and
before the Court of Justice of the European Union and the EFTA Court.

In addition, there are a number of European regional instruments
specifically addressing the settlement of disputes. In 1957, the Council of
Europe adopted the European Convention for the Peaceful Settlement of
Disputes.[17] It has fourteen parties, all but one of which were members
of the Council of Europe in 1957.[18] The Convention was inspired by the
General Act of 1928/1949, and has been criticized.[19] It was invoked by
Liechtenstein (unsuccessfully) in the *Liechtenstein* v. *Germany* case,[20] and

---

[16] Recommendation CM/Rec. (2008) 9 of 2 July 2008, adopted by the Committee of Ministers
of the Council of Europe to member states on the nomination of international arbitrators
and conciliators.

[17] Lucius Caflisch, 'European Convention for the Peaceful Settlement of Disputes (1957)',
in Rüdiger Wolfrum (ed.), *Max Planck Encyclopedia of Public International Law* (Oxford
University Press, 2012).

[18] Austria, Belgium, Denmark, Germany, Italy, Liechtenstein, Luxembourg, Malta, Netherlands, Norway, Slovakia, Sweden, Switzerland, United Kingdom.

[19] See Caflisch, above n. 17.

[20] *Case concerning Certain Property (Liechtenstein* v. *Germany) (Preliminary Objections)*,
[2005] ICJ Rep. 6.

EUROPEAN PERSPECTIVES ON INTER-STATE LITIGATION   137

successfully by Germany in *Jurisdictional Immunities of the State (Germany v. Italy: Greece intervening)*.[21]

In 1992, the Council of Foreign Ministers of the Conference on Security and Co-operation in Europe adopted a Convention on Conciliation and Arbitration (Stockholm Convention).[22] This instrument entered into force on 5 December 1994 and established, with effect from 29 May 1995, a Court of Conciliation and Arbitration based in Geneva. The French jurist, Robert Badinter, has been president of the court since its inception.[23] Participation in the Convention entails no obligation to submit a dispute to arbitration, unless an optional declaration is made,[24] but only to conciliation. Conciliation is described on the court's website as 'the main mechanism offered by the Court'.[25] In the eighteen years since its establishment, no dispute among its thirty-three states parties has been submitted to the court, even for conciliation. The Convention thus remains *lettre morte* – although it may one day awaken to the surprise of some of its parties.[26]

European states and inter-state dispute settlement in practice

All the contentious cases before the PCIJ,[27] and many of those before the ICJ, were between or involved European states. Over half (66) of the 127 cases listed on the ICJ's website (as at October 2013) had at least one European state as party. In thirty-four cases, both parties were European.[28] They were commenced by special agreement (*compromis*), by unilateral

---

[21] *Jurisdictional Immunities of the State (Germany v. Italy: Greece intervening) (Judgment)*, ICJ General List No. 143, 3 February 2012.

[22] Convention on Conciliation and Arbitration (opened for signature 15 December 1992, entered into force 5 December 1994), 1842 UNTS 121; Lucius Caflisch (ed.), *Règlement pacifique des différends entre États* (The Hague: Kluwer, 1998); Helmut Steinberger, 'Organization for Security and Co-operation in Europe, Court of Conciliation and Arbitration', in Rüdiger Wolfrum (ed.), *Max Planck Encyclopedia of Public International Law* (Oxford University Press, 2012).

[23] The Court is composed of a list of conciliators and arbitrators. In addition, it elects a Bureau and the Registrar.

[24] As of November 2012, five states parties had made such a declaration (Denmark, Greece, Macedonia, Malta, Sweden).

[25] Steinberger describes it as 'the central element' of the Convention: Steinberger, above n. 22, [7].

[26] As happened with the 'revival' of the General Act of 1928 at the time of the *Nuclear Tests* cases.

[27] See the list in Ole Spiermann, *International Legal Argument in the Permanent Court of International Justice* (Cambridge University Press, 2005), 405–24.

[28] The figure includes *Monetary Gold*, in which three of the four parties were European states.

138 MICHAEL WOOD

application under the optional clause, or by unilateral application under the European Convention for the Settlement of Disputes or some other jurisdictional title, or without a jurisdictional title.[29]

Of the twenty contentious cases brought before the International Tribunal for the Law of the Sea (ITLOS) in Hamburg (as at October 2013), ten involved one or (in two cases) two European states (or in one case the European Union, which is a party to the United Nations Convention on the Law of the Sea, 1982 (UNCLOS)). Six of these ten cases involved the special procedure before ITLOS for the prompt release of vessels,[30] and two were proceedings for provisional measures pending the constitution of an arbitral tribunal under UNCLOS Annex VII. The remaining two contentious cases involved the European Union[31] and Spain[32] respectively.

It is also interesting to look at pending and past inter-state arbitrations or commissions listed on the website of the Permanent Court of Arbitration (PCA). Seventeen inter-state cases are listed between 1998 and October 2013.[33] Of these, five are between two European states[34] and one is between an African and a European state.[35]

It is difficult to say what motivates states to initiate proceedings, and even more difficult to know why they decide not to initiate proceedings. Determining a state's motives for commencing inter-state litigation is not straightforward. This is so even where a state gives reasons, whether before the court or tribunal (for example in the opening speech of its agent) or elsewhere. Reasons given publicly may not tell the whole story.

---

[29] Since the insertion of Art. 38(5) in the Rules of Court in 1978, such applications are no longer entered in the Court's General List and are not listed on the Court's website, unless and until the proposed respondent consents to the jurisdiction.

[30] Three prompt release cases have been brought against France, two against Russia, and one by Russia (against Australia).

[31] *Conservation and Sustainable Exploitation of Swordfish Stocks (Chile/European Union)*, ITLOS, Case No. 7, 20 December 2000.

[32] *The M/V 'Louisa' Case (Saint Vincent and the Grenadines v. Spain)*, ITLOS, Case No. 18, 10 December 2010.

[33] This figure leaves aside the Eurotunnel arbitration, which was mixed, and one case where the website says 'No further information about these proceedings is available.' Nor does it include arbitrations from the early period of the PCA's activity (1902–35).

[34] *Arbitration between Croatia and Slovenia (Croatia/Slovenia)*, PCA, 4 November 2009; *The MOX Plant Case (Ireland v. United Kingdom) (Order No 6)*, PCA, 6 June 2008; *Iron Rhine Arbitration (Belgium/Netherlands)*, PCA, 20 September 2005; *Arbitration between Netherlands and France (Netherlands/France)*, PCA, 12 March 2004; *OSPAR Arbitration (Ireland v. United Kingdom)*, PCA, 18 June 2001. See generally Permanent Court of Arbitration – Cases, available at www.pca-cpa.org/showpage.asp?pag_id=1029.

[35] *Chagos Archipelago (Mauritius v. United Kingdom)*, PCA, 20 December 2010.

The influence of particular officials, or even law firms, cannot be discounted. Reasons are generally clearer where a case is submitted by agreement. Especially in the latter case, the predominant motive is likely to be to remove a dispute from the political arena, thus reducing tensions between the states concerned, and to solve it definitively, thus permanently removing an irritant.

The cases before the ICJ involving European states may be seen as falling into the following (largely subjective) categories:

– Maritime delimitation cases: *Maritime Delimitation in the Black Sea (Romania v. Ukraine)*; *Maritime Delimitation in the Area between Greenland and Jan Mayen (Denmark v. Norway)*; *Aegean Sea Continental Shelf (Greece v. Turkey)*; *North Sea Continental Shelf (Federal Republic of Germany/Netherlands)*; *North Sea Continental Shelf (Federal Republic of Germany/Denmark)*.

– Those between friendly states aimed at resolving disputes of no great political importance, often with high legal content and interest: *Jurisdictional Immunities of the State (Germany v. Italy: Greece Intervening)*; *Case concerning Certain Property (Liechtenstein v. Germany)*; *Passage through the Great Belt (Finland v. Denmark)*; *Elettronica Sicula S.p.A. (ELSI) (United States of America v. Italy)*; *Barcelona Traction, Light and Power Company, Limited (Belgium v. Spain) (New Application: 1982)*; *Compagnie du Port, des Quais et des Entrepôts de Beyrouth and Société Radio-Orient (France v. Lebanon)*; *Sovereignty over Certain Frontier Land (Belgium/Netherlands)*; *Interhandel (Switzerland v. United States of America)*; *Application of the Convention of 1902 Governing the Guardianship of Infants (Netherlands v. Sweden)*; *Certain Norwegian Loans (France v. Norway)*; *Monetary Gold Removed from Rome in 1943 (Italy v. France, United Kingdom of Great Britain and Northern Ireland and United States of America)*; *Nottebohm (Liechtenstein v. Guatemala)*; *Minquiers and Ecrehos (France/United Kingdom)*; *Ambatielos (Greece v. United Kingdom)*; *Case concerning Rights of Nationals of the United States of America in Morocco (France v. United States of America)*; *Fisheries (United Kingdom v. Norway)*. It is interesting to note that most were submitted by unilateral application, although sometimes this was done by prior arrangement.

– Those involving issues of considerably more political concern: *Questions relating to the Obligation to Prosecute or Extradite (Belgium v. Senegal)*; *Certain Questions of Mutual Assistance in Criminal Matters (Djibouti v. France)*; *Certain Criminal Proceedings in France (Republic of the Congo v.*

France); Fisheries Jurisdiction (Spain v. Canada); Gabčíkovo-Nagymaros Project (Hungary/Slovakia).

- Those involving highly political issues, where jurisdiction was often contested: *Application of the Interim Accord of 13 September 1995 (the former Yugoslav Republic of Macedonia v. Greece); Case Concerning Application of the International Convention on the Elimination of All Forms of Racial Discrimination (Georgia v. Russian Federation);* the many cases involving *Serbia and Montenegro/Yugoslavia; Questions of Interpretation and Application of the 1971 Montreal Convention arising from the Aerial Incident at Lockerbie (Libyan Arab Jamahiriya v. United Kingdom); Case concerning East Timor (Portugal v. Australia); Nuclear Tests (New Zealand v. France); Nuclear Tests (Australia v. France); Fisheries Jurisdiction (Federal Republic of Germany v. Iceland); Fisheries Jurisdiction (United Kingdom of Great Britain and Northern Ireland v. Iceland); Rights of Passage over Indian Territory (Portugal v. India); Anglo-Iranian Oil Co. (United Kingdom v. Iran); Corfu Channel (United Kingdom of Great Britain and Northern Ireland v. Albania).*

- Those which hardly got started, most of which would no longer be entered in the Court's List: *Status vis-à-vis the Host State of a Diplomatic Envoy to the United Nations (Commonwealth of Dominica v. Switzerland);* various *Aerial Incident* cases of the 1950s; *Antarctica (United Kingdom v. Chile); Antarctica (United Kingdom v. Argentina); Electricité de Beyrouth Company (France v. Lebanon).*

Whatever may have been the position in the past, it is unlikely that the attitude of European states towards inter-state litigation is very different from that of states in other regions. It is possible that on balance they (or most of them) may have a more open mind towards inter-state litigation than some states from other regions, although it would be difficult to demonstrate that empirically.

It seems improbable that any European state has a general policy towards inter-state litigation in practice (as opposed to a policy towards the principle of inter-state litigation). Decisions to commence or not to commence litigation are undoubtedly rare, and are likely therefore to be taken ad hoc. Negotiation is surely the preferred way to resolve a dispute. It is probably only when the prospects for a solution through negotiation appear negligible that litigation may be considered; and even then the better course may be to leave the matter unresolved until more propitious times. In the case of maritime delimitation, or border disputes, litigation may have the attraction that neither government will be seen as to have sold the pass.

Decisions to lodge an application against another state are not taken lightly, and are likely to be taken only after a good deal of consultation within government, including the foreign ministry and the highest government lawyers. Among the obvious factors that will be weighed are the existence of jurisdiction, the estimate of success, the effect on bilateral relations, the timing, and the cost of the proceeding (which is often considerable, with virtually no chance of recouping it in the event of success).[36]

If one discounts the early cases that were entered in the General List even though there was no basis of jurisdiction, there are relatively few examples of European states not appearing before the Court, or failing to defend the case. The most recent were forty years ago.[37]

The United Kingdom and inter-state litigation

The United Kingdom has a long history of engagement with the settlement of inter-state disputes through international courts and tribunals. This is an important component of its commitment to the rule of law in international affairs. This engagement concerns both the promotion of international dispute settlement, and participation in proceedings before international courts and tribunals.

In this area of international law, as in others, the United Kingdom has tended to strike a balance between idealism and realism. As is the case with many European states, while much is said about the importance of international dispute settlement, in practice the United Kingdom is rather careful only to do what it sees as in its short-, medium-, or long-term interests. The United Kingdom's position as regards dispute settlement has evolved over time, from what might be called hesitant pioneer in the nineteenth century, to just hesitant in the first half of the twentieth century, to hovering between idealism and realism during the cold war and thereafter.

---

[36] See, e.g., the failed efforts of the United Kingdom to recover from Ireland its very substantial costs in *The MOX Plant Case (Ireland v. United Kingdom) (Order No 6)*, PCA, 6 June 2008.

[37] Albania in *Corfu Channel (United Kingdom v. Albania) (Assessment of Compensation)*, [1949] ICJ Rep. 244; Iceland in *Fisheries Jurisdiction (United Kingdom v. Iceland) (Merits)*, [1974] ICJ Rep. 3 and *Fisheries Jurisdiction (Federal Republic of Germany v. Iceland) (Merits)*, [1974] ICJ Rep. 175; and France in *Nuclear Tests Cases (Australia v. France, New Zealand v. France) (Merits)*, [1974] ICJ Rep. 457.

The Alabama Claims arbitration of 1871–2 is perhaps the most famous example of a case in which the United Kingdom has been involved.[38] It is seen as having initiated a new era in the settlement of disputes between states. But it was not an isolated case. There was something of a tradition of arbitration between the United Kingdom and the United States going back to the Jay Treaty of 1794.[39] Subsequent major arbitrations involving the United Kingdom were the 1872 *Delagoa Bay* arbitration with Portugal,[40] the 1892 *Newfoundland Lobster* arbitration,[41] the 1893 *Behring Sea* arbitration,[42] the 1895 *Costa Rica Packet Case* with the Netherlands,[43] and the 1899 *British Guiana and Venezuela Boundary* arbitration.[44]

The United Kingdom was an active participant in the debates on dispute settlement at the Hague Peace Conferences of 1899 and 1907, which resulted in the 1899 and 1907 Conventions for the Pacific Settlement of International Disputes and in the establishment of the PCA. The United Kingdom also played a significant role in the establishment of the PCIJ, being concerned about a court where the majority of judges would not be from common law systems and being opposed to compulsory jurisdiction. Nevertheless, it has accepted the compulsory jurisdiction of that Court and its successor, the ICJ, almost without break since 1930.[45] Today it is the only permanent member of the Security Council to do so, albeit with some far-reaching reservations. The United Kingdom also regularly accepts optional settlement of disputes clauses in multilateral conventions.

---

[38] J. Gillis Wetter, *The International Arbitral Process: Public and Private*, Vol. I (New York: Oceana Publications, 1979), 3–173; John B. Moore, *History and Digest of International Arbitrations*, Vol. I (Washington, DC: Government Print Office, 1898), 653; Tom Bingham, 'The Alabama Claims Arbitration', (2005) 54 ICLQ 1; Tom Bingham, 'Alabama Arbitration', in Rüdiger Wolfrum (ed.), *Max Planck Encyclopedia of Public International Law* (Oxford University Press, 2012).

[39] Signed on 19 November 1794, 52 *Consolidated Treaty Series*; see Jackson H. Ralston, *International Arbitration from Athens to Locarno* (Stanford: Stanford University Press, 1929). Three arbitrations were provided for under Arts. V, VI and VII of the Treaty: concerning the St Croix river and the boundary with British possessions in North America; obstruction of debts owed to British creditors; and claims arising from the seizure of British ships and cargoes during the War of Independence. This was followed by four arbitrations under the Treaty of Ghent (which ended the Anglo-American war of 1812–14). Great Britain was party to a number of arbitrations in the mid-nineteenth century, including three arbitrations by the Senate of Hamburg between 1856 and 1864 (John Liddle Simpson and Hazel Fox, *International Arbitration* (London: Stevens & Sons, 1959), 5); an arbitration with Venezuela in 1869 (ibid., 6–7); and the *Bulama Island* arbitration with Portugal in 1870 (Moore, above n. 38, 1909).

[40] Moore, above n. 38, 5015.   [41] Ibid., 4939.   [42] Ibid., 495.   [43] Ibid., 4948.

[44] Wetter, above n. 38, vol. III; 92 *British Foreign and State Papers*, 970.

[45] See Wood, above n. 10.

EUROPEAN PERSPECTIVES ON INTER-STATE LITIGATION 143

Between 1914 and 1939, the United Kingdom was much engaged with the PCIJ. The British member of the Advisory Committee of Jurists, Lord Phillimore, was a strong advocate of compulsory jurisdiction, although the British government was opposed. In 1920 (as in 1945), the majority of states favoured compulsory jurisdiction, but the 'great powers' of the day prevailed on each occasion. The optional clause, derived from a proposal by the Brazilian, Raoul Fernandes, was a form of optional compulsory jurisdiction. It then took until 1929 for the United Kingdom to accept the optional clause,[46] and it did so with seven reservations that attracted severe criticisms from, among others, Hersch Lauterpacht.[47] The British declaration had been co-ordinated among the dominions, and contained a British Commonwealth reservation that reflected the Commonwealth *inter se* doctrine.[48] This reservation remains in the UK declaration, and still has effect,[49] even though the *inter se* doctrine itself is 'largely of historic interest'.[50] The reservation was extended in July 2004 to cover countries that had been but were no longer members of the Commonwealth. The United Kingdom's 1929 declaration 'became a pacesetter for other states, and other declarations increased rapidly'.[51]

The United Kingdom has now had a declaration in place, with the exception of a few days between 14 and 18 April 1957, for well over eighty years.[52] The current declaration contains some basic reservations which, with the exception of the Commonwealth exception (for which special reasons continue), may be regarded as a minimum necessary for a

---

[46] Lorna Lloyd, *Peace through Law: Britain and the International Court in the 1920s* (London: Royal Historical Society, 1997). On the United Kingdom and the ICJ generally, see Ian Sinclair, 'International Law: The Court, Commission and Judges', in Erik Jensen and Thomas Fisher (eds.), *The United Kingdom and the United Nations* (London: Macmillan, 1990) 126.

[47] Hersch Lauterpacht, 'The British Reservations to the Optional Clause', (1930) 10 *Economica* 137.

[48] 'Historically, intra-Commonwealth relations were not regarded as international relations. According to the *inter se* doctrine Commonwealth countries were not "foreign" in relation to each other': Charlotte Steinorth, 'Commonwealth', in Rüdiger Wolfrum (ed.), *Max Planck Encyclopedia of Public International Law* (Oxford University Press, 2012), [9].

[49] *Aerial Incident of 10 August 1999 (Pakistan v. India) (Jurisdiction)*, [2000] ICJ Rep. 12, 31 [44].

[50] Steinorth, above n. 48, para. 10.

[51] Leo Gross, 'Compulsory Jurisdiction under the Optional Clause: History and Practice', in Lori Damrosch (ed.), *The International Court of Justice at the Crossroads* (New York: Transnational Publishers, 1987) 20.

[52] For a description of the United Kingdom's nine successive declarations, see Wood, above n. 11.

reasonably prudent declaration. These are a reasonable cut-off date (1974), a twelve-month period to prevent 'surprise' applications, a right to terminate or modify at any time, and an exception for disputes that the parties have agreed to settle by other means. Of these, the right to terminate is perhaps the most contested. It has even been suggested that a declaration with such a reservation is not really an acceptance of compulsory jurisdiction at all. But this is not so. A state making such a declaration is always at risk of a surprise application, since it will not necessarily receive warning. And termination or modification of a declaration to avoid a threatened case is not necessarily without political cost or something to be done lightly.

In the period between 1940 and the present, the United Kingdom seemed to hesitate between idealism and realism. In 1943, it took the initiative in calling for an Informal Inter-Allied Committee of experts to examine the question of the Court,[53] which produced a 'valuable and stimulating – even controversial' report on the future of the PCIJ.[54] In 1944/5, it resisted pressure to make the jurisdiction of the new ICJ truly compulsory. An American author wrote of the United Kingdom's declaration of 18 April 1957 that it 'has the unenviable distinction of including more reservations – no less than fourteen in number – than any other declaration in force and of including a subjective reservation on national security as determined by the United Kingdom which undermines the system of compulsory jurisdiction'.[55]

The United Kingdom's current support for the principle of the peaceful settlement of disputes, as an element in its support for the rule of law in international relations, is clear. But the same could be said nowadays for virtually all members of the United Nations. What does this commitment mean in practice? Can it be said that in principle the United Kingdom supports compulsory third-party dispute settlement, in particular arbitration and judicial settlement? Its statements and actions suggest that it does indeed tend to favour such procedures, or at least is not in principle opposed to them. But it does not do so dogmatically, in all, or virtually all, circumstances. Its approach is more pragmatic. It considers questions

---

[53] Geoffrey Marston, 'The London Committee and the Statute of the International Court', in Vaughan Lowe and Malgosia Fitzmaurice (eds.), *Fifty Years of the International Court of Justice: Essays in Honour of Sir Robert Jennings* (Cambridge University Press, 1996) 40.

[54] Shabtai Rosenne, *The Law and Practice of the International Court, 1920–2005*, 4th edn (The Hague: Martinus Nijhoff, 2006), 51.

[55] Herbert W. Briggs, 'Reservations to the Acceptance of the Compulsory Jurisdiction of the International Court of Justice', (1958) 93 *Hague Recueil* 121, 303.

EUROPEAN PERSPECTIVES ON INTER-STATE LITIGATION 145

such as whether it is realistic to expect states to accept binding dispute settlement in this particular context; whether indeed it makes sense to settle such and such a class of disputes, or a particular dispute, through binding third-party procedures; whether a dispute needs settling at a particular time, and if so whether this can better be achieved by negotiation.

The United Kingdom's record of accepting the jurisdiction of international courts and tribunals through optional dispute settlement protocols and clauses is a good one. Indeed, it has done so in virtually all cases.[56]

Once dispute settlement bodies are established, they can generally rely on the United Kingdom's support. This has long been so in relation to the ICJ (and its predecessor, the PCIJ), but also to certain bodies the establishment of which the United Kingdom did not originally support, such as ITLOS.[57] Support includes adequate resources, and administrative and legal support, and above all the nomination of and support for good candidates.[58] It is not to be measured by participation in contentious cases, which depends on many other factors. But participation in advisory opinion proceedings may indicate the seriousness with which a state takes judicial settlement, and on that score the United Kingdom has a reasonable record.

The United Kingdom has in the past occasionally acted as arbitrator, but this is nowadays unlikely, since that form of arbitration is only likely to arise under very old treaties. More likely is a role in hosting or otherwise providing material support to arbitral proceedings, although with the growing role of bodies like the PCA in offering skilled registry services this is also less likely to be necessary than in the past.

One should not overlook the contribution of UK nationals in their personal capacity, whether as judges, arbitrators, counsel, or registry staff.

---

[56] While not within the scope of this chapter, it is worth noting that, probably to avoid double exposure since it is already a party to the European Convention on Human Rights, the United Kingdom has so far refrained from accepting the jurisdiction of the various human rights committees to accept individual communications, though exceptionally it has done so since 2004 in the case of the Committee on the Elimination of Discrimination against Women (CEDAW).

[57] An exception is the OSCE Court of Conciliation and Arbitration (see section I above), the jurisdiction of which the United Kingdom does not accept.

[58] Michael Wood, 'The Selection of Candidates for International Judicial Office: Recent Practice', in Tasfir M. Ndiaye and Rüdiger Wolfrum (eds.), *Law of the Sea, Environmental Law and Settlement of Disputes: Liber Amicorum Judge Thomas A. Mensah* (The Hague: Martinus Nijhoff, 2007). See also Ruth Mackenzie, Kate Malleson, Penny Martin, and Philippe Sands, *Selecting International Judges: Principle, Process, and Politics* (Oxford University Press, 2010).

Finally, mention should be made of the contribution of writers in the United Kingdom. The latest (seventh) edition of Volume II of *Oppenheim's International Law*, dating from 1951 and the work of Hersch Lauterpacht, contains what is still a useful part, entitled 'Settlement of State Differences'. Perhaps the most accessible up-to-date book on international dispute settlement is that of John Merrills.[59]

In short, it may be thought that the United Kingdom's approach to international dispute settlement has, generally speaking, been informed by a healthy balance of idealism and realism (self-interest). It has not been starry-eyed; nor has it been excessively cautious.

If acceptance of the compulsory jurisdiction of the ICJ is taken as a touchstone of a state's support for dispute settlement, by this measure, the United Kingdom is somewhere in the middle. It has never accepted the jurisdiction of the ICJ without important reservations. At times, indeed, the United Kingdom has had many reservations. Often they are with quite specific purpose, to avoid a particular dispute reaching the Court. Quite a few states (such as Denmark, Finland, Netherlands, Switzerland, but also the Democratic Republic of the Congo, Dominica, Georgia, Guinea-Bissau, Paraguay) accept the jurisdiction with no substantive reservations at all. And many others have fewer reservations than the United Kingdom. But many do not accept it at all.

Conclusion

Any comparison of the relative contribution of states to the peaceful settlement of disputes is bound to be largely impressionistic. One cannot usefully measure a state's support for international dispute settlement in any mathematical or scientific way. But there are certain indicia that one could look to, as reflected above.

There is a tradition of support in Europe for international dispute settlement, albeit hesitant support, stretching back more than a hundred years and in some cases much longer.

European states, at least many of them, are increasingly subject to the jurisdiction of international courts and tribunals. This extends the opportunities to commence litigation *inter se*, but at a time when politically it

---

[59] John G. Merrills, *International Dispute Settlement*, 5th edn (Cambridge University Press, 2011). See also John Collier and Vaughan Lowe, *The Settlement of Disputes in International Law* (Oxford University Press, 1999); Duncan French, Matthew Saul, and Nigel D. White (eds.), *International Law and Dispute Settlement* (Oxford: Hart, 2010).

may be thought that such litigation is less likely, at least between member states of the European Union. Nevertheless, as the *Germany* v. *Italy* ICJ case and a series of cases between Ireland and the United Kingdom show, such litigation is not to be excluded (although EU membership may place limits on litigating outside the EU framework, as Ireland found to its cost in the *MOX Plant* case).

8

Asian perspectives on inter-state litigation

RODMAN R. BUNDY

While Asian states have been fairly active in state-to-state litigation and arbitration over the past fifteen years, it is difficult to draw generalized conclusions about Asian attitudes towards inter-state litigation given the large number and geographical and political diversity of the states involved. Many Asian countries still appear to take a cautious view towards international litigation if measured by the relatively modest number of Asian states that have filed optional clause declarations under Article 36(2) of the Statute of the International Court of Justice (ICJ). Others may be wary of litigation, especially if they have been respondents in cases brought by unilateral application.

Nonetheless, recent trends suggest that some Asian states, particularly members of the Association of Southeast Asian Nations (ASEAN) and certain South Asian states, are becoming more amenable to dispute resolution by means of the ICJ, ad hoc arbitral tribunals (including tribunals constituted under Annex VII to the 1982 United Nations Convention of the Law of the Sea (UNCLOS)) and the International Tribunal for the Law of the Sea (ITLOS). The cases in which these states have been engaged tend for the most part to involve issues of disputed territorial sovereignty, maritime delimitation and matters arising under UNCLOS, although recourse has also been made to courts and tribunals in respect of other kinds of dispute.

Over the past ten years, the ICJ has decided two cases brought by special agreement between ASEAN states concerning disputed sovereignty over territory.[1] In 2005, an Annex VII tribunal issued an Award on Agreed Terms in connection with a land reclamation dispute in and around

---

[1] *Sovereignty over Pulau Ligitan and Pulau Sipadan (Indonesia/Malaysia)*, [2002] ICJ Rep. 625 (*Sovereignty over Pulau Ligitan*); *Sovereignty over Pedra Branca/Pulau Batu Puteh, Middle Rocks and South Ledge (Malaysia/Singapore)*, [2008] ICJ Rep. 12 (*Sovereignty over Pedra Branca*).

the Strait of Johor brought by Malaysia against Singapore.[2] And, on 14 March 2012, ITLOS rendered its judgment in a maritime delimitation case between Bangladesh and Myanmar – the first time ITLOS has decided a delimitation dispute.[3]

Currently, the ICJ has before it Cambodia's request for interpretation of the Court's 1962 judgment in the *Temple of Preah Vihear* case,[4] and the *Whaling in the Antarctic* case brought by Australia against Japan.[5] The maritime delimitation case between Bangladesh and India is also pending before an arbitral tribunal constituted under Annex VII of UNCLOS. In addition, for the first time since the Indus River Treaty was concluded between Pakistan and India in 1960, an arbitral tribunal has been constituted under the dispute resolution clause of that treaty to decide a dispute brought by Pakistan against India concerning a hydroelectric project on a tributary of the Indus River in Kashmir.[6]

When proceedings are instituted by special agreement or a bilateral arbitration agreement, it is reasonable to conclude that both parties to the dispute consider that state-to-state litigation is an appropriate and politically useful means of dispute resolution. In contrast, when litigation is instituted by means of unilateral application, that may indicate a willingness of the applicant state to resort to inter-state litigation, but it does not necessarily mean that the respondent state shares the same view. In such cases, jurisdictional issues generally play a critical role in determining whether the applicant will submit the dispute to a sitting court or tribunal, or to arbitration.

Asian states and the International Court of Justice

Optional clause declarations

Compared with other geographic regions of the world, relatively few Asian states have deposited optional clause declarations under Article 36(2) of

---

[2] *Case concerning Land Reclamation by Singapore in and around the Straits of Johor (Malaysia v. Singapore) (Decision of 1 September 2005)*, 27 RIAA 133.

[3] *Dispute concerning Delimitation of the Maritime Boundary between Bangladesh and Myanmar in the Bay of Bengal (Bangladesh/Myanmar)*, ITLOS, Case No. 16, 14 March 2012 (*Dispute concerning the Bay of Bengal*).

[4] *Request for Interpretation of the Judgment of 15 June 1962 in the Case Concerning the Temple of Preah Vihear (Cambodia v. Thailand)*, ICJ, General List No. 151, 18 July 2011 (*Request for Interpretation of Temple of Preah Vihear*).

[5] *Whaling in the Antarctic (Australia v. Japan)*, ICJ, General List No. 148, 31 May 2010.

[6] *Indus Waters Kishenganga Arbitration (Pakistan v. India)*, PCA, 31 August 2012.

150 RODMAN R. BUNDY

the Statute of the ICJ accepting the compulsory jurisdiction of the Court. Five Asian states currently have optional clause declarations on record: Cambodia, India, Japan, Pakistan, and the Philippines.

The earliest optional clause declaration currently in effect was made by Cambodia on 9 September 1957.[7] In it, Cambodia

> recognize[s] as compulsory ipso facto and without special agreement, in relation to any other State Member of the United Nations, accepting the same obligation, that is to say on condition of reciprocity, the jurisdiction of the said Court in all legal disputes, other than:
> 1. Disputes in regard to which the parties have agreed, or shall agree, to have recourse to some other method of peaceful settlement;
> 2. Disputes which fall exclusively within the jurisdiction of the Kingdom of Cambodia;
> 3. Disputes relating to any matter excluded from judicial settlement or compulsory arbitration by virtue of any treaty, convention or other international agreement or instrument to which the Kingdom of Cambodia is a party.

In 1950, Thailand had also deposited a communication indicating that its 1929 declaration accepting the compulsory jurisdiction of the Permanent Court of International Justice (PCIJ), which had been renewed once in 1940 for a period of ten years, was renewed again for a further ten-year period.[8] Thus, when Cambodia filed its application in October 1959 instituting proceedings against Thailand in the *Temple of Preah Vihear* case, the basis of jurisdiction relied on by Cambodia was grounded on the parties' respective optional clause declarations. Thailand raised preliminary objections to the Court's jurisdiction, but these were not accepted by the Court.[9]

In the meantime, Thailand's optional clause declaration lapsed in 1960 and was not thereafter renewed. There is little doubt that the Court's judgment on the merits of the *Temple* case rendered in 1962 was badly received by Thailand. This may explain why Thailand has not filed a new optional clause declaration during the fifty years since the judgment was handed down. However, whether Thailand's conduct is indicative of a general reluctance among Asian states to have recourse to the ICJ after

---

[7] For the text of Cambodia's declaration see 'Declaration by Cambodia', (1998) 52 *ICJ Yearbook* 88.

[8] For the text of Thailand's 1950 declaration see *Temple of Preah Vihear (Cambodia v. Thailand) (Preliminary Objections)*, [1961] ICJ Rep. 24 (*Temple of Preah Vihear*).

[9] Ibid., 35.

receiving what is perceived to be an unfavourable result is speculative given the lack of a sufficient number of precedents.

With respect to the *Temple* case, on 28 April 2011, Cambodia filed an Application with the Court requesting an interpretation of the 1962 Judgment and a request for provisional measures of protection.[10] With respect to jurisdiction, Cambodia's request was based on Article 60 of the Court's Statute, which provides in relevant part: 'In the event of dispute as to the meaning and scope of the judgment, the Court shall construe it upon the request of any party.'

On 18 July 2011, the Court issued an order indicating provisional measures applicable to both parties.[11] As of the time of writing, the proceedings in the case were still in their written phase. Whether oral hearings were to be convened was a matter within the Court's discretion under Article 98(4) of the Rules of Court. Hearings did ultimately take place and a decision was due towards the end of 2013.

The other optional clause declarations made by Asian states are more restrictive in nature. For example, the declarations filed by Pakistan (1960), the Philippines (1972), India (1974), and Japan (2007) all contain provisions that exclude acceptance of the Court's jurisdiction for disputes in respect of which the other party to the dispute has either accepted the compulsory jurisdiction of the ICJ for or in relation to the purposes of such dispute, or where the acceptance of the Court's compulsory jurisdiction was deposited or ratified less than twelve months prior to the filing of the application bringing the dispute before the Court.[12]

These exclusions reflect a measured approach to the acceptance of the Court's jurisdiction by states that have filed optional clause declarations. As a practical matter, they permit the states concerned to monitor the list of states that have filed such declarations in order to ascertain whether a new declaration may have been filed solely for the purpose of instituting proceedings against them and, if so, to withdraw or modify their own declaration if resolution of the dispute by the ICJ is not desired.

---

[10] *Request for Interpretation of the Judgment of 15 June 1962 in the Case concerning the Temple of Preah Vihear (Cambodia* v. *Thailand)*, ICJ, General List No. 151, 18 July 2011.

[11] *Request for Interpretation of the Judgment of 15 June 1962 in the Case concerning the Temple of Preah Vihear (Cambodia* v. *Thailand) (Order of 18 July 2011)*, ICJ, General List No. 151, 18 July 2011.

[12] This model broadly follows the United Kingdom's declaration which, to the author's knowledge, was the first to include such language.

Interestingly, both India's and Japan's current declarations containing this exclusion differ from previous declarations they had made.

In 1940, India deposited a declaration under Article 36(2) of the Statute that was broader in nature. In the *Rights of Passage* case, Portugal based the Court's jurisdiction on the fact that both parties had accepted compulsory jurisdiction by virtue of their optional clause declarations.[13] While India raised a series of six preliminary objections to the Court's jurisdiction, in its judgment on those objections the Court rejected four and joined the other two to the merits.[14] India's 1940 declaration has now been superseded by its 1974 declaration.

Japan also filed an optional clause declaration in 1958 that did not contain the kind of exclusion discussed above, but that declaration was replaced with a new one in 2007 which broadly followed the model that the United Kingdom used in 1969.

Unilateral applications to the International Court of Justice involving Asian states

Whether due to the absence of a jurisdictional link or for other reasons, relatively few cases have been brought before the ICJ by unilateral application either by an Asian state or against such a state (or, perhaps more accurately, there have been relatively few Asian states that have been parties to such cases). Apart from the *Rights of Passage* and *Temple* cases, both of which date back over fifty years, seven cases involving an Asian state or states have been introduced before the Court on a unilateral basis. Three of those cases were between Pakistan and India, three between Iran and the United States, and one (currently pending) between Australia and Japan. These are briefly discussed below.

In 1971, India filed an application with the ICJ instituting an appeal from certain decisions rendered by the Council of the International Civil Aviation Organization (ICAO) on preliminary objections raised by India in connection with an application and complaint brought before the Council by Pakistan. The basis of jurisdiction was Article 84 of the Chicago Convention.[15] In its judgment, the Court found that it had jurisdiction to

---

[13] *Rights of Passage over Indian Territory (Preliminary Objections)*, [1957] ICJ Rep. 140 (*Rights of Passage*).

[14] Ibid., 152.

[15] Convention on International Civil Aviation (opened for signature 1 December 1944, entered into force 5 March 1947), 15 UNTS 295.

entertain India's appeal, but rejected that appeal on the grounds that the ICAO Council was competent to entertain the application and complaint laid before it by Pakistan.[16]

One other case has been brought before the ICJ by an Asian state on appeal from a decision rendered by the ICAO Council. This was the case concerning the *Aerial Incident of 3 July 1988*, instituted by Iran against the United States in respect of a decision that the ICAO Council issued under the Chicago Convention regarding the destruction by US naval forces of an Iranian civil aircraft flying over the Persian Gulf. In addition to invoking Article 84 of the Chicago Convention as a basis of jurisdiction, Iran also relied on the compromissory clause contained in Article 14(1) of the 1971 Montreal Convention.[17] The United States raised preliminary objections to the Court's jurisdiction, but the case was subsequently discontinued pursuant to a notification submitted by the parties indicating that they had entered into a full and final settlement of the dispute.[18]

In 1973, Pakistan instituted proceedings against India in the *Trial of Pakistani Prisoners of War* case on the basis of the Convention on the Prevention and Punishment of the Crime of Genocide, including the compromissory clause contained in Article IX thereof.[19] Pakistan also sought an order of provisional measures of protection.[20] On 14 December 1973, however, Pakistan submitted a letter to the ICJ which referred to the fact that negotiations with India over the dispute were ongoing and requested that the case be discontinued. Accordingly, on 15 December 1973 the ICJ issued an order placing on record the discontinuance of the proceedings by the government of Pakistan and removing the case from the list.[21]

In addition to being the applicant in the *Aerial Incident of 3 July 1988* case, Iran has been a party to two other ICJ cases: the *United States*

---

[16] *Appeal Relating to the Jurisdiction of the ICAO Council*, [1972] ICJ Rep. 46, 70 [46].

[17] Convention for the Suppression of Unlawful Acts Against the Safety of Civil Aviation (opened for signature 23 September 1971, entered into force 26 January 1973), 974 UNTS 178.

[18] *Aerial Incident of 3 July 1988 (Iran v. United States) (Order of 22 February 1996)*, [1996] ICJ Rep. 9, 9–11.

[19] 'Pleadings', *Trial of Pakistani Prisoners of War (Pakistan v. India)*, [1973] ICJ Rep. 328.

[20] *Trial of Pakistani Prisoners of War (Pakistan v. India) (Order of 13 July 1973)*, [1973] ICJ Rep. 328.

[21] *Trial of Pakistani Prisoners of War (Pakistan v. India) (Order of 15 December 1973)*, [1973] ICJ Rep. 348.

Diplomatic and Consular Staff in Tehran case, in which Iran was the respondent; and the *Oil Platforms* case, in which it was the applicant.[22]

The former case arose out of the hostage crisis. The United States based its claims and the jurisdiction of the Court on the 1961 Vienna Convention on Diplomatic Relations,[23] the Optional Protocol to that Convention concerning the Compulsory Settlement of Disputes,[24] the 1963 Vienna Convention on Consular Relations,[25] the Optional Protocol to that Convention,[26] the 1973 Convention on the Prevention of Crimes against Internationally Protected Persons, including Diplomatic Agents,[27] and the 1955 Treaty of Amity, Economic Relations, and Consular Rights between the United States and Iran.[28]

On 15 December 1979, the Court indicated provisional measures in the case,[29] and on 24 May 1980 it rendered its judgment, finding that Iran had violated, and was still violating, obligations owed by it to the United States under both international conventions in force between the parties and general international law.[30] Iran did not participate in either the written or oral proceedings. Following the conclusion of the Algiers Declarations in January 1981,[31] the United States informed the Court

---

[22] This contribution does not address the numerous cases that have been adjudicated between Iran and the United States, and between Iran and US nationals, that have been decided by the Iran–United States Claims Tribunal established pursuant to the 1981 Algiers Declarations.

[23] Vienna Convention on Diplomatic Relations (opened for signature 18 April 1961, entered into force 24 April 1964), 500 UNTS 95.

[24] Optional Protocol to the Vienna Convention on Diplomatic Relations concerning the Compulsory Settlement of Disputes (opened for signature 24 April 1963, entered into force 21 June 1985), 1400 UNTS 339.

[25] Vienna Convention on Consular Relations (opened for signature 24 April 1963, entered into force 19 March 1967), 596 UNTS 261.

[26] Optional Protocol to the Vienna Convention on Consular Relations concerning the Compulsory Settlement of Disputes (opened for signature 24 April 1963, entered into force 19 March 1967), 596 UNTS 487.

[27] Convention on the Prevention and Punishment of Crimes against Internationally Protected Persons, including Diplomatic Agents (opened for signature 14 December 1973, entered into force 20 February 1977), 1035 UNTS 167.

[28] Treaty of Amity, Economic Relations, and Consular Rights between the United States and Iran, Iran–United States, (signed 15 August 1955, entered into force 16 June 1957), 284 UNTS 93.

[29] *United States Diplomatic and Consular Staff in Tehran (United States v. Iran) (Order of 15 December 1979)*, [1979] ICJ Rep. 7.

[30] *United States Diplomatic and Consular Staff in Tehran (United States v. Iran)*, [1980] ICJ Rep. 44, [95].

[31] Algiers Accords: Declaration of the Government of the Democratic and Popular Republic of Algeria, Iran–United States, 62 ILR 595 (signed and entered into force 20 January 1981).

that it sought the discontinuance of the case, which had yet to address the form and amount of reparation owed by Iran to the United States. On 12 May 1981, therefore, the Court issued an order placing on record the discontinuance of the case and removing it from the list.[32]

The *Oil Platforms* case was brought by Iran against the United States by application dated 2 November 1992.[33] Iran based its claims on the allegation that, by attacking and destroying a number of Iranian offshore oil platforms in 1987 and 1988, the United States had breached the 1955 Treaty of Amity between the two states. Iran relied on the compromissory clause appearing in Article XXI(2) of the treaty for jurisdictional purposes.

At the time, there was a question whether Iran should bring the case before the Court under the Treaty of Amity or before the Iran–United States Claims Tribunal under Point 1 of the General Declaration signed by Iran and the United States on 19 January 1981 and the compromissory clause contained in paragraph 17 of that Declaration.[34] Under Point 1, the United States pledged that it was and from then on would be the policy of the United States not to interfere, directly or indirectly, politically or militarily in Iran's internal affairs.[35] Paragraph 17 of the Declaration provides that, if any dispute arises between the parties as to the interpretation or performance of any provision of the Declaration, either party may submit the dispute to binding arbitration by the Iran–United States Claims Tribunal.[36]

Ultimately, the decision was made by Iran to submit the dispute to the ICJ, in part because the ICJ had previously addressed the provisions of a treaty that were similar in nature to the Treaty of Amity in the *Nicaragua–United States* case.[37]

While the United States raised preliminary objections in the *Oil Platforms* case which were not accepted by the Court,[38] the United States thereafter vigorously defended the case on the merits, unlike in its case against Nicaragua. In its judgment of 6 November 2003, the Court held

---

[32] *United States Diplomatic and Consular Staff in Tehran (United States v. Iran) (Order of 12 May 1981)*, [1981] ICJ Rep. 47.

[33] 'Application Instituting Proceedings', *Oil Platforms (Iran v. United States) (Judgment)*, [2003] ICJ Rep. 161 (*Oil Platforms*).

[34] For the text of the General Declaration, see 1 Iran–US CTR 3.   [35] Ibid., 3.

[36] Ibid., [17].

[37] *Military and Paramilitary Activities in and against Nicaragua (Nicaragua v. United States) (Merits)*, [1986] ICJ Rep. 14. This view reflects the author's personal recollection as counsel to Iran at the time, but does not necessarily represent the views of the government of Iran.

[38] *Oil Platforms (Iran v. United States) (Preliminary Objections)*, [1996] ICJ Rep. 803, [55].

156 RODMAN R. BUNDY

that the United States' actions against the oil platforms could not be justified as measures necessary to protect its essential security interests under the treaty, but that Iran's claims of a breach of the treaty regarding freedom of commerce and navigation between the territories of the parties could not be upheld.[39]

In 1999, Pakistan instituted proceedings against India in the case concerning the *Aerial Incident of 10 August 1999*, in which Pakistan primarily relied on India's 1974 optional clause declaration for establishing the Court's jurisdiction. In its judgment, however, the ICJ ruled that it had no jurisdiction to entertain Pakistan's application in the light of India's 'Commonwealth reservation' contained in sub-paragraph (2) of the first paragraph of its declaration.[40]

The most recent case involving an Asian state to be brought before the ICJ is the case concerning *Whaling in the Antarctic*, which Australia introduced against Japan by means of an application filed on 31 May 2010.[41] In its application, Australia requested the Court to adjudge and declare that Japan is in breach of its international obligations under the International Convention for the Regulation of Whaling in implementing the second phase of its Whale Research Program under Special Permit in the Antarctic. Australia based the Court's jurisdiction on the declarations of acceptance made respectively by Australia, dated 22 March 2002, and by Japan, dated 9 July 2007, in accordance with Article 36(2) of the Court's Statute. The case was, at the time of writing, pending before the Court.

What, if any, conclusions can be drawn from this practice regarding the attitude of Asian states to litigation before the ICJ? First, of the nine cases involving Asian states introduced by means of unilateral application, in only six of them was an Asian state the applicant (Iran twice, Pakistan twice, and India and Cambodia once each). Three of those cases did not reach the merits stage either because the Court lacked jurisdiction (*Aerial Incident of 10 August 1999*) or because the case was discontinued as a result of settlement (*Aerial Incident of 3 July 1988* and *Trial of Pakistani Prisoners of War*). Second, most of the cases in question have tended to relate to particular bilateral relationships. For example, in all three cases in

---

[39] *Oil Platforms*, [2003] ICJ Rep. 161, [125].

[40] *Aerial Incident of 10 August 1999 (Pakistan v India) (Jurisdiction)*, [2000] ICJ Rep. 12, [46], [56] (*dispositif*). In the declaration by India recognizing the jurisdiction of the ICJ reservation was made to '(2) disputes with the government of any State which is or has been a Member of the Commonwealth of Nations'.

[41] 'Application Instituting Proceedings', *Whaling in the Antarctic (Australia v. Japan)*, ICJ, General List No. 148, 31 May 2010.

which Iran has been a party, the other party was the United States. Three other cases have involved disputes between India and Pakistan. And in the *Rights of Passage* case, India was the respondent. Given this small sample size, it is difficult to draw broad conclusions about the readiness of Asian states to take the initiative to have recourse to the Court by filing unilateral applications. In any event, there has never been an ICJ case brought by an Asian state either unilaterally or by special agreement against a non-Asian state apart from the two cases introduced by Iran against the United States.

Cases brought by special agreement

Notwithstanding the practice discussed above, there are signs that at least some ASEAN states are willing by mutual agreement to submit certain kinds of disputes between themselves to the ICJ. Over the past ten years or so, the Court has rendered two judgments in cases concerning disputed sovereignty over land territory (specifically, islands) that ASEAN states submitted to it by special agreement. These are the case concerning *Sovereignty over Pulau Ligitan and Pulau Sipadan* between Indonesia and Malaysia decided by the Court in 2002,[42] and the case concerning *Sovereignty over Pedra Branca/Pulau Batu Puteh, Middle Rocks and South Ledge* between Malaysia and Singapore decided by the Court in 2008.[43]

The *Indonesia/Malaysia* case arose in connection with negotiations between the parties over the delimitation of their continental shelf boundaries, not as an independent, pre-existing sovereignty dispute. In 1969, the parties were able to agree continental shelf boundaries in the Strait of Malacca and the South China Sea.[44] When it came to delimiting the continental shelf boundary off the east coast of Borneo between Sabah and Kalimantan, however, the parties were not able to reach an agreement because of a dispute that then emerged as to which party possessed sovereignty over two small islands in the area of concern: Pulau Ligitan and Pulau Sipadan.

It took the two states almost thirty years to agree to submit the dispute jointly to the ICJ. A special agreement to this effect was signed on 31 May 1997 at Kuala Lumpur and filed with the Registry of the Court on 2

---

[42] *Sovereignty over Pulau Ligitan*, [2002] ICJ Rep. 625.
[43] *Sovereignty over Pedra Branca*, [2008] ICJ Rep. 12.
[44] Jonathan Charney and Lewis Alexander (eds.), *International Maritime Boundaries*, Vol. I (Dordrecht: Martinus Nijhoff, 1993), 1025.

November 1998. In that instrument, the ICJ was requested to determine, on the basis of the treaties, agreements, and other evidence furnished by the parties, whether sovereignty over Pulau Ligitan and Pulau Sipadan belonged to Indonesia or Malaysia.

During the proceedings in the case, the Philippines filed an application for permission to intervene under Article 62 of the Court's Statute.[45] In support of its request, the Philippines argued that the Court was likely to address a number of treaties and other documents in the case that might have a bearing on the Philippines' historical claim to North Borneo. That request was rejected by the Court in 2001 because the Philippines had not demonstrated an interest of a legal nature that might be affected by a decision in the case.[46] The following year, the Court delivered its judgment on the merits of the dispute in which it ruled that sovereignty over the two islands belongs to Malaysia.[47]

There is some anecdotal evidence from the Indonesian side suggesting that, during negotiations, thought was given to submitting the dispute within an ASEAN context under the framework of the 1976 Treaty of Amity and Cooperation in Southeast Asia.[48] However, Malaysia apparently convinced Indonesia that, because Malaysia had a number of boundary or sovereignty disputes with other ASEAN member states, this would not be appropriate. The decision was therefore made to submit the dispute to the Court – the first time that two Asian states had recourse to the ICJ by means of a special agreement.

The *Malaysia/Singapore* case over Pedra Branca/Pulau Batu Puteh, Middle Rocks, and South Ledge also had a long pedigree. The dispute first emerged in 1979, when Malaysia published a map that appeared to depict the island of Pedra Branca situated at the eastern end of the Strait of Singapore as belonging to Malaysia. Singapore protested in 1980.

The parties then entered into a lengthy series of negotiations during the course of which each side prepared, and submitted to the other, documents and arguments supporting its position. The decision to submit the matter to third-party adjudication was not taken until 1994, some fourteen years after the dispute first emerged.[49]

---

[45] 'Application for Permission to Intervene', *Sovereignty over Pulau Ligitan and Pulau Sipadan (Indonesia/Malaysia)*, [2001] ICJ Rep. 575.

[46] Ibid.   [47] *Sovereignty over Pulau Ligitan*, [2002] ICJ Rep. 625, [150].

[48] Treaty of Amity and Cooperation in Southeast Asia (opened for signature 24 February 1976, entered into force 15 July 1976), 1025 UNTS 316.

[49] S. Jayakumar and Tommy Koh, *Pedra Branca, The Road to the World Court* (Singapore: NUS Press, 2009) 20, 32–3.

Thereafter, it took the parties another four years to work out the terms of the special agreement, and still more time before that agreement was notified to the ICJ. One of the issues that needed to be resolved was whether the request to the Court should be limited to the question of sovereignty over Pedra Branca/Pulau Batu Puteh or should include Middle Rocks and South Ledge as well.[50] In addition, Malaysia was also involved at that time in its ICJ case with Indonesia, the special agreement for which had been signed before the Malaysia–Singapore agreement. Malaysia apparently wished to conclude that case before taking up a new case.

Following the Court's judgment in *Indonesia/Malaysia*, the special agreement between Malaysia and Singapore was jointly notified to the Court on 24 July 2003. On 23 May 2008, the Court delivered its judgment, in which it found that sovereignty over Pedra Branca/Pulau Batu Puteh belongs to Singapore, sovereignty over Middle Rocks belongs to Malaysia, and sovereignty over South Ledge (a low-tide elevation) belongs to the state in the territorial waters of which it is located.[51] As recounted by Singapore's agent and another senior government official in a book they wrote about the case,

> The Pedra Branca case was an important development in our bilateral relations with Malaysia. It finally brought closure to this long-standing dispute between the two countries. Beyond bilateral relations, this case served as a good example to the rest of the region on the merits of amicable settlement of disputes through third party adjudication.[52]

Hopefully, these words will resonate with other Asian states, particularly in cases involving disputed sovereignty or maritime boundaries. In both cases that were brought by Asian states pursuant to special agreement, the governments concerned had at their disposal highly competent internal teams as well as experienced teams of foreign counsel. It is this author's impression that, in considering whether to submit their disputes to the Court, Malaysia, Indonesia, and Singapore all took into account the fact that the ICJ had a long track record of resolving territorial disputes on the basis of international law. Even though the final results could not be predicted with certainty, it was reasonably clear from the Court's jurisprudence what principles and rules of international law would apply to determining issues relating to the acquisition and maintenance of title

---

[50] Ibid., 36–7.   [51] *Sovereignty over Pedra Branca*, [2008] ICJ Rep. 12, [300].
[52] Jayakumar and Koh, above n. 49, xviii.

160 RODMAN R. BUNDY

to territory and which state could show the better title to the territory in question.

Arbitration between Asian states

There have been relatively few disputes between Asian states that have been submitted to arbitration, although this trend may be changing as a result of the dispute resolution alternatives provided for under UNCLOS, to which more than twenty Asian states are parties.

Ad hoc arbitration and arbitration under bilateral treaties

The first modern inter-state arbitration between two Asian states was the *Rann of Kutch* case. The genesis of that dispute, which concerned a sector of the boundary between India and Pakistan in the south-western region of the Indian sub-continent, dates back to before the independence of both countries. Following independence, and particularly as a result of hostilities that broke out along the boundary area in April 1965, the issue became more pressing.[53]

British officials were interested in achieving a ceasefire as rapidly as possible, and to this end entered into discussions with both sides in an effort to mediate the dispute. With British assistance, the parties eventually concluded a ceasefire agreement, in which they also consented to arbitration, on 30 June 1965. A three-member tribunal was thereafter constituted in Geneva in early 1966, and the tribunal rendered its award in February 1968.[54] As one author observed at the time with respect to the arbitral proceedings,

> Above all, however, the *Rann of Kutch* arbitration demonstrates that even today a peaceful settlement can be reached in a dispute affecting large

---

[53] J. Gillis Wetter, 'The Rann of Kutch Arbitration', 65 AJIL 346.

[54] *Indo-Pakistan Western Boundary (Rann of Kutch)*, (1968) 17 RIAA 1. More recently, the government of France played a similar role in a dispute between Yemen and Eritrea. In 1995, hostilities between the two countries broke out on the Hanish Islands in the southern Red Sea. France, with the assistance of Ethiopia and Egypt, first helped in brokering an 'Agreement on Principles' in May 1996, in which the two countries agreed in principle to arbitrate their sovereignty dispute over the islands. Subsequently, the French Foreign Ministry acted as a facilitator for the negotiation of a detailed Arbitration Agreement dated 3 October 1996 pursuant to which an arbitral tribunal was established to decide, in two phases, the question of disputed sovereignty and the maritime boundaries between the parties. For a copy of the two awards, see: PCA, *The Eritrea–Yemen Arbitration Awards 1998 and 1999* (The Hague: T. M. S. Asser Press, 2005).

nations which, though superficially insignificant, has been the cause of war. It is therefore to be hoped that it will serve as a precedent for the settlement of other disputes of like character in which an exhaustive and impartial judicial examination may be a proper vehicle for assuring a peaceful resolution of justiciable issues.[55]

With respect to state-to-state arbitration under a bilateral treaty, one recent case deserves mention. On 17 May 2010, Pakistan instituted arbitration proceedings against India under the dispute resolution clauses contained in Article IX and Annexure G of the Indus Waters Treaty 1960.[56] Somewhat unusually, Annexure G to the treaty provides for a mechanism to establish a Court of Arbitration consisting of seven arbitrators to decide certain disputes arising under the treaty. Each party has the right to appoint two arbitrators; the remaining three arbitrators are to be appointed one each from the following categories:

(i) persons qualified by status and reputation to be chairman who may, but need not, be engineers or lawyers;
(ii) highly qualified engineers;
(iii) persons well versed in international law.

The requirement to have at least one engineer on the Court of Arbitration stems from the fact that the Indus Waters Treaty, together with its annexures, contains a large number of technical specifications governing the use of the waters of the Indus system of rivers and the construction of dams and/or hydroelectric projects on those rivers.

Thus far, the Court of Arbitration has issued an Order on Interim Measures dated 23 September 2011 and organized two site visits (possibly a first in international arbitration) to the area of concern in Kashmir.[57] In other respects, the proceedings continue.

The *Indus Waters Kishenganga Arbitration* is the first arbitration brought under the Indus Waters Treaty since its conclusion in 1960. That being said, the treaty also provides for the possibility of determinations to be made by a neutral expert on certain technical points of difference

---

[55] Wetter, above n. 53, 357.

[56] Indus Waters Treaty, India–Pakistan (signed on 19 September 1960, entered into force 12 January 1961), 419 UNTS 125.

[57] The proceedings are confidential, but publicly available information, including the members of the Court of Arbitration and the Order on Interim Measures, may be found on the website of the Permanent Court of Arbitration, which acts as Secretariat to the Court of Arbitration in the case.

that a party may refer under the provisions of the treaty. That mechanism has been used once before. Thus, on 12 February 2007 a neutral expert appointed by the World Bank rendered an Expert Determination on a number of issues referred to him by Pakistan in connection with the Baglihar hydropower plant constructed by India on a tributary of the Indus.[58]

In both instances, the choice of mechanism for invoking third-party settlement was dictated by the provisions of the treaty. In other words, there was no possibility of submitting disputes arising under the treaty to another forum.

Finally, there are media reports suggesting that Singapore and Malaysia may be contemplating ad hoc arbitration in connection with a dispute relating to development charges associated with moving a Malaysian railway station in Singapore to another location and the joint development of several parcels of railway land that would be involved in such a transaction.[59] Details of the arbitration, should it in fact be taking place, are not available. Nor is there as yet any indication whether an institutional body has been appointed to act as registrar in the case. Both states, however, do have international arbitration and litigation experience as a result of their cases before the ICJ and the Annex VII arbitration that Malaysia brought under UNCLOS against Singapore in relation to a land reclamation project along the Strait of Johor.

Judicial proceedings under the UN Convention on the Law of the Sea

Recent practice suggests that a number of Asian states, once again concentrated in South and South-east Asia, are willing to submit disputes arising in connection with the interpretation or application of UNCLOS to third-party arbitration under Annex VII to the Convention or to ITLOS.

Approximately twenty-two Asian states (depending on how one classifies a state as 'Asian') are parties to UNCLOS. Of these, four states have filed 'opt out' declarations under Article 298, indicating that they do not accept compulsory dispute resolution for disputes concerning, *inter alia*,

---

[58] See World Bank, 'Indus Waters Treaty – Articles and Annexures. Baglihar Decision – Expert Determination', 2007, available at http://water.worldbank.org/publications/indus-waters-treaty-articles-and-annexures-baglihar-decision-expert-determination.

[59] See, e.g., 'KTM Land Swap Done but Arbitration for Development Charges', *Malaysia Insider*, 20 September 2010, available at www.themalaysianinsider.com/malaysia/article/ktm-land-swap-done-but-arbitration-for-development-charges/.

Articles 15, 74, and 83 of UNCLOS, dealing with the delimitation of the territorial sea, exclusive economic zone, and continental shelf. These are China, Palau, the Republic of Korea (South Korea) and Thailand.

The very first arbitration instituted under Annex VII to the Convention involved an Asian state (Japan) as the respondent. This was the *Southern Bluefin Tuna* case, brought by Australia and New Zealand against Japan in 1999. Pending the constitution of the arbitral tribunal, both applicant states filed a request for the prescription of provisional measures with ITLOS. On 27 August 1999, ITLOS issued an order finding that, prima facie, the arbitral tribunal to be constituted would have jurisdiction, and indicating certain provisional measures.[60] On 4 August 2000, however, the arbitral tribunal (which had been constituted under Annex VII in the meantime) issued an Award on Jurisdiction and Admissibility in which it decided that it was without jurisdiction to rule on the merits of the dispute. The tribunal therefore revoked the provisional measures that had previously been ordered by ITLOS.[61]

The second case involving an Asian state under the dispute resolution provisions of UNCLOS was commenced by Malaysia against Singapore pursuant to a diplomatic note sent on 4 July 2003, in which Malaysia requested the submission of a dispute concerning certain land reclamation activities that Singapore was undertaking in and around the Strait of Johor to an arbitral tribunal to be established under Annex VII to the Convention. On 5 September 2003, pending the constitution of the arbitral tribunal, Malaysia filed a request for provisional measures with ITLOS under Article 290(5) of UNCLOS.[62]

On 8 October 2003, ITLOS prescribed a series of provisional measures applying to both parties. These included an order for the two states to establish a group of independent experts to conduct a study to determine the effects of Singapore's land reclamation and to propose, as appropriate, measures to deal with any adverse effects.[63]

Malaysia and Singapore did thereafter establish a Group of Experts, which prepared and submitted both an interim report and a final report on the project. Following the issuance of the final report, the parties signed

---

[60] *Southern Bluefin Tuna (Australia and New Zealand v. Japan) (Provisional Measures) (Order of 27 August 1999)*, (1999) 117 ILR 148.

[61] *Southern Bluefin Tuna (Australia and New Zealand v. Japan) (Jurisdiction and Admissibility)*, (2000) 119 ILR 508.

[62] *Land Reclamation by Singapore in and around the Straits of Johor (Malaysia v. Singapore) (Provisional Measures)*, [2003] ITLOS Rep. 10 (*Land Reclamation*).

[63] *Land Reclamation (Order of 8 October 2003)*, [2003] ITLOS Rep. 10, [106].

a settlement agreement on 26 April 2005. Thereafter, on 18 May 2005, the parties jointly submitted a letter to the arbitral tribunal requesting the tribunal to deliver a final award binding on the parties in the terms set out in the settlement agreement.[64] On 1 September 2005, the arbitral tribunal delivered an Award on Agreed Terms attaching the text of the settlement agreement and terminating the proceedings.[65]

With respect to disputes over maritime boundaries in the region, on 8 October 2009 Bangladesh instituted separate arbitral proceedings against Myanmar and India, respectively, pursuant to Article 287 and Annex VII of UNCLOS.

In the *Bangladesh–Myanmar* case, Bangladesh and Myanmar filed declarations on 4 November 2009 and 12 December 2009 consenting to the jurisdiction of ITLOS instead of Annex VII arbitration. This was the first time that ITLOS had been seized of a maritime delimitation case. ITLOS rendered its judgment on 14 March 2012. While that judgment followed the past practice of the ICJ in adopting the 'equidistance/relevant circumstances' rule for determining the course of the maritime boundary, it broke new ground by extending the delimitation line beyond 200 nautical miles from the parties' baselines into areas of outer continental shelf.[66] Both parties to the case appear to be satisfied with the result.

As for the *Bangladesh–India* case, at the time of writing Annex VII proceedings were still in their written phase.

Conclusions

Based on a review of the case precedents, it appears that at least at the regional level a number of Asian states are adopting a more proactive stance with respect to inter-state litigation and arbitration. South and South-east Asian states, in particular, have recently been involved, or are currently involved, in a number of judicial and arbitral proceedings.

In this respect, Singapore's former deputy prime minister and senior minister, S. Jayakumar, has offered insightful views on Singapore's position regarding third-party settlement of bilateral disputes as a result of Singapore's experience in both the *Land Reclamation* and the *Pedra Branca* cases. As Jayakumar observes,

---

[64] *Land Reclamation (Decision of 1 September 2005)*, 27 RIAA 133. [65] Ibid.
[66] *Dispute concerning the Bay of Bengal*, ITLOS, Case No. 16, 14 March 2012.

ASIAN PERSPECTIVES ON INTER-STATE LITIGATION 165

> Not every dispute will have legal overtones or be connected to provisions of agreements. But when they do, and an impasse is reached after bilateral talks, Singapore's consistent position has been to propose that the issue be settled by third-party dispute settlement mechanisms, whether through international arbitration or other methods such as international adjudication, e.g., the International Court of Justice (ICJ). Third-party dispute settlement is an amicable way of resolving intractable issues. Governments can get on with other aspects of bilateral cooperation while the process of resolving that issue gets under way.[67]

Whether these views reflect the perceptions of other Asian states remains to be seen, although recent practice seems to suggest a willingness amongst at least some states to submit sovereignty, delimitation, and law of the sea disputes to third-party resolution.

That being said, there are notable exceptions. For example, despite the fact that both China (Shi, 2003–6) and Japan (Owada, 2009–12) have had one of their nationals serve as president of the ICJ during the past ten years, neither state has instituted proceedings before the Court or under UNCLOS, whether by unilateral application or special agreement. While Japan has been the respondent in two cases brought by non-Asian states (one ICJ case and one Annex VII arbitration), China remains the only permanent member of the Security Council not to have been a party to an ICJ case.

Even with respect to maritime delimitation issues, a number of seemingly intractable disputes remain. For example, a large portion of the Gulf of Thailand remains off-limits for hydrocarbon exploration due to a long-standing dispute between Thailand and Cambodia dating from the early 1970s. The fact that Thailand has not renewed its optional clause declaration and has filed an opt-out declaration under Article 298 of UNCLOS makes it unlikely that this dispute will be resolved by third-party adjudication or arbitration in the near future absent agreement between the parties.

It is also well known that important sovereignty and delimitation issues remain unresolved in the South China Sea and in areas lying further north. In the light of the number of states that are implicated in these disputes, and the absence of sufficient jurisdictional links binding all such states, recourse to third-party dispute resolution may again prove elusive for the time being.

---

[67] S. Jayakumar, *Diplomacy: A Singapore Experience* (Singapore: Straits Times Press, 2011), 176.

9

African perspectives on inter-state litigation

MAKANE MOÏSE MBENGUE

In a speech on January 16th, 1925, President Max Huber stated that on account of its judicial function the Court should rise above the clash of men's interests and men's passions – above those of party, of class, of nation and of race [...] Thus, through its very being the Court retains and cultivates ideas common to the whole of humanity. It is asked of the Court that it should contribute to peace by deciding the disputes submitted to it. Perhaps it will make a yet greater contribution by inculcating a knowledge of that which, after all, unites mankind.[1]

Deconstructing a myth: the African 'mistrust' towards international adjudication

It has been a long road since 1952, when the International Court of Justice (ICJ) rendered its judgment in the *Case Concerning Rights of Nationals of the United States of America in Morocco*.[2] Albeit the 'legal interests of Morocco form[ed] the very subject-matter'[3] of the dispute between France and the United States, Morocco could not be a party to the dispute because of its status at that time as a French protectorate. This situation was not unique to Morocco.[4] It concerned the

---

[1] Speech of President Basdevant, ICJ Pleadings, Oral arguments, Documents, *Reparation for Injuries Suffered in the Service of the United Nations*, Advisory Opinion of 11 April 1949, 46.

[2] *Case concerning Rights of Nationals of the United States of America in Morocco (France v. United States)*, [1952] ICJ Rep. 176.

[3] By reference to the expression used by the ICJ to formulate the 'Monetary Gold principle', *Monetary Gold Removed from Italy in 1943 (Italy v. France, United Kingdom and United States)* (1954) ICJ Rep. 19, 32.

[4] Morocco's legal interests were also the subject matter of disputes before the Permanent Court of International Justice (PCIJ). See *Nationality Decrees in Tunis and Morocco (Advisory Opinion)*, [1923] PCIJ (ser. B) No. 4; *Phosphates in Morocco (Italy v. France)*, [1938] PCIJ (ser. A/B) No. 74. During the PCIJ era, in addition to the two aforementioned cases another case dealt with an African country, namely the Belgian Congo: see *Oscar Chinn (United Kingdom v. Belgium)*, [1934] PCIJ (ser. A/B) No. 63. With respect to inter-state

AFRICAN PERSPECTIVES ON INTER-STATE LITIGATION 167

quasi-totality[5] of African countries that were subject to colonial or other dependent status.[6] It is, then, not surprising that for more than half of the twentieth century, Africa contributed very little to the 'development of modern judicial settlement of international disputes'.[7]

arbitration, African countries were not involved during an important part of the twentieth century. As for proceedings before the PCIJ and the ICJ, some of their interests of a legal nature were occasionally engaged without their being able to be parties to arbitration proceedings. See, e.g., *Deserters of Casablanca (France* v. *Germany)*, PCA, 22 May 1909.

[5] There were some exceptions. Four African countries had been recognized as states by 1945: Egypt, Ethiopia, Liberia, and South Africa. It is interesting to note, for instance, that the third case submitted to the ICJ related to a dispute between France and another African state (Egypt). See ICJ, 'Filing by France of an Application Instituting Proceedings against Egypt', press release 1949/17, 14 October 1949. The case was discontinued following a request from the French government. See *Protection of French Nationals in Egypt, Order of March 29, 1950* [1950] ICJ Rep. 59. Also noteworthy is the fact that Egypt submitted written statements in the fourth and fifth advisory proceedings that the ICJ dealt with in its history. See ICJ Pleadings, Oral arguments, Documents, *Competence of the General Assembly for the admission of a State to the United Nations*, Advisory Opinion of 3 March 1950, 156; ICJ Pleadings, Oral arguments, Documents, *International Status of South-West Africa*, Advisory Opinion of 11 July 1950, 67–71. See also the written statement of the government of Liberia in ICJ Pleadings, Oral arguments, Documents, *Constitution of the Maritime Safety Committee of the Inter-Governmental Maritime Consultative Organization*, 34–85.

[6] On the impact of such status on the participation of African countries to inter-state litigation, see T. O. Elias, *The International Court of Justice and Some Contemporary Problems* (The Hague: Martinus Nijhoff Publishers, 1983), 299. According to the author, 'Africa has in one aspect or another been before the Court since the days of the League of Nations, though unfortunately more often as the object rather than as the subject of international law'. See also A. Mahiou, 'Préface', in D. Perrin, *La Cour internationale de Justice et l'Afrique* (Aix-en-Provence: Presses Universitaires d'Aix-Marseille, 2005), Vol. I, 7: 'D'abord le continent a été présent en tant qu'objet de contentieux, au moment où les puissances coloniales demandaient à la Cour d'indiquer les droits de chacune dans leur course au partage de l'Afrique.'

[7] P. B. A. Ajibola, 'Africa and the International Court of Justice', in C. A. Armas Barea et al. (eds.), *Liber Amicorum 'In Memoriam' of Judge José Maria Ruda* (The Hague: Kluwer Law International, 2000) 353. Nevertheless, there are examples of inter-state arbitration cases involving African states that demonstrate that Africa contributed in a way to the development of international dispute settlement in the first half of the twentieth century and even during the second half of the nineteenth century: see *Arrangement for the Settlement of Differences between the Sultan of Muscat and the Sultan of Zanzibar, and the Independence of their Respective States*, [1861] 28 RIAA 107; *Arbitral award relating to Boundary Delimitation between South-African Republic (Transvaal) and Free State of Orange*, [1870] 28 RIAA 125; *Award as to the boundary between the United Kingdom and the South African Republic (Transvaal)*, [1885] 28 RIAA 185; *Affaire de l'attaque de la caravane du maharao de Cutch (Royaume-Uni contre Éthiopie)*, [1927] 2 RIAA 821; *Salem case (Egypt, USA)*, [1932] 2 RIAA 1161; *L'incident de Walwal (Italie contre Éthiopie)*, [1935] 3 RIAA 1657; *Affaire de la Société Radio-Orient (Etats du Levant sous mandat français contre Egypte)*, [1940] 3 RIAA

168   MAKANE MOÏSE MBENGUE

However, after most African countries gained independence and acceded to international sovereignty, the situation evolved. From then on, African states progressively became fully aware of one of the essential features of their international legal personality: the competence or capacity to bring an international claim.[8] As pinpointed by the ICJ, 'this capacity certainly belongs to the State: a State can bring an international claim against another State. Such a claim takes the form of a claim between two political entities, equal in law, similar in form, and both the direct subjects of international law'.[9] Despite African states not being specifically the addressees of such a statement, it was of the utmost importance for those states. Indeed, it affirmed that accession to statehood would allow African states to have recourse – on an equal basis – to international adjudication in order to preserve their independence and, most of all, to benefit from the protection of the international rule of law.[10] For newly born nations that were economically, socially, and politically among the weakest states within the international community, this was a crucial safety valve. Ultimately it would allow 'the gnat [to have] the temerity to confront the eagle and the lion'.[11]

Temerity from African states is exactly what transpired subsequently. As early as 1960 – at the peak of the wave of independence on the continent – two African states (Ethiopia and Liberia) seized the ICJ of two disputes with South Africa concerning the status of South West Africa. This was the first time that African states initiated contentious proceedings before the ICJ. The judgments of the Court on preliminary objections (1962 and

---

1871; *Administration of certain properties of the State in Libya (Italy v. United Kingdom and United Kingdom of Libya)*, [1952/1953] 12 RIAA 357.

[8] As defined by the ICJ, 'Competence to bring an international claim is, for those possessing it, the capacity to resort to the customary methods recognized by international law for the establishment, the presentation and the settlement of claims. Among these methods may be mentioned protest, request for an enquiry, negotiation, and request for submission to an arbitral tribunal or to the Court in so far as this may be authorized by the Statute.' *Reparation for injuries suffered in the service of the United Nations (Advisory Opinion)*, [1949] ICJ Rep. 174, 177.

[9] Ibid., 177–8.

[10] As argued by Lauterpacht, 'International settlements are incipient international legislation.' Hersch Lauterpacht, *The Development of International Law by the Permanent Court of International Justice* (London: Longman, Green & Co., 1934), 309.

[11] *Questions of Interpretation and Application of the 1971 Montreal Convention arising from the Aerial Incident at Lockerbie (Libyan Arab Jamahiriya v. United States) (Libyan Arab Jamahiriya v. United Kingdom)*, CR/97/20 (translation), Mr El-Murtadi Suleiman, 26, [3.20].

AFRICAN PERSPECTIVES ON INTER-STATE LITIGATION   169

1966)[12] in those cases have been subject to significant commentary,[13] and described as having 'marked a watershed in the role of the Court'.[14] Beyond the legitimate criticisms that can be made of the 1966 judgment of the Court in the *South West Africa Cases*, it appears from the proceedings in those cases that African states are not traditionally opposed to the idea of international adjudication or, more specifically, to subjecting themselves to the jurisdiction of international courts and tribunals. To think the contrary is a misperception.[15] Very early, African states adhered to the idea that international courts and tribunals could be the main driving forces in the promotion and strengthening of the rule of international law.[16]

---

[12] *South West Africa Cases (Ethiopia v. South Africa; Liberia v. South Africa) (Preliminary Objections)*, [1962] ICJ Rep. 319; *South West Africa Cases (Ethiopia v. South Africa; Liberia v. South Africa) (Second Phase)*, [1966] ICJ Rep. 6.

[13] See, e.g., Rosalyn Higgins, 'The International Court and South West Africa: The Implications of the Judgment', (1966) 42 *International Affairs* 573 (repr. in Rosalyn Higgins, *Themes and Theories: Selected Essays, Speeches, and Writings in International Law*, Vol. 2 (Oxford University Press, 2009) 758); G. Fischer, 'Les réactions devant l'arrêt de la CIJ concernant le Sud-ouest africain', (1966) *Annuaire français de droit international* 144; Richard A. Falk, 'The South West Africa cases: an appraisal', (1967) 21 *International Organization* 1; W. Friedman, 'The jurisprudential implications of the South West Africa case', (1967) 6 *Columbia Journal of Transnational Law* 1; Joel Trachtman, 'The South West Africa cases and the development of international law', (1976–7) 5 *Millennium: Journal of International Studies* 292; Georges Abi-Saab, 'The International Court as a World Court', in Vaughan Lowe and Malgosia Fitzmaurice (eds.), *Fifty Years of the International Court of Justice: Essays in Honour of Sir Robert Jennings* (Cambridge University Press, 1996) 3; I. de la Rasilla del Moral, '*Nihil Novum Sub Sole* since the South West Africa Cases? On *Ius Standi*, the ICJ and Community Interests', (2008) 10 *International Community Law Review* 171; M. Kawano, 'The Role of Judicial Procedures in the Process of the Pacific Settlement of International Disputes', (2009) 346 *Collected Courses* 413.

[14] Ajibola, above n. 7, 356.

[15] See, e.g., Antonio Cassese, *International Law in A Divided World* (Oxford: Clarendon Press, 1986), 205. Cassese considered that developing countries were reluctant to accept adjudication. Discussing international arbitration, he nonetheless acknowledged that 'Western countries are very often no less reluctant than other States to resort to [arbitration]'.

[16] See Mahiou, above n. 6, 7. According to the author, 'Les Etats africains ayant pensé que la Cour incarne une justice universelle, elle ne pouvait que les aider à mettre en place un système fondé aussi bien sur le respect du droit que sur la paix et l'harmonie des relations internationales: leur approche du droit international est qu'il ne peut y avoir de règlement harmonieux que par le passage devant le juge qui devient un élément essentiel pour la revendication d'une conscience juridique internationale.' See also the dissenting opinion of Judge Badawi (*Northern Cameroons (Cameroon v. United Kingdom), (Preliminary Objections)*, [1963] ICJ Rep. 150), where he stresses the importance for Cameroon to obtain a 'declaratory judgment' – i.e. to obtain a simple declaration of facts and legal findings concerning irregularities in the administration of the administering authority throughout the period of trusteeship and not a judgment of an executory character.

170   MAKANE MOÏSE MBENGUE

Accordingly, they did not hesitate to participate in landmark advisory proceedings for the United Nations system[17] or to initiate disputes against other African states or non-African states.[18] What prompted a cautious attitude, not to say a 'hostile reaction',[19] of African states vis-à-vis the system of international adjudication (and, in particular, the ICJ), was a feeling of dismay after the 1966 judgment in the *South West Africa Cases*.[20] And here, too, it is a misperception to think that only African states were disappointed by the 1966 judgment of the Court in the *South West Africa Cases*.[21]

'Mistrust' should not be confused with 'distrust'. What occurred after 1966 was mere 'distrust' in the ability of the ICJ properly to defend the peculiar interests of African states.[22] Hence, till the end of the 1970s, African states refrained from submitting disputes to the ICJ through the contentious procedure. Nonetheless, trust in peaceful settlement of disputes through international adjudication has been strongly advocated and reiterated by African nations since their independence.[23] It is a myth to

[17] See, e.g., the written statement submitted by the government of the Republic of Upper Volta (which became independent in August 1960) in ICJ Pleadings, Oral arguments, Documents, *Certain Expenses of the United Nations (Article 17, paragraph 2 of the Charter)*, Advisory Opinion of 20 July 1962, 123–4.

[18] See *Northern Cameroons (Cameroon v. United Kingdom) (Preliminary Objections)*, [1963] ICJ Rep. 15.

[19] Higgins, above n. 13, 774.

[20] See Abi-Saab, above n. 13, 5. Referring to the 1966 judgment, the author explains that 'it thrust the Court into an acute crisis, having shattered the confidence of large parts of the world, particularly the Third World, in the Court as it then was'.

[21] Higgins, above n. 13, 774: 'The dismay expressed, sometimes in terms of great vehemence, has not by any means been limited to Africans.'

[22] A. Mahiou, 'L'Afrique et la CIJ: un bref aperçu de la pratique', in M. Kamga and M. M. Mbengue (eds.), *Liber Amicorum Raymond Ranjeva* (Paris: Pedone 2012) 191. See also G. Abi-Saab, 'Cours général de droit international public', (1987) 207 *Recueil des cours* 9, 255 (where he talks about an 'alleged mistrust' towards judicial settlement) and 257 (where he says that the 1966 judgment in the *South West Africa cases* 'a ébranlé la confiance de larges parties du monde, et surtout du tiers monde, dans la Cour comme elle se présentait à ce moment-là'); Georges Abi-Saab, 'Evolutions dans le règlement des différends économiques depuis la Convention Drago-Porter', in Yves Daudet (ed.), *Topicality of the 1907 Hague Conference, the Second Peace Conference*, Hague Academy of International Law, Workshop, 2007 (The Hague: Martinus Nijhoff, 2008) 191.

[23] See, e.g., the speech of Mr Engo, Assistant Agent for the Federal Republic of Cameroon, 'This Court, Mr President, is a great symbol of hope for all young nations which, conceived by political evolution, have only in the recent past been born into a world imprisoned in confusion and unrest. Its very presence on this international arena gives credence to the existence of these young nations. We are here because we consider this to be the only civilized and desirable way to settle disputes between any two States. We are indeed

consider that African states 'have been suspicious of the established mechanisms of judicial settlement'.[24] Even after the 1966 episode, some African states continued to participate in advisory proceedings before the ICJ,[25] and in such a way to contribute to the development of international law. Furthermore, by the end of the 1970s,[26] twelve African states were already parties to the system of the optional clause under Article 36(2) of the Statute of the ICJ.[27] Today, twenty-two African states have made declarations recognizing the compulsory jurisdiction of the Court. This means that half of the African states that are parties to the system of compulsory jurisdiction became so at a time when African states were wrongly perceived as being suspicious of third-party adjudication.[28] Treaty practice also shows that, at an early stage, African states have been willing to accept dispute settlement clauses in multilateral treaties, in particular, compromissory clauses referring to the ICJ. This is the case for fundamental

delighted that we can, in this way, resolve a dispute without resort to political animosity and perhaps violence'. ICJ Pleadings, Oral arguments, Documents, *Case concerning the Northern Cameroons (Cameroon v. United Kingdom), Preliminary Objections*, Public hearing of 25 September 1963, 314.

[24] Ajibola, above n. 7, 353. See also Perrin, above n. 6, 17 ('le continent fut longtemps considéré – avec l'Asie – comme la région la plus réticente à l'acceptation de la juridiction internationale'). In practice, it is rare to find examples of such a strong suspicion. One can maybe think of the *Décision du Président du Conseil arbitral franco-tunisien (France, Tunisie)*, taken after Tunisian arbitrators decided not to sit in an arbitration under the 1955 General Convention between France and Tunisia, 12 RIAA 271.

[25] See, e.g., the written statement of Nigeria (made on behalf of the Organization of African Unity), ICJ Pleadings, Oral arguments, Documents, *Legal Consequences for States of the Continued Presence of South Africa in Namibia (South West Africa) notwithstanding Security Council Resolution 276 (1970)*, Vol. I, 889–897. See also the oral statement by Mr Elias (Organization of African Unity), ICJ Pleadings, Oral arguments, Documents, *Legal Consequences for States of the Continued Presence of South Africa in Namibia (South West Africa) notwithstanding Security Council Resolution 276 (1970)*, Vol. II, 88. See written statement of Mauritania and written statement of Morocco, ICJ Pleadings, Oral arguments, Documents, *Western Sahara*, Vol. III, 4.

[26] In the present contribution, the end of the 1970s is taken as a critical date since it marks the end of the period during which African states refrained from having recourse to the ICJ. Indeed, in 1978, Tunisia and Libya submitted their dispute over the continental shelf to the ICJ. See Special Agreement between Tunisia and the Libyan Arab Jamahiriya (notified to the Registry of the ICJ on 1 December 1978), ICJ Pleadings, *Continental Shelf (Tunisia/Libyan Arab Jamahiriya)*, Vol. I, 3.

[27] Botswana (16 March 1970), Egypt (22 July 1957), Gambia (22 June 1966), Kenya (19 April 1965), Liberia (20 March 1952), Malawi (12 December 1966), Mauritius (23 September 1968), Somalia (11 April 1963), Sudan (2 January 1958), Swaziland (26 May 1969), Togo (25 October 1979), and Uganda (3 October 1963).

[28] And at a time when Sir Humphrey Waldock had already described the 'Decline of the Optional Clause', (1955–6) 32 BYIL 244.

treaties such as the 1948 Genocide Convention,[29] the 1966 Convention on the Elimination of All Forms of Racial Discrimination,[30] and the 1967 Protocol relating to the status of refugees.[31]

When referring to multilateral treaties, especially noteworthy is the 1965 Convention on the Settlement of Investment Disputes between States and Nationals of Other States (commonly referred to as the ICSID Convention). Despite not dealing purely with inter-state litigation,[32] this instrument, which established the International Centre for Settlement of Investment Disputes (ICSID), is perhaps the first dispute settlement treaty that has been so widely ratified by African states and in record time.[33] Although the ratification of the ICSID Convention does not constitute *ipso jure* consent to ICSID arbitration,[34] the popularity of that

---

[29] By the end of the 1970s the following African states had ratified the Genocide Convention without any reservation to Art. IX: Algeria (1963), Burkina Faso (1965), Democratic Republic of Congo (1962), Egypt (1952), Ethiopia (1949), Gambia (1978), Ghana (1958), Lesotho (1974), Liberia (1950), Mali (1974), Morocco (1958), Tunisia (1956).

[30] By the end of the 1970s, the following African states had ratified the Convention on the Elimination of all Forms of Racial Discrimination without any reservation to Art. 22: Algeria (1972), Botswana (1974), Burkina Faso (1974), Burundi (1977), Cameroon (1971), Cape Verde (1979), Central African Republic (1971), Chad (1977), Côte d'Ivoire (1973), Democratic Republic of Congo (1976), Egypt (1967), Ethiopia (1976), Gabon (1980), Gambia (1978), Ghana (1966), Guinea (1977), Lesotho (1971), Liberia (1976), Mali (1974), Mauritius (1972), Niger (1967), Nigeria (1967), Rwanda (1975), Senegal (1972), Seychelles (1978), Sierra Leone (1967), Somalia (1975), Sudan (1977), Swaziland (1969), Togo (1972), Tunisia (1967), Uganda (1980), Tanzania (1972), and Zambia (1972).

[31] By the end of the 1970s, the following African states had ratified the Protocol relating to the Status of Refugees without any reservation to Art. IV: Benin (1970), Burkina Faso (1980), Burundi (1971), Cameroon (1967), Central African Republic (1967), Congo (1970), Democratic Republic of Congo (1975), Côte d'Ivoire (1970), Djibouti (1977), Ethiopia (1969), Gabon (1973), Gambia (1967), Ghana (1968), Guinea (1968), Guinea-Bissau (1976), Liberia (1980), Mali (1973), Morocco (1971), Niger (1970), Nigeria (1968), Senegal (1967), Seychelles (1980), Somalia (1978), Sudan (1974), Swaziland (1969), Togo (1969), Tunisia (1968), Uganda (1976), Zambia (1969).

[32] Art. 64 is the only provision of the ICSID Convention that provides for inter-state litigation.

[33] By the end of the 1970s, the following African states had ratified the ICSID Convention: Benin (1966), Botswana (1970), Burkina Faso (1966), Burundi (1969), Cameroon (1967), Central African Republic (1966), Chad (1966), Comoros (1978), Democratic Republic of Congo (1970), Republic of Congo (1966), Côte d'Ivoire (1966), Arab Republic of Egypt (1972), Gabon (1966), Gambia (1974), Ghana (1966), Guinea (1968), Kenya (1967), Lesotho (1969), Liberia (1970), Madagascar (1966), Malawi (1966), Mali (1978), Mauritania (1966), Mauritius (1969), Morocco (1967), Niger (1966), Nigeria (1965), Rwanda (1979), Senegal (1967), Seychelles (1978), Sierra Leone (1966), Somalia (1968), Sudan (1973), Swaziland (1971), Togo (1967), Tunisia (1966), Uganda (1966), Zambia (1970).

[34] Consent may be given in a clause included in an investment agreement (e.g., a bilateral investment treaty (BIT)), providing for the submission to the ICSID of future disputes

instrument on the African continent[35] confirms a strong adherence to the idea of international adjudication. It also reveals that the more adjudicatory mechanisms purport to integrate African states' concerns,[36] the more those states would be attracted to them.[37] In other words, 'attractiveness of adjudication' is a key, not to say a determinant, factor in the political choice that would lead an African state to opt in or to opt out of a given judicial or arbitral mechanism.[38] Attractiveness being the *raison d'être* of the ICSID system,[39] it is, then, not surprising that a vast majority

arising out of that agreement or in a *compromis* regarding a dispute which has already arisen. Consent can also be given by a host state in its national investment legislation. On the issue of consent to ICSID arbitration through national investment, see Makane M. Mbengue, 'National Legislations and Unilateral Acts of States', in T. Gazzini and E. de Brabandère (eds.), *The Sources of Rights and Obligations in Transnational Investment Law* (The Hague: Martinus Nijhoff Publishers, 2012) 183. See also Makane M. Mbengue, 'Consent to Arbitration through National Investment Legislations', (2012) 2(4) *Investment Treaty News* 7.

[35] See A. A. Agyemang, 'African States and ICSID arbitration', (1988) 21 *Comparative and International Law Journal of Southern Africa* 177.

[36] The preamble of the ICSID Convention refers to 'the need for international cooperation for economic development, and the role of private international investment therein' (first preambular paragraph of the ICSID Convention).

[37] It is crucial to recall that an African state – i.e. Gabon – was the first state in the history of the ICSID to initiate a claim against a foreign investor (*Government of Gabon* v. *Société Serete*, ICSID Case No. ARB/76/1). For comments on that case, which was discontinued, see I. F. I. Shihata, A. R. Parra, 'The Experience of the International Centre for Settlement of Investment Disputes', (1999) 15 *ICSID Review – Foreign Investment Law Journal* 316. See also M. Toral and T. Schultz, 'The State, a Perpetual Respondent in Investment Arbitration? Some Unorthodox Considerations', in M. Waibel, A. Kaushal, K.-H. L. Chung, and Cl. Balchin (eds.), *The Backlash against Investment Arbitration: Perceptions and Reality* (The Hague: Kluwer Law International, 2010) 589.

[38] Although referring to developing countries in general, see for a similar position in the context of GATT 1947, W. J. Davey, 'Dispute Settlement in GATT', (1987) 11 *Fordham International Law Journal* 90: 'Developing countries have only seldom made use of the dispute settlement system . . . In large part, this seems to be a consequence of their belief that the system is, at best, designed to deal with disputes between the major developed countries. It is thought to be futile for them to invoke the system because GATT will not give a sympathetic ear to their claims and that even if they win their case they will not have the diplomatic or economic muscle to ensure that the decision is implemented'. See also M. L. Busch and E. Reinhardt, 'Developing Countries and GATT/WTO Dispute Settlement', (2003) 37 *Journal of World Trade* 719 (where they assert, 'The underlying presumption, of course, is that developing countries were especially ill-served by GATT's diplomacy').

[39] See ICSID, 'Report of the Executive Directors on the Convention on the Settlement of Investment Disputes between States and Nationals of other States', (1965) 1 ICSID Rep. 25, paras. 9 and 12: 'The creation of an institution designed to facilitate the settlement of disputes between States and foreign investors can be a major step toward promoting an atmosphere of mutual confidence and thus stimulating a larger flow of private

174 MAKANE MOÏSE MBENGUE

of African nations expressed their consent to be bound by the ICSID Convention.

The same infatuation did not extend to the Permanent Court of Arbitration (PCA) for several decades after the independence of most African countries.[40] The Hague Conventions of 1899[41] and 1907[42] were, indeed, conceived as reflecting essentially the concerns of former colonial powers[43] and were concluded at a time when the overwhelming majority of African nations were not members of the international community. Third-party adjudication can never be attractive to a state or group of states when it tends to legitimating or imposing a core of values that are not wholly shared by the said state(s).[44] Indeed, adherence to international

international capital into those countries which wish to attract it... adherence to the Convention by a country would provide additional inducement and stimulate a larger flow of private international investment into its territories, which is the primary purpose of the Convention.'

[40] By the end of the 1970s, only nine African states were members of the PCA, namely Burkina Faso (1961), Cameroon (1961), Democratic Republic of Congo (1961), Egypt (1907), Mauritius (1970), Senegal (1977), Sudan (1966), Swaziland (1970), and Uganda (1966). The other African member states of the PCA are Benin (2005), Eritrea (2003), Ethiopia (2003), Kenya (2006), Libya (1996), Madagascar (2009), Morocco (2001), Nigeria (1987), South Africa (1998), Togo (2004), Zambia (2000), and Zimbabwe (1984). It is interesting to note that there has been a gap of almost thirty years, and sometimes more, between the moment when the first African states became members of the PCA and the time when other African states became members: Benin (2005), Eritrea (2003), Ethiopia (1973), Kenya (2006), Libya (1996), Madagascar (2009), Morocco (2001), Nigeria (1987), South Africa (1998), Togo (2004), and Zambia (2000).

[41] Convention for the Pacific Settlement of International Disputes (signed 29 July 1899, entered into force 4 September 1900), 32 Stat. 1799.

[42] Convention for the Pacific Settlement of International Disputes (signed 18 October 1907, entered into force 26 January 1910), 36 Stat. 2199.

[43] Shabtai Rosenne, *The Hague Peace Conferences of 1899 and 1907 and International Arbitration: Reports and Documents* (The Hague: T.M.C. Asser Press, 2001), xxvi ('All the European Powers with overseas possession of the epoch took part in both Peace Conferences, and the Conventions when ratified were, according to the international law of the time, applicable to all their territories... there is no sign in the records of either Conference of any input from any of the overseas territories or of any consideration of their interests'). See also Martti Koskenniemi, 'The Ideology of International Adjudication and the 1907 Hague Conference', in Yves Daudet (ed.), *Topicality of the 1907 Hague Conference, the Second Peace Conference*, Hague Academy of International Law, workshop, 2007 (The Hague: Martinus Nijhoff Publishers, 2008) 135 ('The 1899 Conference was still a European affair'), and 139 ('The Second Peace Conference was from the beginning to the end, with the brief Russia interlude, an American affair').

[44] G. Oduntan, 'Africa before International Courts: The Generational Gap in International Adjudication and Arbitration', (2004) 5 *The Journal of World Investment and Trade* 979:

AFRICAN PERSPECTIVES ON INTER-STATE LITIGATION   175

adjudication is a matter of ideology.[45] And, so often, ideology aligns with relatedness.

A reality: the African 'ideology' of adjudication

Each continent is governed by different ideological paradigms of adjudication.[46] To a certain extent, African states have moulded an African ideology of international adjudication that is based on two axioms: the 'axiom of regionalization' and the 'axiom of de-legalization'.[47]

The axiom of regionalization

Soon after gaining independence, regionalization of dispute settlement – that is settling disputes at the level of the continent – appeared as the preferred option for African states. The Organization of African Unity (OAU) even had dispute settlement as one of its main institutional objectives. Not surprisingly, the OAU Charter set forth provision for the creation of a Commission of Mediation, Conciliation and Arbitration.[48] The idea was that the Commission of Mediation, Conciliation and Arbitration would have a sort of primary responsibility in the pacific settlement of disputes among African states. Recourse to universal adjudicatory mechanisms like the ICJ would only be a last resort, in situations where a dispute was not referred to the Commission or where the latter would reveal itself inefficient in solving a dispute. This gradual approach has been explicitly

---

'Without prejudice to the many achievements of the PCA in its 104 years of existence, it is possible to argue that its record with relation to Africa has been less than satisfactory.'

[45] See Koskenniemi, who uses the formula 'Adjudication as ideology', above n. 43, 127.

[46] For instance, Europe and the Americas are the sole continents that have concluded general dispute settlement treaties: the American Treaty on Pacific Settlement (signed 30 April 1948, entered into force 6 May 1949), 30 UNTS 84 (commonly known as the Pact of Bogotá) and the European Convention for the Pacific Settlement of Disputes (signed 29 April 1957, entered into force 30 April 1958), 320 UNTS 243.

[47] Albeit very rare in practice, one could also mention an 'axiom of solidarity'. See Abi-Saab, who explains that Ethiopia and Liberia filed applications in the *South West Africa cases* on behalf of African countries. Abi-Saab, 'Cours général', above n. 22, 255.

[48] On this commission, see P. Mweti Munya, 'The Organization of African Unity and Its Role in Regional Conflict Resolution and Dispute Settlement: A Critical Evaluation', (1999) 19 *Boston College Third World Law Journal* 547. The author underlines that 'the complexity of this Commission emphasizes the seriousness with which the founders of the OAU valued dispute resolution by peaceful means'. Ibid., 547.

or implicitly embodied in some treaties concluded between African states.[49]

For the first time, regionalization of dispute settlement coincided with a tendency to create a certain hierarchy between regional diplomatic forums of dispute settlement and universal adjudicatory bodies. Indeed, although the OAU Commission of Mediation, Conciliation and Arbitration could also deal with arbitration, it was in its nature more diplomatic than anything else. This hierarchy can be seen as a logical consequence of the dispute settlement 'culture', not to say ideology, of adjudication in Africa. African states are by definition more attracted to negotiation than to adjudication.[50] Nevertheless, should that trend be perceived as a disdain for judicial resolution of disputes?[51] Or, should preference for diplomacy (i.e., negotiations) or 'mutually agreed solutions' be considered as an African 'exception'? It is difficult to reach hard and fast conclusions.

For instance, with respect to the first query, some scholars emphasize structural reasons to explain the weight that was given in theory to the OAU Commission of Mediation, Conciliation and Arbitration in the

[49] The wording varies according to the treaties at stake. See, e.g., African Convention on the Conservation of Nature and Natural Resources (signed 15 September 1968, entered into force 16 June 1969), 1001 UNTS 4 (Art. XVIII); Act Regarding Navigation and Economic Co-operation between the States of the Niger Basin (signed 26 October 1963, entered into force 1 February 1966), 587 UNTS 9 (Art. 7); Convention creating the Organization for the Development of the Senegal River (signed 11 May 1972), available at http://faolex.fao.org/docs/texts/mul16004.doc (Art. 18); Convention Relating to the Status of the River Gambia (signed 30 June 1978), available at www.fao.org/docrep/w7414b/w7414b0b.htm (Art. 18); Agreement between the Federal Republic of Nigeria and the Republic of Niger Concerning the Equitable Sharing in the Development, Conservation and Use of their Common Water Resources (signed 18 July 1990), available at www.fao.org/docrep/w7414b/w7414b10.htm (Art. 17).

[50] See P. Mweti Munya, 'The International Court of Justice and Peaceful Settlement of African Disputes: Problems, Challenges and Prospects', (1998) 7 *Journal of International Law and Practice* 164. The author explains that 'the first three decades of independent existence of African countries as sovereign states was characterized by an attitude of indifference and lack of faith displayed toward the International Court of Justice. Some scholars found explanations for this supposedly African skepticism towards the International Court of Justice rooted in both the African and Oriental cultures. Both cultures prefer negotiation and consensus as the ideal modes of dispute resolution.'

[51] See, e.g., R. P. Anand, 'Attitudes of the "New" Asian African Countries towards the International Court of Justice', in Frederik E. Snyder and Surakiart Sathirathai (eds.), *Third World Attitudes towards International Law: An Introduction* (The Hague: Brill, 1987) 17: 'It is thought that the policies and attitudes of these newly independent states about international law and relations are affected by their religious and cultural traditions and that these explain their intransigent behavior and attitude, for instance, toward judicial settlement of their international disputes.'

African system of dispute settlement.[52] In practice, the OAU Commission of Mediation, Conciliation and Arbitration never became operational[53] and, therefore, failed to show that African states were more attracted to negotiation than to adjudication compared with any other member states of the international community.

This remark leads to the second question of whether it is an African exception to favour a culture of diplomacy rather than a culture of adjudication. The answer should be negative. True, the resort by African states to international courts and tribunals 'is still an exceptional method';[54] yet 'this is also true for the rest of the members of the international community'.[55] Furthermore, postmodern international adjudication procedures go as far as incorporating diplomacy into adjudicatory processes. Let's think for instance, about the WTO dispute settlement mechanism, which clearly prioritizes diplomacy over adjudication in the settlement of international trade disputes.[56]

Unexpectedly, the failure of the OAU Commission of Mediation, Conciliation and Arbitration did not result in a status quo ante in which African states would reject the establishment of forums where they could settle their disputes through diplomatic means or judicial means. Rather, it was compensated with a sort of 'baby boom' in the creation of regional courts on the African continent. Of course, this is not to say that there is a cause and effect relationship between the non-success of the OAU Commission of Mediation, Conciliation and Arbitration and the proliferation of regional courts and tribunals at the level of the African continent. However, it is noteworthy that the failure of a mechanism that was

---

[52] See J. G. Merrills, *International Dispute Settlement*, 4th edn (Cambridge University Press, 2005), 284 ('the OAU was a much looser type of regional organization with an emphasis on moral rather than legal obligations and on respect for the members' sovereignty').

[53] Ibid. On the failure of the OAU Commission of Mediation, Conciliation and Arbitration, see also T. O. Elias, 'The Commission of Mediation, Conciliation and Arbitration of the Organization of African Unity', (1964) BYIL 336; W. J. Foltz, 'The Organization of African Unity and the Resolution of Africa's Conflicts', in Francis M. Deng and Ira W. Zartman (eds.), *Conflict Resolution in Africa* (Washington, DC: Brookings Institution Press, 1991) 347.

[54] Ibrahim F. I. Shihata, 'The Attitude of New States toward the International Court of Justice', (1965) 19 *International Organization* 222.

[55] Ibid.

[56] See, e.g., Understanding on Rules and Procedures Governing the Settlement of Disputes, Art. 3(7): 'Before bringing a case, a Member shall exercise its judgment as to whether action under these procedures would be fruitful. The aim of the dispute settlement mechanism is to secure a positive solution to a dispute. A solution mutually acceptable to the parties to a dispute and consistent with the covered agreements is clearly to be preferred.'

characterized by its diplomatic features did not bring African states to repeat the experience, but rather to consolidate another path. This path can be designated as 'regionalization of adjudication'. It confirms the fact that African states are not – were never, truly speaking – allergic to international adjudication of disputes. They just prefer, whenever possible, to settle those disputes at the regional level. It can even be said that regional diplomatic means of dispute settlement and regional mechanisms of adjudication evolved in parallel in Africa.

Regionalization of adjudication is today a true axiom of the African 'ideology' of adjudication.[57] Some courts and tribunals, albeit extinct nowadays, were created quite early after decolonization. This is the case of the defunct East African Community Court of Appeal (1967–77), the East African Community Common Market Tribunal (1967–77), the Economic Community of West African States Tribunal (1975–91), and the Court of Justice of the Economic Community of Central African States (1983). Certain other defunct courts were created later on, such as the Court of Justice of the Arab Maghreb Union (1989) and the Court of Justice of the African Economic Community (1991).[58] For the time being, there are at least eight functional regional courts and tribunals: the Common Court of Justice and Arbitration of the Organization for the Harmonization of Corporate Law in Africa (1997), the Court of Justice of the Common Market for Eastern and Southern Africa (1998), the Court of Justice of the African Union (2003), the Court of Justice of the Economic Community of West African States (ECOWAS) (2001), the Court of Justice of the West African Economic and Monetary Union (1996), the East African Court of Justice (2001), the Southern Africa Development Community (SADC) Tribunal (2000),[59] and the African Court of Human and Peoples' Rights. The phenomenon of the proliferation or multiplication of international courts and tribunals is, therefore, an issue that arose not only at the international level but also at the regional level in the case of Africa.

What prompted the increase in the establishment of African courts and tribunals was the desire of African states to keep their 'options

---

[57] See Oduntan, who insists on multiplying regional international courts: G. Oduntan, 'How International Courts Underdeveloped International Law: Political, Economic and Structural Failings of International Adjudication in Relation to Developing States', (2005) 13 *African Journal of International and Comparative Law* 308.

[58] Information provided by the Project on International Courts and Tribunals, 'The International Judiciary in Context', available at www.pict-pcti.org/publications/synoptic_chart/synop_c4.pdf.

[59] Ibid., It should be noted that the SADC Tribunal was de facto suspended in 2010 at the SADC Summit of Heads of State and Government.

open'[60] in the settlement of their disputes. In other words, by promoting the development of regional courts and tribunals, African states were able to design a system of adjudication *à la carte*, where they could decide between relying solely on diplomacy or resorting to regional courts or to universal courts and tribunals. This being said, it is important to underline that adjudication *à la carte* does not only refer to the options that African states allow themselves to use in the context of inter-state litigation. It also encompasses the options in terms of adjudication that African states grant to other subjects of international law or non-state actors in order to challenge an African state.

One thing for sure is that regionalization of adjudication can presumably entail competition between African courts and universal courts. In its turn, the competition, if not well managed, could provoke fragmentation in the interpretation of international law by those different courts and tribunals. But cross-fertilization, or at least informal co-ordination, can arise from the use of different courts at both the African and the universal level. Indeed, it is not to be presumed that African states, by subjecting themselves to regional courts and tribunals, intend to opt out of general international law. Not at all. Regionalization of adjudication implies adaptation as well as adjustment of the application of international law and its interpretation to African realities.[61] It does not implicate any *contracting out* of general international law.

Still, problems of judicial dialogue or divergent interpretations can emerge in practice. For example, the Hissène Habré saga was dealt with, on one hand, by two African courts, the African Court of Human and Peoples' Rights[62] and the ECOWAS Court of Justice, and, on the other

---

[60] Stephen M, Schwebel, 'The Impact of the International Court of Justice', in Boutros Boutros-Ghali (ed.), *Amicorum Discipulorumque Liber: Peace, Development, Democracy* (Brussels: Bruylant, 1998) 667.

[61] See the various contributions in E. A. Ankumah and E. K. Kwakwa (eds.), *African Perspectives on International Criminal Justice*, (Accra-Maastricht-Pretoria: Africa Legal Aid, 2005).

[62] *Michelot Yogogombaye* v. *Republic of Senegal*, African Court of Human and Peoples' Rights, Application No. 001/2008, Judgment of 15 December 2009. In December 2009, the African Court of Human and Peoples' Rights ruled that it had no jurisdiction to hear an application filed in August 2008 against the Republic of Senegal, aimed at the withdrawal of the ongoing proceedings instituted by that state, with a view to charging, trying, and sentencing Hissène Habré. The African Court of Human and Peoples' Rights based its decision on the fact that Senegal had not made a declaration accepting its jurisdiction to entertain such applications under Art. 34(6) of the Protocol to the African Charter on Human and Peoples' Rights on the establishment of an African Court of Human and People's Rights.

hand, by the ICJ. The indirect clash between the ECOWAS Court of Justice and the ICJ deserves to be mentioned.

In a judgment of November 2010,[63] the ECOWAS Court of Justice ruled on an application filed in October 2008, in which Habré – ruler of Chad from 1982 until his overthrow in 1990 – requested the court to find that his human rights would be violated by Senegal if proceedings were instituted against him. Having observed that evidence existed pointing to potential violations of Habré's human rights as a result of Senegal's constitutional and legislative reforms, the ECOWAS Court of Justice ordered Senegal to comply with the principle of non-retroactivity. The ECOWAS Court of Justice stressed that the mandate that Senegal received from the African Union was in fact to devise and propose all the necessary arrangements for the prosecution and trial of Habré to take place 'within the strict framework of special ad hoc international proceedings'. The ECOWAS judgment was, therefore, basically stating that Senegal could not prosecute Habré by submitting his case to its competent authorities for the purpose of prosecution. Only a special tribunal with an international character could do so according to the ECOWAS Court of Justice.

The ICJ, on its side, found that Senegal's duty to comply with its obligations under the Convention against Torture and Other Cruel, Inhuman or Degrading Treatment or Punishment (Convention against Torture) '[could not] be affected by the decision of the ECOWAS Court of Justice'.[64] It thus took a different direction from the ECOWAS Court of Justice and considered that Senegal, by failing to submit Habré's case to its competent authorities for the purpose of prosecution, breached the Convention against Torture.

It is not within the ambit of the present contribution to deal further with issues of judicial consistency, coherence, and dialogue between African courts and tribunals and universal courts. What is crucial to take into account is that regionalization of adjudication at the level of the African continent does not lead to limitations regarding the jurisdiction of universal courts and tribunals. African regional courts might have more weight when a dispute concerns two African states. However, African states do not only interact with other African states. They also interact with other (non-African) states, and through that interaction, African states might have no other choice than to accept the jurisdiction of more universal

---

[63] *Hissène Habré* v. *Republic of Senegal*, ECOWAS Court of Justice, Judgment No. ECW/CCJ/JUD/06/10 of 18 November 2010.

[64] *Questions relating to the Obligation to Prosecute or Extradite (Belgium* v. *Senegal) (Judgment)*, 20 July 2012, [2012] ICJ Rep. __, para. 111.

international courts and tribunals to settle their disputes with those other states.

Even when disputes concern only African states, resistance to universal mechanisms of inter-state adjudication can be exercised if an African state party to a given dispute would prefer to use the regional option. This is exactly the attitude that Nigeria evinced in the *Cameroon* v. *Nigeria* case before the ICJ. Among the preliminary objections raised in that case by Nigeria, one consisted of claiming that the settlement of boundary disputes within the Lake Chad region was subject to the exclusive competence of the Lake Chad Basin Commission, and in this context the procedures of settlement within that Commission were obligatory for the concerned African states. For Nigeria, the exclusive competence of the Lake Chad Basin Commission meant that it was not possible for Cameroon to invoke Nigeria's Declaration recognizing the compulsory jurisdiction of the ICJ (Art. 36(2) of the ICJ Statute).[65] In response, the ICJ recalled what it said in the *Nicaragua* case, according to which 'the Court is unable to accept either that there is any requirement of prior exhaustion of regional negotiating processes as a precondition to seising the Court'.[66] In *Cameroon* v. *Nigeria*, the ICJ went even further and stated that '[w]hatever their nature, the existence of procedures for regional negotiation cannot prevent the Court from exercising the functions conferred upon it by the Charter and the Statute'.[67] It is true that in *Cameroon* v. *Nigeria*, the ICJ was not dealing with a regional court or tribunal; nevertheless, the attitude of the ICJ in *Belgium* v. *Senegal*, discussed above, shows that it would be quite impossible for an African state to oppose the option of a regional court to prevent the ICJ or another 'universal' court or tribunal from exercising jurisdiction when a title of jurisdiction is conferred on the said court or tribunal.

Therefore, options in inter-state litigation might turn out *ex post facto* to be non-options. In particular, that transformation might arise in the African context, where states are sometimes keen to use mechanisms of international adjudication that are 'de-legalized' – that is, that put aside a *legal settlement* in favour of a *political settlement*. Such situations occur because the African perspective of inter-state litigation is also governed by what may be called an 'axiom of de-legalization'.

---

[65] *Land and Maritime Boundary between Cameroon and Nigeria* (*Cameroon* v. *Nigeria*) (*Preliminary Objections*), [1998] ICJ Rep. 275, 304, [61].

[66] *Military and Paramilitary Activities in and against Nicaragua* (*Nicaragua* v. *United States*) (*Jurisdiction and Admissibility*), [1984] ICJ Rep. 392, 440.

[67] *Land and Maritime Boundary between Cameroon and Nigeria*, above n. 65, 307, [68].

182 MAKANE MOÏSE MBENGUE

The 'axiom of de-legalization'

As correctly pinpointed by Judge Schwebel, 'there will always be disputes with a high degree of political or ideological content which States simply do not wish to present, or to have resolved, in legal terms... Often a State is unwilling to submit to adjudication unless it is confident of winning.'[68] This observation sums up quite well the attitude of African states towards international legal disputes that arise in their relations. Quite often, the preferred option of African states has been to seek political settlement rather than legal settlement. And, herein lies the true reason for the failure of the OAU Commission,[69] or for the reluctance of African states to have recourse to third-party adjudication. Maluwa explains:

> [T]he evidence relating to the readiness and willingness of African states to submit their disputes to third-party conflict resolution and management leaves a lot to be desired. And even in the limited area of political or diplomatic settlement, the overriding function of the various *ad hoc* commissions of mediation and conciliation has been merely to act as 'tension reducers' rather than to prescribe definitive solutions to the disputes in question... In general, the *ad hoc* commissions have tended to avoid pronouncing on the international legal rights and wrongs of the disputants or, still less, to apportion *culpa* in all such disputes.[70]

In practice, African states have been keener to use 'solitary diplomacy'[71] (i.e. good offices under the aegis of a head of state) and/or ad hoc mediation or conciliation committees or commissions[72] to settle their disputes. Specifically, in the context of boundary disputes, which is the most common type of dispute between African states, the latter have preferred to

---

[68] Schwebel, above n. 60, 667.

[69] Despite the diplomatic character of the OAU Commission of Mediation, Conciliation and Arbitration, African states were surely suspicious that dispute settlement under the auspices of the Commission would be more a legal type of settlement than a political type of settlement.

[70] T. Maluwa, 'The Peaceful Settlement of Disputes among African States 1963–1983: Some Conceptual Issues and Practical Trends', (1989) 38 ICLQ 299, 316–17.

[71] On this concept see Maluwa, above n. 70, 309. The author gives the following examples of successful mediation under the aegis of a head of state: Emperor Haile Selassie and President Modibo Keita of Mali in the Morocco–Algeria conflict of 1963, President Abbud of Sudan in the Ethiopia–Somalia dispute of 1964, President Mobutu Sese Seko of Zaïre in the Rwanda–Burundi dispute of 1966.

[72] Ibid., 310–13. The author deals with two examples of conciliation commissions involving African states. One, established in 1964 to look into the Congo conflict, comprised Cameroon, Ethiopia, Guinea, Somalia, Nigeria, Egypt, Tunisia, Kenya, and Upper Volta. Another, established in 1966 to reconcile Ghana and Guinea over certain disputes arising from the overthrow of President Nkrumah's government in Ghana, was composed of Kenya, Sierra Leone, and Zaïre.

set up technical boundary committees. These technical committees are also a good illustration of the reluctance of African countries to submit their territorial disputes to international adjudication, and most precisely to the ICJ or to inter-state arbitration. Technical boundary committees are not always composed of lawyers and, if they are, those cohabit with other disciplines. As such, technical boundary committees are, most of the time,[73] governed by the axiom of 'de-legalization' of dispute settlement processes in Africa.

The *Frontier Dispute (Benin/Niger)* case is a perfect illustration of how African states can sometimes postpone for decades the settlement of territorial disputes through international adjudication. It took about forty years for Benin and Niger finally to agree to submit their territorial dispute to the ICJ. Meanwhile, the two states did their best to find a solution outside a courtroom and, in particular, within technical boundary commissions. It is interesting to recall the steps that led Benin and Niger to go before the ICJ, after decades of attempts to 'de-legalize' their territorial dispute. The frontier dispute started with incidents that occurred on the island of Lété on the eve of the independence of Benin and Niger, in 1959 and 1960 respectively. Following those events, the two states set up a process for the friendly settlement of their frontier dispute. In 1961 and 1963, two Dahomey (the former name of Benin)–Niger joint commissions met to discuss the matter. In October 1963, the crisis between Dahomey and Niger deepened, in particular regarding the island of Lété. Each state subsequently published a White Paper containing their respective positions regarding the frontier dispute. However, the issue of sovereignty over the island of Lété was not resolved and there were further incidents in subsequent years, notably in 1993 and 1998. On 8 April 1994, Benin and Niger concluded an agreement to establish a joint commission for the delimitation of their common border, whose terms of reference included the enumeration, collection, and analysis of documents relating to the frontier and the precise establishment thereof. The commission held six meetings between September 1995 and June 2000. Since efforts to arrive at a negotiated solution to the dispute were unsuccessful, the commission

---

[73] There are some exceptions in practice. For instance, the dispute relating to the boundary between Ethiopia and Eritrea was submitted to the Eritrea–Ethiopia Boundary Commission, composed solely of international lawyers (Sir Elihu Lauterpacht, Prince Bola Adesumbo Ajibola, W. Michael Reisman, Judge Stephen Schwebel and Sir Arthur Watts). The Permanent Court of Arbitration served as registry for this commission. See *Decision Regarding Delimitation of the Border Between the State of Eritrea and the Federal Democratic Republic of Ethiopia (Eritrea/Ethiopia)*, Eritrea–Ethiopia Boundary Commission, 13 April 2002, (2002) 41 ILM 1057.

proposed that the two states bring the dispute before the ICJ by Special Agreement. The Special Agreement was signed in Cotonou on 15 June 2001 and entered into force on 11 April 2002.[74] It is interesting to note that, in the case of Benin and Niger, it was the technical boundary commission itself that recommended to both states that they seize the ICJ. Thus this demonstrates that even if African states insist in a particular context on opting for a 'de-legalized' dispute settlement process, the bodies that they put in place can then acknowledge their limits and advocate the use of the third-party adjudication.

However, recourse to technical boundary committees can raise difficulties subsequently when African states decide *in fine* to submit their disputes to third-party adjudication. Indeed, since it is not based on a legal settlement – but, rather, political or technical – African states still attempt to have the work of these commissions *validated* by international courts and tribunals or to use international courts in order to *unfreeze* the process within a given technical committee.

For instance, in the *Continental Shelf (Tunisia/Libya)* case (which was the first African dispute brought before the ICJ after more than ten years of boycott by African countries following the *South West Africa Cases*), the special agreement required the ICJ to clarify the principles and rules of international law that might apply for the delimitation of the area of the continental shelf and to specify precisely the practical way in which the aforesaid principles and rules applied, so as to enable the experts of the two countries to delimit those areas without any difficulties.[75] Both states disagreed on the meaning of the special agreement at this level. According to Tunisia, the ICJ was required to take into account all the elements of fact and law regarding the practical methods and instruments to be used, 'up to the ultimate point before the technical work'.[76] For Libya, the Court was not authorized to carry the matter 'right up to the ultimate point before the purely technical work'[77] and also was 'not invited to set out the specific method of delimitation itself'.[78] It is then clear that from Libya's point of view, the ICJ was supposed to facilitate the technical determination of the continental shelf by the experts of the two countries and not really to proceed with the delimitation itself. The ICJ noted that regardless of the two states' dispute settlement options, the Court is first

---

[74] The historical facts of the case are available in *Frontier Dispute (Benin/Niger)*, [2005] ICJ Rep. 90, 107, [20]–[22].
[75] *Continental Shelf (Tunisia/Libyan Arab Jamahiriya) (Merits)*, [1982] ICJ Rep. 18, 38, [25].
[76] Ibid., 39, [27].   [77] Ibid., 39, [28].   [78] Ibid.

and foremost an organ of law. Consequently, once seized of a contentious case, the Court 'is to render a judgment in a contentious case... which will have therefore the effect and the force attributed to it under Article 94 of the Charter of the United Nations and the said provisions of the Statute and the Rules of Court'.[79] Here is another example of an indirect clash between the willingness of African states to control – this time, through a *compromis* (special agreement) – not only the jurisdiction of an international court but also the international judicial function per se.[80] This is a peculiarity of some of the African territorial disputes submitted to international courts and tribunals, particularly when those states try to create a certain continuum between international courts and tribunals and the (non-legal) work of their technical boundary commissions.

Some international courts and tribunals might see a sort of legal continuum between their activity – which is rooted in international law – and the activity of those 'de-legalized' mechanisms in the African context. In this regard we can consider the *Abyei* arbitration between the government of Sudan and the Sudan People's Liberation Movement/Army. There, the arbitral tribunal was more deferential to the work conducted by the Abyei Boundary Commission (ABC) experts, a body (or a technical boundary commission) that the arbitral tribunal itself qualified as composed of 'individuals known and recognized in the fields of Sudanese and African history, geography, politics, public affairs, ethnography, and culture'.[81] Noteworthy is the fact that the tribunal stressed the characteristics of 'de-legalized' dispute settlement mechanisms in Africa. For example, it indicated that the ABC experts 'were to apply the procedures of "scientific analysis and research" [and that] there was no reference to the application of international law, whether substantive or procedural [in the work of the ABC experts]'.[82] The tribunal also underlined that, 'Unlike traditional judicial or arbitral proceedings, the ABC's procedures were markedly informal ("informal yet businesslike"), the proceedings

---

[79] Ibid., 39–40, [40].
[80] On the international judicial function, see Georges Abi-Saab, 'The Normalization of International Adjudication: Convergence and Divergences', (2010) 43 *New York University Journal of International Law and Politics* 1.
[81] *In the matter of an arbitration before a tribunal constituted in accordance with Article 5 of the Arbitration Agreement between the Government of Sudan and the Sudan People's Liberation Movement/Army on delimiting Abyei Area and the Permanent Court of Arbitration Optional Rules for arbitrating disputes between two parties of which only one is a state, between the Government of Sudan and the Sudan People's Liberation Movement/Army*, PCA, Final award, 22 July 2009, [467].
[82] Ibid., [468].

186   MAKANE MOÏSE MBENGUE

were not conducted in a confrontational fashion, and an atmosphere of cooperation was sought'.[83] Despite those features,[84] the arbitral tribunal went as far as to conclude that the ABC experts as a body had *compétence de la compétence*[85] (like any international court or tribunal), and that the tribunal would follow the 'interpretation' of the ABC experts as long as that interpretation was 'reasonable'[86] (e.g., the interpretation was considered reasonable if the ABC experts did not exceed their mandate).

The approach that was endorsed by the arbitral tribunal in the *Abyei* arbitration remains original, if not unique. It might encourage African states to submit their territorial disputes to international adjudicatory mechanisms should they need an international court and tribunal to strengthen the determinations of their technical commissions, such as a technical boundary commission, or to validate them. 'De-legalized' disputes can sometimes address de facto legal issues[87] and as such can be given more weight when African states resort to international adjudication. For the time being, it seems that there is instead resistance from 'universal' international courts and tribunals to follow African states down that path.

Recently, the ICJ had occasion to state clearly its position vis-à-vis delimitation carried out by African technical boundary commissions. In the *Frontier Dispute (Burkina Faso/Niger)* case, Burkina Faso requested the Court to adjudge and declare that one part of its frontier with Niger followed a course that was already determined by a joint technical commission established in 1997. In other words, for the sake of *res judicata*, Burkina Faso wanted the Court to include in the operative part of its

---

[83] Ibid., [469].

[84] Ibid., [483], where the tribunal concludes as follows: 'Given the ABC's singular characteristics, a majority of the Tribunal has no difficulty in concluding that the ABC possessed important decision-making powers in addition to its fact-finding functions. While the ABC Experts were not lawyers but persons recognized in the fields of "history, geography and other relevant expertise," they were required to arrive at a final and binding decision. Although the Parties did not require the ABC Experts to apply international law or legal reasoning to the delimitation of the boundaries of the Abyei Area but scientific methods, they did require the ABC Experts to arrive at a decision that would resolve the dispute with final and binding consequences. It is this essential decision- making function that, in the view of the Majority, is a defining characteristic of the ABC.'

[85] Ibid., [502]–[503].   [86] Ibid., [504].

[87] Maluwa gives the example of the Lété island dispute between Benin and Niger. He explains, 'Legal arguments were invoked by both parties throughout the duration of the dispute (1960–1965) although what was sought and achieved – partly through direct negotiations between the disputants and partly through the mediation of the *Conseil de l'Entente* – was not a legal settlement as such but a political settlement.' Maluwa, above n. 70, 301, n. 6.

judgment the line of the common frontier fixed by the joint technical commission. According to Niger, since there already existed an agreement between the parties regarding the sector at stake, there was no need for the ICJ to include a reference to the said sector in the operative part of its judgment. For Niger, it was sufficient that the Court took note of the agreement in question in the reasoning of its judgment, 'and settle the only dispute which remains between the Parties, namely that relating to the part of the frontier in respect of which the Joint Technical Commission was unable to conclude its work successfully, and on which the Parties have therefore not been able to reach agreement'.[88]

The ICJ refused categorically to accede to Burkina Faso's request. The Court recalled to Burkina Faso that in the light of the special agreement concluded between Burkina Faso and Niger, the Court was only supposed to 'place on record the Parties' agreement' regarding the delimitation of the frontier made by the Joint Technical Commission, and not 'to delimit itself the frontier according to a line that corresponds to the conclusions of the Joint Technical Commission upon which the two Parties have agreed'.[89] The Court explained that 'it is one thing to note the existence of an agreement between the Parties and to place it on record for them; it is quite a different matter to appropriate the content of that agreement in order to make it the substance of a decision of the Court itself'.[90] It rejected Burkina Faso's request as it considered that the said request exceeded the special agreement between Burkina Faso and Niger. However, noteworthy is the passage of the judgment in which the Court declared that even if the *compromis* requested the Court to do so (that is, to delimit a frontier on the basis of the conclusions of a technical boundary commission), the Court would not give effect to such a request. Indeed, in a powerful dictum the Court stated,

> A special agreement allows the parties to define freely the limits of the jurisdiction, *stricto sensu*, which they intend to confer upon the Court. It cannot allow them to *alter* the limits of the Court's judicial function: those limits, because they are defined by the Statute, are not at the disposal of the parties, even by agreement between them, and are mandatory for the parties just as for the Court itself.[91]

It is interesting to note that this is the second time in its history that the ICJ has emphasized through the formulation of new dicta not only the

---

[88] *Frontier Dispute (Burkina Faso/Niger)*, [2013] ICJ Rep. __, [39].
[89] Ibid., [43].   [90] Ibid.   [91] Ibid., [46] (emphasis added).

limits of its judicial function but also the limits that are imposed on states when taking the option to seize an international court of a dispute. In both cases, it has been in the context of 'African disputes' that the Court has come up with new and strong formulations of those limits. It did so in 1963 in the *Northern Cameroons* case, which can be considered as an African dispute since Cameroon was the applicant state and the subject matter concerned self-determination and territorial issues in Africa. The judgment of the Court in the *Frontier DISPUTE (Burkina Faso/Niger)* not only reiterated what the Court said in 1963,[92] but also added another 'layer of protection' with the above-mentioned dictum.

Concluding remarks

The message sent to African states is clear: no control can be exercised by states over third-party adjudication once they decide to have recourse to it. Bowett once affirmed that 'the basic reason for avoiding legal settlement is simply that states prefer to retain control over the settlement process, so as to ensure that any settlement is acceptable to them or, if that cannot be achieved, that no settlement is reached'.[93] Maluwa went further and advanced the argument that the issue of 'control of the settlement process provide[s] the key to much that is seemingly puzzling in the attitude of African states toward the settlement of disputes, in general'.[94] If 'control' is the *sine qua non* for more adherence to and use by African states of the system of international courts and tribunals, then there is no hope for greater involvement of African states in international adjudication. The reaction of the ICJ to Burkina Faso's request shows that any idea of control is illusory, and, in particular, in a context where the international judicial function has matured.

Moreover, and with all due respect to scholars like Maluwa, it is quite often groundless to think that the main factor that dictates the choice

---

[92] '[E]ven if the Court, when seised, finds that it has jurisdiction, the Court is not compelled in every case to exercise that jurisdiction. There are inherent limitations on the exercise of the judicial function which the Court, as a court of justice, can never ignore. There may thus be an incompatibility between the desires of an applicant, or, indeed, of both parties to a case, on the one hand, and on the other hand the duty of the Court to maintain its judicial character. The Court itself, and not the parties, must be the guardian of the Court's judicial integrity.' *Northern Cameroons (Cameroon v. United Kingdom) (Preliminary Objections)*, [1963] ICJ Rep. 15, 29. See also *Frontier Dispute (Burkina Faso/Niger)*, above n. 88, [45].

[93] Derek W. Bowett, 'Contemporary Developments in Legal Techniques in the Settlement of Disputes', (1983) *Recueil des cours* 181.

[94] Maluwa, above n. 70, 314.

of African states in relation to international adjudication is linked to 'control'. The most important factor is 'confidence'. As Jenks correctly highlighted, 'the essence of the question is confidence: confidence in the stability and adequacy of the law, and confidence in the integrity and predictability of the courts and tribunals administering the law'.[95] Since their accession to sovereignty, African states have progressively built a culture of adjudication. They have put more trust and confidence in third-party adjudication, and thus have had greater recourse to international courts and tribunals (in the sense of universal courts). It cannot be doubted that, in future, African states will be even more involved in international adjudication processes and contribute more actively to the development of international law.

[95] C. W. Jenks, *The Prospects of International Adjudication* (London/New York: Stevens & Sons/Oceana Publications, 1964), 104.

PART III

10

Initiating territorial adjudication: the who, how, when, and why of litigating contested sovereignty

LEA BRILMAYER AND ADELE FAURE

Buy land, they're not making it any more.

Mark Twain

Only a fraction of territorial disputes make it to adjudication. Some are solved through negotiation, through mediation, or through the passage of time; others simply fester. In this chapter, we consider the factors that affect which cases are more likely to be adjudicated. In other words, we look at the 'why' of territorial adjudication. What is it that causes a state (or rather, a pair of states) to decide to take a territorial dispute to binding third-party resolution – that is, to court or arbitration? We also examine the 'who' – namely whether there are trends among the types of state that go to the ICJ or to binding arbitration over land conflicts.[1]

We start out by testing what seem to be commonsensical observations based on simple logic about state interests. First, we examine the 'who'. The winner of the adjudication, other things being equal, ought more often than not to have been the initiating party. The party with the weaker case has no reason to go to litigation, because that will only make it worse off than before the case was heard. If the case goes to court at all, therefore, it would be at the instance of the party with the stronger legal and factual arguments. We further hypothesize that the initiating party will not be in

---

[1] As the problem is framed, territorial adjudications are the 'what', whereas the jurisdictional rules for going to the ICJ or arbitration are the 'how'. The 'who' in this chapter refers to the set of all forty dyads that have gone to the ICJ or arbitration over the last century (the 'when') for territorial disputes. This chapter is in part concerned with the 'who' – namely, whether any predictions can be made about certain attributes of a state and its likelihood of going to or winning an adjudication. Above all, however, this chapter is concerned with 'why' these states seek out adjudication of land disputes.

occupation of the disputed territory: the state that is not in occupation has little, if anything, to lose, while the occupying state has little to gain.[2]

Furthermore, we expect that the state that is less likely to initiate adjudication will also be unwilling to agree to litigation when it is proposed by the other side – and for the same reason. Therefore, it would be reasonable to expect that the decided cases would mainly involve disputes in which jurisdiction was based on the non-initiating party's agreement *ex ante*, rather than a special agreement between the contending states *ex post*.

Then we turn to the 'why'. We posit that states will be motivated to go to binding third-party adjudication only if they believe that things will turn out well for them, or at least that things will turn out *better* than the status quo. Based on this assumption, we predict that states will only initiate adjudication if they have the stronger legal case.

All these assumptions are in theory testable (although with difficulty). And so we then set out to assess them as objectively as possible, given the practical limitations on the data.[3] Our assessment of litigated cases (from the International Court of Justice (ICJ), from the Permanent Court of International Justice (PCIJ), and from reported arbitral awards) mostly, if weakly, support our examination of *who* initiates or wins territorial adjudications. But for our hypothesis of *why* states end up in court, our basic premise that only cases of *ex ante* agreement reach adjudication is wholly upended: by far the larger number of territorial decisions has been a product of special agreement (what we call '*ex post*' consent to jurisdiction).

We turn therefore to more complex models of state interests and motivations to adjudicate in an attempt to identify where the simplistic view must be adjusted. We examine both different types of interest in territory and non-territorial interests that might affect the decision to bring territorial disputes to court or arbitration.

Unfortunately, there are too many variables – and nowhere near enough data points – to develop a genuine empirical theory. What is possible, however, is an appreciation (however impressionistic) of the different types of factors that influence a state's decision to adjudicate. It is interesting to see how far from reality the simple version of the 'conventional wisdom' turns out to be. Suggestions are made throughout, however, about how

---

[2] For a discussion of how this distinguishes territorial from other disputes, see Lea Brilmayer and Natalie Klein, 'Land and Sea: Two Sovereignty Regimes in Search of a Common Denominator', (2001) 33 *NYU Journal of International Law & Politics* 703, 730–31.

[3] For a discussion of the difficulties in conducting this empirical analysis, see the discussion below entitled 'Methodological and definitional problems'.

to adjust the simple premises that at first seem commonsensical, allowing space for nuances that make the premises more complex, but also more realistic.

Some common sense about international territorial adjudication

The premises that underlie decisions about whether to submit a case to an international court just seem like common sense. We start, therefore, by spelling out some basic premises that characterize the subject. From these assumptions we shall make predictions about what we would expect to find in the decided cases.

Basic assumptions

We start by identifying three basic assumptions. The first (the 'uniqueness' assumption) relates to the special nature of territory: land is unique and its loss cannot easily be compensated. The second (the 'maximization' assumption) is that litigation is a strategy for maximizing the state's territory. The third is that states will fight to avoid the jurisdiction of any court or arbitral tribunal that threatens its existing territorial interests (the 'avoidance of jurisdiction' assumption).

Uniqueness of territory

Territorial disputes are especially contentious. Although valued also for economic reasons and for national security, territory provokes extraordinary emotional attachments. Land is unique. There are few things that people care about more than 'their place', and when that attachment is forcibly broken, their grievances are carried undiluted for generations. As a source of conflict, territory is probably rivalled only by religion.

The world has only a fixed amount of territory, unlike most other assets. Territorial disputes are zero-sum in a very fundamental way: what one state wins comes necessarily from what another state loses. And once lost, territory will most likely not be replaceable. Ordinarily, states would not be expected to trade their territorial claims for advantages of other sorts.

Litigation as a maximization strategy

Land is desirable, and states want more of it. No matter how dedicated the diplomacy, compromise is difficult to fashion, and sometimes the only alternatives are war and law. Given the obvious disadvantages of war, third-party adjudication has obvious attractions. States use adjudication as a tool to accomplish their objective of territorial acquisition. They seek a tribunal with jurisdiction when they have positive objectives to attain, and seek to avoid the jurisdiction of tribunals when they have something to lose.

Avoidance of jurisdiction

Compared with domestic law, few international legal cases make it to court. The chief reason is the limited jurisdiction of international tribunals, judicial or arbitral. Because jurisdiction is consent-based, third-party adjudication must be attractive to both parties if it is to present a viable solution.

It seems clear that litigation should be appealing only to a state that expects to gain something from it. Whether a state expects to benefit from adjudication depends on two things: its evaluation of the status quo prior to the initiation of litigation, and its expectations about the international tribunal's decision. States' expectations about that change in status, we expect, will determine a state's willingness to adjudicate. Because territorial disputes are zero-sum, however, the likelihood is that anything appealing to one of the disputants will for that very reason not appeal to the other – and this problem forms the central puzzle with which this chapter is concerned.

These three assumptions are so simple and obvious that it seems hard to imagine that they might not be accurate. But (as we shall see) they have testable implications that are not all borne out by the facts. We compared the implications of these assumptions to the existing body of adjudicated territorial cases over the last century, and the two are not entirely consistent.

International adjudication: courts, tribunals, and jurisdictional rules

We have taken as our pool of relevant data all 'territorial cases' with reported arbitral or judicial awards in the last hundred years. Maritime delimitations are not included unless the case has a land territory component as well. The earliest of these territorial disputes is 1911, and a few are sufficiently recent that, at the time of writing, the decision has not been announced.

Territorial disputes form a substantial but not overly large part of the ICJ's docket. As of 2012, the Court had decided around 140 cases, total, in all areas of international law. Of these, 114 were contentious cases; the other twenty-six were brought pursuant to the Court's advisory jurisdiction.[4] Of these 114 contentious cases, seventeen were territorial sovereignty disputes, which puts disputes over territory at around 15 per cent of the Court's docket. There have been, in addition, another twenty-two territorial disputes resolved by arbitration since 1911.

Jurisdiction over contentious cases at the ICJ is established in one of three ways. Pursuant to Article 36(2) of the Statute of the Court (the 'optional clause declaration'), a state may sign on to the ICJ's jurisdiction as a general matter, and will thereafter be permitted to sue and be sued by other states that have also subjected themselves to the ICJ's jurisdiction. Second, under Article 36(1), a state may become a party to a treaty that contains an acceptance of the ICJ's jurisdiction for cases arising under that treaty. A case brought under either of these two types of jurisdiction can be started with a unilateral application. Finally, Article 36(1) allows two states possessed of an international legal dispute to sign a special agreement referring their dispute to the ICJ. In other words, this mechanism allows states to agree to adjudication *after* the dispute has arisen.

Because arbitrations are heard by ad hoc tribunals, created specifically for the purpose of deciding a particular case, the jurisdictional rules are different. Some cases are brought under generalized treaties that provide for the arbitration of disputes that arise under them; such provision for arbitration is common under bilateral investment treaties. There are also a small number of multilateral substantive agreements, such as the United Nations Convention on the Law of the Sea (UNCLOS), which specify arbitration as a dispute resolution mechanism.[5]

For arbitration, however, it is much more common for the arbitration agreement to be written *after* the dispute arises. This is particularly the case for territorial disputes, for which there are few substantive mechanisms comparable to UNCLOS that might commit parties generally to arbitration in disputes over territory. Instead, arbitration is chosen by the parties to a particular territorial dispute as a solution to that dispute, and that one alone.

The importance of this jurisdictional structure will become clearer as the incentives to litigation are explored. Ad hoc arbitrations are different from standing courts in some respects, but there are also important similarities. This is particularly the case with ICJ jurisdiction derived from special agreement, which most nearly resembles agreements to arbitrate.

---

[4] ICJ, Cases, 8 October 2012, available at www.icj-cij.org/docket.
[5] See UNCLOS, Part XV, Arts. 279–299, especially Art. 287(1)(c) (arbitration). See generally Natalie Klein, *Dispute Settlement in the UN Convention on the Law of the Sea* (Cambridge University Press, 2005).

Methodological and definitional problems

International law is a challenging area for data collection – in particular with respect to the collected jurisprudence of international tribunals (judicial and arbitral). The jurisprudence of territorial disputes is no exception. Most importantly, the number of cases is limited – we consider forty such disputes – and so it is frequently not possible to collect enough instances of a hypothesis to test its validity.

The reported opinions, additionally, often do not reveal the whole story; and the judges or arbitrators, as well as historians and international law scholars, may have a motivation for telling what they know about the story with a slant. With arbitration in particular, the pleadings are unlikely to be publicly available. The answers to some of the questions we ask are subjective; and even when they permit objective answers, the answers may not be black and white, but a matter of degree. The scientist does not stand a chance.

In addition to these methodological problems are the definitional problems that stem from the absence of a standard terminology. Three terms whose interconnections will turn out to be important require definition: 'initiating party', 'winner', and 'occupier'. These turn out to be more complex concepts than might appear; and this complexity bears substantial responsibility for our inability to make crisp statistical judgements.

'Initiating party' or 'initiator'

By 'initiating party', or 'initiator', we mean the party who starts the case as a formal legal matter. In domestic law, this would be the person referred to as the plaintiff, and no great subtlety would be required to figure out which party that was. But international adjudication is quite different from domestic law in one respect: both sides have to consent before adjudication can occur. Thus international cases tend towards greater symmetry of party structure, undermining the meaningfulness of attempts to distinguish which state was active at the outset and which state reactive.

In many cases, it would be possible to claim plausibly that both states were 'initiators'. We shall count cases where both states give their consent to adjudicate at the outset of the litigation (as opposed to prior to the arising of the dispute) as lacking an initiator. As will be discussed below, these would be cases filed by 'special agreement' or arbitrations initiated by a compromise. Such cases are formally symmetric, in that both states have given consent to the adjudication with full knowledge of what, specifically, they are agreeing to. Thus neither state party is the one that brings the case to the court or arbitral tribunal. These are to be contrasted with cases where a general state agreement made prior to a particular dispute is the basis for jurisdiction; in such cases, the adjudication can be commenced by the application of a single party.

The sole exception that we make to characterize all formally symmetric cases as not having an initiator is where one side formally contested the court or tribunal's jurisdiction. We consider this sufficient evidence of opposition to treat the other party as the true initiator. This exception will not apply in very many cases, because (as noted above) cases are formally symmetric where they are brought by special agreement (for ICJ cases) or *compromis* (for arbitration). In such cases, it is likely to be uncommon for a party to contest jurisdiction.

We note one key difficulty in using the terminology in this way: even in cases of formally equal involvement in starting the case, the motivation may be far from symmetric. Even where the agreement to litigate is formally symmetric, one state may have been more aggressive or more enthusiastic in pushing the dispute towards litigation. Such cases would be of considerable interest to add to our study, but the question of asymmetric motivation cannot be resolved without considerable (and possibly unreliable) inside information.[6] Where such information is available, we cautiously include it after first analysing the data about formal asymmetry.

'Occupier'

A second problematic term is 'occupier'. The 'occupier' is the state in control of the disputed territory at the moment the dispute enters the adjudication phase; it is, naturally, entirely possible for both parties to a

---

[6] Take, for instance, the Rann of Kutch arbitration between India and Pakistan in 1966 to resolve a boundary dispute that followed the Indo-Pakistani War. India was said to be hostile to arbitration and had been resisting it for the prior decade. Jonathan Colman, 'Britain and the Indo-Pakistani Conflict: The Rann of Kutch and Kashmir', (1965) 37 *Journal of Imperial & Commonwealth History* 465, 470–1. Pakistan, on the other hand, had shown itself willing to take the dispute to arbitration. Mukund Untawale, 'The Kutch–Sind Dispute: A Case Study in International Arbitration', (1974) 23 ICLQ 818, 824. Still, whether Pakistan qualifies as 'pro-litigation' is not very clear. Likewise, the winner is not so easy to determine. The arbitral panel upheld 90 per cent of India's claim over the Rann of Kutch marshes, which some have read as meaning that India obtained the better outcome. Colman, above, 470. However, Pakistan obtained the most controversial areas – namely, the most 'usable' land – and was satisfied with the outcome, whereas India indicated displeasure with the award. Untawale, above, 829, 838. Although there were indications that the parties could fit into some of our boxes, we judged it prudent not to apply classifications in such relatively uncertain cases. Accordingly, this case (among others) was excluded from our analysis.

dispute to be in occupation of different parts of the disputed territory. Some disputed territory is unoccupied; other disputed territory may have occupants of a particular nationality, but no sign of official presence. As we use the term, neither of these would count as 'occupied' and neither has an 'occupier'. We limit that term to areas that fall somehow under the state's physical control, even if minimally. This usage does not require that the 'occupier' be a foreigner (as in the laws of war, where a hostile army occupies the territory of another state). A state can occupy its 'own' territory or it can occupy another state's territory, so far as our meaning of the word requires.

Occupation in this sense is often a matter of degree. In particular, one state's hold on the territory may be precarious and it may be a judgement call how much longer it will be in occupation. But there will be some cases in which the question has a relatively clear answer, and in such cases the status of the disputed territory is worth noting.

'Winner'

Likewise, determining the 'winner' of a territorial adjudication is fraught with peril. Decisions wholly recognizing the claims of one state against another are rare. This is particularly the case where the value attached by a state to a particular piece of land is subjective (a point to which we shall return).[7]

For the purposes of our analysis, however, it is highly desirable to be able to determine, if only roughly, which state came out ahead in adjudication. In certain cases the result is unequivocally in favour of one state; it is straightforward to classify the states in dispute as winners or losers. In judgments where the main bone of contention is awarded clearly to one state, that state is considered as having 'won', even when the judgment favours the 'loser' on certain other issues. Where one of the two parties strenuously disputed a judgment while another accepted it readily, we treated this as a sign, however imperfect, that the state that accepted it was more a winner.

When we could not be reasonably certain which state could be characterized as winning, we classified the case as having no clear winner. To illustrate: in the *El Salvador/Honduras* case, the ICJ decided in 1992 that, of the roughly 440 sq km of land at stake, El Salvador would be awarded 140, and Honduras would get 300. At first glance, it seems as if El Salvador did not come out ahead. But perhaps El Salvador's 140 sq km were the

---

[7] See scenario 4, discussed further below.

most valuable of the disputed land. Or, perhaps El Salvador's initial claim to the territory that Honduras was awarded was not made in good faith but simply to enlarge El Salvador's claim for strategic purposes; in that case, for El Salvador to lose that part of its claim would not matter as much to it. Where such uncertainties make assessments controversial, we refrained from classifying either state as a 'winner' or a 'loser'.

For this reason, the universe of cases which we could use to examine our hypotheses was reduced to those with fairly stark contrasts in the results. However, while our rough classifications mask a great deal of complexity, they still allow us to examine whether certain preliminary patterns emerge.

Basic hypotheses and empirical observations on international adjudication

With these cautionary provisos in mind, we formulated four distinct hypotheses to test. They are:

Hypothesis 1: All else being equal, the initiating party is expected not to be in occupation of the disputed territory.

Hypothesis 2: All else being equal, the occupying state should be more likely to prevail in the adjudication.

Hypothesis 3: All else being equal, the international tribunal should tend to rule in favour of the initiating party.

Hypothesis 4: Territorial disputes should be more likely to reach adjudication as a result of ex ante *agreements.*

For each of these, we shall first explain why it might follow from the basic premises described above. We then assess the consistency with existing awards, and then provide concrete illustrations of that consistency or inconsistency.

As will appear, none of these is strongly borne out by the examination of existing judicial or arbitral awards. The first three are weakly consistent with our examination of the last hundred years' worth of cases, subject to our methodological caveats noted above. However, the data firmly reject our fourth hypothesis.

We conclude that there is enough divergence between these hypotheses and the empirical results that the next goal should be to identify where in our basic premises the 'self evident' logic is actually erroneous. The last section of this chapter raises some questions in that regard, and points towards some possible answers.

Hypothesis 1: All else being equal, the initiating party is expected not to be in occupation of the disputed territory

As a preliminary matter, we would expect the party that initiates the case in court not to be occupying the disputed territory. The occupying state has a greater interest in preserving the status quo; seeking international adjudication could jeopardize its control over the territory. It would thus be against the occupying state's interests to seek adjudication. In contrast, the state not in possession could only improve its position by seeking binding dispute resolution; if the tribunal rules against it, it is not much worse off than it was before the process started.

Accordingly, we would expect, more often than not, to see non-occupying states as initiators – if the territory at stake is occupied at all. This is a 'soft' conclusion; it describes a tendency that might be overcome by competing pressures in the opposite direction. But it describes what we might rationally expect, other things being equal.

One of the main difficulties in assessing the empirical situation is that the sample size is too small to yield interesting generalizations. States that formally initiate litigation are relatively few; as will be shown below, most cases are the result of negotiations leading to special agreements (or the arbitration analogue thereof), which lack a 'formal' initiator and purport to be mutual. Our dataset yielded only nine cases,[8] two of them arbitrations, where a state formally instituted proceedings (or where, for procedural reasons, there is not technically a 'formal' initiator, but where one state contested the tribunal's jurisdiction enough to deem the other party to be an initiator). Of the subset of nine cases with formal initiators, only five featured a party clearly in occupation of the disputed territory: the ICJ cases of *Nicaragua* v. *Honduras*, *Costa Rica* v. *Nicaragua*,

---

[8] *Certain Activities carried out by Nicaragua in the Border Area (Costa Rica v. Nicaragua)*, ICJ, General List No. 150, 18 November 2010 (*Certain Activities*); *Territorial and Maritime Dispute (Nicaragua v. Colombia) (Preliminary Objections)*, [2007] ICJ Rep. 832 (*Territorial and Maritime Dispute*); *Territorial and Maritime Dispute between Nicaragua and Honduras in the Caribbean Sea (Nicaragua v. Honduras)*, [2007] ICJ Rep. 659 (*Caribbean Sea*); *Land and Maritime Boundary between Cameroon and Nigeria (Cameroon v. Nigeria: Equatorial Guinea intervening)*, [2002] ICJ Rep. 303 (*Land and Maritime Boundary*); *Temple of Preah Vihear (Cambodia v. Thailand) (Merits)*, [1962] ICJ Rep. 6 (*Temple of Preah Vihear*); *Maritime Delimitation in the Area between Greenland and Jan Mayen (Denmark v. Norway)*, [1993] ICJ Rep. 38 (*Jan Mayen*); *Maritime Delimitation and Territorial Questions between Qatar and Bahrain (Qatar v. Bahrain) (Merits)*, [2001] ICJ Rep. 40 (*Qatar and Bahrain*); *The Boundary Case between Honduras and Nicaragua (Honduras/Nicaragua)*, (1906) 11 RIAA 101; *Argentine–Chile Frontier Case (Argentina/Chile)*, (1966) 16 RIAA 109 (*Argentine–Chile Frontier Case*).

Cameroon v. *Nigeria*, and *Cambodia* v. *Thailand*, as well as the PCIJ case of *Denmark* v. *Norway*. In each of these cases, the initiator was the party out of possession – as we had expected, given the incentives of each party. However, with such a limited subset, the conclusions we can draw are limited, even anecdotally.

If we expand our view to include soft evidence that one of the two parties was very reluctant to proceed to arbitration and required serious coaxing and/or threatening to agree, the same pattern seems to apply. 'Symmetric' cases – in other words, cases that were ostensibly the product of a joint agreement to proceed to court – that feature one reluctant party approximate the dynamics of formally initiated cases. One party is clearly more in favour of adjudication; we would assume that, in these cases as well, this may be because they have more to gain (or, equivalently, less to lose) from legally binding resolution. In other words, the more enthusiastic party in symmetric cases – if one can be identified from the context and the associated literature – should not be in occupation of the disputed territory. In addition to the five formally initiated cases named above, we can identify approximately six more cases where both an occupier and an asymmetry in the willingness to adjudicate can be discerned. In all but (arguably[9]) two of these cases, the more reluctant party tended also to be the one in occupation of the disputed land. And if we look at the whole set of parties where there was an identifiable asymmetry in the desire for adjudication – just about twenty cases – regardless of whether there was an identifiable occupier, the fact that, at most, two featured 'occupiers' in favour of litigation is telling (see Table 10.1).

Naturally, this is still a small sample size; there are likely even more territorial cases from the last century featuring either one state pressuring the other to adjudicate, and/or particularly reluctant parties. Whether or not we could categorize the cases as such depended on whether the primary or secondary literature revealed such aspects of the litigation and its run-up. In turn, some of the cases demonstrating a strong imbalance in the states' willingness to litigate did not feature a clear occupier of the disputed territory, so they could not be included in this count. Nonetheless,

---

[9] The two cases where 'occupiers' were in favour of litigation do not feature particularly strong or obvious cases of occupation. Nonetheless, we chose to include both cases (*UK/France* and *Costa Rica/Panama*) as having identifiable occupiers in order to cast as wide a net as possible in demonstrating the scarcity of cases where occupiers were pro-litigation.

Table 10.1 *Cases where there was an identifiable asymmetry in the desire for adjudication*

Non-occupying state is pro-litigation	Occupying state is pro-litigation
Nicaragua v. *Colombia* (2012)[1]	*United Kingdom*/France (1953)[3]
Nicaragua v. *Honduras* (2007)[2]	*Costa Rica*/Panama (1914)[4]
Cameroon v. *Nigeria* (2002)	
Qatar/*Bahrain* (2001)	
Libya/Chad (1994)	
Cambodia v. *Thailand* (1962)	
Siam/*France* (1947)	
Denmark v. *Norway* (1933)	
Chile/Peru (1925)	

Note: the state whose name is given in italics is the occupying state. The date in parentheses is the year the case was decided.

[1] Nicaragua's complaint was premised on Colombia's claim of dominion over the maritime space in which the islands and keys are located. Although Colombia did not have boots on the ground in the contested islands in the Caribbean Sea, we decided to classify Colombia as the occupying state because its more powerful navy exclusively patrolled the area and regularly blocked access and stopped Nicaraguan vessels. Christina Stegemoller, 'Nicaragua v. Colombia', (2005) 11 *Law & Business Review of the Americas* 127, 133. Colombia's control over the territory in question appeared tighter and exclusive of Nicaraguan nationals, in such a way that we believe that an 'occupier' qualifier would be the better representation of the facts on the ground.

[2] Honduras was reported to have had troops on South Cay (Cayo Sur) at the time Nicaragua instituted proceedings.

[3] France and the United Kingdom quibbled over the ownership of islands and rocks in what was called the Minquiers and Ecrehos group. Only a small number of these islands were habitable, and even fewer were inhabited at the time of the dispute. On one of the islands the Minquiers group (Maîtresse), the government of the British Crown dependency of Jersey had set up a slipway, a custom house, a house 'for the Bailiff of Jersey,' and a flagstaff. See D. H. N. Johnson, 'The Minquiers and Ecrehos Case', (1954) 3 ICLQ 189, 206–7. Jersey fishermen lived in wooden huts on the island half the year. In the Ecrehos group, Maître island was inhabited by a certain Lord Trent of Nottingham; Marmotière featured twelve huts inhabited by Jerseymen half the year (for fishing and holidays) as well as a custom house, a slipway, and a flagstaff maintained by the States of Jersey; and finally Blanc island was home to a large house owned by a Jersey national. Ibid. Thus, at the time of the case's submission to the court, the occupation and administration of the island appeared to have been primarily British.

Table 10.1 (*cont.*)

[4] The territory in dispute was an area along the Panama–Costa Rica border that had already been arbitrated by the then president of France, Émile Loubet, in 1900 (when Panama was still part of Colombia). Costa Rica contested what was known as the 'Loubet award' because it gave part of Costa Rica's territory to Panama, but the issue went no further until early 1909. At that point, the United States wanted title to be quieted along the border, as land-owning Americans in the contested region could not settle their own claims until the latent territorial disagreement between Panama and Costa Rica was decided. For an overview of the case see L. H. Woolsey, 'Boundary Disputes in Latin-America', (1931) 25 AJIL 324, 329. The Loubet award had awarded the disputed area to Panama – a result that Costa Rica contested – but Costa Rica had retained de facto control over it. Acknowledging this, and since Panama did not want to go back to arbitration, the United States indicated that it would treat the area as belonging to Costa Rica. Ibid. Eventually the United States pressured a reluctant Panama into going to arbitration; the arbitrator, Chief Justice White of the United States Supreme Court, found in favour of Costa Rica.

the trend we see provides some support, if only anecdotal, to our hypothesis that the parties desirous of adjudication are almost never those in occupation of the disputed territory.

Sometimes the classifications are difficult to make. For instance, in the convoluted Qatar/Bahrain dispute, identifying the 'occupier' was a complex task. Both states were in occupation of some of the contested territories: Bahrain occupied the Hawar islands and Qatar occupied Zubarah, a small region on the north-west coast of Qatar. Nonetheless, the Hawar islands appear to have been the main bone of contention, and there does not seem to have been much question as to, ultimately, which state would receive Zubarah. According to one commentator, 'since Bahrain was in possession of the territory, Qatar had little to lose by going to Court'.[10] For these reasons, the occupation of the Hawar islands appears to be the more relevant factor to examine when classifying which state occupied the territory at stake. And, indeed, although both parties came close to signing a special agreement,[11] Qatar unilaterally applied to institute proceedings

---

[10] Maurice Mendelson, 'The Curious Case of *Qatar* v. *Bahrain* in the International Court of Justice', (2001) BYBIL 183.

[11] Bahrain had signed a preliminary agreement (the 'Doha minutes') with Qatar in late 1990 that contained a clause whereby the parties could go to the ICJ if the dispute over the Hawar islands and Zubarah (among some other areas) was not resolved by May 1991.

before the ICJ under Article 36(1), while Bahrain fought tooth and nail to avoid the ICJ's jurisdiction. To Qatar's dismay, the ICJ, by twelve votes to five, awarded the Hawar islands to Bahrain.[12]

Classification difficulties aside, the above results suggest that we rarely see occupying states in favour of litigation. One explanation could be that occupying states always have (or think they have) the weaker legal case, although the results in the section below indicate that, if anything, occupying states tend to win more often than lose. Rather, the fact that occupying states rarely initiate or push for adjudication suggests that, even when they believe they have the stronger legal case, they still do not believe that it is in their interests to litigate.

Hypothesis 2: All else being equal, the occupying state should
be more likely to prevail in the adjudication

As explained above, we expect that occupying states would not ordinarily have a motivation to seek adjudication. In contrast, the state not in occupation of the disputed territory has less to lose from an adjudication; it may then be more tempted to try cases that are a long shot, or at least a longer shot than the occupying party would be willing to risk, all else being equal. This would create a selection bias, resulting in more disputes where the occupier had a strong legal case reaching adjudication.

There may also be an independent reason why the occupying state might be expected to win more, on average, than the non-occupier. Hypothetically, international tribunals could be tempted to rule in favour of the occupier. Considering the difficulties inherent in transferring sovereignty to one party when the land is controlled by the other, and the fact that the buy-in of the occupier is key to implementing the award, there may

---

Due to a difference in translation, the clause could be understood as allowing either a unilateral submission to the ICJ by one party or a submission if *both* parties so agreed. Bahrain made the former argument to contest Qatar's unilateral submission of the dispute to the ICJ, but to no avail: the ICJ found that it had jurisdiction over the case. It is believed that Bahrain, in signing the Doha minutes, did not think it could be brought to court on the sole initiative of Qatar. See Mendelson, above n. 100, 210.

[12] However, identifying a 'winner' in this case (for use in hypothesis 3) was also complicated by the fact that the award was not unambiguously in favour of one party over another. Technically, the award appears 'symmetric' – Bahrain got the Hawar islands and Qatar got Zubarah – such that deciding a winner injects an element of subjectivity that is not as present as in, say, the Preah Vihear temple dispute between Thailand and Cambodia (see note 188 below). However, it is generally understood that the award tipped in favour of Bahrain, as Qatar's arguments were generally given short shrift. See, e.g., Colter Paulson, 'Compliance with Final Judgments of the International Court of Justice since 1987', (2004) 98 AJIL 434, 454.

INITIATING TERRITORIAL ADJUDICATION   207

be some institutional pressure, at the margin, for the tribunal to find in favour of the occupier.

For instance, this dynamic may have been at play in the 1911 Walvis Bay arbitration between Great Britain and Germany. Germany had challenged Great Britain's possession of a strategic deep-water bay on what is now the Namibian coast. Over Germany's objections, Great Britain had been in possession of the Walvis Bay port since 1878.[13] Under the auspices of the King of Spain, a professor of international law at the University of Madrid was selected to arbitrate the dispute. He found in favour of Great Britain, the state in possession of the Walvis Bay port. The arbitral award stated:

> Considering that, as exception has not been taken to the continued posses-
> sion on the part of Great Britain of the [disputed] territory . . . it is necessary
> to accept the fact of possession, cited by the British Government, and to
> see in it not only a proof of the sense in which the [British] Proclamation
> of Annexation was always interpreted . . . but also the evidence of a wish
> to acquire, and of an effective occupation, by which in any case British
> sovereignty could have been established over the zone in dispute, before
> the adjacent territory was placed under the protection of Germany.[14]

The arbiter's language suggests that the fact of Great Britain's occupation played into his understanding of the legal rights at stake.

The empirical results are consistent with this hypothesis but cannot be said to constitute strong evidence in favour of it. Of the approximately thirteen cases where both a clear winner and occupier could be discerned, nine saw the occupier winning. Table 10.2 lists the thirteen cases broken down by whether the award favoured the occupier.

Hypothesis 3: All else being equal, the international tribunal should tend to rule in favour of the initiating party

We might also expect that the initiating party is more likely to win. The fact that it files a case shows that it expects to win, and it has greater familiarity with the strength of its case than anyone else.

As noted above, there are only nine cases featuring formal 'initiators' – quasi 'plaintiffs', so to speak. Of these nine, six have identifiable 'winners', two are still pending, and one (the Argentine–Chile 'Frontier Case' arbitration) lacked a clear winner.[15] In the universe of six cases with formal initiators and identifiable winners, four – namely *Cameroon* v. *Nigeria*,

---

[13] *The Walfish Bay Boundary Case (Germany/Great Britain)*, (1911) 11 RIAA 267.
[14] Ibid., 307–8.   [15] See scenario 4, discussed further below.

Table 10.2 *Cases where both a clear winner and occupier could be discerned*

Occupying state wins	Occupying state loses
Nicaragua v. *Honduras* (2007)	Cameroon v. *Nigeria* (2002)
Qatar/*Bahrain* (2001)	Egypt/*Israel* (1988)
Botswana/Namibia (1999)	Cambodia v. *Thailand* (1962)
United Kingdom/France (1953)	Denmark v. *Norway* (1933)
France/Siam (1947)	
Bolivia/*Paraguay* (1938)	
Peru/*Chile* (1925)	
Costa Rica/Panama (1914)	
Germany/*Great Britain* (1911)	

Note: The party in italics is the state in occupation. The date in parenthesis is the year the case was decided.

Cambodia v. *Thailand*, *Denmark* v. *Norway*, and the *Honduras–Nicaragua* arbitration of 1960 – feature the initiator winning the case.

The sample size of formal initiators and identifiable winners, at six, is too small to identify any kind of trend. So, as we did earlier, we used soft evidence to expand the set of 'initiators' to include those cases where there was a distinct asymmetry in the desire to go to adjudication. While a state may not technically be an initiator, we can identify in these cases a state that is more 'pro-litigation' while the other state is more reluctant to proceed to adjudication. The results suggest that where there is a more pro-litigation state, that state has a mildly higher probability of success. Of the thirteen cases where there was both a reasonably identifiable state pushing for litigation (versus a more reluctant state) *and* a reasonably identifiable winner, the initiator tended to win. In nine of these cases the pro-litigation state 'won' at the hands of the arbitral tribunal or the ICJ. In only four cases did the pro-litigation state end up losing (Table 10.3).

Hypothesis 4: Territorial disputes should be more likely to reach adjudication as a result of *ex ante* agreements

States know, when they agree to adjudicate, that one of them is destined to lose.[16] Given this rather obvious observation, why do both states do it? In particular, for any given decision resolving a territorial dispute, why

[16] Certainly, one can imagine Gordian knot-style cases where a disputed territory is, quite simply, divided equally between both parties. This may have occurred in the dispute over

INITIATING TERRITORIAL ADJUDICATION 209

Table 10.3 *Cases with identifiable initiator, broken down by winner*

Initiating state (or pro-litigation state) wins	Initiating state (or pro-litigation state) loses
Cameroon v. Nigeria (2002)	*Nicaragua* v. Honduras (2007)[1]
Indonesia/*Malaysia* (2002)	*Qatar*/Bahrain (2001)
Libya/*Chad* (1994)	France/*Siam* (1947)
Cambodia v. Thailand (1962)	*Peru*/Chile (1925)
Honduras v. Nicaragua (1958)	
United Kingdom/France (1953)	
Denmark v. Norway (1933)	
Saudi Arabia/*Yemen* (1931)	
Costa Rica/Panama (1914)	

Note: The party in italics is the state in favour of litigation. The date in parenthesis is the year the case was decided.

[1] This ICJ case concerned the question of sovereignty over overlapping maritime claims in the Caribbean Sea, which included several islands. Nicaragua unilaterally instituted proceedings in 1999 against Honduras; it is speculated that Nicaragua had filed this claim to mitigate the effects of a recent agreement between Honduras and Colombia that recognized Colombian sovereignty over islands that Nicaragua also claimed. (See below for more detail.) In the end, the ICJ set a maritime boundary roughly halfway between the two countries' claims, and Honduras received sovereignty over the handful of islands at stake. Honduras might, strictly speaking, have won the territorial part of the award, but it is not clear whether, on the whole, Honduras or Nicaragua came out 'ahead' – especially since Nicaragua's goal was to disrupt the treaty between Honduras and Colombia.

did the state with the weaker case agree to go to court? This question is meaningful; in international law, unless both states agree, there will not be any litigation. Several commonsensical explanations for how the losing party ends up in court are discussed in the next section; they help to pinpoint deficiencies in the initial basic assumptions.

But, even without altering our initial premises, an important answer can be given. It merely requires asking, at what point was consent to jurisdiction given? It need not have been given with the present territorial

the Agacher Strip, where the ICJ split the strip in half between Mali and Burkina Faso. This pattern is uncommon, however. See Gino Naldi, 'The Case Concerning the Frontier Dispute (Burkina Faso/Republic of Mali): *Uti Possidetis* in an African Perspective', (1987) 36 ICLQ 893.

dispute in mind, because it could have been the product of a general consent many years earlier. If consent was given before the dispute had even crystallized, then one cannot assume anything about the states' willingness to litigate this particular case.[17]

To answer this question, therefore, we might simply posit that territorial disputes will more often be brought through *ex ante* consent. Once a territorial dispute bubbles up, we expect that it would be very difficult to get the consent of both parties to submit the dispute to an international tribunal. As discussed above, a party must believe that it has a strong legal case – one that would lead to a situation that is better than the status quo – to agree to adjudication. However, when it comes to land, both sides cannot 'win' the territory: there is only one piece of land. Both sides know this.

Accordingly, the party with the weaker legal case should never agree to adjudicate, and thus – since the consent of both parties is required – a post-dispute agreement to go to arbitration or to submit the case to the ICJ should almost never occur. In particular, in cases where there is a party especially in favour of adjudication, the basis for jurisdiction should nearly always be an *ex ante* agreement. This is because the pro-litigation party has (or thinks it has) a better case, so its opponent would be foolish to sign a special agreement when it sees the other party so willing to go before a tribunal. This leaves us in a state of the world where adjudications of territorial disputes between states arise primarily out of optional clauses or pre-dispute treaties. In this world, arbitrations and special agreements to go to the ICJ are rare, as these agreements would typically be formed *after* a dispute arises, in a context where the parties better understand their chances of winning.[18]

---

[17] Although, technically, a state could breach its *ex ante* agreement and refuse to litigate, it is far more likely that such states will be pressured into adjudication than states that have made no such agreement.

[18] The ICJ case between Cambodia and Thailand regarding sovereignty over the eleventh-century temple of Preah Vihear presents a convenient example of *ex ante* consent. In the first half of the nineteenth century, the exact location of the border in relation to the temple became a subject of intense disagreement. In 1954, following the departure of the French from Cambodia, Thai forces occupied Preah Vihear to enforce Thailand's claim. Cambodia brought an application to the ICJ pursuant to the optional clause (Art. 36(2)) of the ICJ Statute. The ICJ subsequently rejected Thailand's preliminary objection to its jurisdiction. (Thailand claimed it had only recognized the general jurisdiction of the PCIJ, and that this recognition of jurisdiction had ended when the PCIJ dissolved). In 1962, in a 9–3 vote, the ICJ found that the temple was located in Cambodia. As Thailand's attempt to refuse the jurisdiction of the ICJ demonstrates, the party with the weaker legal case – here, Thailand –

INITIATING TERRITORIAL ADJUDICATION 211

But the data do not support this prediction. Of the eighteen cases handled by the ICJ or PCIJ, twelve were brought by special agreement[19] and only six due to a pre-existing agreement.[20] In one case (*Bahrain/Qatar*), there was disagreement over whether a special agreement existed and was adequate to ground jurisdiction; the ICJ decided in the affirmative. Furthermore, of the twenty-two arbitrations that occurred in the last century, only one (or arguably two) was arbitrated as a result of a pre-existing agreement,[21] while the remaining twenty/twenty-one resulted

did not actually wish to have the ICJ decide the case. Nevertheless, it eventually relented (although it has since reoccupied parts of the Temple, flouting an ICJ order to vacate the site). *Temple of Preah Vihear (Cambodia v. Thailand) (Merits)*, [1962] ICJ Rep. 6.

[19] *Frontier Dispute (Burkina Faso/Niger)*, ICJ, General List No. 149, 14 September 2010; *Sovereignty over Pedra Branca/Pulau Batu Puteh, Middle Rocks and South Ledge (Malaysia/Singapore)*, [2008] ICJ Rep. 12; *Frontier Dispute (Benin/Niger)*, [2005] ICJ Rep. 90; *Sovereignty over Pulau Ligitan and Pulau Sipadan (Indonesia/Malaysia)*, [2002] ICJ Rep. 625; *Kasikili/Sedudu Island (Botswana/Namibia)*, [1999] ICJ Rep. 1045; *Territorial Dispute (Libya/Chad)*, [1994] ICJ Rep. 6; *Land, Island, and Maritime Frontier Dispute (El Salvador/Honduras; Nicaragua intervening)*, [1992] ICJ Rep. 350 ('*Land, Island, and Maritime Frontier Dispute*'); *Frontier Dispute (Burkina Faso/Mali)*, [1986] ICJ Rep. 554; *Sovereignty over Certain Frontier Land (Belgium/Netherlands)*, [1959] ICJ Rep. 209; and *Minquiers and Ecrehos (France/United Kingdom)*, [1953] ICJ Rep. 47. In the case of *Arbitral Award Made by the King of Spain on 23 December 1906 (Honduras v. Nicaragua)*, [1960] ICJ Rep. 192, the parties had reached an ambiguously worded agreement to submit the dispute to the ICJ in 1957, which, to the extent that it qualifies as an agreement to go to the ICJ, is one that was made after the dispute arose. Shabtai Rosenne, *Interpretation, Revision, and Other Recourse from the International Judgments and Awards* (Leiden: Martinus Nijhoff Publishers, 2007), 147. Likewise, in the *Legal Status of the South-Eastern Territory of Greenland (Denmark v. Norway)*, [1933] PCIJ (Ser. A/B) No. 53, the parties agreed to submit their dispute to the PCIJ after it had arisen.

[20] *Certain Activities*, ICJ, General List No. 150, 18 November 2010; *Territorial and Maritime Dispute*, [2007] ICJ Rep. 832; *Caribbean Sea*, [2007] ICJ Rep. 659; *Land and Maritime Boundary*, [2002] ICJ Rep. 303; *Temple of Preah Vihear*, [1962] ICJ Rep. 6; *Qatar and Bahrain*, [2001] ICJ Rep. 40. Of these six cases, two were brought pursuant to Art. 36(1) ('treaties and conventions in force'), two were brought pursuant to Art. 36(2) (optional clause declarations, which is to say compulsory jurisdiction), and two were brought under both Art. 36(1) and 36(2).

[21] Namely the *Argentine–Chile Frontier Case*, (1966) 16 RIAA 109. The two countries had signed a General Treaty of Arbitration on 28 May 1902, stating that the UK government would serve as arbitrator if disputes arose. Decades later, Chile instituted proceedings in the *Frontier Case* under Art. 5 of the General Treaty. Arguably, the later *Beagle Channel* arbitration between Argentina and Chile, which was also rooted in the 1902 General Treaty of Arbitration, can also be seen as an '*ex ante*' arbitration. However, in that case, both Argentina and Chile had in July 1971 signed an Agreement to Arbitrate the Beagle Channel Controversy, which can be seen in and of itself as a sort of special agreement. This contrasts with the unilateral application of Chile for arbitration in the *Frontier Case* under Art. 5 of the 1902 General Treaty, which did not require the agreement of both states.

from a decision to go to arbitration that occurred after the dispute began. This means that of the forty territorial cases in the last century (listed in Annex 1), only seven or eight cases arose as a result of pre-existing agreements. In other words, the large majority of territorial adjudications were the result of *ex post* agreements to submit the dispute to an international tribunal.

This pattern of results suggests that common intuitions are not correct. A substantial majority of disputes are brought to court by both parties acting jointly – either through a special agreement at the ICJ or by agreement to go to arbitration. These data are puzzling: they clash with the above hypothesis that, in any state dyad, one state would be unwilling to take territorial disputes to adjudication, leaving only states with *ex ante* agreements to populate the dockets.

Of course, many states may not have the option of relying on the ICJ's optional clause, as its use depends on whether both parties to the dispute have signed it.[22] Likewise, many bordering states may not have signed treaties with each other providing for the ICJ or arbitration in case of disputes. Accordingly, it appears normal that there should be a limited number of *ex ante* cases. What is surprising is the fact that there are so many more *ex post* cases, where we would expect few. However, it is conceivable that the majority of *all* territorial disputes (including all those that never went to court) in fact failed to reach adjudication because one state feared losing in court, and that what we are witnessing are the exceptions, not the rule. In other words, what appears to be a large number of *ex post* cases is in fact an exception, because an untold number of conflicts never reached adjudication. Such an interpretation would sit better with our initial hypothesis that only those states that agreed on adjudicating conflicts prior to a dispute should be going to court.

Still, thirty-three *ex post* cases (out of forty) is not a small number. Simply put, these data are not consistent with a general unwillingness to take territorial disputes to adjudication, especially when the consent of both sides is necessary. The motivating question here, then, is *why* two countries would agree to go to the ICJ or arbitration after a dispute emerges. In the section below, we explore potential explanations for the pattern of *ex post* agreement that we see actually taking place.

---

[22] To date, sixty-seven countries have accepted the ICJ's jurisdiction as compulsory under Art. 36(2). See International Court of Justice, Declarations Recognizing the Jurisdiction of the Court as Compulsory, available at www.icj-cij.org/jurisdiction/?p1=5&p2=1&p3=3. Of the *ex post* cases, only one featured both parties having opted into the optional clause (namely *Caribbean Sea*, [2007] ICJ Rep. 659).

Revisiting the basic assumptions about why states adjudicate territorial disputes

Our discussion began with three assumptions; from these some basic predictions were made, and the predictions were tested against the relatively small number of cases in which territorial awards have been given. Although our hypotheses about the 'who' were at least anecdotally supported by our review of cases, the 'why' remains elusive. Our overarching premise – that states lacking *ex ante* agreements to go to adjudication should never end up in court – was upended by the fact that a significant majority of adjudicated cases are submitted to court through special agreements (or their arbitral analogue). Thus our basic premises must be flawed in some respect. As discussed below, it turns out – perhaps unsurprisingly – that our assumptions were not so much incorrect as insufficiently nuanced.

First, the uniqueness assumption goes too far and needs to be moderated. It all but categorically rejects the possibility that taking on a potential loss of territory (by agreeing to adjudication) is ever justified, except perhaps as a quid pro quo for gaining other territory. The second assumption – that litigation is a way to maximize territory – overlooks the different ways in which territorial gains and losses might be measured. And, with respect to our third assumption about avoidance of jurisdiction, we need to insert the possibility of asymmetric information and irrational or short-sighted actors.

In each of the three sub-sections below, we re-examine the three initial assumptions in the context of identifiable reasons for which states have chosen adjudication in the past. Each of these scenarios adds complexity to our overly simple 'zero-sum' model by analyoing diotinct motivations to go to adjudication. None of them is, independently, enough to explain the entire rationale of a state's decision to consent to adjudication; however, they break down distinct reasons that, in various combinations, may trigger a state to seek adjudication.

The uniqueness assumption

First, we consider the 'uniqueness assumption', which assigns unique value to every piece of territory. From this premise, it seemed a natural conclusion that outside certain unusual and probably anachronistic situations – a colonial power exchanging land with other colonial powers, or a state relinquishing land that another state took by war in conquest – states do not (when they have any choice in the matter) compromise, bargain away, or exchange pieces of land.[23] This is not merely because of economic or strategic value – as important as those might be – but also because of the value that a state's citizens are likely to attach to it. For some of the state's citizens, this particular place will be 'home'. For others, it may be a matter of national pride not to relinquish sovereignty. Relinquishing territory is never popular.

This creates an uncompromising attitude towards any sort of 'solution' to a territorial dispute such as adjudication. If pieces of land are too uniquely valuable to consider relinquishing, arguments that some other sort of benefit or advantage would justify submitting to third-party dispute resolution will be rejected. The parties will be stuck in a 'zero sum' mentality that hardly encourages compromise. Treating territory as unique means that it cannot be bartered for other sorts of value that the international order has to offer.

The wider the options for making deals, conversely, the better the chance at a win-win solution. The prospect that both states might come out ahead changes the calculation about whether to take a territorial dispute to arbitration or to court. This expectation would go far towards explaining why states take disputes to court while knowing that one will lose. It turns out that, in certain contexts, there is indeed scope for win-win solutions.

The motivations for litigating a particular territorial dispute therefore change when the possibility of exchange for other values is admitted. If it becomes an open possibility that loss or relinquishment of territory can be compensated by other sorts of assets, then these other assets will be factored into a state's decision about whether to file a case, or to go along with some other state's filing of a case. We shall examine three categories of benefit that might compensate for loss of territory: the benefit that a state gets from its own agreement to put an end to the conflict; the benefit that a state gets as compensation from the other disputing party; and the benefit that a state gets from third parties.

Scenario 1: the peace dividend

The peace dividend scenario rejects the characterization of the dispute as a zero-sum game by considering a particular kind of non-territorial

---

[23] Under current conditions, the most frequent reason for loss of territory seems now to be success by secessionist movements. On an interpretation of secessionism as being a disguised claim to territory, see generally Lea Brilmayer, 'Secession and Self-Determination: A Territorial Interpretation', (1991) 16 *Yale Journal of International Law* 177.

advantage that might be an adequate inducement to litigate. The inducement is the advantages (to both sides) of peaceful resolution of the dispute. The peace dividend can take many forms. For instance, lives and property will not be lost to military conflict. Trade and investment between the countries and from third-party states may increase in volume once the dangers of a violent conflict have passed. Border areas will be more secure and peaceful.

An example of the 'peace dividend' scenario is the conflict over the Taba strip at the border between Egypt and Israel. Egypt and Israel vehemently disputed the ownership of this 1 sq km piece of desert, which Israel had kept when it withdrew from the rest of the Sinai in 1982. Except for an upscale tourist beach resort along the Red Sea, Taba was largely valueless. Yet for some time it created an impasse in the normalization of relations between the two countries after the 1967 Six Day War.

Egypt demanded to have the dispute resolved by arbitration, which Israel – perhaps sensing that arbitration would not decide in its favour and facing significant popular resistance – was reluctant to accept.[24] However, Israel had a long-standing interest in making peace in the region, and the thaw with Egypt was the most significant progress it had made. The dispute over Taba threatened to derail the process of the normalization of Egyptian–Israeli relations.[25] The arbitral tribunal largely ruled in Egypt's favour, and the Taba strip returned to Egyptian control in 1989.

Scenario 2: side payments

In the 'peace dividend' scenario, each party receives a benefit from its own agreement to resolve the dispute through adjudication. There, the incentive to undertake the risk of adjudication comes largely from a state's own motivation to change its behaviour and seek peace. A similar scenario involves incentives that come from promises made by the other party to the dispute. Unlike the 'peace dividend', the 'side payments' scenario involves a quid pro quo, where something is given in exchange for another's assuming the risk of relinquishing a right to territory. By agreeing to adjudication, a state runs the risk of losing its claim to land;

---

[24] See, e.g., Dan Fisher, 'Taba's 2 Residents Divided: Israeli–Egyptian Quarrel Echoed at Disputed Beach', *Los Angeles Times*, 15 January 1986.

[25] Eventually consenting to arbitration, the Israeli government insisted that the two sides agree before the arbitration to free access rights to Taba (among other such rights) for the country that lost the arbitration. See ibid. Note that this is also an example of the 'side payments' scenario; as explained above, there may be many causal factors to a decision to adjudicate boundary disputes.

under this scenario, the decision to run that risk is justified by a non-territorial benefit that the other state provides.

The payment can in theory take any form; it would just be a matter of linking the territorial dispute to any other, possibly unrelated, issue that the payee values. Such arrangements can be hard to identify, as they may be the result of undisclosed diplomatic negotiations. The quid pro quo may never be made public. Evidence of exchange, however, is sometimes discernible. In the *Minquiers and Ecrehos* case between France and the United Kingdom, for example, a 'side payment' of sorts seems to have been made.

France and the United Kingdom had had a cordial but long-standing dispute over the tiny Minquiers and Ecrehos island groups in the English Channel, which had some worth due to valuable fisheries in the area. France only agreed to bring the case by special agreement to the ICJ on condition that the United Kingdom first sign an agreement that gave fisheries rights to both countries, regardless of outcome.

> [I]t eventually proved possible to agree on a reference of the sovereignty question by means of a Special Agreement, although the French Government made it a condition of such a step that the fishery question should also be simultaneously and definitively settled... By insisting upon the simultaneous conclusion of a Fishery Agreement along these lines, the French Government, who had always appeared to be more concerned with the fishery question than with the sovereignty question, had therefore substantially secured their position, even if the decision on sovereignty should go against them. This had the beneficent result that it was possible for both parties to argue the sovereignty question more purely on its merits.[26]

The Fishery Agreement granted equal rights to French and UK fishermen around the islands, except within small zones immediately off the islands that would be reserved to whomever was awarded sovereignty. By making this resource agreement a condition precedent to agreeing to the ICJ's jurisdiction, France secured its rights to the valuable fisheries, even though the ICJ ultimately found unanimously that sovereignty over the Minquiers and Ecrehos groups belonged to the United Kingdom. The United Kingdom's concession of these rights can be seen as a 'payment' to France for its participation. This example indicates that positive value (sufficient to drive a common preference for adjudication) can be supplied from a source extrinsic to the particular dispute.

---

[26] D. H. N. Johnson, 'The Minquiers and Ecrehos Case', (1954) 3 ICLQ 189, 206–7.

Another example of a state effectively trading a claim to land for a non-land benefit arose in the conflict between Siam (now Thailand) and France immediately after the Second World War. During the war, the Vichy government of France had been pressured to relinquish sovereignty over 20,000 square miles of Laotian and Cambodian territories to Siam. Following the end of the war, the French government pushed aggressively for Siam to return these territories. France allegedly threatened to veto Siam's application to the United Nations if the territories were not returned.[27] Confronted with this threat and the possibility of outright war, Siam agreed to cede the territories back to France under the condition that a conciliation commission arbitrate Siam's claims in the future.[28] In this sense, Siam appears to have ceded territory for non-territorial value.

Scenario 3: third-party involvement

The benefits that lure reluctant states to adjudication are sometimes supplied by third parties. Intervention by third-party governments has many times played a role in getting parties to the ICJ or arbitration. For instance, many of the cases in South America saw considerable involvement – some would say meddling – by the United States. In the *Costa Rica–Panama* arbitration of 1914, the United States pushed hard for the parties to go to arbitration because it wanted resolution of a latent territorial dispute in order to settle conflicting American claims to land in the region.[29] Panama, in particular, was reluctant to consent to arbitration, but eventually yielded to US pressure;[30] the United States was also the arbitrator in this case.

In a distinct variant of the 'international pressure' scenario, it appears that third-party considerations influenced Nicaragua to file a case at the ICJ against Honduras. Apparently, Nicaragua felt threatened by a treaty signed between Honduras and Colombia regarding maritime delimitations that recognized Colombian ownership of islands that Nicaragua contested.[31] Since Nicaragua could not interfere in a bilateral treaty, it

---

[27] S. H., 'Musical Chairs in Siam', (1949) 5 *World Today* 378, 383.
[28] 'Siam to Return Disputed Provinces to the French', *Indian Express*, 14 October 1946.
[29] L. H. Woolsey, 'Boundary Disputes in Latin-America', (1931) 25 AJIL 324, 329.
[30] Ibid.
[31] Martin Pratt, 'The Maritime Boundary Dispute between Honduras and Nicaragua in the Caribbean Sea', (2001) 9 *IBRU Boundary and Security Bulletin* 108, 109–10. See also Alexandra Hudson, 'UN Court Hears Nicaragua Honduras Border Row Case', Reuters, 5 March 2007; 'Nicaragua-Honduras Sea Border Set', *BBC News*, 8 October 2007.

instead resorted to contesting its border with Honduras in an attempt to undermine the effects of the Colombia–Honduras treaty.[32]

Foreign pressures may also create intangible reasons for states to select arbitration in the form of parties' interest in maintaining a good international image.[33] In the *Libya/Chad* conflict, for example, Colonel Mu'ammer Qaddafi, the then Libyan leader, is thought to have decided to proceed with the ICJ – and then mostly comply with its decision awarding the Aouzou Strip to Chad – due in part to such concerns.[34] In the 2002 *Malaysia/Singapore* case concerning sovereignty over Pulau Ligitan and Pulau Sipadan, islands in the Celebes Sea, Malaysia insisted on going to the ICJ rather than seeking any kind of regional dispute settlement. This was allegedly motivated by a Malaysian concern regarding vested interests of regional states, and the fact that it was involved in other territorial disputes with some of those states; showing a commitment to international law in this case would improve its prospects in the other cases.[35]

Litigation as a strategy for maximizing territory

The second of our initial assumptions was that states use adjudication to maximize their interests. Read in conjunction with the first premise, it means that states' objectives are all about maximizing territory. For the same reasons that we recognized a need to reformulate the 'territory is unique' premise, we need to revisit the 'states go to court to maximize their territory' premise. And, as with the first assumption, the second is not so much mistaken as lacking in nuance.

What needs refinement is the understanding of what 'winning' means. There are ways of defining 'winning' that allow both sides to win. Where the competing states have different ways of evaluating the territory that they are awarded, the game more nearly resembles a variable sum than a zero-sum game – even though a fixed amount of territory is at stake. There are several ways in which this can happen.

---

[32] Pratt, above n. 31.

[33] In other instances, however, international considerations can work *against* adjudication: for example, in *Qatar and Bahrain*, [2001] ICJ Rep. 40, Saudi Arabia exerted pressure to keep the dispute settlement process in the Middle East. Mendelson, above n. 100, 195.

[34] Paulson, above n. 12, 438–9.

[35] David Ong, 'Case between Indonesia and Malaysia Concerning Sovereignty over Pulau Ligitan and Pulau Sipadan', (1999) 14 *International Journal of Marine & Coastal Law* 399, 413.

Scenario 4: subjective value

It is easy to lose track of everything other than the conventional 'zero-sum' interpretation of litigation. There is a fixed amount of property, and whatever is given to one cannot be given to the other. But, as noted earlier, recognizing that the world of incentives includes more than just territory makes litigation potentially positive-sum. When non-territorial values are taken into account, a benefit to one side is not necessarily a loss of the same magnitude to the other.

Our point here goes one step further; it is that *even if the only thing of value that might change hands is territory*, the end result might still be positive-sum. The reason is that territory has subjective as well as objective value. The consequences of recognizing that value is subjective are illustrated by a classic example from a beginners' negotiations class. Two siblings are fighting over one orange. Their parent is asked to determine how to resolve the problem. After talking to the two parties, the parent finds out that the older sibling wants the rind from the orange to bake a cake, while the younger sibling wants to eat the inside of the orange. Thus, the orange can be split between its peel and its flesh in a way that satisfies both siblings' desires, rather than the suboptimal fifty-fifty division.

States may assign value differently because of their attachment to, or need for, different things. One state may value a piece of land for historical, symbolic, or similar reasons. Perhaps one state cares about, say, a particular historical monument on the territory, while the other state wants the territory for its water resources or effect on maritime zones. The 1966 Argentine–Chile *Frontier Case* arguably presents one such example. In that case, the British government, acting as arbitrator, found that 70 per cent of the disputed territory should be awarded to Argentina, whereas only 30 per cent would be attributed to Chile, the initiator of the case. However, despite this uneven partition, it remains unclear whether this result would be considered a win for Argentina or for Chile. According to a contemporaneous observer, 'Satisfaction was expressed by Argentina that seven-tenths of the disputed area had been awarded to them, but Chile was equally content that the valleys in which Chilean nationals had settled were allotted to the Chilean side of the frontier.'[36]

Another potential example might be suggested by the *Minquiers and Ecrehos* case discussed above, where France appeared more concerned

---

[36] J. A. Steers, 'The Queen's Award: Review', (1967) 133 *Geography Journal* 57.

about its fisheries rights whereas the United Kingdom wanted to ensure its sovereignty over the rocky islets. Although the ICJ awarded the islands to the United Kingdom, France had already obtained recognition of its fishing rights, more or less in exchange for agreeing to proceed to the ICJ.

These cases illustrate the possibility of subjective value making an otherwise zero-sum dispute into a positive-sum dispute. If one portion of a disputed territory carries with it the economic benefits associated with land (including maritime rights) while the remainder is valued for subjective reasons (e.g., historical reasons or because the region is home to some of a country's citizens), then a division that recognizes this difference in subjective valuation is win-win. Even knowing that it might not get everything that it felt entitled to, a state could overall decide that the odds of winning are high enough to justify adjudication.

Scenario 5: evaluating a 'win'

Another way in which an otherwise zero-sum dispute may have positive-sum attributes would be where the states value differently what is at stake in the dispute. One state may care more about the absolute amount of territory that it wins, while another might care more about the fact that it has won a higher percentage of what it claimed. Then, if the two states make different claims to territory, both of them might end up claiming victory – a 'win-win' result.

For example, as in the *Frontier Case*, assume that there is a piece of land 100 sq km in size. If state A is awarded 70 sq km then there will be 30 sq km left to be awarded to state B. The dispute appears to be zero-sum.

But what if states don't define their interests that way? They might instead define victory in terms of being awarded a high percentage of what they were claiming. So in the dispute that the two states are considering submitting to adjudication, state B has a choice. It might attempt to exaggerate what it claims, on the theory that doing this will maximize its overall amount of territory taken. Or it might frame its claims cautiously in order to minimize the loss to which it is potentially exposed. Without knowing how states evaluate different distributions – absolute amounts, percentage of amount claimed, percentage of currently occupied area that it will receive, and so on – it is not possible to state with confidence that a dispute is zero-sum.

It is simple enough to find cases where one of the parties made excessive claims over territory. For instance, in the *Siam/France* arbitration, Siam negotiators made extensive claims over more than a third of French

Indochina,[37] claims that were seen as being 'exorbitant' and 'difficult if not impossible' to justify.[38] However, it is difficult to determine, in cases of inflated demands, whether the extensive claim was made for strategic reasons (with expectations that the court would award less than what was demanded), or whether it was made in good faith, if ambitiously. In many cases, probably, there is a mixture of both – a mixture that the participants themselves may not be able to untangle, and certainly would not be willing to reveal.

Scenario 6: political cover

Some states may strategically choose to go to court to obtain domestic political cover for *losing* territory. A government may wish to cease a territorial conflict with a neighbour, but would not be able simply to concede the territory at stake without losing face in front of its constituents. Accordingly, a state might agree to adjudicate a case – knowing full well that they will lose – if they believe that this would mitigate or displace domestic displeasure at relinquishing territory. In this way, a court-sanctioned loss of territory might be more domestically palatable than an agreement to concede territory in the first instance.

Such a dynamic appeared to have been at work in the above-mentioned *Siam/France* case. According to contemporaneous news sources, Siam was aware that it would ultimately have to relinquish the contested Laotian and Cambodian territories it had obtained from Vichy France in 1941.[39] Allegedly to save face, the government had attempted to get the United Nations to arbitrate the case, 'largely because the Siamese government, knowing that their surrender to France [was] inevitable, wished to be "compelled" to yield rather than to seem to surrender'.[40] France would

---

[37] *Report of the French–Siamese Conciliation Commission, decision of 27 June 1947*, (1947) 28 RIAA 433, 439.

[38] Kobkua Suwannathat-Pian, 'Thai Wartime Leadership Reconsidered: Phibun and Pridi', (1996) 27 *Journal of Southeast Asian Studies* 166, 171. The French–Siamese Conciliation Commission found that Siam's bold claim exceeded the commission's competence and ruled largely in France's favour.

[39] George Weller, 'Asiatic "Balkans" Boiling in French, Siamese Dispute', *Youngstown Vindicator* (Youngstown, Ohio), 28 August 1946; 'Question of Siam–Indochina Border before UN Potentially Explosive', *Palm Beach Post*, 18 July 1946: 'Now Siamese leaders privately admit the United Nations almost certainly will return these territories to France, but they believe that if the decision is made by the United Nations and not in direct negotiation with France the Siamese government may escape political disaster.'

[40] Weller, above n. 39.

have none of it, however, and so Siam was forced to concede control over the territory in exchange for an agreement to arbitrate at a later point.

Avoidance of jurisdiction

The empirical data did not support our third assumption. This was that a state would resist the jurisdiction of any court or arbitral tribunal that it perceived to threaten its territorial interests. And in any given case, due to the (assumed) zero-sum nature of the dispute, one of the parties should recognize that only one of them could prevail in a territorial dispute. Since the jurisdictional rules of international courts require the consent of both parties, this tendency would limit the number of cases going to court. From this, we expected that the only way to get jurisdiction by mutual consent in practice would be to achieve agreement prior to the point at which the dispute had crystallized. Yet, when the cases were examined, we saw that for both arbitration and ICJ adjudication, most of the decided cases came by way of special agreement.

We have already seen several reasons for the observed pattern. States may value things other than territory, which may not be zero-sum and which may draw them into adjudication even though they risk losing the territorial claim. In addition, states may value different things about the territory they claim, so that while the division of territory is zero-sum, the value that the states assign to the territory may be variable-sum (and potentially positive). Again, the result is that states may be drawn into adjudication by a promise that both will come out ahead – even though the reward is a fixed parcel of land that must be divided between the two.

The final set of explanations arises out of the third premise. As with the first, the reason for the lack of consistency with decided cases is that the original statement of the basic principle is too rigid. What must be taken into account in describing the interplay between jurisdictional rules and the parties' incentives is the effect of imperfect information. When states base decisions on their perceptions about which side will win – relative to the real probabilities of particular outcomes – the chance of achieving consent between them is greatly enhanced.

Scenario 7: the eternal optimist

The first way in which this scenario can come about is that states may overestimate the likelihood that they will win. Although each knows that there is a fixed amount of territory to be divided, and that one or the other of them will come away disappointed, each expects that the disappointed party will be its opponent. While a bit paradoxical, the result is that while each knows that only one will gain the particular piece of territory, both assume that they will be better off if the case goes to litigation.

This might be labelled the 'eternal optimist' scenario. It is not difficult to find cases in which the parties seem to have made exactly these assumptions. One of these is the *Beagle Islands* arbitration between Argentina and Chile in 1977. The Beagle Channel is a narrow strait at the southernmost tip of South America that separates the main island of Tierra del Fuego from other, smaller islands. The sovereignty of the eastern part of the Beagle Channel was in dispute, namely regarding the three islands of Picton, Lennox, and Nueva. Together, these islands were only about a dozen square miles in surface area, but, triggering a 200-nautical mile exclusive economic zone, they brought to whoever owned them control over 30,000 square maritime miles reputed to be rich in halieutic and hydrocarbon resources.[41] The dispute caused friction between Argentina and Chile for over a century, and was marked by a number of failed arbitration attempts.[42]

The parties eventually agreed to submit the dispute to arbitration by the United Kingdom.[43] Much to Argentina's dismay, Chile was essentially awarded the entire territory it had claimed, namely the three islands in dispute. This award took Argentina by surprise. According to one Argentine diplomat familiar with the matter, 'the court's award stunned the government. Argentine diplomats expected that, at worst, the court would allow Argentina one island.'[44] Argentina tried to circumvent the award through bilateral discussions and then by stepping up its military presence in the Beagle Channel, but when this proved truitless, it simply declared the award null. Argentina had clearly thought that its chances of a positive outcome were high, which explains its acceptance of an *ex post* agreement; it was thereafter taken aback by the unfavourable outcome.

Scenario 8: kicking the can down the road

What makes scenario 7 plausible is that the states have incomplete information; if they knew the eventual outcome, this would most likely make

---

[41] Malcolm Shaw, 'The Beagle Channel Arbitration Award', (1978) 6 *International Relations* 415, 416.

[42] James Garrett, 'The Beagle Channel Dispute: Confrontation and Negotiation in the Southern Cone', (1985) 27 *Journal of Interamerican Studies & World Affairs* 81, 89.

[43] Note that while this case was being prepared for arbitration, Argentina and Chile signed a new treaty holding that future territorial cases would go to the ICJ.

[44] Garrett, above n. 42, 93.

an agreement to adjudicate very hard for one of them – the eventual loser – to accept. But ignorance of the future makes possible the agreement of both parties to go to court.

A similar scenario might be called 'kicking the can'. In this final scenario, two states with a boundary dispute sign a treaty in which they agree to resolve their differences together, with a last resort (or, perhaps, threat) of going to the ICJ or arbitration if negotiations fail. States may make such agreements, not believing – or, if the spectre of adjudication is far enough down the road, not caring – that they may fail to resolve their differences within the allotted time.[45] The dispute then proves more difficult to resolve than anticipated, and, over time, the deadline approaches. At this point, a state that committed itself via treaty to adjudication may feel that its hands are tied: it is more difficult and politically costly to turn down a proposal to adjudicate when a state had committed to do so in the past than in the first instance. In this manner, a state reluctant to submit a territorial dispute to a tribunal may still feel forced to adhere to its treaty obligations.

Several examples of this 'kicking the can' scenario present themselves. One of these is the above-mentioned *Qatar/Bahrain* dispute. In the run-up to litigation, Bahrain strongly objected to going to the ICJ. After a series of failed negotiations to sign a special agreement, the two states signed minutes at the 1990 meeting of the Gulf Co-operation Council in Doha providing that they would continue negotiations, but that if the dispute persisted beyond May 1991, the parties could go to the ICJ.

May 1991 came and went, and Qatar unilaterally instituted proceedings at the ICJ. Bahrain vigorously contested the ICJ's jurisdiction, contending principally that the envisaged special agreement had never been agreed to and that – based on a technicality relating to the English and Arabic versions of the minutes – *both* parties needed to consent to the ICJ's jurisdiction.[46] The ICJ found that it did have jurisdiction and, as described earlier, proceeded to decide the case on the merits. Bahrain clearly had no desire to go to the ICJ and might not have even realized that it was exposing itself to unilateral application when it signed the Doha minutes.[47] (If Bahrain simply did not understand the legal implications of signing

---

[45] States might even choose to include such a clause in order to stimulate the parties to an agreement so as to foreclose a potentially riskier outcome. There may be benefits to signing a treaty with a last-resort adjudication clause in the present, and the risk of ending up in adjudication may be (or seem) low at the time, such that states that would not normally agree to adjudicate the dispute may still sign such a treaty.

[46] Mendelson, above n. 10, 19?   [47] Ibid., 210–11.

the minutes, this could reveal yet another distinct explanation for why states go to adjudication over territorial disputes: sheer mistake.)

The violent conflict between Libya and Chad in the 1970s–90s may yield another example of the 'kicking the can' scenario. The Aouzou Strip, a slice of land at the border between Libya and Chad, was believed by both countries to contain valuable uranium deposits. At the direction of Colonel Qaddafi, Syria took over parts of the strip in 1973. As of the late 1980s, Libya had taken quite a severe beating at the hands of Chadian forces, such that Qaddafi reached out to negotiate a peace settlement. A key part of the resulting 1990 agreement was the decision to submit the dispute to the ICJ if the parties could not resolve the conflict within a year.[48] In the face of international pressure to proceed to the ICJ, and also allegedly sure of his legal claim,[49] Qaddafi allowed the case to proceed before the ICJ – which awarded the entire Aouzou Strip to Chad. Here, too, Libya appears to have got 'stuck' in a commitment to go to the ICJ, even though it was not keen to do so.

In the above two examples, Bahrain and Libya did not 'kick the can' very far down the road: both ended up compelled to go to court within a year. Some states push the last resort of litigation further out. For instance, Honduras and El Salvador ended up at the ICJ as the result of an earlier mutual agreement whereby a Joint Frontier Commission would have five years to resolve the conflict before it would be submitted to the ICJ.[50]

Conclusion

One of the reasons for asking what induces states to litigate territorial claims – as opposed to states fighting them out or letting them stagnate – is simply to learn how best to encourage them to do so. The international community at large has a strong interest in the peaceful resolution of disputes, and one of the chief causes of violent conflict is territorial disputes. We would all benefit if it were somehow possible to ensure that territorial disputes could be resolved through legal processes, rather than conflict.

---

[48] Paulson, above n. 12, 440. A month after the agreement, a coup deposed the leader of Chad and brought into power a man much more to Colonel Qaddafi's liking. It is said that Qaddafi believed that, as a result, the dispute would no longer proceed to the ICJ but rather come to an end through bilateral talks; Qaddafi was allegedly surprised when Chad continued to press its claim before the ICJ.

[49] Ibid.   [50] *Land, Island, and Maritime Frontier Dispute*, [1992] ICJ Rep. 350.

In international law, the chief impediment to adjudication is the need to obtain both states' consent. Consent can be difficult to achieve because states appreciate full well that there will be losers as well as winners and that losing a territorial case is a serious matter. There is no real consolation for having to relinquish territory. These are the sentiments that we have tried to identify in the discussion of our fundamental assumptions. The uniqueness assumption maintains that states will not generally be willing or able to justify the loss of territory because some other, non-territorial value was promoted by the decision to litigate. The assumption that a state's goal in litigation is to maximize its share of the disputed territory leads to a conflictual definition of state interests, because what one state gains, another loses. And, according to our final assumption, the impact of these observations on jurisdiction is that once the dispute arises, states' willingness to agree to adjudicate will be limited. The one with the weaker case should have no interest in submitting to jurisdiction, and therefore would only be vulnerable to suit if it has agreed to jurisdiction generally, prior to the dispute's crystallization.

After observing that a century's worth of territorial disputes do not really seem to bear out these predictions, we returned to our premises to re-examine the source of this divergence. This reassessment presented a somewhat more optimistic view of the utility of international territorial litigation. First, states do take into account other values besides territory alone; they can be induced to litigate by the hope of achieving more peaceful relations with their neighbours and greater esteem in the eyes of the world community. Second, even those states that value territory above other objectives may still be induced to litigate by a 'win-win' expectation. While territory is zero-sum in the sense that litigation is an 'either/or' matter – either State A gets the territory or State B does – the differences in valuation may still be sufficient to make some distributions positive-sum. However, we noticed in particular that states in occupation of territory typically end up winning in court, but that they tend to be most reluctant to adjudicate in the first place. Persuading states in occupation of contested territory to proceed to adjudication would likely enhance the number of territorial adjudications. And since states tend to proceed to adjudication largely as a result of *ex post* agreements – often as a result of international pressure and/or last-resort clauses – there is significant scope for third-party encouragement of this form of dispute resolution, even when a dispute has already crystallized.

Finally, differences in attitude or in access to information can make states more willing to take a chance with litigation. They may both be more optimistic in their assessment of winning than the legal merits warrant; they may also be using agreement to jurisdiction as an (unsuccessful) effort at delay. This third category of reasons to litigate is problematic in comparison to the first two, because at the end of the case, the disappointed litigant may refuse to co-operate. This is not so much of a problem with the first two categories (receiving non-land benefits from litigation and 'win-win' situations), because the positive-sum aspects of the dispute can survive the rendering of an unfavourable award.[51] That said, states that have made a public commitment to go to court more likely feel pressure to follow through with their pronouncement, relative to states that have made no such commitment.

The good news is that there are ways to increase the appeal of litigation. Judges or arbitrators can actively search for win-win solutions and might even consider making it clear that they have done so. The bad news, however, is that this approach to the judging function runs up against the principle that cases should be decided on the legal and factual merits. But that is a very big question, which must be reserved for another day.

---

[51] Note that this assumes that the judges or arbitrators will actually identify and implement the positive-sum aspects of the dispute. They might fail to understand which features of the dispute matter more to the different parties – or they might not care – and the result would be negative-sum or still zero-sum.

228 LEA BRILMAYER AND ADELE FAURE

Annex 1 *Territorial cases in the last century*

Parties	Case name	Date of decision
Costa Rica v. Nicaragua	*Certain Activities carried out by Nicaragua in the Border Area*	pending
Burkina Faso/Niger	*Frontier Dispute*	2013
Nicaragua v. Colombia	*Territorial and Maritime Dispute*	2012
Government of Sudan–Sudan People's Liberation Movement/Army	*Abyei Arbitration*	2009
Malaysia/Singapore	*Sovereignty over Pedra Branca/Pulau Batu Puteh, Middle Rocks and South Ledge (Malaysia/Singapore)*	2008
Nicaragua v. Honduras	*Case Concerning Territorial and Maritime Dispute between Nicaragua and Honduras in the Caribbean Sea (Nicaragua v. Honduras)*	2007
Benin/Niger	*Frontier Dispute (Benin/Niger)*	2005
Cameroon v. Nigeria	*Land and Maritime Boundary between Cameroon and Nigeria (Cameroon v. Nigeria: Equatorial Guinea intervening)*	2002
Indonesia/Malaysia	*Sovereignty over Pulau Ligitan and Pulau Sipadan (Indonesia/Malaysia),*	2002
Eritrea–Ethiopia	*Delimitation and demarcation of their common border*	2002
Qatar/Bahrain	*Maritime Delimitation and Territorial Questions between Qatar and Bahrain*	2001
Botswana/Namibia	*Kasikili/Sedudu Island (Botswana/Namibia)*	1999
Eritrea–Yemen	*Territorial Sovereignty and Scope of Dispute (Hanish Islands)*	1998
Libya/Chad	*Territorial Dispute (Libyan Arab Jamahiriya/Chad)*	1994
Argentina–Chile	*'Laguna del Desierto' case*	1994
El Salvador/Honduras	*Land, Island and Maritime Frontier Dispute (El Salvador/Honduras: Nicaragua intervening)*	1992
Egypt–Israel	*Location of boundary markers in Taba*	1988

Annex 1 (*cont.*)

Parties	Case name	Date of decision
Burkina Faso/Mali	*Frontier Dispute (Burkina Faso/ Republic of Mali)*	1986
Argentina–Chile	*Beagle Channel*	1977
India–Pakistan	*The Indo-Pakistan Western Boundary (Rann of Kutch)*	1968
Argentina–Chile	*Frontier Case*	1966
Cambodia v. Thailand	*Case concerning the Temple of Preah Vihear (Cambodia* v. *Thailand), Merits*	1962
Belgium/Netherlands	*Case concerning Sovereignty over certain Frontier Land (Belgium/Netherlands)*	1959
Honduras v. Nicaragua	*Arbitral Award Made by the King of Spain on 23 December 1906 (Honduras* v. *Nicaragua)*	1960
France/UK	*The Minquiers and Ecrehos case (France/United Kingdom)*	1953
India–Pakistan	*Boundary disputes relating to Interpretation of the report of the Bengal Boundary Commission (Radcliffe Award)*	1950
Siam–France	*Report of the French–Siamese Conciliation Commission*	1947
Ecuador–Peru	*Zamora–Santiago sector (Maranon Basin) of their common boundary*	1945
Romania–Hungary	*Territory ceded by Romania to Hungary*	1940
Bolivia–Paraguay	*Chaco case – boundary delimitation*	1938
Czechoslovakia–Hungary	*Establishing their common boundary*	1938
Guatemala–Honduras	*Honduras borders*	1933
Denmark v. Norway	*Legal Status of Eastern Greenland*	1933
Saudi Arabia–Yemen	*Aaroo Mountain*	1931
United States–Netherlands	*Island of Palmas*	1928
Peru–Chile	*Tacna–Arica border case*	1925
Colombia–Venezuela	*Border case – common border fixed by arbitral award of the Crown of Spain of 16 March, 1891*	1922
Portugal–Netherlands	*Case of Timor Island enclaves*	1914
Costa Rica–Panama	*Over Loubet Award* (1900 arbitration)	1914
Germany–United Kingdom	*The Walfish Bay Boundary Case*	1911

11

Why litigate a maritime boundary?
Some contributing factors

COALTER G. LATHROP

All coastal states have a maritime boundary relationship with at least one neighbouring state. These relationships often involve overlapping claims to the same ocean area, necessitating a maritime boundary to separate the area of one coastal state from that of another. To date, fewer than 200 of the approximately 430 potential maritime boundaries worldwide have been delimited (and some only partially),[1] leaving well over 200 latent or active maritime boundary disputes still to be resolved.[2] Of those disputes that have been resolved, the vast majority have been resolved by negotiation. However, a significant minority of these disputes have been resolved by litigation.[3] So far, litigation has accounted for the settlement of twenty-one disputed maritime boundaries, with three additional cases pending at the time of writing.[4]

---

[1] Victor Prescott and Clive Schofield, *The Maritime Political Boundaries of the World*, 2nd edn (Leiden: Martinus Nijhoff, 2005), 218: 'Of these 427 potential maritime boundaries, only about 168 (39 per cent) have been formally agreed, and many of these only partially'.

[2] Tallies of delimited and potential maritime boundaries vary with time and methodology. Regardless of methodology, it is safe to say that over half of the maritime boundaries in the world are not yet agreed.

[3] Here, the term 'litigation' includes both adjudication and arbitration. Political scientists working in the field of international dispute settlement often take the approach of 'treating the two [arbitration and adjudication] as functionally similar'. Todd L. Allee and Paul K. Huth, 'Legitimizing Dispute Settlement: International Legal Rulings as Domestic Political Cover', (2006) 100(2) *American Political Science Review* 219, 220.

[4] The twenty-one cases, counting both *North Sea* cases, in which an international maritime boundary dispute was addressed if not completely resolved, are as follows: *North Sea Continental Shelf (Federal Republic of Germany/Denmark; Federal Republic of Germany/Netherlands) (Judgment)*, [1969] ICJ Rep. 3 (*North Sea*); *Beagle Channel (Argentina/Chile) (Award)*, [1977] 21 RIAA 57; *Continental Shelf (United Kingdom/France) (Award)*, [1977] 18 RIAA 3; *Dubai–Sharjah Border (Dubai/Sharjah) (Award)*, [1981] repr. in (1993) 91 ILR 543; *Continental Shelf (Tunisia/Libyan Arab Jamahiriya) (Merits)*, [1982] ICJ Rep. 18; *Delimitation of the Maritime Boundary in the Gulf of Maine Area (Canada/United States) (Judgment)*, [1984] ICJ Rep. 246; *Continental Shelf (Libyan Arab Jamahiriya/Malta) (Merits)*, [1985] ICJ Rep. 13; *Délimitation de la frontière maritime entre la Guinée et la Guinée-Bissau (Guinée/Guinée-Bissau)*, [1985] 19 RIAA 149 (unofficial English translation

Maritime boundary disputes, like territorial sovereignty or land boundary disputes, implicate core sovereignty concerns.[5] This may account for the relatively few instances in which states have delegated decision-making authority to a third party. Much of the literature that is most relevant to maritime boundary dispute resolution involves studies of the more robust and longer-standing practice in the field of land boundary dispute resolution.[6] Although similar in nature, the two categories of dispute and their subject matter are not identical. Maritime boundary relationships tend to be younger than land boundary relationships because the regime that created these relationships is derivative of and subsequent

---

available in 25 ILM 252 [1986]); *Délimitation de la frontière maritime entre la Guinée-Bissau et le Sénégal (Guinée-Bissau/Sénégal) (Award)*, [1989] 20 RIAA 121 (unofficial English translation available as Annex to Application of Guinea-Bissau instituting proceedings before the ICJ, available at www.icj-cij.org/docket/files/82/11289.pdf) (*Guinée-Bissau v. Sénégal*); *Délimitation des Espaces Maritimes entre le Canada et la République Française (Canada/France) (Award)*, [1992] 21 RIAA 267 (unofficial English translation available [1992] 31 ILM 1149); *Maritime Delimitation in the Area between Greenland and Jan Mayen (Denmark v. Norway) (Judgment)*, [1993] ICJ Rep. 38 (*Jan Mayen*); *Maritime Delimitation (Eritrea/Yemen) (Second Phase)*, [1999] 22 RIAA 335; *Maritime Delimitation and Territorial Questions between Qatar and Bahrain (Qatar v. Bahrain) (Merits)*, [2001] ICJ Rep. 40; *Land and Maritime Boundary between Cameroon and Nigeria (Cameroon v. Nigeria: Equatorial Guinea intervening) (Merits)*, [2002] ICJ Rep. 303; *Barbados v. Trinidad and Tobago (Award)*, [2006] 27 RIAA 147; *Guyana v. Suriname (Award)*, UNCLOS Arbitral Tribunal, 17 September 2007; (2008) 47 ILM 164, available at www.pca-cpa.org/upload/files/Guyana-Suriname%20Award.pdf; *Territorial and Maritime Dispute between Nicaragua and Honduras in the Caribbean Sea (Nicaragua v. Honduras) (Judgment)*, [2007] ICJ Rep. 659; *Maritime Delimitation in the Black Sea (Romania v. Ukraine) (Judgment)*, [2009] ICJ Rep. 61 (*Black Sea*); *Delimitation of the Maritime Boundary between Bangladesh and Myanmar in the Bay of Bengal (Bangladesh/Myanmar) (Judgment)*, ITLOS, Case No. 16, 14 March 2012, available at www.itlos.org/fileadmin/itlos/documents/cases/case_no_16/1 C16_Judgment_14_02_2012.pdf; *Territorial and Maritime Dispute (Nicaragua v. Colombia) (Judgment)*, ICJ, General List No. 124, 19 November 2012.

The three pending cases, in order of initiation date, are: 'Application Instituting Proceedings', *Maritime Dispute (Peru v. Chile)*, ICJ, General List No. 137, 16 January 2008; *Bangladesh v. India*, UNCLOS Arbitral Tribunal, 8 October 2009 (*Bangladesh v. India*); *Arbitration between Croatia and Slovenia (Croatia v. Slovenia)*, PCA, 13 April 2012.

[5] 'The sea boundary question . . . lies at the very heart of sovereignty', wrote Gamble in 1976 about plans at that point in the negotiations of UNCLOS to limit the applicability of the dispute settlement provisions in specific situations. John King Gamble, Jr, 'The Law of the Sea Conference: Dispute Settlement in Perspective', (1976) 9 *Vanderbilt Journal of Transnational Law* 323, 331. Indeed, maritime boundary disputes are one of a few categories of dispute for which states may declare that they do not accept the compulsory procedures entailing binding decisions as provided in Part XV, Section 2. See United Nations Convention on Law of the Sea (opened for signature 10 December 1982, entered into force 16 November 1994), 1833 UNTS 3 (UNCLOS), Art. 298(1)(a).

[6] See further Chapter 10 in this volume.

to the much older territorial sovereignty regime. Exclusive coastal state sovereign rights and jurisdiction in areas beyond a narrow territorial sea is a twentieth-century invention that is still coming into full effect as coastal states continue to claim sovereign rights and jurisdiction in larger areas of the ocean, including the seabed and subsoil of the continental shelf as permitted under the current law of the sea.[7] Being young, many of these maritime boundary relationships have not had the opportunity to mature, setting the law and practice of maritime boundary dispute resolution in an early to mid-life developmental stage. From this vantage point, we can assess past practice while watching the development of the dispute resolution process as it continues to unfold.

Contributing to the relative youth of these disputes has been the only recent interest in and ability to exploit valuable hydrocarbon resources on the continental shelf, the land-based version of which has been accessible for centuries. These strategic offshore resources have been at the centre, and often acted as the trigger point, in most of the maritime boundary disputes that have reached litigation.[8]

Other differences between territorial and maritime disputes include the modes of acquisition of title, the sources and rules of law defining rights and obligations in maritime areas, and the procedural and substantive rules which drive the resolution of disputes concerning maritime areas. The differences between the law of territorial acquisition and the acquisition of maritime rights and the manner in which they are secured may impact the costs associated with the non-resolution of maritime boundary disputes. Brilmayer and Klein have argued that, unlike land, which has direct consumption value, is susceptible to occupation, and for which effective occupation may create title, maritime resources, unless they are consumed directly by the coastal state, require marketable title in order to be valuable.[9] Marketable title is created by operation of law, specifically through the application of the rules of maritime delimitation in negotiation or litigation. Until such resolution, the resources in disputed maritime areas may be of little or no value to the coastal states concerned.

---

[7] See, e.g., the ongoing process of making submissions to the Commission on the Limits of the Continental Shelf pursuant to UNCLOS, Art. 76 and Annex II.

[8] Some exceptions include *Jan Mayen*, in which fisheries resources were the main issue, and *El Salvador/Honduras*, in which the land boundary and island sovereignty issues were the primary considerations.

[9] Lea Brilmayer and Natalie Klein, 'Land and Sea: Two Sovereignty Regimes in Search of a Common Denominator', (2000–1) 33 *NYU Journal of International Law and Policy* 703, 732–4.

Various approaches have been taken to resolve maritime boundary disputes under vastly different sets of circumstances. Nonetheless, these disputes share several general characteristics. As with most disputes that arise on the international plane, parties to the negotiation or litigation of a maritime delimitation dispute face a co-ordination problem in which neither party may unilaterally compel negotiation or litigation. This is a function of a consent-based legal system. Those parties also face a co-operation or distribution problem in the division of overlapping claims to maritime area, which is often perceived as a zero-sum game. Moreover, like other international disputes over high-saliency subject matter, maritime boundary dispute resolution plays out at two levels: at the international level, where the disputant states interact, and at the national level, where domestic constituencies exert influence over the decision makers who represent the state on the international plane.[10]

The main questions addressed in this chapter are why and under what circumstances – given the alternatives of negotiation and non-resolution – do states choose to resolve their maritime boundary disputes through litigation? This chapter begins by setting out the maritime disputes in which one or both states have decided to litigate. The introduction to the cases is followed by some thoughts on the relationship between the two modes of dispute resolution addressed herein – negotiation and litigation. The answers to the questions raised above will be influenced first and foremost by the jurisdictional context in which the parties find themselves. Specifically, does an international court or tribunal enjoy adjudicative jurisdiction over the parties with respect to the dispute, and, if so, how was this jurisdiction created? A lack of jurisdiction must be considered one of the constraints, if not the primary constraint, on the decision to litigate in the international legal system. Jurisdiction on the basis of ad hoc and *ante hoc* consent is briefly discussed in the context of maritime delimitation. If litigation is an option, many contributing factors could bear on the litigation decision-making process. The literature is then reviewed to expose several of the important factors. It is posited that, together, these factors contribute to a state's assessment of the costs of non-resolution, negotiated resolution, and litigated resolution. On the basis of this assessment of perceived costs states will pursue the lowest-cost option. However, because litigation is a bilateral process requiring the consent of both parties, the lowest-cost option for one

---

[10] Robert D. Putnam, 'Diplomacy and Domestic Politics: The Logic of Two-Level Games', (1988) 42 *International Organization* 427.

234 COALTER G. LATHROP

state may be blocked by the non-consent of the other. This brings the jurisdictional bases back into the analysis and allows a distinction to be made between the important contributing factors in the presence of ad hoc and *ante hoc* consent. This chapter finishes with some brief concluding remarks.

The cases

Maritime boundary cases are frequently found on the dockets of international courts and tribunals. Writing in the early 1990s, Charney stated that 'there has been more litigation before the International Court of Justice (ICJ) on maritime boundaries than any other single subject'.[11] That trend has continued, with many more maritime boundary cases arriving on the Court's docket in the subsequent decades. The ICJ has been presented with sixteen cases involving a disputed maritime boundary since the two inaugural *North Sea* cases, including the maritime boundary case currently pending before the Court between Peru and Chile.[12] The International Tribunal for the Law of the Sea (ITLOS) has now ruled on its first maritime boundary dispute in the litigation between Bangladesh and Myanmar. Eight ad hoc tribunals have been formed to consider maritime boundary disputes.[13] By definition, the adjudicative jurisdiction in these cases arose from ad hoc consent embodied in a *compromis* or arbitration agreement. The arbitration between Croatia and Slovenia is the most recent example in this category. Finally, four arbitration tribunals have

[11] Jonathan I. Charney, 'Introduction', in Jonathan I. Charney and Lewis M. Alexander (eds.), *International Maritime Boundaries* (Dordrecht: Martinus Nijhoff, 1993), Vol. I, xxiii, xxvii.

[12] The ICJ reached a judgment with respect to the disputed maritime boundary in thirteen of the sixteen cases; see above n. 4 for those thirteen cases. In the case between Greece and Turkey, the ICJ found that it did not have jurisdiction to entertain the Greek application; see *Aegean Sea Continental Shelf (Greece v. Turkey) (Jurisdiction)*, [1978] ICJ Rep. 3 (*Aegean Sea*). In the case between El Salvador and Honduras, El Salvador asked the ICJ to delimit a maritime boundary in the Gulf of Fonseca. The Court declined to do so; see *Land, Island and Maritime Frontier Dispute (El Salvador/Honduras: Nicaragua intervening) (Merits)*, [1992] ICJ Rep. 351. In the case between Guinea-Bissau and Senegal, the ICJ did not reach a judgment on the merits; see *Maritime Delimitation between Guinea-Bissau and Senegal (Guinea-Bissau v. Senegal)*, discontinued by Order of the Court, 8 November 1995. Nonetheless, these three cases are important here for what they tell us about the decision making that led to the filing of the case. The delimitation outcome is not relevant to this analysis.

[13] See above n. 4 for the eight ad hoc arbitrations, including the arbitration pending between Croatia and Slovenia.

been formed pursuant to the United Nations Convention on the Law of the Sea (UNCLOS) Annex VII to hear maritime boundary disputes.[14] In this category, *Land Reclamation* did not reach judgment on the merits, and *Bangladesh* v. *India* is ongoing.

The total number of maritime boundary litigations that have been initiated, if not concluded, is twenty-eight.[15] With the exception of trade and investment disputes, disputed maritime boundaries are one of the most litigated subjects in the field of public international law, rivalling land boundary disputes and disputes concerning state responsibility. Nonetheless, in absolute terms, there have been relatively few maritime boundary litigations. The number pales in comparison to maritime boundary disputes resolved by negotiation, and the cases provide only a small sample size consisting of units with widely divergent facts and circumstances. To the extent that these disparate cases can be usefully compared and contrasted in order to discern important considerations in the decision to litigate, it seems that the forum is a less important factor than the jurisdictional posture of each case, specifically whether jurisdiction was based on the ad hoc or *ante hoc* consent of the parties.

When the twenty-eight maritime delimitation cases are ordered chronologically, with forum and the jurisdictional basis in mind, two interesting trends are revealed. The first is the trend towards decentralization of the international judiciary. Although the ICJ shared the caseload with ad hoc tribunals nearly from the start, the new UNCLOS institutions – ITLOS and Annex VII arbitration tribunals – are now also available and are being utilized by states to resolve their maritime boundary disputes. This trend towards a multi-forum dispute settlement system will come as no surprise to international legal scholars, especially those concerned with the proliferation of dispute settlement bodies and the potential for fragmentation within the international legal system.

The second trend is more stark. The word 'trend' does not capture the abrupt shift in the late 1980s away from litigation on the basis of

---

[14] See above n. 4 for citations to three of the cases that have been instituted pursuant to UNCLOS Part XV and Annex VII. The case between Malaysia and Singapore, in which Malaysia complained of the impact of land reclamation projects on, *inter alia*, the undelimited boundary in the Johor Strait, was terminated before the tribunal reached a decision on the merits; see *Land Reclamation by Singapore in and around the Straits of Johor (Malaysia* v. *Singapore)*, [2003] ITLOS Rep. 10; [2005] 27 RIAA 133 (*Land Reclamation*).

[15] Recalling that what is important in this study is the pre-litigation decision-making process of one or both states, this count includes those maritime boundary cases that did not end in a judgment on the merits and may not have proceeded past a jurisdictional challenge.

ad hoc consent and towards litigation on the basis of *ante hoc* consent. During the two decades between the 1967 start of the *North Sea* cases to the 1986 start of *El Salvador/Honduras*, fourteen maritime boundary cases were initiated, thirteen of them on the basis of ad hoc consent. The one exception, *Aegean Sea*, initiated by Greece in 1976, did not proceed on the merits for lack of jurisdiction. In contrast, in the two and a half decades since 1986, only two of the fifteen maritime boundary cases have been brought on the basis of ad hoc consent, *Eritrea/Yemen* and *Croatia/Slovenia*. The remaining thirteen were brought on the basis of *ante hoc* consent of the parties.[16] For the first twenty years of modern maritime delimitation, 93 per cent of maritime delimitation cases were brought on the basis of ad hoc consent. Since 1986, only13 per cent of these cases have been brought on that basis.

Part of this shift may be explained by the 1994 entry into force of UNCLOS, with its compulsory dispute settlement procedures.[17] Five of the post-1986 cases based jurisdiction in the *ante hoc* consent created upon becoming party to UNCLOS, but more traditional bases of jurisdiction were used in eight of these cases, including declarations made under Article 36(2) of the Statute of the ICJ and compromissory clauses in bilateral and multilateral treaties. The shift away from ad hoc consent may also be a function of increasingly clear approaches that will be applied in maritime boundary litigations. Specifically, courts and tribunals have set out a three-step methodology for reaching an equitable delimitation. With clarity and certainty states may better predict an outcome and compare that likely outcome to the status quo. Perhaps this shift away from a reliance on ad hoc consent is an early sign of what Kingsbury calls 'a new paradigm of routinised litigation and judicial governance' in inter-state dispute settlement.[18] Perhaps it indicates a growing confidence among potential litigants in the ability of the international judiciary to

---

[16] This analysis may overemphasize the superficial or formal aspects of jurisdiction in these cases and underplay the possibility of 'tacit ad hoc consent' that may be masked by form, but it is undeniable that the practice of active consent building through the negotiation and agreement of a *compromis* to structure and to bring a case has fallen off significantly in the past twenty-five years.

[17] It should be noted that, pursuant to Art. 298, maritime boundary disputes may be excluded from compulsory procedures entailing binding decisions. Approximately twenty-five of the 164 states parties to UNCLOS have elected to exclude these disputes.

[18] Kingsbury sees this new paradigm emerging in international human rights, trade, and criminal tribunals, but contrasts it with 'the traditional paradigm of episodic international (inter-state) dispute settlement by tribunals'. Benedict Kingsbury, 'International Courts: Uneven Judicialisation in Global Order', in James Crawford and Martti Koskenniemi

render clear, predictable decisions in maritime delimitation cases, with which respondent states are likely to comply even in the absence of ad hoc, contemporaneous consent.

The relationship between negotiation and litigation

While some maritime boundary disputes have been settled through litigation, most of them have been settled through negotiation. Many resolutions have involved both litigation and negotiation. No single pattern emerges in the relationship between negotiation and litigation considered in the light of these cases. However, several general observations may be made. First, negotiation and litigation are not mutually exclusive. Second, a unidirectional, step-by-step progression from dispute to negotiation to litigation to resolution should not be taken for granted. Third, notwithstanding the second observation, generally litigation may not occur without some prior negotiation. And, fourth, outcomes in negotiations may impact future outcomes in litigation and vice versa.

Negotiation and litigation are not mutually exclusive. Parallel negotiation during litigation, although not often successful in resolving the dispute, is not unknown. As the ICJ wrote in one of its first 'maritime boundary' cases,

> The jurisprudence of the Court provides various examples of cases in which negotiations and recourse to judicial settlement have been pursued *pari passu*. Several cases... show that judicial proceedings may be discontinued when such negotiations result in the settlement of the dispute. Consequently, the fact that negotiations are being actively pursued during the present proceedings is not legally any obstacle to the exercise by the Court of its judicial function.[19]

(eds.), *The Cambridge Companion to International Law* (Cambridge University Press, 2012) 201, 210.

[19] *Aegean Sea*, [1978] ICJ Rep. 3, 12. See also *Military and Paramilitary Activities in and against Nicaragua (Nicaragua v. United States of America) (Jurisdiction and Admissibility)*, [1984] ICJ Rep. 392, 440: '[T]he Court considers that even the existence of active negotiations in which both parties might be involved should not prevent... the Court from exercising [its functions]'; *Land and Maritime Boundary between Cameroon and Nigeria (Cameroon v. Nigeria) (Preliminary Objections)*, [1998] ICJ Rep. 275, 304 (*Cameroon v. Nigeria (Preliminary Objections)*): 'Finally, the Court has not been persuaded that Nigeria has been prejudiced as a result of Cameroon's having instituted proceedings before the Court instead of pursuing negotiations which, moreover, were deadlocked when the Application was filed.'

This approach was taken in *Land Reclamation*, during which the parties continued to negotiate in order to arrive at a resolution of their dispute. As it happened, the negotiation outpaced the parallel litigation and the parties settled before the initiation of the written stage.[20] The parties in *Guinea-Bissau* v. *Senegal* also reached a negotiated solution while their maritime boundary case was pending before the ICJ. That litigation was subsequently discontinued. The United Kingdom and France engaged in litigation concerning one part of their maritime boundary – the southwest approaches to the English Channel and in the vicinity of the Channel Islands – while setting aside for negotiation the rest of their boundary through the Channel, the Strait of Dover and into the southern North Sea. In short, litigation does not preclude negotiation and may be superseded by it.[21]

Some boundary relationships do follow a clear progression from recognition of a dispute, to negotiation, to litigation, to resolution by decision of the body hearing the case, but this progression is neither necessary nor always followed. The dispute between Canada and France, ultimately resolved in *St. Pierre and Miquelon*, did follow this pattern, as have many others. Canada's 1966 issuance of hydrocarbon exploration permits on the continental shelf precipitated the dispute.[22] This was followed by over two decades of negotiation during which the territorial sea boundary between Newfoundland and St Pierre and Miquelon was agreed in 1972.[23] A mediator was appointed in the late 1980s. On the basis of the mediator's report, the parties signed their arbitration agreement in 1989, and the arbitration award establishing the boundary between Canada and France was issued in 1992. In other instances, the progression has not been so clear or unidirectional. In the *North Sea* cases, negotiation preceded and followed litigation. There the parties asked the ICJ: 'What principles and rules of

---

[20] See *Land Reclamation*, [2005] XXVII RIAA 133.

[21] As Lowe notes, 'A judgment in a case is only one element in the process of dispute settlement; and it is not necessarily either the final or the most important element.' Vaughan Lowe, 'The Interplay between Negotiation and Litigation in International Dispute Settlement', in Tafshir Malick Ndiaye and Rudiger Wolfrum (eds.), *Law of the Sea, Environmental Law and Settlement of Disputes, Liber Amicorum Judge Thomas A. Mensah* (Leiden: Martinus Nijhoff, 2007) 235, 236–7.

[22] Jan Schneider, 'Canada–France (St Pierre and Miquelon)', in Jonathan I. Charney and Lewis M. Alexander (eds.), *International Maritime Boundaries* (Dordrecht: Martinus Nijhoff, 1998), Vol. III, 2141, 2143.

[23] Agreement between the Government of Canada and the Government of the French Republic Concerning Their Mutual Fishing Relations off the Atlantic Coast of Canada (signed and entered into force 27 March 1972), 862 UNTS 209.

international law are applicable to the delimitation as between the Parties of the areas of the continental shelf in the North Sea which appertain to each of them beyond the partial boundary' negotiated earlier in near shore areas?[24] The Court's 1969 judgment setting out those principles was followed by two years of negotiations resulting in agreed maritime boundaries in the North Sea among the three litigants-turned-negotiants in 1971.[25]

There are also examples in which the litigation did not resolve all outstanding issues in the maritime boundary relationship, thus requiring subsequent negotiations to fully resolve the dispute. This normally results from jurisdictional constraints placed on the court or tribunal by the parties. For example, the chamber of the Court in *Gulf of Maine* was not asked to resolve, and did not resolve, a section of the maritime boundary in the inner Gulf or the section of the boundary beyond 200 nautical miles from the nearest state. Likewise, the Annex VII tribunal in *Guyana v. Suriname* delimited the maritime boundary only to the 200 nautical mile limit. In both of these cases the coastal states have claimed or could claim continental shelf beyond 200 nautical miles, the delimitation of which would require further negotiation.

Notwithstanding that negotiation may be carried out in parallel with or may follow litigation, some negotiation is, de facto, a necessary precondition of litigation. Clearly, in order to arrive at a *compromis*, the parties must have negotiated the terms of that agreement. In fact, in all maritime boundary cases heard on the basis of ad hoc consent there were attempts to resolve substantive disagreements by negotiation prior to litigation. However, in the context of ad hoc consent to litigate, substantive negotiations are not required. This is so, in part, because the legal dispute which the court or tribunal is asked to resolve will normally have been defined by the parties in the *compromis*.

In contrast, some degree of substantive negotiation may be required in those cases brought by means other than *compromis*. Such negotiations may be necessary in order to identify and define the dispute on which the court or tribunal is asked to rule, or may be required as a formal precondition to the adjudicative jurisdiction of the court or tribunal. Whether negotiation is a prerequisite of litigation may depend on the forum, the basis of jurisdiction, and the applicable law. The ICJ has not

---

[24] *North Sea*, [1969] ICJ Rep. 3, 6 (quoting Art. 1 of the Special Agreements).

[25] Lowe notes that here the ICJ 'is in effect acting in support of a negotiated solution to the dispute'. Lowe, above n. 21 at 241.

240   COALTER G. LATHROP

made diplomatic negotiation a formal prerequisite in all cases, but it has asked 'whether . . . the dispute between the Parties has been defined with sufficient precision for the Court to be validly seised of it'.[26] Prior negotiation by the parties may serve the purpose of so defining the dispute.[27] Beyond defining the dispute, some prior negotiation may be a formal precondition of litigation in the compromissory clause on which jurisdiction is founded. UNCLOS dispute settlement provisions contain such a condition,[28] and the compromissory clause invoked by Romania against Ukraine in *Black Sea* clearly required negotiation prior to accessing the ICJ.[29]

To the extent that state practice influences decision making in international courts and tribunals, negotiated maritime boundary agreements should have some impact on litigation outcomes.[30] The reverse seems more certain – that the decisions of courts and tribunals in boundary litigation will influence approaches taken in subsequent negotiation. Charney observes:

> Developments in the jurisprudence strongly influence the course of interstate negotiations and the resulting delimitation agreements. Diplomats know that – more than for any other area of international law – resort to third-party dispute settlement is a real possibility for maritime boundary disputes. This awareness limits the positions they may credibly take during negotiations by devaluing those that would be untenable if presented for third-party dispute settlement. Based thus on circumscribed negotiating positions, the agreements reflect those restraints.[31]

---

[26] *Cameroon* v. *Nigeria (Preliminary Objections)*, [1998] ICJ Rep. 275, 322. But see Jonathan I. Charney, 'Progress in International Maritime Boundary Delimitation Law', (1994) 88 AJIL 227, 254: assessing this issue in the *Jan Mayen* case, Charney concludes 'the obligation to establish the maritime boundary by agreement was construed as merely a preliminary obligation'.

[27] *Cameroon* v. *Nigeria (Preliminary Objections)*, [1998] ICJ Rep. 275.

[28] Natalie Klein, *Dispute Settlement in the UN Convention on the Law of the Sea* (Cambridge University Press, 2005), 31: 'Prior to the resort to compulsory procedures entailing binding decisions, States parties must have recourse to alternative methods of dispute settlement.'

[29] See para. 4(h) of the Additional Agreement quoted in *Black Sea*, [2009] ICJ Rep. 61, 70: 'If these negotiations shall not determine the conclusion of the above-mentioned agreement in a reasonable period of time, . . . [the parties] have agreed that the problem of delimitation . . . shall be solved by the UN International Court of Justice, at the request of any of the parties.'

[30] These negotiated agreements carry less weight when characterized as political solutions, devoid of the *opinio juris* required to assert them as evidence of custom. Charney points to 'the diversity of these boundary settlements' as one reason why they may not be very influential in litigation. Charney, above n. 26, 228.

[31] Ibid.

WHY LITIGATE A MARITIME BOUNDARY?

While these observations are undoubtedly correct, the power of previous litigation outcomes to influence negotiating positions in a subsequent dispute must also depend on the likelihood of that dispute ever reaching litigation. This, in turn, will depend on the availability of adjudicative jurisdiction.

Jurisdiction to litigate

The relationship between negotiation and litigation exists in the shadow of jurisdictional constraints. One cannot discuss the decision to litigate in the international legal system without addressing the question of adjudicative jurisdiction of international courts and tribunals. At the most basic level, if one of the disputant states has not consented to the jurisdiction of an international court or tribunal for the purpose of resolving a maritime boundary dispute, litigation of the dispute is not an option. Of the many factors that may influence a state's decision to litigate a maritime boundary, adjudicative jurisdiction must be the most important. This is not to say that when jurisdiction does exist a state will always choose litigation, but when jurisdiction is not available, neither is litigation.[32] When considering the many other factors which may contribute to the decision to litigate a maritime boundary, this predominant factor must be borne in mind.

Consenting to the jurisdiction of an international court or tribunal for the resolution of a maritime boundary dispute is a sovereignty-compromising, self-binding[33] delegation by the state to an international body with respect to a core sovereignty issue. As such, litigation is not typically an avenue of first resort. It is not surprising that states are reluctant to grant such consent, and this may account for the relatively low proportion of maritime boundary disputes resolved through litigation.[34]

---

[32] In the absence of adjudicative jurisdiction, a state that prefers litigation may seek to negotiate for the establishment of jurisdiction through ad hoc consent of the opposing party.

[33] See Karen J. Alter, 'Delegating to International Courts: Self-Binding vs. Other-Binding Delegation', (2008) 71 *Law and Contemporary Problems* 37: distinguishing 'self-binding' delegation of decision-making authority by a state to an international court or tribunal from 'other-binding' delegation by a legislative body to the judiciary thereby binding other, usually private, actors.

[34] Allee and Huth, above n. 3, 223: 'For all of the aforementioned reasons, in most instances state leaders will prefer a strategy of bilateral concession-making [negotiation] to a legal dispute settlement [litigation]'.

The consent required to create jurisdiction in international law comes in several forms. How that jurisdiction is created plays into the analysis of the other factors that may influence the decision to litigate. The two general bases of adjudicative jurisdiction considered here are jurisdiction arising from ad hoc consent of the parties and jurisdiction arising from *ante hoc* consent of the parties.[35]

As noted above, in the majority of the cases brought before 1986 consent of the parties was given ad hoc. In these cases there was 'contemporary mutual agreement . . . to submit that very dispute to the [court or tribunal] for delimitation'.[36] Such agreements usually take the form of a *compromis* setting out, among other things, the applicable law and scope of the dispute. The *compromis* often represents a significant negotiating effort in its own right, and, in the context of the decision to litigate, it represents the commitment of *both* parties to resolve their dispute though litigation instead of negotiation.

This co-operative, contemporaneous, express, and mutual approach to establishing adjudicative jurisdiction may be contrasted with situations in which jurisdiction is founded on the *ante hoc* consent of the parties. In those maritime boundary cases the basis for jurisdiction has been the *ante hoc* consent of the parties expressed in Article 36(2) declarations to the ICJ,[37] the Pact of Bogotá,[38] the dispute settlement provisions of UNCLOS,[39] and the compromissory clause in a bilateral treaty.[40] Initiating a case in reliance on the *ante hoc* consent of the respondent state has,

---

[35] Of course, a respondent state may waive its jurisdictional objections and thereby consent to the jurisdiction of the court or tribunal to hear the merits of the case. A court or tribunal may exercise jurisdiction with this informal *post hoc* grant of ad hoc consent on the principle of *forum prorogatum*. Maritime boundary litigation has not yet witnessed the successful reliance on prorogated consent, but this is another potential jurisdictional avenue into litigation. To improve the chances that this approach would succeed, states might be expected to engage in prior discussions in order to establish agreement not to object to jurisdiction.

[36] Charney, above n. 26, 254.

[37] See *Guinea-Bissau* v. *Senegal*, [1989] 20 RIAA 121; *Cameroon* v. *Nigeria (Preliminary Objections)*, [1998] ICJ Rep. 275; *Jan Mayen*, [1993] ICJ Rep. 38; *Nicaragua* v. *Honduras*, [1992] ICJ Rep. 351.

[38] See *Nicaragua* v. *Honduras*, [1992] ICJ Rep. 351; *Nicaragua* v. *Colombia*, *Peru* v. *Chile*, above n. 4.

[39] See *Land Reclamation*, [2005] 27 RIAA 133; *Barbados* v. *Trinidad and Tobago*, [2006] 27 RIAA 147; *Guyana* v. *Suriname*, *Bangladesh/Myanmar*, and *Bangladesh* v. *India*, above nn. 4 and 14.

[40] *Black Sea*, [2009] ICJ Rep. 61.

at times, taken the form of an ambush in which an applicant state sues a respondent relying on a basis of jurisdiction of which the respondent state may have been unaware,[41] or which the respondent state assumed, because the states were engaged in active negotiations, would not be exercised without further notice.[42] As a result, jurisdiction (or at least the scope of subject-matter jurisdiction asserted by the applicant state) has often been challenged in these cases.[43] One observable effect of the use of *ante hoc* consent is the *ex post facto* withdrawal from adjudicative jurisdiction by the respondent.[44] A more insidious effect of cases brought without contemporaneous ad hoc consent, and perhaps one that could damage the international judicial system over the long term, is the *ex ante* pre-emptive withdrawal of potential respondent states from compulsory adjudicative jurisdiction in anticipation of cases that could be brought by neighbours.[45]

---

[41] Nigeria's first preliminary objection to the jurisdiction of the Court was that 'Cameroon, by lodging the Application on 29 March 1994 [*before* the UN Secretary-General transmitted copies of Cameroon's 36(2) declaration of 3 March 1994], violated its obligations to act in good faith, acted in abuse of the system established by Article 36, paragraph 2, of the Statute, and disregarded the requirement of reciprocity established by Article 36, paragraph 2, of the Statute and the terms of Nigeria's Declaration of 3 September 1965.' *Cameroon v. Nigeria (Preliminary Objections)*, [1998] ICJ Rep. 275, 284–5. The Court rejected Nigeria's first preliminary objection. Ibid., 325.

[42] See, e.g., Letter from Runaldo Venetiaan, President of Suriname, to Bharrat Jagdeo, President of Guyana, 23 March 2004, Preliminary Objections Memorandum of Suriname, *Guyana v. Suriname*, Annex I, 23 May 2005, available at www.pca-cpa.org/upload/files/SMem%20Annexes%2001-10.pdf: 'Since the discussions in the Joint Border Commissions of the two countries were still in progress, this action is viewed as premature and not in the spirit of our cooperation expressed during your visit to Suriname in 2002.'

[43] See, e.g., the jurisdictional challenges in the cases between Greece and Turkey, Qatar and Bahrain, Cameroon and Nigeria, Guyana and Suriname, and Nicaragua and Colombia.

[44] See, e.g., Declaration of Nigeria, 30 April 1998, 2013 UNTS 507 (amending the earlier Declaration to accept several dispute types, including 'disputes in respect of which any party to the dispute has accepted the jurisdiction of the Court by a Declaration deposited less than Twelve Months prior to the filing of an Application' and delimitation disputes); Declaration of Colombia, 5 December 2001, 2166 UNTS 3 (terminating acceptance of compulsory jurisdiction the day before Nicaragua's Application in *Nicaragua v. Colombia*).

[45] This effect is difficult to identify. Since Malaysia instituted proceedings against Singapore in July 2003, only eight states have declared that they do not accept compulsory jurisdiction with respect to maritime delimitation under the dispute settlement procedures of UNCLOS. However, six of these eight made their Art. 298 declarations after ratification, indicating a certain level of attention to the issue of jurisdiction and a specific intention to withdraw from that jurisdiction.

The factors

If adjudicative jurisdiction is available through a *compromis* or by virtue of pre-existing consent – that is to say, once litigation is a realistic option – then the question may be asked, what factors influence the decision to litigate a maritime boundary dispute? It seems that many of these factors are not legal but political in nature,[46] and they appear to include a wide range of considerations, some of which have been studied in depth.

Several authors have attempted to tease out the important factors contributing to the decision to litigate. LaTour et al. investigated dispute settlement preferences among undergraduate students and law students along a spectrum of increasing third-party involvement from negotiation ('bargaining') to litigation ('arbitration' and 'autocratic decision making').[47] Three factors were considered as determinants of procedural choice: temporal urgency; the presence or absence of a judgmental standard, such as a rule or tradition; and whether the parties' interests are aligned or opposed ('outcome correspondence'). The LaTour study found that preference for high levels of third-party involvement increase '(1) when outcomes are noncorrespondent [interests are not aligned], (2) when a standard is available, and (3) when there is time pressure'.[48] In most maritime boundary disputes party interests tend to be in direct conflict, suggesting that of LaTour's three factors the existence of a standard and a sense of temporal urgency would be the main considerations in a decision to litigate a maritime boundary.

The substantive standard for maritime delimitation is loose: delimitation 'must be effected on the basis of international law in order to achieve an equitable solution'.[49] This standard has been tightened up over the years by the development of a three-step procedural approach to the creation of an equitable maritime delimitation. In the first step, a provisional equidistance line is constructed. In the second step, relevant circumstances that may require an adjustment of the provisional line are considered. In the third step, a test of proportionality is administered to

---

[46] Sir Arthur Watts, 'Preparation for International Litigation', in Tafshir Malick Ndiaye and Rudiger Wolfrum (eds.), *Law of the Sea, Environmental Law and Settlement of Disputes, Liber Amicorum Judge Thomas A. Mensah* (Dordrecht: Martinus Nijhoff, 2007) 327, 328: 'But essentially the decision [to litigate] is a political one, in which many non-legal factors play their part'.

[47] Stephen LaTour et al., 'Some Determinants of Preference for Modes of Conflict Resolution', (1976) 20 *Journal of Conflict Resolution* 319.

[48] Ibid., 349.

[49] *Bangladesh/Myanmar*, above n. 4, [25] (paraphrasing UNCLOS, Arts. 74 and 83).

WHY LITIGATE A MARITIME BOUNDARY? 245

check for inequity. Over time, the list of relevant circumstances that might be considered in the second step has been pared down. While this does not allow states to make perfect predictions of outcome, it has increased certainty by narrowing the range of possible outcomes and rationales for those outcomes. Following LaTour, we might expect litigation to increase if this standard is further refined.

LaTour's third factor, temporal urgency, appears to be important as well. Although international litigation can seem quite slow when compared with domestic litigation, it tends to be less drawn out than negotiation. Negotiations may be quite protracted when positions have hardened or when one party prefers non-resolution. For example, negotiation of the maritime boundary between Bangladesh and Myanmar began in the mid-1970s and continued for over three decades without reaching a resolution. When Bangladesh initiated litigation in October 2009, the dispute was resolved in two and half years with ITLOS's decision in March 2012. In maritime boundary delimitation, temporal urgency often arises in the context of resource use, specifically the exploration and exploitation of offshore hydrocarbons. Urgency can be created by resource-related conflict events, such as when specific drilling activity is opposed by the threat or use of force,[50] or by the realization that the opportunity costs of non-resolution are rising with the price of oil.

Fischer discerns several additional factors that have been considered by applicant states in a study based on confidential interviews with individuals personally involved in or familiar with decisions to litigate before the ICJ.[51] Fischer investigated the pre-litigation phases of four disparate cases brought before the ICJ between 1967 and 1976,[52] and found three

---

[50] As Feldman notes, 'Nothing could be more inflammatory than drilling on the continental shelf claimed by another state.' Mark D. Feldman, 'The Tunisia–Libya Continental Shelf Case; Geographic Justice or Judicial Compromise?', (1983) 77 AJIL 219, 234. In fact, *Libya/Malta* was precipitated, in part, by an escalation related to offshore oil resources. McDorman reports that 'Libyan warships surrounded the [Malta-licensed] oil rig and forcefully halted its drilling operations.' Ted L. McDorman, 'The Libya–Malta case: Opposite States Confront the Court', (1986) 24 *Canadian Yearbook of International Law* 335, 337. A similar sequence of events led to the institution of proceedings in *Guyana* v. *Suriname*. See *Guyana* v. *Suriname*, above n. 4, [263]–[273] (discussing June 2000 CGX oil rig incident).

[51] Dana D. Fischer, 'Decisions to use the International Court of Justice: Four Recent Cases', (1982) 26 *International Studies Quarterly* 251.

[52] *Nuclear Tests (Australia* v. *France, New Zealand* v. *France) (Merits)*, [1974] ICJ Rep. 253, 457; *Fisheries Jurisdiction (United Kingdom* v. *Iceland)*, [1974] ICJ Rep. 3; *Fisheries Jurisdiction (Federal Republic of Germany* v. *Iceland)*, [1974] ICJ Rep. 175; *North Sea Continental Shelf Cases (Federal Republic of Germany* v. *Denmark; Federal Republic of Germany* v.

factors that were considered by each applicant state. In each case, the applicant state considered that ample time had been spent exhausting all other forms of peaceful dispute settlement ('time and diplomacy'), considered the dispute within the state's overall foreign policy context ('dispute and context'), and considered the likelihood of a good outcome ('probability of winning/losing').[53] Presumably, if the applicant had considered that any of these three factors were not in its favour, the applicant would have been more likely to prefer an approach other than litigation.

With respect to time and diplomacy, the maritime delimitation cases seem to support Fischer's findings. In most cases, significant effort has been made prior to litigation to resolve the dispute by some other means, usually negotiation. Prior to their litigation in *Gulf of Maine*, the United States and Canada engaged in 'more than five years of intensive high-level negotiations which failed to reach an agreed result'.[54] Some disputes take much more time to reach litigation. The maritime boundary in *Nicaragua v. Colombia*, for example, is closely tied to a 1928 treaty allocating insular territory in the south-western Caribbean Sea.

Fischer's overall foreign policy factor, while undoubtedly paramount, is difficult to quantify. By definition, maritime boundary disputants are neighbouring states. As such, disagreement about the location of a maritime boundary is likely to be one of many past or current disagreements between those proximate states. In the circumstance of adjacent states, those neighbours will also share a land border, a possible source of additional disputes. Argentina and Chile, the parties to the *Beagle Channel* maritime delimitation case, share one of the world's longest land borders, which itself has been the subject of several litigations.[55] Trade relationships across land borders would also fall under this category of foreign policy considerations.[56] We must assume that long-term neighbours have

---

Netherlands), [1969] ICJ Rep. 3; *Trial of Pakistani Prisoners of War* (*Pakistan v. India*), [1973] ICJ Rep. 328.

[53] Fischer, above n. 51, 255–61.

[54] David A. Colson, 'Canada–United States (Gulf of Maine)', in Jonathan I. Charney and Lewis M. Alexander (eds.), *International Maritime Boundaries*, Vol. I (Dordrecht: Martinus Nijhoff, 1993) 401.

[55] Marcelo G. Kohen, 'The "Laguna del Desierto" Case between Argentina and Chile', (1993) 1 *International Boundaries Research Unit, Boundary and Security Bulletin* 70.

[56] Simmons cites figures that 'suggest that arguments over territory may exact a high opportunity cost in terms of trade'. Beth A. Simmons, 'Capacity, Commitment, and Compliance: International Institutions and Territorial Disputes', (2002) 46 *Journal of Conflict Resolution* 829, 832.

WHY LITIGATE A MARITIME BOUNDARY? 247

all aspects of their bilateral relationship firmly in mind when deciding to litigate their maritime boundary.

The probability of winning specific issues in a delimitation case may influence the decision to litigate. The ability to predict a 'win' on a particular issue is increased by the refined procedural standard discussed above. In the context of maritime delimitation, the particular issue might be the effect of an island on the course of the maritime boundary or the likelihood that a specific location, such as a disputed drilling site, would end up on one or the other side of the litigated line. The effect of small islands is a common cause of maritime disputes. This problem featured prominently in *Black Sea* with respect to Serpents' Island and in *Bangladesh* v. *Myanmar* with respect to Saint Martin's Island. In both cases, the island was given no effect on the boundary beyond the territorial sea, resulting in 'wins' on that issue for Romania and Myanmar respectively. A specific drilling location was the trigger and subsequently the focal point for Guyana in its case against Suriname. The tribunal in *Guyana* v. *Suriname* noted that 'Guyana now has undisputed title to the area where the incident occurred'[57] – a quote that was trumpeted by Guyana's legal team after the decision,[58] despite the fact the Suriname won other aspects of the case. Some of these 'wins' may have been predicted prior to litigation and may have influenced decisions to litigate.

Allee and Huth mine a large data set related to the resolution of territorial disputes worldwide in the period 1919 to 1995 to test their hypothesis that 'leaders will seek legal dispute settlement [litigation] in situations where they anticipate sizeable domestic political costs should they attempt to settle a dispute through the making of bilateral, negotiated concessions'.[59] The authors expect that the avoidance of these costs will be a contributing factor only when both sides face high domestic political costs of concession making.[60] According to the study, domestic political costs rise when leaders 'are highly accountable to domestic political opposition'[61] and the dispute is 'highly salient

---

[57] *Guyana* v. *Suriname*, above n. 4, [451].

[58] Foley Hoag LLP, 'Foley Hoag Helps Republic of Guyana Assert Sovereignty over Oil- and Gas-Rich Seas in Maritime Dispute with Neighboring Suriname', 2007, available at www.foleyhoag.com/newscenter/presscenter/2007/09/20/foley-hoag-helps-republic-of-guyana.aspx.

[59] Allee and Huth, above n. 3, 219.   [60] Ibid., 225.

[61] That is, when leaders face strong domestic political opposition and leaders are from states with democratic institutions. Ibid., 225–6.

to domestic audiences'.[62] Others have speculated that 'saving face' may contribute to the decision to litigate.[63] To the extent that face must be saved before a domestic audience, the Allee and Huth study may provide the empirical support for this idea.

Simmons asks a similar question about the decision of Latin American states to litigate territorial disputes and arrives at a similar answer: states choose to litigate in order 'to achieve results that cannot be realized through negotiations and domestic decision making alone'.[64] Here, the domestic explanation is couched in terms of assessments of pay-offs from litigated versus negotiated solutions,[65] but the basic conclusion is the same. Like Allee and Huth, Simmons finds that litigation may be used as an end run around 'domestic political blockage' under certain circumstances.[66]

Conscious of alternative explanations for the decision to access the international judicial system, the Allee and Huth and Simmons studies incorporate realist control variables. Both confirm the realist view that a military imbalance or power asymmetry between the parties makes litigation less attractive to the more powerful party and litigation less likely than negotiation as a mode of dispute settlement.[67] However, they find that other realist factors have no significant impact on the choice

---

[62] That is, when disputed territory involves ethnic co-nationals, the dispute adversary is an enduring rival, and the states have taken a previous hard-line stance. Ibid., 226–7.

[63] Arthur W. Rovine, 'The National Interest and the World Court', in Leo Gross (ed.), *The Role of the International Court of Justice* (Dobbs Ferry: Oceana Publications, 1976) 313, 323: 'The Court is also useful for its face-saving or accommodation functions.'

[64] Simmons, above n. 56, 831: asking 'why do governments sometimes allow third parties to make authoritative rulings on their actions and policies?'

[65] As Simmons explains, the decision to litigate 'happens because some groups expect arbitration to provide higher payoffs than political concessions; they believe they will win in court, but even if the outcome is the same as the negotiated deal, there is a strong preference to defer to an authoritative body rather than to a political-military rival'. Ibid., 846.

[66] Ibid., 839.

[67] Allee and Huth, above n. 3, 232: '[T]he disparity in military power establishes a situation in which the stronger side has considerable bargaining leverage over the weaker party'; Simmons, above n. 56, 839: 'The greater the asymmetry between countries, the greater the expected value of a political settlement for the larger country, making arbitration unlikely'. But see Fischer, above n. 51, 258, who indicates one explanation given for the *Fisheries Jurisdiction* case brought by the United Kingdom and Germany (clearly the more powerful parties) against Iceland: '[Britain] agreed with Germany that using the Court was the easiest way of avoiding the appearance of two big states "bullying" a small one.' A modern example of this dynamic is currently unfolding in the South China Sea between China and its less powerful neighbours.

of dispute settlement. The existence of common security ties between the parties, which should decrease the likelihood of litigation, had no impact on the decision.[68] States would also be expected to avoid litigation in disputes with serious national security implications. However, both studies found that this factor had no impact on the decision to litigate.[69]

Flexibility may be another factor in the decision whether to negotiate or litigate. One of the advantages of negotiation is flexibility with respect to timing and range of solution, which is usually lost once a dispute is brought to litigation. Courts and tribunals apply the applicable law and are unable to make political side payments or consider issue linkage.[70]

Familiarity with international litigation procedures and forums may contribute to decisions to litigate by states with previous international litigation experience. Five states – Germany, Libya, Guinea-Bissau, Nicaragua, and Bangladesh – have each been involved in, and in most instances have initiated, two maritime delimitation cases with, respectively, Denmark and the Netherlands, Tunisia and Malta, Guinea and Senegal, Honduras and Colombia, and Myanmar and India. For those states claiming that they are at the back of a coastal concavity and therefore zone-locked by their neighbours to either side (Germany, Guinea-Bissau, and Bangladesh) there may have been some strategic advantage to bringing these cases at the same time or even, as in the case of Germany, to the same forum in order to demonstrate the cut-off effect caused by both neighbours' maritime areas when considered together. But it is also possible that familiarity with a forum played some role in the decision. Nicaragua is a good example of a state that is familiar with the ICJ, having appeared in The Hague in four cases before initiating its maritime delimitation cases against Honduras and Colombia.

---

[68] Allee and Huth, above n. 3, 232.

[69] Ibid.; Simmons, above n. 56, 840: 'There is no evidence that high stakes strip governments' desire to commit to arbitration.'

[70] Klein would likely agree that this is an important factor in the decision to litigate. She writes that 'Coastal States may wish to negotiate boundary agreements rather than refer matters to third parties, as the States concerned are able to take into account human and resource conditions that have been ignored in boundaries settled through adjudication or arbitration.' Klein, above n. 28, 255 (footnotes omitted). See also Prosper Weil, 'Geographic Considerations in Maritime Delimitation', in Jonathan I. Charney and Lewis M. Alexander (eds.), *International Maritime Boundaries* Vol. I (Dordrecht: Martinus Nijhoff, 1993) 115, 121: 'While there are legal norms binding on the courts, there are no legal norms restricting the contractual freedom of states in this area.'

Economies of scale may be a consideration for states with multiple maritime delimitation disputes. Efficiency may be increased if one legal team can address two cases at the same time. In addition to Germany, whose two cases were joined into a single proceeding, Guinea-Bissau and Bangladesh each maintained largely the same legal teams to litigate two simultaneous cases. Nicaragua's maritime cases have overlapped significantly in terms of timing and personnel, and Libya's maritime cases, although sequential, were argued by essentially the same team each time.

According to this limited review, the factors that may contribute to a decision to litigate include urgency of resolution, the existence of a standard, whether all diplomatic options have been exhausted, the larger foreign policy context in which the dispute is situated, assessments of the likely outcomes, avoidance of domestic political costs, power asymmetry between the parties, flexibility of process and solution, familiarity with procedure and forum, and economies of scale. Parties would be expected to make assessments of the costs and benefits of litigation on the basis of these factors. However, it should be appreciated that the two parties may not share the same assessment of each factor. For example, the cost of litigation may be high for the more powerful state, because it would lose a negotiating advantage, but for the less powerful state, litigation – by neutralizing the strategic disparity – might be the low-cost option. With respect to urgency, one state might want an immediate resolution while the other would be content to draw the process out. Of course, the foreign policy context and the domestic political pressures differ significantly from state to state. Finally, the existence of a standard may increase certainty, but if it increases the certainty of a loss it would also increase the cost of litigation for the likely loser.

Other factors, many of them related to those already listed, might be considered as well, such as strategic and tactical concerns; reputational consequences; anticipated duration of the dispute resolution processes; degree of delegation or loss of party autonomy with respect to rules, timing, and decision makers; control of information within the process; financial expenses coupled with personnel and budgetary constraints; finality of a solution; and expected levels of compliance with the outcome. With each of these factors come potential costs and benefits, the assessments of which will not always be identical as between the parties to a dispute.

Any government involved in a serious assessment of its options would try to take the items on this laundry list into account in some form of multivariate cost–benefit analysis. It is, perhaps, unrealistic to posit the state as a unitary actor,[71] much less a rational actor capable of quantifying the costs or benefits of litigation and negotiation on the basis of such a wide range of disparate factors. However, decisions to litigate (well-considered or haphazard) are ultimately made, and those decisions do bind the state, unitary or otherwise.

Some structure is provided in the following section in an attempt to ground this litany of possible factors in a conceptual framework with particular regard to maritime boundary disputes.

Party preferences and dispute settlement decisions

A state will opt for the resolution of a dispute when the perceived costs of non-resolution exceed those of resolution. Implicit in this truism is the notion that both options – resolution and non-resolution – are actually available. This does not take into account the perceived costs of the other party which may differ and thus remove an option, usually resolution. In other words, it should not be assumed that an unresolved maritime boundary dispute would always be perceived as suboptimal for both states at the same time.[72] When non-resolution is preferred by one state, stalemate is likely to ensue. However, when resolution is preferred by both states, their preferences may be further refined to account for the choice between modes of resolution: a state will opt to litigate a dispute when the perceived costs of negotiation exceed those of litigation. Here again we must consider that dispute resolution is a bilateral process and that cost–benefit assessments may differ between the disputants, leading to different preferences. This brief exercise sets up the three options that, in the abstract, might be available to, and which could be preferred by, the disputant states: non-resolution, negotiated resolution, and litigated resolution.

In fact these three options are not always available, and, in the case of inter-state dispute settlement, are often unavailable. Negotiation may be effectively unavailable if one of two states is recalcitrant, and litigation will

---

[71] Putnam, above n. 10, 433: '[A]s all experienced negotiators know, . . . the unitary-actor assumption is often radically misleading'.

[72] Simmons, above n. 56, 847: It is assumed that governments 'want to solve a problem that, unresolved, constitutes a "suboptimality"'. Rovine notes, however, that resolution is not always optimal. Rovine, above n. 63, 322: 'There are of course occasions when the reverse is true – that is to say, a continuation of the dispute is preferred even to a clear win in Court.'

be unavailable without the consent of both states. Availability of litigation brings us back to the question of jurisdiction, which, being based on the consent of states is a function of their preferences. The matrix in Figure 11.1 below sets out the preferences of hypothetical state A and state B in order to conceptualize the likely dispute outcomes in a variety of preference configurations. It is apparent that preferences will drive the likely mode of dispute resolution, but may also account for the creation of adjudicative jurisdiction by ad hoc consent where preferences match or the use of *ante hoc* consent where they do not. Moreover, the preferences of one or both states may change over time, with the consequence that the likely outcome will change as well.

It bears repeating that the majority of maritime boundaries are not yet resolved. Depending on the states' preferences and the availability of adjudicative jurisdiction, unresolved maritime boundary disputes might be situated in any box other than 2B and 3C. Without knowing the preferences of the states involved, it is difficult to know where within this matrix a particular unresolved dispute might best be placed. Sometimes state preferences may be gleaned from news reports. In recent reporting from Asia, the Philippines has expressed a preference for litigation before ITLOS while China has expressed a preference for resolution through bilateral negotiation, indicating that this unresolved maritime dispute is probably situated in the 2C/3B category.[73] At the time of *Aegean Sea*, Greece clearly preferred litigation while Turkey preferred negotiation or non-resolution, placing that unresolved dispute in the 2C/3B or 1C/3A category as of 1976. However, recent reporting indicates a shift in Greek and Turkish preferences towards 2B (negotiated resolution) with hints of a possible resolution in 3C (litigated resolution).[74]

Generally, the disputes in the 1A category tend to be dormant or potential disputes in areas of no particular interest to either state. Here, mutual disinterest may result in the shared perception that the opportunity costs of non-resolution are low. Most maritime boundary relationships start in

---

[73] See Jerry E. Esplanada, 'Philippines Getting Ready to Take Dispute With China to Int'l Tribunal', *Philippine Daily Inquirer*, 2012, available at globalnation.inquirer.net/35475/philippines-getting-ready-to-take-dispute-with-china-to-int'l-tribunal; Pia Lee-Brago, 'China Opposes Taking Dispute to Int'l Tribunal', *Philippine Star*, 2012, available at www.philstar.com/Article.aspx?articleId=800424&publicationSubCategoryId=63.

[74] International Crisis Group, 'Turkey and Greece: Time to Settle Aegean Dispute', Europe Briefing No. 64, 2011, available at www.crisisgroup.org/en/regions/europe/turkey-cyprus/turkey/B64-turkey-and-greece-time-to-settle-the-aegean-dispute.aspx at 3 September 2012: 'Their foreign ministries have met more than 50 times for "exploratory talks" since 2002, with a view to taking the continental shelf dispute and possibly other unresolved matters to the ICJ.'

Preferences of state B	Preferences of state A		
	1. Non-resolution	2. Negotiated resolution	3. Litigated resolution
A. Non-resolution	1A. Dispute remains unresolved	2A. Protracted negotiations with no resolution	3A. Dispute remains unresolved OR Litigated resolution if *ante hoc* consent by B
B. Negotiated resolution	1B. Protracted negotiations with no resolution	2B. Negotiated resolution	3B. Dispute remains unresolved OR Negotiated resolution with suboptimal result for A OR Litigated resolution if *ante hoc* consent by B
C. Litigated resolution	1C. Dispute remains unresolved OR Litigated resolution if *ante hoc* consent by A	2C. Dispute remains unresolved OR Negotiated resolution with suboptimal result for B OR Litigated resolution if *ante hoc* consent by A	3C. Litigated resolution

Figure 11.1 Likely dispute outcome based on preferences of state A and state B

1A. The shift out of 1A may occur with the increasing scarcity of a resource, such as fish, or the discovery of a valuable resource, such as oil or gas. In an ideal world, the shift would occur along the bias from 1A to 2B, where the states would arrive at a negotiated solution. And, in fact, this is the progression that many maritime boundary relationships have followed.[75] Without more information it is difficult to know whether a negotiated resolution is best categorized in 2B, where the negotiated resolution was preferred by both states, or in 2C or 3B, where the negotiated solution was suboptimal for the state that preferred, but could not access, a litigated resolution.

After a dispute is brought to litigation it may be easier to discern the preferences involved. Litigated resolutions arrived at on the basis of ad hoc consent indicate a shared preference for litigation as manifested in the *compromis*. Litigation based on ad hoc consent is easy to distinguish from litigated resolutions that rely on *ante hoc* consent of a respondent state that might otherwise have preferred non-resolution or negotiated resolution. Although reliance on *ante hoc* consent may indicate that the respondent state did not prefer litigation, it is possible that the use of *ante hoc* consent masks a preference for litigation on the part of the respondent. Preliminary objections to jurisdiction add clarity to the respondent's true preference for something other than litigation. The three different preference configurations under which a litigated resolution might occur – both states prefer litigation (3C); one state prefers litigation and one state prefers negotiation (2C and 3B); one state prefers litigation and one state prefers non-resolution (1C and 3A) – are addressed in turn.

Resolution by litigation on the basis of *ad hoc* consent has been the dispute outcome in half of the litigated international maritime boundary disputes. States parties to these disputes clearly preferred resolution over non-resolution, and ultimately preferred litigation over negotiation. Often these litigations were preceded by years of negotiation both on the substantive matters in dispute and on the procedure to be applied in litigation, that is, in the negotiation of the *compromis*. The main question here is what factors contributed to the mutual change in preferences from negotiation to litigation and moved these parties from the negotiating table to the courtroom?

In these instances, the parties faced a true choice between negotiation and litigation, and together they agreed that litigation would achieve something that negotiation could not or would not under the

---

[75] As of 2010 there were approximately 165 maritime boundary relationships, which had been resolved, fully or partially, by negotiation.

circumstances. That is to say, the two states shared the perception that the cost of litigation would be lower than the cost of negotiation. A shared desire to reduce their respective domestic audience costs provides the most convincing explanation for the decision to move a dispute from negotiation to litigation.

Negotiating states expect to make some concessions during the course of the negotiating process. In maritime boundary litigation, where the substantive rule is 'to achieve an equitable solution', states also expect (or should expect) that they will not prevail on their full claim before a court or tribunal. As demonstrated by their prior negotiating efforts, these states prefer resolution and know that concessions must be made in order to achieve that goal. In these circumstances, the decision between negotiation and litigation is a matter of choosing by what process and, more importantly, by whom, those concessions will be made.[76] If, in this two-level game, the cost of making negotiated concessions on the international plane is increased by the domestic audience costs generated for a state leader or political party at the national level, those costs may be reduced, if not avoided entirely, by delegating decision-making authority to a third party.[77] As with the assessment of costs elsewhere, the perspective of both parties must be taken into account. The move from negotiated resolution to litigated resolution becomes 'relatively more attractive only in those situations in which state leaders on both sides face considerable domestic costs for making negotiated concessions'.[78] When this does happen – when both states shift preferences from negotiation to litigation – they may create jurisdiction by their mutually agreed, ad hoc consent.[79]

---

[76] See Allee and Huth, above n. 3, 223: 'The primary difference between the two options, then, lies with the process by which concessions are made and the different costs and benefits associated with each option.' Lowe notes that 'the aim of litigation might be such that it is essential to proceed to a determination of the merits of the case, regardless of its strength. (This is said to be the case in some boundary disputes, where neither State may wish to give away in negotiations even a tiny part of what has been claimed as national territory, but both States may be content to allow a tribunal to award part of its claimed territory to the other Party . . . It is often convenient to blame everything on the lawyers).' He adds that 'Some States, after all, consciously choose adjudication in order to shift the responsibility for compromising on national territorial claims away from the Government and on to an international tribunal': Lowe, above n. 21, at 241, 246.

[77] Allee and Huth, above n. 3, 219: '[State] leaders who anticipate significant domestic audience costs for the making of voluntary, negotiated concessions are likely to seek the "political cover" of an international legal ruling.'

[78] Ibid., 225.

[79] This moment has been characterized as 'a plateau in the bargaining process where both sides agree that the settlement of the dispute is more important than the relative distribution of objectives resulting from the final decision'. William D. Coplin, 'The World Court

This progression from 2B (agreement to negotiate) to 3C (agreement to litigate) stands in contrast to the other progressions that could ultimately end in a litigated resolution under different jurisdictional constraints. For those litigations initiated on the basis of *ante hoc* consent, it is more likely that the preferences of the disputant states did not match, and that only one state – the applicant state – preferred litigation while the respondent state preferred non-resolution (1C/3A) or a negotiated resolution (2C/3B). In a consent-based system, these mismatched preferences will result in a stalemate, a negotiated resolution that is suboptimal for one party, or a litigated resolution if the respondent state has provided *ante hoc* consent to jurisdiction. When, under these circumstances, the dispute is resolved by litigation, the decision to litigate will have been made unilaterally and the factors that contributed to that decision should be considered from the applicant state's perspective alone.

Here the domestic explanation seems less powerful than it is when the decision to litigate is made in the context of shared litigation preferences.[80] When litigation occurs in the context of mismatched preferences the choice to delegate decision-making authority to a third party is not made by mutual agreement. Unlike cases brought by *compromis* in which both parties take an active role in framing their dispute, choosing their forum, and creating the jurisdiction under which that forum will hear their case, cases litigated on the basis of *ante hoc* consent result from unilateral action by the applicant state. The decision makers in such a state might look inward to consider domestic audience costs, but here the decision to litigate may be more strongly influenced by outward-looking concerns regarding the actions or postures of the neighbouring state. The common thread in maritime boundary cases brought on the basis of *ante hoc* consent appears to be the applicant state's need to overcome a potentially prejudicial, high-cost status quo resulting from non-resolution of the dispute. In these situations, litigation has been used by the applicant state to break an unfavourable stalemate.

A high-cost status quo may arise from the coastal geography of the disputant states. States that find themselves at the back of a coastal

---

in the International Bargaining Process', in R.W. Gregg and M Barkim (eds.), *The United Nations and its Functions* (Princeton: Van Nostrand, 1968) 313, 329, quoted in Fischer, above n. 51, 265.

[80] However, when the respondent state does in fact prefer litigation, being sued on the basis of *ante hoc* consent given by a previous government would provide even more domestic political cover in the respondent state than would the creation of ad hoc consent in which the current government would take an active role.

concavity and which are therefore disadvantaged and even zone-locked by the application of the equidistance method[81] may resort to litigation in an attempt to 'break out'. Germany and Guinea-Bissau managed this prejudicial situation by negotiating *compromis* with both neighbours and litigating on that basis. In contrast, Bangladesh and Cameroon brought their disputes to litigation on the basis of *ante hoc* consent against Myanmar and India, and against Nigeria[82] respectively. The presence of islands, which, as a matter of entitlement, are equivalent to mainland territory,[83] can create stalemates when a state gives its islands full weight against the neighbour's mainland coast in a delimitation negotiation. Romania faced this situation in the Black Sea with respect to Ukraine's Serpents' Island. Romania brought that dispute to litigation on the basis of Ukraine's *ante hoc* consent.

In addition to coastal geography, state and state-authorized conduct in the disputed area may begin to establish an unfavourable status quo for the weaker or less active state. Power asymmetry may contribute, in particular when naval and law enforcement actions are undertaken by the more powerful state in areas claimed by the other state. Oil and gas leasing, exploration and exploitation practices may begin to create a prejudicial body of conduct. Fisheries licensing, state-sanctioned fishing, and fisheries-related law enforcement may be a factor as well. The establishment of a negotiated boundary between one of the potential litigant states and a third state may also contribute to the prejudicial status quo against which an applicant state feels compelled to move.

Some examples from the cases illustrate these points. The Greek initiation of *Aegean Sea* appears to have been in direct response to seismic work by the Turkish research vessel *Mta-Sismik I*.[84] This work would have reinforced several years of related oil and gas practice that was prejudicial to Greece's maritime boundary position in this area. In *Guyana* v. *Suriname*, the combination of hydrocarbon exploration by Guyana and law

---

[81] Equidistance is the presumed delimitation method in the territorial sea in the absence of special circumstances or historic title. See UNCLOS, Art. 15. Although there is no presumption in favour of equidistance in zones beyond the territorial sea, equidistance is normally the starting point of boundary analyses in those zones and may be the basis of the negotiating position of the state favoured by equidistance.

[82] Cameroon may have wished to initiate proceedings against its other neighbour, Equatorial Guinea, but that state took pre-emptive action to remove itself from adjudicative jurisdiction by filing a declaration under UNCLOS, Art. 298, declaring that it does not accept jurisdiction with respect to maritime boundaries.

[83] See UNCLOS, Art. 121.   [84] *Aegean Sea*, [1978] ICJ Rep. 3, 10.

enforcement activity by Suriname in response led Guyana to initiate litigation on the basis of the dispute settlement provisions of UNCLOS. Nicaragua's initiation of *Nicaragua* v. *Honduras* was precipitated by the establishment of a maritime boundary between Honduras and Colombia that bolstered Honduras's maritime claim against Nicaragua, specifically by Honduran plans to ratify that agreement. Oil and gas practice that coincided with the Honduran claim may also have contributed to this situation. Lastly, in *Land Reclamation*, Singapore's baseline-altering land reclamation projects in the Johor Strait contributed to Malaysia's decision to litigate before an Annex VII tribunal. These cases contain diverse histories and a variety of contributing factors, but in each the applicant state attempted, through litigation, to overcome an existing (or developing) state of affairs that could not be overcome by other means. Presumably, the applicant's perceived cost of litigation was lower than the cost of non-resolution or the cost of a suboptimal negotiated solution.

Conclusions

Why do states decide to litigate their maritime boundary disputes and what factors are most likely to contribute to that decision? The information that might provide an authoritative and conclusive answer to these questions is concealed in the internal memoranda and unrecorded discussions among key decision makers in the foreign policy branches of governments around the world. Nonetheless, inductive reasoning applied to the facts surrounding litigated maritime boundary disputes results in the following conclusions.

The primary factor in the decision to litigate must be the availability of this option in the first place, which in turn depends on the consent of both disputant states to the adjudicative jurisdiction of an international court or tribunal. The decision by two states co-operatively to establish jurisdiction by ad hoc consent manifested in a *compromis* or special agreement arises from shared preferences – first, to resolve the disputed maritime boundary and, second, to do so through litigation. Those preferences are a function of the costs and benefits associated with a variety of political, legal, financial, reputational, strategic, and other factors. Disputes are most likely to be litigated if the preference to litigate is shared by the disputant states. However, if the preferences are mismatched, litigation may still occur if, first and foremost, jurisdiction is available and then only if the cost of litigation as perceived by the applicant state is lower than the cost of non-resolution or of a suboptimal negotiated resolution.

When states have a true choice between negotiated resolution and litigated resolution, the avoidance of domestic political costs must factor heavily into the decision to litigate. However, when litigation has occurred on the basis of *ante hoc* consent, in many instances the applicant state's decision to litigate appears to have been triggered by a need to overcome an unfavourable status quo.

12

Litigating law of the sea disputes using the UNCLOS dispute settlement system

MD. SAIFUL KARIM

The interpretation and application of the United Nations Convention on the Law of the Sea (UNCLOS or Convention)[1] may be the source of many disputes.[2] UNCLOS introduced an à la carte menu for dispute settlement with a number of options for international dispute resolution, including a compulsory procedure entailing binding decisions.[3] While drafting this ambitious and complex system of dispute settlement, the drafters had to negotiate many delicate compromises to secure a system for the uniform interpretation of the Convention.[4] This compulsory dispute settlement system was treated by developing countries as a means of safeguarding their interests from the political, economic, and military pressures of the powerful developed countries.[5]

The aim of this chapter is to explore why litigation using the UNCLOS dispute settlement system may, or may not, be a preferred mode of settlement for law of the sea disputes. Like other international law disputes, law of the sea disputes can be settled through litigation in the International Court of Justice (ICJ) or other available forums without using the UNCLOS dispute settlement system. However, due to space limitations and to avoid repetition of other chapters in this book, this chapter focuses

---

[1] United Nations Convention on the Law of the Sea (opened for signature 10 December 1982, entered into force 16 November 1994), 1833 UNTS 3 (UNCLOS).

[2] Robin R. Churchill and Alan V. Lowe, *The Law of the Sea*, 3rd edn (Manchester University Press, 1999), 447.

[3] For a detailed discussion on the UNCLOS dispute settlement system see generally Natalie Klein, *Dispute Settlement in the UN Convention on the Law of the Sea* (Cambridge University Press, 2005); Andronico O. Adede, *The System for Settlement of Disputes under the United Nations Convention on the Law of The Sea: A Drafting History* (Dordrecht: Martinus Nijhoff, 1986).

[4] Adede, above n. 3, 241; Klein, above n. 3, 52.

[5] Robin R. Churchill, 'Some Reflections on the Operation of the Dispute Settlement System of the UN Convention on the Law of the Sea During its First Decade', in David Freestone, Richard Barnes, and David M. Ong (eds.), *The Law of the Sea: Progress and Prospects* (Oxford University Press, 2006) 388, 389; Klein, above n. 3, 52.

only on the UNCLOS dispute settlement system. In doing so, it examines the extent to which the UNCLOS dispute settlement system provides a comprehensive mechanism for law of the sea litigation. After providing a general overview on the limitations of the UNCLOS dispute settlement system, this chapter will explore the factors behind decisions to pursue litigation using the UNCLOS dispute settlement system by examining some recent disputes as examples.

This chapter argues that strategic decisions to litigate under UNCLOS are highly influenced by a number of issues, including, inter alia, jurisdictional certainty, economic and political interests, and the reputation of the parties. It also argues that there is an increasing tendency of states to resort to litigation for the settlement of law of the sea disputes. The next part of this chapter presents a general overview on litigation concerning the law of the sea. The chapter then presents a brief introduction to the UNCLOS dispute settlement system, and also examines the jurisdictional limitations of the UNCLOS dispute settlement system and its impact on litigation strategy. The final part examines the extralegal factors in the litigation decision-making process, focusing mainly on the economic, political, reputational, and other issues of national interest.

Litigating law of the sea disputes

As noted earlier, dispute settlement options for the law of the sea can broadly be divided into two categories: the general dispute settlement system under international law and the UNCLOS dispute settlement system. Article 33 of the UN Charter imposes an obligation on parties to a dispute involving international peace and security to seek a solution 'by negotiation, enquiry, mediation, conciliation, arbitration, judicial settlement, resort to regional agencies or arrangements, or other peaceful means of their own choice'.[6] International dispute settlement mechanisms can be divided into two main groups. Non-binding or diplomatic processes constitute the first group. In these systems, parties control the whole procedure and retain the right to accept or reject a proposed settlement. For the other group, arbitration and judicial settlement procedures are binding. The formal and legal procedures of dispute settlement are primarily based on consent.[7] For the purposes of this chapter, both

---

[6] United Nations Charter, Art. 33(1).
[7] Ian Brownlie, *Principles of Public International Law*, 7th edn (Oxford University Press, 2008), 701.

proceedings in international judicial institutions and ad hoc arbitration will be treated as litigation.

A large number of international disputes related to the law of the sea are resolved through non-binding negotiation, and states mostly prefer this approach over third-party dispute settlement.[8] Nevertheless, the law of the sea is one of the most frequently litigated areas of international law.[9] The very first case of the ICJ, the *Corfu Channel Case*,[10] concerned the law of the sea, as did the first case of the ICJ's predecessor, the Permanent Court of International Justice (PCIJ).[11] States have shown a general propensity to resolve their law of the sea disputes through litigation and, of those cases, a majority have concerned maritime boundary disputes.[12] As will be seen later in this chapter, states are also gradually showing their interest in the International Tribunal for the Law of the Sea (ITLOS or Tribunal), despite some bottlenecks created by the jurisdictional framework of the Tribunal.

Starting from the first case of the PCIJ, the *SS Wimbledon*, states have sought recourse to litigation in international judicial institutions for the settlement of disputes involving various issues of the law of the sea, including baselines, bays, and territorial waters,[13] straits used for international navigation,[14] maritime boundaries,[15] sovereignty over islands or other maritime features,[16] navigational rights,[17] fisheries and marine

---

[8] Ted L. McDorman, 'Global Ocean Governance and International Adjudicative Dispute Resolution', (2000) 43 *Journal of Ocean and Coastal Management* 255, 257.

[9] Donald R. Rothwell and Tim Stephens, *International Law of the Sea* (Oxford: Hart, 2010), 442.

[10] *Corfu Channel Case (United Kingdom v. Albania)*, [1949] ICJ Rep. 4.

[11] *SS Wimbledon*, [1923] PCIJ (ser. A) No. 1.

[12] More than a quarter of the contentious cases in the ICJ are directly or indirectly related to the law of the sea, and most of the law of these cases is related to maritime boundary rules. See ICJ, List of Contentious Cases, available at www.icj-cij.org/docket/index.php?p1=3&p2=3. See further Chapter 11 in this volume.

[13] E.g., *Gulf of Fonseca Case (El Salvador/Nicaragua)*, Central American Court of Justice, 9 March 1917; *Fisheries Case (United Kingdom v. Norway)*, [1951] ICJ Rep. 116; *Land, Island and Maritime Frontier Dispute (El Salvador/Honduras: Nicaragua intervening)*, [1992] ICJ Rep. 350.

[14] E.g., *Corfu Channel Case*, [1949] ICJ Rep. 4.

[15] E.g., *North Sea Continental Shelf Cases (Federal Republic of Germany v. Denmark; Federal Republic of Germany v. Netherlands)*, [1969] ICJ Rep. 3; *Maritime Delimitation and Territorial Questions between Qatar and Bahrain (Qatar v. Bahrain)*, [2001] ICJ Rep. 40; *Dispute concerning Delimitation of the Maritime Boundary between Bangladesh and Myanmar in the Bay of Bengal (Bangladesh/Myanmar)*, ITLOS, Case No. 16, 14 March 2012.

[16] E.g., *Sovereignty over Pedra Branca/Pulau Batu Puteh, Middle Rocks and South Ledge (Malaysia v. Singapore)*, [2008] ICJ Rep. 12.

[17] E.g., *Volga Case (Russian Federation v. Australia) (Prompt Release)*, ITLOS, (2003) 42 ILM 159.

living resources,[18] criminal jurisdiction and flag state jurisdiction on the high seas,[19] and protection of the marine environment.[20]

Apart from international judicial institutions, ad hoc arbitration has been widely used for law of the sea litigation. The history of using arbitration is undoubtedly older than the history of litigation in international judicial institutions. Some of the early arbitrations included the 1872 *Alabama Claims* arbitration between the United States and the United Kingdom regarding neutrality and warfare at sea, the 1889 *Bering Sea* fur seals arbitration between the United States and the United Kingdom relating to the rights of United States in the Bering Sea and the preservation of fur seals; and the 1935 *SS I'm Alone* arbitration between Canada and the United States regarding hot pursuit of a Canadian vessel. Despite the establishment of a number of permanent judicial institutions, arbitration is still a popular mechanism for law of the sea litigation. For example, three out of four cases reported in one of the most recent volumes of the United Nations Reports of International Arbitral Awards are directly related to the law of the sea.[21] In fact, arbitration has been introduced as the default choice in the UNCLOS compulsory dispute settlement system in the absence of a declared choice of forum.[22]

Against this background discussion on litigation relating to the law of the sea, the next section discusses the specialized dispute settlement system created by UNCLOS.

The UNCLOS dispute settlement system

UNCLOS encourages parties to use non-binding means like negotiation and conciliation for the peaceful settlement of disputes. Where parties have failed to settle their disputes by these non binding procedures, the Convention provides for compulsory procedures entailing binding decisions. Article 287 gives the parties the option to choose any one or more

---

[18] E.g., *Fisheries Jurisdiction (United Kingdom v. Iceland) (Merits)*, [1974] ICJ Rep. 3; *Fisheries Jurisdiction (Federal Republic of Germany v. Iceland) (Merits)*, [1974] ICJ Rep. 175; *Southern Bluefin Tuna Case (New Zealand v. Japan; Australia v. Japan) (Provisional Measures)*, ITLOS, Case No. 3 & 4, (1999) 117 ILR 148.

[19] E.g., *SS Lotus Case (France v. Turkey) (Judgment)*, [1927] PCIJ (ser. A) No. 10.

[20] E.g., *The MOX Plant Case (Ireland v. United Kingdom) (Provisional Measures)*, ITLOS, Case No. 10, 3 December 2001.

[21] United Nations, *Reports of International Arbitral Awards Vol. XXVII* (New York: United Nations, 2008), iii.

[22] UNCLOS, Art. 287.

of the following procedures: ITLOS,[23] the ICJ, an arbitral tribunal constituted in accordance with Annex VII,[24] and a special arbitral tribunal constituted in accordance with Annex VIII.[25]

These courts or tribunals each have jurisdiction over any dispute concerning the interpretation or application of UNCLOS.[26] However, the disputes relating to a coastal state's exercise of sovereign rights can be submitted to compulsory dispute resolution only when the coastal state violates the following:

- freedom of navigation;
- the right of over-flight or the right of laying of submarine cables and pipelines; or in regard to other internationally lawful uses of the sea specified in Article 58;
- where the coastal state is exercising its jurisdiction in a manner inconsistent with marine environmental rules and standards introduced by the Convention or adopted by competent international organizations or diplomatic conferences in accordance with the Convention.[27]

This binding dispute resolution process is subject to a number of exceptions. Disputes arising from marine scientific research in the exclusive economic zone (EEZ) and disputes related to fisheries, including the determination of the total allowable catch in the EEZ, are excluded from compulsory procedures entailing binding decisions. Moreover, states can also opt out of compulsory processes for disputes concerning sea boundary delimitations and historic bay titles; military and certain law enforcement activities; and matters in respect of which the Security Council is exercising its functions.[28] These exceptions may have a significant impact on the jurisdiction of the UNCLOS dispute settlement system. This issue will be discussed in more detail in a later section of this chapter.

The compulsory dispute settlement system also anticipates incidental proceedings to provide speedy and interim remedies for disputing parties, including a system for provisional measures and for the prompt release

---

[23] ITLOS is a creation of UNCLOS. ITLOS constitutes twenty-one independent judges having 'recognised competence in the field of the law of the sea'. UNCLOS, Annex VI.

[24] UNCLOS, Annex VII, see also John Collier and Vaughan Lowe, *The Settlement of Disputes in International Law: Institutions and Procedures* (Oxford University Press, 2000), 90–1.

[25] UNCLOS, Annex VIII; see also Collier and Lowe, above n 24, 91–2.

[26] UNCLOS, Art. 288(1).

[27] UNCLOS, Art. 297(1)(a) and 1(c); also see Collier and Lowe, above n. 24, 92–93.

[28] UNCLOS, Art. 298.

of vessels and crew members. If a dispute submitted to any of the above-mentioned courts and tribunals is prima facie considered to be within the jurisdiction of that court or tribunal, then the latter can prescribe provisional measures.[29] Similarly, if a state party detains a vessel, the flag state can apply to any of the above-mentioned courts or tribunals agreed on by the disputing parties or, failing such an agreement, to ITLOS for prompt release of the vessel if the detaining state has not complied with the provisions of UNCLOS related to the prompt release of the vessel or its crew on the posting of a reasonable bond or other financial security.[30] The Convention contains two such provisions addressing the prompt release of a vessel arrested for alleged illegal fishing in the EEZ of a coastal state[31] and the prompt release of a vessel arrested by a port or coastal state for marine environmental pollution.[32] The prompt release procedure is inapplicable to other vessel arrests. According to Article 292, the prompt release of vessels may only be ordered if 'it is alleged that the detaining state has not *complied with the provisions of this Convention* for the prompt release of the vessel or its crew upon the posting of a *reasonable* bond or other financial security' (emphasis added). The drafting history of Article 292 also clearly supports the suggestion that this provision 'did not apply to all cases of detention' and it was only applicable 'to the cases expressly provided for in the substantive part of the Convention'.[33]

The incidental proceedings may be a source of interaction between different judicial institutions. There are examples where two institutions exercised jurisdiction in the same case. In the *Land Reclamation* case,[34] ITLOS exercised its jurisdiction over provisional measures and an Annex VII arbitral tribunal finally settled the case. A similar situation arose in the *Southern Bluefin Tuna* cases.[35] This jurisdiction is neither competitive nor concurrent. ITLOS is allowed to issue provisional measures that may or may not be finally confirmed by the subsequent adjudicative or arbitral body.[36]

---

[29] UNCLOS, Art. 290.   [30] UNCLOS, Art. 292.
[31] UNCLOS, Art. 73.   [32] UNCLOS, Art. 226.
[33] Myron H. Nordquist, Shabtai Rosenne, and Louis B. Sohn, *United Nations Convention on the Law of the Sea 1982: A Commentary, Vol. V* (Dordrecht: Martinus Nijhoff, 1988), 68–9.
[34] *Land Reclamation by Singapore in and around the Straits of Johor* (*Malaysia* v. *Singapore*), (2005) 27 RIAA 133; [2003] ITLOS Rep. 10.
[35] *Southern Bluefin Tuna Case (New Zealand* v. *Japan; Australia* v. *Japan) (Provisional Measures)*, ITLOS, Case No. 3 & 4, 27 August 1999.
[36] UNCLOS, Art. 290(5).

There is the possibility that new and emerging maritime disputes will be brought under the UNCLOS dispute settlement mechanism.[37] However, experience since 1996 has shown that the UNCLOS dispute settlement system has a number of limitations and that it is not comprehensive. These limitations may be a significant factor in the decision to litigate using this system. The next section briefly examines the major jurisdictional limitations of the UNCLOS dispute settlement system.

Jurisdictional limitations of the UNCLOS dispute settlement system and its impact on litigation strategy

Whether the party initiating litigation has the best possibility of winning the case is a key issue. As observed by one commentator, litigation is 'at best a zero-sum game and often the outcome is lose-lose'.[38] One of the main factors in the litigation decision-making process is jurisdictional certainty.[39] If there is any jurisdictional uncertainty, a state may be reluctant to seek recourse to international litigation. It is very common that a case may go through two phases: preliminary objections to jurisdiction and admissibility, and consideration of the merits of the case. If a case fails at the preliminary stage due to jurisdictional limitations or admissibility, it is unlikely to give the expected result to the party initiating the litigation. Confidence in the jurisdictional competence of the relevant court or tribunal is therefore a critical factor in litigation strategy.

The UNCLOS dispute settlement system has a number of limitations that may discourage a party from initiating compulsory procedures entailing binding decisions. If a dispute is submitted to the UNCLOS dispute settlement system without the consent of one party, it may face a jurisdictional challenge on the basis of three different grounds.[40] These grounds comprise propositions that (i) the alleged dispute does not involve any issue of interpretation and application of UNCLOS; (ii) another tribunal or procedure has priority over the UNCLOS compulsory dispute settlement system; and (iii) consensual procedures as introduced in Part XV, Section 1 of the Convention have not been exhausted.[41] All these issues

---

[37] One such issue may be climate change. See Meinhard Doelle, 'Climate Change and the Use of the Dispute Settlement Regime of the Law of the Sea Convention', (2006) 37 *Ocean Development and International Law* 319.

[38] Andrew Serdy, 'Paradoxical Success of UNCLOS Part XV: A Half-Hearted Reply to Rosemary Rayfuse', (2005) 36 *Victoria University Wellington Law Review* 713, 715.

[39] See further Chapter 2 in this volume.   [40] Churchill, above n. 5, 399.   [41] Ibid.

are linked with provisions of UNCLOS, which are discussed below along with their practical application in various judicial decisions.

The first issue mentioned above is linked with Article 279, which clearly states that the UNCLOS dispute settlement system is only applicable in the case of disputes concerning the application and interpretation of the Convention. The UNCLOS dispute settlement system will not be available in the case of law of the sea disputes that derive from the interpretation and application of customary international law or other treaties if there is no corresponding provision in UNCLOS. However, if a dispute involves both UNCLOS and other treaties or customary international law, the UNCLOS dispute settlement system will be applicable. In *Southern Bluefin Tuna*, Japan argued that the dispute was related solely to the interpretation and application of the Convention for the Conservation of Southern Bluefin Tuna 1993 (CCSBT).[42] In its provisional measures decision, ITLOS did not accept this proposition.[43] The Tribunal was of the opinion that, under Articles 64 and 116–119, states parties to UNCLOS have an international obligation to co-operate directly or through international organizations in the conservation of highly migratory species including southern bluefin tuna.[44] Thus the dispute may be treated as a dispute related to the interpretation and application of UNCLOS.[45] In the jurisdiction phase of the case, the Annex VII arbitral tribunal held a similar view.[46] In the *MOX Plant* case, the United Kingdom argued that Ireland's case was not admissible, as the dispute relating to authorization and construction of the MOX plant was one regarding the interpretation and application of the Convention for the Protection of the Marine Environment of North-East Atlantic (OSPAR Convention) and the EC and other European treaties, as well as directives adopted under those treaties. Consistent with its previous decision, ITLOS rejected this proposition at the provisional measures stage.[47] The indication from the jurisprudence of ITLOS on this issue thus far is that it may not be a serious limitation to using the UNCLOS dispute settlement system for the settlement of law of the sea disputes that

---

[42] *Southern Bluefin Tuna Case (New Zealand v. Japan; Australia v. Japan) (Provisional Measures)*, ITLOS, Case No. 3 & 4, 27 August 1999, [46].

[43] Ibid., [55]. [44] Ibid., [48], [49]. [45] Ibid., [55].

[46] *Southern Bluefin Tuna Case (New Zealand v. Japan; Australia v. Japan) (Provisional Measures)*, ITLOS, Case No. 3 & 4, 27 August 1999, [47]–[52]. However, the tribunal found that it lacked jurisdiction in this case for another reason, which will be discussed below. See notes 50–55 below.

[47] *The MOX Plant Case (Provisional Measures)*, ITLOS, Case No. 10, 3 December 2001, [50], [51].

268   MD. SAIFUL KARIM

implicate other international obligations.[48] As a result, states should not be dissuaded from resorting to litigation under UNCLOS.

The next issue is whether another tribunal or procedure has priority over the UNCLOS compulsory dispute settlement system. Two articles of UNCLOS are related to this issue: Articles 281 and 282. Article 281 provides that if states decide to settle their dispute using other peaceful means of dispute settlement of their own choice, the UNCLOS compulsory dispute settlement system will only be applicable if no settlement is reached through recourse to such means and the agreement between the parties does not exclude any further procedure. According to Article 282, if the parties to a dispute have agreed through a general, regional, or bilateral agreement or otherwise that such a dispute shall be submitted to a procedure that entails a binding decision, that procedure shall apply in lieu of the UNCLOS dispute settlement procedures unless the parties to the dispute otherwise agree.

Article 281 was mainly relied on in the *Southern Bluefin Tuna, Land Reclamation,* and *Barbados/Trinidad and Tobago* cases. In *Southern Bluefin Tuna,* the Annex VII tribunal decided that the CCSBT constituted an agreement of the kind referred to in Article 281.[49] The tribunal also decided that the dispute between the parties was still an unsettled dispute under the CCSBT, and UNCLOS therefore excluded recourse to any further procedure.[50] This interpretation of the tribunal has been considered very controversial,[51] and attracted significant debate.[52] One issue

---

[48] Churchill, above n. 5, 401.

[49] *Southern Bluefin Tuna Case (New Zealand v. Japan; Australia v. Japan) (Provisional Measures),* ITLOS, Case No. 3 & 4, 27 August 1999, [63].

[50] Ibid.

[51] Alan Boyle, 'Southern Bluefin Tuna Arbitration', (2001) 50 ICLQ 447. See also Churchill, above n. 5, 403.

[52] See generally Boyle, above n. 51; Leah Sturtz, 'Southern Bluefin Tuna Case: Australia and New Zealand *v.* Japan', (2001) 28 *Ecology Law Quarterly* 455; Barbara Kwiatkowska, 'The Australia and New Zealand *v.* Japan Southern Bluefin Tuna (Jurisdiction and Admissibility) Award of the First Law of the Sea Convention Annex VII Arbitral Tribunal', (2001) 16 *International Journal of Marine and Coastal Law* 239; Tim Stephens, 'A Paper Umbrella which Dissolves in the Rain? Implications of the Southern Bluefin Tuna Case for the Compulsory Resolution of Disputes Concerning the Marine Environment', (2001) 6 *Asia Pacific Journal of Environmental Law* 297; Barbara Kwiatkowska, 'The Southern Bluefin Tuna (New Zealand *v.* Japan; Australia *v.* Japan) Cases', (2000) 15 *International Journal of Marine and Coastal Law* 1; Tim Stephens, 'The Limits of International Adjudication in International Environmental Law: Another Perspective on the Southern Bluefin Tuna Case', (2004) 19 *International Journal of Marine and Coastal Law* 177, 187; Douglas M. Johnston, 'Fishery Diplomacy and Science and the Judicial Function', (1999) 10 *Yearbook of International Environmental Law* 33; Jacqueline Peel, 'A Paper Umbrella which

is whether the CCSBT is an agreement of the kind referred to in Article 281 of UNCLOS. The dispute settlement system under Article 16 of the CCSBT is related to disputes arising under the CCSBT, whereas the UNCLOS dispute settlement system is for disputes arising from the interpretation and application of UNCLOS. However, the tribunal decided that distinguishing these two systems of dispute settlement 'would be artificial',[53] and Article 16 of the CCSBT provided for 'an agreement by the parties to seek settlement of the instant dispute by peaceful means of their own choice'.[54] The next issue was whether Article 16 of the CCSBT excluded any further procedure. Article 16 did not do so explicitly, but the tribunal found that Article 16 was comparable to such provisions as Article XI of the Antarctic Treaty 1959, and held that 'it is obvious that these provisions are meant to exclude compulsory jurisdiction'.[55] However, this interpretation is not beyond doubt, as observed by Alan Boyle:

> It is entirely obvious that Article 16 of the CCSBT is meant to exclude compulsory jurisdiction over disputes under that Convention, but it is far from obvious that it is meant also to exclude compulsory disputes under UNCLOS. With all due respect to the learned arbitrators, this assertion simply lacks conviction.[56]

He is also of the opinion that Article 281 was never intended to have the meaning attributed to it in this case.[57] The tribunal's interpretation may have a far-reaching impact on the UNCLOS dispute settlement system. This decision has further shown that the practical nature of this compulsory dispute settlement system can only be revealed through practice and that the apparent nature of the UNCLOS dispute settlement as a compulsory and comprehensive dispute settlement system is a myth.[58] The

---

Dissolves in the Rain? The Future for Resolving Fisheries Disputes under UNCLOS in the Aftermath of the Southern Bluefin Tuna Arbitration', (2002) 3 *Melbourne Journal of International Law* 53; Bill Mansfield, 'Letter to the Editor: The Southern Bluefin Tuna Arbitration: Comments on Professor Barbara Kwiatkowska's Article', (2001) 16 *International Journal of Marine and Coastal Law* 361; Bill Mansfield, 'Compulsory Dispute Settlement after the Southern Bluefin Tuna Award', in Alex G. Oude Elferink and Donald R. Rothwell (eds.), *Oceans Management in the Twenty-First Century: Institutional Frameworks and Responses* (Dordrecht: Martinus Nijhoff, 2004) 255.

[53] *Southern Bluefin Tuna Case (New Zealand v. Japan; Australia v. Japan) (Provisional Measures)*, ITLOS, Case No. 3 & 4, 27 August 1999, [53]–[65].
[54] Ibid., [54].   [55] Ibid., [58].   [56] Boyle, above n. 51, 449.   [57] Ibid.
[58] See generally Shirley V. Scott, 'The Contribution of the LOS Convention Organizations to its Harmonious Implementation', in Alex G. Oude Elferink and Donald R. Rothwell (eds.), *Oceans Management in the Twenty-First Century: Institutional Frameworks and Responses* (Dordrecht: Martinus Nijhoff, 2004) 313.

270 MD. SAIFUL KARIM

tribunal itself indicated as such and concluded that the UNCLOS dispute settlement system 'falls significantly short of establishing a truly comprehensive regime of compulsory jurisdiction entailing binding decisions'.[59] This interpretation of UNCLOS may be very critical to states in deciding in favour of litigation using the UNCLOS dispute settlement system. The decision has created serious uncertainty that makes litigation using the UNCLOS dispute settlement system a less attractive option for states in areas where there are some ambiguities in UNCLOS provisions regarding the applicability of the UNCLOS dispute settlement system.

The application of Article 281 was also raised by Singapore in the provisional measures stage of the *Land Reclamation* case, arguing that the parties were engaged in a negotiation to settle the dispute. However, ITLOS rejected this proposition as the parties had agreed that the negotiations were without prejudice to Malaysia's right to continue proceedings in the Annex VII arbitral tribunal.[60]

In the *MOX Plant Case*, the United Kingdom also relied on these provisions of UNCLOS. In the provisional measures stage, it argued that the main elements of the dispute were covered by the dispute settlement procedures of the OSPAR Convention and the EC and Euratom treaties, which had been, or would be, initiated by Ireland, and so no jurisdiction was available under the UNCLOS dispute settlement system.[61] ITLOS rejected this argument, stating that the dispute settlement systems of those treaties dealt with disputes arising from the interpretation and application of those treaties rather than disputes related to the interpretation and application of UNCLOS. ITLOS decided that Article 282 was not applicable in these types of situation.[62] However, the Annex VII tribunal later suspended proceedings because of the possibility of proceedings in the European Court of Justice (ECJ). According to Churchill, it was not clear whether the tribunal suspended its proceedings as an application of Article 282 or for another reason.[63] The tribunal stated:

> [Taking into account] considerations of mutual respect and comity which should prevail between judicial institutions both of which may be called

---

[59] *Southern Bluefin Tuna Case (New Zealand v. Japan; Australia v. Japan) (Provisional Measures)*, ITLOS, Case No. 3 & 4, 27 August 1999, [62].

[60] *Land Reclamation by Singapore in and around the Straits of Johor (Malaysia v. Singapore) (Provisional Measures)*, [2003] ITLOS Rep. 10, [49] (*Land Reclamation Case*).

[61] *The MOX Plant Case (Provisional Measures)*, ITLOS, Case No. 10, 3 December 2001, [41]–[44].

[62] Ibid., [49]–[53].   [63] Churchill, above n. 5, 404.

LITIGATING LAW OF THE SEA DISPUTES

upon to determine rights and obligations as between two states, the Tribunal considers that it would be inappropriate for it to proceed further with hearing the Parties on the merits of the dispute in the absence of a resolution of the problems referred to. Moreover, a procedure that might result in two conflicting decisions on the same issue would not be helpful to the resolution of the dispute between the Parties.[64]

However, Crawford has stated that the tribunal decision was because of Article 281 of UNCLOS, citing the claim by European Commission that if the ECJ has exclusive jurisdiction pursuant to Article 292 of the EC Treaty, the Annex VII tribunal would be without jurisdiction by virtue of Article 281 of UNCLOS.[65] The ECJ ultimately decided that Ireland had violated Article 292 of the EC Treaty by initiating the case under the UNCLOS dispute settlement system.[66] The ECJ held that it was the only court competent to decide on EC law, which includes UNCLOS.[67] Consequently, Ireland had to withdraw the case from the UNCLOS arbitral tribunal.[68]

However, recent jurisprudence shows that the approach to the interpretation of Article 281 may have shifted. In *Barbados* v. *Trinidad and Tobago*, which concerned a maritime boundary delimitation dispute, another Annex VII arbitral tribunal observed that 'it would appear that Article 281 is intended primarily to cover the situation where the Parties have come to an *ad hoc* agreement as to the means to be adopted to settle the particular dispute which has arisen'.[69] According to Kwiatkowska, this clarification may be very significant, considering the very broad interpretation of the term 'peaceful means' under Article 281 by the *Southern Bluefin Tuna* arbitration.[70] However, whether this clarification is evident enough or how it has removed the ambiguity created by the *Southern Bluefin Tuna* arbitration is not fully clear. The decision for litigation using

---

[64] *The MOX Plant Case (Ireland v. United Kingdom) (Order No. 3)*, PCA, 24 June 2003), [28]. See also Volker Roben, 'The Order of the UNCLOS Annex VII Arbitral Tribunal to Suspend Proceedings in the Case of the MOX Plant at Sellafield: How Much Jurisdictional Subsidiarity?', (2004) 73 *Nordic Journal of International Law* 223.

[65] James Crawford, 'Continuity and Discontinuity in International Dispute Settlement: An Inaugural Lecture', (2010) 1 *Journal of International Dispute Settlement* 3, 21.

[66] *Commission of the European Communities* v. *Ireland* (Case C-459/03), [2006] ECR I-4635.

[67] Ibid.

[68] *The MOX Plant Case (Ireland v. United Kingdom) (Order No. 6)*, PCA, 6 June 2008).

[69] *Arbitration between Barbados and the Republic of Trinidad and Tobago*, (2006) 45 ILM 800, [200](ii). See generally Barbara Kwiatkowska, 'Barbados/Trinidad and Tobago Award on Jurisdiction and Merits', (2007) 101 AJIL 149, 151–2.

[70] Barbara Kwiatkowska, 'The 2006 Barbados/Trinidad and Tobago Award: A Landmark in Compulsory Jurisdiction and Equitable Maritime Boundary Delimitation', (2007) 22 *International Journal of Marine and Coastal Law* 7, 24.

MD. SAIFUL KARIM

Table 12.1 *Declarations under Article 298 concerning optional exceptions to compulsory dispute settlement (total number of parties: 166[1])*

Exception	Number of states
Maritime boundaries and historic title	29
Military activities	20
Law enforcement activities relating to marine scientific research and fishing within the EEZ	19
Disputes in respect of which the UN Security Council is exercising its functions	17

[1] United Nations, Chronological lists of ratifications of, accessions and successions to the Convention and the related Agreements as at 20 September 2013 (4 November 2013), available at www.un.org/Depts/los/reference_files/chronological_lists_of_ratifications.htm.

the UNCLOS dispute settlement is still a difficult one in certain circumstances.

Another limitation of the UNCLOS dispute settlement system is the permitted exceptions to compulsory jurisdiction set out in Articles 297 and 298 of UNCLOS. Article 297 deals with the general exceptions applicable to all parties, while Article 298 deals with optional exceptions of which parties may choose to avail themselves. Both the general and optional exceptions may be very critical issues in respect of the compulsory jurisdiction of the UNCLOS dispute settlement system.

As can be seen from Table 12.1, a small number of countries have made declarations availing themselves of the optional exceptions to compulsory procedures. These statistics, however, do not conclusively diminish the impediments these provisions may impose because other states can make such a declaration at any time.[71]

The foregoing discussion makes it clear that the UNCLOS dispute settlement system has a number of jurisdictional limitations. It is pertinent to discuss whether these jurisdictional limitations have any role in the process of decision making in relation to litigation. Legal certainty is one of the critical factors in litigation strategy; if there is a fear that litigation may not be successful due to the jurisdictional limitations of the forum, a state is likely to be unwilling to use that forum. This becomes a critical issue when different forums for litigation are available, as may be elaborated

---

[71] UNCLOS, Art. 298.

by reference to Australia's recently initiated case against Japan regarding Japanese whaling.[72]

As noted above, Australia was unsuccessful in the *Southern Bluefin Tuna* arbitration because the tribunal constituted under Annex VII of UNCLOS found that it lacked jurisdiction. It is pertinent to discuss whether Australia's experience in the *Southern Bluefin Tuna* arbitration has any relevance to Australia's decision to refer the *Whaling* case to the ICJ instead of to arbitration under UNCLOS. At least one expert was of the opinion that the most likely possibility for Australia was to initiate proceedings under UNCLOS, arguing that Japan's whaling activities were in violation of the high seas marine living resources conservation provisions of UNCLOS.[73] However, Australia in fact initiated litigation in the ICJ.[74] Interestingly, Australia did not rely on UNCLOS in its application to the ICJ, but referenced other conventions, including the Convention on International Trade in Endangered Species of Wild Fauna and Flora (CITES)[75] and the Convention on Biological Diversity (CBD).[76]

The question then arises of why Australia preferred the ICJ to the UNCLOS dispute settlement system. One reason may be its previous experience. Australia likely thought that Japan might challenge the jurisdiction of the UNCLOS dispute settlement system. However, unlike the CCSBT, the International Convention for the Regulation of Whaling[77] does not have a dispute settlement clause, and Article 281 would not therefore have applied. However, broader legal issues may arise. In order to use the UNCLOS dispute settlement system and hence UNCLOS provisions for the conservation of the living resources of the high seas, Australia might have been put in the politically undesirable position of re-defining part of its claimed EEZ in the Antarctic as high seas.[78]

---

[72] *Whaling in the Antarctic (Australia v. Japan)*, ICJ, General List No. 148, 31 May 2010.

[73] Natalie Klein, 'Whales and Tuna: The Past and Future of Litigation between Australia and Japan', (2009) 22 *Georgetown International Environmental Law Review* 143, 193.

[74] 'Application Instituting Proceedings', *Whaling in the Antarctic (Australia v. Japan)*, ICJ, General List No. 148, 31 May 2010.

[75] Convention on International Trade in Endangered Species of Wild Fauna and Flora (opened for signature 3 March 1973, entered into force 1 July 1975), 999 UNTS 243 (CITES).

[76] Convention on Biological Diversity (opened for signature 5 June 1992, entered into force 29 December 1993), 1760 UNTS 79 (CBD).

[77] International Convention for the Regulation of Whaling (opened for signature 2 December 1946, entered into force 10 November 1948), 161 UNTS 72.

[78] Ruth Davis, 'Enforcing Australian Law in Antarctica: The HSI Litigation', (2007) 8 *Melbourne Journal of International Law* 142.

The litigation strategy of a state may be different where the UNCLOS dispute settlement system is the only available forum for litigation. This issue may be demonstrated by using as an example the *Chagos Archipelago Arbitration* between Mauritius and the United Kingdom. In this case, Mauritius decided to use the UNCLOS dispute settlement regime despite the possibility that the United Kingdom would challenge jurisdiction on a number of grounds.[79] For example, this dispute may involve the determination of title to land territory.[80] It is a hotly debated issue whether the UNCLOS dispute settlement system extends to disputes over title to land.[81] This problem could easily be solved by initiating litigation in the ICJ, which has general jurisdiction. However, the ICJ was not an available forum because both Mauritius and the United Kingdom accepted conditionally the compulsory jurisdiction of the ICJ under Article 36(2) of its Statute.[82] One such condition excludes litigation with another member of the Commonwealth.[83] In this situation, the UNCLOS dispute settlement system is the only available forum for Mauritius and had to be relied upon despite some jurisdictional uncertainty.

The jurisdictional limitations associated with the compulsory procedures available under UNCLOS indicate that states may avoid litigation under this regime, particularly when other avenues for dispute settlement are available. While states clearly saw advantages in having compulsory procedures entailing binding decisions available for a variety of law of the sea disputes, there was not a broad consensus that litigation should be available in all instances, either because of the subject matter of the particular dispute or because alternative agreement had been reached on the appropriate avenue for dispute settlement. The legal parameters, particularly as manifested in jurisdictional limitations, are therefore highly influential, if not decisive, in determining whether a state will turn to litigation for disputes relating to rights and responsibilities under UNCLOS. There is also a range of extralegal factors influencing decision making and these are next addressed.

---

[79] Peter Prows, 'Mauritius Brings UNCLOS Arbitration Against The United Kingdom Over The Chagos Archipelago', ASIL Insights, 5 April 2011, available at www.asil.org/insights110405.cfm.

[80] Ibid.   [81] Ibid.

[82] ICJ, Declarations Recognizing the Jurisdiction of the Court as Compulsory, available at www.icj-cij.org/jurisdiction/index.php?p1=5&p2=1&p3=3.

[83] Ibid.

Extralegal factors in decision making for litigation over law of the sea disputes

When considering the large number of international disputes that exist, it is clearly rare for litigation to be used for the settlement of a dispute in international affairs.[84] The motivation of a state in initiating international litigation is a very important area of focus. On the other hand, it is equally important to know why a state makes a decision *not* to initiate international litigation.[85]

Despite some jurisdictional limitations, the UNCLOS dispute settlement system has been used in a number of law of the sea disputes. As can be seen from Table 12.2, the UNCLOS dispute settlement system has been invoked in twenty-nine cases involving contentious proceedings. However, some Annex VII arbitrations and applications to ITLOS for provisional measures are related to the same disputes.

Previous experience shows that there are a number of factors underlying using or not using the UNCLOS dispute settlement system, including jurisdictional uncertainty (discussed above), national interest, political relationships, reputation, and economic issues. Some of these are legal issues and some extralegal. This section focuses on the latter, and will show that legal certainty or the possibility of winning the case are not the only factors in the litigation decision-making process. Other factors may also play a critical role.

Economic issues and international litigation as domestic political cover

States may seek recourse to the UNCLOS dispute settlement system if they have failed to reach an agreement after negotiation.[86] As discussed above, UNCLOS introduced a system whereby states are obliged to accept compulsory jurisdiction for certain issues when becoming parties to the treaty. While the Convention has allowed for opting out of the compulsory dispute settlement system for certain disputes, some states have shown a passive acquiescence by not doing so and have created room for another disputant party to initiate litigation. As can be seen in Table 12.1, above, a

---

[84] Terry D. Gill, *Litigation Strategy at the International Court: A Case Study of the Nicaragua v. United States Dispute* (Dordrecht: Martinus Nijhoff, 1989), 47.

[85] Dana D. Fischer, 'Decisions to Use the International Court of Justice: Four Recent Cases', (1982) 26 *International Studies Quarterly* 251, 252.

[86] UNCLOS, Art. 286.

Table 12.2 *Litigation using the UNCLOS dispute settlement system*

Annex VII Arbitration

Total	Maritime boundary delimitation	Marine pollution	Marine protected area	Conservation of marine living resources	Maritime jurisdiction	Navigational rights/right of the flag state
10	3	2	1	1	1	2

ITLOS

Total	Prompt release	Provisional measures	Navigational rights/ right of the flag state	Conservation of marine living resources	Maritime boundary delimitation
19	9	5	3	1	1

small number of states have made declarations opting out of the compulsory dispute settlement system. Some states did not opt out in respect of maritime boundary delimitation, even where there was every possibility that a neighbouring country might initiate proceedings against them. It will be interesting to know what prompted those states to embark on this strategy. It is not possible to identify the causes conclusively, but there appear to be two main factors behind this decision, namely economic need and international litigation as domestic political cover.

Economic need may be a vital factor in the litigation decision-making process. This issue can be examined by using maritime delimitation under the UNCLOS dispute settlement system as an example. One of the main reasons for one party initiating this litigation and the other party not opting out of the compulsory dispute settlement system is the economic need to explore and exploit hydrocarbons in a settled and well-defined maritime area. As mentioned by the foreign minister of Guyana in *Guyana v. Suriname*, 'At every stage and at every level, we sought to impress on our Surinamese colleagues the need to ensure that the cause of development in our maritime space was not held hostage to dispute on delimitation.'[87] A similar tone can be recognized from the statement by the foreign minister of Bangladesh in the Bangladesh and Myanmar maritime boundary case:

> The absence of defined maritime boundaries with Myanmar or India has undermined our ability to exploit this much needed resource. Our difficulties are compounded by the far-reaching maritime claims of our neighbours. The resolution of this case in a manner that achieves an equitable solution in the areas beyond 12 miles provides an opportunity for us to realize our full potential.[88]

Settled maritime boundaries are needed for both parties to exploit resources. However, their boundary could be settled through bilateral agreement. Why did these states resort to litigation rather than a bilateral agreement? The answer to this question may be the political reality of the region.

In some regions it may be very difficult to negotiate a bilateral agreement with neighbouring countries because of internal political pressures. It has been demonstrated by political scientists that when governments

---

[87] PCA, Hearing Transcripts – December 2006, Day 1, 7 December 2006, available at http://server.nijmedia.nl/pca-cpa.org/upload/files/1207%20Day%201%20no%20header.pdf.

[88] ITLOS, *Oral Proceedings 8 September 2011 Verbatim Records (Bangladesh/Myanmar)*, 8 September 2011, available at www.itlos.org/fileadmin/itlos/documents/cases/case_no_16/PV_11-2_09_08_E__am.pdf.

'face strong domestic political opposition they are more likely to seek the settlement of international disputes through international legal mechanisms as opposed to concessions in bilateral negotiations'.[89] It is not uncommon for opposition political parties to create domestic political pressure on the government by claiming that a bilateral agreement is not in the best interests of the country. This issue will be elaborated below using the Bangladesh–India relationship as an example.

For Bangladesh and India to sign a bilateral treaty is very difficult – because of the political situation in both countries rather than the subject matter of the proposed treaty. For example, both countries recently signed an agreement to exchange enclaves of one country's territory completely surrounded by the other.[90] This agreement met with serious criticism by the main opposition political party in India.[91] When there is a serious objection from an opposition party, signing a treaty with a neighbouring country presents the considerable risk of it becoming an issue in the next election. On another occasion, the Indian government was unable to sign a water-sharing treaty with Bangladesh with regard to a transboundary river because of strong opposition from one of its own coalition partners.[92] Reaching political consensus to sign a treaty with a neighbouring country is a very difficult task and sometime just impossible.

Against this backdrop a bilateral agreement demarcating maritime boundaries would not be easily achieved. However, it does not mean that states will immediately choose international litigation if a bilateral

---

[89] Todd L. Allee and Paul K. Huth, 'Legitimizing Dispute Settlement: International Legal Rulings as Domestic Political Cover', (2006) 100 *American Political Science Review* 219, 225.

[90] 'Border Agreements: The End of the Enclaves', *Economist*, 7 September 2011, available at www.economist.com/blogs/banyan/2011/09/border-agreements. People of these political enclaves, which are a remnant of the partition of British India in 1947, have been suffering for last sixty years because of their de facto statelessness. They are prevented from any administrative contact with their home country. Reece Jones, 'Sovereignty and Statelessness in the Border Enclaves of India and Bangladesh', (2009) 28 *Political Geography* 373.

[91] 'India's opposition Bharatiya Janata Party (BJP) has tried to present the enclaves as symbols of Indian territorial inviolability and an opportunity to flaunt its Hindu-nationalist credentials and to attack what it sees as the ruling Congress Party's weak spot', *Economist*, above n. 90.

[92] Pallab Bhattacharya, 'Teesta Deal Has to Wait Delhi Tells Dhaka; Insists No Himalayan Rivers to be Inter-linked', *Daily Star*, 8 May 2012, available at www.thedailystar.net/newDesign/news-details.php?nid=233262; Nasim Firdaus, 'Slipping on the Slippery Slopes of the Teesta', *Daily Star*, 8 September 2011, available at www.thedailystar.net/newDesign/news-details.php?nid=201504.

agreement is not possible. For example, India has shown long-standing opposition to third-party dispute settlement in respect of transboundary river water sharing because, even if the issue is not resolved, there is no direct negative economic impact on India. By contrast, an unresolved maritime boundary may have an adverse economic impact because it is not possible to explore hydrocarbons in such circumstances.[93] We may conclude this part by saying that economic need and uncertainty in reaching a bilateral agreement due to domestic political pressure may have prompted India not to opt out of the UNCLOS compulsory dispute settlement system for sea boundary disputes, creating the opportunity for Bangladesh to institute the proceedings.

Apart from economic factors, a number of other extralegal factors may play a critical role in dispute settlement strategy, including, inter alia, reputation and national interests. These issues will be discussed below.

Reputation and national interests

Reputation and national interests may also be critical factors in deciding whether (or not) to initiate litigation. This issue will be examined using two prompt release proceedings in ITLOS, namely the *Volga Case*,[94] and the *Hoshinmaru* case.[95]

In the *Volga* prompt release proceedings, the Russian Federation announced that it would initiate separate proceedings against Australia for violations of Article 111 and Article 87(1)(a) of UNCLOS.[96] A ship is entitled to compensation if it 'has been stopped or arrested ... in circumstances which do not justify the exercise of the right of hot pursuit'.[97] In its prompt release application, the Russian Federation stated that it intended to invite Australia to accept the jurisdiction of ITLOS for a separate proceeding for violation of Article 111 of UNCLOS. ITLOS is Australia's preferred forum pursuant to its declaration under Article 287.[98] Alternatively, the Russian Federation might have referred the dispute to Annex

---

[93] See generally Lea Brilmayer and Natalie Klein, 'Land and Sea: Two Sovereignty Regimes in Search of a Common Denominator', (2001) 33 *New York University Journal of International Law and Politics* 703.

[94] *Volga Case (Russian Federation v. Australia) (Prompt Release)*, ITLOS, (2003) 42 ILM 159.

[95] *Hoshinmaru (Japan v. Russian Federation) (Judgment)*, ITLOS, Case No. 14, 6 August 2007.

[96] *Volga Case (Russian Federation v. Australia) (Prompt Release)*, ITLOS, Case No. 11, 23 December 2002, [25].

[97] UNCLOS, Art. 111(8).   [98] See generally Collier and Lowe, above n. 24, 92–93.

VII arbitration.[99] However, Russia did not initiate such arbitration. A discussion of the reasons behind its decision is illuminating.

There were three possible legal uncertainties regarding the alleged violation of Article 111 of UNCLOS. First, whether there was any violation of Article 111 at all. Second, even if there was a violation, whether jurisdiction existed over the Russian claim. This issue arose because of a Russian declaration under Article 298 of the Convention. Finally, there was Russia's standing as a flag state. However, none of these legal uncertainties was significant; in a previously published article I put forward the proposal that there was no serious legal impediment in this matter.[100] Perhaps the main reason behind Russia's decision was not the legal uncertainty, but concerns that lay elsewhere. Notably, there was no real Russian national interest at stake in this dispute and the issue could have negatively impacted on the national image of Russia. As stated by Judge ad hoc Shearer in his dissenting opinion in the *Volga Case*,

> It is notable that in recent cases before the Tribunal, including the present case, although the flag State has been represented by a State agent, the main burden of presentation of the case has been borne by private lawyers retained by the vessel's owners.[101]

In many prompt release cases, the flag state is in fact that of a flag of convenience.[102] Where real national interest is involved, the approach of the parties in the proceedings may be totally different. This can be seen by comparing the situation in *Volga* with that in *Hoshinmaru*.[103]

In *Hoshinmaru*, Japan initiated a prompt release proceeding against Russia for the release of its vessel of that name. The Russian authorities detained the *Hoshinmaru* in Russia's EEZ, where it was licensed to fish. Although it possessed a fishing licence, Russia alleged that, in breach of the licence, one type of fish had been substituted for another. This case

---

[99] *Volga Case (Russian Federation v. Australia) (Prompt Release)*, ITLOS, Case No. 11, 23 December 2002. [25].

[100] M. S. Karim, 'Conflicts over Protection of Marine Living Resources: The "Volga Case" Revisited', (2011) 4 *Goettingen Journal of International Law* 101.

[101] *Volga Case (Russian Federation v. Australia) (Prompt Release)*, ITLOS, Case No. 11, 23 December 2002, dissenting opinion of Judge ad hoc Ivan Shearer, [19].

[102] A huge number of ships operate under flags of convenience or are registered in what are otherwise called open registries. About 70 per cent of the total tonnage of the world's merchant fleet is registered outside the owner's domicile. The major open registry counters in the world are Panama, Liberia, Marshall Islands, Bahamas, Cyprus, Antigua and Barbuda, Saint Vincent and the Grenadines, and Cayman Islands.

[103] *Hoshinmaru (Japan v. Russian Federation) (Judgment)*, ITLOS, Case No. 14, 6 August 2007, [27]–[35].

differs from *Volga* in that the vessel was fishing legally in the Russian EEZ but had allegedly infringed the conditions of its licence, whereas the *Volga* was not entitled to be in the Australian EEZ.

Unlike in *Volga*, all the crew members of the *Hoshinmaru*, including the master of the ship, were of Japanese nationality and the vessel was legally and beneficially owned by a Japanese company.[104] The national interest of Japan was seriously at stake in this case, because the nineteen Japanese crew members were imprisoned by the Russian Federation. The interest of Japan was so great that a member of the Japanese legal team was later bestowed a national honour for 'playing an indispensable role in the maintenance of Japan's *national interests* as an ocean state'.[105]

In this case, as there were serious national interests involved, Japan was represented by a very strong legal team including legal luminaries such as Professor Vaughan Lowe.[106] Russia was also represented by a legal team of such standing, including Professor Vladimir Golitsyn, who later became a judge of the Tribunal. As both Japan and Russia had real national interest at stake both countries were represented by lawyers retained by the state, not private lawyers retained by the shipowner. The situation was totally different in the *Volga* case, as can be seen if we compare the oral presentation of Russia with that of Australia. As Australia's national interest was at stake, the country was represented by the most senior government lawyers as well as the globally renowned public international law expert, Professor James Crawford. On the other hand, the presentation on behalf of Russia was given mainly by private lawyers retained by the shipowner.[107] The agent for Russia said very little about the prompt release of the *Volga*. Although he gave a brief introduction to the issue in his first presentation, in his second presentation he mainly replied to the Australian allegation of Russian inaction as a member of the Commission for the Conservation of Antarctic Marine Living Resources (CCAMLR), and as a flag state in the conservation of the Patagonian toothfish. His presentation was mainly focused on Russia's future interests, not specifically on the plight of the *Volga*.

---

[104] Ibid., [27].

[105] Embassy of Japan, London, 'Japanese Government Honours Professor Alan Vaughan Lowe', 18 December 2008, available at www.uk.emb-japan.go.jp/en/japanUK/decoration/081212lowe.html (emphasis added).

[106] Professor Vaughan Lowe represented Japan as a counsel in the *Southern Bluefin Tuna* arbitration also.

[107] *Volga Case (Russian Federation v. Australia) (Prompt Release)*, ITLOS, Case No. 11, 23 December 2002, [19] (ad hoc Judge Shearer).

It was quite clearly and convincingly explained in the *Volga* case that Russia actually had no real control of the *Volga* except for providing the flag. The vessel was beneficially owned by someone who was not a resident in Russia,[108] and was operated by a Jakarta-based group engaged in illegal fishing in the CCAMLR area.[109] This assertion was supported by an affidavit of the master of the *Volga*'s sister ship, the *Lena*, which had been detained by the Australian authorities just before the *Volga*.[110] To institute another proceeding against Australia would have been a low priority for Russia, which had no real national interest in the vessel.

In the proceedings for prompt release, counsel for Russia were silent on one issue. They never claimed that the *Volga* was not engaged in illegal fishing in the Australian EEZ, but mainly placed emphasis on the technical issue of the legality of hot pursuit.[111] Another interesting point is that no action was taken to challenge the forfeiture of the *Lena*. The only difference between the *Volga* and the *Lena* was that the *Volga* was arrested a few hundred metres outside the Australian EEZ. Both vessels were engaged in the same type of activities.[112] On the other hand, from the very beginning of the proceedings, Australia presented a substantial amount of evidence in support of its allegation of illegal fishing by the vessel. There was very little moral basis for Russia to initiate proceedings against Australia for violation of Article 111 of the Convention.

Even if the Russian Federation were to win a case on the legality of Australia's actions under Article 111, its image might be tainted by such a case. Russia is not widely regarded as a 'flag of convenience' country, but, unfortunately in the case of the *Volga*, the Russian relationship with the vessel was tenuous. Had Russia initiated further proceedings, Australia could have highlighted this issue. Although the legal consequence of this emphasis is not particularly great, it would have been costly for Russia in respect of reputation. As a member of the CCAMLR, it would have been embarrassing for Russia if unlawful activities of the vessel carrying its flag were revealed and circulated more widely. As mentioned by Crawford, 'when one commences proceedings, one lays oneself open

---

[108] ITLOS, *Volga Case*, Minutes of Public Sitting, available at www.itlos.org/case_documents/2008/document_en_312.pdf, 44–5.

[109] Ibid.   [110] Ibid., 45.   [111] Ibid., 74.

[112] As Crawford observed, 'It seems, with respect, that the shipowner would have nothing to say if there was no doubt about the Article 111 issue, but why should the shipowner be able to rely on Article 111? What virtue is it to the shipowner that it was arrested in one place or another when the substance of the issue against the shipowner is flagrant, repeated, unlawful depredations against an endangered species?' Ibid., 76.

to criticism'.[113] Even in the *Volga* proceedings, Russia's performance as a member of CCAMLR was convincingly questioned by Australia.[114] Australia's very comprehensive presentation in the prompt release proceedings warned Russia of the danger of initiating further proceedings relating to the same issue. Doing so would have jeopardized Russia's reputation and image as a member of the CCAMLR and a permanent member of the United Nations Security Council. Perhaps these were the main factors behind Russia's decision not to sue Australia again on the *Volga* issue.

Conclusion

This chapter has shown that states may use or be reluctant to use litigation for the settlement of law of the sea disputes for a variety of reasons, including jurisdictional certainty, economic interest, political interest, reputation, and other national interests. However, this is an explorative study and does not necessarily present conclusive findings. Many other factors (covert or open) may play a role in the decision-making process. The settlement of disputes concerning the law of the sea most often involves very complex legal issues. While states are showing a general tendency to use litigation as a mechanism for the settlement of law of the sea disputes, self-interest remains the main factor in the decision-making process. However, the term 'self-interest' should not be interpreted narrowly. An enlightened self-interested state will consider all aspects of legal and extralegal issues, including reputational and political cost, and hence sometimes not pursue litigation even if there is legal certainty of winning the case. This chapter can be concluded by saying that, despite some limitations, states are showing an increasing interest in using the dispute settlement procedures available under UNCLOS, including litigation.

[113] Ibid., 34. [114] Ibid.

13

International environmental disputes: to sue or not to sue?

TIM STEPHENS

International environmental law has largely shaken off doubts as to its status as a legitimate body of legal rules and principles, and is widely recognized as having as much entitlement to specialized labelling as other fields of public international law such as 'international human rights', 'international trade law', the 'international law of the sea' or 'international refugee law'.[1] Although in a post-ontological era international environmental law is not a complete code, nor does it operate in isolation from other bodies of international law. Environmental issues may arise in many international legal contexts, including in other specialized fields, as seen most clearly in the ongoing debates surrounding the consistency of national health and environmental regulations with World Trade Organization (WTO) rules. This regime complexity greatly complicates the task of analysing in a general or abstract way the litigation of international disputes,[2] including those having an environmental dimension.

There is seldom, if ever, a *pure* environmental dispute, and instead environmental issues and environmental norms will normally intersect with other international legal and policy domains. As Romano puts it, 'the polymorphic nature of environmental disputes makes a wide variety of

---

Some elements of this chapter draw on the author's contribution to the Final Report of the International Law Association's Committee on International Law on Sustainable Development (2012), relating to the role of international courts and tribunals in advancing the principle of sustainable development.

[1] Report of the Study Group of the International Law Commission: Fragmentation of International Law: Difficulties Arising from the Diversification and Expansion of International Law, UN Doc. A/CN.4/L.682, [8].

[2] See generally James Crawford and Penelope Nevill, 'Relations between International Courts and Tribunals: The "Regime Problem"', in Margaret A. Young (ed.), *Regime Interaction in International Law: Facing Fragmentation* (Cambridge University Press, 2012) 235.

fora potentially usable, which are almost impossible to list'.[3] Against the backdrop of this complex international legal terrain, the purpose of this chapter is to assess the options available to states for pursuing their environmental foreign policy objectives through litigation in international courts or arbitral institutions.[4] In the light of the significant increase in the frequency of litigation on environmental questions in the International Court of Justice (ICJ) and other international judicial bodies, the chapter suggests several reasons why states are ever more willing to turn to 'legalized' (i.e. judicial) modes of enforcement over diplomatic (i.e. political) ones.

Weighing the options to litigate international environmental disputes

Factors at play in the decision to litigate

The decision by a government to litigate on the international plane is not straightforward, and involves the balancing of a number of factors, some of which may overlap or are in tension.[5] Klein has noted that relevant factors in the decision to sue may include economic concerns, historical considerations, the existence and function of relevant international organizations, the nature and intensity of domestic public interest, scientific and other evidentiary uncertainties, calculations of national interest, and the character of the relevant legal norms.[6] Also of importance will be an applicant state's assessment of the chances of success, and of the legal and political implications that may flow from a successful or an unsuccessful outcome.

Whether in a particular dispute the factors identified by Klein are relevant and the weight accorded to them by governments depend to a considerable extent on the character of the dispute, and on the political

---

[3] Cesare Romano, 'International Dispute Settlement', in Daniel Bodanksy, Jutta Brunnée, and Ellen Hey (eds.), *The Oxford Handbook of International Environmental Law* (Oxford University Press, 2007) 1036, 1055.

[4] States remain the primary, and in many contexts sole, actors capable of pursuing international environmental litigation, although there are some opportunities for civil society to influence the process, or in specific contexts (e.g., the United Nations human rights treaty body system) to instigate proceedings on their own motion: Linda A. Malone and Scott Pasternack, *Defending the Environment: Civil Society Strategies to Enforce International Environmental Law*, rev. edn (Washington, DC: Island Press, 2005).

[5] Natalie Klein, 'Whales and Tuna: The Past and Future of Litigation between Australia and Japan', (2008–9) 21 *Georgetown International Environmental Law Review* 143, 150.

[6] Ibid.

system and culture in the state concerned. Liberal theorists of international law (in an extrapolation of the democratic peace theory) have posited that such internal political differences have a flow-on effect in terms of international litigation choices, with democratic states generally more willing than authoritarian governments to litigate.[7] Yet even among democratic states there are significant variations both in the foreign policy priorities that are considered important, the process by which decisions are made about these priorities, and the way in which to implement them. Not all democratic states are as attuned to environmental concerns as others, even though, as Dryzek has argued, democratic governance is a *sine qua non* for the effective protection of the ecological systems on which humanity depends.[8]

An influential conceptual framework for examining how domestic pressure has a bearing on government decisions to litigate is supplied by Putnam's concept of the 'two-level game'.[9] Putnam's model describes the dynamics of foreign policy engagement by liberal democracies. Like other governments, including undemocratic regimes, democratic governments must negotiate and co-operate with other governments on the international plane in order to achieve their objectives. Yet in advancing their foreign policy agenda, democratic governments must also negotiate with influential societal actors on the domestic plane and satisfy the electorate at large if they are to remain in office. The designs of the executive and the will of the electorate are not always in alignment – witness for instance the decision of some democratic governments to join the invasion of Iraq in 2003 despite overwhelming public opposition.[10] However, democratic governments will, according to Putnam, usually seek to acknowledge and accommodate civil society concerns.

There is a growing body of evidence in the context of environmental diplomacy to support this liberal theory of foreign policy decision making.[11] However, again, there are important exceptions, such as

---

[7] L. R. Helfer and A. M. Slaughter, 'Toward a Theory of Effective Supranational Adjudication', (1997) 107 *Yale Law Journal* 273.

[8] John S. Dryzek, *The Politics of the Earth: Environmental Discourses* (Oxford University Press, 2005), 234–5.

[9] Robert D. Putnam, 'Diplomacy and Domestic Politics: The Logic of Two-Level Games', (1988) 42 *International Organization* 427.

[10] Gerry Simpson, 'The War in Iraq and International Law', (2005) 6 *Melbourne Journal of International Law* 167.

[11] Eric Neumayer, 'Do Democracies Exhibit Stronger International Environmental Commitment? A Cross-Country Analysis', (2002) 39 *Journal of Peace Research* 139.

INTERNATIONAL ENVIRONMENTAL DISPUTES   287

Canada's withdrawal in late 2011 from the Kyoto Protocol,[12] despite the fact that support among Canadians for a binding climate treaty remains strong.[13] Turning to international litigation specifically, the importance of pressure from domestic constituencies is evidenced by several decisions to bring key environmental cases before the ICJ. Strong domestic opposition within Australia and New Zealand to French nuclear tests in the Pacific was a major reason why the litigation in the *Nuclear Tests* cases[14] was commenced, despite the slim chances of its succeeding.[15] Similarly, a grass-roots environmental movement in Hungary that staged a series of protests beginning in the 1980s, and which had the support of key institutions including the Hungarian Academy of Science, succeeded in reversing the Hungarian government's support for the dam and dredging project on the Danube,[16] and led to Hungary instituting proceedings against Slovakia in the *Gabčíkovo-Nagymaros Project* case.[17] More recently, civil society protests (which included a blockade of an international bridge) in Argentina against a pulp mills project being undertaken in Uruguay on the Uruguay river provided key support for the decision by Argentina to commence proceedings against Uruguay in the ICJ in the *Pulp Mills* case.[18] Similarly the *Whaling in the Antarctic* case made good a pre-election commitment made by the Rudd government in Australia to seek an end to Japanese whaling in the Southern Ocean, and leaked US diplomatic cables indicate that the litigation decision was specifically aimed at responding to public pressure.[19]

---

[12] Kyoto Protocol to the United Nations Framework Convention on Climate Change (opened for signature 11 December 1997, entered into force 16 February 2005), 1771 UNTS 107.

[13] Shawn McCarthy, 'Support for Climate Action Still Strong in Canada, Poll Finds', *Globe and Mail*, 30 November 2011.

[14] *Nuclear Tests (Australia v. France) (Interim Measures)*, [1973] ICJ Rep. 99; *Nuclear Tests Cases (Australia v. France, New Zealand v. France)*, [1974] ICJ Rep. 253 and 457; *Request for an Examination of the Situation in Accordance with Paragraph 63 of the Court's Judgment of 20 December 1974 in Nuclear Tests (New Zealand v. France)*, [1995] ICJ Rep. 288.

[15] Tim Stephens, *International Courts and Environmental Protection* (Cambridge University Press, 2009), 138.

[16] Miklós Sükösd, 'Democratization, Nationalism and Eco-Politics: The Slovak-Hungarian Conflict over the Gabčíkovo-Nagymaros Dam System on the Danube', in Eileen Petzold-Bradley, Alexander Carius, and Arpád Vincze (eds.), *Responding to Environmental Conflicts: Implications for Theory and Practice* (Norwell, MA, and Dordrecht: Kluwer Academic, 2001) 225.

[17] *Gabčíkovo-Nagymaros Project (Hungary/Slovakia) (Merits)*, [1997] ICJ Rep. 7.

[18] *Pulp Mills on the River Uruguay (Argentina v. Uruguay)*, [2010] ICJ Rep. 28.

[19] Philip Dorling, 'Whaling Plan Was to Divert Public', *The Age*, 5 January 2011.

288 TIM STEPHENS

First-order versus second-order issues

Despite the growing importance to governments of environmental concerns, prompted in large part by the influence exerted by environmental mass movements, it is often the case that environmental matters are relegated to the periphery in inter-state diplomacy,[20] and this has implications for international environmental litigation.

In contrast to major issues of state, most notably those connected with national security, environmental issues have tended to be considered as second- or lower-order issues.[21] Hence states have often endured environmental harm at the hands of other states, and have seldom sought to elevate environmental disputes from the diplomatic to international legal arena. There are some well-known exceptions, including the *Trail Smelter* case[22] between Canada and the United States concerning air pollution from a metals smelter in British Columbia, but these tend to prove the rule by virtue of their rarity. Other serious instances of transboundary harm, such as the Chernobyl incident in 1986, which led to increased levels of radioactivity across Europe, and the Indonesian forest fires in the late 1990s, which produced a haze of dangerous particulate matter that lingered over the region for many months, attracted intense diplomatic attention, but never developed into legal disputes, let alone into claims before international courts.[23]

Although environmental questions are often marginalized in interstate diplomacy, they can be brought to the fore when closely connected to first-order issues. A classic example of this linkage is seen in the context of the Antarctic, in respect of which the 1959 Antarctic Treaty,[24] and the Antarctic Treaty System built on it, balances and links security and environmental values: the demilitarization of the continent, the promotion of co-operative scientific research, and the comprehensive protection of the Antarctic environment (including through the prohibition on mining).[25] The increasingly prominent discourse of 'environmental security' captures the reality that many environmental matters can be viewed

---

[20] Stewart Firth, *Australia in International Politics: An Introduction to Australian Foreign Policy*, 2nd edn (Crows Nest: Allen & Unwin, 2005), ch. 11.

[21] For an overview of the distinction in the context of US foreign policy see Sam C. Sarkesian, John Allen Williams, and Stephen J. Cimbala, *US National Security: Policymakers, Processes and Politics*, 4th edn (Boulder: Lynne Rienner, 2008), 9.

[22] *Trail Smelter Arbitration (United States* v. *Canada)* (1938 and 1941), 3 RIAA 1911.

[23] Daniel Bodansky, *The Art and Craft of International Environmental Law* (Cambridge, MA: Harvard University Press, 2010), 247.

[24] Antarctic Treaty (opened for signature 1 December 1959, entered into force 23 June 1961), 402 UNTS 71.

[25] Donald R. Rothwell, 'Sovereignty and the Antarctic Treaty', (2010) 46 *Polar Record* 17.

INTERNATIONAL ENVIRONMENTAL DISPUTES   289

through the first-order foreign policy objective of national security.[26] Climate change, the gravest of environmental threats to humanity, not only is an environmental problem but also poses challenges to regional and global security, and threatens the very existence of a number of small island states.[27] It may also be noted that natural resource issues have often been treated as first-order issues. While disputes over living and non-living resources are today viewed increasingly in terms of 'sustainability and the limits of resource use',[28] the hard substratum underlying such disputes is the competition between states for economically valuable living and non-living resources.

A given environmental dispute may be viewed quite differently by the litigating states in terms of its relevance to first-order foreign policy objectives. For instance, in the *Whaling in the Antarctic* case,[29] Australia contends that by undertaking its large-scale 'scientific' whaling programme in international waters, Japan is in breach of several general obligations of international environmental law, including the moratorium on commercial whaling adopted under the International Convention for the Regulation of Whaling.[30] Hence for Australia the case goes to the somewhat abstract question of global whale conservation, rather than being a core issue as the integrity of the Australian environment. The case is viewed very differently by the Japanese government, as one that challenges Japan's foreign policy priority to retain access to the greatest possible share of marine living resources so as to ensure the security of food supplies for the Japanese population.[31]

---

[26] Rita Floyd, *Security and the Environment: Securitisation Theory and US Environmental Security Policy* (Cambridge University Press, 2010), 61 ff

[27] Alan Dupont and William J. Reckmeyer, 'Australia's National Security Priorities: Addressing Strategic Risk in a Globalised World', (2012) 66 *Australian Journal of International Affairs* 34, 39 (noting that 'Pacific Island nations see climate change as an existential security threat rather than a manageable environmental problem'). See also Natalie Klein, *Maritime Security and the Law of the Sea* (Oxford University Press, 2011) 320 (observing that climate change 'may prompt greater emphasis on marine environmental security than exists at present').

[28] Rosalyn Higgins, 'Natural Resources in the Case Law of the International Court', in Alan Boyle and David Freestone (eds.), *International Law and Sustainable Development: Past Achievements and Future Challenges* (Oxford University Press, 1999) 87, 111.

[29] 'Application Instituting Proceedings', *Whaling in the Antarctic (Australia v. Japan)*, ICJ, General List No. 148, 31 May 2010.

[30] Opened for signature 2 December 1946, entered into force 10 November 1948, 161 UNTS 72.

[31] Midori Kagawa-Fox, 'Japan's Whaling Triangle – The Power Behind the Whaling Policy', (2009) 29 *Japanese Studies* 404, 405. See also Jun Morikawa, *Whaling in Japan: Power, Politics and Diplomacy* (London: Hurst, 2009).

290   TIM STEPHENS

Strategic and tactical international environmental litigation

That environmental disputes are generally considered to be lower-order foreign policy priorities has implications for the ways in which states go about resolving them. As they are likely to be seen as less serious than major disputes concerning core sovereignty or security issues, there is less pressure on states to resolve environmental disputes, and consequently they can be left to languish indefinitely. On the other hand, precisely because they are perceived to be of lesser significance, there are fewer political impediments to submitting environmental disputes for independent arbitration or adjudication. While states will never be indifferent to the result of international litigation, given the reputational costs associated with a loss, they may not be as concerned about an adverse finding as they may be in relation to other matters perceived to be more vital to the state.

States may therefore seek to bring somewhat speculative environmental cases for tactical, or even strategic, reasons to achieve defined foreign policy objectives, including as one technique for catalysing a negotiated solution. Examples include the *Nuclear Tests* cases brought by Australia and New Zealand against France in relation to the latter's nuclear testing programme in the South Pacific. The litigation had a very limited likelihood of succeeding in terms of generating a clear legal outcome, given the untested nature of the legal norms invoked. However, it was part of a broader international 'public relations' strategy that led, ultimately, to the cessation of French nuclear testing in the Pacific.[32] Another example is the *Southern Bluefin Tuna* case.[33] Although brought by Australia and New Zealand on far clearer legal grounds than those relied on in the *Nuclear Tests* cases, the matter foundered when an arbitral tribunal concluded that it did not have jurisdiction over this dispute relating to a Japanese 'experimental fishing program' for the endangered southern bluefin tuna. Nonetheless, although on one view it was a clear 'loss' for the applicants, the litigation is credited with moving the parties towards a negotiated solution to the impasse over allowable catches, and fishing quotas, within the Commission for the Conservation of Southern Bluefin Tuna.[34] As Lowe has observed, even if successful, 'Litigation is never an end in itself:

---

[32] For discussion see Stephens, above n. 15, 137–50.

[33] *Southern Bluefin Tuna (New Zealand v. Japan; Australia v. Japan) (Provisional Measures)*, (1999) 117 ILR 148; *Southern Bluefin Tuna (New Zealand v. Japan; Australia v. Japan) (Jurisdiction and Admissibility)*, (2000) 119 ILR 508.

[34] Bill Mansfield, 'The Southern Bluefin Tuna Arbitration: Comments on Professor Kwiatkowska's Article', (2001) 16 *International Journal of Marine and Coastal Law* 361.

it is always a means to an end . . . a step towards a solution of the problem, rather than a complete solution in itself.'[35]

International environmental litigation must therefore be understood by reference to the broader political context of 'environmental statecraft' in which it takes place.[36] Cases are seldom, if ever, brought purely to achieve legal objectives, and instead are often part of the 'theatre' of environmental diplomacy. Death has observed in this regard that 'Environmental sustainability – like justice – must be *seen* to be done, and [global environmental] summits are one of the primary sites where this performance is played out'.[37] International environmental litigation, particularly that which is unlikely to produce a clear legal outcome, can be viewed in a similar light, as serving to 'depoliticize' important environmental disputes and instead move them to an arena where they can be played out in a more genteel manner and where, regardless of the result, the parties can point to the case as having been resolved by an independent umpire.

The growth of international environmental litigation

The traditional view

The mainstream view among international relations commentators has been that international litigation plays next to no useful role in achieving the objectives set by multilateral environmental agreements. Rather than turning to bilateral, winner-takes all, confrontational approaches to advancing environmental objectives, it is posited that achieving regional or global environmental goals requires the formation of environmental regimes that incorporate a system of incentives, reciprocal obligations, and self-enforcement.[38] From this perspective, litigation is viewed not only as ineffective but also as a sign of regime failure. This view has been forcefully put by a number of commentators over several decades,[39] and more recently by Bodansky, who argues that traditional dispute settlement 'plays

---

[35] Vaughan Lowe, 'The Function of Litigation in International Society', (2012) 61 ICLQ 209, 221.

[36] Scott Barrett, *Environment and Statecraft: The Strategy of Environmental Treaty-Making* (Oxford University Press, 2003), 63–64.

[37] Carl Death, 'Summit Theatre: Exemplary Governmentality and Environmental Diplomacy in Johannesburg and Copenhagen', (2011) 20 *Environmental Politics* 1, 2 (emphasis in original).

[38] Ibid.

[39] Abram Chayes and Antonia Handler Chayes, *The New Sovereignty: Compliance with International Regulatory Agreements* (Cambridge, MA: Harvard University Press, 1995), 205: 'A century of experience with international adjudication leads to considerable scepticism

a negligible role in the implementation of international environmental law'.[40] Far more important to the effectiveness of international environmental law, the argument goes, is the design of treaties that can pull states into compliance through a range of mechanisms, including reporting, monitoring, and, if need be, the use of supervisory institutions such as compliance procedures.[41]

The emergence of compliance procedures is in large part a response to the perceived failures of inter-state litigation as a tool for environmental governance.[42] The first such procedure was established to supervise compliance with the Montreal Protocol on Substances that Deplete the Ozone Layer,[43] and others have since emerged in a host of environmental regime settings.[44] In contrast with courts, which are normally turned to only in the event of a breach of an obligation, compliance procedures are more proactive, and preventive, in their focus. They seek to assist parties in meeting their obligations, including by facilitating the provision of technical and other assistance. In several regimes, compliance procedures have been very active, and appear to have been quite successful in promoting more faithful adherence to an environmental regime. Importantly, these compliance procedures have tended to complement, rather than replace, traditional mechanisms of dispute settlement.

The flourishing of international environmental litigation

States now appear more willing than at any previous stage in history to litigate disputes concerning natural resources and environmental protection. After only a handful of cases throughout most of the twentieth century, the tempo of litigation on environmental questions accelerated from the 1970s, and such cases now comprise a substantial proportion of the dockets of several courts, most notably the ICJ. This is all the more remarkable given that international environmental regimes have increasingly turned away from judicial settlement as a preferred dispute

about its suitability as an international dispute settlement method and, in particular, as a way of securing compliance with treaties.'

[40] Bodansky, above n. 23, 247.   [41] Ibid., 250.

[42] Karen N. Scott, 'Non-compliance Procedures and Dispute Resolution Mechanisms under International Environmental Agreements', in Duncan French, Matthew Saul, and Nigel D. White (eds.), *International Law and Dispute Settlement: New Problems and Techniques* (Oxford: Hart, 2010) 223, 233.

[43] Opened for signature 16 September 1987, entered into force 1 January 1989, 1522 UNTS 29.

[44] Scott, above n. 42, 259–61.

settlement option in favour of compliance procedures as an alternative, 'softer', mechanism for managing and avoiding disputes.

Of the thirteen cases in the ICJ's docket, three are concerned directly with environmental issues: *Construction of a Road in Costa Rica along the San Juan River (Nicaragua v. Costa Rica)*,[45] *Aerial Herbicide Spraying (Ecuador v. Colombia)*,[46] and *Whaling in the Antarctic (Australia v. Japan)*.[47] A fourth case, *Request for interpretation of the Judgment of 15 June 1962 in the Case Concerning the Temple of Preah Vihear (Cambodia v. Thailand)*,[48] also has some relevance, as it is concerned, in part, with the protection of a culturally significant site inscribed in 2008 on the World Heritage List.[49] And, perhaps most significantly, in 2010 the Court handed down a decision that made express reference to a core principle of international environmental law, 'sustainable development', in *Pulp Mills on the River Uruguay*.[50]

There is a range of reasons why states now appear more inclined to litigate environmental questions in international courts. Commonly cited explanations include the existence of a growing number of judicial forums (the 'proliferation' of international courts)[51] and increased familiarity with international litigation across several policy domains (including human rights, trade, and foreign investment). Two developments appear to be of particular importance for explaining the flourishing of international environmental litigation: (i) the increasing 'depth' of international environmental law – that is, the greater clarity and stringency of international environmental standards – and (ii) the emergence of a detailed and demanding body of procedural requirements, including those relating to environmental impact assessment (EIA).

---

[45] *Construction of a Road in Costa Rica along the San Juan River (Nicaragua v Costa Rica)*, ICJ, General List No. 152, 23 January 2012.

[46] *Aerial Herbicide Spraying (Ecuador v. Colombia)*, [2008] ICJ Rep. 174.

[47] 'Application Instituting Proceedings', *Whaling in the Antarctic (Australia v. Japan)*, ICJ, General List No. 148, 31 May 2010.

[48] ICJ, General List No. 151, 18 July 2011.

[49] It should also be noted that one of the thirteen cases in the ICJ's docket is *Gabčíkovo-Nagymaros Project (Hungary/Slovakia)*; this litigation has been in abeyance, however, since 1998, when Slovakia requested an additional judgment because of the alleged unwillingness of Hungary to implement the 1997 judgment of the Court. Hungary has not formally replied to this request by filing a written statement with the Court.

[50] *Pulp Mills on the River Uruguay (Argentina v. Uruguay)*, [2010] ICJ Rep. 28.

[51] See Chester Brown, 'The Proliferation of International Courts and Tribunals: Finding Your Way through the Maze', (2002) 3 *Melbourne Journal of International Law* 453.

TIM STEPHENS

The increasing depth of international environmental rules

Many areas of international environmental law impose only general and flexible standards rather than laying down clear rules of conduct, placing courts in a difficult position should they be asked to examine them (they will be criticized for 'judicial activism' if they hold states to a high standard, yet will be labelled handmaidens to state interests if they do not).[52]

When confronted with a choice between rigid environmental rules and more flexible environmental standards, states will tend to prefer the latter, as they impose fewer constraints on state behaviour.[53] However, in a growing range of contexts in international environmental law there are highly detailed rules susceptible to judicial examination. By way of illustration, a comparison may be drawn between the 1933 Convention Relative to the Preservation of Fauna and Flora in their Natural State that, in Article 3(1), encourages states to 'explore forthwith the possibility of establishing . . . national parks and strict natural reserves', with the exceptionally exacting and elaborate norms in the global regime for controlling oil and other pollution from vessels (MARPOL).[54]

The existence of a body of international environmental law built on multilateral agreements of universal importance (and widespread ratification), and which is given conceptual structure and meaning by influential soft-law instruments including the Rio Declaration,[55] makes it possible for states to litigate with greater certainty as to the likelihood of a successful outcome. Yet the growing sophistication and clarity of international environmental law raises something of a conundrum with respect to its impact on state decisions whether or not to litigate. It might be expected that a set of clearer legal standards should lead to fewer disputes and less litigation, as states will be more confident of their legal rights, and

---

[52] Natalie Klein, 'Settlement of International Environmental Law Disputes', in Malgosia Fitzmaurice, David M. Ong, and Panos Merkouris (eds.), *Research Handbook on International Environmental Law* (Cheltenham: Edward Elgar, 2010) 379, 390.

[53] Benedict Kingsbury, 'Global Environmental Governance as Administration: Implications for International Law', in Daniel Bodanksy, Jutta Brunnée, and Ellen Hey (eds.), *The Oxford Handbook of International Environmental Law* (Oxford University Press, 2007) 63, 70.

[54] 1973 International Convention for the Prevention of Pollution from Ships, as Modified by the Protocol of 1978 Relating Thereto (opened for signature 17 February 1978, entered into force 2 October 1983), 1340 UNTS 62. For an account of the operation of this regime in practice see Ronald B. Mitchell, *International Oil Pollution at Sea: Environmental Policy and Treaty Compliance* (Cambridge, MA: MIT Press, 1994).

[55] United Nations Declaration on Environment and Development, UN Doc. A/CONF 151/5/Rev 1 (1992).

will not need to seek the assistance of a third party to determine their content and scope. By contrast, a very unclear body of law will present states with a high degree of risk and uncertainty should they litigate, as the outcome cannot be predicted with any real assurance or certainty. In such circumstances, states will be understandably reluctant to turn to an international court because of the loss of control over the process and the outcome, and the absence of mechanisms to reverse the effect of unwelcome court decisions.[56] In the most extreme circumstances, the dispute will be effectively non-justiciable because of the absence of judicially manageable standards.

The answer to the riddle that an increasingly deep body of international environmental law may help to set the conditions for greater international litigation can be found in the existence of a spectrum of types of environmental obligation, between – at one end of the continuum – those regimes that are shallow, unclear, or undemanding, and – at the opposite terminus – those regimes that are deep, clear, and onerous. As environmental rules become clearer the opportunities for litigation will increase, as the bounds for judicial determination become more certain. However, while there is greater predictability, in the spectrum between deep and shallow obligations there remains some level of uncertainty, which can be resolved by agreement between the parties themselves or via the process of delegation to an independent umpire. When the specificity and clarity of an environmental rule passes a certain point such that the way in which a norm operates is not open to any real debate, litigation as a tool for resolving uncertainty by providing authoritative interpretation becomes unnecessary. Nonetheless, there remains a further and obvious consideration when weighing the decision to litigate, which is that even when the law is certain states may not adhere to it. In such circumstances, litigation becomes primarily an enforcement mechanism, to bring a wayward state into compliance, rather than one that seeks to delegate a law-making function from states to an international court.

The increasing importance of procedural environmental standards

One manifestation of the 'deepening' of international law touching on environmental issues that creates the conditions for environmental litigation is the increasing salience of procedural obligations in environmental governance. The distinction between procedural and substantive norms

---

[56] Lowe, above n. 35, 215.

has been remarked on in a range of contexts in international law, including recently by the ICJ in *Jurisdictional Immunities of the State*[57] in respect of the distinction between rules of state jurisdictional immunity (which are inherently procedural) and *ius cogens* prohibitions against war crimes and crimes against humanity (which are substantive in character).[58]

The procedure/substance distinction has especial relevance to international environmental law, in part because improving the process whereby governments make decisions having transboundary environmental impacts is generally less contentious than imposing new substantive environmental regulations. Analysing international environmental law from the perspective of procedural obligations also brings to bear the many insights gleaned from the 'global administrative law' project. As Kingsbury has explained, there is a host of administrative law concepts that are relevant to global environmental governance, including accountability, reasoned deliberation, professional expertise, and local knowledge.[59]

As Ong has observed, there are 'well-established procedural obligations in public international law for States to notify, inform and consult ... other States about potentially damaging trans-frontier activities'.[60] Indeed, procedural rules have been a core part of international environmental law from its inception, and have been commented on in early disputes. For instance, in the *Lake Lanoux* case,[61] decided in 1957, an arbitral tribunal found that France was required to consult with Spain in relation to a hydroelectricity project that affected Spain as a downstream riparian state. In more recent years, this somewhat amorphous duty to consult has been buttressed by more detailed procedural rules, including EIA. Particularly important has been the work of the International Law Commission (ILC) in its Draft Articles on Prevention of Transboundary Harm from Hazardous Activities.[62]

The reinvigoration of interest in the procedural dimensions of environmental decision making provides a new avenue for international environmental litigation. It also aligns practice in litigation on the international

---

[57] *Jurisdictional Immunities of the State (Germany v. Italy; Greece intervening) (Judgment)*, ICJ General List No. 143, 3 February 2012.

[58] Ibid.   [59] Kingsbury, above n. 53, 65.

[60] David M. Ong, 'Procedural International Environmental Justice? The Evolution of Procedural Means for Environmental Protection: From Inter-State Obligations to Individual-State Rights', in Duncan French (ed.), *Global Justice and Sustainable Development* (Leiden and Boston, MA: Martinus Nijhoff, 2010) 137, 137.

[61] *Lake Lanoux case (France/Spain)*, (1957) 12 RIAA 285.

[62] Report of the International Law Commission, 53rd Session, 366, UN Doc. A/56/10 (2001).

plane with developments that have occurred in many domestic legal systems over a lengthy period. The judicial review of administrative decisions affecting the environment is a mainstay of environmental law in many municipal legal systems.[63] The engagement by international courts with procedural issues is akin in a general sense to the judicial review by domestic courts of administrative decisions on matters of environmental planning and assessment.

In several cases stretching back to the 1970s, the ICJ has been called on to consider what could be regarded as the pre-eminent procedural rule of international environmental law: the obligation to undertake EIA. EIA may be defined in various ways and incorporates a variety of elements.[64] However, at its core, it is, as defined in the 1991 Convention on Environmental Impact Assessment in a Transboundary Context,[65] a 'procedure for evaluating the likely impact of a proposed activity on the environment'. Until recently, applicants in international disputes have had little or no success in claims based on EIA, or asserted deficiencies in undertaking an EIA. In the 1995 *Nuclear Tests* case,[66] New Zealand contended that France had violated a customary international law obligation to undertake an EIA of the potential effects of underground nuclear testing on the marine environment in the South Pacific. France did not contest the principle, but argued instead that its assessment was adequate. The Court itself did not venture a view, as it found that it had no jurisdiction to reopen the original *Nuclear Tests* case, given that it concerned atmospheric testing and New Zealand was now raising a complaint regarding underground testing.

Shortly afterwards, in the *Gabčíkovo-Nagymaros* case,[67] which did proceed to a full examination of the merits, the Court stopped short of embracing EIA as a rule of customary international law and did not

---

[63] See generally Louis J. Kotzé and Alexander R. Paterson, *The Role of the Judiciary in Environmental Governance: Comparative Perspectives* (Alphen aan den Rijn: Kluwer Law International, 2009).

[64] For a helpful overview of the elements of contemporary EIA see Warwick Gullett, 'Transboundary Environmental Impact Assessment in Marine Areas', in Robin Warner and Simon Marsden (eds.), *Transboundary Environmental Governance in Inland, Coastal and Marine Areas: Asian and Australian Perspectives* (Farnham: Ashgate, 2012).

[65] Opened for signature 25 February 1991, entered into force 10 September 1997, 1989 UNTS 310.

[66] *Request for an Examination of the Situation in Accordance with Paragraph 63 of the Court's Judgment of 20 December 1974 in Nuclear Tests (New Zealand v. France)*, [1995] ICJ Rep. 288.

[67] *Gabčíkovo-Nagymaros Project (Hungary/Slovakia) (Merits)*, [1997] ICJ Rep. 7.

specifically mention EIA in its judgment. While not invoking EIA by name, the ICJ's majority judgment was clearly sympathetic to the concept. It observed that 'environmental risks have to be assessed on a continuous basis',[68] and encouraged the parties 'to look afresh' at the effects that the Danube dams project would have on the environment and consider ways to mitigate these impacts consistent with the 1977 Joint Development Treaty and 'new norms and standards' of international environmental law that had emerged in recent decades.[69] Judge Weeramantry, in his separate opinion, considered EIA expressly. He argued that a continuing obligation to carry out EIA was imported into the joint development treaty between the litigants.[70] He also held that the obligation was a general principle of international environmental law, as a specific application of the more general principle of caution that must be read into treaties that have a significant impact on the environment.[71]

The *Gabčíkovo-Nagymaros* case signalled an important shift, in that the ICJ was evidently receptive to arguments concerning the procedural dimensions of international environmental law. The case marked the first occasion on which the court made express reference to sustainable development, yet no judgment was made on whether the joint project on the Danube between Hungary and Slovakia, or its unilateral variation by Slovakia, was, or was not, sustainable. This was despite the large body of evidence before the Court pointing to the damaging environmental impacts of the diversion of Danube waters from ecologically important floodplains. Instead, the ICJ essentially deferred the adjustment of the balance between environmental protection and economic development to the parties themselves according to the bilateral treaty between them that set out the joint venture. Hence the Court effectively adopted a *procedural* approach to sustainable development, avoiding debates as to its substantive content and instead focusing on ways in which environmental governance can be improved by improving the processes of that management in a transboundary context.

There was a further step forward in the judicial recognition of procedural environmental rules in the *Pulp Mills* case. That case related primarily to the scope and operation of a bilateral river treaty, the 1975 Statute of the River Uruguay (1975 Statute).[72] As a consequence, the opportunities

---

[68] Ibid., [112].   [69] Ibid., [140].

[70] Ibid., 113 (Vice-President Weeramantry).   [71] Ibid., 112.

[72] Opened for signature 26 February 1975, entered into force 18 September 1976, 1295 UNTS 340.

satisfaction; this is not the proper way to pay due regard to the interrelation of procedure and substance.

Another recent decision to examine procedural obligations is the advisory opinion of the International Tribunal on the Law of the Sea (ITLOS) in *Responsibilities and Obligations of States Sponsoring Persons and Entities with Respect to Activities in the Area (Seabed Mining Advisory Opinion).*[78] Before turning to consider the implications of this opinion, some observations may be made about how the dispute settlement system of the 1982 United Nations Convention on the Law of the Sea[79] (UNCLOS), including ITLOS, is conducive to international environmental litigation.[80]

First, the jurisdiction of ITLOS, and the other dispute settlement bodies to which states parties to UNCLOS may refer disputes under Part XV, is more stable than that of the ICJ. This is because UNCLOS establishes a wide-ranging and generally compulsory system of dispute settlement. Second, most aspects of UNCLOS, including key environmental protection and resource management obligations, may be subject to compulsory settlement, allowing states to commence proceedings without seeking the specific consent of a respondent. For these reasons, it can be expected that the Part XV system of dispute settlement will be one of the more important forums for litigating international environmental disputes. However, at least until the *Seabed Mining Advisory Opinion,*[81] ITLOS has in fact shown some caution in its approach to sustainability questions.[82] This may be due in part to the criticism that the very creation of the Tribunal generated (and which to some extent ITLOS continues to provoke).[83]

Without question, the most significant decision of ITLOS relating to environmental issues is one of its most recent, the *Seabed Mining Advisory Opinion,* which was adopted unanimously by the Seabed Disputes Chamber of ITLOS and has been described by Freestone as 'historic'[84] from the perspective of international environmental law. The opinion was

---

[78] *Responsibilities and Obligations of States Sponsoring Persons and Entities with Respect to Activities in the Area (Seabed Mining Advisory Opinion)* (2011) 50 ILM 458.

[79] Opened for signature 10 December 1982, entered into force 16 November 1994, 1833 UNTS 397.

[80] See generally Natalie Klein, *Dispute Settlement in the UN Convention on the Law of the Sea* (Cambridge University Press, 2005).

[81] *Seabed Mining Advisory Opinion* (2011) 50 ILM 458.   [82] Stephens, above n. 15, 102.

[83] Jillaine Seymour, 'The International Tribunal for the Law of the Sea: A Great Mistake?', (2006) 13 *Indiana Journal of Global Legal Studies* 1.

[84] David Freestone, 'Responsibilities and Obligations of States Sponsoring Persons and Entities with Respect to Activities in the Area', (2011) 105 AJIL 755, 759. See also Duncan French, 'From the Depths: Rich Pickings of Principles of Sustainable Development and

sought by the International Seabed Authority Council on the prompting of Nauru and Tonga to ascertain the rights and duties of states, particularly developing countries, when they sponsor exploration of minerals on the deep seabed or the 'Area', which is declared by Part XI of UNCLOS to be part of the common heritage of humankind. The *Seabed Mining Advisory Opinion* turned on the interpretation of provisions of Part XI of UNCLOS, the 1994 Implementation Agreement (1994 Agreement),[85] and regulations adopted by the International Seabed Authority (the Mining Code).[86] These impose a range of stringent environmental controls on prospecting, exploration, and mineral exploitation activities, and in its opinion the Seabed Disputes Chamber was able to confirm their scope and operation. As such, care must be taken to understand the particular regulatory context of the *Seabed Mining Advisory Opinion* rather than rushing to judgment on its general significance.[87]

Despite this caveat, the decision will undoubtedly assume general importance in the implementing of procedural environmental obligations and in illustrating the value of international litigation. Specifically in relation to EIAs, the chamber found that states sponsoring mining contractors were under a due diligence obligation to ensure contractors conduct an EIA as required by the 1994 Agreement.[88] States were also under a direct obligation to conduct an EIA, as this is required by UNCLOS and by customary international law. In this context, the chamber referred approvingly to the *Pulp Mills* case.[89]

The chamber also made the more general observation that its 'functions . . . set out in Part XI of the Convention, are relevant for the good governance of the Area'.[90] This underscores the vital role that the chamber has, under UNCLOS and the 1994 Agreement, in supervising the performance not only of the International Seabed Authority but also of states parties. This model of judicial oversight of a regime with a strong environmental focus is unique in international environmental law, although it may be noted that other courts, including the ICJ, possess advisory jurisdiction and could be turned to assist international bodies perform their functions in relation to environmental issues more effectively.

General International Law on the Ocean Floor – the Seabed Disputes Chamber's 2011 Advisory Opinion', (2011) 26 *International Journal of Marine and Coastal Law* 525.

[85] Opened for signature 28 July 1994, entered into force 28 July 1996, 1836 UNTS 42.

[86] The Mining Code is available on the ISBA website: www.isa.org.jm/en/documents/mcode.

[87] Freestone, above n. 84, 566.   [88] 1994 Agreement, Annex 1 (7).

[89] *Seabed Mining Advisory Opinion* (2011) 50 ILM 458, [147].   [90] Ibid., [29].

LITIGATION IN CASES CONCERNING THE USE OF FORCE   309

the violent repression of Kosovo's ethnic Albanians was NATO's first 'out of area' military operation not authorized by the UN Security Council, and it demonstrated NATO's pursuit of a new role after the cold war. While the military operation was still under way, Serbia and Montenegro brought actions against ten NATO states for their use of force. It had at least an arguable case that NATO's military action was unlawful, but lack of jurisdiction prevented a decision.

Land and Maritime Boundary between Cameroon and Nigeria

Cameroon's case against Nigeria concerning their boundary dispute included claims about the ongoing use of force.[18] It claimed that Nigeria was responsible for the violation of Article 2(4) of the UN Charter and of the principle of non-intervention, because it had mounted full-scale invasions of Cameroon's territory, followed by occupation, and it had also been responsible for minor frontier incidents. Although the Court ruled on the delimitation of the boundary, it avoided a decision on the legality of the use of force.

Application of the International Convention on the Elimination of All Forms of Discrimination (Georgia v. Russia)

In this case, Georgia argued that Russia had violated the Convention on Elimination of Racial Discrimination (CERD) through its forcible interventions in South Ossetia and Abkhazia. It brought its action on 12 August 2008 while the conflict, which had broken out on 7/8 August, was continuing. The Court held that it did not have jurisdiction to decide the case.[19]

Provisional Measures

In all these cases, the weaker claimant state that had unilaterally begun proceedings also requested provisional measures in order to prevent irreparable harm resulting from the use of force.[20] Certain members of the ICJ

---

[18] Land and Maritime Boundary between Cameroon and Nigeria (Cameroon v. Nigeria: Equatorial Guinea intervening) (Merits), [2002] ICJ Rep. 303.

[19] Case Concerning Application of the International Convention on the Elimination of All Forms of Racial Discrimination (Georgia v. Russian Federation) (Preliminary Objections), [2011] ICJ Rep. __.

[20] Provisional measures were also requested in Frontier Dispute (Burkina Faso/Mali) (Provisional Measures), [1986] ICJ Rep. 3, and Application of the Convention on the Prevention

314   CHRISTINE GRAY

hear the case. There is clearly no general willingness on the part of states
to take this type of case to a binding third-party settlement, and few such
cases have reached a decision on the merits by the ICJ or by an arbitral
tribunal.

The first case on the use of force: the Corfu Channel *case*

Nevertheless, the ICJ's first case concerned the use of force; this was the
Corfu Channel case between the United Kingdom and Albania.[42] The
United Kingdom claimed that Albania was responsible for the blowing
up of British warships by mines in Albanian waters; Albania initially
challenged the Court's jurisdiction, but subsequently reversed its position
and counterclaimed that the United Kingdom had violated its sovereignty
by sending naval vessels into its waters to search for evidence as to who
had laid the mines that had blown up its ships. This case established
that the use of force was a suitable subject matter for the new Court.
Indeed the UN Security Council had recommended to the parties that they
refer their dispute to the ICJ.[43]

Moreover, the ICJ took a strict view on the substantive law. It held Albania responsible for the blowing up of the British warships because it knew
of the presence of the mines and had failed to warn international shipping.
On Albania's counterclaim, the Court held unanimously that the United
Kingdom's forcible intervention had violated Albania's sovereignty. The
Court's approach in this case could be seen as an encouragement to states
victims of the unlawful use of force to litigate; it strongly affirmed the
prohibition of forcible intervention in the Charter era. The case delivers
a particularly strong message for weaker states.[44] In a famous passage the
Court rejected the United Kingdom's special pleading that it was using
force only to assist the Court in obtaining evidence. It said,

> The Court cannot accept such a line of defence. The Court can only regard
> the alleged right of intervention as the manifestation of a policy of force,
> such as has, in the past, given rise to most serious abuses and such as

It did challenge the admissibility of the claims in so far as they involved actions by
Rwanda. The Court rejected this argument. *Armed Activities on the Territory of the Congo
(Democratic Republic of the Congo* v. *Uganda)*, [2005] ICJ Rep. 168, [196]–[204].
[42]   *Corfu Channel Case (UK* v. *Albania) (Merits)*, [1949] ICJ Rep. 4.
[43]   *Corfu Channel (United Kingdom* v. *Albania) (Preliminary Objections)*, [1948] ICJ Rep. 15,
17; *Corfu Channel Case (UK* v. *Albania) (Merits)*, [1949] ICJ Rep. 4, 6.
[44]   In its pleadings Albania had stressed its military weakness and the need for international
law on the use of force to be equally applicable to all states, weak and strong alike.

LITIGATION IN CASES CONCERNING THE USE OF FORCE   315

> cannot, whatever be the present defects in international organization, find a place in international law. Intervention is perhaps still less admissible in the particular form it would take here; for, from the nature of things, it would be reserved for the most powerful States, and might easily lead to perverting the administration of international justice itself.[45]

The Court also rejected the UK claims to be acting in self-protection or self-help.

However, the Court was cautious in its language. It made no express reference to Article 2(4) of the UN Charter, and simply held in general terms that the United Kingdom had violated Albania's sovereignty. It said that this declaration was sufficient satisfaction for Albania. Some judges were critical of the Court's restraint in this regard and called on it to take a more assertive role as the principal judicial organ of the UN.[46] This cautious choice of language is apparent also in later cases. The reluctance to make a more forceful denunciation of the wrong-doing state may show intent to avoid questions about the Court's relationship with the UN Security Council. It may also indicate a respect for the sensitivities of states parties intended to encourage states to use the ICJ. However, there is no sign that states responded to such (implicit) encouragement.

The Nicaragua *case (1986): a turning point for the court*

After its decision on the merits in *Corfu Channel*, the ICJ decided no further cases on the use of force until *Nicaragua*. That is, from 1949 to 1986 – the period of the cold war – no case on the use of force reached a decision on the merits. Then Nicaragua made its application to the ICJ. It challenged the legality of the forcible intervention by the United States against the left-wing government that had overthrown the repressive regime supported by the United States. The United States challenged the admissibility of Nicaragua's application; it argued that cases concerning the ongoing use of force were not suitable for the ICJ.[47] There were problems with the establishment of the facts.[48] Questions of breaches of

---

[45] *Corfu Channel Case (UK v. Albania) (Merits)*, [1949] ICJ Rep. 4, 35.

[46] Judges Azevedo, Ecer, Krylov, and Alvarez.

[47] *Nicaragua – Jurisdiction*, [1984] ICJ Rep. 392, [84]–[108].

[48] Ibid., [99]: 'The resort to force during ongoing armed conflict lacks the attributes necessary for the application of the judicial process, namely a pattern of legally relevant facts discernible by the means available to the adjudicating tribunal, establishable in conformity with applicable norms of evidence and proof, and not subject to further material evolution during the course of, or subsequent to, the judicial proceedings.'

against Rwanda and Burundi after it became apparent at the provisional measures stage that there was no real chance of jurisdiction on the merits. *Aerial Incident of 3 July 1988 (Iran v. USA)* was withdrawn after the parties agreed to discontinue the case; the United States paid compensation to Iran for the shooting down of the Iran Airbus by the USS *Vincennes* without acknowledging a breach of international law.[58] In this instance, it seems likely that the bringing of the case had helped to produce a settlement; the setting out of Iran's argument in its pleadings had made clear the strength of its case.

In several other cases directly concerning the legality of the use of force, the ICJ found it had no jurisdiction.[59] In all these cases, the dissenting opinions suggested that the Court could conceivably have come to a different conclusion and found jurisdiction by adopting a more radical approach. The two most controversial cases in which the Court denied jurisdiction were the *Legality of Use of Force* cases, and *Georgia v. Russia*. In the latter, Georgia argued that Russia had violated the Convention on Elimination of Racial Discrimination (CERD) through its forcible interventions in South Ossetia and Abkhazia. At the provisional measures stage, Russia argued that the case was not really about racial discrimination; if there were a dispute, it would relate to the use of force and the principles of territorial integrity and self-determination. Thus Russia said that the Court had no jurisdiction in the case.[60] The Court rejected this argument and by eight votes to seven awarded provisional measures. However, at a later stage after a full hearing it found by ten votes to six that it had no jurisdiction.[61]

There were also other cases in which claims of violations of international law arose out of the use of force, but in which the Court did not go into this question. Thus two cases on genocide arose out of the use of force; the claimant states asserted in their applications that there

---

[58] *Aerial Incident of 3 July 1988 (Iran v. United States) (Order of 22 February 1996)*, [1996] ICJ Rep. 9.

[59] *Aerial Incident of 27 July 1955 (Israel v. Bulgaria) (Preliminary Objections)*, [1959] ICJ Rep. 127; *Aerial Incident of 10 August 1999 (Pakistan v. India) (Jurisdiction)*, [2000] ICJ Rep. 12; *Armed Activities on the Territory of the Congo (New Application: 2002) (Democratic Republic of the Congo v. Rwanda) (Jurisdiction and Admissibility)*, [2006] ICJ Rep. 6.

[60] *Case Concerning Application of the International Convention on the Elimination of All Forms of Racial Discrimination (Georgia v. Russian Federation) (Provisional Measures)*, [2008] ICJ Rep. 353, [95]–[98].

[61] *Case Concerning Application of the International Convention on the Elimination of All Forms of Racial Discrimination (Georgia v. Russian Federation) (Preliminary Objections)*, [2011] ICJ Rep. —.

had been an unlawful use of force, but they were not able to claim for this directly because of the limited scope of the Court's jurisdiction.[62] In *Cameroon* v. *Nigeria*, the question of the legality of the use of force arose as a side issue in a boundary case, but the ICJ avoided the issue. After it had determined the land boundary, it simply held that Nigeria should withdraw its military forces from the areas under Cameroonian sovereignty. It did not assign responsibility for any unlawful use of force and it did not require Nigeria to provide guarantees of non-repetition. Nigeria had argued that Cameroon had been wrong to introduce responsibility for use of force issues in a boundary case; Cameroon's approach would make the eventual resolution of boundaries more difficult. The Court did not expressly accept Nigeria's argument, but its decision not to pronounce on the legality of use of force apparently indicates some support for this view.

Thus it is very clear from this overview that the ICJ has not gone out of its way to assert jurisdiction in cases concerning the use of force. There is no sign that the ICJ is willing openly to take the position that as the principal judicial organ of the UN it has the responsibility to maintain international peace and security and so to go out of its way to assert jurisdiction in all cases involving the use of force. It found that it had no jurisdiction in *Legality of Use of Force* and *Pakistan* v. *India*, and it avoided the question of the use of force in *Cameroon* v. *Nigeria*. Therefore it is clear to states that litigation on the use of force is only exceptionally going to be a realistic prospect.

Controversial assertions of jurisdiction by the ICJ in cases concerning the use of force

However, in a few cases, the ICJ's assertion of jurisdiction to decide on the legality of use of force has been controversial. In *Corfu Channel*, it initially relied on the contentious doctrine of implied consent or *forum prorogatum*. The United States as respondent state challenged the Court's jurisdiction in *Nicaragua* and *Oil Platforms*. In both these cases, the Court's decision to assert jurisdiction proved very controversial; the Court seemed keen to pronounce on the legality of the use of force over

---

[62] *Application of the Convention on the Prevention and Punishment of the Crime of Genocide (Croatia* v. *Serbia)*, [2008] ICJ Rep. 412; *Application of the Convention on the Prevention and Punishment of the Crime of Genocide (Bosnia and Herzegovina* v. *Serbia and Montenegro) (Provisional Measures)*, [1993] ICJ Rep. 3, 325.

320 CHRISTINE GRAY

the objections of the United States. In both cases, it might have been possible for the Court reasonably to have found that it had no jurisdiction to rule on the use of force. In both cases, the ICJ seemed determined to overcome all obstacles in order to pronounce on the US use of force. However, even if these decisions were to encourage other states to bring actions against the United States for unlawful use of force, there would today be little prospect of the Court's having jurisdiction because of the US actions to limit its exposure to such actions following *Nicaragua*.

Nicaragua

In *Nicaragua*, the Court asserted jurisdiction under both the optional clause and a bilateral Treaty of Friendship, Commerce and Navigation. It took a flexible approach in holding that Nicaragua had accepted the optional clause jurisdiction despite technical flaws in its acceptance. It was not sympathetic to the US attempt to deprive the ICJ of jurisdiction under the optional clause by making a new reservation just three days before Nicaragua brought its claim. It did not accept that the US reservations stopped it from hearing the case. As regards the 1956 Treaty of Friendship, Commerce and Navigation, the Court held that even such a primarily commercial treaty could allow it to deal with disputes concerning the use of force: it was for the claimant state to show that a particular use of force violated the treaty.[63]

The United States refused to participate in the proceedings after it lost at the jurisdictional stage; it announced that it was withdrawing from the case.[64] It said that the proceedings were a misuse of the Court for political purposes, and reasserted its position that the conflict in Central America was not a narrow legal dispute, but an inherently political problem that was not appropriate for judicial resolution. It claimed that much of the evidence that would establish Nicaragua's aggression was of a highly sensitive intelligence character. The United States would not 'risk national security by presenting such sensitive material in public or before a Court that includes two judges from Warsaw Pact nations'.[65] It pointed out that only the United Kingdom out of the other permanent members of the Security Council had accepted the optional clause. It argued that the

---

[63] *Military and Paramilitary Activities in and against Nicaragua (Nicaragua v. United States) (Jurisdiction and Admissibility)*, [1984] ICJ Rep. 392, [77]–[83]; [1986] ICJ Rep. 14, [270]–[282].
[64] Secretary of State Schultz's Letter and Related Documents, (1985) 24 ILM 246, 249.
[65] Ibid., 248.

Court's decision raised a basic issue of sovereignty: the right of a state to defend itself or to participate in collective self-defence against aggression was an inherent sovereign right that could not be compromised by an inappropriate proceeding before the ICJ. Thus the United States was claiming that its use of force should be beyond external scrutiny. It also suggested that the ICJ was in danger of politicization against the interests of Western democracies. It then terminated its acceptance of the optional clause,[66] and also the Treaty of Friendship.[67] It has not concluded any further friendship and commerce treaties giving jurisdiction to the ICJ. After the 1986 judgment against it on the merits, the United States vetoed a series of Security Council resolutions calling for compliance with the judgment, and it did not in fact so comply.[68]

However, the outspoken US attacks on the judgment did not focus on the Court's statements on the law on the use of force. There had been broad agreement between the parties on the substance of the law; their dispute arose over its application. This contrasts with the US reaction to the next ICJ decision against it, the *Oil Platforms* case.

Oil Platforms

The Court's assertion of jurisdiction in *Oil Platforms* was also very controversial. Another bilateral treaty, the Treaty of Amity between the United States and Iran, provided the sole basis for jurisdiction in this case. The Court was not wholly receptive to Iran's arguments. It rejected Iran's most far-reaching claim that the Court had jurisdiction under Article I of the Treaty of Amity, which provided for firm and enduring peace and friendship between Iran and the United States. Because the treaty was concerned with commercial matters this general provision could not be read as incorporating general rules of international law into the treaty and allowing claims for the use of force. However, Iran also accused the United States of violation of Article X on freedom of commerce by its attacks on Iranian oil platforms. The Court interpreted the treaty as giving it jurisdiction to consider the legality of the use of force by the United States.[69] In marked contrast to *Nicaragua*, the US continued to take part

---

[66] US Department of State, Letter and Statement Concerning Termination of Acceptance of ICJ Compulsory Jurisdiction (7 October 1985), (1985) 24 ILM 1742.

[67] Diplomatic Notes Concerning Economic Sanctions and Termination of FCN Treaty, (1985) 79 ILM 811, 815.

[68] 1986 UNYB 186, 191; Schulte, above n. 27, 197–205, 400.

[69] *Oil Platforms (Iran v. United States) (Preliminary Objections)*, [1996] ICJ Rep. 803.

in proceedings even after it had failed to persuade the Court to deny jurisdiction.

The Court's approach at the merits stage was strongly challenged by dissenting and separate opinions. The first and stronger criticism was that the Court had misused its discretion as to the order in which to deal with the issues in a case; it was wrong to choose to deal with the possible defence for its use of force under Article XX before it considered whether there had actually been a breach of Article X on freedom of commerce.[70] This choice enabled the Court to examine whether the United States had acted in self-defence, to conclude that it had not, and to hold in its dispositif that the US actions were not justified under the treaty, even though such findings were not logically necessary for its decision. The Court explained its choice of order by saying that the original dispute between the parties related to the legality of the actions of the United States in the light of international law on the use of force. The United States had argued before the Court, and outside it, that its actions were justified as self-defence.[71] Moreover, 'the self-defense issues presented in this case raise matters of the highest importance to all members of the international community'.[72] It seems very clear that the Court was keen to pronounce on the use of force in this case.

The second and much weaker criticism was that the Court was not justified in considering the law of self-defence in its interpretation of Article XX, which says that the treaty 'does not preclude the application of measures ... necessary to protect essential security interests'.[73] The United States argued that the Court did not need to address the issue of self-defence; its jurisdiction was limited to the interpretation and application of the words of Article XX. This article allowed the United States to make a subjective determination as to what was necessary to protect essential security interests. Again, the United States was trying to argue that the Court should not consider its right of self-defence, as it had in *Nicaragua*. However, Article XX could obviously not be interpreted to allow a use of force that did not constitute lawful self-defence; it would not be possible for a bilateral treaty to give a state party such a right to use force, and the United States did not make such a claim. Accordingly,

---

[70] See *Oil Platforms (Iran v. United States) (Judgment)*, [2003] ICJ Rep. 161, separate opinions of Judges Parra-Aranguren, Buergenthal, and Owada.

[71] *Oil Platforms (Iran v. United States) (Judgment)*, [2003] ICJ Rep. 161, 180 [37].

[72] Ibid., [38].

[73] Ibid., separate opinions of Judges Higgins, Kooijmans, Buergenthal, and Owada.

LITIGATION IN CASES CONCERNING THE USE OF FORCE   323

the Court held that the general rules of treaty interpretation required it to consider the relevant rules of international law on the use of force. Those judges who supported the majority view on this point said that it was important for the ICJ as the principal judicial organ of the UN expressly to reaffirm international law on the use of force at a difficult time, namely that of the lead-up to the 2003 invasion of Iraq.[74]

The US response to this judgment was very different from its earlier attack on the Court after the *Nicaragua* judgment. Its tone was much more measured. US State Department Legal Adviser William Taft set out the US position in an article.[75] This was an attempt to preserve the US position on the substance of the law, and in particular on the scope of self-defence. The United States, under President George W. Bush, advocated a wide and controversial view of the right of self-defence. Although much of the Court's reasoning should be read in the light of the special facts of the case, the United States was still concerned to put its position on the record and to reject the Court's limitations on the right of self-defence in case they were taken as being of general significance beyond the facts of the case. Taft regretted the Court's decision to pronounce on the issue of self-defence at all. 'Even more regrettable, however, is the fact that there are statements in the Court's opinion that might be read to suggest new and unsupported limitations on the ability of States to defend themselves from armed attacks.'[76] In particular, Taft criticized the Court for its narrow view of armed attack and for its insistence that measures taken in self-defence must be proportional to the particular act immediately preceding the defensive measures rather than proportional to the overall threat being addressed. These issues were crucial in the context of the 'global war on terror'.

Arbitral awards on the use of force

The two arbitration awards that addressed the legality of the use of force also made controversial decisions on the scope of their jurisdiction. After the large-scale conflict between Eritrea and Ethiopia, two of the poorest

---

[74] Interestingly, the division between the judges as to whether the Court should pronounce on the legality of the US use of force against Iran mirrored that between their states on the use of force against Iraq.

[75] W. H. Taft, 'Self-Defense and the *Oil Platforms* Decision', (2004) 29 *Yale Journal of International Law* 295: This may be taken as the official position of the United States, as there is no disclaimer that the article is only Taft's personal view.

[76] Ibid., 306.

324 CHRISTINE GRAY

states in the world, they turned to arbitration to settle the boundary dispute that had led to the conflict.[77] They also set up a Claims Commission to handle claims for violations of humanitarian law. In its *Partial Award: Ethiopia's Jus ad Bellum Claims 1–8*, the Eritrea–Ethiopia Claims Commission interpreted the arbitration agreement as allowing it to decide not only claims for violations of humanitarian law, but also claims on the legality of the use of force.[78] It did so despite the express words of the agreement that 'The commission shall not hear claims arising from the cost of military operations, preparing for military operations, or the use of force, except to the extent that such claims involve violations of international humanitarian law'.[79] The tribunal found Eritrea responsible for the initiation of the 1998–2000 conflict. In a somewhat surprising decision, it held that Eritrea had violated Article 2(4) of the UN Charter, even though it was using force to defend its own territory.[80] It went on to make the first award of damages in such a case since *Corfu Channel.*[81]

In *Guyana* v. *Suriname*, the parties were bound to resort to arbitration under the terms of UNCLOS. The tribunal took a wide view of its jurisdiction to decide on the interpretation or application of UNCLOS.[82] It held that it could pronounce not only on the maritime boundary dispute between the parties, but also on Guyana's claim against Suriname for unlawful use of force in violation of its duty to settle disputes by peaceful means. On the merits, it held that Suriname had violated not only UNCLOS, but also the UN Charter and general international law obligations to settle disputes by peaceful means because of its use of armed force to threaten a Guyanese vessel and oil rig. The tribunal held that Suriname's actions were 'more akin to threat of military action rather than mere

---

[77] *Decision Regarding Delimitation of the Border Between the State of Eritrea and the Federal Democratic Republic of Ethiopia (Eritrea/Ethiopia)* (Eritrea–Ethiopia Boundary Commission, 13 April 2002), (2002) 41 ILM 1057.

[78] *Ethiopia's Jus ad Bellum Claims 1–8 (Ethiopia v. Eritrea)*, (2006) 45 ILM 430.

[79] Ibid., 432, [5].

[80] For a critical account of this award, see Christine Gray, 'The Eritrea/Ethiopia Claims Commission Oversteps its Boundaries', (2006) 17 EJIL 699.

[81] However, the tribunal did not accept Ethiopia's claim that Eritrea was liable to pay compensation for *all* the harm caused by the 1998–2000 conflict. Eritrea was liable only where its specific acts were the proximate causes of the harm. See Eritrea–Ethiopia Claims Commission, Decision No. 7, Guidance regarding *Jus ad Bellum* Liability, 2007, available at www.pca-cpa.org/upload/files/EECC_Decision_No_7.pdf; and *Ethiopia's Damage Claims (Ethiopia v. Eritrea) (Final Award)* (2009) 26 RIAA 631. See also Michael J. Matheson, 'Eritrea–Ethiopia Claims Commission', *ASIL Insight*, 1 September 2009, Vol. 13, Issue 13.

[82] *Guyana v. Suriname (Award)* (UNCLOS Arbitral Tribunal, 17 September 2007), (2008) 47 ILM 164.

LITIGATION IN CASES CONCERNING THE USE OF FORCE   325

law enforcement'.[83] However, it rejected Guyana's claim for over US\$33 million, as the damages had not been proved.[84]

These cases provide a striking contrast with the caution of the ICJ in the *Cameroon* v. *Nigeria* case. In that boundary case, the ICJ did not expressly pronounce on the responsibility of Nigeria for the illegal use of force arising out of its occupation of territory subsequently held to belong to Cameroon. The tribunal in *Guyana* v. *Suriname* directly addressed the question whether there was a general principle that state responsibility was irrelevant to boundary disputes. It held that there was no such principle. This seems theoretically correct, but its approach in this case could discourage other states from turning to arbitration in boundary cases following a conflict.

Advisory opinions on the use of force

Other disputes on the use of force have reached the ICJ through requests for advisory opinions. When states believe that there is a breach of international law on the use of force, but there is no prospect of contentious litigation, they may exceptionally turn to the UN Security Council or General Assembly or other authorized bodies to secure a vote (by simple majority) to request an opinion from the ICJ. Also, when states believe that the Security Council is not carrying out its primary responsibility for the maintenance of international peace and security because of the shared position of the permanent members or because of a veto by one of those five states, they may turn to the General Assembly to seek a technically non-binding but authoritative advisory opinion on a question concerning the use of force.

In the three requests for advisory opinions dealing with the law on the use of force, as in contentious cases, states have challenged the Court's jurisdiction. The World Health Organization (WHO) and the UN General Assembly requested opinions on the legality of nuclear weapons, and the General Assembly requested an opinion on the *Consequences for States of the Construction of a Wall in the Palestinian Occupied Territory*. It was argued by states which opposed the giving of these opinions that the Court did not have jurisdiction under Article 96 of UN Charter because the question was not within the scope of the activities of the requesting

---

[83] Ibid., 231, [445].   [84] Ibid., [452].

326   CHRISTINE GRAY

body and was not a legal question.[85] The Court accepted this argument in the WHO case and refused its request for an opinion.[86]

It was a coalition of NGOs that initiated the World Court Project to put a question on the legality of nuclear weapons to the ICJ.[87] Nuclear and non-nuclear states were divided on the legality of the possession and use of nuclear weapons, and on the obligations of states parties to the Nuclear Non-Proliferation Treaty. The Non-Aligned Movement took up the case and secured the passage of resolutions requesting an opinion in both the WHO and the UN General Assembly. They were optimistic that the ICJ would rule against the legality of nuclear weapons and that such a ruling would strengthen their campaign for nuclear disarmament. However, the end result did not clearly support their position and may have made it less likely that states would seek advisory opinions on such general questions on the use of force in the future.

The General Assembly was deeply divided on the question whether to ask for an opinion; it passed the vote requesting an opinion with 78 in favour, 43 abstaining and 38 against. It asked 'Is the threat or use of nuclear weapons in any circumstances permitted under international law?' Many states made statements to the ICJ on this controversial issue. Seven states, including four nuclear weapons states (the United States, the United Kingdom, France, and Russia), argued that the ICJ should just refuse an opinion. They argued that the matter was not one for the General Assembly, but for the Security Council. Moreover, they claimed that an opinion would not actually assist the General Assembly, but would interfere with disarmament negotiations being carried on elsewhere in the UN. Nevertheless, the Court followed its own previous jurisprudence in giving an opinion. It would not second-guess the General Assembly as to the usefulness of an opinion and there were no sufficiently compelling reasons to prevent it from giving an opinion. However, it is notorious that when the Court came to look at the substance of the question, its opinion on the legality of the use of force was unclear.[88]

---

[85] *Legality of the Threat or Use of Nuclear Weapons (Advisory Opinion)*, [1996] ICJ Rep. 226, [11]; *Wall Opinion*, [2004] ICJ Rep. 136, [15]–[17].

[86] *Legality of the Use by a State of Nuclear Weapons in Armed Conflict (Advisory Opinion)*, [1996] ICJ Rep. 66.

[87] For an account of the background, see Judge Oda's dissenting opinion, *Legality of the Threat or Use of Nuclear Weapons (Advisory Opinion)*, [1996] ICJ Rep. 226, 330 paras. 5–14.

[88] Paragraph E included the statement, 'However, in view of the current state of international law, and of the elements of fact at its disposal, the Court cannot conclude definitively

The second advisory opinion which dealt with the use of force was the *Wall* opinion. The General Assembly had previously condemned Israel's construction of the wall on the occupied West Bank as unlawful, but there was no prospect of action by the Security Council after the United States repeatedly used its veto to block a similar resolution.[89] The League of Arab States then turned to the General Assembly to request an opinion from the Court, and the vote to request an opinion was carried, with 90 in favour, 8 abstaining, and 74 against.[90] Again, states were divided as to whether this was an appropriate use of the Court, and twenty states made statements arguing that it should refuse an opinion. However, only Israel argued that the construction of the wall was lawful.

Israel refused to participate in the proceedings before the Court. It argued that the question was really a dispute between two parties and should not be the subject of an advisory opinion without Israel's consent. It was not a matter for the General Assembly, but for the Security Council. Most disingenuously, it argued that an opinion would interfere with the political process.[91] The Court was not persuaded by these claims and issued an opinion. In contrast with the *Nuclear Weapons* opinion, its central holding was unanimous and quite clear – that the building of the wall on occupied Palestinian territories was unlawful. In the course of its opinion, the Court addressed the use of force in a brief paragraph because Israel had tried to justify its construction of the wall on the basis of self-defence.[92] The significance of this brief and rather obscure section of the opinion has been the subject of much conjecture.

Thus, exceptionally, states have sought advisory opinions as a substitute for contentious litigation before the ICJ. They have done so in frustration at the failure of the Security Council to act. However, states have been divided as to whether this is a proper use of the Court. The ICJ, as the principal judicial organ of the UN, has shown itself unwilling to refuse an opinion even on the most controversial issues. Here, as with contentious cases, accusations that the requests for opinions have been politically

---

whether the threat or use of nuclear weapons would be unlawful or lawful in an extreme circumstance of self-defence, in which the very survival of a State would be at stake.' *Legality of the Threat or Use of Nuclear Weapons* (Advisory Opinion), [1996] ICJ Rep. 226.

[89] See the account in *Wall Opinion*, [2004] ICJ Rep. 136, [18]–[23].

[90] Illegal Israeli Actions in Occupied East Jerusalem and the Rest of the Occupied Palestinian Territory, UN Doc. A/RES/ES-10/14 of 12 December 2003.

[91] *Wall Opinion*, [2004] ICJ Rep. 136, [51]–[54]; Israel Written Statement to the Court, 29 January 2004, at 114.

[92] *Wall Opinion*, [2004] ICJ Rep. 136, [139].

motivated have not swayed the Court to refuse an advisory opinion. However, the advisory nature of its opinions and the Court's approach in these two cases have meant that the Court's pronouncements on the legality of use of force in these two cases were general (and somewhat obscure) rather than specific. Moreover, it has proved difficult to secure compliance with these non-binding opinions.

Conclusion

Primary responsibility for the maintenance of international peace and security lies with the UN Security Council. However, the Security Council as a political organ has not in general taken it upon itself to pronounce expressly on the legality of particular instances of the use of force. Also, there is no hope of Security Council action against the interests of permanent members involved directly or indirectly in the use of force. Accordingly, states may turn to the ICJ in cases against permanent members, as Nicaragua, Iran, Yugoslavia, and Georgia have done. Since *Nicaragua*, developing states have also turned to the ICJ against other developing states in cases on the use of force where they are confident of the strength of their position, as in *DRC* v. *Uganda* and *Pakistan* v. *India*. A judgment in their favour, even in the absence of compliance by the respondent state, will strengthen their political position domestically and internationally. However, there is no willingness of respondent states to litigate on the use of force; they have contested jurisdiction and/or admissibility in almost all the cases on the use of force. States have not concluded special agreements to submit disputes on the use of force to the ICJ or to arbitration tribunals. Advisory opinions provide no more than a very partial alternative mechanism for litigation of issues involving the use of force.

In cases on the use of force the stakes are high: the respondent state will win or lose; there is little room for compromise. Even the measured language of the ICJ has not led to any greater willingness to litigate. When a respondent state resists the Court's jurisdiction – or attempts to lodge new reservations before a case, in order to prevent the Court from hearing an impending case – it might reasonably be deduced that it is not confident about the strength of the legal justification for its use of force. The ICJ has been consistent in its approach to international law on the use of force throughout the changing political circumstances since the Second World War. It has repeatedly referred to its own earlier decisions on the use of

LITIGATION IN CASES CONCERNING THE USE OF FORCE   329

force, in particular to its judgment in *Nicaragua*, and has reaffirmed its findings in the case. That is, the Court's position on the use of force has been predictable. It has taken a strict view on the prohibition on the use of force and on the scope of self-defence. It has avoided controversial questions such as anticipatory self-defence,[93] and the right to use force against non-state actors in third states.[94] So states that have relied on a wide view of the right to use force are unlikely to be willing to resort to the Court, or to accept its jurisdiction as respondent state.[95]

[93] It expressly said that it was not called on to consider this issue in *Military and Paramilitary Activities in and against Nicaragua (Nicaragua v. United States) (Merits)*, [1986] ICJ Rep. 14, [194], and *Armed Activities on the Territory of the Congo (Democratic Republic of the Congo v. Uganda)*, [2005] ICJ Rep. 168, [143].

[94] It avoided these questions in *DRC v. Uganda* and in the *Wall Opinion*.

[95] Israel, which also takes a wide view of the right to use force, used to have a reservation on the use of force; it subsequently terminated its acceptance of the optional clause. It seems possible that recent German and Djibouti reservations to the optional clause have stemmed from their involvement in US or NATO military actions. However, the United Kingdom has made no such reservation.

15

Adjudicating armed conflict

JOHN R. CROOK

International laws and customs regulating the initiation[1] and conduct of armed conflicts have been around for a long time,[2] but their observance has largely depended on shared cultural values, reciprocity, or the threat of reprisal. Participants in conflicts have observed the rules (if they have) in the hope or expectation that the opposing party would practise comparable restraint, or because they feared the consequences if they did not.

For about the last 150 years, there have been episodic efforts to utilize mechanisms shaped or influenced by law – particularly arbitration and litigation, but also including forms of inquiry – as additional means of promoting compliance and sanctioning non-compliance with the rules governing armed conflict. This chapter sketches some of these efforts. It suggests factors that led to resort to use of these mechanisms, and briefly considers the practical challenges involved in using them to address legal claims stemming from the chaos and brutality of armed conflict.

Adjudication has deep historic roots

International law rules regulating neutrality and the initiation and conduct of armed conflicts were applied with some frequency in international dispute settlement mechanisms throughout the late nineteenth and early twentieth centuries. Mixed claims commissions charged with resolving claims of states based on injuries to their nationals during revolutions

---

[1] At the risk of modest overlap with Chapter 14, this discussion mentions a few cases involving the law of neutrality and the law regulating resort to force (*jus ad bellum*) as well as the law governing the conduct of hostilities (*jus in bello*). Past tribunals have sometimes applied multiple bodies of law in a single case without distinguishing between them.

[2] See, e.g., Theodor Meron, *Henry's Wars and Shakespeare's Laws: Perspectives on the Law of War in the Late Middle Ages* (Oxford: Clarendon Press, 1993); Theodor Meron, *Bloody Constraint: War And Chivalry In Shakespeare* (Oxford University Press, 1998).

and other violent upheavals were a familiar feature of the nineteenth-century diplomatic landscape. Decisions to create these mechanisms often reflected great disparities of power. Weaker states saw the mixed commissions as a lesser evil than having a stronger power's marines take over their customs houses. The commissions also reflected the nineteenth century's enthusiasm for adjudication as a powerful tool for adjusting inter-state disputes on the basis of law – indeed, as the road to global peace.[3]

Nineteenth-century internationalists' enthusiasm for adjudication was fanned by the success of the famous *Alabama Claims* arbitration.[4] The tale is familiar. The Confederate States of America commissioned construction of several powerful commerce raiders in British shipyards. American officials complained to the British government about the vessels, but several were launched and had departed before official action was taken. The British-built raiders inflicted enormous damage on northern merchantmen and whalers. The most successful was the CSS *Alabama*, built by John Laird Sons and Company of Liverpool.[5] Before the *Alabama* was sunk by the USS *Kearsarge* off Cherbourg in June 1864, she took more than sixty prizes, worth approximately $6,000,000, then a huge sum.[6] In total, the Confederate raiders took 300 ships.[7]

Unresolved US claims for the damage wrought by the Confederate commerce raiders were prominent among the issues roiling US–UK relations during and after the American Civil War. Ultimately, in the 1871 Treaty of Washington, the two powers agreed to arbitrate these claims along with disputed fisheries and boundaries issues.[8] In Article VI of the treaty, the British side in effect conceded liability for violations of the law of neutrality, agreeing that the arbitral tribunal should apply as governing

---

[3] John W. Foster, *Arbitration and the Hague Court* (Boston: Houghton, Mifflin, 1904); David D. Caron, 'War and International Adjudication: Reflections on the 1899 Hague Peace Conference', (2000) 94 AJIL 4.

[4] Foster, above n. 3, 9; Mary Ellen O'Connell, 'Arbitration and Avoidance of War: The Nineteenth-Century American Vision', in Cesare P. Romano (ed.), *The Sword and the Scales: The United States and International Courts and Tribunals* (Cambridge University Press, 2009) 30, 36–7.

[5] Jessup attributes a critical British government delay in blocking the departure of the *Alabama* to Lady Harding, wife of Sir John Harding, Law Officer of the Crown. Lady Harding kept from Sir John, who was failing mentally, the US evidence that the *Alabama* was a warship ready to sail: Phillip C. Jessup, *The Price of International Justice* (New York: Columbia University Press, 1971), 4–5. See also Amanda Foreman, *World On Fire: An Epic History of Two Nations Divided* (London: Penguin Books, 2011), 279.

[6] 'Naval History and Heritage Command', CSS *Alabama*, 2011, available at www.history. navy.mil/branches/org12-1.htm.

[7] O'Connell, above n. 4, 35.   [8] Jessup, above n. 5, 2–7.

rules that a neutral government must use due diligence 'to prevent the fitting out, arming, or equipping, within its jurisdiction, of any vessel which it has reasonable ground to believe is intended to cruise or to carry on war against a Power with which it is at peace; and also to use like diligence to prevent' its departure. (The British government denied that these rules were in existence at the time, but agreed that the tribunal should nonetheless apply them.)

Given the parties' agreement on the governing rules in Article VI, the remaining issues primarily concerned the extent of compensable damages. There was not much factual dispute regarding the circumstances of *Alabama*'s construction or the extent of direct damages she and other British-built raiders inflicted on northern shipping. Instead, the issue of primary concern was whether indirect damages were compensable, with the US side claiming extensive consequential damages, such as increased insurance costs and even the costs of prolonging the war.[9] Under heavy pressure from the tribunal,[10] the United States did not pursue its consequential damages claims, leaving the tribunal to find that Britain was liable for direct losses inflicted by the *Alabama* and other raiders to the amount of $15,500,000 in gold.

Over the ensuing decades, dozens of mixed claims commissions were created to consider claims for injuries to claimant countries' nationals, often including claims involving military operations during civil wars or insurrections.[11] Many of their awards applied international law rules regulating the conduct of military operations. An example was the *Claim of Heirs of Jules Brun*, decided by a Franco-Venezuelan commission created in 1902 to hear claims arising from revolutionary events in Venezuela.[12] Brun, a French national, lived in a town briefly occupied by revolutionary forces. Brun was shot and mortally wounded by a government soldier as he closed his window shutters. The umpire, a canny, competent, if now largely forgotten, Vermont lawyer named Frank Plumley, concluded that the government forces had a special duty to protect innocent civilians, and that no military necessity justified the shot that killed poor Brun. 'A

---

[9] Marjorie M. Whiteman, *Damages in International Law* (Washington, DC: Government Printing Office, 1943) Vol. III, 1773 5.

[10] Ibid., 1773; Foreman, above n. 5, 812.

[11] Jackson H. Ralston, *International Arbitration from Athens to Locarno* (Stanford University Press, 1929), 194–249.

[12] Jackson H. Ralston, *Report of French Venezuelan Mixed Claims Commission of 1902* (Washington, DC: Government Printing Office, 1906), 5.

ADJUDICATING ARMED CONFLICT

state of war, a battle, or skirmish excuses only those [civilian] casualties which are unavoidable.'[13]

In the two decades prior to the First World War, governments also turned to arbitration to resolve inter-state disputes involving resorts to force. In 1899, Germany, the United Kingdom, and the United States agreed to arbitrate claims stemming from British and US bombardments and other military operations during a civil war in Samoa.[14] The arbitrator, King Oscar II of Sweden and Norway, ruled that British and US uses of force were not legally justified, and that the two powers were liable for the resulting damage.[15] In 1905, Great Britain and Russia resorted to a commission of inquiry to assess responsibility after Russia's trigger-happy Baltic fleet, racing for the Pacific to face near-annihilation by the Japanese navy at the battle of Tsushima, opened fire on a British fishing fleet on the Dogger Bank in the North Sea.[16] Contemporary observers credited the commission with averting war between the two powers, although this perhaps overstates things. Several of the Permanent Court of Arbitration's early cases involved violations of neutral rights, as Italian naval vessels intercepted, boarded, and seized French ships suspected of carrying contraband or Turkish troops during Italy's war in Libya.[17]

The carnage of the First World War dimmed faith in arbitration as the pathway to world peace, but, even after the war, arbitration was used to address some types of claim stemming from the conflict. The German-American Mixed Claims Commission, created under the post-war US–German Treaty of Berlin,[18] heard a claim on behalf of the Lehigh Valley Railroad Company against Germany stemming from German agents' sabotage of the railroad's munitions terminal on Black Tom Island in New

---

[13] Ibid.

[14] Convention between United States, Germany, and Great Britain Relating to Settlement of Samoan Claims, 7 November 1899, in William Malloy, *Treaties, Conventions, International Acts, Protocols And Agreements Between The United States And Other Powers, 1776–1909*, Vol. II (Washington, DC: Government Printing Office, 1910), 1589; see *Samoan Claims (Germany, Great Britain, United States)*, 9 RIAA 15, 21.

[15] *Samoan Claims (Germany, Great Britain, United States)*, 9 RIAA 15, 23.

[16] Nissim Bar-Yaacov, *The Handling of International Disputes by Means of Inquiry* (London: Oxford University Press for the Royal Institute of International Affairs, 1974), 48–60; P. Hamilton, H.C. Requena, L. van Scheltinga, and B. Shifman (eds.), *The Permanent Court of Arbitration: International Arbitration and Dispute Resolution, Summaries of Awards, Settlement Agreements and Reports* (The Hague: Kluwer Law International, 1999), 297–302.

[17] Hamilton et al., above n. 16, 88–97.

[18] Charles Bevans, *Treaties and Other International Agreements of the United States of America 1776–1949*, Vol. 8 (Washington, DC: Government Printing Office, 1971), 145.

York Harbor in 1916 (while the United States was neutral) and a second claim involving sabotage of a factory in New Jersey. The commission's umpire eventually ruled for the claimant in 1939, after finding that Germany offered false evidence leading to a 1930 decision in its favour.[19] The *Black Tom* case illustrates two crucial vulnerabilities of inter-state arbitration if a party is determined to frustrate the proceedings. As noted, the tribunal found that Germany's defence leading to a favourable 1930 decision rested on fraudulent and perjured evidence.[20] (While not all states are as cynical as Germany seems to have been, even generally law-abiding states can be tempted to fudge.[21]) Further, the proceedings were threatened when the arbitrator appointed by Germany refused to participate further, although this did not prevent the umpire from ruling against Germany.[22]

Thus there is a rich history of the use of adjudication and related mechanisms to address claims of state responsibility for violations of international law involving uses of force. These efforts seem to have been most successful in situations involving events limited in geographic scope and time, or where central facts were not disputed. In cases involving disputed facts, it is noteworthy that parties often utilized panels of naval and military officers, and not legally trained persons, to assess the facts.[23] As will be discussed below, fact-finding often is a central challenge in disputes regarding compliance with international humanitarian law.

Individual criminal responsibility for violations of international humanitarian law

Following the Second World War, matters moved in another direction. In the immediate aftermath of the war, the victors made energetic use of

---

[19] Lester H. Woolsey, 'The Arbitration of the Sabotage Claims Against Germany', (1939) 33 AJIL 737.

[20] Ibid., 738.

[21] Recently declassified documents indicate that British officials refused the International Court of Justice's request to see the sailing orders of the Royal Navy ships that struck mines in the Corfu Channel for fear the orders would prejudice Britain's legal position, not to protect naval secrecy: Anthony Carty, 'The Corfu Channel Case – and the Missing Admiralty Orders', (2004) 3 *Law and Practice of International Tribunals* 1, 3–4.

[22] Woolsey, above n. 19, 738–9; Stephen M. Schwebel, *International Arbitration: Three Salient Problems* (Cambridge: Grotius, 1987), 216–26.

[23] Bar-Yaacov, above n. 16, 60 (Dogger Bank inquiry conducted by five admirals); ibid., 160–1 (three naval officers conduct inquiry into German submarine's sinking of Spanish ship *Tiger*); ibid., 173 (four naval officers on five-person commission inquiring into German submarine's sinking of Netherlands ship *Tubantia*).

courts and tribunals to assess *individual* criminal responsibility for large-scale violations of humanitarian law, rather than non-criminal responsibility of states under the law of state responsibility. As is well known, the victors created post-war military tribunals to try major Axis leaders, notably the International Military Tribunal at Nuremberg and the Tokyo Tribunal. They also conducted hundreds of trials in other courts created under occupation authority. Many of the defendants were technically war criminals, charged with violations of the 1899 and 1907 Hague Conventions and the 1929 Geneva Conventions. However, some high-ranking defendants were also charged with and convicted of offences not previously known to international law: crimes against humanity and crimes against peace.[24]

Although these post-war proceedings posed novel challenges, they were much simpler than subsequent criminal tribunals in one crucial respect. The Nazi regime and its servants seem to have had a powerful urge to document their activities. Allied forces captured great masses of these records at the end of the war. These captured documents, photographs, and other evidentiary materials provided much of the evidence against many defendants, simplifying the prosecutors' task of proving their cases.[25]

The international military tribunals marked an important shift in focus, to international enforcement of individual responsibility for violations of humanitarian law. Unlike the situation at the end of the First World War, Germany and Japan were totally defeated. Their capitals and great cities were in ruins, and their territory was under military occupation. Given the totality of Axis defeat, there seems to have been little appetite among the Allies to pursue any sort of formal determination or declaration that the enemy states had violated international law along the lines of Article 231 of the Treaty of Versailles, the 'war guilt' clause.[26] For all practical purposes, the enemy states had ceased to function. Nevertheless, persons acting under their authority had committed acts of extraordinary brutality, cruelty, and extent. The complete Allied victory gave the Allies broad latitude to create tribunals to try these persons, to define

---

[24] Geoffrey Best, *Law and War since 1945* (Oxford: Clarendon, 1994), 180–3.
[25] Nancy Armoury Combs, *Fact-Finding without Facts: The Uncertain Evidentiary Foundations of International Criminal Convictions* (Cambridge University Press, 2010), 11.
[26] *Treaty of Versailles* (signed 28 June 1919, entered into force 10 January 1920), 225 Consol. TS 188, Art. 231 provided that 'The Allied and Associated Governments affirm and Germany accepts the responsibility of Germany and her allies for causing all the loss and damage to which the Allied and Associated Governments and their nationals have been subjected as a consequence of the war imposed upon them by the aggression of Germany and her allies.'

336   JOHN R. CROOK

the tribunals' jurisdiction,[27] and to overcome legal concerns (notably *nulla poena sine lege*[28]) by political decisions. Tribunals were selective in enforcement: offences by the Allies were not considered.[29]

The impressive precedent of the Nuremberg tribunal was not repeated for almost five decades. While Article VI of the Genocide Convention anticipated the creation of an 'international penal tribunal', none ensued. The cold war dominated global politics. Occasional attempts by Western powers and their allies to use legal mechanisms to pursue questionable uses of force by the other side failed.[30] And, neither superpower was inclined to pursue transgressions by its own supporters.[31] Moreover, events revealed significant shortcomings in the substance of the law. Armed conflict in the post-war years typically did not match the model of inter-state conflict for which the legal rules of the 1949 Geneva Conventions were carefully crafted. Instead, conflicts largely took the form of real (or contrived) wars of national liberation or other conflicts waged by non-state entities.[32]

The 1990s brought a dramatic shift, marked by greatly increased interest in and support for using international criminal law in response to violations of humanitarian law. The cold war was over, and the process of decolonization largely so. This changed political climate created political space for states and non-state entities to look critically at brutal behaviour that went unchallenged in previous decades, particularly conduct occurring within the borders of a state. The success of the ensuing global movement to promote individual criminal responsibility is symbolized by the creation of the International Criminal Court, an institution with a 2011 budget of €103 million and a prosecution staff of 218.[33]

The key event in this process was the UN Security Council's May 1993 decision to create the International Criminal Tribunal for the Prosecution

---

[27] Best, above n. 24, 400.

[28] Michael P. Scharf, *Balkan Justice: The Story behind the First International War Crimes Trial since Nuremberg* (Durham, NC: Carolina Academic Press, 1997) 12, 70–1.

[29] Lori F. Damrosch, 'Enforcing International Law through Non-forcible Measures', (1997) 269 *Recueil des cours* 13, 239.

[30] Efforts by Israel, the United Kingdom, and the United States to challenge Bulgaria's 1955 downing of a civilian airliner in the ICJ failed: Terry D. Gill (ed.), *Rosenne's The World Court: What It Is and How It Works*, 6th edn (Leiden: Martinus Nijhoff, 2003), 156–7.

[31] Michael J. Matheson, *Council Unbound: The Growth of UN Decision Making on Conflict and Postconflict Issues after the Cold War* (Washington, DC: United States Institute of Peace, 2006), 200.

[32] Best, above n. 24, 207.

[33] Reuters, 'Member Countries Fight over International Court's Budget', 2011, available at http://newsandinsight.thomsonreuters.com/Legal/News/2011/12_-_December/ Member_countries_fight_over_international_court_s_budget/.

of Serious Violations of International Humanitarian Law in the former Yugoslavia (ICTY).[34] With the end of the cold war and the demise of the Soviet Union, Russia did not use its veto to shield its former collaborators in the former Yugoslavia from scrutiny, allowing the Security Council to make an innovative and unprecedented use of its powers to create an international criminal tribunal predicated on Chapter VII of the United Nations Charter.[35] The decision to create the ICTY was driven by outside powers' frustration and distress at widespread atrocities in the conflicts in the former Yugoslavia, coupled with their unwillingness to use significant force to try to stop them. Williams and Scharf describe the tribunal as a 'judicial placebo', suggesting that 'the members of the Security Council embraced the norm of justice mainly as a public relations device'.[36] As described by a former senior US State Department lawyer actively involved in the tribunal's creation,

> By the second half of 1992 . . . the international community had become so appalled by the widespread atrocities being committed in the former Yugoslavia and so frustrated by its inability to effectively deal with the conflict through other means that a consensus began to develop in favor of some form of international prosecution of those responsible.[37]

The ICTY was followed soon after by the Security Council's creation of the International Criminal Tribunal for Rwanda (ICTR).[38] The ICTR again reflected an after-the-fact response by the international community to a vicious genocide that outside powers were not prepared to stop with military force.[39]

Analysis of the history and jurisprudence of the ICTY, the ICTR, and other international and mixed criminal tribunals[40] that have followed is far beyond this scope of this chapter. However, the institutions have had important effects and taught important lessons:

- They have set important new precedents for the individual responsibility of senior military and political leaders for violations of international

---

[34] SC Res. 827, UN SCOR, 48th sess., 3217th mtg, UN Doc. S/RES/827 (25 May 1993).

[35] Matheson, above n. 31, 200–4.

[36] Paul R. Williams and Michael P. Scharf, *Peace with Justice? War Crimes and Accountability in the Former Yugoslavia* (Maryland: Rowman & Littlefield Publishers, 2002), 91–92, 100.

[37] Matheson, above n. 31, 200–1.

[38] SC Res. 955, UN SCOR, 49th sess., 3453rd mtg, UN Doc. S/RES/955 (8 November 1994).

[39] Matheson, above n. 31, 204–205.

[40] These include the Extraordinary Chambers of the Courts of Cambodia, the Special Tribunal for Lebanon, and the Special Court for Sierra Leone, all of which incorporate international and domestic law into their governing statutes and include both national and international judges: Matheson, above n. 31, 221–2.

humanitarian law. As the ICTY's website observes, that tribunal 'has laid the foundations for what is now the accepted norm for conflict resolution and post-conflict development across the globe, specifically that leaders suspected of mass crimes will face justice'.[41]

- The tribunal's decisions have filled lacunae in the law, clarifying and expanding old rules and creating some new ones, notably including areas such as crimes of sexual violence. The ICTY, for example, established or reinforced precedents that 'there could be individual criminal responsibility for war crimes in internal armed conflict, that rape constitutes a war crime and a crime against humanity, and that military and civilian leaders could be criminally responsible for the acts of subordinates over whom they exercise effective control'.[42]
- The tribunals' procedures have heightened public, professional, and scholarly awareness of international humanitarian law. These institutions have helped to spawn and sustain large and vigorous scholarly and civil society communities committed to the principle of individual accountability. Civil society was a powerful force leading to the creation of the ICC.[43]

However, these tribunals' experiences also convey important warnings about the challenges and limitations of attempting to apply humanitarian law norms in criminal prosecutions.

- Establishing international institutions to assess criminal responsibility has typically proved to be slow and difficult, for reasons that are practical, legal, political, or a mixture of all.[44] Melding different systems of criminal prosecution, trial procedure, evidence, and sentencing[45] into a workable system has been challenging, and the results have not always been satisfactory.
- The elaborate institutions required to mount and administer effective prosecutions can be very expensive. The ICTY's budget for 2010–11 was

---

[41] International Criminal Tribunal for the former Yugoslavia, 'About ICTY', available at www.icty.org/sections/AbouttheICTY.

[42] Williams and Scharf, above n. 36, 117.

[43] See, e.g., Coalition for the International Criminal Court, available at www.iccnow.org.

[44] On the protracted political struggle to select the ICTY's first prosecutor see Williams and Scharf, above n. 36, 106–9.

[45] Neha Jain, 'Introductory Note to Extraordinary Chambers in the Courts of Cambodia: Co-Prosecutors' Notice of Appeal against the Judgment of the Trial Chamber in the Case of Kaing Guek Eav *Alias* Duch', (2010) 49 ILM 1683.

US$301,895,900 – a very large sum, although reduced from the previous budget of over \$342 million.[46] The criminal tribunals' high costs have led important governments facing financial stringency at home, including the ICC's largest donors, to press for budgetary discipline and greater efficiency.[47]

- Proof of guilt to the high standards required for criminal conviction has required massive and protracted proceedings. Prosecutors in the trial of Duško Tadić, the first case heard by the ICTY, presented seventy-five witnesses over a four-month period: two expert witnesses, fourteen 'policy' witnesses, and fifty-nine eyewitnesses.[48] The cases also demonstrate the difficulties of identifying persons responsible for brutal acts in remote places years previously. These are heightened for tribunals addressing the aftermath of armed conflict, which Best rightly describes as marked by 'the fog of lies, rumors, myths and misunderstandings'.[49] Prosecutors and defence counsel have had to overcome challenges posed by ongoing conflicts, lack of local co-operation (or, indeed, active local opposition), chaotic local conditions, and limited infrastructure in places like Rwanda.[50]

- As Nancy Combs' important recent work shows, fact-finding can be difficult and highly uncertain.[51] Tribunals addressing events in some areas in Africa and other less developed areas must base their fact-finding largely on oral testimony by local witnesses who often are unfamiliar with Western notions of time, distance, numbers, sequence, and causation.[52] Combs explains that witnesses' testimony is often unreliable for cultural and other reasons; in some parts of the world, consistency and truthfulness in speech are not necessarily recognized or valued.[53] Even if witnesses see the need to speak the truth and seek to do so, their testimony is often blurred as counsels' questions and

---

[46] ICTY, 'The Cost of Justice', 19 December 2011, available at www.icty.org/sid/325; Report of the International Court of Justice 1 August 2009–31 July 2010, UN GAOR, 56th sess., Supp. No. 4, UN Doc. A/65/4 (1 August 2010), 59: The budget of the ICJ for its 2009–10 fiscal year was one-sixth of this amount – US\$51,010,200.

[47] Reuters, above n. 33.

[48] Williams and Scharf, above n. 36, 120, 171; ibid., 205, 207–8: in all, 125 witnesses testified over the course of a seven-month trial that generated over 6,000 pages of transcripts.

[49] Best, above n. 24, 382.

[50] Matheson, above n. 31, 206: 'Because of the scope and character of the crimes committed, the multilingual character of the proceedings, and the logistics involved, investigations and trials were inevitably more complex, expensive, and time consuming than ordinary criminal proceedings.'

[51] Combs, above n. 25.   [52] Ibid., 21–148.   [53] Ibid., 106–48.

340 JOHN R. CROOK

the witness's answers pass through one, two, or even three layers of imperfect interpretation.

- Some cases have not been models of procedural good order. Some, indeed, raise questions about the basic fairness of the proceedings. In *Tharcisse Muvunyi* v. *Prosecutor*, the defendant was charged in the ICTR with participating in genocidal attacks at a hospital. The evidence did not establish his personal participation, but the trial chamber nevertheless convicted him of responsibility for genocide committed by his subordinates, a charge not included in the indictment he was called to answer. (The ICTR Appeals Chamber unanimously overturned Muvunyi's conviction on this and other counts, although it remanded an incitement charge for retrial.)[54]
- International criminal tribunals depend on the co-operation of states to gain custody of persons facing charges; non-co-operation can frustrate the process. Thus Omar Hassan Ahmad al Bashir, the president of Sudan, remains at liberty and able to travel to some other countries, notwithstanding the ICC's March 2009 warrant of arrest against him.[55]

State responsibility for violations of international humanitarian law

In parallel with the development of international institutions to enforce individual criminal responsibility, there have been less publicized instances of recourse to international legal institutions applying international humanitarian law and related rules in assessing state responsibility under international law.

The International Court of Justice

Professor Gray's chapter addresses cases in which the ICJ has examined questions involving the initiation and conduct of internal and international armed conflicts.[56] To avoid duplication, comments here are limited to a few points regarding the Court's approach to fact-finding in cases involving uses of armed force.

---

[54] Susana Sácouto and Katherine Cleary, 'Introductory Note to the International Criminal Tribunal for Rwanda: Tharcisse Muvunyi v. Prosecutor', (2008) 47 ILM 875.

[55] Michael P. Scharf, 'Introductory Note to the International Criminal Court's Arrest Warrant for Omar Al Bashir, President of the Sudan', (2009) 48 ILM 463.

[56] See Chapter 14 in this volume.

Like some other observers, I see fact-finding – particularly in the confused and murky circumstances of armed conflicts – as one of the Court's
greatest challenges.[57] Scholars have highlighted the issue.[58] Concern about
the Court's uses of evidence led the British Institute of International and
Comparative Law to commission a thorough and thoughtful 2009 study
of the issue.[59] Judge Schwebel's 1984 dissent in *Nicaragua* v. *United States*[60]
identified serious problems with fact-finding in that case – concerns on
which Schwebel recently expanded in a comment in the *American Journal
of International Law* accusing Nicaragua of committing a fraud on the
ICJ by knowingly submitting false evidence denying its support for anti-
government forces in El Salvador.[61] Some US State Department lawyers
still bear psychological scars from the Court's approach to evidence in
Oil Platforms.[62] Judge Buergenthal highlighted the shortcomings of the
factual record underlying the majority opinion in the *Wall* advisory opinion case.[63] The Court's fact-finding in *Bosnia* v. *Serbia* has received much
criticism.

Some recent ICJ presidents have wrestled with these issues, but their
efforts have created new problems. In brief, the ICJ seems to be settling on
principles that discount much of the evidence that a respondent state –

[57] John R. Crook, 'Fact-Finding in the Fog: Determining the Facts of Upheavals and Wars in
Inter-state Disputes', in Roger Alford and Catherine Rogers (eds.), *The Future of Investment
Arbitration* (Oxford University Press, 2009) 313.

[58] Thomas M. Franck, 'Fact-Finding in the International Court of Justice' in Richard Lillich
(ed.), *Fact-Finding before International Tribunals* (Ardsley, NY: Transnational, 1991) 1,
11–17.

[59] Anna Riddell and Brendan Plant, *Evidence before the International Court of Justice* (London:
British Institute of International and Comparative Law, 2009).

[60] *Military and Paramilitary Activities in and against Nicaragua (Nicaragua* v. *United States)
(Merits)*, [1986] ICJ Rep. 14, 259 (Judge Schwebel); Stephen M. Schwebel, 'Three Cases of
Fact-Finding by the International Court of Justice', in Richard Lillich (ed.), *Fact-Finding
before International Tribunals* (Ardsley, NY: Transnational, 1991) 1, 11–17.

[61] Stephen M. Schwebel, 'Celebrating a Fraud on the Court', (2012) 106 *American Journal of
International Law* 102.

[62] *Oil Platforms (Iran* v. *United States) (Judgment)*, [2003] ICJ Rep. 161, 195 [71]: 'The main
evidence that the mine struck by the USS *Samuel B. Roberts* was laid by Iran was the
discovery of moored mines in the same area, bearing serial numbers matching other
Iranian mines, in particular those found aboard the vessel *Iran Ajr* . . . This evidence is
highly suggestive, but not conclusive.'

[63] *Legal Consequences of the Construction of a Wall in the Occupied Palestinian Territory
(Advisory Opinion)*, [2004] ICJ Rep. 136 *(Wall)*, 240 [1] (Judge Buergenthal): 'I am
compelled to vote against the Court's findings on the merits because the Court did not
have before it the requisite factual bases for its sweeping findings; it should therefore have
declined to hear the case.'

342 JOHN R. CROOK

or an applicant – may have available in cases involving armed conflict. The Court's fullest expression of its approach appears in *Congo* v. *Uganda*:

> 61. The Court will treat with caution evidentiary materials specially prepared for this case and also materials emanating from a single source. It will prefer contemporaneous evidence from persons with direct knowledge. It will give particular attention to reliable evidence acknowledging facts or conduct unfavourable to the State represented by the person making them... The Court will also give weight to evidence that has not, even before this litigation, been challenged by impartial persons for the correctness of what it contains ...
>
> ...
>
> 65. ... Uganda has also furnished the Court with a notarized affidavit of the Chief of Staff of the UPDF... This affidavit is stated to have been prepared in November 2002, in view of the forthcoming case before the International Court of Justice. The Court recalls that it has elsewhere observed that a member of the government of a State engaged in litigation before this Court – and especially litigation relating to armed conflict – 'will probably tend to identify himself with the interests of his country'... The same may be said of a senior military officer of such a State, and 'while in no way impugning the honour or veracity' of such a person, the Court should 'treat such evidence with great reserve'...
>
> ...
>
> 68. Nor can the truth... be established by extracts from a few newspapers, or magazine articles, which rely on a single source... on an interested source... or give no sources at all... The Court has explained in an earlier case that press information may be useful as evidence when it is 'wholly consistent and concordant as to the main facts and circumstances of the case'... but that particular caution should be shown in this area. The Court observes that this requirement of consistency and concordance is not present in the journalistic accounts ... [64]

This is all well and good, except that in cases involving armed conflict, the primary – and perhaps only – sources of evidence available to either party may be those that the ICJ discounts. Military operations are often conducted far from public view, in remote places away from the eyes of dispassionate observers. Sworn declarations by officials prepared for the purposes of litigation, perhaps supplemented by print or video journalists' accounts, may be the only means available to prove key facts. If the ICJ

---

[64] *Armed activities on the Territory of the Congo (Democratic Republic of the Congo* v. *Uganda) (Judgment)*, [2005] ICJ Rep. 160.

ADJUDICATING ARMED CONFLICT

believes these must be given short shrift, a party with a meritorious claim or defence may be left in dire straits.

The Court's distaste for evidence originated by the parties has led it to rely heavily on evidence developed by others. In *Congo* v. *Uganda*, it relied on UN reports and on an official investigation conducted in Uganda to justify key findings.[65] In the *Genocide Convention* case, it relied on findings made by the ICTY and a report on Srebrenica prepared by the Secretary-General.[66] In the *Wall* advisory opinion case, it relied heavily on a dossier prepared by the Secretary-General.[67] Relying on facts found by other bodies offers the ICJ a way forward, but it poses significant risks. There may well not be reliable outside observers, or (as with many reports prepared by the International Committee of the Red Cross) the observers will not share what they know. In any case, the ICJ has limited ability to assess the quality of information others assemble, the collectors' biases, or the integrity or accuracy of the collection process.

The United Nations Compensation Commission

The United Nations Compensation Commission (UNCC) is by far history's largest effort to address claims for widespread violations of international law, including many claims involving violations of international humanitarian law.[68] Although the UNCC has received limited public and scholarly attention, as of October 2011 it has paid out over US$34 billion in compensation to over a million and a half individuals, companies, and governments injured as the result of Iraq's 1990 invasion and subsequent occupation of Kuwait.[69]

The UNCC was created by Security Council action during the unique brief period following the fall of the Berlin Wall, when the United States and the Soviet Union co-operated to an unparalleled degree.[70] The

---

[65] Ibid.

[66] *Application of the Convention on the Prevention and Punishment of the Crime of Genocide (Bosnia and Herzegovina* v. *Serbia and Montenegro) (Judgment)*, [2007] ICJ Rep. 43.

[67] *Legal Consequences of the Construction of a Wall in the Occupied Palestinian Territory (Advisory Opinion)*, [2004] ICJ Rep. 136.

[68] Veijo Heiskanen, 'The United Nations Compensation Commission', (2003) 296 *Recueil des Cours* 259; Matheson, above n. 31, 168–80.

[69] United Nations Compensation Commission, Status of Processing and Payment of Claims, 2012, available at www.uncc.ch/status.htm.

[70] Matheson, above n. 31, 5–6. The Security Council resolutions underpinning the UNCC, decisions of the Commission's Governing Council, and other relevant documents are in

commission's success in channelling compensation to large numbers of injured claimants rested on the use of unusual mass claims procedures intentionally designed to avoid the claim-by-claim assessments central to most international adjudication. Instead, the UNCC processed most of its claims through innovative administrative processes created to address large numbers of similarly situated claimants in groups, not case by case.[71]

In the resolutions creating the UNCC, the Security Council declared Iraq to be responsible under international law for direct injuries resulting from its 1990 invasion of Kuwait and the ensuing occupation; many of these injuries (although not all) involved violations of international humanitarian law. Given the Security Council's action, the Commission was not required to make legal determinations of liability, although it had to assess whether particular types of injury satisfied the Security Council's directive to limit claims to those for 'direct' injury. Instead, the Commission's governing council focused on developing criteria defining large groups of claimants who suffered similar types of injury as the result of the invasion and occupation. These types of claim were denominated with letters ranging from 'A' (for the simplest claims for small fixed amounts, primarily by low-paid foreign workers displaced by the invasion) to much larger 'E' (business, including oil company claims) and 'F' (government claims, notably huge claims by Kuwait and Saudi Arabia for environmental damage). Different procedures were developed for each type of claim, with the level of evidence required, the degree of scrutiny given to individual claims, and the extent of Iraq's participation increasing as the amounts at issue increased.[72]

Some of the mass claims techniques developed by the UNCC were later adapted for use in several of the mass claims processes created to address claims stemming from the Holocaust and Germany's forced labour programmes during the Second World War.[73] Similar techniques

---

Marco Frigessi di Rattalma and Tullio Treves, *The United Nations Compensation Commission: A Handbook* (The Hague: Kluwer Law International, 1999).

[71] Norbert Wühler, 'Institutional and Procedural Aspects of Mass Claims Settlement Systems: The United Nations Compensation Commission', in International Bureau of the PCA (ed.), *Institutional and Procedural Aspects of Mass Claims Settlement Systems* (The Hague: Kluwer Law International, 2000) 17.

[72] Christopher S. Gibson, 'Mass Claims Processing: Techniques for Processing over 400,000 Claims for Individual Loss at the United Nations Commission', in Richard Lillich (ed.), *The United Nations Compensation Commission: Thirteenth Sokol Colloquium* (Irvington, NY: Transnational, 1995) 155.

[73] John R. Crook, 'Mass Claims Processes: Lessons Learned over Twenty-Five Years', in International Bureau of the PCA (ed.), *Redressing Injustices through Mass Claims Processes: Innovative Responses to Unique Challenges* (Oxford University Press, 2006) 41, 48–53.

have been used in some national programmes.[74] However, there has not been another similar large-scale mass international claims programme following any subsequent armed conflict, and none seems likely. (The Eritrea–Ethiopia Claims Commission (discussed below) briefly considered attempting such a programme, but abandoned the idea for lack of time and resources.)

The primary reason why the UNCC experience will not often be copied in international settings is brutally practical. Mass claims programmes are complex and expensive to design and implement. There is little reason to go to the effort and expense of designing such a system, and to raise the hopes of potential claimants, without reasonable likelihood of substantial, steady funding to pay approved claims.[75] Such funding was available in the unusual situation of the UNCC and Iraq in the 1990s. Iraq has large oil resources. It was resoundingly defeated in a war in which it was almost universally condemned as an aggressor. The international community, acting through the Security Council, gave strong and sustained support to the claims programme, not least because it benefited claimants from dozens of countries, including over a million from developing countries. Similar favourable conditions will not often occur.

The Eritrea–Ethiopia Claims Commission

Between 1998 and 2000, Ethiopia and Eritrea waged a bitter war that an informed observer estimates to have taken 100,000 lives.[76] The war's underlying causes are complex and the immediate causes disputed, but the intensity of the conflict is clear.

Unlike many contemporary conflicts, the war between Eritrea and Ethiopia was largely conducted between well-organized regular armed forces operating under clear chains of command and following established bodies of doctrine. After almost two years of fighting, a successful offensive in May and June of 2000 took the Ethiopian army deep into Eritrean territory. With large areas of Eritrea occupied by Ethiopian forces, the

---

[74] Kenneth R. Feinberg, 'Final Report of the Special Master of the September 11th Victim Compensation Fund Vol. 1', in International Bureau of the PCA (ed.), *Redressing Injustices through Mass Claims Processes: Innovative Responses to Unique Challenges* (Oxford University Press, 2006) 325.

[75] Crook, above n. 73, 57–8.

[76] Martin Plaut, 'The Conflict and its Aftermath', in Dominique Jacquin-Berdal and Martin Plaut (eds.), *Unfinished Business: Eritrea and Ethiopia at War* (New Jersey: Red Sea Press, 2004) 119.

parties in June 2000 concluded a ceasefire agreement.[77] In December 2000, they agreed on a treaty formally ending hostilities and creating three mechanisms intended, in different ways, to address the war's causes and consequences.[78] Article 3 of the December 2000 Agreement called for an inquiry under the auspices of the Organization of African Unity '[i]n order to determine the origins of the conflict'. That process never got under way. Article 4 created a commission to determine the much disputed boundary between the two countries. And, Article 5.1 created a five-member commission to address each party's claims for damages under the law of state responsibility:

> The mandate of the Commission is to decide through binding arbitration all claims for loss, damage or injury by one Government against the other, and by nationals (including both natural and juridical persons) of one party against the Government of the other party or entities owned or controlled by the other party that are (a) related to the conflict ... and (b) result from violations of international humanitarian law, including the 1949 Geneva Conventions, or other violations of international law.

Over the course of almost nine years, the commission heard and issued awards resolving all of both parties' claims for billions of US dollars in compensation.[79] I was one of the party-appointed members of this commission,[80] so it is not appropriate for me to comment in detail on the proceedings or on the awards in particular claims. However, some general comments may be in order regarding the possible relevance of the commission's experience elsewhere.

Jurisdiction

This tribunal was unusual in that, with limited exceptions, jurisdiction was not an issue. Article 5 contains a broad grant of jurisdiction; while not clear in every respect, it provided an agreed foundation for most of the parties' claims. I do not know why Eritrea and Ethiopia took the unusual

---

[77] Ibid., 104–7.

[78] United States Institute of Peace, Agreement between the Government of the Federal Democratic Republic of Ethiopia and the Government of the State of Eritrea, 12 December 2000, available at www.usip.org/files/file/resources/collections/peace_agreements/eritrea_ethiopia_12122000.pdf.

[79] All the tribunal's awards and decisions are in *Reports of the International Arbitral Awards Volume XXVI* (New York: United Nations, 2008). They are also available on the website of the PCA, www.pca-cpa.org.

[80] The Commission was chaired by Professor Hans van Houtte; Ms Lucy Reed and I were appointed by Eritrea; Dean James Paul and Judge George Aldrich were appointed by Ethiopia. With a single exception, all the tribunal's awards were unanimous.

step of agreeing to a tribunal with such a broad mandate soon after their bitter war. The tribunal proceedings offered no answers. Perhaps lawyers from the US Department of State (familiar with the workings of international claims processes and with their occasional value as a means of putting difficult issues off to the future) suggested this course to the two countries' negotiating teams. At the time, the parties were bitterly divided, as they remain today. They faced an angry array of issues they could not resolve through direct negotiations. Referring these to separate law-based institutions for later resolution by third parties perhaps offered the way forward.

Determining the law

Determining the facts usually presented the commission with much greater challenges than determining the law to be applied. Indeed, the parties' briefs usually converged regarding the international legal rules to be applied in particular claims. The 1998–2000 war was an international armed conflict, waged by conventional armies, and so the commission did not face the limitations and lacunae associated with the law of non-international armed conflicts. Ethiopia was party to the 1949 Geneva Conventions at all relevant times. Eritrea acceded in August 2000, after hostilities had ended. Nevertheless, both parties typically operated on the premise that relevant rules of the 1949 Geneva Conventions should be applied, presumably as expressions of customary international law. The tribunal followed their lead. Both parties also sometimes invoked the rules of Additional Protocol I to the Geneva Conventions as reflecting contemporary customary international law, but the customary status of some Protocol rules was not agreed upon, leaving the commission to decide.[81]

While identifying the governing rules generally was not a challenge, the clarity of particular rules and the difficulty of applying them varied. For some claims, the rules and their application were straightforward. Thus, in considering both parties' prisoner of war claims, the commission found ready guidance from the Third Geneva Convention's detailed

---

[81] *Western Front, Aerial Bombardment and Related Claims – Eritrea's Claims 1, 3, 5, 9–13, 14, 21, 25 & 26 (Eritrea v. Ethiopia) (Partial Award)*, (2005) 26 RIAA 291 (*Western Front Partial Award*), 328–30, [98]–[105]: the tribunal finds that attacks on a reservoir supplying water to a city in a harsh desert region violate Article 54 of Geneva Protocol 1, which prohibits attacks on 'objects indispensable to the survival of the civilian population, such as . . . drinking water installations'.

regime for the treatment of prisoners of war (POWs). Some minor elements of this regime, such as Article 60's requirement that detaining powers grant POWs a monthly advance of pay equivalent to a specified number of Swiss francs, do not mesh easily with the realities of a conflict between two poor African states. Nevertheless, the Third Geneva Convention's rules provided effective standards to assess both parties' claims. Ethiopia's claims against Eritrea emphasized physical mistreatment of POWs; Eritrea's claims against Ethiopia stressed enforced political indoctrination. For both types of claim, the Third Geneva Convention provided effective yardsticks.[82]

Both parties were able to develop substantial bodies of evidence after their respective POWs were released and debriefed and had received physical and psychological examinations. Nevertheless, additional evidence would have been useful, so the commission sought access to reports of POW camp visits by delegates of the International Committee of the Red Cross. However, in keeping with its traditions of confidentiality, the ICRC would not allow these to be used.[83] This sounds a cautionary note for other situations where the ICRC or other humanitarian organizations may be the best sources of evidence about violations of humanitarian law, but may not be prepared to provide that evidence.

Not all humanitarian law rules were as straightforward in application as the Third Geneva Convention. Important rules governing the conduct of military operations, such as those regulating targets and precautions in attack, often require detailed assessments of the facts of an event. These assessments frequently involve matters of judgement regarding complex and unfamiliar military matters as to which most civilian arbitrators have no knowledge or experience. The tribunal thus may have been fortunate that it did not face many claims requiring assessments of the legality of particular targets or the conduct of particular attacks. Indeed, disagreement as to whether a power plant near the Eritrean city of Assab was a legitimate military target led to the only split decision in the commission's history.[84]

As noted, the commission's greatest challenges involved determining the facts. Armed conflicts are chaotic. They involve large, complex and

---

[82] *Prisoners of War – Eritrea's Claim 17 (Eritrea v. Ethiopia) (Partial Award)*, (2003) 26 RIAA 23 (*Prisoners of War Eritrea's Claim 17*); *Prisoners of War – Ethiopia's Claim 4 (Ethiopia v. Eritrea) (Partial Award)*, (2003) 26 RIAA 73.

[83] *Prisoners of War Eritrea's Claim 17*, (2003) 26 RIAA 23, 42–3, [50]–[53].

[84] *Western Front Partial Award*, (2005) 26 RIAA 291, 332–6, [111]–[123]; ibid., 346–9 (President Van Houtte).

confusing events that usually take place over expanses of space and time. Many crucial events occur in remote places. Witnesses (if they exist, survive, can be found, and are willing to co-operate) often see only a small fragment of a complex event. Accordingly, fact-finders must try to assemble a mosaic, but one with important pieces missing.[85]

This task is made more difficult because parties to a conflict often become committed to radically different conceptions of what happened, leading to frequent clashes of testimony even among witnesses who may believe they speak the truth.[86] Things become more complicated if, as in the *Black Tom* arbitration, a government fabricates evidence.[87] And, as recent experience in the ICTY reminds us, some unscrupulous counsel may procure perjured or false testimony.[88] All of this makes evidence from unbiased non-party sources potentially quite valuable, if it can be found. In this regard, one of the parties in the Eritrea–Ethiopia cases made effective use of commercial satellite imagery, including before-and-after overhead images of towns and villages damaged during the conflict. In several claims, this provided important corroboration of eyewitness testimony.[89]

Claims involving rape and sexual abuse posed particular fact-finding difficulties. Victims are understandably loath to provide evidence, especially in societies like Eritrea and Ethiopia where sexual assault cannot be spoken of. Fortunately, unlike some other contemporary conflicts, the record in the Eritrean and Ethiopian claims contained

> no suggestion, much less evidence, that either Eritrea or Ethiopia used rape, forced pregnancy or other sexual violence as an instrument of war. Neither side alleged strategically systematic sexual violence against civilians in the course of the armed conflict and occupation of Central Front territories.

---

[85] Crook, above n. 57, 323–4.

[86] Consider the inconsistent eyewitness accounts of the outbreak of the battle of Lexington, the opening battle of the American Revolutionary War in 1775. Lexington was a small engagement, involving relatively few troops, in a small place, over a short time. Nevertheless, multiple eyewitnesses (doubtless thinking they spoke the truth) described very different versions of the event. Christopher Hibbert, *Redcoats and Rebels: The American Revolution through British Eyes* (New York: Avon Books, 1991), 31–2.

[87] Woolsey, above n. 19, 738–9.

[88] ICTY, 'Trial Chamber Accepts Plea Agreement in Trial of Jelena Rašić for Contempt of the Tribunal', press release, JKE/CS/PR1475e, 31 January 2012: Ms Rašić procured a false witness statement from a witness in exchange for €1,000 in cash.

[89] See, e.g., *Central Front – Eritrea's Claims 2, 4, 6, 7, 8 & 22 (Partial Award)*, (2004) 26 RIAA 115.

350   JOHN R. CROOK

Each side did, however, allege frequent rape of its women civilians by the other's soldiers.[90]

In some situations, the testimony of medical personnel who treated victims provided important evidence regarding the occurrence of such rape by soldiers. The commission also adopted a modified standard of proof in assessing rape claims. 'Given...heightened cultural sensitivities, in addition to the typically secretive and hence unwitnessed nature of rape, the Commission [did not require] evidence of a pattern of frequent or pervasive rapes' as a predicate to liability.[91]

Conclusions

I have reservations about the future prospects for adjudication as an effective means to establish state responsibility for claimed violations of international humanitarian law.

The five-hundred-pound gorilla in the room is jurisdiction. Like it or not, in most circumstances, the jurisdiction of any process created to address these issues will rest on both participants' consent, be they states or non-state entities. It can happen. Great Britain and the United States agreed to arbitrate the Alabama Claims to eliminate a long-running irritant in their relations.[92] Ethiopia and Eritrea agreed to arbitrate their boundary and claims disputes because both needed a definitive end to hostilities; arbitration allowed them to declare peace while deferring key issues. There may be future cases like Iraq in 1991, involving a state so badly defeated that it will whisper consent to escape the threat of renewed combat. Nevertheless, I suspect these precedents will rarely be repeated. Most states or non-state entities emerging from armed conflict – consider Georgia and Russia – are not disposed to settle complaints about the conduct of the conflict in orderly ways.

A second limitation is the limited capacity of the procedures of adjudication to capture and digest events as large, complex, and often chaotic as armed conflicts. Moreover, the litigation process forces both parties to commit to, and seek to prove, their respective visions of what happened. This can lessen the room for diplomatic negotiation and even intensify controversy. In this regard, modern states have shown little appetite for using neutral third parties to conduct inquiries into disputed events,

[90] Ibid., 132 [36].   [91] Ibid., 132 [40].
[92] Foreman, above n. 5, 809–11.

notwithstanding past successes of such techniques in cases like the Dogger Bank dispute. Article 90 of Protocol I to the Geneva Conventions creates a standing International Humanitarian Fact-Finding Commission that can be authorized to conduct inquiries into alleged breaches of the Geneva Conventions.[93] That commission has never been called on to conduct an inquiry.

Adjudication is extremely expensive in time and money, and in the demands it can place on the time of senior leaders. As noted above, the trial of a single defendant in the ICTY, Duško Tadić, took 125 witnesses, 7 months and 6,000 pages of transcript. The Eritrea–Ethiopia Commission considered only selected slices of a two-year war, but took nine years; even this pace put both countries' legal teams under massive pressure.

Yet another issue is the limited ability of legal processes to provide truly effective remedies for the consequences of war. Arbitral tribunals can declare that one side or another violated international law. They can even attempt to put a price tag on the resulting damage, as the Eritrea–Ethiopia Commission sought to do.[94] However, they have no means of enforcing damages awards, or of creating wealth that will allow countries emerging from war to pay them.

There is a further troubling point. Armed conflicts cause deaths and damage. However, many of those deaths and much of that damage can result from actions that are entirely lawful under humanitarian law. Thus they provide no basis for recovery under the law of state responsibility. This makes international law a limited and potentially haphazard tool if a state's goal is to address comprehensively the physical and human damage caused by war.[95]

A final comment: with the disappearance of compulsory military service in almost all democracies, the number of judges or arbitrators and counsel with military experience is nearing the vanishing point. This leaves counsel and decision makers in any future tribunals to make difficult and sometimes technical judgments in areas where they have no training or life experience.

---

[93] International Humanitarian Fact-Finding Commission, available at www.ihffc.org/index. asp?Language=EN&page=home.

[94] *Eritrea's Damages Claims (Eritrea v. Ethiopia) (Final Award)*, (2009) 26 RIAA 505; *Ethiopia's Damage Claims (Ethiopia v. Eritrea) (Final Award)*, (2009) 26 RIAA 631.

[95] It is not appropriate for me to address the argument sometimes advanced to the effect that a party that makes the first move in an armed conflict in violation of the *jus ad bellum* bears international legal responsibility for all of the ensuing damage. A form of this argument was made by Ethiopia and rejected by the tribunal.

For all of these reasons, states considering resort to adjudication to address claims of violations of international humanitarian law should look with a critical eye at whether it will offer an effective resolution of the issues at hand. The processes of international adjudication are not well suited to dealing with the sorts of fact-finding challenge often posed by armed conflicts. Particularly in cases involving disputes about large and complex events, adjudication may not be a solution.

16

Human rights as a subject of international litigation

IVAN SHEARER

The development of international human rights law, and of avenues of redress for breaches of that law, has been rapid – indeed, revolutionary – since 1945. The Universal Declaration of Human Rights, adopted by the United Nations General Assembly in 1948, sounded the clarion call.[1] Even though the response to it was initially slow (with the notable exception of the adoption in 1950 by the Council of Europe of the European Convention on Human Rights), since 1965 there has appeared a multitude of international instruments regarding human rights and mechanisms, at the regional and international levels, to monitor application of human rights in practice and to allow, in some cases, individuals to pursue remedies against states violating those rights.

The term 'litigating', however, is not apt in the case of all these developments. The scene is more diffuse. As Professor Shelton has put it,

> Having emerged hesitatingly following the Second World War and then expanded rapidly in recent years, [international human rights law] displays an uneven proliferation of international complaints mechanisms and techniques that has created a mixture of remedies drawn from the traditional law of state responsibility for injury to aliens, from domestic legal systems, and from the different views of judges about the role of tribunals in affording relief to victims of state abuse. Remedies range from declaratory judgments to awards of widely differing amounts of compensatory damages to orders for specific state action. It is rare to find a reasoned decision articulating the principles on which a remedy is afforded.[2]

The greatest strides in opening up the prospects of remedies to individuals through litigation, in the strict sense of the term, are to be seen in the establishment of three regional courts: the European Court of Human

[1] For a comprehensive account of its genesis see Mary Ann Glendon, *A World Made New: Eleanor Roosevelt and the Universal Declaration of Human Rights* (New York: Random House, 2001).
[2] Dinah Shelton, *Remedies in International Human Rights Law* (Oxford University Press, 1999), 1.

353

Rights (established in 1950, and inaugurated as a full-time court in 1998), the Inter-American Court of Human Rights (established in 1969), and the African Court of Human and Peoples' Rights (established in 1998).[3] Subject to certain conditions, individuals may bring actions in those courts against member states. Each has distinctive features and each has a wide literature to explain its workings and disseminate its jurisprudence. The present chapter will not attempt even to summarize the work of those courts,[4] but will confine itself to an examination of the topic from the perspective of the majority of states in the world which are not parties to such regional arrangements. The question for them, and their citizens, is what procedures are available at the universal level for the vindication of human rights and why those procedures have been established.

The body of international (as distinct from regional) human rights law is strikingly rich in its range of international mechanisms for the resolution of issues of violations of human rights, even though these fall below the level of litigation in the strict sense of that term. The diversity of international mechanisms, indeed, is unique to the field of human rights law. This diversity reflects, on the one hand, the emergence of the individual as a subject of international law, rather than as an object of it, which is the position of the individual in relation to other branches of international law, and, on the other hand (and arguably negatively), the aversion of states to subject themselves to binding dispute resolution in matters traditionally regarded as lying within their exclusive domestic jurisdiction.

In addition to these mechanisms, for those states accepting the jurisdiction of the International Court of Justice (ICJ) and of certain other tribunals, there may be avenues of direct invocation of human rights in a truly litigious process, leading to a binding result. These instances, however, are infrequent, and likely to remain so, owing to the need to found jurisdiction on the consent of the parties. Nevertheless, there have been some significant recent developments in international judicial practice respecting human rights.

---

[3] For recent developments see Kate Parlett, *The Individual in the International Legal System* (Cambridge University Press, 2011), 327–35; Olivier De Schutter, *International Human Rights Law* (Cambridge University Press, 2010), ch. 11.

[4] See, e.g., David Harris, Michael O'Boyle, and Colin Warbrick, *The Law of the European Convention on Human Rights*, 2nd edn (Oxford University Press, 1999); Thomas Buergenthal and Dinah Shelton (eds.), *Protecting Human Rights in the Americas*, 4th edn (Kehl-am-Rhein: N. P. Engel Verlag, 1995); Malcolm David Evans and Rachel Murray, *The African Charter on Human and Peoples' Rights*, 2nd edn (Cambridge University Press, 2008).

This chapter will examine the following areas of activity, or potential activity:

1. State responsibility for acts violating human rights.
2. The modern evolution of human rights law and proposals for an international court of human rights.
3. The human rights treaty monitoring system.
4. The right of individual petition under the human rights treaty monitoring system.
5. Inter-state complaints under the human rights treaty-monitoring system.
6. The UN Human Rights Council and Universal Periodic Review (UPR).
7. The complaints mechanisms of the UN Human Rights Council.

It will appear from this examination that certain forms of dispute resolution regarding human rights have emerged, each with its own distinctive character, providing limited forms of redress for violations of human rights.

State responsibility for acts violating the rights of foreign citizens

The reports of international courts and of arbitral tribunals are replete with examples of states bringing actions against other states alleging that the rights of their citizens have been violated in the territory of the respondent state. However, the rights invoked tend to be restricted to limited categories of rights traditionally regarded as protected under the law of state responsibility.[5] Thus cases very often relate to the confiscation, or nationalization without adequate compensation, of the property of a foreign investor, or interference in other respects with the rights accorded to the citizens of the other under customary international law or bilateral treaties of establishment, commerce, and navigation.[6] Such examples have been commonplace since the late nineteenth century. A few cases have involved wider questions of human rights, where it has been alleged that the respondent state has failed to give adequate personal protection to the foreign citizen, such as by way of failing to investigate and bring to justice perpetrators of murder, arson, and so on; conditions of imprisonment; or failure to provide redress in its courts. In the past, most of these cases were brought before temporary arbitral commissions or ad hoc arbitral

---

[5] See further Chapter 19 in this volume.
[6] See further Chapter 18 in this volume.

356   IVAN SHEARER

tribunals, established on a bilateral basis between the parties. A recent example, productive of significant jurisprudence, has been the Iran–US Claims Tribunal. Increasingly, cases involving investment disputes are brought before panels convened under the International Convention for the Settlement of Investment Disputes (ICSID), an initiative of the World Bank. A large number of states are parties to that convention. Occasionally, cases involving the rights of individual citizens may reach the ICJ, such as the *Nottebohm* (expropriation of property and wrongful expulsion) case.[7] The *Namibia* (breach of the terms of the Mandate by applying the discriminatory policies of apartheid)[8] and *Genocide Convention*[9] cases raised important human rights issues, but in special contexts. Mention should also be made of the *LaGrand*[10] and *Avena*[11] cases, which concerned the failure of state authorities in the United States to inform foreign nationals facing trial (and ultimately execution) of their rights of access to consular assistance, although the rights invoked derived from the Vienna Convention on Consular Relations and not from the general body of human rights law.

The cases also reflect the traditional view that international law applies between states, and that individuals may assert rights under that law against other states only through the mediation of their own national state. It is entirely within the discretion of the national state whether to espouse the cause of a citizen. In doing so, the state is asserting that a violation of the rights of one of its citizens is an injury to itself. In general, before the claim is espoused, injured citizens must have availed themselves of any remedies available in the delinquent state (the rule of exhaustion of local remedies). The espousal of claims is also linked to the right of diplomatic protection. On that basis, and without necessarily resorting to litigation (which often may not be possible in the absence of any dispute resolution machinery accepted by both states), representations on the diplomatic plane may be made about the treatment of citizens arrested, or tried, including the threat of capital punishment.

A recent decision of the ICJ has opened up the entire body of international human rights law as a basis for an international claim, beyond

---

[7] *Nottebohm Case (Liechtenstein v. Guatemala)*, [1955] ICJ Rep. 4.

[8] *Legal Consequences for States of the Continued Presence of South Africa in Namibia (South West Africa) notwithstanding Security Council Resolution 276 (1970)* (Advisory Opinion), [1971] ICJ Rep. 16.

[9] *Application of the Convention on the Prevention and Punishment of the Crime of Genocide (Bosnia and Herzegovina v. Serbia and Montenegro) (Judgment)*, [2007] ICJ Rep. 43.

[10] *LaGrand (Germany v. United States) (Merits)*, [2001] ICJ Rep. 466.

[11] *Avena and Other Mexican Nationals (Mexico v. US)*, [2004] ICJ Rep. 12.

HUMAN RIGHTS AS A SUBJECT OF INTERNATIONAL LITIGATION   357

the traditional categories of injury subject to diplomatic protection. In the case of *Ahmadou Sadio Diallo*,[12] which concerned the treatment by the Democratic Republic of Congo (DRC) of a businessman of Guinean nationality by way of arrest, ill-treatment in detention, and expulsion, the Court had regard to the International Covenant on Civil and Political Rights and the African Charter on Human and Peoples' Rights. The ICJ held that the DRC had violated both these instruments and was obliged to compensate Guinea for the injurious consequences to the individual of those violations.[13] This very significant decision moved the Court's focus beyond the traditional view of state responsibility as confined to acts violating the minimum standard of treatment of aliens to the entire corpus of accepted international human rights law. Already, in its judgment of 2007 on the preliminary objections made by the DRC, the Court declared that 'owing to the substantive development of international law over recent decades in respect of the rights it accords to individuals, the scope *ratione materiae* of diplomatic protection, originally limited to alleged violations of the minimum standard of treatment of aliens, has subsequently widened to include, *inter alia*, internationally guaranteed human rights'.[14] A commentator has noted of this decision that 'As *Diallo* shows, diplomatic protection and human rights pull in the same direction – the former does so within the traditional state–state framework, the latter within the more recent state–individual framework.'[15] The same commentator draws especial attention to the separate opinion of Judge Cancado Trindade, who summarizes the effect of the decision in the following pithy way:

> The subject of the rights that the Court has found to have been breached by the respondent State in the present case is not the applicant State: the subject of those rights is Mr. A. S. Diallo, an individual. The procedure for the vindication of the claim originally utilized (by the applicant State) was that of diplomatic protection, but the substantive law applicable in the present case, – as clarified after the Court's Judgment of 2007 on Preliminary Objections, in the course of the proceedings (written and oral phases) as to the merits – is the International Law of Human Rights.[16]

[12] *Ahmadou Sadio Diallo (Republic of Guinea* v. *Democratic Republic of the Congo) (Merits)*, [2010] ICJ Rep. 639.

[13] Ibid., [74]–[75].

[14] *Ahmadou Sadio Diallo (Republic of Guinea* v. *Democratic Republic of the Congo) (Preliminary Objections)*, [2007] ICJ Rep. 582, [39].

[15] Eirik Bjorge, 'Ahmadou Sadio Diallo (Republic of Guinea v. Democratic Republic of the Congo)', (2011) 105 AJIL 534, 539.

[16] *Ahmadou Sadio Diallo (Republic of Guinea* v. *Democratic Republic of the Congo) (Merits)*, [2010] ICJ Rep. 639, separate opinion of Judge Cançado Trindade, [223].

358   IVAN SHEARER

This view of the case should also be seen alongside the separate opinion of
Judge Simma in the earlier case of *Armed Activities on the Territory of the
Congo*.[17] Uganda had complained, in its counterclaim, of the treatment
by the DRC of its diplomats and other nationals present in Congolese
territory. It pleaded its case on the basis of the traditional substantive law
of state responsibility and on the law of diplomatic relations, and the ICJ
decided the case on those restricted bases.[18] Judge Simma, however, would
have had the ICJ go further. He declared that Uganda would have had
standing to bring, and the Court jurisdiction to entertain, a claim based
on both international humanitarian law and international human rights
law, and, moreover, even in relation to individuals not of its nationality.[19]
In this view, he was fortified by the well-known dictum of the Court in
the *Barcelona Traction* case referring to obligations owed *erga omnes*,[20]
which are, by their very nature, the concern of all states and in which all
states can be held to have a legal interest in their protection.

    Thus the recent jurisprudence of the ICJ in relation to the protection
of human rights can rightly be regarded as 'a sea change'.[21] Clearly the
growth in recognition of the substantive corpus of international human
rights law is increasingly supported by enforcement mechanisms, including litigation.

The modern evolution of human rights law and proposals for an International Court of Human Rights

With the object of implementing the objectives of the UN Charter to promote human rights,[22] the UN General Assembly established the Commission on Human Rights in 1946. The first task of the commission was to
negotiate the Universal Declaration of Human Rights, which was adopted

---

[17] *Armed Activities on the Territory of the Congo (Democratic Republic of the Congo v. Uganda)*,
    [2005] ICJ Rep. 168.
[18] Ibid., [306]–[317].   [19] Ibid., separate opinion of Judge Simma, [17].
[20] *Barcelona Traction, Light and Power Company Ltd (Belgium v. Spain) (Second Phase)*,
    [1970] ICJ Rep. 3, 32.
[21] Bjorge, above n. 15, 539. No such sea change is evident in relation to the doctrine of
    state immunity before national courts, where the ICJ has ruled that it does not become
    inapplicable in relation to violations of norms of human rights and international human-
    itarian law, even of *jus cogens* norms; *Jurisdictional Immunities of the State (Germany v.
    Italy: Greece intervening) (Judgment)*, ICJ General List No. 143, 3 February 2012, [97].
[22] UN Charter, Arts. 1(3), 55, 56.

HUMAN RIGHTS AS A SUBJECT OF INTERNATIONAL LITIGATION   359

on 9 December 1948.[23] Thereafter, the commission worked on the drafts of a more detailed elaboration of human rights to which a court was to be attached. This work was, however, impeded by the advent of the cold war, which rendered agreement impossible as between the Western powers and the states allied to the Soviet Union. Less ambitious aims were realized by the adoption, and opening for signature in 1966, of the twin Covenants on Human Rights: the International Covenant on Economic, Social and Cultural Rights (ICESCR),[24] and the International Covenant on Civil and Political Rights (ICCPR).[25] The ICESCR was couched largely in aspirational terms, committing states only to the progressive realization of the rights expressed therein, such as the rights to education, health, and social services. By contrast, the ICCPR was couched in peremptory terms investing individuals with such rights as the right to a fair trial, the prohibition of torture, and the freedom of conscience and belief. The separation of the ICESCR from the ICCPR thus made it easier for some states to adhere to the former while demurring to the latter.[26]

It is important to remember, however, that even for states that are not parties to the covenants (and especially the ICCPR) the Universal Declaration contains the essence of all important human rights and that its norms have been regarded as having entered the corpus of customary international law, binding on all states. There is thus no escape from the reach of basic international human rights law. This is reflected not only in state practice but also in the recently introduced process of the Universal Periodic Review (UPR) in the UN Human Rights Council, in which the record of observance of human rights by all UN member states is reviewed every four years. The UPR process provides that the record of all states is to be reviewed against the standards of the Universal Declaration, together with any human rights instruments of a conventional nature to which they have voluntarily subscribed.

---

[23] GA Res. 217A (III), UN GAOR, 3rd sess., 183rd plen. mtg, UN Doc. A/810 (10 December 1948).

[24] Opened for signature 16 December 1966, entered into force 3 November 1976, 993 UNTS 3.

[25] Opened for signature 16 December 1966, entered into force 23 March 1976 (except for Art. 41, which entered into force on 28 March 1979), 999 UNTS 171.

[26] The UN Office of Legal Affairs in 1999 gave an opinion that once ratified it was not possible for a state to withdraw from the ICCPR, since the contractual nature of the ICCPR is qualified by its character as expressing the rights of people rather than of states. This opinion was rendered following the purported denunciation of the ICCPR by the Democratic People's Republic of Korea (DPRK). The DPRK appears to have accepted this ruling, for it duly presented its regular report to the Human Rights Committee in 2001.

It was not possible in 1966 to agree on the creation of a court of human rights or any other enforcement mechanism of a binding nature. Instead, the covenants provided for the establishment of monitoring committees to which all states parties were obliged to report regularly. Those committees were invested with the power to make observations and recommendations to the reporting states after having considered their reports, material gathered from other sources, and the results of a public hearing of the state delegation presenting its initial and subsequent periodic reports. The possibility of individual complaints being brought by citizens against their own states that the terms of the covenants were not being observed was opened up through the attachment of optional protocols to the covenants, requiring acceptance by states separately from that of the covenants themselves.

It is worth noting in passing that what could have grown out of the Universal Declaration as a universal institution, had it not been for the cold war, is illustrated by the geographically confined European Convention on Human Rights, adopted by the Council of Europe in 1950. Its provisions are not only derived from the Universal Declaration but are strikingly similar in many respects to the wording later adopted in the ICCPR. The most significant difference, however, is that the European Convention provides for a European Court of Human Rights with compulsory jurisdiction, to which individuals have a right of access. Proposals for an international court of human rights were not revived until 2005, since when once more they have been met with resistance.[27]

After 1948, the UN Commission on Human Rights turned its attention to the drafting of particular human rights instruments in treaty form, dealing with certain aspects of human rights in greater detail. These included provision for the creation of an expert monitoring committee in respect of each covenant, the purpose of which is to receive regular reports on the implementation of the instrument concerned by each of the states parties. In addition to the twin covenants mentioned above, these instruments were the Convention for the Elimination of Racial Discrimination (1965),[28] the Convention for the Elimination of Discrimination against

---

[27] Michael O'Flaherty and Clare O'Brien, 'The Reform of the United Nations Treaty Bodies: A Critique of the High Commissioner's Concept Paper', (2007) 7 *Human Rights Law Review* 141, 172.

[28] International Convention on the Elimination of All Forms of Racial Discrimination (opened for signature 21 December 1965, entered into force 4 January 1969), 660 UNTS 195.

Women (1979),[29] the Convention against Torture (1984),[30] the Convention on the Rights of the Child (1989),[31] the Convention on Migrant Workers (1990),[32] the Convention on Persons with Disabilities (2006),[33] and the Convention on Enforced Disappearance (2006).[34]

The human rights treaty monitoring system

The monitoring system devised by the Commission on Human Rights for inclusion in the instruments amplifying the Universal Declaration[35] appeared first in the International Convention for the Elimination of All Forms of Racial Discrimination,[36] adopted in December 1965 (and therefore shortly before the adoption of the twin covenants of 1966). The convention created a Committee on the Elimination of Racial Discrimination consisting of eighteen experts, elected from among the nominees of the states parties, 'who shall serve in their personal capacity, consideration being given to equitable geographical distribution and to the representation of the different forms of civilization as well as of the principal legal systems'.[37] The term of office is four years, but members may be re-elected to further terms. The committee's main task is to consider the initial, and subsequent periodic, reports of the states parties on 'the legislative, judicial, administrative or other measures which they have adopted and which

[29] Convention on the Elimination of All Forms of Discrimination against Women (opened for signature 1 March 1980, entered into force 3 September 1981), 1249 UNTS 13.

[30] Convention against Torture and Other Cruel, Inhuman or Degrading Treatment or Punishment (opened for signature 10 December 1984, entered into force 26 June 1987), 1465 UNTS 85.

[31] Convention on the Rights of the Child (opened for signature 20 November 1989, entered into force 2 September 1990), 1577 UNTS 3.

[32] International Convention on the Protection of the Rights of All Migrant Workers and Members of their Families (opened for signature 18 December 1990, entered into force 1 July 2003), 2220 UNTS 3.

[33] Convention on the Rights of Persons with Disabilities (opened for signature 13 December 2006, entered into force 3 May 2008), 2515 UNTS 3.

[34] International Convention for the Protection of All Persons from Enforced Disappearance (opened for signature 20 December 2006, entered into force 23 December 2010), UN Doc. A/61/488.

[35] See generally Philip Alston and James Crawford (eds.), *The Future of UN Human Rights Treaty Reporting* (Cambridge University Press, 2000). On the Dublin Statement on the Process of Strengthening the UN Human Rights Treaty Body System (2009) (available at www.nottingham.ac.uk/hrlc/documents/specialevents/dublinstatement.pdf), see Michael O'Flaherty, 'Reform of the UN Human Rights Treaty Body System: Locating the Dublin Statement', (2010) 10 *Human Rights Law Review* 319.

[36] 660 UNTS 195, Arts. 8–10.   [37] Ibid., Art. 8(1).

give effect to the provisions of the Convention'.[38] The committee is then mandated to 'report annually', through the UN Secretary-General, on its activities and 'may make suggestions and general recommendations based on the examination of the reports and information received from the states parties. Such suggestions and general recommendations shall be reported to the General Assembly together with comments, if any, from states parties'.[39] Bearing in mind the aversion of many states to exposing themselves to criticism in international forums, this was as far as the drafters thought they could go, if the instruments were to attract a sufficient degree of support.

The monitoring mechanism thus established in the Racial Discrimination Convention was followed in the twin Covenants of 1966 and in the subsequent human rights conventions to 2006. The monitoring role of the committees was, however, significantly modified in practice through the adoption of rules of procedure by these committees. In the first place, the committees began to require that a delegation from the reporting state party appear before the committee, sitting in either Geneva or New York, to formally present the report and, if necessary, update it, and to answer questions or requests for further information from individual committee members. Second, in addition to 'bundling' all reports into one annual report to the UN General Assembly, the committees began to issue concluding observations and recommendations at the conclusion of the oral examination of each state party's report. These changes had the effect of making the reporting process more stringent, and – to an extent – more adversarial. They have been included in the body of the later human rights instruments, beginning with the 1984 Torture Convention. Thus it would appear that many states earlier unwilling to face up to direct criticism of their human rights records have acquiesced in a more intrusive role of the committees.

While not expressed in binding terms in the instruments, the committees regard their concluding observations, reports, and suggestions in relation to the reports of states parties as carrying weight. If they are not acted on, the state party concerned will be asked to explain its failure on the next occasion that it appears before the committee. Although hitherto not invoked in practice, in extreme cases of failure to remedy an egregious breach of the relevant convention, a state party may be called up early out of the usual cycle of periodic reporting to present a special report to the committee.

---

[38] Ibid., Art. 9(1).   [39] Ibid., Art. 10(1).

The obligation of preparing and presenting regular reports to up to nine committees places a heavy burden on states parties, especially on developing states with limited resources. No sooner has one report been completed than another is due. In an effort to reduce that burden, and to streamline its procedures, the Human Rights Committee has instituted a system of focused reports, based on questions devised by the committee and sent in advance to the reporting party.[40]

The monitoring system under the UN-sponsored human rights conventions is not a dispute settlement procedure as such. The committees do not assume a confrontational role, or act as fact-finding bodies. The Human Rights Committee, for example, regularly stresses the relationship between itself and reporting states parties as 'a dialogue', in the course of which it offers constructive criticism of a reporting state's human rights record, based on all information known to it. This information includes the reports of non-governmental organizations (NGOs), many of which have studied particular country situations in great detail. Nevertheless, the concluding observations adopted by the various committees and their recommendations and calls for reform are adopted in the public arena, and thus reflect the concerns raised by both citizens of the reporting state and by concerned international organizations (such as Amnesty International and Human Rights Watch). To this extent the procedures amount to a quasi-adversarial process.

The right of individual petition under the human rights treaty monitoring system

In contrast to the indirect method of critically evaluating a state's human rights record represented by the reporting system, a more direct method of evaluation was instituted in the human rights conventions adopted after 1948. This method was indeed radical, since it allowed, subject to certain conditions, individual citizens, or groups of citizens, to bring a complaint to the committees alleging that their own national state had violated the rights to which they were entitled under the relevant convention. Not only did this innovation allow for a remedy where it was impossible to find redress at the local level, but it radically transgressed the traditional status of individuals under international law as one of objects rather than

---

[40] Human Rights Committee, Focused Reports Based on the Replies to Lists of Issues Prior to Reporting (LOIPR): Implementation of the New Optional Reporting Procedure, 99th sess., UN Doc. CCPR/C/99/4 (29 September 2010).

subjects of that law. However, the political sensitivity of a right of direct access by individuals to an international instance was reflected in the subjection of the petition procedure to a number of conditions, above all to the condition that the state party must have explicitly accepted the procedure under optional provisions included in, or attached to, the conventions.[41]

A right of individual petition first appeared in the 1965 Racial Discrimination Convention. Article 14 of the Convention provides:

> A State party may at any time declare that it recognises the competence of the Committee to receive and consider communications from individuals or groups of individuals within its jurisdiction claiming to be victims of a violation by that State party of any of the rights set forth in this Convention. No communications shall be received by the Committee if it concerns a State party which has not made such a declaration.

This right of communication was reproduced in the two covenants of 1966 and in all the subsequent conventions, but with certain significant modifications. In the first place, the Racial Discrimination Convention requires that a state accepting this procedure

> establish or indicate a body within its national legal order which shall be competent to receive and consider petitions from individuals within its jurisdiction who claim to be victims of a violation of any of the rights set forth in this Convention and who have exhausted other available local remedies.[42]

There is no requirement in the covenants or any of the subsequent conventions for this interposition of a special national body. First, it was probably thought unnecessary, since the rule of exhaustion of local remedies applies under all.[43] In the second place, communications are treated confidentially by the committee under the Racial Discrimination Convention.[44] The nature of the allegations is made known to the state party, but not

---

[41] See generally on the significance of the petitions (complaints) procedures Christian Tomuschat, *Human Rights: Between Idealism and Realism*, 2nd edn (Oxford University Press, 2008), 193–4; Alex Conte and Richard Burchill, *Defining Civil and Political Rights: The Jurisprudence of the Human Rights Committee*, 2nd edn (Farnham: Ashgate, 2009), 2–3, 17; Henry Steiner and Philip Alston, *International Human Rights in Context*, 2nd edn (Oxford University Press, 2000), 738–40.

[42] 660 UNTS 195, Art. 14.

[43] On the evidential burden in demonstrating exhaustion of local remedies, see Bernard Robertson, 'Exhaustion of Local Remedies in International Human Rights Litigation – the Burden of Proof Reconsidered', (1990) 39 ICLQ 191–6.

[44] 660 UNTS 195, Art. 14(4), 6(a).

the identity of the complainant, unless he or she agrees. Third, the committee is empowered only to make 'suggestions and recommendations' to the state party and the complainant.[45] Summaries of the cases are reported on an annual basis to the UN General Assembly. However, it appears that, in recent times, complainants have been happy to have their identities revealed, and the conclusions of the committee are thus published under the complainants' names. The complaints procedure under the other conventions, although conducted in private session, allows for the publication of the resulting decisions. Fourth, the opening up of an optional right of individual complaint has, since 1965, been contained in an optional protocol annexed to the convention, rather than contained in the body of the convention itself. The only human rights convention under the UN system not containing a right of individual petition is the 1989 Convention on the Rights of the Child.

The individual complaints procedure under the ICCPR Optional Protocol, for example, works as follows. The procedure is entirely written. There is no right of personal appearance before the committee, or by counsel (although lawyers sometimes assist a complainant in formulating their written statements.) The claimant (termed an 'author' in the practice of the committee) submits a statement of the alleged violation, identifying the relevant right under the ICCPR. The claim need not follow a particular form, although guidance on the submission of complaints is available from the website of the UN High Commissioner for Human Rights. The Petitions Unit of the Office of the High Commissioner in Geneva, having satisfied itself that the complaint raises an issue under the ICCPR and that the complainant has been personally affected by the alleged violation (generalized complaints in the nature of an *actio popularis* – e.g., a claim that jail conditions are generally intolerable – are not admissible), then brings the complaint to the attention of the state party concerned, requesting 'written explanations or statements clarifying the matter and the remedy, if any, that may have been taken by that State'.[46] The Petitions Unit is advised in less straightforward cases by a member of the committee designated as Rapporteur for New Communications, who also has the power to order provisional measures in cases of urgency (e.g., an imminent imposition of the death penalty, or a deportation). The

---

[45] Ibid., Art. 14(7)(b).

[46] Optional Protocol to the International Convention on Civil and Political Rights (opened for signature 16 December 1966, entered into force 23 March 1976), 999 UNTS 171, Art. 4.

366

IVAN SHEARER

reply of the respondent state party is required to be forthcoming within six months,[47] but in practice the procedure often moves more slowly, with reminders needed. On receipt of the state party's reply the complainant is permitted to make observations on that response, to which the state party has a further opportunity to reply. While most complaints are processed to the point where they are ready for consideration by the committee within two to four years, some cases take longer because of delays in receipt of responses. With the 'pleadings' closed, a working group of the committee, consisting of between five and ten members, considers a draft decision on admissibility or the merits. In that work it is assisted by lawyers (mostly young) working in the Petitions Unit. The case then moves to the plenary committee, where the draft decision prepared by the working group may or may not be approved. Both the working group and the plenary committee work in individual petition cases in private session. The committee may (i) find the case inadmissible by reason of its incompatibility with the provisions of the ICCPR or of the Optional Protocol, or for failure to exhaust domestic remedies; (ii) dismiss the case after a consideration of the merits; or (iii) find a violation. In the last event, in presenting its decision (termed 'views') to the state party and to the individual concerned, it directs the state party to provide a remedy for the violation, which often includes monetary compensation.[48]

The Human Rights Committee has taken a nuanced position as to the legal status of its 'views' in cases under the Optional Protocol.[49] While the committee is not a court, it has recently noted that its views 'exhibit some important characteristics of a judicial decision. They are arrived at in a judicial spirit, including the impartiality and independence of Committee members, the considered interpretation of the language of the Covenant, and the determinative character of the decisions'.[50] Without stating in so many words that its views are binding on the state to which they are directed, the committee regards them as 'an authoritative determination

---

[47] Ibid., Art. 4(2).

[48] For a detailed examination of the procedure, and for a comprehensive survey of the decisions of the committee in Optional Protocol cases, see Sarah Joseph, Jenny Schultz, and Melissa Castan, *The International Covenant on Civil and Political Rights: Cases, Materials and Commentary*, 2nd edn (Oxford University Press, 2004). See also Jacob Th. Moeller and Alfred de Zayas, *United Nations Human Rights Committee Case Law 1977–2008* (Kehl-am-Rhein: N. P. Engel Verlag, 2009).

[49] Human Rights Committee, General Comment No 33: The Obligations of States Parties under the Optional Protocol to the International Covenant on Civil and Political Rights, 94th sess., UN Doc. CCPR/C/GC/33 (5 November 2008).

[50] Ibid., [11].

by the organ established under the Covenant itself charged with the interpretation of that instrument. These views derive their character, and the importance which attaches to them, from the integral role of the Committee under both the Covenant and the Optional Protocol.'[51] Reliance is also placed by the committee on the duty of states parties under Article 2(3)(a) of the ICCPR to ensure an effective remedy to those whose rights have been violated, and also on the principle of good faith in carrying out their duty to co-operate with the committee in the discharge of its functions under the Optional Protocol.[52] The complaints procedure is thus, in the committee's view, tantamount to litigation with an 'authoritative' decision resulting.

Notwithstanding that the surprisingly large number of 114 out of a total of 167 states parties to the ICCPR (as at 5 January 2012) have become parties to the Optional Protocol, its invocation by individuals in those states has been uneven. Some states are known to discourage complaints being made against them,[53] or threaten retaliation against those who do so. In other states, the procedure is not widely known. A large number of Western European states accept the procedure, even though they are also parties to the European Convention on Human Rights, so that complainants have the option of going to the European Court of Human Rights, where they may obtain a legally binding decision. It would seem that an important factor is the widespread knowledge of the procedure among lawyers in developed countries. For example, in the case of Australia, as at November 2008, 105 cases had been registered at the Office of the High Commissioner as ready for consideration by the Human Rights Committee. Of these, violations were found in twenty-four cases, no violation in six, thirty-two cases were found inadmissible, twenty-eight were discontinued by the complainants, and fifteen cases were pending. Additional communications are in the course of processing by the Petitions Unit prior to formal registration, and show no sign of abating. It can therefore be concluded that the complaints procedure stands as a welcome substitute for litigation where no other mechanisms are available.

---

[51] Ibid., [13].   [52] Ibid., [14]–[15].

[53] On the misunderstanding that the views of the committee were technically binding, the chief justice of Sri Lanka declared in 2006, in the case of *Singarasa v. The Attorney-General*, that it was 'unconstitutional' for citizens to resort to the committee, since this would be to acknowledge an authority superior to the established courts of the country. N. S. Rodley, 'The Singarasa case: Quis custodiet: A test for the Bangalore Principles of Judicial Conduct', (2008) 41 *Israel Law Review* 41.

Inter-state complaints under the human rights treaty monitoring system

A procedure potentially offering a form of direct dispute resolution between states was created in the Racial Discrimination Convention and included in all subsequent instruments. Article 11 of the convention provides that:

> 1. If a State party considers that another State party is not giving effect to the provisions of this Convention, it may bring the matter to the attention of the Committee. The Committee shall then transmit the communication to the State party concerned. Within three months, the receiving State shall submit to the Committee written explanations or statements clarifying the matter and the remedy, if any, that may have been taken by the State.
>
> 2. If the matter is not adjusted to the satisfaction of both parties, either by bilateral negotiations or by any other procedure open to them, within six months after the receipt by the receiving State of the written communication, either State shall have the right to refer the matter again to the Committee by notifying the Committee and also the other State . . .

Articles 12 and 13 then proceed to establish an ad hoc Conciliation Commission, comprising five persons (not being members of the committee), which shall present a report to the chairman of the committee embodying its findings of fact and containing recommendations for the amicable solution of the dispute. The states concerned are to indicate within three months whether they accept those recommendations. Thereafter, the committee shall communicate the report of the commission and the declarations of the states parties concerned to the other states parties to the convention.

Thus far, this inter-state dispute resolution procedure has not been invoked in practice. While available generally under the Racial Discrimination Convention, it was made subject to special acceptance in Article 41 of the ICCPR, and in subsequent instruments. It was rumoured that Australia and New Zealand were contemplating invoking the procedure under the ICCPR against Zimbabwe after the flawed elections in 2005, but were dissuaded from doing so. Perhaps its general non-use may be attributed to the reluctance of states to point the finger at others, where few if any diplomatic advantages may be gained. Also it is sometimes remarked that 'people who live in glass houses should not throw stones'. But egregious cases should surely not be passed over in silence.

The UN Human Rights Council and the Universal Periodic Review

The Human Rights Council was established in 2006 to replace the Commission on Human Rights by UN General Assembly resolution 60/251.[54] The commission had, in the view of many, run its course in the promotion of new human rights conventions. What was needed was not more conventions but better enforcement of the existing conventions. Moreover, the commission of fifty-three members had descended into an arena of conflict and unseemly debate, in which little of substance was being achieved. Thus high hopes were first held out for the establishment of a new body that would have a more specific mandate. Unfortunately, this hope has been somewhat disappointed to date.

Included in the mandate of the Human Rights Council is the direction to 'undertake a universal periodic review, based on objective and reliable information, of the fulfilment by each State of its human rights obligations and commitments in a manner which ensures universality of coverage and equal treatment with respect to all States'.[55]

The process of the Universal Periodic Review (UPR) began in 2008. UN Secretary-General Ban Ki-moon stated that the UPR process 'has great potential to promote and protect human rights in the darkest corners of the world'.[56] The major steps forward from the perspective of the monitoring of human rights, compared with the treaty body system under the individual specialized conventions, are (i) that the review is truly universal in the sense that all UN member states would be reviewed periodically, quite independently of their obligations, or lack of them, under other reporting procedures; and (ii) their record of adherence to the norms established under the Universal Declaration of Human Rights, 1948, constitutes a fundamental standard of measurement, in addition to obligations under the particular conventions to which states under review have voluntarily subscribed.

---

[54] See generally Kevin Boyle, 'The United Nations Human Rights Council: Origins, Antecedents and Prospects', and Nigel Rodley, 'The United Nations Human Rights Council, Its Special Procedures and Its Relationship with the Treaty Bodies: Complementarity or Competition?', in Kevin Boyle (ed.), *New Institutions for Human Rights Protection* (Oxford University Press, 2009).

[55] GA Res. 60/251, UN GAOR, 60th sess., 72nd plen. mtg, UN Doc. A/RES/60/251 (15 March 2006), para. 5(e).

[56] In opening the 4th session of the Human Rights Council, 12 March 2007: Office of the High Commissioner for Human Rights, 'Universal Periodic Review', available at www.ohchr.org/EN/HRBodies/UPR/Pages/UPRMain.aspx.

The programme of review provides for the examination of sixteen UN member states at each of the three sessions of the Human Rights Council held annually. In this way, the human rights records of all 193 member states were examined by the end of 2011.

The reviews are conducted by a working group which, despite its name, consists of all forty-seven members of the council. Membership of the council consists of representatives of elected state members, unlike the independent expert individuals elected to the committees under the UN treaty body system. UN member states that are not members of the council may also attend and take part as observers. The process is assisted by a 'troika' of three members of the council who act as rapporteurs. Separate troikas are selected by ballot for each state to be reviewed. NGOs may submit information to the working group but may not otherwise participate in the examination. The duration of each examination is fixed at three hours. Shortly after the examination the troika prepares an 'outcome report' which allows for the participation of the reviewed state. The outcome report then returns to the working group for adoption, during which the reviewed state may indicate its acceptance or rejection of particular findings or recommendations. The report then goes to a plenary session of the council for adoption, at which the reviewed state is permitted to make further statements, and to answer questions. Members of the council and observer states, as well as NGOs, may also make statements at this point.

While this process seems good in principle, in practice it has proven to be disappointing. It is evident from the records of the examinations of a number of states reviewed thus far by the council that some poorly performing states tend to be given an easy time in their oral examination by other poorly performing states, which will stress their accomplishments in the face of alleged economic or political difficulties rather than condemn their failures. A few states (and some NGOs) will deal more directly and frankly with the reviewed state's shortcomings. On the whole, however, and bearing in mind the limited time allowed for the process, the final reports in relation to each state reviewed are reasonably balanced. Adverse findings and recommendations are expressed in moderate language, and harsh condemnation is avoided. Prospects for a more rigorous examination of reports in the second cycle of reviews (2012–16) seem to be indicated by an examination of the Human Rights Council's conduct of reviews in the last year of the first cycle by Human Rights Watch.[57]

---

[57] Human Rights Watch, 'Keeping the Momentum: One Year in the Life of the UN Human Rights Council', September 2011.

Some have suggested that the introduction of the UPR in the Human Rights Council might replace the work of the nine specialized committees in monitoring compliance with the various human rights instruments.[58] It is evident that the task of attending to the reporting obligations that states have assumed under up to nine instruments is onerous, especially for developing countries. Moreover, each report requires attendance by a state delegation for its presentation in either Geneva or New York, at which the delegation is called on to respond to questions asked by the relevant committee, thus draining valuable financial resources. On the other hand, it is argued that to relegate all monitoring under the treaty system to the council may run the danger of both minimizing and politicizing the process.[59] The expert committees retain a wealth of experience and depth of knowledge difficult to replicate in a large political body. Moreover, the individual complaints procedures would be difficult to conduct in a body such as the Human Rights Council, especially the maintenance and development of a coherent jurisprudence.

While it is important to note the addition of the Human Rights Council as part of the architecture of the international human rights system, the council at most provides a third-order avenue of redress for individual violations of human rights through the publicity attending the UPR process. The limited complaints mechanisms, yet to be established, are described below.

The complaints mechanisms of the UN Human Rights Council[60]

In 2007, the Human Rights Council established a working group to review the previous complaint system instituted under the replaced Human Rights Commission, known as the 1503 Procedure (named after the number of the resolution establishing it). The council intends to establish a comparable but revised procedure. The intention of the complaint procedure is 'to address consistent patterns of gross and reliably attested violations of all human rights and all fundamental freedoms occurring in any part of the world and under any circumstances'.[61] Complaints may be made by individuals or by groups. It is confidential in its nature

---

[58] O'Flaherty and O'Brien, above n. 27.   [59] Ibid.

[60] Office of the High Commissioner for Human Rights, Human Rights Council Complaint Procedure, available at www2.ohchr.org/english/bodies/chr/complaints.htm.

[61] Human Rights Council, UN GAOR, 62nd sess., Supp. No. 53, A/HRC/RES/5/1 (18 June 2007).

IVAN SHEARER

'with a view to enhancing co-operation with the State concerned'.[62] There are three layers of consideration. A complaint first goes to the Working Group on Communications of the Council, which consists of five qualified independent experts nominated by each of the five UN regional groups (Africa, Asia, Latin America and the Caribbean, Eastern Europe, and Western Europe and Others). Having ascertained its admissibility and whether, on the merits, it would appear to qualify as revealing a consistent pattern of gross and reliably attested violations, the communication passes to the Working Group on Situations. This group also consists of five expert and independent members, nominated in the same manner as the Working Group on Communications. The Working Group on Situations may then make recommendations to the council on the course of action to take.

Thus far, there appear to have been no such matters before the council. In principle, the design promises hope of effective action, since it does not involve states having to accuse other states of these patterns of violation. However, the political realities in the council – as in the UN generally – tend to dictate that effective, or, indeed, any, action is selective. It has been pointed out many times that Israel, for example, is more often criticized than any other state in the council. It remains to be seen whether the complaints procedure being established under the new UN Human Rights Council offers the prospect of a veiled inter-state dispute resolution procedure, with individuals or groups standing as proxies for states.

Conclusions

Direct inter-state dispute resolution in the matter of human rights is mostly lacking in the international system. The principal reason why the indirect methods under the monitoring systems described above have been preferred is that a majority of states are still not prepared to accept the challenge to state sovereignty represented by compulsory procedures leading to binding and enforceable decisions. This 'neuralgic' aversion is felt not only among small states with weak social institutions and struggling economies and among states in transition from authoritarian modes of governance, but also among some developed states whose legal

---

[62] Ibid.

orders and political traditions are resistant to dictation from external bodies.[63]

Notwithstanding this 'neuralgia', it is remarkable that so many states have accepted the second-order level of monitoring and complaints procedures contained in the bodies established for the international community as a whole in the field of human rights. It might be observed that, at first, the compromise of state sovereignty represented by the twin covenants and the first of the specialized conventions seemed relatively slight. A majority of states were willing to profess their commitment to human rights ideals and to co-operate with the treaty bodies in a spirit of goodwill. Practical advantages were thought to flow from such a demonstration of international 'good citizenship' in the shape of trade, investment, tourism, and other forms of interaction with the international community. Once confidence had been established in the integrity of these bodies, the incremental increase in the intrusiveness of their procedures into the realm of domestic jurisdiction appears to have been accepted, more through acquiescence than through overt acceptance. That said, it remains true that most parties to the conventions containing monitoring and complaints mechanisms regard decisions taken by those bodies as recommendatory only, and full compliance is disappointingly low.[64] Indeed, for some states, adherence to their human rights treaty obligations may be seen as little more than window-dressing.

It is important to note, however, that a significant number of states are also parties to regional human rights conventions, especially the European and Inter-American conventions, under which binding and enforceable decisions may be obtained.

It remains to be seen whether the general complaints procedures being established under the Human Rights Council for large-scale violations of human rights will be effective, with individuals, groups and NGOs standing as proxies for states in a quasi-litigious procedure.

For the time being there is little or no prospect of the establishment of an International Court of Human Rights along the lines of the European Court of Human Rights, nor of a court with optional jurisdiction to take over the complaints procedures of the existing nine treaty bodies. Such a

---

[63] For the attitude of the United States see John F. Murphy, *The United States and the Rule of Law in International Affairs* (Cambridge University Press, 2004), 42, 329–32.

[64] For example, the rate of satisfactory compliance with the views of the Human Rights Committee was estimated in 2002 to be approximately 30 per cent: David Harris, *Cases and Materials on International Law*, 7th edn (London: Sweet & Maxwell, 2010), 565 n. 149.

proposal would be expensive to realize, especially in the absence of likely support from the UN's major financial contributors, and would appear to lack widespread political support.

However, there is further room for improving the work of the existing committee structures and procedures in order to make them more efficient and effective. As their workload increases there is a case to be made for lengthier sitting periods and for paying their members adequate compensation. Their procedures could be further streamlined in order to reduce the burden of reporting by states. The backlog of individual complaints, especially before the Human Rights Committee, may have to be addressed by the institution of a screening process through which only cases raising issues of general significance for the interpretation of the law, or especially egregious violations, are dealt with by the committee.

17

The WTO dispute settlement system and underlying motivating factors for adjudication

M. RAFIQUL ISLAM

The institutionalized international trade law developed since the Second World War is contractual, composed of international agreements between trading countries. The orderly governance of contractual rights and obligations and satisfactory resolution of differences in conducting trade relationships necessitated the creation of a dispute settlement process under the General Agreement on Tariffs and Trade (GATT) in 1947.[1] Its conciliatory and consensus approach of diplomatically negotiated dispute settlement to the mutual satisfaction of the disputant members favoured powerful members who bent the system to their undue advantage at the expense of less powerful members. Rampant unilateralism and defiance of GATT disciplines by powerful members underscored the urgency of overhauling the dispute settlement system. There thus emerged a demonstrated need for a rule-based, adjudicative, and binding form of dispute resolution capable of providing strong multilateral remedies and effective enforcement. Against this backdrop, the eighth round of multilateral trade negotiations within the GATT framework – the Uruguay Round – commenced in 1986 and eventually adopted the Understanding on the Rules and Procedures Governing the Settlement of Disputes (DSU)[2] in 1992, establishing the dispute settlement system (DSS) of the World Trade Organization (WTO).

The DSS is the cornerstone of the WTO, providing the normative framework and constitutional guarantees of trading rights and duties of all WTO members, particularly assuring special security to economically

---

[1] General Agreement on Tariffs and Trade (opened for signature 30 October 1947, entered into force 1 January 1948), 55 UNTS 194.

[2] WTO, *The Legal Text: The Results of the Uruguay Round of Multilateral Trade Negotiations* (Cambridge University Press, 2000), 354.

disadvantaged members.[3] It is premised on certain proclaimed policy objectives to be pursued to overcome the inadequacies and unfairness of the GATT system. The Uruguay Round Preparatory Committee in its 1986 meetings recognized the existing power asymmetry and need for legal protection for the less powerful by preserving rights over might in the enforcement of assumed commitments and obligations. The Ministerial Declaration of September 1986 launching the Uruguay Round unequivocally set these policy agenda,[4] which are reiterated in DSU provisions.[5] The DSS purports to achieve these goals by being independent, legalistic, adjudicative, and formal. It seeks to promote its credibility and predictability by deciding disputes on their merits and effectiveness by prohibiting infractions, enforcing rules and disciplines, monitoring compliance, and securing specific performance promptly *for the benefit of all members*.[6] It is these desirable policy goals that generated expectations and euphoria among WTO members, which expressed their fundamental faith in and general consensus on the DSS at the Uruguay Round.

An examination of these policy aspects reflected through performance suggests that the DSS is surely an improvement on GATT, and many WTO members have benefited from it. Indeed, the DSS has been used more frequently than any other inter-state dispute settlement system, since January 1995 dealing with some 435 disputes by 4 April 2012.[7] This high rate of litigation in the DSS is discernibly attributable to the very approach of the WTO to trade dispute settlement. It treats a dispute over trade nullification and/or impairment as arising out of and in the course of, and is limited to, the trade relationships between the disputant parties concerned. Such a dispute is not an internationally wrongful act and entails no state responsibility under international law. This approach makes it politically and diplomatically expedient for WTO members to continue their support for the DSS. Most WTO members are inherently

---

[3] Julio Lacarte-Muro and Petina Gappah, 'Developing Countries and the WTO Legal and Dispute Settlement System: A View from the Bench', (2000) 3 *Journal of International Economic Law* 401.

[4] Ministerial Declaration on the Uruguay Round, GATT Doc. No. MIN 86/6, 20 September 1986; *GATT Newsletter*, No. 43, January–February 1987, 6.

[5] Marrakesh Agreement Establishing the World Trade Organization (opened for signature 15 April 1994, entered into force 1 January 1995), 1867 UNTS 3, Annex 2 (DSU), Arts. 4(10), 8(10), 12(10–11), 21(7–8), 24.

[6] Terence Stewart (ed.), *The GATT Uruguay Round: A Negotiating History (1986–1992)* (Deventer: Kluwer, 1993), Vol. II, 2697–811.

[7] World Trade Organization, Chronological List of Disputes Cases, available at www.wto.org/english/tratop_e/dispu_e/dispu_status_e.htm at 4 June 2012.

protectionist and self-serving, and this instinct can still be pursued in the DSS. Its legal framework and modus operandi are obliquely susceptible to power, which invariably favours powerful members.[8] The GATT-style political leverage and economic clout can still defy legal obligations with impunity and influence the outcomes of disputes. This opportunity for power-induced stratagem as an influential factor in the DSS, and its inability to force compliance with rulings are important underlying motivating factors for the frequent use of the DSS. The policy euphoria of receiving proclaimed legal protection to salvage their trading rights and interests, which may otherwise be lost, is a crucial consideration of some developing members in their continuing reliance on the DSS. Members that do not belong to either group are the non-users of the DSS and happen to be the majority. The DSS is popular only in terms of the actual number of disputes, involving only a minority of members. The hybrid operation of the DSS, accommodating both legal and power-sponsored outcomes, explains why it has been dealing with so many disputes.

This chapter addresses this critical point on the motivations for reliance on litigation in the WTO by considering different stages of the DSS and how these stages benefit some members seeking to utilize litigation to their advantage and disenfranchise others. Resource-rich and powerful parties are in an advantageous position at every stage of the WTO dispute settlement system. The mandatory consultative process allows them to use their political clout and market power to arrive at a negotiated settlement on their terms or otherwise to go passively through the motions of consultation with the strategy of settling the dispute in resource-intensive panel and appeal phases, which often are beyond the capacity of the majority of members. There is no institutional or centralized mechanism for the enforcement of dispute settlement rulings, and it is left to the winning parties to induce compliance. As a result, powerful winning parties are in a better position to secure compliance from comparatively weaker losing parties. If both sides are powerful, the process of implementation of the ruling becomes almost never-ending. There are ample instances of powerful parties unduly procrastinating regarding, and not complying with, the specific performance required by the ruling, with impunity. The authorized sanction to induce compliance with rulings is overly skewed to the advantage of powerful parties, which can retaliate through authorized trade sanction measures against comparatively less powerful parties. However, the latter cannot afford to utilize authorized sanctions against

---

[8] For an outline of the DSS see the discussion in Chapter 1 of this volume.

the former for fear of retaliation in other bilateral trading sectors. Moreover, any trade sanctions by the latter makes no economic sense as it would have almost no impact on the economy of the former. With all these systemic advantages, powerful developed members and a few developing members with increasing market shares dominate the WTO dispute settlement system. Confronted with systemic disadvantages, resource constraints, and cost–benefit considerations, the overwhelming majority of members find no incentive to litigate at the WTO to redress the impairment and/or nullification of their legitimate trading rights and economic interests.

There are crucial policy objectives in providing a legalistic adjudicative system propelled by effective and prompt enforcement, but these remain elusive for the majority of members and the DSS thus remains beyond their reach after seventeen years of operation. The legitimate trading rights and opportunities of the majority continue to be eclipsed in the shadow of power and lack of legal protection in dispute resolution, causing insurmountable barriers for many to access justice under the DSS. The lacklustre balance of trading rights and opportunities between the most and least-advantaged has rendered the DSS largely a monopoly of powerful members. Litigation within the context of international trade disputes can therefore be seen as a tool of power, primarily available for use by a small portion of WTO members. Reforms to overcome these policy failures warrant urgent attention to promote the systemic value and sustainability of the DSS.

Policies and realities pertaining to the institution of proceedings

Causes of action

The DSS resolves disputes arising from the defiance of WTO objectives, and rules and disciplines contained in various covered agreements, causing the nullification and/or impairment of trading rights, interests, and benefits that could legitimately be accrued under any WTO agreements. Its sole purpose is to end the WTO-inconsistent trade policies, practices, and measures of members. This preponderance of contractual orientation distinguishes the DSS from the notion of dispute resolution under general international law, which involves identifying internationally wrongful acts and entails state responsibility. Every infringement, impairment, or nullification of rights, benefits, and interests of members by the non-performance of contractual objectives, obligations, and commitments by another are presumed WTO-inconsistent trade policy, practice, and

THE WTO DISPUTE SETTLEMENT SYSTEM 379

measure and can legally constitute a sufficient ground for a prima facie dispute for resolution under the DSS. Actual trade losses or damages sustained by WTO-inconsistent practices appear at best corroborative, rather than substantive, evidence of impairment or nullification. Such losses are looked at technically in a product- or sector-specific piecemeal way regardless of the positive implications for other stakeholders and the economy holistically. This policy is pursued to protect competitive trade benefits in a given product or sector that may well be uncompetitive, rather than focusing on the total volume of trade. This cause of action has the potential of according priority to protection over liberalization, the antithesis of the WTO.

This product- or sector-specific determination of impairment and/or nullification as a cause of action does not always reflect the economic realities of WTO members. Numerous dumping/anti-dumping disputes are examples in point. The DSS decides these disputes pursuant to the Anti-Dumping Agreement,[9] which presumes that dumping has price-discriminatory and trade distortive effects on the competitive environment of the market. The dumping of a product unfairly and adversely affects the competitive strength of the same or like domestic product in the dumped market. Anti-dumping duties may be levied to offset any impairment or nullification suffered by the competing domestic industry. This rationale to sustain market competition makes no economic sense and is at odds with the policy aims of multilateral trade liberalization under the WTO. One of these aims is to provide consumers with the widest possible variety of products at the cheapest possible prices. Dumping by foreign producers serves this interest of domestic consumers. The domestic producers of the same or like product may suffer a loss due to dumping, but this loss may be compensated or even outweighed by the gains of domestic consumers of the dumped product. In the case of perishable primary goods, the alternative to their dumping is to leave them to waste at the expense of agriculture exporting countries, which invariably suffer loss due to fluctuating and low agricultural prices in the world market. Dumping perishable goods may well be a humane act for many hunger- and famine-stricken net-food-importing least-developed countries (LDCs). Yet anti-dumping cases at the WTO have been prolific.

The rationale for pursuing impairment or nullification actions as a result of dumping is product-specific, not economy-specific. These cases

---

[9] Marrakesh Agreement Establishing the World Trade Organization (opened for signature 15 April 1994, entered into force 1 January 1995), 1867 UNTS 3, Annex 1 A (Anti-Dumping Agreement).

focus narrowly, solely on the effects of the dumped product on a domestic competitor. Account is not taken of the beneficial effect of dumping on the importing economy as a whole, nor the positive effects of increased competition, welfare gains of domestic consumers, effects of anti-dumping duties on the domestic importer of the dumped product, and the state of competition in the domestic market. A national economy-wide cost–benefit approach with the broad public interest and right of domestic consumers would go a long way in balancing the policy rationale for impairment or nullification as a cause of action. There are credible studies with empirical evidence that it is not dumping, but anti-dumping, which is trade protectionist, monopolistic, and a threat to competition in the domestic market.[10] A state can launch a dumping investigation at will and impose anti-dumping duties arbitrarily on a competing foreign product as disguised protectionism in favour of its uncompetitive product/sector. It is this scope for the pursuit of protectionism that explains why the DSS is inundated with anti-dumping disputes (about a quarter of total disputes).[11]

Mandatory consultations

Preponderant weight is accorded to the peaceful settlement of trade disputes through consultations between disputing parties. It affords opportunities for the parties to engage in friendly negotiations to appreciate better the factual and legal dimensions of their dispute and arrive at a mutually satisfactory amicable settlement. It also aims at averting formal legal proceedings and ruling against a member responsible for the abrogation of WTO obligations and commitments. This pragmatic and conciliatory approach is a recognized means of the pacific settlement of disputes in international law embodied in Article 33 of the UN Charter. But the reality in most trade disputes is somewhat different.

---

[10] OECD Committee on Competition Law and Policy, 'Competition Policy and Antidumping', OECD Official Study Paper No. DAFFE/CLP/WP1 (95) 9 (Paris: 1995); S. Hutton and M. Trebilcock, 'An Empirical Study of the Application of Canadian Anti-dumping Laws: A Search for Normative Rationales', (1990) 24 *Journal of World Trade* 128; Christopher Corr, 'Trade Protection in the New Millennium: The Ascendancy of Anti-dumping Measures', (1997) 18 *Northwestern Journal of International Law and Business* 49.

[11] World Trade Organization, above n. 7: of a total of 438 disputes as of 12 June 2012, 90 disputes concern anti-dumping issues. Brink Lindsey and Daniel J. Ikenson, *Antidumping Exposed: The Devilish Details of Unfair Trade Law* (Washington, DC: Cato Institute, 2003).

The DSU consultative process is essentially political, not legalistic and judicial, in nature. Except for the time limitation of sixty days,[12] there are no strict operational rules and procedures to induce the parties to engage in meaningful consultations. The DSU contains certain procedural rules of special and differential (S & D) treatment favourable to developing members in the form of faster process, longer time frames, and legal aids. Developing countries' particular problems and interests are required to be given 'special attention' in consultations.[13] A consultation request to the Dispute Settlement Body (DSB) is a precondition for receiving any S & D treatment. This very first step requires adequate legal knowledge of making a nullification and/or impairment case, selecting a viable ground, the feasibility of lodging a complaint, hiring experts, and keeping pace with the phases of consultations. Many developing members lack all these essential pre-consultation resources, and there is no WTO assistance available for them. The descriptive requirement of giving 'special attention' to developing members contains no operative element to render it a mandatory obligation. There is no surveillance mechanism to know whether the parties are adhering to the S & D treatment requirement in consultations. Neither panel nor Appellate Body (AB) reports clarify the legal status of the term 'special attention', which is often conveniently ignored by developed members.[14] As a result, the requirement of S & D treatment in consultations appears to be no more than a best-endeavour, upholding only a hollow commitment.

Disputants are reluctant to take consultation seriously due to their preconceived experience of ineffective GATT negotiations, which reflected the relative power position of the parties rather than the merits of the dispute. They often prefer rule-based mandatory rulings for the withdrawal of WTO-inconsistent trade measures. While undertaking consultations is compulsory, arriving at a resolution through consultations is not. Either party may potentially abuse the process by treating it as a formality and as a cooling-off period prior to an automatic legalistic solution by the panel and appeal process.

Domestic policy preferences in developed members to move disputes to the panel process often influence the outcome of consultations.[15]

---

[12] DSU, Art. 4.   [13] DSU, Art. 4(10).

[14] Valentina Delich, 'Developing Countries and the WTO Dispute Settlement System', in Bernard Hoekman et al. (eds.), *Development, Trade and the WTO: A Handbook* (New York: Council on Foreign Relations, 2002) 71, 73.

[15] Duane W. Layton and Jorge O. Miranda, 'Advocacy before WTO Dispute Settlement Panels in Trade Remedy Cases', (2003) 37 *Journal of World Trade* 71.

Developing members see it as no more than a diplomatic process, which has the propensity to allow them to evade WTO obligations and commitments with impunity. Developing members are vulnerable in consultations, particularly with those developed members that are the suppliers of foreign investments, loans, and aids to the former. Concerns for their non-trade interests may dictate the consultation process and mask the legitimate rights of developing members, which have too much to lose by seriously pursuing their legal rights in consultations. Empirical evidence reveals that 'rich complainants are much more likely to get defendants to concede... than poor complainants.'[16] The DSS is yet to address this practical difficulty of an entry-level barrier, inhibiting the underdog in consultation from accessing remedies. Given that the role of extralegal considerations remains largely unabated and obscured, trade disputes are not easily settled through consultations. In fact, powerful parties often remain passive in consultations as a deliberate strategy to settle the dispute in subsequent resource-intensive legal processes (panel and appeal stages). This approach may well be intuitively appealing as apolitical and good for developing members. However, the reality is somewhat different, as both panel and appeal processes are yet to dissipate the power dynamics in proceedings and the implementation of rulings. Thus the very first step of dispute settlement is susceptible to the influence of power, which the DSS stands for eradicating.

Confidentiality

Confidentiality is pursued at all stages of the DSS. The secrecy of the process, the underlying policy of mediation, is observed in consultations. Panels meet in closed session and treat all deliberations and documents confidentially. Appeal proceedings are held in confidence, opinions are anonymous, and reports are prepared in the absence of the parties. This confidentiality is intended to protect the integrity and interests of the process and parties.[17] However, the release of panel and AB decisions to WTO members prior to their adoption by the DSB and the practice of parties of making their own written pleadings public are signs of improved access and transparency of the DSS. Nonetheless, the proceedings are open only for the parties (complainant and respondent), including formal third

---

[16] Marc L. Busch and Eric Reinhardt, 'Developing Countries and GATT/WTO Dispute Settlement', (2003) 37 *Journal of World Trade* 731.

[17] DSU, Art. 17(10).

THE WTO DISPUTE SETTLEMENT SYSTEM 383

parties with qualified access.[18] Other entities, non-party WTO members, non-WTO members, non-state entities such as non-governmental organizations (NGOs), and individuals, however interested in a given dispute, do not have any intervener status and remain largely in the dark unless they are able to join formally as third parties. This policy increases participation but not the transparency of the dispute settlement process to public observation and knowledge. It creates a shell of confidentiality that deprives many stakeholders and the public at large greater insight into what is judged as fair or unfair in the outcome of a given dispute.

The issue of public access and transparency of the DSS was addressed in *Shrimp-Turtle* in terms of the admissibility of *amicus curiae* briefs submitted by NGOs. The panel found that the acceptance of unsolicited *amicus curiae* submissions from NGOs went beyond its right to 'seek' information under DSU Article 13. The AB reversed the panel finding as being unnecessarily narrow and technical and thus undermining the broad fact-finding powers of the panel in the interest of 'an objective assessment of the fact' under DSU Article 11.[19] The AB also contemplated the scope of DSU Article 12, which allows a panel to create procedures deviating from the default procedures in DSU Annex 3, and concluded that the combined effect of DSU Articles 12 and 13 granted the panel broad powers of inquiry to discharge its obligations.[20] The AB explicitly affirmed its authority to accept and consider *amicus* submissions in *Carbon Steel*,[21] and in *Asbestos* introduced a Special Procedure including criteria according to which entities might apply for leave to submit a brief to the AB.[22]

There are strong legal policy arguments around this development, ranging from unprincipled and unsolicited participation, undermining the inter-governmental framework of the WTO, and bias against developing countries to procedural delay, inefficient use of judicial resources, and

---

[18] Circumscribed by its limited access to the panel proceedings and difficulties in oral proceedings, although third-party access to an AB hearing is full.

[19] DSU, Art. 11.

[20] Appellate Body Report, *United States – Import Prohibition of Certain Shrimp and Shrimp Products*, WTO Doc. WT/DS58/AB/R (6 November 1998).

[21] Appellate Body Report, *United States – Imposition of Countervailing Duties on Certain Hot-Rolled Lead and Bismuth Carbon Steel Products Originating in the UK*, WTO Doc. WT/DS138/AB/R (7 June 2000).

[22] Appellate Body Report, *European Communities – Measures Affecting Asbestos and Asbestos-Containing Products*, WTO Doc. WT/DS135/9 (8 November 2000); WT/DS135/AB/R (12 March 2001) [52] (*Asbestos*).

384 M. RAFIQUL ISLAM

breach of confidentiality of proceedings.[23] But there is nothing in the DSU or Appellate Review Working Procedures[24] that specifically prohibits the panel or AB from accepting or considering *amicus* briefs. *Amicus* submissions may be an external and additional source of information, which may assist them in reaching an objective and fair decision. *Amicus* briefs unrelated to the parties submitted pursuant to the procedural rules and admitted on careful scrutiny are likely to promote the overriding policy values of objectivity, fairness, transparency, and due process in the assessment of disputant matters. The AB has granted the right to submit *amicus* briefs with no guarantee of their admission and consideration. The AB rejected all applications for *amicus* briefs in *Asbestos*[25] and *Sardines*[26] on the pretext that the applicants failed to comply with the requirements of the Special Procedure. The manner in which the AB granted the right to submit *amicus* briefs in *Asbestos* represents a form of access or participation which can be confused with transparency. Moreover, 'the fact that such a brief has never had any perceptible influence on the result of a case has led to scepticism about their value and heightened cynicism about WTO transparency'.[27] The *Asbestos* decision is not necessarily helpful in developing a coherent and orderly process of *amicus* briefs and/or intervener in the proceedings. It deals with the transparency issue inadequately, only by way of widening participation in disputes, which falls short of achieving the public openness of the process.

Greater openness of the proceedings is crucial for the wider public good implications of decisions on such issues as the environment, human rights, public health, the food crisis, green technology transfer, and corporate culture. The DSS exercises jurisdiction over many trading areas having socio-cultural ramifications. Its policy of confidentiality based on the narrowly focused exclusivity of trade is both inadequate and unsustainable at a time when a broad spectrum of public reactions in favour of social inclusion and economic justice is going from strength to

---

[23] Robert Howse, 'Membership and its Privileges: The WTO, Civil Society and the Amicus Brief Controversy', (2003) 9 *European Law Journal* 496, 503; Steve Charnovitz, 'Opening the WTO to Nongovernmental Interests', (2000) 24 *Fordham International Law Journal* 173.

[24] Appellate Review Working Procedures, WTO Doc. WT/AB/WB/6 (16 August 2010) (WTO Dispute Settlement: Appeals Procedures).

[25] *Asbestos*, WTO Doc. WT/DS135/9; WT/DS135/AB/R.

[26] Appellate Body Report, *European Communities – Trade Description of Sardines*, WTO Doc. WT/DS231/AB/R (6 September 2002).

[27] Donald McRae, 'What Is the Future of WTO Dispute Settlement?', (2004) 7 *Journal of International Economic Law* 12.

THE WTO DISPUTE SETTLEMENT SYSTEM 385

strength. The less transparent the DSS appears, the more it suffers from a legitimacy crisis. There has been a welcome yet circumscribed move towards open public hearings in recent years.[28] The ongoing global financial crises triggered by confidential dealings of many financial institutions have generated widespread public cynicism about the credibility of those institutions making decisions in confidence. The DSS is better off by not being one of those institutions. Its obsession with confidentiality must be abandoned in favour of open and public hearings to be made available worldwide through information and communication technologies. This would provide public education in WTO members, particularly developing countries and LDCs, in their legal-capacity building for greater and informed participation in the DSS.

Transparency can expose the proceedings of the DSS to all stakeholders, and show how it is being exploited by powerful WTO members to the grave detriment of developing countries and LDCs. Such exposure can have a deterrent effect on decisions to litigate and may trigger reforms of the system, which were promised and are now long overdue.

Policies and realities pertaining to remedies and enforcement

Effective remedies

The recommendations of panels and the AB of specific performance to bring any WTO-inconsistent measures into conformity are usually adopted by the DSB as its rulings, which are binding on the disputant parties. The DSS provides two important remedies for prevailing parties to enforce rulings: compensation for delays in the implementation of rulings and retaliation for non-compliance with rulings.[29] Compensation is voluntary for the offending member, which can maintain its WTO-inconsistent measures temporarily and compensate the member that suffers loss as a result of non-compliance. Moreover, the offending member risks DSB-authorized trade sanctions in the form of suspended concessions or cross-retaliation if it refuses to implement the ruling or pay compensation.

The DSS remedies operate only prospectively, requiring compliance with WTO obligations by rectifying WTO-inconsistent measures. This

---

[28] The public viewing of hearings takes place only by live closed-circuit television in a separate room, requiring physical presence in that room in Geneva.
[29] DSU, Art. 19, 22.

policy of prospectiveness does not necessarily provide an effective remedy and ensure specific performance for prevailing members. Compensation appears to accommodate the exercise of sovereignty and compliance through incentives. However, the amount and process of compensation are largely contingent on the agreement of the parties, which can put winners at the mercy of defaulters. Being voluntary and temporary, compensation lacks enough force to induce offenders to comply. The DSU provides no remedy for the past losses or injuries suffered by prevailing members during the period from the time of imposition of WTO-inconsistent measures to the time of their withdrawal. This lack of restoration of the balance of negotiated concessions interrupted by non-compliance is a major policy failure, rendering compensation a flawed and dysfunctional remedy.[30] The lack of remedy for past injuries and the availability of 'a reasonable amount of time'[31] to withdraw WTO-inconsistent measures encourage members, particularly powerful members, to breach their obligations almost with impunity in order to protect uncompetitive domestic industries.

The ineffectiveness of the WTO remedies may be demonstrated through what happened between Australia/New Zealand and the United States in *Lamb Meat*.[32] In 1999, the United States imposed safeguard measures (tariff rate quota), initially for three years, on the importation of lamb meat from Australia and New Zealand, which was perceived as a serious threat to the US lamb meat industry. Australia challenged and prevailed in a DSB ruling in May 2001.[33] The United States successfully pleaded for 'a reasonable amount of time' to remove its WTO-inconsistent trade measures. Facing further extension of its losses, Australia negotiated an agreement with the United States in September 2001, in which the latter agreed to withdraw its punitive tariffs from 15 November 2001.[34] From its imposition in 1999, the illegal measure continued for almost three years until November 2001. It was not the DSS remedies, but a bilateral deal that ended the dispute. The diplomatically negotiated withdrawal offered

---

[30] John H. Jackson, 'International Law Status of WTO Dispute Settlement Reports: Obligations to Comply or Option to "Buy Out"', (2004) 98 AJIL 123.

[31] DSU, Art. 19.

[32] Appellate Body Report, *United States – Safeguard Measures on Imports of Fresh, Chilled or Frozen Lamb Meat from New Zealand and Australia*, WTO Doc. WT/DS177AB/R, WT/DS178/AB/R (1 May 2001).

[33] Ibid.

[34] Department of Foreign Affairs and Trade, 'US to Remove Lamb Tariffs on 15 November', press release, 1 September 2001.

faster redress for Australia than the pursuit of further WTO action against the United States. The United States pursued the tactic of delaying the withdrawal of its measure and succeeded in continuing tariff protection to its lamb meat industry, which the DSB had found structurally inefficient. Australia won the dispute but its lamb meat industry suffered serious economic injury during 1999–2001,[35] without having any right of redress due to the unavailability of compensation for past injuries. The United States lost the dispute but succeeded in extending the rules of remedy to its advantage for nearly three years, during which period its uncompetitive lamb meat industry flourished.[36]

Trade retaliation or sanctions are authorized by the DSB in the form of withdrawing equivalent concessions against defaulters unwilling to stop their WTO-inconsistent measures and/or pay compensation to winners sustaining injuries due to non-compliance. This remedy is given to winners as a last resort to pressurize and induce defaulters to comply with WTO obligations. In reality, though, retaliation hardly provides an effective remedy to secure specific performance, due to its self-contradictory policy base and gerrymandering implementation. The authorized retaliation through trade restrictive countermeasures is overtly inconsistent with the trade liberalization objective of the WTO. The existing WTO-inconsistent measures of defaulters are trade-restrictive enough, which the DSB has ruled must be lifted to promote trade liberalization. The authorized imposition of equivalent trade-restrictive countermeasures by retaliating members does not dismantle the barriers already in place. Instead, it creates further barriers, multiplies protectionism, and renders trade liberalization doubly difficult. Retaliation tends to correct one wrong by using another, and the two wrongs do not make it right. It is essentially a trade-protectionist policy camouflaged in the form of a remedy. The implementation process of authorized sanctions is overly skewed to the advantage of winning powerful parties, which can retaliate against

---

[35] Australian Farmers' Federation, 'The United States Action Cost Australian Lamb Industries over $30 million', *Telegraph* (Sydney), 2 September 2001, 2.

[36] The US lamb meat industry partially recovered, mainly due to a massive assistance package of US$142.7 million that the United States negotiated with Australia and New Zealand as a condition of the withdrawal of US punitive tariffs. Larry V. Fedorov, *US Agricultural Trade: Trends, Policy and Direction* (Hauppauge, NY: Nova Science Publishers, 2003), 65. However, this partial recovery in production did not improve market share due to the strong US dollar and weak Australian and New Zealand dollars. Keithly G. Jones, 'Trends in the US Sheep Industry', Agriculture Information Bulletin No. 787, United States Department of Agriculture, January 2004, 27.

losing weaker parties to force compliance. But the latter, as winners, cannot afford to utilize authorized sanctions against losing powerful states for fear of retaliation in other bilateral trading sectors. Moreover, trade sanctions imposed by weaker parties make no economic sense, as they would have almost no impact on the economy of powerful parties. This dynamic reinforces the point that WTO litigation is a viable option only for a minority of members.

Retaliation is more a self-harm than self-help remedy, as it proves detrimental to most retaliating members. Raising trade barriers against defaulters would reduce the export markets and trade-induced income of retaliating members through price increases of the targeted products in the domestic market and decrease welfare gains from trade liberalization for the consuming public. On a cost–benefit comparison between the continuation of its illegal measures and retaliation, a powerful defaulter may find compliance unattractive when the economic and political benefits of defiance outweigh the cost of compliance. The defaulter may choose to continue its illegal measures and invite retaliation, an alternative option that has become the monopoly of powerful defaulters to the detriment of comparatively weaker retaliating members. The DSU does not allow retaliation, separately or collectively, by members other than the authorized retaliating member against the defaulting member. Developing countries with smaller trade volumes are generally disadvantaged, as their imposed sanctions are largely ineffective in generating any pressure on powerful economies to induce compliance. By contrast, retaliation by powerful members can have dire consequences for developing members. Thus the cost of retaliation is far greater for retaliating developing members than defaulting powerful members. It is this cost–benefit consideration that influences developing and LDC members not to resort to the WTO litigation process.

This point was amply shown in *Bananas*,[37] where the DSB authorized the United States and Ecuador to impose sanctions on the European Communities (EC) to induce compliance. The United States immediately implemented the authorization by imposing punitive tariffs on selected EC products. But Ecuador did not dare to impose the authorized sanctions

---

[37] Panel Report, *European Communities – Regime for the Importation, Sale and Distribution of Bananas*, WTO Doc. WT/DS27/R (22 May 1997); Appellate Body Report, *European Communities – Regime for the Importation, Sale and Distribution of Bananas*, WTO Doc. WT/DS27/AB/R, AB-1997-3 (9 September 1997); Recourse to Arbitration under DSU, Art. 22(6), WTO Doc. WT/DS27/ABR (1999); WT/DS27/ABR/ECU (2000), paras. 170, 173; Minutes of the DSB Meetings, WTO Doc. WT/DSB/M/80 (26 June 2000) para. 49.

THE WTO DISPUTE SETTLEMENT SYSTEM 389

on the EC for fear of cross-retaliation in other sectors of Ecuador's export interests. The DSS provides no protection whatsoever for Ecuador against potential EC tit-for-tat actions. Ecuador attempted in vain to resolve the dispute through a negotiated agreement with the EC in 2001. The EC's discriminatory banana regime continued for fifteen years, despite its being ruled illegal, first in 1997 and then in thirteen subsequent rulings,[38] costing Ecuador over US$100 million a year in extra tariff payments to the EC.[39] Eventually, the Latin American countries and the EC notified the WTO on 15 December 2009 that they had concluded the Framework Agreement on Trade in Bananas, which amicably resolved the dispute and thus bypassed the authorized retaliation.[40] The United States participated in the negotiations leading to the agreement but declined to be a party.[41] Instead, the United States preferred to retain the authorized sanction against the EC. In its bid to undermine the banana agreement, the United States threatened to adopt 'extra-WTO' counter-retaliation against Costa Rica and Colombia by launching its Super 301 investigation and withdrawing US trade preferences granted under the Andean Trade Preference Act 1991.[42]

In marked contrast to *Bananas*, where the United States took full advantage of the authorized retaliation, it subverted the authorized retaliation it faced in *Gambling*.[43] The DSB authorized retaliation for Antigua and Barbuda against the United States. In a bid to circumvent the retaliation, the United States notified the WTO of its withdrawal of commitments on gambling and betting services under Article XXI of the General Agreement on Trade in Services (GATS).[44] This meant that the entire adjudication and implementation process of this dispute came under the full control

---

[38] Sébastien Falletti, 'EU Looks at Doha to Solve Banana Dispute', EUROPOLITICS, 2008, available at www.europolitics.info/eu-looks-at-doha-to-solve-banana-dispute-artr148044-42.html at 21 August 2012.

[39] Dispute Settlement Body, Minutes of Meeting Held in the Centre William Rappard on 22 December 2008, WTO Doc. WT/DSB/M/261 (6 March 2009), para. 62.

[40] Geneva Agreement on Trade in Bananas, WTO Doc. WT/L/784 (15 December 2009).

[41] Raj Bhala and David Gantz, 'WTO Case Review 2009', (2010) 27 *Arizona Journal of International and Comparative Law* 94.

[42] Chad P. Bown, *Self-Enforcing Trade: Developing Countries and WTO Dispute Settlement* (Washington, DC: Brookings Institution Press, 2009), 61.

[43] Appellate Body Report, *United States – Measures Affecting the Cross-Border Supply of Gambling and Betting Services – Recourse by Antigua and Barbuda to DSU, Art. 22:6 on the Understanding of Rules and Procedures Governing the Settlement of Disputes*, WTO Doc. WT/DS285/ARB (21 December 2007).

[44] Modification of Schedules: Invocation by the United States of Article XXI of the General Agreement on Trades and Services (GATS), WTO Doc. S/L/293 (2007).

390   M. RAFIQUL ISLAM

of the United States, the offender, and the DSS lacks any sort of procedure to compel the United States to comply with the adverse ruling. The sanctions authorized in *Gambling* remain in limbo, presumably to be settled through a bilateral agreement between the parties.

Of the twenty-one authorized retaliation rulings so far, only four have been implemented.[45] In these four cases, the retaliating members were developed members (the United States and the European Communities) with substantial market and bargaining power to create real threats to offenders. The *Lamb Meat, Bananas,* and *Gambling* disputes suggest that the DSS remedies work for comparatively powerful parties and that weaker parties are forced to reach a bilaterally negotiated settlement after a protracted and costly legal battle. In all cases, it was the powerful party's stand, not the DSS, which dictated the outcomes. The economic consequences of such lacklustre remedies for fragile economies dependent on a few exportable products could be irreparable. A domestic economic slump might occur as a result of the loss of traditional markets and established trade routes, reduced competitiveness, and the waste of perishable and seasonal crops and meat. Such economic losses undermine the ability of many members to continue their litigation against powerful members under the DSS. Even the Sutherland Report on the decade of operation of the WTO highlighted the reform of this asymmetric remedy of retaliation and its ineffectiveness for weaker WTO members.[46]

Effective remedies for trade violations require punitive measures backed by the strict enforcement of compliance through specific performances, not a fallback position such as compensation as a means of buying off obligations. Effective remedies must also embrace collective and/or institutionalized enforcement, like the enforcement measures

---

[45] The United States retaliated against the European Communities in *Bananas,* above n. 37; Panel Report, *Measures Concerning Meat and Meat Products (beef hormones),* WTO Doc. WT/DS26/R/USA; Appellate Body Report, *Measures Concerning Meat and Meat Products* WT/DS26/AB/R (13 February 1998). The European Communities retaliated against the United States: Panel Report, *United States – Tax Treatment for "Foreign Sales Corporations",* WTO Doc. WT/DS108/RW (20 August 2001); Appellate Body Report, *United States – Tax Treatment for "Foreign Sales Corporations",* WTO Doc. WT/DS108/AB/R, AB-1999-9 (24 February 2000); Decision by the Arbitrator, *Tax Treatment for "Foreign Sales Corporations" – Recourse to Arbitration by the United States under Article 22.6 of the DSU and Article 4.11 of the SCM Agreement,* WT/DS108/ARB, (30 August 2002); Appellate Body Report, *United States – Definitive Safeguard Measures on Imports of Wheat Gluten from the European Communities,* WT/DS166/AD/R, AB-2000-10 (19 January 2001).

[46] P. Sutherland et al., *The Future of the WTO; Addressing Institutional Challenges in the New Millennium* (Geneva: WTO, 2004), 54.

under Chapter VII of the UN Charter, in cases where the individual action of the retaliating member is insufficient to induce compliance. The exaction of automatic, mandatory, and punitive compensation from the offender, backed by collective or institutional enforcement, until it removes the illegal measures would create economic incentives for compliance and effect the cessation of and reparation for proven injuries. The DSS simply cannot institutionally remain inactive and rely solely on retaliating or injured members to implement its rulings. As it stands, its compensation and retaliation are anything but effective remedies to induce compliance with rulings. So long as these institutional inadequacies in affording effective trade remedies are not rectified through reforms, they will continue to militate in favour of developed members and against developing and LDC members, exacerbating the lopsided participation of these last two in the WTO litigation process.

The prompt dispensation of justice

The prompt resolution of disputes backed by a strict time frame for completing all phases of proceedings is a major improvement over the GATT system. If the WTO-stipulated time frame is followed, an illegal measure should be removed within twenty-six months of the date of request for consultations.[47] The policy of a prospective remedy contradicts the policy of prompt resolution because there is no carrot or stick to induce prompt compliance, which may be undertaken within an open-ended 'reasonable period', with no compensation or retaliation. Delayed compliance with DSB rulings has become a common feature in developed members, notably the United States, the EC, Japan, Canada, and Australia, where 20 per cent of rulings are implemented with an average delay of thirteen months, 10 per cent are the subject of disputes over their implementation, and 10 per cent remain unimplemented.[48] This dilatory and failed implementation of 40 per cent of rulings is anything but a prompt dispensation of justice – a proclaimed objective of the DSU – with serious economic consequences for winning parties, particularly

---

[47] The DSU provides two months for consultations, one month for panel establishment, nine months for panel report, forty-five days for appeal, three months for the appellate body, fifteen days for adoption, and nine months for illegal barrier withdrawal, therefore totalling twenty-six months.

[48] William J. Davey, 'Implementation in WTO Dispute Settlement: An Introduction to the Problems and Possible Solutions', Trade and Industry Discussion Paper Series 05-E-013, Research Institute of Economy, March 2005, 3, 4, 9.

developing states and LDCs, in the absence of any DSU provision for the recovery of past damages. The resolution of disputes between powerful members continues endlessly, exemplified by the almost never-ending *Bananas* and *Beef Hormones* cases, due to their spurious legal wrangling and obfuscation, blocking each other's actions to exonerate themselves from WTO obligations, a luxury that most developing and LDC members cannot afford.

The tendency not to comply within the specified time limit is fairly common among the major users of the DSS. In contrast to the Australian position in *Lamb Meat*, the DSB held in 1998 that the Australian ban on raw salmon imports from Canada lacked appropriate scientific risk assessment and was WTO-inconsistent under the Sanitary and Phytosanitary Agreement.[49] On the face of the continuing Canadian threats of trade retaliation, Australia had immediately to enter into negotiations with Canada to reach an agreement, effective 1 June 2000, ending the dispute.[50] Facing the US threat of retaliation in 1998 against the subsidised Howe Leather Company in Victoria, Australia was forced not only to stop its subsidies but to collect all previous subsidies from the company.[51] On both occasions, Australia became a perpetrator of delayed implementation of DSB rulings. Its initial measures of compliance were found inadequate in the arbitration proceedings under the DSU Article 21(5).[52] The *Salmon* ruling was implemented on 16 May 2000, long after the permissible reasonable period for compliance had expired, on 6 July 1998. The *Automotive Leather* ruling due for implementation on 14 September 1999 was not implemented until 24 July 2000.[53] Cost-intensive procrastination and power differences are used to stretch the limits of DSU rules in order to achieve desirable outcomes in disputes between unequal members, due to their disparities in resource and standover capacity. There is also a discernible trend emerging in the practice of panels, the AB, and disputant parties to seek additional time beyond the DSU limits. Recent

---

[49] Panel Report, *Australia – Measures Affecting Importation of Salmon*, WT/DS18/R (6 November 1998); Appellate Body Report, *Australia – Measures Affecting Importation of Salmon*, WT/DS18/AB/R (20 October 1998).

[50] DFAT, 'Australia's Relationship with the WTO', Canberra, 26 September 2001, 50.

[51] Panel Report, *Australia – Subsidies Provided to Producers and Exporters of Automotive Leather*, WT/DS126/R (16 June 1999).

[52] *Australia – Recourse to DSU Article 21.5 by Canada*, WTO Doc. WT/DS18/RW (18 February 2000); *Australia – Recourse to DSU Article 21.5 by U.S.*, WTO Doc. WT/DS126/RW (21 January 2000).

[53] Davey, above n. 48, 8, 20.

examples of such delays in completing the specific phases of proceedings and reporting are many.[54]

The prompt resolution of situations where a member is unjustly deprived of its legitimate benefits by another's illegal measures is imperative for the effective functioning of the DSS and the maintenance of an appropriate balance between the rights and obligations of members. But compelling powerful members to comply with their assumed contractual obligations and compelling specific performance in the face of adverse rulings is a real challenge for the DSS. These members exploit DSU loopholes and caveats to work out trade-offs and face-saving formulas to circumvent or circumscribe their obligations. The DSS thus by conduct and default condones the wilful defiance of its rulings, leading to undue enrichment by defaulters at the expense of winners, who become victims for being compliant. The dilatory dispensation of settlement contributes to the backlog of disputes, and undermines the concept of their prompt resolution for the benefit of all.

Policies and realities pertaining to equal access to justice

The participation of developing countries

A rule-based, legalistic, and adjudicative DSS has been conceived of as a guarantor to ensure the exercise of recognized rights and to prevent abuses and defiance of those rights. Such a centralized institutional check is indispensable in a multilateral trading system dominated by economic clout and hegemonic powers. In reality, however, the DSS does not necessarily provide equal access to justice for all. In balancing the costs and benefits of litigation, many developing and LDC members choose to endure the nullification and/or impairment of their trading rights and interests without lodging any complaint with the DSS.[55]

Developing members are entitled to certain specific procedural S & D treatment by way of there being at least one panellist hearing their case from any developing member,[56] additional time to prepare and present their cases,[57] and panel reports being required to indicate explicitly the form in which the S & D treatment has been granted.[58] But developing members face difficulties in receiving the S & D treatment under these

---

[54] Appellate Body Annual Report for 2005, WTO Doc. WT/AB/5 (25 January 2006) 8–10.
[55] Trade Policy Review: Mauritius, WTO Doc. WT/TPR/G/90 (2001) (Report by Government).
[56] DSU, Art. 8(10).   [57] DSU, Art. 12(10).   [58] DSU, Art. 12(11).

394 M. RAFIQUL ISLAM

provisions because of the lack of specificity. It is not obvious whether they are substantive or procedural requirements, and whether the panel should apply them only when the issue is raised by developing members or can apply them on its own initiative, even when they are not raised by developing members. These ambiguities have led panellist and arbitrators to disregard the grant of special treatment to developing members in the majority of disputes. The same is the situation with DSU Article 21(2), requiring particular attention to be paid to matters affecting developing countries' interest in determining the 'reasonable period of time' for bringing WTO-inconsistent measures to conformity. This determination in the arbitration process, under DSU Article 21(3)(c), is crucial for developing members, which need a longer time as the implementing party and the shortest possible implementation period as the complaining party. Of the 13.8 per cent of disputes in which developing members sought special treatments all but two[59] were unsuccessful.[60]

DSU Article 24 sets out some features allowing for flexibility for LDCs, none of which has brought them any benefit due to the insurmountable structural barriers of the DSS. During its seventeen years of operation, Bangladesh is the only LDC to have brought a consultation request against India in an anti-dumping dispute; it was resolved at that stage in 2006 and this was possible only due to the availability of subsidized legal fees from the Advisory Centre on WTO Law (ACWL).[61] Apart from this

[59] Panel Report, *India – Quantitative Restrictions on Imports of Agriculture, Textile and Industrial Products*, WTO Doc. WT/DS90/R (1999), [5(8)]–[5(10)], granted an extra eleven days to India to prepare its first written submission; Decision by Arbitrator, *European Communities – Export Subsidies on Sugar – Arbitration under DSU Article 21(3)(c)*, WTO Doc. WT/DS265/33, WT/DS266/33, WT/DS283/14 ARB (28 October 2005), [2], paid special attention to the interests of Brazil and Thailand in determining the implementation time.

[60] Eduardo Pérez Motta and Mateo Diego-Fernández, 'If the DSU Is "Working Reasonably Well", Why Does Everybody Want to Change It?', in Dencho Georgiev and Kim Van der Borght (eds.), *Reform and Development of the WTO Dispute Settlement System* (London: Cameron May, 2006) 298. Examples include Panel Report, *Mexico – Measures Affecting Telecommunications Services*, WTO Doc. WT/DS204/R (2004) [4(180)]–[(190)], [242]; *Mexico – Taxes on Soft Drinks*, WTO, Dispute Settlement Reports 2006, vol. 1, 261; Decision by Arbitrator, *United States – Sunset Reviews of Anti-Dumping Measures on Oil Country Tubular Goods from Argentina – Arbitration under Article 21.3(c) of the Understanding of Rules and Procedures Governing the Settlement of Disputes*, WTO Doc. WT/DS268/12, ARB-2005-1/18 (7 June 2005) [47]–[48], [52]; Decision by Arbitrator, *Indonesia – Certain Measures Affecting the Automobile Industry – Arbitration under Article 21.3(c) of the DSU*, WTO Doc. WT/DS54/15, WT/DS55/14, WT/DS59/13, WT/DS64/12 ARB (7 December 1998), [24]; *Gambling*, above n. 43, arbitral award, paras. 26, 57, 59, 60.

[61] *India – Antidumping Measures on Batteries from Bangladesh*, WT/DS306/1, G/L/669, G/ADP/D52/1 (2004); WT/DS306/2, G/L/669/Add.1, G/ADP/D52/2 (2006); M. Taslim,

THE WTO DISPUTE SETTLEMENT SYSTEM   395

solitary case, LDCs are virtually excluded from the DSS. It is not a mere idiosyncrasy of forty-eight LDCs that they have had no occasion to invoke the DSS. There are deep-rooted reasons for their absence, which the LDC Group ventilated to the DSB:

> [T]his is definitely not because these countries have had no concerns worth referring to the DS[S], but rather due to the structural and other difficulties that are posed by the system itself.[62]

According to an empirical study of the dispute settlement record for the period 1995–2005, the percentage ratio of disputes initiated by developed and developing members was 70:30 and 75:25 at the panel stage.[63] The participation of developing members has worsened during 2006–9, when there were twelve 'main users' bringing 85 per cent of the total complaints.[64] Of the total 400 disputes during 1995–2009, an examination of state participation shows that only fifteen members have been the consistent major users, as complainants in 354 and respondents in 333 disputes.[65] The United States and the EC have overwhelmingly been the top two users (the United States as a complainant in 93 and a respondent in 107, a total of 200 cases; and the EC as a complainant in 81 and a respondent in 66, a total of 147 cases).[66] Taking all participation (complainant, respondent, and third party) during the first fifteen years into account, far fewer than one-third of WTO members, mostly developed and a few advanced developing members, use the DSS and more than two-thirds, mostly poor developing and LDC members, are absolute non-users. The overall participation of developing countries in the DSS started to decline at the beginning of the WTO era compared with

'WTO and Indo-Bangladesh Trade Dispute', *Financial Express* (Dhaka), 3 January 2008, 25; M. Taslim, 'How the DSU Worked for Bangladesh: The First LDC to Bring a WTO Claim', in Gregory Shaffer and Ricardo Melendez-Ortiz (eds.), *Dispute Settlement at the WTO: The Developing Country Experience* (Cambridge University Press, 2010) 230.

[62] LDC Group Proposal to the DSB Special Session on the DSU, WTO Doc. TN/DS/W/17 (9 October 2002).

[63] Roderick Abbot, 'Are Developing Countries Deterred from Using the WTO Dispute Settlement System? Participation of Developing Countries in the DSM in the Years 1995–2005', Working Paper No. 1, European Centre for International Political Economy, 2007.

[64] WTO, 'Table of Disputes by Members', available at www.wto.org/english/tratop_e/dispu_e/dispu_by_country_e.htm 11 January 2010.

[65] Ibid., Bhala and Gantz, above n. 41, 90.

[66] The main users in order of magnitude are United States (200), EC (147), Canada (48), Brazil (38), India (38), Mexico (35), Argentina (31), Japan (28), South Korea (27), Chile (23), China (23), Australia (17), Thailand (16), Philippines (10), and Turkey (10). Bhala and Gantz, above n. 41, 90.

396 M. RAFIQUL ISLAM

their participation under the GATT era. In view of the constraints facing developing countries, a study reveals that (i) they are 'one-third less likely to file complaints against developed states under the WTO than they were under the post-1989 GATT regime'; and (ii) 'the fraction of cases targeting [them] has risen dramatically from 19 to 33 percent', suggesting that they are 'up to five times more likely to be subject to a complaint under the WTO'.[67]

There are obvious reasons for the circumscribed participation of most developing countries. The institutional structure of the WTO is inherently diplomatic and adversarial in nature, where power politics and a cut-throat culture of advancing self-interest at the cost of others play a dominant, if not decisive, role in decision making. This self-serving and pragmatic participatory approach of powerful members circumscribes the opportunity for any meaningful participation by weaker members, which have too much to lose to be able to voice their marginalized trading plight. The 'green room'[68] informal negotiating practice isolates and manipulates poor members by trade-offs and 'arm twisting' through aid and loans; and allows the powerful to use their market strength to coerce and block decisions until they are satisfied that their interests are protected.[69] There was little active participation by weak members at the time of the creation of the WTO,[70] and the institution has since done almost nothing to

---

[67] Marc L. Busch and Eric Reinhardt, 'Testing International Trade Law: Empirical Studies of GATT/WTO Dispute Settlement', in Daniel L. M. Kennedy and James D. Southwick (eds.), *The Political Economy of International Trade Law* (Cambridge University Press, 2002) 457, 466–7. DSS complaints against developing countries in 1995–2001 were 37 per cent of the total compared with 8 per cent during GATT: Bernard Hoekman and Michel Kostecki, *The Political Economy of the World Trading System: The WTO and Beyond* (Oxford University Press, 2002), 394–5.

[68] This is a meeting room adjacent to the office of the WTO Director General. Informal meetings among major players invited by the Director General are held in this room to iron out their differences on a given trade issue under consideration in multilateral negotiations. Most developing and LDC members are usually not invited: Dilip K. Das, *Global Trading System at the Crossroads: A Post-Seattle Perspective* (London: Routledge, 2001), 38–41; Peter Van Den Bossche, *Law and Policy of the WTO* (Cambridge University Press, 2005), 131–2.

[69] Fatoumata Jawara and Aileen Kwa, *Behind the Scenes at the WTO: The Real World of International Trade Negotiations* (London: Zed Books, 2001).

[70] Will Martin and L. Alan Winters, *The Uruguay Round and the Developing Countries* (Cambridge University Press, 1996); Donnatella Alessandrini, *Developing Countries and the Multilateral Trading Regime: The Failure and Promise of the WTO's Development Mission* (Oxford: Hart Publishing, 2010); T. N. Srinivashan, *Developing Countries in the Multilateral Trading System* (Boulder: Westview Press, 2000); Constantine Michalopoulos, *Developing Countries in the WTO* (Houndmills: Palgrave, 2001); Aaditya Mattoo and

alleviate the difficulties they face in playing a proactive role. Developing states have not been able to overcome the institutional disadvantages of multilateral trade under the WTO.

The limitations of weaker members are also partly responsible for their inability to utilize the DSS. They lack human resources in terms of trade law expertise and private support from their export industries to prepare a DSS complaint. They cannot afford to deploy a constant squad of efficient WTO legal experts and diplomats at the WTO Secretariat to fight in a competitive and costly legal battle. Nor do they have existing or emerging markets with the volume and variety of exports crucial for their trading partners. Exorbitant litigation costs, the value of the legal action, and collateral hassles for accruable gains from ineffective DSS remedies are some of the factors that often lead them to opt for trade losses over greater economic losses through WTO litigation.[71] This explains why no complaint has yet been lodged by any African member, developing countries and LDCs alike.[72] The western African countries, being the major producers and exporters of cotton, sustained serious loss due to US export subsidies for upland cotton. But in *US – Subsidies on Upland Cotton*,[73] it was Brazil that challenged the US trade distorting subsidies at the DSS and prevailed. The west African countries had sufficient grievances in terms of economic injuries[74] – indeed, far more than Brazil – to become

---

Arvind Subramanian, 'The WTO and the Poorest Countries: The Stark Reality', (2004) 3 *World Trade Review* 385.

[71] Panel Report, *Japan – Measures Affecting Consumer Photographic Film and Paper (Fuji-Kodak)*, WTO Doc. WT/DS44/R (31 March 1998). The combined litigation costs were US$12,000,000. Gregory Shaffer, *Defending Interests: Public–Private Partnership in WTO Litigation* (Washington DC: Brookings Institution Press, 2003), 38; Håkan Nordstrom, 'The Cost of WTO Litigation, Legal Aid and Small Claim Procedures', paper presented at a conference on WTO Dispute Settlement and Developing Countries: Implications, Strategies, Reforms, Center for World Affairs and the Global Economy, University of Wisconsin, 20–21 May 2005.

[72] Only Egypt, Senegal, and South Africa participated as respondents, WTO Dispute Settlement: Disputes by Country, above n. 64.

[73] Panel report, *United States – Subsidies on Upland Cotton*, WTO Doc. WT/DS267/R (8 September 2004); Appellate Body Report, *United States – Subsidies on Upland Cotton*, WTO Doc. WT/DS267/AB/R (3 March 2005).

[74] Cotton accounted for 77 per cent of Benin's exports: Trade Policy Review: Benin, WTO Doc. WT/TPR/S/131 (2004); 57 per cent of Burkina Faso's, African Development Bank and OECD 2004, *African Economic Outlook 2003/2004, Country Studies: Burkina Faso*; and 18 per cent of Mali's: Trade Policy Review: Mali, WTO Doc. WT/TPR/S/133 (2004); Kevin Watkins, 'Cultivating Poverty: The Impact of US Cotton Subsidies on Africa', Briefing Paper No. 30, Oxfam Australia, 2002; Hilton E. Zunckel, 'The African Awakening in US – Upland Cotton', (2005) 39 *Journal of World Trade* 1071, 1086.

complainants themselves with independent claims. Of all the west African cotton-exporting members, only Benin and Chad joined the dispute as third parties with limited claims to match with, and depend on, Brazil's claim. They secured spillover benefits from the outcome of the dispute but only to the limited extent of Brazil's claim, which was far less than the benefits they could have achieved as complainants. Their third-party participation and limited benefits were made possible by the assistance (in the form of subsidized legal fees) from the ACWL.[75]

The lack of effective remedies and prompt enforcement and fear of non-trade retaliation remain major concerns for developing countries and LDCs contemplating litigation.[76] They fear that while they may legally prevail in the DSS over a powerful defaulter, the latter may engage in extra-WTO reprisals by curtailing development or military aid and limiting preferential market access. This is not an empty fear, as international trade diplomacy is littered with such threats, which can have a chilling effect on many developing countries' willingness to initiate a case, and eventually press them into inaction. For them, it is not just the merit of the case to be taken into account but also shunning it to balance and preserve bilateral economic ties with powerful members.[77] The combined effect of the WTO's structural limitations and those of the developing countries themselves prevent many from resorting to the DSS when their legitimate trading rights and interests are impaired and/or nullified. Thus the DSU provisions on S & D treatment for developing countries and LDCs in reality remain largely cosmetic rather than substantive.

Conclusion

The WTO is meant to be maximizing the participation of its members in the DSS as a means of resolving their trade disputes. Because of the

---

[75] Advisory Centre on WTO Law, 'Report on Operations', (Report, 2010), 4; C. Brown, *Self-Enforcing Trade: Developing Countries and WTO Dispute Settlement* (Washington, DC: Brookings Institution Press, 2009), 157; G. Yusuf, 'The Marginalisation of African Agricultural Trade and Development: A Case Study of the WTO's Efforts to Cater to African Agricultural Trading Interests, Particularly Cotton and Sugar', (2009) 17 *African Journal of International & Comparative Law* 213; Fulvio Maria Palombino, 'Judicial Economy and Limitation of the Scope of the Decision in International Adjudication', (2010) 23 *Leiden Journal of International Law* 909.

[76] Busch and Reinhardt, above n. 67, 457 and 467.

[77] Timothy Stostad, 'Trappings of Legality: Judicialization of Dispute Settlement in the WTO, and its Impacts on Developing Countries', (2006) 39 *Cornell International Law Journal* 811, 826–7; Christina L. Davis and Sarah Blodgett Bermeo, 'Who Files? Developing Country Participation in GATT/WTO Adjudication', (2009) 71 *Journal of Politics* 1033.

particular features of the DSS, the strength of litigation in terms of the number of cases does not offer evidence of maximum participation. Barely a handful of powerful and major developing trading members comprise the avid users of the DSS; this is not necessarily a cause of concern. However, the reasons for and manner of such involvement render it part of the problem of lopsided participation. These frequent users manage with impunity to operate within the system more equally than others. They more often than not implement favourable rulings through their economic strength, and procrastinate or even defy unfavourable rulings by exploiting DSS flaws and caveats. Their frequent use is attributable not so much to their love of the rule of law and of justice, but to the lure of the opportunity for might to prevail over right in the DSS. The overwhelming majority of members, which lack market power, usually fall victim to the DSS flaws and caveats for want of adequate systemic protection, and are either infrequent users or non-users of the DSS. Nonetheless, these members remain faithful, albeit frustratingly, to the DSS and its rulings, which offer limited interest for them as prevailing parties. The rulings afford them a solid basis for bargaining their way to a negotiated settlement. It would have been exceedingly difficult, if not impossible, for them to achieve negotiated settlements with powerful defaulters without these rulings. In most disputes they negotiated in vain to arrive at settlements at the pre-consultation and consultation stages. Moreover, the fear of covert trade and overt non-trade retribution, and the liberalization of trade under the auspices of WTO as one of the conditions of IMF and World Bank loans, leave hardly any palatable options for many developing countries other than to stay in the system. It is presumably the accommodation of the blend and interplay of law, power, politics, international relations, and diplomacy in the DSS that still gives the system some relevance to WTO members, developed, developing, and LDC alike.

The DSS has succeeded in resolving many disputes and in providing remedies involving a minority of members. However, its lack of protection, inoperative S & D treatment, flawed remedies, and lacklustre enforcement are barriers to the overwhelming majority of members attempting to access justice. Its enforcement regime suffers from pragmatism and permissiveness that often rely on reconciliation over adjudication and the standover power of the winning parties over centralized institutional arrangement. The circumvention by powerful members of the development of a uniform and predictable compliance standard remains unabated, to the grave detriment of weaker members. Its credibility and effectiveness are often overshadowed by its inability to compel powerful members to implement unfavourable rulings. Providing S & D treatment during the proceedings and protection in enforcement to weak parties are not merely procedural matters but substantive rights warranted by the notion of natural justice.[78] The DSS is meant to be different from its GATT predecessor in taking seriously the substantive issue of inequality of disputant parties in rendering justice for the benefit of all members – a transition that is yet to happen. Long overdue reforms to the congenital imbalance of the DSS in providing and ensuring distributive economic justice to all members have successively been stultified by the political horse-trading of influential users over the past seventeen years. Should the ongoing failure to balance the rights and opportunities of the most and least powerful persist unabated, the DSS may be relegated to a star chamber of hollow policy idealism and the survival of the fittest.

[78] Asif Qureshi, 'Participation of Developing Countries in the WTO Dispute Settlement System', (2003) 47 *Journal of African Law* 194.

18

Resolving international investment disputes

CHESTER BROWN

One of the more striking developments in the international legal order in recent years is the prominence that has been achieved by international investment law, and, in particular, the growth in the settlement of international investment disputes by international arbitration. This is not to say that disputes concerning international investments had never before been the subject of international dispute settlement proceedings; the many mixed claims commissions of the late 1800s and early 1900s largely concerned the treatment by states of foreign nationals and their property,[1] and some of the better known cases before the Permanent Court of International Justice (PCIJ) and its successor, the International Court of Justice (ICJ), such as the *Factory at Chorzów* case,[2] the *Barcelona Traction* case,[3] and the *Elettronica Sicula* case,[4] were essentially investment claims that were brought by way of diplomatic protection.[5] But the real growth in the litigation of international investment disputes has come about largely as a result of the reliance by investors on bilateral investment treaties (BITs). These are treaties which, in addition to providing for substantive standards of protection, typically provide investors with a right to bring a claim in international arbitration against the host state of its investment, if the investor considers that the host state has breached obligations that it owes under the BIT.[6]

---

[1] See, e.g., Abraham H. Feller, *The Mexican Claims Commissions: 1923–1934* (Germantown: Periodicals Service Company, 1935).

[2] *Certain German Interests on Polish Upper Silesia (Germany v. Poland) (Merits)*, [1926] PCIJ (ser. A) No. 7; *Factory at Chorzów (Germany v. Poland) (Indemnity)*, [1928] PCIJ (ser. A) No. 17.

[3] *Barcelona Traction, Light and Power Company Ltd (Belgium v. Spain) (Second Phase)*, [1970] ICJ Rep. 3.

[4] *Elettronica Sicula SpA (United States v. Italy)*, [1989] ICJ Rep. 15.

[5] For a more recent example, see *Ahmadou Sadio Diallo (Republic of Guinea v. Democratic Republic of Congo) (Preliminary Objections)*, [2007] ICJ Rep. 582; *(Merits)*, [2010] ICJ Rep. 639.

[6] It now appears to be accepted that the substantive standards of protection under BITs are obligations that are owed by the states parties to investors of the other state's nationality: see

BITs are not recent innovations; the first such treaty was entered into between Germany and Pakistan in 1959.[7] Yet it was not until 1987 that the first claim was brought under a BIT, and the award of the arbitral tribunal in that case – which found that Sri Lanka was obliged to pay compensation to the Hong Kong-based investor – was rendered in 1990.[8] And the real growth in the presentation of claims under investment treaties followed the Argentine financial crisis of 2001–2, which has spawned around forty investment treaty claims against the Argentine Republic.[9]

Today, investment treaty arbitration is a vibrant and rapidly developing area of practice for public international lawyers, and the UN Conference on Trade and Development (UNCTAD) has reported that, as at the end of 2011, there had been 450 known claims under BITs and multilateral investment treaties.[10] While public international law was once the preserve of lawyers in ministries of foreign affairs and academics, private lawyers today practise in this field which, like other areas of public international law, does not exist as a self-contained system, but has multiple interactions with issues arising under general international law, such as issues of jurisdiction and admissibility, the law of treaties, and the law of state responsibility.

The focus of this chapter is the relationship between the substantive body of international investment law and the procedures for the settlement of investment disputes. There are two features of this relationship which merit attention: the first of these is the contribution of arbitral tribunals constituted under BITs and other investment treaties to the development of international investment law; and the second is the question whether international arbitration is the most appropriate method

especially Zachary Douglas, 'The Hybrid Foundations of Investment Treaty Arbitration', (2003) 74 *British Yearbook of International Law* 151, 182; see also *Occidental Exploration and Production Company* v. *Republic of Ecuador*, [2005] EWCA Civ. 1116, [14]–[20].

[7] Germany–Pakistan BIT, signed 25 November 1959, Bundesgesetzblatt, Pt II, No. 33 (6 July 1961), 793.

[8] *Asian Agricultural Products Ltd* v. *Sri Lanka*, (1997) 4 ICSID Rep. 246.

[9] See, e.g., Christina Binder, 'Changed Circumstances in International Law: Interfaces between the Law of Treaties and the Law of State Responsibility with a Special Focus on the Argentine Crisis', in Christina Binder, Ursula Kriebaum, August Reinisch, and Stephan Wittich (eds.), *International Investment Law for the 21st Century: Essays in Honour of Christoph Schreuer* (Oxford University Press, 2009) 608, 609; see also Chester Brown, 'Investment Arbitration as the "New Frontier"', (2009) 28 *Arbitrator and Mediator* 59; and Ignacio Suarez Anzorena, 'Multiplicity of Claims under BITs and the Argentine Case', (2005) 2 *Transnational Dispute Management* 20.

[10] UNCTAD, Latest Developments in Investor-State Dispute Settlement, UNC-TAD/WEB/DIAE/IA/2010/3 (April 2012), 1.

RESOLVING INTERNATIONAL INVESTMENT DISPUTES 403

for the settlement of investment disputes. In addressing these issues, this chapter first provides an introduction to the origins and nature of international investment law and the substantive standards of protection in BITs, and also identifies the types of investment disputes (investor–state, as well as inter-state) that might arise. It then considers the possible methods of settling international investment disputes. It is argued that the decisions of arbitral tribunals have significantly developed the substance of international investment law, and that international arbitration remains an appropriate means of settling investment disputes, although alternative methods of settling disputes may be preferable for reasons of cost, efficiency, and the achievement of balanced outcomes.

The nature of international investment law

Origins and development

Although the first BIT was not signed until 1959, international investment law has a much longer history. States had, for instance, developed the practice of including provisions dealing with the protection of property and economic interests in treaties that were concluded in the aftermath of hostilities dating at least as far back as the Treaty of Utrecht in 1713.[11] It was, however, the advent of significant volumes of world trade in the early 1800s that saw states focus on the need for some form of international protection for their (and their nationals') economic interests.[12] Some states had already begun entering into friendship, commerce, and navigation treaties (FCN treaties) in the late 1700s; one such country was the United States, whose Treaty of Amity and Commerce with France of 1778 was possibly the first 'modern' FCN treaty.[13] Many other

---

[11] See, e.g., Treaty of Peace and Friendship between Great Britain and Spain, signed 13 July 1713, 28 Consol. TS 295, Arts. VII, VIII, IX, XV; see further Chester Brown, 'Introduction: The Development and Importance of the Model Bilateral Investment Treaty', in Chester Brown (ed.), *Commentaries on Selected Model Investment Treaties* (Oxford University Press, 2013) 1.

[12] Kenneth Vandevelde, *Bilateral Investment Treaties: History, Policy, and Interpretation* (Oxford University Press, 2010), 19–31.

[13] Treaty of Amity and Commerce between the United States and France, 6 February 1778, 46 Consol. TS 417. For discussion of the United States' FCN treaties see, e.g., Robert Wilson, 'Property Protection Provisions in United States Commercial Treaties', (1951) 45 AJIL 83; Hermann Walker, 'Modern Treaties of Friendship, Commerce and Navigation', (1957) 42 *Minnesota Law Review* 805; Vandevelde, above n. 12, 19–59; Kenneth Vandevelde, *United States International Investment Agreements* (Oxford University Press, 2009), 19; and Lee

countries – including the United Kingdom,[14] Netherlands,[15] Colombia,[16] Germany,[17] Italy,[18] Japan,[19] Latvia,[20] and the Soviet Union[21] – also embarked on programmes for the negotiation of FCN treaties.

FCN treaties were general economic treaties, which typically focused on 'the protection of property rights and the business interests of foreigners', rather than investments.[22] Hundreds of FCN treaties were concluded by states up until the 1960s and, although their content varied, they usually contained guarantees concerning the right of access to the territory of the other state party; most favoured nation (MFN) treatment with respect to taxes and trade; and sometimes national treatment.[23] These FCN treaties were not, however, concluded in a vacuum of applicable rules of international law on the treatment of aliens and the protection of foreign property. Customary international law and general principles of law contained rules on the protection of aliens, although the precise content of these rules generated much disagreement among states, the views of developed, capital-exporting states usually differing from the views of developing, capital-importing states.[24] For instance, a number of developed states considered that aliens should be treated in accordance

Caplan and Jeremy Sharpe, 'United States', in Chester Brown (ed.), *Commentaries on Selected Model Investment Treaties* (Oxford University Press, 2013) 755.

[14] Chester Brown and Audley Sheppard, 'United Kingdom', in Chester Brown (ed.), *Commentaries on Selected Model Investment Treaties* (Oxford University Press, 2013) 697.

[15] Nico Schrijver and Vid Prislan, 'Netherlands', in Chester Brown (ed.), *Commentaries on Selected Model Investment Treaties* (Oxford University Press, 2013) 535.

[16] Jose Antonio Rivas, 'Colombia', in Chester Brown (ed.), *Commentaries on Selected Model Investment Treaties* (Oxford University Press, 2013) 183.

[17] Rudolf Dolzer and Yun-I Kim, 'Germany', in Chester Brown (ed.), *Commentaries on Selected Model Investment Treaties* (Oxford University Press, 2013) 289.

[18] Federico Ortino, 'Italy', in Chester Brown (ed.), *Commentaries on Selected Model Investment Treaties* (Oxford University Press, 2013) 321

[19] Shotaro Hamamoto and Luke Nottage, 'Japan', in Chester Brown (ed.), *Commentaries on Selected Model Investment Treaties* (Oxford University Press, 2013) 347; see also Shuji Yanase, 'Bilateral Treaties of Japan and Resolution of Disputes with Respect to Foreign Direct Investment', in Albert J. van den Berg (ed.), *International Commercial Arbitration: Important Contemporary Issues* (Leiden: Kluwer, 2003) 426.

[20] Martins Paparinskis, 'Latvia' in Chester Brown (ed.), *Commentaries on Selected Model Investment Treaties* (Oxford University Press, 2013) 425.

[21] Vandevelde, above n. 12, 49.

[22] Andrew Newcombe and Lluis Paradell, *Law and Practice of Investment Treaties: Standards of Treatment* (Leiden: Kluwer, 2009), 41.

[23] Vandevelde, above n. 12, 21–23; see also Brown, above n. 11.

[24] Jeswald Salacuse, *The Law of Investment Treaties* (Oxford University Press, 2010), 46; Stephan Schill, *The Multilateralization of International Investment Law* (Cambridge University Press, 2009), 25–8.

with an 'international minimum standard' which was set by international law, rather than the peculiarities of national legal systems.[25] For their part, developing states tended to consider that it was sufficient for foreigners to be accorded 'national treatment', regardless of what standard of treatment applied to nationals.[26] These debates continued to rage throughout the decolonization era of the 1960s and 1970s, and were the subject of a series of UN General Assembly resolutions.[27] In the light of these disagreements, as well as the adverse effect of post-war settlements on private foreign investments, states and private organizations set about exploring ways of reaching agreement in the form of treaties on the applicable standards of protection that would apply to their nationals who made investments abroad, and their property.

Efforts to reach multilateral agreement

Various diplomatic efforts were made in the twentieth century to negotiate a multilateral treaty for the protection of foreign investment. Early initiatives had, however, failed; these included proposals at the League of Nations in 1928 and the Havana Conference of 1948.[28] In 1948, a non-governmental organization, the International Law Association (ILA), published the Draft Statutes of the Arbitral Tribunal for Foreign Investment and the Foreign Investment Court, although these, too, were not adopted.[29] Another proposal by a non-governmental organization, the

---

[25] See, e.g., Elihu Root, 'The Basis of Protection to Citizens Residing Abroad', (1910) 4 AJIL 517, 521–2.

[26] This view was perhaps most prominently put in the writings of the Argentine jurist and Minister for Foreign Affairs, Carlos Calvo: see especially Carlos Calvo, *Le Droit international théorique et pratique*, 5th edn (1896), Vols. 1–6, cited in Salacuse, above n. 24, 49.

[27] These included the Resolution on Permanent Sovereignty over Natural Resources, GA Res. 1803(XVII)/17 UN GAOR, 17th sess., Supp. No.17, UN Doc. A/5217 (14 December 1962); the Declaration on the Establishment of a New International Economic Order, GA Res. 3201(S-VI), UN GAOR, 6th Special sess., UN Doc. A/RES/S-6/3201 (1 May 1974), in which states declared that they had 'full permanent sovereignty' over their natural resources; and the Charter of Economic Rights and Duties of States, GA Res. 3281(XXIX), UN GAOR, 29th sess., Supp. No. 31, UN Doc. A/RES/29/3281.

[28] Newcombe and Paradell, above n. 22, 15–20; Schill, above n. 24, 31–5; and Stanley Metzger, 'Multilateral Conventions for the Protection of Private Foreign Investment', (1960) 9 *Journal of Public Law* 133.

[29] UNCTAD, *International Investment Agreements: A Compendium*, Vol. III (New York: United Nations, 1996), 259; Newcombe and Paradell, above n. 22, 21.

Germany-based Society to Advance the Protection of Foreign Investments, was the International Convention for the Mutual Protection of Private Property Rights in Foreign Countries of 1957, but this was regarded as being too ambitious.[30] In 1959, the Abs-Shawcross Draft Convention on Investments Abroad was jointly proposed by Hermann Abs, the chairman of the Deutsche Bank, and Lord Hartley Shawcross, the former Attorney General of the United Kingdom, but this, too, did not garner sufficient support to be considered as a basis for a multilateral treaty.[31] In 1961, Professors Louis Sohn and Richard Baxter of Harvard Law School published the Harvard Draft Convention on the International Responsibility of States for Injuries to Aliens, which set out 'to codify with some particularity the standards established by international law for the protection of aliens and thereby to obviate, as far as possible, the necessity of looking to customary international law'.[32] Much of the Harvard Draft Convention reflected customary international law, and various provisions were later included in the ILC's Articles on State Responsibility. However, states did not adopt the Harvard Draft Convention as the basis of a multilateral treaty. In the following year, 1962, the Organization for Economic Cooperation and Development (OECD) issued the Draft Convention on the Protection of Foreign Property for comment, and it was then reissued with minor amendments in 1967.[33] The OECD Draft Convention did not gain enough support for adoption as a multilateral convention, which was due to the opposition of many developing countries, as well as the reluctance of some less developed members of the OECD to be bound by the provisions.[34]

At the same time, a number of other initiatives resulted in multilateral treaties dealing with foreign investment, although these did not establish substantive rules. One of these was the Convention on the Settlement of Investment Disputes between States and Nationals of Other States (ICSID Convention), which established the International Centre for Settlement of Investment Disputes (ICSID), and provided a framework for the settlement of such disputes and rules of procedure to be used in the conciliation

---

[30] Rudolf Dolzer and Christoph Schreuer, *Principles of International Investment Law* (Oxford University Press, 2008), 18.

[31] Schill, above n. 24, 35–6; Chester Brown, 'The Evolution of the Regime of International Investment Agreements: History, Economics and Politics', in Marc Bungenberg, Jörn Griebel, August Reinisch, and Stephan Hobe (eds.), *International Investment Law* (Baden-Baden: Nomos, forthcoming).

[32] Louis Sohn and Richard Baxter, 'Responsibility of States for Injuries to the Economic Interests of Aliens', (1961) 55 AJIL 545, 547.

[33] Newcombe and Paradell, above n. 22, 30–31.   [34] Ibid., 30; Schill, above n. 24, 38–39.

RESOLVING INTERNATIONAL INVESTMENT DISPUTES 407

and arbitration of such disputes.[35] Although there was disagreement on the substantive rules of international investment law, the then General Counsel of the World Bank, Aron Broches, proposed the creation of a neutral mechanism for the resolution of investment disputes, and ICSID was the result;[36] the ICSID Convention quickly gathered enough ratifications to enter into force, and today it has 147 states parties.[37] Another initiative resulted in the Multilateral Investment Guarantee Agency Convention (MIGA Convention), which established an international organization (MIGA) which aimed to support foreign investment flows by offering an insurance scheme for foreign investors in developing countries.[38] ICSID and MIGA have been immensely successful in, respectively, facilitating the resolution of international investment disputes, and providing insurance to stimulate cross-border flows of capital. But, as noted above, neither of these multilateral treaties provide any guidance on the substantive rules of foreign investment protection, which was the object of the Abs-Shawcross Convention, the Harvard Draft Convention, and the OECD Draft Convention. The failure of these multilateral initiatives – which would later be repeated in the abandonment of the negotiations for a Multilateral Agreement on Investment in 1998[39] – led states to turn to the bilateral approach.

The emergence of bilateral investment treaties

Germany was the first state to embark on a programme of negotiating BITs, in 1959, and other states – including France (1960), Switzerland (1960), the Netherlands (1963), Italy (1964), the Belgo-Luxembourg Economic Union (1964), Sweden (1965), Denmark (1965), and Norway (1966) – soon followed suit,[40] with other states commencing BIT

---

[35] *Convention on the Settlement of Investment Disputes between States and Nationals of other States* (opened for signature 18 March 1965, 575 UNTS 159, entered into force 14 October 1966) ('ICSID Convention'); see Schill, above n. 24, 44–7; and Christoph Schreuer, Loretta Malintoppi, August Reinisch and Anthony Sinclair, *The ICSID Convention: A Commentary*, 2nd edn (Cambridge University Press, 2009).

[36] Newcombe and Paradell, above n. 22, 27; Ibrahim Shihata, 'Toward a Greater Depoliticisation of Investment Disputes', (1986) 1 *ICSID Review – Foreign Investment Law Journal* 1.

[37] Figures taken from the ICSID website: www.worldbank.org/icsid.

[38] Convention Establishing the Multilateral Investment Guarantee Agency (MIGA Convention), available at www.miga.org, Arts. 11–22; Schill, above n. 24, 48.

[39] Schill, above n. 24, 53–8.

[40] See, e.g., Vandevelde, above n. 12, 54–5; Newcombe and Paradell, above n. 22, 42–3.

408 CHESTER BROWN

programmes later, including the United Kingdom (1975),[41] Austria (1976),[42] Japan (1977),[43] and the United States (1977).[44] Treaty making was initially relatively slow, with fewer than 400 BITs being concluded between 1959 and 1989, but in the next fifteen years, around 2,000 BITs were concluded.[45] UNCTAD has reported that, as at the end of 2011, there were 2,833 BITs in existence,[46] and states are continuing to negotiate BITs and other international investment agreements.[47] In addition, there are today a growing number of multilateral agreements in force which contain investment protections, such as the North American Free Trade Agreement,[48] the Energy Charter Treaty,[49] and the ASEAN–Australia–New Zealand Free Trade Agreement.[50]

BITs typically follow a standard structure, and include provisions that set out definitions and outline the BIT's scope of application, provisions that contain the substantive obligations on the states parties, and provisions that set forth dispute settlement procedures.[51] In order to fall within a BIT's scope of protection – and therefore within the jurisdiction of an arbitral tribunal constituted under the BIT – the putative claimant must be an 'investor' within the meaning of the BIT (jurisdiction *ratione personae*), the putative claimant must have made an 'investment' within the meaning of the BIT (jurisdiction *ratione materiae*), and the investment

---

[41] Brown and Sheppard, above n. 14.

[42] August Reinisch, 'Austria', in Chester Brown (ed.), *Commentaries on Selected Model Investment Treaties* (Oxford University Press, 2013) 15.

[43] Hamamoto and Nottage, above n. 19.

[44] Caplan and Sharpe, above n. 13; Vandevelde, above n. 12, 56–7.

[45] Vandevelde, above n. 13, 64.

[46] UNCTAD, *World Investment Report 2012: Towards a New Generation of Investment Policies* (New York: United Nations, 2012), 84.

[47] UNCTAD reported that in 2011, forty-seven international investment agreements were concluded, consisting of thirty-three BITs and fourteen other agreements (free trade agreements or economic partnership agreements including provisions on investment). Ibid.

[48] North American Free Trade Agreement (signed 17 December 1992, entered into force 1 January 1994), 32 ILM 289.

[49] Energy Charter Treaty (opened for signature 17 December 1994, entered into force 16 April 1998), 34 ILM 360.

[50] ASEAN–Australia–New Zealand Free Trade Agreement, signed 27 February 2009, available at www.dfat.gov.au/fta/aanzfta/index.html; see especially Vivienne Bath and Luke Nottage, 'The ASEAN Comprehensive Investment Agreement and ASEAN-Plus: The ASEAN–Australia–New Zealand Trade Area and the PRC–ASEAN Investment Agreement', in Marc Bungenberg, Jörn Griebel, August Reinisch and Stephan Hobe (eds.), *International Investment Law* (Baden Baden: Nomos, forthcoming).

[51] Schill, above n. 24, 70–88.

must also fall within the BIT's temporal protection (jurisdiction *ratione temporis*).[52] The definition of 'investor' varies from one BIT to another, but it usually includes natural persons and legal persons that have the nationality of a state party to the BIT; in the case of legal persons, this usually includes companies and other entities that are incorporated or organized under the laws of one state party to the BIT.[53] The term 'investment' is typically defined in broad terms, to include, for instance, 'every kind of asset' that is owned or controlled by an investor, and is usually stated as including an enterprise or company, shares and rights of participation in a company, bonds and debentures, rights under contracts, claims to money and other performance having a financial value, and intellectual property rights.[54] As for the temporal protection of investment treaties, most BITs apply to investments made both before and after the BIT's entry into force, but do not apply to disputes that arose prior to the BIT becoming effective.[55] Some BITs stipulate that they only apply to investments made after a certain date.[56] Most BITs also provide protection for investments for a certain period of time after they have been terminated (if such termination takes places unilaterally). For instance, under Article XV(7) of the Canada–Slovak Republic BIT, the substantive protections remain effective for fifteen years after the BIT's unilateral termination.

Substantive standards of protection in bilateral investment treaties

The typical claim that is made by an investor under a BIT is that the host state has violated one or more of the obligations that it owes under

---

[52] See also ibid., 71.

[53] E.g., the Austria–South Korea BIT, Art. 1(2), defines 'investor' as meaning '(a) any natural person who is a national of either Contracting Party in accordance with its laws and regulations and makes an investment in the other Contracting Party's territory; (b) any juridical person or commercial partnership constituted in accordance with the laws and regulations of either Contracting Party, having its seat in the territory of this Contracting Party and making an investment in the other Contracting Party's territory'.

[54] E.g., the United Kingdom–Egypt BIT, Art. 1(a) defines 'investment' as meaning 'every kind of asset and in particular, though not exclusively, includes: (i) movable and immovable property and any other property rights such as mortgages, liens and pledges; (ii) shares, stocks and debentures of companies or interests in the property of such companies; (iii) claims to money or to any performance under contract having a financial value; (iv) intellectual property rights and goodwill; (v) business concessions conferred by law or under contract, including concessions to search for, cultivate, extract or exploit natural resources'.

[55] E.g., Finland–Azerbaijan BIT, Art. 14; Schill, above n. 24, 73.

[56] E.g., Australia–Hungary BIT, Art. 2(1), states that it only applies to 'investments made after 31 December 1972'.

the treaty to the investor. Although the content of BITs is by no means uniform, there are a number of substantive standards of protection that are usually included, which are considered in the following paragraphs. These substantive protections are often included in BITs that do not provide much by way of detail or guidance to arbitral tribunals in how they are to be applied; many BITs are relatively short documents of only seven to ten pages (in contrast to more recent BITs and investment chapters in free trade agreements (FTAs), which can run to over forty pages).[57] The following section does not purport to provide an exhaustive analysis of the application or interpretation of these standards of protection, but seeks to illustrate in general terms the circumstances in which they might be invoked.

One such standard of protection is the obligation to accord 'fair and equitable treatment' (FET) to investments of investors.[58] This is usually understood to be a treaty-based formulation of the minimum standard of treatment under customary international law, although its precise relationship with the customary international law standard remains controversial.[59] The FET standard has been the subject of much consideration by arbitral tribunals, and its application depends on the facts and circumstances of each case. Recent arbitral practice suggests that it may be breached if the host state of the investment acts in a way which is 'arbitrary, grossly unfair, unjust, or idiosyncratic', engages in conduct which is 'discriminatory',[60] or acts in a way which is inconsistent with the investor's legitimate expectations.[61]

---

[57] Cf., e.g., the United Kingdom–Egypt BIT (1975), which is eight pages long, with the United States–Uruguay BIT (2005), which is fifty pages in length.

[58] See, e.g., United Kingdom–Malaysia BIT, Art. 2(2).

[59] E.g., *Glamis Gold Ltd* v. *United States (Award)*, UNCITRAL, 8 June 2009, [559]–[627]; *Chemtura Corporation* v. *Canada (Award)*, UNCITRAL, 2 August 2010, [111]–[123]; *Biwater Gauff (Tanzania) Ltd* v. *Tanzania (Award)*, ICSID Arbitral Tribunal, Case No. ARB/05/22, 24 July 2008, [586]–[603]; *Saluka Investments BV* v. *Czech Republic (Partial Award)*, UNCITRAL, 17 March 2006, [279]–[309].

[60] *Waste Management, Inc.* v. *Mexico (No 2) (Award)*, ICSID Arbitral Tribunal, Case No. ARB(AF)/00/3, 30 April 2004, [98]: '[T]he minimum standard of fair and equitable treatment is infringed by conduct attributable to the State and harmful to the claimant if the conduct is arbitrary, grossly unfair, unjust or idiosyncratic, is discriminatory and exposes the claimant to sectional or racial prejudice, or involves a lack of due process leading to an outcome which offends judicial propriety – as might be the case with a manifest failure of natural justice in judicial proceedings or a complete lack of transparency and candour in an administrative process'.

[61] *Saluka Investments BV* v. *Czech Republic (Partial Award)*, UNCITRAL, 17 March 2006, [300]–[308]; see also *Joseph Charles Lemire* v. *Ukraine (Jurisdiction and Liability)*, ICSID Arbitral Tribunal, Case No. ARB/06/18, 14 January 2010, [284].

A second standard of protection typically found in BITs is the obligation on the host state to accord 'full protection and security' to investments of investors.[62] This obligation is primarily concerned with failures by the state to provide physical protection for the investor's property and protect it from actual damage, caused either by state officials or by the actions of others where the state has failed to exercise due diligence.[63]

A third commonly found obligation on host states is the obligation not to expropriate the investments of investors unless certain conditions are met, which usually include requirements that the measure be for a public purpose, be non-discriminatory, and accompanied by the payment of prompt, adequate, and effective compensation.[64] The protection against expropriation in BITs usually applies both to direct expropriations (where the host state adopts a measure which transfers title of an investor's property to the host state, as happened in, e.g., the Libyan oil nationalization cases),[65] and to indirect expropriations (where arbitral jurisprudence remains unsettled, but it might be said that the measure does not deprive the investor of title to its property, but it nonetheless has the effect of substantially depriving the investor of its ability to exercise rights over its investment).[66] At all times, it is important to distinguish between compensable expropriations and non-compensable regulatory measures adopted for a public purpose within the police powers of the host state.[67]

A fourth typically found substantive protection is the obligation on host states to accord national treatment to investors and their investments. This

---

[62] See, e.g., Netherlands–Bulgaria BIT, Art. 3(1).

[63] See, e.g., *Asian Agricultural Products Ltd* v. *Sri Lanka*, (1997) 4 ICSID Rep. 246, [78]–[86]; *Wena Hotels Ltd* v. *Egypt* (2004) 6 ICSID Rep. 89, [84]–[95]; and *Saluka Investments BV* v. *Czech Republic (Partial Award)*, UNCITRAL, 17 March 2006, [483]–[484]; but see also *Azurix* v. *Argentina (Award)*, ICSID Arbitral Tribunal, Case No. ARB/01/12, 14 July 2006, [408]; and *Siemens AG* v. *Argentina*, ICSID Arbitral Tribunal, Case No. ARB/02/8, 6 February 2007, [303].

[64] See, e.g., Croatia–Hungary BIT, Art. 5(1).

[65] *BP* v. *Libya*, (1977) 53 ILR 297; *Libyan American Oil Company (LIAMCO)* v. *Libya*, (1977) 62 ILR 140; and *Texaco/Calasiatic* v. *Libya*, (1977) 53 ILR 389 (on these cases see Christopher Greenwood, 'State Contracts in International Law: The Libyan Oil Arbitrations', (1982) 53 *British Yearbook of International Law* 27).

[66] See, e.g., the various factors identified by the NAFTA tribunal in *Fireman's Fund Insurance Co* v. *Mexico (Award)*, ICSID Arbitral Tribunal, Case No. ARB(AF)/02/1, 17 July 2006, [176].

[67] E.g., *Methanex Corporation* v. *United States (Final Award)*, UNCITRAL, August 2005, Part IV, Ch. D, [7]; *Fireman's Fund Insurance Company* v. *Mexico (Award)*, Arbitral Tribunal, ICSID Case No. ARB(AF)/02/1, 17 July 2006, [176(j)].

is usually expressed in such a way as to entitle investors to treatment which is 'no less favourable' than the treatment which is accorded to nationals or companies of the host state.[68] The national treatment obligation has been applied by investment treaty tribunals by comparing the treatment accorded to foreign investors with that to local investors in the same business sector of the economy.[69] As the tribunal in *Nykomb Synergetics Technology Holdings AB v. Latvia* observed, 'in evaluating whether there is discrimination in the sense of the Treaty one should only "compare like with like"'.[70] The tribunal proceeds to determine whether the foreign investor is treated differently from the national investor, and finally considers, if the treatment is indeed different, whether there is any justification for the differential treatment.[71]

A fifth standard of protection is the obligation to accord MFN treatment, and this generally requires that investors from that state receive treatment no less favourable than the treatment enjoyed by investors from other states.[72] The effect of including an MFN clause in BITs is that they act as a 'potent ratchet' by which the obligations assumed by host states can become greater than what is actually agreed in a particular BIT.[73] This is because an investor can generally rely on the MFN provision in 'its' treaty to obtain more beneficial treatment than the host state may have agreed to grant investors from another state, in a different BIT. There is a divergence of views among arbitral tribunals, scholars, and practitioners as to whether an MFN clause in a BIT can be understood as only applying to the substantive standards of protection, or whether it also extends to any additional procedural rights, such as the investor–state arbitration provision.[74] This matter remains unresolved, and tribunals have regarded

---

[68] See, e.g., Netherlands–Paraguay BIT, Art. 3(2).

[69] E.g., *SD Myers v. Canada (Partial Award)*, UNCITRAL, 13 November 2000, [250].

[70] *Nykomb Synergetics Technology Holdings AB v. Latvia (Award)*, UNCITRAL, December 2003, [34].

[71] *Saluka Investments BV v. Czech Republic (Partial Award)*, UNCITRAL, 17 March 2006, [313].

[72] See, e.g., Switzerland–Chile BIT, Art. 4(2).

[73] Campbell McLachlan, Laurence Shore, and Matthew Weiniger, *International Investment Arbitration* (Oxford University Press, 2007), 254.

[74] A number of tribunals have held that the MFN provision can be used to obtain the benefit of a more favourable investor–state arbitration provision (see, e.g., *Maffezini v. Spain (Jurisdiction)*, ICSID Arbitral Tribunal, Case No. ARB/97/7, 25 January 2000, [64]; and *Gas Natural SDG SA v. Argentina (Jurisdiction)*, ICSID Arbitral Tribunal, Case No. ARB/03/10, 17 June 2005, [49]), while other tribunals have disagreed with this approach (*Salini Costruttori SpA and Italstrade SpA v. Jordan (Jurisdiction)*, ICSID Arbitral Tribunal, Case No. ARB/02/13, 9 November 2004, [119]; see also *Plama Consortium Ltd v. Bulgaria*

it as a matter of treaty interpretation in each individual dispute; as the tribunal in *Renta 4 SVSA* v. *Russian Federation* put it, it is 'necessary to proceed BIT by BIT'.[75]

A sixth standard of protection often found in BITs is the 'observance of undertakings' obligation, or the so-called 'umbrella clause'.[76] The standard is generally formulated in rather broad terms as requiring the host state of the investment 'to observe any obligation it may have entered into with regard to investments of nationals or companies of the other Contracting Party'.[77] Although the case law remains unsettled, the effect of the umbrella clause would appear to be that it elevates to the international plane any contractual obligations that the host state may owe the investor.[78]

The foregoing section is not an exhaustive review of the substantive protections that are found in BITs, and nor does it purport to provide a comprehensive analysis of how these protections might be applied from one case to another. However, it can be said that these provisions are relatively common (with one author suggesting that the commonality in the content of BITs has contributed to the 'multilateralization' of international investment law),[79] and it is also apparent that their interpretation and application has been developed in the practice of investment treaty tribunals. This is not a static field; every week brings with it the publication of one or two more investment treaty awards that are immediately scoured by scholars and practitioners for their contribution to the developing jurisprudence on the interpretation of investment treaties.[80]

(Jurisdiction), ICSID Arbitral Tribunal, Case No. ARB/03/24, 8 February 2005, [223]). For a recent review of the arbitral case law, see Zachary Douglas, 'The MFN Clause in Investment Arbitration: Treaty Interpretation off the Rails', (2011) 2 *Journal of International Dispute Settlement* 97; Schill, above n. 24, 121–96.

[75] *Renta 4 SVSA* v. *Russian Federation (Preliminary Objections)*, UNCITRAL, 20 March 2009, [94].

[76] On the 'umbrella clause' see especially Anthony Sinclair, 'The Origins of the Umbrella Clause in the International Law of Investment Protection', (2004) 20 *Arbitration International* 411.

[77] See, e.g., UK Model BIT, Art. 2(2).

[78] E.g., *Noble Ventures, Inc.* v. *Romania (Award)*, ICSID Arbitral Tribunal, Case No. ARB/01/11, 12 October 2005, [51]–[61]; *SGS Société Général de Surveillance SA* v. *Philippines (Jurisdiction)*, ICSID Arbitral Tribunal, Case No. ARB/02/6, 29 January 2004, [113]–[129]; see also *BIVAC* v. *Paraguay*, ICSID Case No. ARB/07/9, 29 May 2009, [159]–[161].

[79] Schill, above n. 24, 70–1.

[80] Many investment treaty awards (as well as other international investment law-related materials) can be accessed on the website maintained by Professor Andrew Newcombe, available at http://italaw.com.

414   CHESTER BROWN

Types of dispute

Investor–state disputes

Because the obligations under BITs are typically owed by the states parties to the investors of the other state's nationality, disputes that arise under BITs are usually investor–state disputes, where an aggrieved investor considers that the host state of its investment has adopted a measure, or taken some action, that constitutes a breach of its obligations under the BIT. The investor–state dispute settlement provisions of BITs usually require that there be a 'dispute' concerning an investment, although there is some variation in the formulation used. For instance, the Germany–China BIT refers in Article 9(1), the investor–state dispute settlement provision, to 'any dispute concerning investments between a Contracting Party and an investor of the other Contracting Party'.[81] This can be contrasted with the (arguably more narrow) language of Article 7(1) of the United Kingdom–Chile BIT, which covers 'disputes, which arise within the terms of this Agreement'.[82] In another example, the United States–Georgia BIT provides a prescriptive definition of the term 'investment dispute' (in respect of which the states parties agree to the BIT's dispute settlement procedures) as 'a dispute between a Party and a national or company of the other Party arising out of or relating to an investment authorization, an investment agreement or an alleged breach of any right conferred, created or recognised by this Treaty with respect to a covered investment'.[83]

In order for an investor–state claim to be brought under a BIT, the action or omission that has allegedly had an adverse effect on the investment must be attributable to the government of the host state in accordance with the international law of state responsibility.[84] Claims have been presented under BITs arising out of a wide range of facts and circumstances, including the adoption by a state of emergency measures that resulted in the cancellation of contractually agreed guarantees regarding the payment of tariffs;[85] the failure by a state's judiciary to provide due process to a foreign investor, the denial of justice by a state's judicial system, or the state's failure to provide 'effective means' of asserting

---

[81] Germany–China BIT (2003), Art. 9(1).   [82] United Kingdom–Chile BIT, Art. 7(1).

[83] United States–Georgia BIT, Art. IX(1).

[84] As for which see especially James Crawford, *The International Law Commission's Articles on State Responsibility: Introduction, Text and Commentaries* (Cambridge University Press, 2002), 91–123.

[85] See, e.g., *CMS Gas Transmission Company* v. *Argentina (Award)*, ICSID Arbitral Tribunal, Case No. ARB/01/8, 12 May 2005.

claims;[86] the unjustified termination by a state of a mining licence;[87] the termination by a state of an import licence;[88] and the introduction of a legislative ban on the production and sale of certain products.[89] In these claims, investors have alleged that the host state has breached a range of the substantive standards of protection under the BIT, the content of which has been described above. Of course, not all claims are successful; UNCTAD has reported that of the known concluded cases, approximately 40 per cent were decided in favour of the state, 30 per cent were decided in favour of the claimant, and 30 per cent were settled.[90]

Inter-state disputes

Because BITs are agreements between states, they typically also provide for an inter-state dispute settlement procedure. For instance, the Sweden–Bolivia BIT provides in Article 7 for '[a]ny dispute between the Contracting Parties concerning the interpretation or application of this Agreement' to be settled by negotiations between the governments of the two contracting parties, and if the dispute cannot be so settled, it is to be submitted to international arbitration.[91] Inter-state disputes under BITs are, however, rare. This is likely a product of the fact that one of the very purposes of negotiating BITs was to confer rights on individual investors to present claims themselves, rather than relying on their state of nationality to do so; by conferring the right on individual investors to assert claims, such disputes are depoliticized, and there is less possibility that the disputes will affect the bilateral relationship between the two states.

There have, however, been at least three known inter-state claims presented under BITs. First, in *Empresas Lucchetti SA and Lucchetti Peru SA* v.

---

[86] See, e.g., *Loewen Group, Inc. and Raymond Loewen* v. *United States (Award)*, ICSID Arbitral Tribunal, Case No. ARB(AF)/98/3, 26 June 2003; *Chevron Corporation and Texaco Petroleum Company* v. *Ecuador (Partial Award on Merits)*, UNCITRAL, 30 March 2010; *White Industries Australia Ltd* v. *Republic of India (Final Award)*, UNCITRAL, 30 November 2011.

[87] See, e.g., *Oxus Gold plc* v. *Kyrgyz Republic*; see Luke Eric Peterson, 'Kyrgyz Republic Settles BIT Claim with UK Miner, Oxus', *IA Reporter*, 16 May 2008, available at www.iareporter. com/articles/20091001_96.

[88] *Middle East Cement Shipping and Handling Co.* v. *Egypt (Award)*, ICSID Case No. ARB/99/6, 12 April 2002.

[89] *Methanex Corporation* v. *United States (Final Award)*, UNCITRAL, August 2005.

[90] UNCTAD, 'Latest Developments in Investor–State Dispute Settlement', *IIA Issues Note No. 1*, March 2011, 2, available at http://unctad.org/en/Docs/webdiaeia20113_en.pdf.

[91] Sweden–Bolivia BIT, Art. 7.

Peru, an investor–state claim, the respondent requested that the proceedings be suspended 'in view of the fact that "Claimants' Request for Arbitration [was] . . . the subject of a concurrent state-to-state dispute between the Republic of Peru and the Republic of Chile",[92] but the tribunal did not suspend the proceedings, and it appears that the inter-state claim was discontinued.[93] Second, an inter-state dispute between Italy and Cuba, in which Italy complained of the mistreatment of certain Italian investors in Cuba, was the subject of an ad hoc arbitral award of 1 January 2008.[94] Third, Ecuador commenced inter-state dispute settlement proceedings against the United States, and this claim principally concerned the interpretation and application of Article II(7) of the Ecuador–United States BIT, under which the states parties agree to provide 'effective means of asserting claims and enforcing rights with respect to investment, investment agreements, and investment authorizations', following the interpretation of that provision by a tribunal in an investor–state dispute.[95] This inter-state claim has reportedly been rejected on jurisdictional grounds.[96]

In addition to these three inter-state claims under BITs, the states parties to the North American Free Trade Agreement (NAFTA) have issued 'Notes of Interpretation of Certain Chapter 11 Provisions', in which they provided guidance on issues of transparency and clarification of the content of Article 1105, although the issue of these notes did not result from a 'dispute' between the states parties to NAFTA.[97]

There is little controversy about the inter-state dispute settlement procedures that are typically included in BITs and other international investment agreements. There has, in contrast, been much discussion about the various methods by which investor–state disputes are settled, and the remainder of this chapter focuses on the procedures for the settlement of investor–state disputes.

---

[92] *Empresas Lucchetti SA and Lucchetti Peru SA v. Peru (Award)*, ICSID Case No. ARB/03/4, 7 February 2005, [7].

[93] Ibid., [9].   [94] *Italy v. Cuba (Final Award)*, UNCITRAL, 1 January 2008, [48].

[95] *Chevron Corporation and Texaco Petroleum Company v. Ecuador (Interim Award)*, UNCITRAL, 1 December 2008.

[96] Luke Eric Peterson, 'United States Defeats Ecuador's State-to-State Arbitration: Will Outcome Dissuade Argentine Copycat Case?', *IA Reporter*, 2 September 2012, available at www.iareporter.com/articles/20120903_3.

[97] NAFTA Free Trade Commission, Notes of Interpretation of Certain Chapter 11 Provisions, 31 July 2001.

Methods for settling investor–state disputes

Generally

Investor–state arbitration as the typical method of settling disputes

It has already been noted that BITs, in addition to substantive standards of protection, typically confer on investors a procedural protection, being the ability to assert a claim (usually in international arbitration) directly against the host state of the investment, if the investor considers that the host state has breached its obligations under the treaty. It might be argued that the existence of compulsory procedures for the settlement of investor–state disputes is just as important as the actual substantive standards of protection typically afforded by BITs, since they provide a means for the investor to vindicate its rights under the treaty, and enforce compliance by the host state with its obligations.[98] As UNCTAD has stated, from the perspective of investors,

> Having means at their disposal to ensure the host country's compliance with the obligations under BITs increases the level of certainty regarding the business environment in which investors operate in the host country. In addition, this mechanism ensures that the dispute is decided on legal grounds, thus separating legal from political considerations.[99]

Despite the importance placed on the availability of investor–state dispute settlement procedures, the first BIT – the Germany–Pakistan BIT (1959) – did not include an investor–state dispute settlement provision, providing only that any disputes concerning the interpretation or application of the BIT could be referred to the ICJ, with both parties' agreement, but if there was no such agreement, then an arbitral tribunal would decide such disputes.[100] The first BIT to include such a provision was the Indonesia–Netherlands BIT of 1968, although, like the Abs–Shawcross Draft Convention of 1959 and the OECD Draft Convention of 1967, this only provided for investor–state arbitration on the basis that the contracting state on the territory of which a national of the other contracting state makes or intends to make an investment 'shall assent to any demand on the part of such national ... to submit, for conciliation or arbitration, to

---

[98] See, e.g., Salacuse, above n. 24, 354.

[99] UNCTAD, *Bilateral Investment Treaties 1995–2006: Trends in Investment Rulemaking* (New York: United Nations, 2007), 100.

[100] Germany–Pakistan BIT, Art. 11(2)(b).

418   CHESTER BROWN

[ICSID]'.[101] This was, therefore, a qualified or imperfect form of consent to investor–state arbitration. The first BIT to include unqualified consent to investor–state arbitration would appear to be the Italy–Chad BIT of 1969;[102] this introduced the possibility of depoliticized dispute settlement between investors and host states, without the need for the investor's state of nationality to be involved.

The most important element of the investor–state arbitration provision is the host state's consent to international arbitration. This must identify the types of dispute that are within the host state's consent, but also, which is of greater interest for present purposes, the means by which disputes are to be settled, which is invariably by international arbitration, although most BITs provide that efforts must be made to settle disputes by negotiation in the first instance.[103] In some BITs, the scope of the host state's consent to investor–state arbitration is quite broad; it may be formulated as extending to 'any dispute concerning investments', such as in the Germany–China BIT,[104] which is arguably more expansive than, for instance, 'any dispute ... concerning the interpretation or application of this Agreement', which is the corresponding provision for the settlement of inter-state disputes in the same treaty.[105] In other BITs, the host state's consent is more clearly prescribed.[106]

There are various institutions and sets of procedural rules that can be employed for international arbitration, such as the procedures established under the ICSID Convention, the Rules of Arbitration of the United Nations Commission on International Trade Law (UNCITRAL), and the Rules of the Arbitration Institute of the Stockholm Chamber of Commerce (SCC). Some BITs offer a choice among these various sets of rules, while others provide only for the possibility of one set of arbitration rules being employed in investor–state claims. For instance, Article 8 of the United Kingdom–Singapore BIT provides exclusively for ICSID arbitration.[107] In contrast, Article 26(4) of the Energy Charter Treaty provides for a range of options, namely international arbitration under the ICSID Convention,

---

[101] Netherlands–Indonesia BIT (1968), Art. 11, as cited in Newcombe and Paradell, above n. 22, 44–5. This has since been replaced by a Netherlands–Indonesia BIT signed on 6 April 1994, which entered into force on 1 July 1995, in which both states provide their unqualified consent to investor–state arbitration.

[102] Italy–Chad BIT (1969), Art. VII; cited in Newcombe and Paradell, above n. 22, p. 45.

[103] Vandevelde, above n. 12, 433; e.g., Germany–China BIT, Art. 9(1)–(2).

[104] Germany–China BIT, Art. 9(1).   [105] Ibid., Art. 8(1).

[106] See, e.g., United States–Georgia BIT, Art. IX(1).

[107] United Kingdom–Singapore BIT, Art. 8.

RESOLVING INTERNATIONAL INVESTMENT DISPUTES

international arbitration under ICSID's 'Additional Facility' Rules, which extend ICSID's jurisdiction to disputes where only one of the relevant states is a state party to the ICSID Convention, UNCITRAL arbitration, and arbitration under the Rules of Arbitration of the Stockholm Chamber of Commerce.[108]

Expressions of disquiet about investor–state arbitration

In recent years a number of states, members of civil society, and other stakeholders have voiced concerns about the investment treaty regime, including doubts about the 'legitimacy' of investment treaty arbitration and the existence of treaty provisions that confer on private actors the right to challenge measures adopted by sovereign states.[109] The perceived problems with investor–state arbitration include the 'regulatory chill' created by investor–state arbitration, which sees states refraining from the adoption of regulatory measures due to the fear of inviting claims under BITs;[110] inconsistent decisions that have been rendered by arbitral tribunals;[111] alleged conflicts of interest where arbitrators may also act as counsel in other pending claims;[112] the lack of transparency in international arbitration;[113] and the difficulties with multiple and parallel

---

[108] Energy Charter Treaty (signed 17 December 1994, entered into force 16 April 1998), 2080 UNTS 95, Art. 26(4).

[109] See, e.g., Susan Franck, 'The Legitimacy Crisis in Investment Treaty Arbitration: Privatising Public International Law through Inconsistent Decisions', (2005) 73 *Fordham Law Review* 1521; M. Sornarajah, 'A Coming Crisis: Expansionary Trends in Investment Treaty Arbitration', in Karl Sauvant (ed.), *Appeals Mechanisms in International Investment Disputes* (Oxford University Press, 2008) 39; and Michael Waibel et al. (eds.), *The Backlash against Investment Arbitration* (Alphen aan den Rijn: Kluwer Law, 2010). For a contrary view see Devashish Krishan, 'Thinking about BITs and BIT Arbitration: The Legitimacy Crisis that Never Was', in Todd Weiler and Freya Baetens (eds.), *New Directions in International Economic Law: In Memoriam Thomas Wälde* (Dordrecht: Martinus Nijhoff, 2011) 107.

[110] Kyla Tienhaara, 'Regulatory Chill and the Threat of Arbitration: A View from Political Science', in Chester Brown and Kate Miles (eds.), *Evolution in Investment Treaty Law and Arbitration* (Cambridge University Press, 2011) 606.

[111] Cf., e.g., *CMS Gas Transmission Company* v. *Argentina (Award)*, ICSID Arbitral Tribunal, Case No. ARB/01/8, 12 May 2005, [353]–[94], [468]; and *LG&E* et al. v. *Argentina (Liability)*, ICSID Arbitral Tribunal, Case No. ARB/02/1, 3 October 2006, [226]–[266]. On this issue see Michael Waibel, 'Two Worlds of Necessity in ICSID Arbitration: *CMS* and *LG&E*', (2007) 20 *Leiden Journal of International Law* 637.

[112] E.g., Philippe Sands, 'Conflict and Conflicts in Investment Treaty Arbitration: Ethical Standards for Counsel', in Chester Brown and Kate Miles (eds.), *Evolution in Investment Treaty Law and Arbitration* (Cambridge University Press, 2011) 19.

[113] E.g., Micah Burch, Luke Nottage, and Brett Williams, 'Appropriate Dispute Resolution for Australia–Japan and Asia–Pacific Commerce in the 21st Century', (2012) 35 *University*

proceedings that result from arbitral tribunals being established as ad hoc bodies for individual disputes.[114]

In the light of these and other issues, some states have announced their intention to withdraw from obligations under investment treaties. On 2 May 2007, Bolivia submitted a notice denouncing the ICSID Convention, which took effect six months later.[115] In January 2008, Ecuador declared that it intended to terminate several of its BITs,[116] and on 6 July 2009, it too announced its denunciation of the ICSID Convention.[117] Venezuela had already terminated its BIT with the Netherlands,[118] and on 24 January 2012, it also announced that it was denouncing the ICSID Convention.[119] But the states walking away from investment treaty obligations did not just include Latin American countries, which may have watched the experience of Argentina with some nervousness. In 2007, Norway issued a revised Draft Model BIT in which it sought to balance substantive protections for investors with recognition of public goods.[120] In 2009, the Czech Republic, the respondent to at least

---

    of New South Wales Law Journal 1013; Natalie Bernasconi-Osterwalder, 'Transparency and Amicus Curiae in ICSID Arbitrations', in Marie-Claire Cordonnier-Segger, Markus Gehring, and Andrew Newcombe (eds.), *Sustainable Development in World Investment Law* (Alphen aan den Rijn: Kluwer International, 2011) 189; and Luke Nottage and Kate Miles, '"Back to the Future" for Investor–State Arbitrations: Revising Rules in Australia and Japan to Meet Public Interests', (2009) 26 *Journal of International Arbitration* 25.

[114] E.g., *CME Czech Republic BV* v. *Czech Republic (Partial Award)*, UNCITRAL, 13 September 2001; *CME Czech Republic BV* v. *Czech Republic (Final Award)*, UNCITRAL, 14 March 2003; *Ronald Lauder* v. *Czech Republic (Final Award)*, UNCITRAL, 3 September 2001; see McLachlan, Shore, and Weiniger, above n. 73, 117–26.

[115] ICSID, 'Bolivia Submits a Notice under Article 71 of the ICSID Convention', News Release, 16 May 2007, available at https://icsid.worldbank.org/ICSID/FrontServlet?requestType=CasesRH&actionVal=OpenPage&PageType=AnnouncementsFrame&FromPage=NewsReleases&pageName=Announcement3.

[116] Namely, its BITs with Cuba, Dominican Republic, El Salvador, Guatemala, Honduras, Nicaragua, Paraguay, Romania, and Uruguay: UNCTAD, *World Investment Report 2010: Investing in a Low-Carbon Economy* (Geneva: United Nations, 2010), 85.

[117] ICSID, 'Ecuador Submits a Notice under Article 71 of the ICSID Convention', News Release, 9 July 2009, available at https://icsid.worldbank.org/ICSID/FrontServlet?requestType=CasesRH&actionVal=OpenPage&PageType=AnnouncementsFrame&FromPage=NewsReleases&pageName=Announcement20.

[118] UNCTAD, above n. 116, 86.

[119] ICSID, 'Venezuela Submits a Notice under Article 71 of the ICSID Convention', News Release, 26 January 2012, available at https://icsid.worldbank.org/ICSID/FrontServlet?requestType=CasesRH&actionVal=OpenPage&PageType=AnnouncementsFrame&FromPage=Announcements&pageName=Announcement100.

[120] Norway Model BIT (2007), available at http://italaw.com. In 2009, the Draft Model BIT was withdrawn: International Institute for Sustainable Development, 'Norwegian

RESOLVING INTERNATIONAL INVESTMENT DISPUTES 421

nineteen investment treaty claims, initiated the termination process for its intra-EU BITs.[121] And in April 2011, the Australian government published a 'Trade Policy Statement' in which it stated that:

> In the past, Australian Governments have sought the inclusion of investor–state dispute resolution procedures in trade agreements with developing countries at the behest of Australian businesses. The Gillard Government will discontinue this practice. If Australian businesses are concerned about sovereign risk in Australian trading partner countries, they will need to make their own assessments about whether they want to commit to investing in those countries.[122]

Already in 2004, Australia and the United States had signed a free trade agreement which included a chapter on investment protection, but did not include an investor–state dispute settlement provision.[123] Australia had subsequently entered into other free trade agreements with such provisions,[124] but in February 2011, Australia and New Zealand signed a Protocol on Investment to the Australia–New Zealand Closer Economic Relations Trade Agreement, which did not include an investor–state dispute settlement provision. Likewise, the Malaysia–Australia Free Trade Agreement, which was signed on 22 May 2012, includes a chapter with

Government Shelves its Draft Model Bilateral Investment Treaty', *Investment Treaty News*, 8 June 2009, www.iisd.org/itn/2009/06/08/norway-shelves-its-proposed-model-bilateral-investment-treaty/.

[121] UNCTAD, above n. 116, 86 (although the Czech Republic's decision may have been motivated principally by issues arising in EU law). For the number of investment treaty claims faced by various states, see UNCTAD, 'Latest Developments in Investor–State Dispute Settlement', IIA Issues Note No. 1, April 2012, 17–18, available at http://unctad.org/en/PublicationsLibrary/webdiaeia2012d10_en.pdf.

[122] Australian Government, 'Trade Policy Statement: Trading our Way to More Jobs and Prosperity', April 2011, 14, available at www.dfat.gov.au. For detailed commentary and critique see especially Jürgen Kurtz, 'Australia's Rejection of Investor–State Arbitration: Causation, Omission, and Implication', (2012) 27 *ICSID Review – Foreign Investment Law Journal* 65; Luke Nottage, 'Throwing the Baby out with the Bathwater: Australia's New Policy on Treaty-Based Investor–State Arbitration and Its Impact in Asia', (2013) 37 *Asian Studies Review* 253.

[123] Australia–United States Free Trade Agreement (signed 18 May 2004, entered into force 1 January 2005), available at www.dfat.gov.au/fta/.

[124] E.g., Thailand–Australia Free Trade Agreement (signed 5 July 2004, entered into force 1 January 2005), available at www.dfat.gov.au/fta/; Australia–Chile Free Trade Agreement (signed 30 July 2008, entered into force 6 March 2009), available at www.dfat.gov.au/fta/; and ASEAN–Australia–New Zealand Free Trade Agreement (signed 27 February 2009, entered into force 1 January 2010), available at www.dfat.gov.au/fta/. On Australia's practice in entering into BITs and FTAs, see Mark Mangan, 'Australia's Investment Treaty Program and Investor–State Arbitration', in Luke Nottage and Richard Garnett (eds.), *International Arbitration in Australia* (Sydney: Federation Press, 2010) 191.

investment protections, but does not include an investor–state dispute settlement provision.[125]

In the light of the concerns expressed by some states and stakeholders regarding the appropriateness of investor–state dispute settlement provisions, it is apposite to consider other ways in which investment disputes might be resolved. In this regard, it is useful to recall Article 33(2) of the Charter of the United Nations, which is of course primarily relevant for disputes which threaten the maintenance of international peace and security. This provides that 'The parties to any dispute ... shall, first of all, seek a solution by negotiation, enquiry, mediation, conciliation, arbitration, judicial settlement, resort to regional agencies or arrangements, or other peaceful means of their own choice.'[126] Not all these methods of dispute resolution will apply to international investment disputes; an investor may be unlikely, for instance, to seek the establishment of a fact-finding commission of enquiry to facilitate the settlement of a dispute concerning its investment. However, it provides an indication of the other methods that might be used to settle investment disputes.[127]

Alternatives to investor–state arbitration

Negotiation

An alternative method of settling investor–state disputes is for the investor to seek to resolve the matter in direct negotiations with the host state. Negotiations, also referred to as 'consultations', or attempts at 'amicable settlement', are invariably the best method of resolving disputes; it is the means by which 'the large majority of international disputes are settled'.[128] Many investment treaties that contain an investor–state dispute settlement provision make it compulsory for the disputing parties to seek to resolve the dispute in negotiations before international arbitration can

---

[125] Malaysia–Australia Free Trade Agreement (signed 22 May 2012, entered into force 1 January 2013), available at www.dfat.gov.au, Arts. 12(4), 12(5), 12(7), and 12(8).

[126] UN Charter, Art. 33(2).

[127] See also UNCTAD, 'Exploring Alternatives to Investment Treaty Arbitration and Other Dispute Prevention Policies', first draft for discussion, 2009, available at www.unescap.org/tid/projects/tisiln-unctad.pdf; and Jeswald Salacuse, 'Is There a Better Way? Alternative Methods of Treaty-Based, Investor–State Dispute Resolution', (2008) 31 *Fordham International Law Journal* 138, 162.

[128] John Collier and Vaughan Lowe, *The Settlement of Disputes in International Law: Institutions and Procedures* (Oxford University Press, 1999), 20.

be initiated.[129] An example is provided by the Germany–China BIT, which provides in Article 9:

> (1) Any dispute concerning investments between a Contracting Party and an investor of the other Contracting Party should as far as possible be settled amicably between the parties in dispute.
> (2) If the dispute cannot be settled within six months of the date when it has been raised by one of the parties in dispute, it shall, at the request of the investor of the other Contracting Party, be submitted for arbitration.[130]

It is of course possible for investment disputes to be resolved in the course of direct negotiations, and because of the requirement in some BITs for there to be a period of negotiations, it has been observed that 'virtually all disputes go through a period of negotiation before either reaching settlement or advancing to a formal investor–state arbitration'.[131] Because such negotiations are typically confidential, there are no statistics on negotiated settlements of investor–state disputes,[132] although it seems that 30 per cent of known investment treaty disputes have been settled through negotiations rather than through awards issued by arbitral tribunals.[133]

The likelihood of negotiations being successful in settling the investor–state dispute will depend on many factors that will be specific to the facts and circumstances of the case. These would include, for instance, the interest of the investor in continuing to make investments in the host state; whether the investor has other investments in that state; and the desire for both disputing parties to avoid extended and costly litigation (which may make it more likely that the disputing parties will settle);

---

[129] Vandevelde, above n. 12, 433. Most BITs with an inter-state dispute settlement provision also provide that the states parties are to seek to resolve such disputes by negotiation (or 'through the diplomatic channel') prior to any further dispute settlement methods being initiated; see, e.g., UK–Azerbaijan BIT, Art. 9(1). In addition to including an inter-state dispute settlement procedure, some BITs provide in a separate provision that the states parties are to 'consult promptly' with each other 'to resolve any disputes in connection with the Treaty, or to discuss any matter relating to the interpretation or application of the Treaty', e.g., United States–Grenada BIT, Art. V. Some BITs even put inter-state negotiations or consultations on an institutional footing, and provide for the creation of an inter-state commission to review the implementation of the BIT: e.g., Canada–Peru BIT, Art. 50.

[130] Germany–China BIT, Art. 9(1), 9(2).   [131] Salacuse, above n. 24, 357.

[132] Ibid., 357.

[133] UNCTAD, above n. 90, 2. See also Salacuse, above n. 24, 364, citing Jack Coe, 'Toward a Complementary Use of Conciliation in Investor–State Disputes – A Preliminary Sketch', (2005) 12 *University of California Davis Journal of International Law and Policy* 8.

424 CHESTER BROWN

the determination of the host state to persist with the implementation of the measure it has adopted; and whether there has been a complete breakdown in the relationship between the investor and the host state (which would make it less likely that a settlement would be achieved); as well as the comparative strength of the parties' legal cases, and the ability of the parties to afford the costs of international arbitration proceedings.

Mediation

Mediation is another possible method of settling investor–state disputes, and given its prevalence as a means of settling international commercial disputes, there would appear to be good reason for considering its use in investor–state disputes as well.[134] However, it would seem that its use in the context of investment treaty disputes is quite rare. The International Bar Association (IBA) formed a sub-committee on mediation of investor–state disputes in October 2007, which had the mandate:

> To examine the current use of mediation in relation to investor–state disputes, to determine whether wider use would benefit the investor–state dispute system in general (or discrete types of participants who use it in particular), to identify and assess obstacles to wider use of investor–state mediation, and to propose concrete measures that might be pursued to increase resort to mediation for investor–state disputes should our initial findings make such proposals appropriate.[135]

The IBA sub-committee produced Draft Rules on the Mediation of Investor–State Disputes in March 2012. Although the use of mediation in investor–state disputes seems to be in an early stage of consideration, it is clear that its use would have to be agreed to by both parties to the dispute, as mediation is typically not included in BITs. Parties to investor–state disputes may see mediation assisting the achievement of an early resolution to the dispute, at what would usually be considerably less cost to the parties. But the fact that it does not, as yet, appear to have been embraced by parties to investor–state disputes suggests that the same factors that dictate whether negotiations will achieve a settlement may also apply

---

[134] See, e.g., Margrete Stevens and Ben Love, 'Investor–State Mediation: Observations on the Role of Institutions', in Arthur Rovine (ed.), *Contemporary Issues in International Arbitration and Mediation: The Fordham Papers 2009* (Leiden: Brill, 2010), as well as the other contributions to the *Fordham Papers 2009*; and Jack Coe, 'Settlement of Investor–State Disputes through Mediation – Preliminary Remarks on Process, Problems and Prospects', in Doak Bishop (ed.), *Enforcement of Arbitral Awards against Sovereigns* (New York: Juris Publishing, 2009) 73.

[135] Cited in Stevens and Love, above n. 134.

RESOLVING INTERNATIONAL INVESTMENT DISPUTES 425

to mediation; in this sense, once negotiations have finished (without a resolution), parties may prefer to proceed directly to international arbitration, which will result in a final and binding settlement of the dispute. However, it is too early to predict whether the adoption in October 2012 of the IBA Rules for Investor–State Mediation may change the behaviour of disputing parties.

Conciliation

Another possibility is for investment disputes to be resolved by conciliation. Conciliation is a process with the participation of a third party that does not result in a binding decision, but rather aims to produce a recommendation that may be adopted by the disputing parties as the terms of an agreed settlement. Some BITs provide for the settlement of investor–state disputes by conciliation (albeit where the parties to the dispute agree).[136] So, Article 9 of the United Kingdom–India BIT provides that:

> (2) Any dispute which has not been amicably settled within a period of six months from written notification of a claim may be submitted to international conciliation under the Conciliation Rules of the United Nations Commission on International Trade Law, if the parties to the dispute so agree.
> (3) Where the dispute is not referred to international conciliation, or where it is so referred but conciliation proceedings are terminated other than by the signing of a settlement agreement, the dispute may be referred to arbitration . . . [137]

The ICSID Convention contains provisions to facilitate the conciliation of investor–state disputes, and these provisions illustrate the nature of the conciliation process.[138] For instance, Article 34(1) of the ICSID Convention provides that the conciliation commission that is constituted for the particular dispute has a 'duty' to 'clarify the issues in dispute between the parties', and to 'endeavour to bring about agreement between them on mutually acceptable terms'.[139] The commission may, at any stage of the proceedings, 'recommend terms of settlement to the parties', to which they are to give 'their most serious consideration'.[140] Under Article 35 of the ICSID Convention, parties to conciliation proceedings are

---

[136] Ibid.   [137] United Kingdom–India BIT, Art. 9(2), 9(3).
[138] See, e.g., Malcolm Holmes and Chester Brown, *The International Arbitration Act 1974: A Commentary* (Sydney: LexisNexis, 2011), 282–7.
[139] ICSID Convention, Art. 34(1).
[140] On the functioning of the Commission, see Schreuer et al., above n. 35, 443–52; and see especially the view of Lord Wilberforce, the sole conciliator in *Tesoro* v. *Trinidad and*

426 CHESTER BROWN

generally not entitled to invoke or rely on any statements made in the course of the conciliation before an arbitral tribunal or court.[141] The purpose of this provision is to ensure that parties to conciliation proceedings can discuss their dispute candidly and flexibly, without the fear that any position adopted, or offer of settlement proposed, by them in the conciliation might later be used against them in subsequent proceedings, should the conciliation fail to result in an agreed settlement of the dispute.[142]

Despite the availability of conciliation as a means of settling investor–state disputes, it does not appear to have been a popular method; there have been relatively few conciliations under the ICSID Convention, with only six requests for conciliation having been registered.[143] Its underutilization may reflect the reality that once parties have embarked on formal dispute settlement proceedings, it is seen as more desirable for that process to result in a final and binding award, rather than a recommendation which will have to be adopted and implemented by the parties.

International commercial arbitration

It may be possible for the investor to submit the dispute to be settled by international commercial arbitration where it has entered into some form of concession contract with the government of the host state of the investment, and has included an arbitration clause in the concession contract. In the event that the government of the host state has committed a breach of its contractual obligations, the investor would be able to initiate international arbitration proceedings. Such concession contracts are also referred to as 'investment agreements' or 'host government agreements', and are common for long-term investments concerning natural resources, as well as other large-scale projects, such as the construction of major infrastructure facilities and the provision of certain services to the host

---

Tobago, ICSID Arbitral Tribunal, Case No. CONC/83/1, 27 November 1985, as extracted in Schreuer et al., above n. 35, 446.

[141] ICSID Convention, Art. 35.   [142] Schreuer et al., above n. 35, 453–4.

[143] *SEDITEX* v. *Madagascar (No. 1)*, ICSID Arbitral Tribunal, Case No. CONC/82/1, 20 June 1983; *Tesoro* v. *Trinidad and Tobago*, ICSID Arbitral Tribunal, Case No. CONC/83/1, 27 November 1985; *SEDITEX* v. *Madagascar (No. 2)*, ICSID Arbitral Tribunal, Case No. CONC/94/1, 19 July 1996; *TG World Petroleum Ltd* v. *Niger*, ICSID Arbitral Tribunal, Case No. CONC/03/1, 8 April 2005; *Togo Eléctricité* v. *Togo*, ICSID Arbitral Tribunal, Case No. CONC/05/1, 6 April 2005; *SFSAM* v. *Central African Republic*, ICSID Arbitral Tribunal, Case No. CONC/07/1, 13 August 2008.

RESOLVING INTERNATIONAL INVESTMENT DISPUTES 427

state, such as pre-shipment inspection services.[144] From the creation of ICSID in 1966 until 1987, all the claims that were submitted to ICSID tribunals were claims brought under concession contracts containing an ICSID arbitration clause.

Investors who have negotiated a concession contract with an arbitration clause may bring a claim under the contract, but such investors may also be able to present a claim under an applicable investment treaty, assuming that they can satisfy the relevant jurisdictional conditions, including that they are an 'investor' within the meaning of the investment treaty, and that they have an 'investment' that falls within the investment treaty's scope of protection.[145] The reasons why an investor may decide to present a claim under a BIT rather than under the contract will vary from case to case, but it may be, for instance, that the international commercial arbitration would be 'seated' in the host state of the investment, and therefore susceptible to the supervisory jurisdiction of that country's national courts, and the investor may have concerns that the involvement of those courts may create delays or difficulties for the investor's claim in international commercial arbitration.

Complex issues have arisen in several investment treaty claims where the respondent state has argued that the investment treaty dispute is in reality a contractual dispute, and that the investor has sought to present its contractual claims as claims under a BIT.[146] Investment treaty tribunals have typically concluded that the same conduct by a host state can give rise to claims for breach of contract as well as claims for breach of treaty;

---

[144] E.g., *RSM Production Corporation* v. *Grenada (Award)*, ICSID Arbitral Tribunal, Case No. ARB/05/14, 13 March 2009; see also the Libyan oil nationalization cases, which were claims under concession contracts: *BP* v. *Libya*, 53 ILR 297 (1977); *Libyan American Oil Company (LIAMCO)* v. *Libya*, (1977) 62 ILR 140; and *Texaco/Calasiatic* v. *Libya* (1977) 53 ILR 389 (on these cases, see Greenwood, above n. 65).

[145] E.g., the following ICSID claims were brought under BITs, although the underlying investment consisted at least in part of rights under a contractual agreement with the host state: *Compañía de Aguas del Alconquija SA and Vivendi Universal SA* v. *Argentine Republic (Award)*, (2004) 25 ILR 1, which concerned a concession contract for the supply of water services; *ADC Affiliate Ltd and ADC & ADMC Management Ltd* v. *Hungary*, ICSID Arbitral Tribunal, Case No. ARB/03/16, 2 October 2006, which concerned the construction of a new terminal at Budapest airport; and *SGS Société Générale de Surveillance SA* v. *Paraguay*, ICSID Arbitral Tribunal, Case No. ARB/07/29, Award of 10 February 2012, which arose out of a contract for the provision of pre-shipment inspection services.

[146] See, e.g., James Crawford, 'Treaty and Contract in Investment Arbitration', (2008) 24 *Arbitration International* 351; Yuval Shany, 'Contract Claims vs Treaty Claims: Mapping Conflicts between ICSID Decisions on Multisourced Investment Claims', (2005) 99 AJIL 835.

as the ICSID tribunal in *Impregilo SpA* v. *Pakistan* held, 'Even if the two perfectly coincide, they remain analytically distinct, and necessarily require different enquiries.'[147]

National courts

A further possibility for the settlement of investor–state disputes is for the investor to submit such disputes to a national court, which has the benefit of not requiring the consent of the disputing parties in order to take jurisdiction over the claim. There are, however, certain obstacles that need to be considered in referring investor–state disputes to national courts.

For instance, the national courts of the investor's home state, or the courts of a third state, may not be able to assume jurisdiction over a claim against a foreign sovereign state due to the operation of the rules of state immunity, which generally protect states from the jurisdiction of the courts of foreign states. Even though the doctrine of state immunity has been significantly eroded since the days of 'absolute' immunity, there are related doctrines, such as the 'act of state' doctrine, which may serve to render the actions and omissions of foreign states non-justiciable before national courts.[148] Although the application of these doctrines may differ from one country to another, these rules are likely to pose difficulties for an investor. This means that the national courts that would ordinarily have jurisdiction over a claim against a state are the courts of that state itself. And in a situation where an investor has not concluded a concession contract with the host state, which includes an arbitration clause, or where there is no applicable BIT, the national courts of the host state of the investment may be the only forum open to the investor to bring a claim without the assistance of the investor's state of nationality.

Even where there is an applicable BIT, it might be a requirement of the investor–state dispute settlement provision in that treaty that the claim is first submitted to the courts of the host state. For instance, Article 8(1) of the United Kingdom–Argentina BIT provides that where a dispute with regard to an investment which arises under the BIT has not been settled

---

[147] *Impregilo SpA* v. *Pakistan (Jurisdiction)*, ICSID Arbitral Tribunal, Case No. ARB/03/3, 22 April 2005, [258].

[148] See especially Hazel Fox, 'International Law and Restraints on the Exercise of Jurisdiction by National Courts of States', in Malcolm Evans (ed.), *International Law*, 3rd edn (Oxford University Press, 2010) 340.

RESOLVING INTERNATIONAL INVESTMENT DISPUTES 429

by negotiation, that dispute 'shall be submitted, at the request of one of the Parties to the dispute, to the decision of the competent tribunal of the Contracting Party in whose territory the investment was made'.[149] Under Article 8(2), the dispute can then only be submitted to international arbitration in the following circumstances:

> (a) if one of the Parties so request, in any of the following circumstances:
>> (i) where, after a period of eighteen months has elapsed from the moment when the dispute was submitted to the competent tribunal of the Contracting Party in whose territory the investment was made, the said tribunal has not given its final decision;
>> (ii) where the final decision of the aforementioned tribunal has been made but the Parties are still in dispute;
> (b) where the Contracting Party and the investor of the other Contracting Party have so agreed.[150]

Accordingly, in order to commence investor–state arbitration proceedings under the United Kingdom–Argentina BIT, an investor must, on the face of the BIT, first litigate in the courts of the host state for eighteen months, or have a final decision from those courts which has not settled the dispute (in the absence of any agreement to the contrary).[151]

Other BITs also provide that the investor may submit the dispute to the local courts, but that if this is done, it is taken to be a final choice of the investor in favour of the local courts over international arbitration. In the language of investment treaty arbitration, the provision operates as a 'fork in the road',[152] in the sense that the provision implements the *electa una via* principle.[153] So, Article 13 of the Australia–Argentina BIT provides in relevant part that:

> 1. Any dispute which arises between a Contracting Party and an investor of the other Contracting Party relating to an investment shall, if possible, be settled amicably. If the dispute cannot so be settled, it may be submitted, upon request of the investor, either to:

---

[149] United Kingdom–Argentina BIT, Art. 8(1).   [150] Ibid., Art. 8(2).

[151] Tribunals have reached differing views as to whether strict compliance with such provisions is in all cases necessary: cf. *BG Group plc* v. *Argentine Republic (Final Award)*, UNCITRAL, 24 December 2007; and *ICS Inspection and Control Services Ltd* v. *Argentine Republic (Jurisdiction)*, PCA, 10 February 2012.

[152] E.g., *Compañía de Aguas del Alconquija SA and Vivendi Universal SA* v. *Argentine Republic (Decision of Annulment)*, (2004) 6 ICSID Rep. 340, [36]–[43].

[153] On this principle, see especially Yuval Shany, *The Competing Jurisdictions of International Courts and Tribunals* (Oxford University Press, 2003), 212–17.

(a) the competent tribunal of the Contracting Party which has admitted the investment; or

(b) international arbitration in accordance with paragraph 3 of this Article.

2. Where an investor has submitted a dispute to the aforementioned competent tribunal of the Contracting Party which has admitted the investment or to international arbitration in accordance with paragraph 3 of this Article, this choice shall be final.[154]

Even where the local courts might be available to a foreign investor, there may be legal impediments to the submission of an investment dispute to the local courts, or reasons why the investor would be reluctant to follow this course. First, it is not necessarily the case that the investor will be able to frame a justiciable cause of action before the local courts. This will depend on the relevant measure that has been adopted by the host state, but the law of the host state might not, for instance, permit the investor to seek the judicial review of administrative decisions, and may not provide for any form of protection for property (such as the payment of compensation in the event of an expropriation). Where this is the case, it would not appear likely that the investor's claim before the local courts would meet with success. Second, where the cause of action does not exist as a matter of local law, but there is an applicable BIT, the BIT may set out the relevant claim (such as FET, or expropriation, as per the substantive standards of protection in the treaty). However, the obligations on the host state under the BIT may not have been implemented in domestic law, and the treaty itself may not be susceptible of direct application in the domestic legal system; this is the case in 'dualist' legal systems. Third, investors may also face challenges of a different order before the national courts of the host state. As Professor Salacuse has observed, 'local courts may lack judicial independence and might be subject to the control of the host government, depriving the investor of an impartial forum'; in addition, those courts 'may harbour prejudice towards foreign investors'.[155] A further consideration is that the court systems in certain developing countries are overburdened, with a heavy backlog of cases.[156] For these reasons, bringing proceedings before the local courts may not be an attractive option for the foreign investor.

---

[154] Australia–Argentina BIT, Art. 13(1), 13(2).   [155] Salacuse, above n. 24, 358.

[156] See, e.g., the complaints of the investor in *White Industries Australia Ltd* v. *Republic of India (Final Award)*, UNCITRAL, 30 November 2011.

Inter-state dispute settlement (diplomatic protection)

Where efforts to settle the dispute by negotiation have failed, in the absence of any agreement by the host state to submit the dispute to mediation, conciliation, or international arbitration, where the local courts have failed to provide a remedy, and where the investor is unable itself to present a claim under a BIT, the investor is left with the need to enlist the help of its state of nationality to seek a satisfactory settlement of the dispute with the host state.[157] This involves the investor's state of nationality deciding to 'espouse' the claim of the investor, and present it at the international level against the host state that has allegedly breached its international obligations in accordance with the rules of diplomatic protection.[158] The claim may be presented against the host state either by seeking resolution of the dispute through diplomatic channels; by invoking an inter-state dispute settlement provision in an applicable BIT (which would usually provide for the arbitration of inter-state disputes); or by submitting the claim to, for instance, the ICJ, assuming that it has jurisdiction over the dispute.

For many years diplomatic protection was the only means open to an individual to have his or her claim asserted against the state alleged to have committed an internationally wrongful act. It was historically associated with the practice of gunboat diplomacy, where powerful states would implement a blockade of the ports of the state having allegedly committed an internationally wrongful act towards the powerful state's nationals. States have in the past espoused a number of investment claims and submitted them to the PCIJ and ICJ,[159] although this has occurred relatively infrequently in recent years.

Despite the experience of states in exercising diplomatic protection and espousing claims of their nationals, this is not a preferred way of

---

[157] See, e.g., Salacuse, above n. 24, 358–9.

[158] Report of the International Law Commission, UN GAOR, 58th sess., Supp. No. 10, UN Doc. A/61/10 (1 May–9 June and 3 July–11 August 2006), Art. 1: '[D]iplomatic protection consists of the invocation by a State, through diplomatic action or other means of peaceful settlement, of the responsibility of another State for an injury caused by an internationally wrongful act of that State to a natural or legal person that is a national of the former State with a view to the implementation of such responsibility'.

[159] *Certain German Interests on Polish Upper Silesia (Germany v. Poland) (Merits)*, [1926] (ser. A) No. 7; and *Factory at Chorzów (Germany v. Poland) (Indemnity)*, [1928] (ser. A) No. 17; *Barcelona Traction, Light and Power Company Ltd (Belgium v. Spain) (Second Phase)*, [1970] ICJ Rep. 3; *Elettronica Sicula SpA (United States v. Italy)*, [1989] ICJ Rep. 15; and *Ahmadou Siado Diallo (Republic of Guinea v. Democratic Republic of Congo)*, [2011] ICJ Rep. 103.

432 CHESTER BROWN

settling investment disputes, for several reasons. First, the investor's state of nationality is not obliged to espouse the claim of one of its nationals; 'the decision to espouse a claim or not, and to pursue it vigorously or not, is completely within the discretion' of the investor's state of nationality,[160] which means that the investor has no guarantee that it will be offered any assistance at all. Second, a key difficulty with diplomatic protection is that it has the effect of 'politicizing' investment claims, as it becomes an inter-state dispute and has to be dealt with as part of the broader bilateral diplomatic relationship between the investor's state of nationality and the home state. This makes diplomatic protection claims unattractive for the investor's state of nationality, and investors also tend to dislike this feature of diplomatic protection claims, for the resolution of the investment dispute may become a bargaining chip in the bilateral relationship, and the investor's state of nationality may decide not to press the claim if it would jeopardize other interests (such as co-operation on security, or trade).[161] This leads to a third problem with diplomatic protection claims, namely that once the investor's state of nationality has espoused the claim, 'it effectively "owns" it', meaning that it 'controls how the claim will be made, what settlement it will accept, and whether any portion of the settlement will be paid to the aggrieved national'.[162] And, finally, the espousal of diplomatic protection claims invariably leads to an increased burden for a state in its diplomatic work. For these reasons, investors as well as states tend to view diplomatic protection of investment claims as a last resort.

Concluding remarks

There are a number of conclusions that can be drawn regarding the relationship between the substantive field of international investment law and the methods of settling investor–state disputes.

The first conclusion is that the resolution of investment treaty disputes by international arbitration has led to the substantive development of international investment law. As was noted above, most BITs are rather skeletal in their content, and leave much to be interpreted and applied by investment treaty tribunals. Although there have been a number of high-profile instances where investment treaty tribunals have reached divergent conclusions, the decisions that have emanated from investment treaty tribunals have arguably led to the creation of what might be described

---

[160] Salacuse, above n. 24, 358.   [161] Ibid.
[162] Ibid.; see also *Mavrommatis Palestine Concessions*, [1924] PCIJ (ser. A) No. 2, 12.

as a form of '*jurisprudence constante*'. One investment treaty tribunal has expressed the following view on the relevance of past decisions of other tribunals:

> The Tribunal is not bound by previous decisions of ICSID tribunals. At the same time, it is of the opinion that it should pay due regard to earlier decisions of such tribunals. The Tribunal is further of the view that, unless there are compelling reasons to the contrary, it ought to follow solutions established in a series of consistent cases, comparable to the case at hand, but subject of course to the specifics of a given treaty and of the circumstances of the actual case. By doing so, it will meet its duty to seek to contribute to the harmonious development of investment law and thereby to meet the legitimate expectations of the community of states and investors towards certainty of the rule of law.[163]

The second conclusion that can be drawn is that although there are various methods of settling investment disputes, the method that has been included in the overwhelming majority of BITs is international arbitration, and there have been 450 known investment treaty claims since the first such claim was launched in 1987.[164] There are various 'alternative' methods of settling investor–state disputes – such as negotiation, mediation, and conciliation – and each of these methods may be more appropriate than international arbitration, for much the same reasons that they are often preferred in the context of domestic disputes: they are usually more flexible, more efficient, and less expensive methods of settling disputes, and ordinarily enable the interests of both parties to be taken into account in seeking a resolution, rather than adopting a 'winner-take-all' approach, which is often the hallmark of formal and binding forms of third-party adjudication. Further alternatives also exist, as disputing parties can agree to one of the various hybrid forms of dispute settlement, such as 'med-arb', and 'arb-med' (which, respectively, essentially involve the disputing parties referring their dispute to mediation first, and then to arbitration if mediation fails; or, alternatively, to arbitration, but with the arbitrator assisting in facilitating the settlement of the dispute).[165] Yet – with the exception of negotiation – these methods of settling investment disputes have not been embraced by investors.

---

[163] *Bayindir* v. *Pakistan (Award)*, ICSID Arbitral Tribunal, Case No. ARB/03/29, 27 August 2009, [145].

[164] *Asian Agricultural Products Ltd* v. *Sri Lanka*, (1997) 4 ICSID Rep. 246.

[165] On 'med-arb', see especially Nigel Blackaby and Constantine Partasides with Alan Redfern and Martin Hunter, *Redfern and Hunter on International Arbitration*, 5th edn (Oxford University Press, 2009), 47–8. For a discussion of 'arb-med', see that in Gabrielle

The settlement of disputes by international commercial arbitration is also a possibility, although this is only open to those investors who have entered into a concession contract with the host state and included an arbitration clause for the settlement of disputes. The availability of national courts presents another option for the settlement of investment disputes, but they are not an ideal forum for a number of reasons. There may be difficulties in framing an appropriate cause of action before the local courts of the host state, and the investor may also have concerns about the impartiality or independence of the local courts of the host state, as well as the speed at which justice is administered in that country.

Finally, investors (and states alike) are unlikely to wish to revert to a situation where investment disputes are resolved at the inter-state level by diplomatic protection claims. Indeed, one of the benefits of investors having direct recourse to international arbitration was that states no longer had to become involved in investment disputes, and the investment dispute was, in most cases, separated from the bilateral relationship and depoliticized.

It follows from this that until such time as another, more preferable method of settling investment disputes presents itself, it is difficult to see what form of dispute settlement might replace international arbitration as an acceptable alternative in all cases. It is clear that in the absence of any investor–state dispute settlement provision in an investment treaty, the default option – assuming that the dispute is not settled by negotiation, or before any national courts – is for the investor to request the diplomatic protection of its state of nationality. But this solution – for the reasons described above – would not seem to be desirable from any of the stakeholders' perspectives.

This chapter has considered the relationship between international investment law and the methods that are employed to resolve investment disputes. It has examined the contribution of investment treaty tribunals to the development of international investment law, and has also reviewed the various available methods of settling investment disputes. The practice of arbitral tribunals is recognized as being influential in contributing to the body of substantive rules, but the ability of investors to submit disputes to international arbitration has proved to be controversial.

Kaufmann-Kohler, 'When Arbitrators Facilitate Settlement: Towards a Transnational Standard', (2009) 25 *Arbitration International* 187.

Questions remain, however, as to what other method might be employed for the satisfactory settlement of investment disputes. It is apparent that there are complex policy issues to be addressed by states as they consider their ongoing and future investment treaty and free trade agreement negotiations.

19

Dispute settlement options for the protection of nationals abroad

NATALIE KLEIN

The treatment and protection of nationals abroad is an issue that has long been of concern in international law. Traditionally referred to as the treatment of aliens, international law has articulated standards to which states would be held in dealing with the business interests and personal safety of foreigners within their borders. The violation of these standards has resulted on occasions in considerable tension between the states concerned.[1] The claims of nationals, taken up by their states, have been redressed in a variety of ways, and could lead to aggressive tactics, including the use of force. Litigation, particularly in the form of claims commissions and arbitrations, was historically promoted as an alternative to the use of force for dealing with the claims of nationals mistreated abroad.

In considering how litigation is currently used for the protection of nationals abroad, it is important to identify at the outset the categories of claim that are likely to arise. This step is essential because international law has developed beyond broad standards on the treatment of aliens into complex rules reflecting the different activities in which individuals engage in overseas jurisdictions. Moreover, account must be taken of the more particular, or detailed, standards of treatment that have now emerged. Having established the categories of claim, it is then possible to assess the avenues available to address harm suffered by nationals abroad. These options are quite elaborate, and are commonly linked to the substantive body of law offering different protections. Beyond this, states have a right of diplomatic protection – the right of a state to take up a national's claim and assert that right against another state as if it was

---

[1] See Enrico Milano, 'Diplomatic Protection and Human Rights before the International Court of Justice: Re-fashioning Tradition?', (2004) 35 *Netherlands Yearbook of International Law* 85, 86–7.

DISPUTE SETTLEMENT OPTIONS   437

its own.[2] The right of diplomatic protection is predominantly asserted at the point when a state is proceeding to international judicial avenues.[3]

Ultimately, litigation plays an important part in resolving disputes over the protection of nationals abroad, but it will be seen that inter-state litigation features less prominently than other forms of adjudication or arbitration. It could therefore be posited that the ascent of individuals as subjects of international law has reduced reliance on inter-state litigation for the protection of nationals abroad. This approach reduces diplomatic tension that may otherwise ensue from direct confrontations between the states concerned. Further, the availability of a remedy may be construed as a fundamental dimension to human rights protections,[4] and it is therefore more appropriate for individuals to pursue their own dispute settlement

---

[2] The Permanent Court of International Justice articulated this right of diplomatic protection as follows:

> By taking up the case of one of its subjects and by resorting to diplomatic action or international judicial proceedings on his behalf, a State is in reality asserting its own rights – its right to ensure, in the person of its subjects, respect for the rules of international law. The question, therefore, whether the present dispute originates in an injury to a private interest, which in point of fact is the case in many international disputes, is irrelevant from this standpoint. Once a State has taken up a case on behalf of one of its subjects before an international tribunal, in the eyes of the latter the State is sole claimant.

Mavrommatis Palestine Concessions Case (Greece v. *United Kingdom) (Jurisdiction)*, [1924] PCIJ (ser. A) No. 2, 12. The International Law Commission adopted a set of draft articles on diplomatic protection in 2006. See Report of the International Law Commission, UN GAOR, 58th sess., Supp. No. 10, UN Doc. A/61/10 (1 May–9 June and 3 July–11 August 2006) (ILC Articles on Diplomatic Protection), [13–100]. Art. 1 of those articles refers to 'diplomatic protection consist[ing] of the invocation by a State, through diplomatic action or other means of peaceful settlement, of the responsibility of another State for an injury caused by an internationally wrongful act of that State to a natural or legal person that is a national of the former State with a view to the implementation of such responsibility'. Ibid., 24. This definition was accepted as reflecting customary international law in *Ahmadou Sadio Diallo (Republic of Guinea* v. *Democratic Republic of the Congo) (Preliminary Objections)*, [2007] ICJ Rep. 582 (*Diallo – Preliminary Objections*), [39].

[3] See Annemarieke Künzli, 'Exercising Diplomatic Protection: The Fine Line between Litigation, Démarches and Consular Assistance', (2006) 66 *ZaöRV* 321, 323. The ILC has taken the view that the line between diplomatic protection and consular assistance is unclear. See ILC Articles on Diplomatic Protection, 27. The ILC has noted, however, that diplomatic protection tends to reflect a remedial function, whereas, in seeking to stop nationals being the victims of internationally wrongful acts, consular assistance is primarily preventive. Ibid.

[4] This right is enshrined in Art. 2(3) of the International Covenant on Civil and Political Rights (opened for signature 16 December 1966, entered into force 23 March 1976), 999 UNTS 171 (ICCPR).

438   NATALIE KLEIN

channels. In either instance, litigation provides an important, albeit last resort, option for resolving claims of nationals harmed abroad.

Categories of claim

The treatment and protection of nationals abroad arise in diverse contexts. As a starting point, all individuals are now internationally recognized as the bearers of human rights protections. The International Court of Justice (ICJ) has recognized that there has been an expansion in the range of protections offered to individuals as follows:

> [O]wing to the substantive development of international law over recent decades in respect of the rights it accords to individuals, the scope *ratione materiae* of diplomatic protection, originally limited to alleged violations of the minimum standards of treatment of aliens, has subsequently widened to include, *inter alia*, internationally guaranteed human rights.[5]

Human rights are thus clearly a source of rights for individuals and can be used as a reference point for challenging their treatment at the hands of a foreign government.

By way of example, members of the so-called Bali Nine, who challenged their death sentences before the Indonesian Constitutional Court, referred to human rights standards enshrined in the International Covenant on Civil and Political Rights (ICCPR). The Bali Nine were a group of young Australians arrested in Bali, Indonesia, for attempting to traffic large quantities of heroin into Australia.[6] Some of the drug couriers as well as the two ringleaders of the operation were sentenced to death.[7] While the challenge to the Constitutional Court was necessarily based on the terms

---

[5] *Diallo – Preliminary Objections*, [39].

[6] For discussion of various legal aspects of their arrest, prosecution, and sentencing, see Lorraine Finlay, 'Exporting the Death Penalty? Reconciling International Police Cooperation and the Abolition of the Death Penalty in Australia', (2011) 33 *Sydney Law Review* 95, 96–9.

[7] Andrew Chan and Myuran Sukumaran, the purported ringleaders, were both sentenced to death. Scott Rush, one of the drug couriers, was initially sentenced to a life imprisonment. This sentence was then changed to a death sentence. See Ronli Sifris, 'Balancing Abolitionism and Cooperation on the World's Scale: The Case of the Bali Nine', (2007) 35 *Federal Law Review* 81, 83. In his final appeal in 2011, Rush was successful in having his death sentence commuted. Matt Brown, 'Scott Rush Escapes Death Penalty', *ABC News* (online), 27 May 2011, available at www.abc.net.au/news/stories/2011/05/10/3213037.htm. Si Yi Chen, Tach Duc Thanh Nguyen, and Matthew Norman, who were arrested in a hotel where the drug couriers had been prepared for their trip, also initially received life sentences, which were then upgraded to death sentences, only to have their life sentences reinstated in 2008. Natalie Zerial, 'Decision No. 2–3/PUU-V/2007 [2007] (Indonesian Constitutional Court)', (2007) 14 *Australian International Law Journal* 217, 218–19.

of the Indonesian Constitution, the arguments of the applicants extended into the standards and meaning of the right to life as articulated and interpreted under the ICCPR.[8] Treatment in detention and due process rights in any country can also be benchmarked against international human rights standards during national court proceedings.

International human rights standards could also be invoked to the extent that the treatment of nationals abroad entails discriminatory action on the part of the state. Policies may be put in place that deliberately single out particular racial or national groups. It may be the case that the members of a minority group singled out in this regard are in any event nationals of the state concerned, so that their situation is of less relevance for this particular examination. The treatment of these minority groups is of course more pertinent if they still hold the nationality of their state of origin, and it is more complex if they are dual nationals[9] or, alternatively, stateless.[10]

Another category of claims is derived from foreign investors. Indeed, many of the early claims relating to the treatment of aliens concerned how businesses and other investments had been harmed by the state. This harm might be a result of expropriation or nationalization of business interests, or of changes in laws that prejudice, sometimes deliberately, the operation of the business. Failures by states to meet their financial commitments in relation to foreign investments have been, and continue to be, particularly problematic. Investment protection has evolved into a very distinct body of law in its own right within international law.[11]

Claims may also arise from nationals abroad in the context of armed conflicts. While the laws of naval warfare, for example, have typically protected the interests of neutrals, especially their commercial interests,[12]

---

[8] *Decision Number 2–3/PUU-V/2007 (Petition by Scott Anthony Rush)*, [2007] Constitutional Court of the Republic of Indonesia, 93, 100–2, available at www.mahkamahkonstitusi. go.id/putusan/putusan_sidang_eng_PUTUSAN%202_PUU_V_07%20%20Hukuman% 20Mati%20(Eng).pdf. For discussion see Zerial, above n. 7.

[9] This group can only be assisted by the state of the nationality with which they have the predominant ties against the other state of nationality. ILC Articles on Diplomatic Protection, Art. 7.

[10] If individuals are stateless then there is no state to which they can turn to take up their claims against the state treating them in contravention of international human rights standards. In this situation, the human rights mechanisms available for conduct within a particular state would be most relevant. These are discussed in more detail in Chapter 16 in this volume.

[11] See further Chapter 18 in this volume.

[12] See, e.g., Louise Doswald-Beck (ed.), *San Remo Manual on International Law Applicable in Armed Conflicts at Sea* (Cambridge University Press, 1995), Arts. 67–71, Arts. 146–52.

440 NATALIE KLEIN

the more common situation today is that individuals caught up in an armed conflict will be accorded protections as civilians.[13] The nationality of the individuals may not be a central issue. It becomes more relevant when belligerent states choose to take actions against foreign nationals holding the nationality of their enemy state. Those actions might entail detention, expulsion, or confiscation of property. An example is the steps taken by both Ethiopia and Eritrea against the nationals of the other state when a border conflict erupted between these neighbours in 1998. In that conflict, Ethiopia pursued a policy of mass expulsion, not only of all Eritreans within Ethiopia but also of Ethiopians of Eritrean national origin.[14] These claims were ultimately resolved by a claims commission established by the peace accords ending the border conflict.[15]

A final grouping of claims is broad, and is intended to cover all nationals abroad who require consular assistance. Consular assistance is of course relevant to anyone caught up in an armed conflict overseas, or who has a foreign investment harmed, or who is being subjected to human rights violations. However, consular assistance is also germane if a national loses their passport, is a victim of crime, or is caught up in a tsunami, earthquake, or other natural disaster. These diverse scenarios prompt a range of responses from the state of nationality, which may be dependent on their resources, or the level of representation in another state, or the relationship enjoyed between the states concerned. The more controversial area in this regard has been consular assistance for individuals who are arrested or detained while overseas. This focus is obvious from the series of cases brought against the United States in relation to the Vienna Convention on Consular Relations.[16]

---

[13] These protections are codified in Geneva Convention (IV) relative to the Protection of Civilian Persons in Time of War (signed on 12 August 1949, entered into force 21 October 1950), 75 UNTS 287, and elaborated on in Protocol Additional to the Geneva Conventions of 12 August 1949, and Relating to the Protection of Victims of International Armed Conflicts (signed on 8 June 1977, entered into force 7 December 1978), 1125 UNTS 3.

[14] For discussion see Wendy Pitcher Wilson, 'The Deportation of "Eritreans" from Ethiopia: Human Rights Violations Tolerated by the International Community', (1998) 24 *North Carolina Journal of International Law and Commercial Regulation* 451.

[15] Agreement between the Government of the Federal Democratic Republic of Ethiopia and the Government of the State of Eritrea, 12 December 2000, Eritrea–Ethiopia, 40 ILM 260 (2000 Agreement), Art. 5. The work of the EECC is available through the Permanent Court of Arbitration, available at www.pca-cpa.org/showpage.asp?pag_id=1151.

[16] Vienna Convention on Consular Relations (opened for signature 24 April 1963, entered into force 19 March 1967), 596 UNTS 261. The cases were *Vienna Convention on Consular Relations (Paraguay v. United States of America) (Provisional Measures)*, [1998] ICJ Rep. 248; *LaGrand (Germany v. United States of America) (Merits)*, [2001] ICJ Rep. 466; *Avena*

In relation to these diverse categories of claim, it should be acknowledged that individual circumstances necessarily affect what body of law is available and/or relevant for the protection of that individual. A national may generally rely on protections recognized under customary international law, but there may also be regional obligations or other treaty requirements potentially relevant as between the foreign national and the state that has failed in its duties of protection.

The status of the individual may also be relevant. A national abroad who is a diplomat is therefore covered by a series of international rights and obligations relevant to the diplomatic corps. Someone who is a member of a national military force, or who is a peacekeeper or otherwise associated with the work of the United Nations, will also have other protections by virtue of their status. For example, a peacekeeper will likely be covered by a status of forces agreement in place between the United Nations and the host country of the peacekeeping operation.[17] The peacekeeper would also potentially be protected by standards set out in the UN Convention on the Safety of United Nations and Associated Personnel.[18]

There is clearly no 'one size fits all' approach for states when responding to the treatment and protection of nationals abroad. As a result, there are many avenues available to both the individuals concerned as well as the states of nationality in deciding how to pursue claims when rights are alleged to have been violated.

Avenues available for redressing claims

When considering the avenues available to protect nationals abroad, it can be acknowledged in the first instance that states may seek to resort to force.[19] Certainly the United States claimed that it had a right of self-defence in its invasion of Grenada as well as its invasion of Panama in the 1980s, because the United States was seeking to protect its nationals who

---

and Other Mexican Nationals (Mexico v. United States of America) (Judgment), [2004] ICJ Rep. 12.

[17] A model status of forces agreement was adopted by the General Assembly in 1990: Model UN Status of Forces Agreement, A/45/594. The rights and obligations of UN employees and agents are also set out in the Convention on the Privileges and Immunities of the United Nations (signed on 13 February 1946, entered into force 17 September 1946), 21 UNTS 1418.

[18] Convention on the Safety of United Nations and Associated Personnel (signed 9 December 1994, entered into force 15 January 1999), 2051 UNTS 363.

[19] The ILC in its articles excluded this possibility by reference to states resorting to 'peaceful means' for the purposes of diplomatic protection. ILC Articles on Diplomatic Protection, Art. 1. See discussion in Milano, above n. 1, 93.

had been harmed there, or were perceived to be threatened with harm.[20] Forcible rescue missions have also been undertaken or contemplated when nationals are being held hostage in another state.[21] Examples of such practice include the attempted rescue mission by the United States of its nationals held hostage in its diplomatic and consular premises in Iran,[22] the French rescue of nationals held by Somali pirates,[23] and the Israeli mission to free hostages held at the Entebbe airport in Uganda.[24]

Most commonly, there is an expectation that any national injured or harmed abroad will first pursue remedies with national authorities and before local judiciaries. This requirement is consistent with respect for state sovereignty, and is reflected in the rule of exhaustion of local remedies.[25] Demanding that foreign nationals seek redress within the state concerned prior to an international claim being pursued is consistent with respect for the sovereignty of a state and non-interference in the domestic affairs of a state. If a foreign national has suffered an injury then the state should be afforded the opportunity to correct or otherwise respond before the issue escalates into an international incident.

Where individuals have the opportunity to pursue claims to international human rights courts or international human rights committees, then a prerequisite of those claims is that local remedies are exhausted.[26] There are exceptions to this requirement – such as undue delay, that there are no reasonably available local remedies to provide redress, and that the

---

[20] See, e.g., Ved P. Nanda, 'The Validity of United States Intervention in Panama under International Law', (1990) 84 AJIL 494; Tom J. Farer, 'Panama: Beyond the Charter Paradigm', (1990) 84 AJIL 503.

[21] See generally Natalino Ronzitti, *Rescuing Nationals Abroad through Military Coercion and Intervention on the Grounds of Humanity* (Dordrecht: Martinus Nijhoff, 1985).

[22] *Case Concerning United States Diplomatic and Consular Staff in Tehran (United States of America v. Iran)*, [1980] ICJ Rep. 3, 43–4. See also Kristen E. Eichensehr, 'Defending Nationals Abroad: Assessing the Lawfulness of Forcible Hostage Rescues', (2008) 48 *Virginia Journal of International Law* 451, 453–6.

[23] See, e.g., Xan Rice and Lizzy Davies, 'Hostage Killed as French Storm Yacht Held by Somali Pirates', *Guardian*, 11 April, 2009, available at www.guardian.co.uk/world/2009/apr/10/hostage-killed-as-french-storm-pirate-yacht.

[24] See Eleanor C. McDowell, 'United Nations: Security Council Debate and Draft Resolutions Concerning the Operation to Rescue Hijacked Hostages at the Entebbe Airport', (1976) 15 ILM 1224.

[25] This requirement was articulated in Art. 7 of the ILC Articles on Diplomatic Protection.

[26] E.g., First Optional Protocol to the International Covenant on Civil and Political Rights (opened for signature 16 December 1966, entered into force 23 March 1976), 999 UNTS 302, Art. 5(2)(b); European Convention on Human Rights (opened for signature 4 November 1950, entered into force 3 September 1953), 213 UNTS 222, Arts. 26 and 27(3).

injured person is manifestly excluded from pursuing local remedies.[27] It is at least notable that individual access to international human rights courts or committees reflects a willingness on behalf of states to create judicial, or judicial-like, forums to respond to human rights violations.[28] The use of these forums for individuals may be limited, however, if the individual is in a region not covered by a regional human rights mechanism,[29] or the state violating the individual's rights is not party to the relevant human rights treaty or, if a party, has excluded recourse to third-party dispute settlement.[30]

To illustrate this point, there is the case of Jock Palfreeman, an Australian arrested in Sofia, Bulgaria, and convicted of murder with hooliganism.[31] As Bulgaria is a member of the Council of Europe and a party to the European Convention on Human Rights,[32] Palfreeman has claimed that there were due process violations in the conduct of his trial,[33] and may ultimately seek to refer his case to the European Court of Human Rights if his appeals before Bulgarian courts are unsuccessful. For the purposes of the European human rights system, Palfreeman's nationality as an Australian is irrelevant, because the Court is concerned with actions that occur on the territory of its member states.[34] As Bulgaria's judicial system has been subjected to considerable criticism for its corruption and failures in due process,[35] it is a useful, if not vital, avenue for Palfreeman to pursue. By contrast, Van Nguyen, an Australian arrested and convicted on a drug trafficking charge carrying a mandatory death sentence in Singapore, did not have access to any regional human rights court, or to any UN human rights committee.[36]

---

[27] ILC Articles on Diplomatic Protection, Art. 15.

[28] See discussion in Chapter 16 in this volume.

[29] Notably Asia-Pacific and the Middle East.

[30] States may enter reservations to the relevant clause in the human rights treaty, or not become party to the optional protocol that otherwise provides access to a committee monitoring compliance with the instrument.

[31] For discussion see Natalie Klein, 'David Hicks, Stern Hu, Scott Rush, Jock Palfreeman and the Legal Parameters of Australia's Protection of its Citizens Abroad', (2011) 35 *Melbourne University Law Review* 134, 154–7.

[32] Bulgaria ratified the European Convention on Human Rights on 7 September 1992.

[33] Simon Palfreeman, 'Father's Summing Up of the Case', 3 December 2009, available at www.abc.net.au/news/documents/2009/20091203_palfreeman.pdf.

[34] European Convention on Human Rights, Art. 1 (referring to 'everyone within their jurisdiction').

[35] See, e.g., Juanita Riaño, Finn Heinrich, and Robin Hodess, 'Global Corruption Barometer', report, Transparency International, 2009, 6.

[36] For discussion, see Li-Ann Thio, 'The Death Penalty as Cruel and Inhuman Punishment before the Singapore High Court? Customary Human Rights Norms, Constitutional

444 NATALIE KLEIN

While the national seeks to exhaust their local remedies, the state of their nationality may undertake diplomatic démarches.[37] Although a right of diplomatic protection does not arise until local remedies are exhausted, the state of the affected individual may communicate with the state concerned to ensure, for example, that any trial is pursued promptly. In the case of an Australian, David Hicks, who was imprisoned in Guantánamo Bay, the Australian Attorney-General at the time sought assurances from the United States that it would not seek the death penalty in Hicks's case, that Australia would be able to seek his extradition to Australia to serve any sentence, that Hicks would have confidential access to his lawyer and that Australian officials would be permitted to monitor his trial.[38] The United Kingdom went further and sought the release of its nationals from Guantánamo Bay.[39] The relief afforded to individuals is clearly dependent on the relationship between the countries involved, as well as the state's particular concern for the individuals at issue.[40]

Nationals who are injured or harmed abroad may also benefit from consular assistance. Article 36(1) of the Vienna Convention on Consular Relations requires that states inform a detained individual of their right to contact their consulate, and that the state arresting or detaining an individual notify the consulate of that individual. Article 36(2) then requires states to give full effect to this obligation for the purposes intended. While duties of notifying or informing may not seem very significant, in some circumstances they can be the difference between life and death.

The case of Angel Breard, a Paraguayan national arrested in the United States for a capital offence and never informed of his right to contact his consulate, provides a poignant example. Rather than plea bargain, Breard chose to confess on the stand because in Paraguay it helps to throw

---

Formalism and the Supremacy of Domestic Law in Public Prosecutor v. Nguyen Tuong Van (2004)', (2004) 4 *Oxford University Commonwealth Law Journal* 213.

[37] Künzli, above n. 3, 323.

[38] Natalie Klein and Lise Barry, 'A Human Rights Perspective on Diplomatic Protection: David Hicks and His Dual Nationality', (2007) 13 *Australian Journal of Human Rights* 1, 17–18.

[39] 'Timeline: Guantánamo Bay Britons', *BBC News* (online), 27 January 2005, available at http://news.bbc.co.uk/2/hi/uk_news/3545709.stm. See also Klein, above n. 32, 140.

[40] The British practice can be contrasted to the Chinese attitude vis-à-vis Uighur detainees held in Guantánamo Bay. Even though the United States determined that many of them in fact posed no threat, they could not be returned to China because China considered them to be terrorists and the individuals concerned feared persecution if they were returned to China. See David Johnston, 'Uighurs Leave Guantánamo for Palau', 31 October 2009, available at www.nytimes.com/2009/11/01/world/asia/01uighurs.html.

yourself on the mercy of the court.[41] In the United States, it ensured that he was convicted and ultimately executed. Paraguay challenged the United States' violation of consular rights before the International Court of Justice (ICJ), arguing that if such assistance had been available then Paraguayan consular officials could have explained how the US criminal justice system operates.[42] An early guilty plea might have resulted in a life sentence rather than a death sentence.

The obligations under the Vienna Convention on Consular Relations are then elaborated on by some states through bilateral treaties. Australia and China have entered into such an agreement. The reasons for doing so included ensuring improved notification of the arrest or detention of Australian nationals, clarity around the treatment of Australian nationals of Chinese ethnic origin who were also born in China, and clarifying rights of access of consular officials to arrested or detained Australian nationals.[43] The United States has also entered into more than seventy bilateral agreements, which frequently include obligations regarding notifying consular offices if a national is detained by one of the states concerned.[44]

Through each of these points, what may be illustrated is that there is a variety of avenues available to ameliorate or redress the treatment and protection of nationals abroad. As such, inter-state litigation is obviated through the availability of other means of resolving claims. The term *inter-state* litigation is used quite deliberately in this instance. Individuals accessing regional human rights courts or international human rights committees could fall within international litigation broadly understood.

Equally, when we consider the protection of foreign investors then there is again a lack of examples of inter-state litigation. On the other hand, there is an extremely vibrant international arbitration practice around investment treaty disputes. The development of bilateral investment treaties, as

---

[41] See Linda Jane Springrose, 'Strangers in a Strange Land: The Rights of Non-Citizens under Article 36 of the Vienna Convention on Consular Relations', (1999) 14 *Georgetown Immigration Law Journal* 185, 195.

[42] Application of the Republic of Paraguay, 3 April 1998, available at www.icj-cij.org/docket/files/99/7183.pdf.

[43] Agreement on Consular Relations between Australia and the People's Republic of China (signed 8 September 1999, entered into force 15 September 2000), 2169 UNTS 494; Joint Standing Committee on Treaties, Parliament of Australia, Report 28: Fourteen Treaties tabled on 12 October 1999 (1999), 99–100.

[44] United States Department of State, Consular Notification and Access, 3 September 2010, available at http://travel.state.gov/pdf/cna/CNA_Manual_3d_Edition.pdf, 69–72 (listing the countries with bilateral agreements containing provisions on consular notification and access).

NATALIE KLEIN

well as free or preferential trading agreements with investment chapters, has empowered individuals (natural or juridical persons) to assert their rights directly against the host state. This dispute settlement mechanism is not premised on any requirement of exhaustion of local remedies. Rather, the bilateral investment treaty may specify that an investor has a choice of the local courts or international arbitration and once one option is selected it precludes recourse to the other. These are referred to as the 'fork in the road' clauses.[45]

The sophisticated legal system that has developed around investor–state disputes arguably reflects international recognition of the utility of judicial mechanisms to resolve claims arising from the treatment of investments. The availability of international arbitration is an integral form of protection; and may be viewed as important as the substantive rules of protection.

A final avenue in terms of redressing the claims of nationals mistreated abroad is through the role of civil society. Activist groups, particularly through the use of social media, can have an important effect on influencing political opinion at home and abroad. As government decision making on how to address the claims of their nationals abroad can be decisive as to the level of protection afforded, this sort of political pressure may be an important factor. In the context of armed conflict, the role of the International Committee of the Red Cross (ICRC) is essential in ensuring that prisoners of war are accorded international standards of treatment, and the ICRC may also have a role in monitoring and advocating in relation to the detention and expulsion of foreign nationals during times of armed conflict.

The above discussion has indicated that *inter-state* litigation may ultimately not be essential in light of the variety of mechanisms and requirements in place to resolve claims. The availability of regional human rights courts and international commissions, as well as the investor–state dispute settlement mechanism, do stand out as areas where international litigation has clearly been identified as a useful means of dispute settlement and access to these mechanisms has been devolved to the individuals concerned. Although state engagement in establishing or permitting access to these avenues remains critical, the referral to procedures other than direct state-to-state confrontation would have undoubted political utility.

---

[45] For discussion on the use of local remedies in relation to investment disputes, see Christoph Schreuer, 'Calvo's Grandchildren: The Return of Local Remedies in Investment Arbitration', (2005) 4 *Law and Practice of International Courts and Tribunals* 1.

As such, states have a clear interest in promoting the use of alternative avenues for resolving the variety of claims.

The role of claims commissions

Among the potential avenues available to individuals injured when overseas, access to a claims commission has proven an important tool to resolve disputes. The creation of claims commissions through an inter-state agreement has empowered individuals to seek redress for injuries suffered at the hands of a foreign government.[46] These claims commissions have often been established between the states concerned at a point when there was a critical mass of complaints requiring resolution.[47] Sometimes states would opt for lump-sum settlements to avoid any drawn-out commission proceedings.[48] The use of claims commissions could be seen as a de facto form of inter-state litigation, given the crucial state role in establishing these commissions for individuals to use.

Why states would opt for the establishment of a claims commission is a complex question. In reviewing the past practice of international claims settlements, Bederman has observed:

> Aggrieved states seeking compensation for their nationals in the aftermath of hostilities or revolutionary events typically have constituted these claims institutions. With a few notable exceptions, stronger nations have imposed them upon weaker ones. Although the terms of many of the treaties establishing the claims settlements were nominally reciprocal (that is, nationals of both parties could bring claims), in practice, this was rarely the case.[49]

In this regard, claims commissions could be perceived as victor's justice.

---

[46] The 1794 Jay Treaty included two claims commissions, one addressing vessel seizures by the United Kingdom or French privateers, and another dealing with debts owed to the United Kingdom. See further Chapter 6 in this volume.

[47] Bederman has defined international claims commissions as:

> an arbitration (1) established by agreement of two or more States, (2) to adjust a class of claims within a specified competence, (3) brought or espoused by nationals of the parties, and which (4) actually rendered an award on some or all of those claims. (David J. Bederman, 'The United Nations Compensation Commission and the Tradition of International Claims Settlement', (1994) 27 *NYU Journal of International Law* 1, n. 2).

[48] This practice has been thoroughly addressed in Burns H. Weston et al., *International Claims: Their Settlement by Lump Sum Agreements* 1975–1995 (Dordrecht: Martinus Nijhoff, 1999).

[49] Bederman, above n. 47, 3.

448   NATALIE KLEIN

One early example of this practice concerned Mexico, one of the states most frequently engaged in this process.[50] Mexico's engagement has been variously attributed to its revolutionary past, an assertive northern neighbour, and being the home of many European investments.[51] The United States and Mexico undertook claims commission processes in 1839, 1868, and 1923. Many US nationals had business interests in Mexico and complaints were frequently made to the US State Department about their treatment throughout the 1830s.[52] Mexico's economic crisis in the 1830s led to claims being raised by the United Kingdom and France, as well as the United States.[53] Some of the US claims were settled by the 1839 commission, but unredressed claims continued to be a source of tension. Also relevant in US–Mexican relations at the time was conflict over the boundary, and the US interest in expanding the Texas boundary into Mexico.[54] With the failure to resolve outstanding claims of US nationals in Mexico, the United States declared war on Mexico in 1846. Obtaining reparations for US nationals was cited as the prime reason for the war, rather than any expansionist agenda.[55] A further claims commission was thus established after the war. The power dynamics existing between these states at the relevant time lends weight to Bederman's characterization of claims settlement practice as 'coercive, unilateral, and fundamentally inequitable'.[56]

Estimates of the number of international claims commissions that have existed vary, depending on the characteristics ascribed to any particular proceeding. Approximately eighty international claims commissions operated during the 1800s, with another thirty or so in place in the first half of the 1900s.[57] Following the Second World War there was less reliance on this mechanism, particularly because of perceived deficiencies in eventually resolving the claims concerned, the length of time taken, and the perceived inequities between the parties involved.

The circumstances leading to some of the more recent claims commissions have been varied. First, the Iran–US Claims Tribunal was established as part of a broader settlement enshrined in the Algiers Declarations,

---

[50] Mexico was party to ten claims processes. John R. Crook, 'Thoughts on Mass Claims Processes', (2005) 99 *American Society of International Law Proceedings* 80, 80.
[51] Bederman, above n. 47, 5. See also Crook, above n. 50, 80; Peter M. Jonas, 'William Parrott, American Claims, and the Mexican War', (1992) 12 *Journal of the Early Republic* 213, 213.
[52] Jonas, above n. 51, 223.   [53] Ibid., 221–2.   [54] Ibid., 233.
[55] 'President Polk's War Message', ibid., 237.
[56] Bederman, above note 47, 6. John Crook has referred to them as 'offering "rough justice"'. Crook, above n. 50, 80.
[57] Crook, above n. 50, 80.

which secured the release of US hostages held in Iran and unblocked Iranian assets that had been frozen by a number of countries.[58] The establishment of the tribunal was necessary to resolve outstanding claims by US nationals against Iran and vice versa, as well as claims *ex contractu* between the United States and Iran, and property disputes concerning the deposed shah of Iran. The extent of claims involved underlined that a formal mechanism would facilitate the resolution of these cases. Moreover, the composition of the tribunal, which allowed for equal representation of nationals from the United States and Iran as well as the involvement of neutral arbitrators,[59] and the jurisdictional limitations imposed on the tribunal, for example placing the hostage crisis itself outside the subject-matter jurisdiction of the tribunal,[60] gave each state confidence in the way in which the tribunal would operate.

The experience of the Iran–US Claims Tribunal has been highly influential in subsequent claims commission practice. This influence has partly been evident in the substantive law that has developed through the decisions of the tribunal and the development of procedural rules through the interpretation and application of the UNCITRAL Model Rules, and because of the many 'graduates' of the tribunal who subsequently worked on other claims commissions.[61] To the extent that it may be speculated that states will be more likely to resort to this form of litigation when they have some level of certainty as to the running of the procedure and the resolution of particular substantive questions of law, the ability to draw on the lessons of other commissions may well be a relevant consideration.

Bederman's depiction of claims commissions as a victor's prize may still be warranted when considering the United Nations Compensation Commission (UNCC). This commission was imposed on Iraq following the conflict that resulted from Iraq's invasion of Kuwait in 1990. Security Council Resolution 687 of 1991 provided that Iraq was 'liable under international law, for any direct loss, damage, including environmental damage and the depletion of natural resources, or injury to foreign

---

[58] See General Declarations and Claims Settlement Declaration, (1981) 20 ILM 224.

[59] The tribunal consists of three US and three Iranian nationals, each appointed by their respective governments, and three neutrals or third-country members who are appointed by the government-appointed members. Cases would be heard primarily by tribunals of three members, with one neutral, one US national, and one Iranian national.

[60] Claims Settlement Declaration, Art. II(1). A further limitation included upholding choice of forum clauses in contracts that clearly selected Iranian courts as the forum for dispute settlement. Ibid.

[61] Crook, above n. 50, 81.

450 NATALIE KLEIN

Governments, nationals and corporations, as a result of Iraq's unlawful invasion and occupation of Kuwait'.[62] This resolution was adopted pursuant to the mandatory authority of the Security Council under Chapter VII of the UN Charter.

As a result of this resolution, Iraq's liability was determined and the only question for resolution was the extent of reparations that would be payable to all the claimants. Claims were divided into six categories; four of which related to injuries suffered by individuals, whereas the other two related to damage to businesses and to states or international organizations. Payments to individuals were largely expedited and were paid when issues of causation and valuation were met.[63] One reason for facilitating a rapid resolution of claims was that earlier commissions had experienced considerable delay and some cases were left unresolved.[64] There was considerable political momentum behind the operation of the UNCC following Iraq's defeat and the resurgence of the UN Security Council at the end of the cold war. The process followed has been described as 'hybrid political-judicial' and as administering 'rough justice'.[65] Many pragmatic determinations could be made by the UNCC, particularly as there was no Iraqi representation within that body.[66]

A third recent example is the Eritrea–Ethiopia Claims Commission (EECC), established under the 2000 Agreement. The border war concluded by this treaty had been fought on three main fronts, and gave rise to a range of claims relating to the conduct of hostilities. The jurisdiction of the EECC was stated under Article 5(1) as follows:

> The mandate of the Commission is to decide through binding arbitration all claims for loss, damage or injury by one Government against the other, and by nationals (including both natural and juridical persons) of one party against the Government of the other party or entities owned or controlled by the other party that are (a) related to the conflict that was the subject of the Framework Agreement, the Modalities for its Implementation and the Cessation of Hostilities Agreement, and (b) result from violations of international humanitarian law, including the 1949 Geneva Conventions, or other violations of international law.

---

[62] UN Security Council Resolution 687, April 3, 1991, UN Doc. S/RES/1991/687, para. 16.
[63] See further Francis E. McGovern, 'Dispute System Design: The United Nations Compensation Commission', (2009) 14 *Harvard Negotiation Law Review* 171, 178–9.
[64] Bederman, above n. 47, 17–18.   [65] McGovern, above n. 63, 177.
[66] Bederman, above n. 47, 10. Iraq was granted the right to present comments on claims, however. Ibid.

Under the 2000 Agreement, the states clearly expected that a large number of individual claims would be presented to the EECC.[67] However, the states ultimately presented nearly all of these claims on behalf of the individuals concerned, and the EECC therefore addressed a series of inter-state disputes concerning violations of the law of armed conflict, as well as human rights violations and other violations of international law.[68]

The EECC was one of several mechanisms established between Eritrea and Ethiopia in bringing their border war to a close; a boundary commission was also established to delimit and demarcate the boundary between the two states,[69] and there was also to be an 'investigation . . . carried out by an independent, impartial body appointed by the Secretary General of the OAU [Organization of African Unity], in consultation with the Secretary General of the United Nations and the two parties'.[70] The inclusion of a claims commission in the overall settlement can be seen as an important element for redressing outstanding grievances between the states because of acts perpetrated by each state during the war.[71] These matters needed to be resolved, in addition to a formal boundary delimitation between the parties, to encourage the restoration of a positive relationship between the two states.

A further question may be posed as to why a third party was required to litigate these differences between Eritrea and Ethiopia, rather than establishing a lump-sum settlement as satisfaction for the claims. Lump-sum settlements are best utilized when the parties are reasonably clear as to the liability of the state concerned and they are able to negotiate an appropriate amount of reparations. Such settlements are also more easily

---

[67] The EECC was mandated under the 2000 Agreement 'to adopt such methods of efficient case management and mass claims processing as it deems appropriate'. 2000 Agreement, Art. 5(10).

[68] Natalie Klein, 'State Responsibility for International Humanitarian Law Violations and the Work of the Eritrea–Ethiopia Claims Commission So Far', 47 *German Yearbook of International Law* 214 (2004); J. Romesh Weeramantry, 'Eritrea Ethiopia Claims Commission Partial Awards Regarding Civilian Claims for Violations of International Humanitarian Law and Human Rights Law', (2006) 100 AJIL 201.

[69] 2000 Agreement, Art. 4.   [70] Ibid., Art. 3(2). This body was not established, however.

[71] For example, Eritrea was concerned with settling, inter alia, the claims of the Eritreans and Ethiopians of national origin who had been expelled and had their property confiscated, and Ethiopia sought redress for economic losses suffered as a result of the war, as well as reparations for Eritrean conduct during the war, including the bombing of a school in a town near the border.

reached when the nationals of only one state have a claim.[72] The claims existing between Eritrea and Ethiopia were extensive, and liability was contested between the parties in a separate phase of proceedings before the EECC, prior to any determinations of the amount of compensation owed.[73] In the light of the extent of disagreement between the states over the liability for alleged violations of international humanitarian law and other international law obligations, resort to a neutral third-party forum becomes a more apparent choice.

John Crook has observed that claims commissions 'offer the greatest benefits where there is a distinctive combination of factors: (a) large numbers of similarly situated people have suffered similar injuries, (b) some body has made an authoritative judgment that such injuries entitle the victims to compensation, and (c) an underlying political consensus and adequate resources support the process'.[74] This observation tends to suggest that there must be a decision on, or a strong presumption in favour of, liability before the procedure is instituted. While that was clearly not the case for the EECC, such characteristics could be drawn from the UNCC experience, as well as other more recent claims commission processes (such as those related to the Holocaust and the resolution of housing claims in Bosnia and Herzegovina and in Kosovo).

While individuals may be given direct access to international proceedings through claims commissions, state involvement remains apparent. Ultimately, varied circumstances behind the establishment of claims commissions makes it difficult to draw broad conclusions as to why it may be a preferred mechanism for resolving disputes concerning the treatment of nationals abroad. Some of the modern practice suggests that being able to sequester a particular matter of contention through an ostensibly neutral process removes the issue from the (usually) ongoing bilateral dynamic between the states involved. While there may be questions of sovereign importance addressed by the commission (such as questions of dual nationality before the Iran–US Claims Tribunal, and responsibility for the use of force decided by the EECC), there is scope for the commission

---

[72] Bederman, above n. 47, 26. Bederman has also pointed to the use of claims commissions where there is no dispute settlement provision in contracts that are at issue, which may otherwise have opened up the possibility of resolving disputes through international commercial arbitration. Ibid., 27.

[73] The decisions are set out on the website of the Permanent Court of Arbitration, available at www.pca-cpa.org/showpage.asp?pag_id=1151.

[74] Crook, above n. 50, 83.

DISPUTE SETTLEMENT OPTIONS 453

to operate outside the glare of the direct, ongoing, relationship of the
states concerned.

A continuing role for inter-state litigation

Beyond claims commissions, inter-state adjudication or arbitration may
be possible where jurisdiction exists between the states concerned.[75]
Moreover, the absence of treaty commitments may limit the options
available to individuals to seek redress for their claims. In this context,
'Diplomatic protection conducted by a State at inter-State level remains
an important remedy for the protection of persons whose . . . rights have
been violated abroad.'[76]

For a state to exercise its right of diplomatic protection, a series of
requirements must be met. These requirements are particularly tested in
the context of inter-state litigation, where a defendant state may challenge the admissibility of claims presented by a state asserting the right
of diplomatic protection. These requirements for the exercise of the right
of diplomatic protection have been set out in the ILC articles on diplomatic protection,[77] and include the exhaustion of local remedies[78] and
establishing the proper nationality of the claim.[79]

---

[75] The Permanent Court of International Justice addressed at least ten contentious cases
involving the exercise of diplomatic protection: *Mavrommatis Palestine Concessions Case
(Greece v. United Kingdom) (Jurisdiction)*, [1924] PCIJ (ser. A) No. 2; *Certain German
Interests in Polish Upper Silesia (Germany v. Poland) (Merits)*, [1926] (ser. A) No. 7; *Factory
at Chorzów (Germany v. Poland) (Indemnity)*, [1928] PCIJ (ser. A) No. 17; *SS Lotus Case
(France v. Turkey)*, [1927] PCIJ (ser. A) No. 10; *Payment of Various Serbian Loans Issued
in France (France v. Yugoslavia)*, [1929] PCIJ (ser. A) No. 20; *Phosphates in Morocco
(Italy v. France)*, [1938] PCIJ (ser. A/B) No. 74; *Panevezys-Saldutiskis Railway (Estonia v.
Lithuania)*, [1938] PCIJ (ser. A/B) No. 75; *Société Commerciale de Belgique (Belgium v.
Greece)*, [1939] PCIJ (ser. A/B) No. 78.
[76] ILC Articles on Diplomatic Protection, 26. See also Francisco Orrego Vicuna, 'Changing
Approaches to the Nationality of Claims in the Context of Diplomatic Protection and
International Dispute Settlement', in Sabine Schlemmer-Schulte et al. (eds.), *Liber Amicorum Ibrahim F. I. Shihata: International Finance and Development Law* (The Hague:
Kluwer Law International, 2001) ('A residuary role for diplomatic protection seems more
adequate to the extent that this mechanism might only intervene when there are no
international procedures directly available to the affected individual').
[77] The ILC's work on diplomatic protection has been subject to considerable academic
scrutiny. See, e.g., Alain Pellet, 'The Second Death of Euripide Mavrommatis? Notes on
the International Law Commission's Draft Articles on Diplomatic Protection', (2008) 7
Law and Practice of International Courts and Tribunals 33; Milano, above n. 1.
[78] ILC Articles on Diplomatic Protection, Arts. 14 and 15.   [79] Ibid., Arts. 4–8.

454   NATALIE KLEIN

Successful challenges to the admissibility of claims brought on the basis of diplomatic protection have prevented resolution of disputes on the merits. For example, the *Interhandel* dispute was inadmissible because of Switzerland's failure to exhaust local remedies in the United States;[80] Liechtenstein lacked standing because of an absence of a genuine link to its national in *Nottebohm*;[81] and Belgium lacked standing to take up the claim of shareholders in a company incorporated in Canada in *Barcelona Traction*.[82]

A more recent decision of the ICJ addressing diplomatic protection was *Ahmadou Sadio Diallo*.[83] The background to this case concerned Diallo, a national of Guinea who had resided in the Democratic Republic of the Congo (DRC) for over thirty years. Diallo had founded two companies in the DRC and was the manager and an *associé* of both. After Diallo had sought to recover monies owed to the companies by the state, as well as by public and private companies, he was deported to Guinea following his arrest and imprisonment.

In instituting proceedings before the ICJ, Guinea asserted that Diallo's rights under the Vienna Convention on Consular Relations had been denied, and further claimed on the basis of diplomatic protection that Diallo's rights as an individual and as an *associé* of the companies had been violated in relation to human rights standards as well as 'a minimum standard of civilization'.[84] The DRC claimed at the preliminary objections stage that Diallo had not exhausted local remedies and that Guinea further lacked standing to assert diplomatic protection of the companies because those companies were not incorporated under Guinea's laws.[85] The ICJ rejected the first objection, but upheld the second objection.

In addressing the second objection, the role of the ICJ in resolving the claims of foreign investors was particularly in the spotlight. In the 1970 decision of *Barcelona Traction*, the Court had determined that Belgium lacked standing to bring a claim on behalf of Belgian shareholders against Spain when the company in question was incorporated in Canada.[86] While the ICJ indicated in *Barcelona Traction* that there might be circumstances

---

[80] *Interhandel Case (Switzerland v. United States) (Preliminary Objections)*, [1959] ICJ Rep. 6.

[81] *Nottebohm Case (Liechtenstein v. Guatemala)*, [1955] ICJ Rep. 4.

[82] *Barcelona Traction, Light and Power Company Ltd (Belgium v. Spain) (Second Phase)*, [1970] ICJ Rep. 3 (*Barcelona Traction*).

[83] *Diallo – Preliminary Objections*, above n. 2; *Ahmadou Sadio Diallo (Republic of Guinea v. Democratic Republic of the Congo) (Merits)*, [2010] ICJ Rep. 639 (*Diallo – Merits*).

[84] *Diallo – Preliminary Objections*, above n. 2, [28].   [85] Ibid., [32].

[86] For discussion on the ongoing relevance of *Barcelona Traction* in the light of state practice, see Lawrence Jahoon Lee, '*Barcelona Traction* in the 21st Century: Revisiting its Customary

allowing the state of nationality of shareholders to bring claims on their behalf,[87] *Diallo* reaffirmed the primary position of the state of incorporation of the companies as the basis for exercising the right of diplomatic protection.[88] This restrictive position of the ICJ is not reflected in bilateral investment treaties, which typically expand the possible range of claimants through the definition of 'investor'. As such, the potential use of inter-state litigation for the protection of juridical persons, already limited by the consensual basis of jurisdiction, remains more likely to occur in the context of investor–state arbitrations because of the restricted bases of standing for states under the customary rules of diplomatic protection.

At the merits stage, the *Diallo* case reflects the application of international human rights law[89] and rights relating to consular assistance in the context of inter-state litigation. In applying the ICCPR and the African Charter on Human and Peoples' Rights (African Charter) to the facts surrounding Diallo's treatment, the ICJ took into account the jurisprudence of the Human Rights Committee, as well as the African Commission on Human and Peoples' Rights, the European Court of Human Rights and the Inter-American Court of Human Rights.[90] The ICJ considered that this was appropriate 'to achieve the necessary clarity and the essential consistency of international law, as well as legal security, to which both the individuals with guaranteed rights and the States obliged to comply with treaty obligations are entitled'.[91] In doing so, the Court has ensured

---

and Policy Underpinnings 35 Years Later', (2006) 42 *Stanford Journal of International Law* 237, 247–55.

[87] *Barcelona Traction*, above n. 82, [93]. These possibilities arise where the company no longer exists, the corporation has the nationality of the state causing the injury, or where direct rights are infringed. Stephen J. Knight and Angus J. O'Brien, '*Ahmadou Sadio Diallo (Republic of Guinea* v. *Democratic Republic of the Congo)*: Clarifying the Scope of Diplomatic Protection of Corporate and Shareholder Rights', (2008) 9 *Melbourne Journal of International Law* 151, 152–3.

[88] *Diallo – Preliminary Objections*, above n. 2, [89]–[90]. See further discussion in Alberto Alvarez-Jiménez, 'Foreign Investors, Diplomatic Protection and the International Court of Justice's decision on Preliminary Objections in the *Diallo* Case', (2007–8) 33 *North Carolina Journal of International Law and Commercial Regulation* 437, 450–3; Annemarieke Vermeer-Künzli, '*Diallo* and the Draft Articles: The Application of the Draft Articles on Diplomatic Protection in the *Ahmadou Sadio Diallo* Case', (2007) 20 *Leiden Journal of International Law* 941, 946–9.

[89] Guinea claimed violations of Art. 13 and Art. 9 of the ICCPR, as well as violations of Art. 21, Art. 14 and Art. 6 of the African Charter on Human and Peoples' Rights.

[90] *Diallo – Merits*, above n. 83, [66]–[68].

[91] Ibid., [66]. It is notable that the Court's findings on certain human rights violations were unanimous. Ibid., [165].

456 NATALIE KLEIN

that there is continuity and consistency in the remedies available for individuals, provided a state is willing to take up the individual's claims on the basis of diplomatic protection.[92]

Diallo further affirmed that the violation of individual rights enshrined under the Vienna Convention on Consular Relations could be adjudicated before the ICJ, even though a state must still present these claims. There is an optional protocol to the Vienna Convention on Consular Relations, to which 173 states are currently parties, allowing for resort to the ICJ for disputes relating to the interpretation or application of this treaty.[93] As previously mentioned, three cases were filed against the United States in relation to the consular rights of foreign nationals on death row: *Case Concerning the Vienna Convention on Consular Relations, LaGrand*, and *Avena and other Mexican Nationals.*

The *Case Concerning the Vienna Convention* was instituted by Paraguay on behalf of Angel Breard, who had not been informed of his right to consular assistance. Paraguay sought provisional measures from ICJ, but after Breard's death sentence was carried out Paraguay terminated the proceedings.[94]

In *LaGrand*, Germany brought a case against the United States for violation of Germany's rights, as well as the rights of the LaGrand brothers, who were not informed of their right to contact German consular officials when detained and arrested for a capital offence. Germany successfully secured an order for provisional measures from the Court prior to the execution of the second brother,[95] but the United States failed to prevent the execution as required.[96] Unlike Paraguay, Germany continued its case against the United States, adding to its claim the United States' failure to abide by the Court's provisional measures as a further violation of international law.

Germany presumably continued the case because of its opposition to the death penalty and because of the principles at stake. As the United

---

[92] In his separate opinion, Judge Cancado Trinidade reflected on the role of the Court in providing substantive human rights protection, whereas diplomatic protection was the means by which such protection could be afforded. *Diallo – Merits*, above n. 83, Separate Opinion of Judge Cancado Trinidade, Part III.

[93] Optional Protocol to that Convention concerning the Compulsory Settlement of Disputes (opened for signature 24 April 1963, entered into force 21 June 1985), 1400 UNTS 339.

[94] *Vienna Convention on Consular Relations (Paraguay v. United States of America), (Order of 10 November 1998)*, [1998] ICJ Rep. 426.

[95] *LaGrand (Germany v. United States) (Provisional Measures)*, [1999] ICJ Rep. 9.

[96] At the merits stage of the case, the Court confirmed that its provisional measures orders were binding on states. *LaGrand*, above n. 16, [109].

States had conceded the violation of its obligation to notify the LaGrand brothers of their consular rights, Germany did not have much to lose in continuing the litigation. In the end, Germany secured a holding that required the United States to provide a remedy to affected nationals:

> [A]n apology would not suffice in cases where the individuals concerned have been subjected to prolonged detention or convicted and sentenced to severe penalties. In case of such a conviction and sentence, it would be incumbent upon the United States to allow the review and reconsideration of the conviction and sentence by taking account of the violation of the rights set forth in the Convention. The obligation can be carried out in various ways. The choice of means must be left to the United States.[97]

The United States also provided assurances of non-repetition and under-took to institute a broad and detailed programme to ensure that its law enforcement officials would adhere to the international requirements under the Vienna Convention.[98]

Mexico brought the third of these cases against the United States. Given that Germany had already proceeded in its case against the United States and the Court had indicated an appropriate remedy, the question may well arise as to why an additional case was warranted. Unlike Germany, Mexico had over fifty of its nationals on death row, and these nationals were alive and at various stages of appeal at the time the case was submitted.[99] Like Germany, Mexico's position was strongly against the death penalty. To assist its nationals in the United States, Mexico set up legal offices specifically to assist Mexican nationals charged with capital offences.

While Mexico clearly had an interest in the protection of these nationals in the United States, it is reasonable to state that the issue was not the most critical between Mexico and the United States at the time. However, it was also a time when the presidents of the United States and of Mexico enjoyed a strong relationship. Mexico seemingly decided to take a moral stand on this particular issue. Certainly there had been strong support from within central and south America, as evidenced by the earlier advisory opinion on the issue by the Inter-American Court of Human Rights.[100]

---

[97] Ibid., [125].   [98] Ibid., [124].

[99] The ICJ concluded that there was no requirement to exhaust local remedies. See below nn. 104–107 and accompanying text.

[100] *Right to Information on Consular Assistance in the Framework of the Guarantees of the Due Process of Law*, Inter-American Court of Human Rights, Advisory Opinion No. 16, 1 October 1999.

458 NATALIE KLEIN

In *Avena*, the ICJ recognized that rights were held directly by Mexico as well as by the individuals concerned, and the state could therefore pursue both claims before the Court.[101] It has been suggested that in doing so, Mexico was representing the rights of its nationals, as opposed to taking up those claims and 'in reality asserting its own rights'.[102] This perspective supports the idea that there will be a basis on which states can resolve disputes through inter-state litigation over the violation of individual rights suffered by their nationals abroad.

Moreover, in these circumstances the requirement to exhaust local remedies did not apply because the Court focused on the interdependence of the claims submitted on behalf of Mexico for injury suffered directly and through the Mexican nationals.[103] In this situation, the ICJ considered that where there was such a convergence of interests, the foreign nationals would not be required to exhaust local remedies.[104] This new exception was established over a finding that the remedies within the United States were ineffective,[105] or limiting an exception to the special circumstances of the case.[106] The creation of another exception to the requirement to exhaust local remedies could therefore be construed as broadening the instances of states pursuing inter-state claims for violations of the consular rights (or other rights) of nationals abroad.

It is perhaps enough to demonstrate that there remains an interest among states in pursuing inter-state litigation when the stakes are high enough. But the number of inter-state cases does pale in comparison with the pursuit of investor–state cases.

Conclusion

Given that there are often political, economic, or other interests at stake between the countries concerned, the availability of inter-state litigation may become a useful bargaining tool in seeking to redress the concerns of nationals injured overseas. Ultimately, the diversity of avenues available for individuals may obviate the need to rely on state assistance. This

---

[101] *Avena*, above n. 16, [40].
[102] As characterized in *Mavrommatis*, above n. 2. See also Pellet, above n. 77, 48–50.
[103] *Avena*, above n. 16, [40].   [104] Ibid.
[105] This approach was supported by Judge Tomka. Ibid., Separate Opinion of Judge Tomka, [11]–[13].
[106] An approach preferred by Judges Ranjeva, Vereshchetin, and Parra-Aranguren. Ibid., Declaration of Vice President Ranjeva, [11]–[13]; Separate Opinion of Judge Vereshchetin, [12]–[13]; Separate Opinion of Judge Parra-Aranguren, [23]–[28].

situation would be preferable, given the state-centric focus that otherwise pervades rules relating to the rights of states to act on behalf of individuals. As states are not required to take action for their nationals, the more options available to the individuals themselves makes it more likely that a remedy for their injuries may be achieved.

20

Litigating international law disputes: where to?

CESARE P. R. ROMANO

The chapters in this book have tried to map which states, or groups of states, resort to international litigation and under what circumstances; the areas of international law and relations where most litigation seems to occur; and factors limiting the occurrence of international litigation. They yield a rich portrait of the actual state of international litigation at this time in history, a portrait with lights and many shadows. Indeed, despite the plethora of international adjudicative bodies created across time and regions, international judicialization (i.e. the creation and use of international adjudicative bodies) is still remarkably uneven.[1]

First, while there are regions of the globe where there are multiple, overlapping, international adjudicative bodies, there are others where there are none. While some states have accepted the jurisdiction of multiple international adjudicative bodies, others have accepted none. Second, patterns of utilization are inconsistent. Even where there are international adjudicative bodies, often they are used more frequently by certain actors than others. Third, certain areas of international relations have been judicialized significantly more than others.

As some wise person once said, 'Prediction is very difficult, especially about the future.'[2] It is all the more difficult when events are still tumultuously unfolding. After all, the big bang in the history of international adjudication took place only about two decades ago, at the end of the cold war – a few minutes ago in the timescale of the history of international law.

---

[1] For an overview of the uneven state of international judicialization, see Benedict Kingsbury, 'International Courts: Uneven Judicialization in Global Order', in James Crawford and Martti Koskenniemi (eds.), *The Cambridge Companion to International Law* (Cambridge University Press, 2012) 203; Cesare Romano, 'The Shadow Zones of International Judicialization', in Cesare Romano, Karen Alter, and Yuval Shany (eds.), *The Oxford University Press Handbook of International Adjudication* (Oxford University Press, 2013) 90.

[2] Attributed to Neil Bohr (but also to Yogi Bear and Mark Twain). See, e.g., Niels Bohr, Wikipedia: the Free Encyclopedia, available at http://en.wikipedia.org/wiki/Niels_Bohr.

Be that as it may, at the risk of being derided by future generations of scholars, I will venture on some risky predictions.

These days it is popular to wonder whether international litigation has reached a high-water mark.[3] How many more international adjudicative bodies can be created? How much more international litigation can there be? The sense of saturation probably stems from comparison with the not-too-distant past when international courts could be counted on one hand, and litigation was a sporadic event, rarely grabbing headlines.

Will there be more international courts and tribunals in the future? The short answer is a qualified yes. States create international courts either because they need them to do something they cannot do unilaterally or through other means (e.g., the International Criminal Court), or because they are unhappy with the existing international courts (e.g., the International Tribunal for the Law of the Sea (ITLOS) was created as a reaction to the shortcomings of the International Court of Justice (ICJ)). These two factors driving the multiplication of international courts will remain. The question is where and what kinds of new international courts we are likely to see in the not-too-distant future.

Currently, at the global level there are only four judicial bodies active: the ICJ, the World Trade Organization (WTO) Dispute Settlement System; the ITLOS; and the International Criminal Court (ICC). Beside these, there are a number of global international arbitral bodies, the two most important of which are the Permanent Court of Arbitration and the International Center for the Settlement of Investment Disputes.

Granted, none of these is truly global, for none has jurisdiction actually extending to all states. That is either because the organization to which the judicial body is attached does not have universal membership (e.g., the WTO), or the treaty creating the judicial body has not attracted universal ratification (e.g., the ICC), or because, while the organization does have universal (or virtually universal) membership (e.g., the UN), the judicial bodies attached to it (e.g., the ICJ or ITLOS) have jurisdiction only insofar as states have expressly accepted it. Looking at the future from where I am writing, of the four global adjudicative systems the only one that seems to have a reasonable chance of becoming truly universal is the WTO Dispute Settlement System, because of the gravitational effect that the WTO is gaining by now having included in its membership all significant world economies. Despite the aspiration of its founders, the

---

[3] See, for instance, Vaughan Lowe, 'The Function of Litigation in International Society', (2012) 61 ICLQ 209, 210.

462 CESARE P. R. ROMANO

ICC does not seem capable of achieving universal membership for several decades, if ever.

At this time in history, perceptible changes in the global distribution of power among major states and shifts in the dominant approaches to the international legal order put in question the prospects of governance through major new comprehensive global legal regimes.[4] As a consequence, this diminishes the chances of witnessing the creation of new courts under such treaties. Presently, no new adjudicative body with global scope is in the making. The last 'global court' was the ICC, a turn-of-the-millennium adjudicative body. While a World Court of Human Rights would be desirable, if not necessary, to ensure that everyone has access to a binding international remedy, the project still needs to gain sufficient traction among governments to start taking the long road towards actual establishment.[5]

That being said, the global level has traditionally been difficult terrain for judicialization. Most international adjudicative bodies that populate the current scene have sprung up at the regional or sub-regional level. If new courts are going to be created, it is at this level that we shall find them. Thus it is safe to say that more regional economic integration agreements will be negotiated. Most will feature some type of adjudicative body, either with marked judicial features and mimicking the European Court of Justice (ECJ), or with more pronounced arbitral features along the lines of the North American Free Trade Agreement (NAFTA)/WTO model.[6] It is hard to imagine a United States–European Union free trade agreement – a much talked-about project these days – without some sort of dispute settlement arrangement.

Gazing at the puzzle of international adjudicative bodies, one can spot several gaps. For instance, one could imagine that one day, besides regional human rights courts in Europe, the Americas and Africa, there will be one or more in Asia, or at least some of its sub-regions. There are some

---

[4] Kingsbury, above n. 1, 223.

[5] Manfred Nowak, 'It's Time for a World Court of Human Rights', in Cherif Bassiouni and William Schabas (eds.), *New Challenges for the UN Human Rights Machinery: What Future for the UN Treaty Body System and the Human Rights Council Procedures?* (Mortsel, Belgium: Intersentia, 2011) 17; Julia Kozma, *A World Court of Human Rights, Consolidated Statute and Commentary* (Vienna: Neuer Wissenschaftlicher Verlag, 2010); Cesare Romano, 'Can You Hear Me Now? Making the Case for Extending the International Judicial Network', (2009) 9 *Chicago Journal of International Law* 233, 267–8.

[6] Karen Alter, 'The Global Spread of European Style International Courts', (2012) 35 *West European Politics* 135; Karen Alter, *The New Terrain of International Law: Courts, Politics, Rights* (Princeton University Press, 2013).

encouraging signals that South-East Asia might be heading in that direction, and maybe the Arab world might one day have a regional human rights court, too.[7] It would also not be implausible to imagine a regional human rights court gathering together the various island nations of the Pacific.[8] Also, more human rights courts might emerge as a reaction to the shortcomings of existing courts.

In the criminal field, the future is likely to see more hybrid international criminal courts.[9] These ad hoc exercises in national/international justice fill a niche and help an accountability gap. As stated before, the ICC does not enjoy, and will likely never enjoy, universal membership. It also does not have retrospective jurisdiction, since it can only adjudicate on events that took place after 1 July 2002. For these reasons alone, hybrid international courts will continue to be the most dynamic – albeit quite dysfunctional – part of the international criminal judicial landscape.

More international adjudicative bodies might result from the judicialization of quasi-judicial bodies. There are dozens of international commissions, panels, and sundry bodies that exercise functions very similar to those of international courts and tribunals, the only difference being that the outcome of their proceedings is not legally binding on the parties.[10] The two largest orders are those of human rights bodies and the non-compliance procedures of multilateral environmental treaties. Again, if it were not for the non-binding nature of their decisions, they would be indistinguishable from international adjudicative bodies. At least in the case of some, such as the Human Rights Committee, the distinction is becoming blurred.[11] Giving them binding powers would obviate the need to create new and expensive international adjudicative bodies.

In sum, if the establishment of more adjudicative bodies is unlikely, at least at the breakneck pace of the past two decades, the increase in caseload and judicial output of existing adjudicative bodies is likely to continue. First, by and large there is an excess capacity in the so-called international judicial system that has not yet been tapped. Second, patterns of utilization

---

[7] Romano, above n. 1.   [8] Romano, above n. 8, 264 ff.

[9] Cesare Romano and Théo Boutrouche, 'Tribunaux pénaux internationalisés: état des lieux d'une justice "hybride"', (2003) 107 *Revue générale de droit international public* 109.

[10] Cesare Romano, 'A Taxonomy of International Rule of Law Institutions', (2011) 2 *Journal of International Dispute Settlement* 241, 260.

[11] See, in general, International Law Association, 'Final Report on the Impact of Findings of the United Nations Human Rights Treaty Bodies', Berlin Conference on International Human Rights Law and Practice, 2004.

are significantly twisted, with a handful of actors being repeat users while most are rare participants or not participants at all.

In terms of docket size, the ICJ seems to have all the cases it can handle. It is difficult to imagine it busier than it is for two reasons. The first is the fact that it is open only to sovereign states and that there are only slightly fewer than 200 of those in the world. To this, one should add its considerable jurisdictional limits. Many states have not accepted its jurisdiction, are not party to a treaty giving it jurisdiction, and do not show any inclination to do so ad hoc. China is but one example. How many cases can those states that did accept its jurisdiction or are willing to do so ad hoc be expected to litigate in a given year? The second reason is that as it is currently organized and operates it cannot handle a docket larger than it does currently. Since time and again the ICJ has proven to be impervious to reform – bar a few cosmetic retouches – it is, and will remain, a forum where states can now and then turn for the settlement of certain kinds of disputes – a noteworthy forum because of its unique role and position within the UN – but with this structural limit it will surely not become the pivot of an international judiciary as many of its disciples would like it to be.

Granted, more states could and should be involved in litigation before the ICJ. Since 1946, as at the time of writing 152 cases have been submitted to it.[12] Altogether, slightly fewer than half of the states of the world (ninety) have been either applicants or respondents, or joint submitters. The United States is by far the most frequent user with twenty-three cases (thirteen as applicant, nine as respondent, and one by ad hoc agreement), to be followed by the United Kingdom and France with thirteen each (respectively seven, five, and one, and five, seven, and one). Yugoslavia would be next, but the figures are debatable. It would total eleven cases, but only if one adds those of Yugoslavia, Serbia, and Serbia-Montenegro, and counts individually the volley of cases it filed against several NATO members in 1999. Then there is the first developing country, Nicaragua, with nine cases (six and three), followed by Germany and Belgium with seven each (respectively three, two, and two, and four, two, and one).

The most noticeable thing, however, is that of those ninety states that have been involved in cases before the ICJ, seventy-eight have four or fewer cases to their name and sixty, two or less. In other words,

---

[12] International Court of Justice, List of All Cases, available at www.icj-cij.org/docket/index.php?p1=3.

utilization of the ICJ is quite diffuse, but, at the same time, only a handful of countries are repeated users. The most glaring absence from the list is China, a permanent member of the UN Security Council, which has so far disdained the principal judicial organ of the UN. All Russia, another permanent member, has to its name is being respondent in a case brought by Georgia (and the ICJ eventually found that it did not have jurisdiction),[13] and, if one counts those of the USSR, four cases that were brought by the United States for the downing of aircraft did not go anywhere.[14]

The fact that the United States, the United Kingdom, and France together have appeared in about one case in three brought before the ICJ, and the cold attitude of the superpowers-to-be (China, Brazil, Russia, and India, but also Indonesia, South Africa, South Korea, and Japan), should give much pause to those who wish the ICJ to be the pivot of the international judicial system.[15] Again, patterns of utilization suggest that it is, and will remain, at best a useful tool to settle certain kinds of disputes mostly by a select group of serial users, but not much else.

States will continue to generate relatively considerable amounts of international litigation. For instance, in this book, Coalter Lathrop told us that maritime boundary delimitations might be a significant source of litigation in the years to come.[16] After all, fewer than 200 of the approximately 430 potential maritime boundaries worldwide have been delimited (and some only partially).[17] However, he also told us that negotiation is by far the tool most frequently used to delimit maritime boundaries. So far litigation has accounted for the settlement of just two dozen maritime boundaries.[18] Moreover, most of those few disputed boundaries that will be litigated will most likely be litigated through arbitration, not before the ICJ or ITLOS.

The WTO, another adjudicative system open only to states, could well see more litigation. As Rafiqul Islam told us, the overwhelming majority of cases litigated in the WTO are between the superpowers of international

---

[13] *Case Concerning Application of the International Convention on the Elimination of All Forms of Racial Discrimination (Georgia v. Russian Federation) (Preliminary Objections)*, [2011] ICJ Rep. __.

[14] *Aerial Incident of 7 October 1952 (United States v. USSR)*, [1956] ICJ 9; *Aerial Incident of 4 September 1954 (United States v. USSR), Order*, [1958] ICJ Rep. 158; *Aerial Incident of 7 November 1954 (United States v. USSR), Order*, [1959] ICJ Rep. 276; *Treatment in Hungary of Aircraft and Crew of United States of America (United States v. USSR), Order*, [1954] ICJ Rep. 99.

[15] Romano, above n. 1.   [16] See Chapter 11 in this volume.   [17] Ibid.   [18] Ibid.

trade (i.e. the United States, the European Union, and Japan).[19] Because of the reliance on countermeasures as the tool to enforce judgments in the WTO, developing countries, and most of all the least developed countries, do not participate. This largely untapped pool, together with expansion in the overall membership and China climbing the curve, will likely make the docket of the WTO dispute settlement system (panels and Appellate Body) rise.

At the same time, litigation might decrease in other areas. As Chester Brown explained, the number of bilateral investment treaties has gone from zero in 1959 to 2,833 at the end of 2011.[20] At the same time, litigation of investment disputes under bilateral investment treaties has gone from zero in 1987 to 450 in 2011.[21] That is a phenomenal growth, by any standard. However, as Brown also explains, in recent years there has been a marked move away by states, developed and developing, east, west, north, and south, from similar dispute settlement clauses or agreements, a fact which, all other things being equal, will necessarily affect overall litigation numbers.[22]

The same warped patterns of utilization can be found in the case of ICSID, one of the many forums that can be used to litigate investment disputes.[23] To date, it is reported that 250 arbitrations have been completed and 169 are pending.[24] Counting both completed and pending cases, a total of 107 states have been involved in ICSID litigation – almost invariably as respondents, the rationale for the mechanism being to give investors an impartial forum to litigate disputes with states. This is a considerable participation rate. However, of these, more than half (fifty-six) have been involved in just two or fewer cases, and eighty-nine in five or fewer cases. Just 10 per cent of states have been involved in 44 per cent of the total (182 cases). They are Argentina, which tops the list with fifty cases (twenty-five completed and twenty-five pending), Venezuela, Egypt, Mexico, Ecuador, Peru, Ukraine, Hungary, Romania, and the Democratic Republic of the Congo. Most of the Argentine cases stem from one single event – its default on sovereign debt of 2001. Likewise, most of Venezuela's cases stem from anti-business steps taken by the government of the late Hugo Chávez. Even controlling for that, the large majority of cases have been brought against a handful of states. From the plaintiff's side, utilization is likewise very spread and concentrated at the same time. Only twenty-four companies have used ICSID more than once. Among

---

[19] See Chapter 17 in this volume.   [20] See Chapter 18 in this volume.   [21] Ibid.
[22] Ibid.   [23] Romano, above n. 1.   [24] See 'Cases', https://icsid.worldbank.org/.

the most frequent users are two oil companies (Mobil and Shell), which have used the system repeatedly through their various subsidiaries, and Impregilo, an Italian infrastructure company. All others have just one or two cases to their name.

The greatest potential for growth in litigation, however, is to be found not in forums open only to states, or to states and corporations, but in those forums where individuals have access. Granted, the caseload of the European Court of Human Rights has reached gargantuan proportions. In 2012, it reported 128,100 cases pending.[25] The number might very well keep on growing. Awareness of the existence of the court and specialized knowledge in how to seize it has constantly grown in Europe, particularly in eastern Europe. However, it is obvious that the number of cases has far outstripped the court's capacity to process them. The process of reform of the court to stem the flood started several years ago. The entry into force of Protocol 14, after years of stalling and blackmailing by Russia, has given the court some limited powers to limit the number of cases it will have to decide, but much more radical reforms will need to be undertaken, lest the court asphyxiate under the weight of its own success.

On a different scale, the same could be said of the Inter-American Court of Human Rights. Since 1988, when it handed down its first judgment on the merits, the court has decided about 150 cases. In the last few years, the tempo of the growth of its docket has picked up, and now it receives about twenty to twenty-five cases a year. The increased number of cases brought before the court is the result of reforms that have taken place at the level of the Inter-American Commission on Human Rights, the feeder of cases to the Court.[26] The commission's docket has grown exponentially during the past decade. In 2011, it reported having received 1,658 cases (petitions) for that year.[27] In 1999, the number was 581.[28] As in Europe, growing numbers reflect growing awareness of the existence of this remedy and how to access it. It will certainly grow exponentially,

---

[25] European Court of Human Rights, Annual Report (2012), 147 (Statistical Information).
[26] 'If the State in question has accepted the jurisdiction of the Inter-American Court ... and the Commission considers that the State has not complied with the recommendations of the report ... it shall refer the case to the Court, *unless there is a reasoned decision by an absolute majority of the members of the Commission to the contrary*' (emphasis added). Inter-American Commission on Human Rights, Rules of Procedure, Art. 45(1), as amended during the Commission's 137th regular session, held from 28 October to 13 November 2009, and entered into force on 31 December 2009.
[27] Inter-American Commission on Human Rights, Annual Report (2011), Chapter 3.b, Table A.
[28] Inter-American Commission on Human Rights, Annual Report (1999), Chapter 3.b.

unless the system is reformed. As a matter of fact, at the time of writing, a quarrelsome process of discussion of possible reform of the commission has started, spearheaded by certain Latin American states that would like to see the Inter-American system of protection of human rights made less accessible and probably less incisive.[29]

Yet, as the history of all international adjudicative bodies shows, once individuals are given access, they eventually develop a penchant for litigation. The number of cases brought is initially small, as knowledge of the existence of these mechanisms and how to use them is limited. But as cases are brought and litigated, knowledge expands. This is the only plausible explanation behind the seemingly odd statistics of certain human rights quasi-judicial bodies. For instance, in the case of the Committee Against Torture (CAT), Switzerland, Sweden, and Canada are respectively first, second and third on the list of countries against which most complaints ('communications' in such bodies' parlance) have been brought (respectively 135, 111, and 82).[30] Of the sixty-four states that have accepted the jurisdiction of the committee for complaints by individuals, thirty-four states have never been the object of a complaint, many of which have a less than stellar human rights record. For instance, although Russia accepted the jurisdiction of the committee in 1991, up to the time of writing there has been only one complaint brought against it.[31]

Of all the UN human rights quasi-judicial bodies, only the Human Rights Committee has a total docket of note (2,145 cases in its history), while those of the others range from zero (Rights of Persons with Disability) to twenty-seven (Discrimination against Women – CEDAW) to forty-five (Racial Discrimination).[32] Considering the fact that these are bodies of the United Nations, not regional organizations, and that several dozen states have accepted their jurisdiction to receive individual communications (e.g., 115 in the case of the Human Rights Committee; 102 for CEDAW; 64 for Torture and 54 for Racial Discrimination), these numbers will certainly grow if and when awareness of these mechanisms

---

[29] See 'Consultation to Actors of the Inter-American System for the Protection of Human Rights', available at www.oas.org/en/iachr/strengthening/consultation.asp.

[30] 'Status of Communications Dealt With by the CAT under Article 22 Procedure (24/07/2012)', available at www2.ohchr.org/english/bodies/petitions/StatisticalInformation.htm (statistical survey, CAT 48th session).

[31] Ibid.

[32] 'Communications/Complaints Procedures', www2.ohchr.org/english/bodies/complaints. htm.

becomes as commonplace as that of the European Convention on Human Rights and the Inter-American systems.[33]

Thus, far from having reached the high-water mark, on aggregate international litigation has just taken off. But what does this mean for the international legal system as a whole? If one thinks of international adjudication merely as a dispute-settlement exercise, obviously these developments are mildly interesting or plainly immaterial. In the end, it does not matter where – nationally or internationally – and how – through adjudication or diplomacy – disputes are settled or rights are recognized, as long as they are. Every act of adjudication is a story in itself. Litigation is essentially a retrospective, private exercise, mostly for the benefit of the parties.

But litigation has another important public dimension. It not only looks backwards, to see who was right and who was wrong in doing whatever was done. It is also system-building and forward-looking. Consider the significant public, *erga omnes*, effects of international adjudication. Only a clueless legal scholar would nowadays affirm that decisions of international adjudicative bodies do not add to the fabric of international law. Nowadays, more so than before, international courts and tribunals contribute to the making of international law by weaving webs of precedents, imbuing treaties with meaning, and, generally, by establishing new reference points for legal argument.[34] Judicial decisions frequently amount to influential arguments in later legal discourse. This is patent in all fields of international law. Whoever wants to formulate an argument about human rights anywhere in the world, before any human rights body, will hardly do so without drawing on the rich jurisprudence of the European Court of Human Rights. Normative assessments of international judicial law-making aside, international adjudication's significant role in thickening at least some fields and questions of international law is today beyond dispute.[35]

So far, two dozen international courts have issued about 37,000 binding legal judgments – 90 per cent of them since 1990 – not to mention thousands of arbitral awards.[36] This mass of judicial reasoning cannot easily be relegated to the ancillary role that the canonical sources of international

---

[33] Ibid.

[34] See Armin von Bogdandy and Ingo Venzeke, 'The Spell of Precedents: Lawmaking by International Courts and Tribunals', in Cesare Romano, Karen Alter, Yuval Shany (eds.), *The Oxford University Press Handbook of International Adjudication* (Oxford University Press, 2013) 503.

[35] Ibid.   [36] Alter, *New Terrain*, above n. 6.

470 CESARE P. R. ROMANO

law claim it should have. Yet, as the body of international adjudicative precedents mushrooms, the question of who litigates, and, even more importantly, the question of *who does not litigate*, raise important normative issues.

As I have written elsewhere, the 'goods' that international adjudicative bodies produce (e.g., the judgments, awards, and orders, the settlement, the predictability, and the stability that they bring, etc.) are 'global public goods'.[37] In short, and to keep it simple, *public goods* are goods whose use by one person does not reduce their availability for others (non-rivalrous), and, once created, it is impossible (or too costly) to exclude third parties from their benefits (non-excludable).[38] A textbook example of a public good is a street sign. It will not wear out, even if large numbers of people are looking at it, and it would be extremely difficult, costly, and inefficient to limit its use to only one or a few persons and try to prevent others from looking at it, too. Likewise, the decision of an international court is non-rivalrous and non-excludable. It is non-rivalrous in the sense that if an adjudicative decision is relied on by an actor it does not diminish the chance of another actor to invoke it in the same way. The more a precedent is invoked, the more confidently parties in disputes will invoke it to argue their own cases persuasively. Additionally, international judicial precedents are non-excludable because they have *erga omnes* effects, as just explained. While the dispositive part of a judgment speaks only to the parties in the case in question, the reasoning leading to the dispositive and the dicta add to the body of international precedent. They speak to all categories of international actors (sovereign states, international organizations, and so on) in all places, at all times.

Conversely, *private goods* are both excludable and rivalrous. I can buy a cake and have exclusive property rights over it (excludable). Once I have eaten it, no one else can enjoy that same cake (rivalrous). The award of an

---

[37] Cesare Romano, 'The United States and International Courts: Getting the Cost–Benefit Analysis Right', in Romano, *The Sword and the Scales: The United States and International Courts and Tribunals* (Cambridge University Press, 2009) 419, 433; Cesare Romano, 'International Courts and Tribunals: Price, Financing and Output', in Stefan Voigt, Max Albert, and Dieter Schmidtchen (eds.), *International Conflict Resolution, Vol. 23: Conferences on New Political Economy/Jahrbuch für neue Politische Ökonomie* (Tübingen: Mohr Siebeck, 2006) 189, 189–91. On 'global public goods' see Inge Kaul, Isabelle Grunberg, and Marc A. Stern (eds.) *Global Public Goods: International Cooperation in the 21st Century* (Oxford University Press, 1999).

[38] Paul A. Samuelson, 'The Pure Theory of Public Expenditure', (1954) 36 *Review of Economics and Statistics* 387; Paul A. Samuelson, 'A Diagrammatic Exposition of a Theory of Public Expenditure', (1955) 37 *Review of Economics and Statistics* 350.

arbitral tribunal that is kept secret, and thus does not contribute to the body of international law, is also an example of a private good. It benefits the parties but no one else.[39]

The fundamental problem of public goods is the 'free-rider'. The cost of international litigation is high. It includes financial and political costs. The financial costs are those of creating and maintaining operative adjudicative bodies and of the lawyers to actually litigate. The political costs include the reduction in sovereignty, the risk of being exposed to litigation, if the adjudicative body in question has compulsory jurisdiction, and the risk of losing the case, to name just the most obvious ones. Because public goods are non-excludable, they provide benefits equally to those who bear the costs of producing the good and those who do not. Free-riders do not bear the costs of producing the good, but reap the benefits.

As we saw, so far in history, the cost of creating the international adjudicative infrastructure and justifying its existence by using it has been shouldered by a relatively small group of actors. Like every other state they pursue their own national interest, but unlike most of their peers they understand the long-term benefits of having an international legal system that is sustained by a network of adjudicative bodies that interpret and apply its rules. Frequent users of the international adjudicative system – be they states, large corporations, human rights advocacy groups, or even the lawyers who actually litigate cases – are interested not only in whether they win or lose a particular case, but also in *how* they win it or lose it.[40] They understand that international litigation always has the effect of reasserting and reinforcing the institutions of international law through which the dispute is pursued, and in this way strengthening the international legal system as such.[41] Thus, asking why states litigate, or when, or under what circumstances, is just a starting point. We need to start talking also about why states should do so, and what can be done to enlarge participation beyond the small circle of the usual repeat players. As the mapping exercise is being completed, the next challenge is to enter solidly into normative terrain.

---

[39] To be precise, economists would call it a 'club good'. Club goods are non-rivalrous (or largely non-rivalrous), but excludable. See, for instance, James M. Buchanan, 'An Economic Theory of Clubs', (1965) 32 *Economica* 1.

[40] Lowe, above n. 3, 213.   [41] Ibid.

INDEX

Abraham, Judge, 93
Abyei Boundary Commission experts, 185
Abs–Shawcross Draft Convention on Investments Abroad, 406, 417
'act of state' doctrine, 43, 44, 45, 46
Advisory Centre on WTO Law, 36, 394
Africa, proliferation of regional courts and tribunals, 177, 178, 182
African Charter on Human and Peoples' Rights, 11, 455
African Commission on Human and Peoples' Rights, 455
African Court of Human and Peoples' Rights, 11, 179, 354
African states, 166–89, 308
  Abyei Boundary Commission experts, 185
  alleged mistrust of international adjudication, 166
  boundary disputes, 180, 182, 183, 184, 185
  commitment to peaceful settlement of disputes, 170
  culture of diplomacy, 177, 182
  decisions to enter into litigation, 188
  and the Hague Convention, 174
  and the ICJ, 171
  and the ICSID Convention, 172
  'ideology' of adjudication, 175–88
  independence, 168
  international legal personalities of, 168
  and international treaties, 172
  regionalization of adjudication, 175–81

African Union Border Programme, 38
An Agenda for Peace, 132
al Bashir, Omar Hassan Almad, 340
Al-Khasawneh, Judge, 300–1
Algiers Declarations, 154, 448
aliens, protection of, 404, 436–58
  applicable law, 441
  in an armed conflict, 440
  avenues available to redress claims, 441–7, 459
  categories of claims, 436, 438–41
  claims commissions, 447–53
  and consular assistance, 440, 444
  dispute settlement options for, 436–58
  forcible rescue missions, 442
  foreign investors' claims, 439
  and human rights, 437
  and inter-state litigation, 445, 453–8
  by litigation, 436
  rule of exhaustion of local remedies, 442, 458
  status of the individual, 441
  and treatment of minority groups, 439
Allsop, Justice, 51–2
Amnesty International, 363
Annan, Kofi, 132
Antarctic Treaty, 52
Antarctic Treaty System, 26, 288
arbitration, 4–7, 261, 333
  ability to specify the applicable law, 5
  ad hoc tribunals, 197
  advantages of, 4
  Anglo-American commissions, 4
  between Asian states, 160–4

472

awards on the legality of the use of force, 323–5
choice of arbitrators, 5
collection of data on, 198
effectiveness of, 7
enforcement of decisions, 7
in inter-state disputes, 7
international commercial arbitration, 426–8
limitations of, 7
mixed arbitrations, 7
procedural arrangements, 5
situations in which it is used, 4
and use of force, 333
vulnerabilities of, 334
arbitration agreements, 5, 197
model rules, 6
procedural arrangements, 5
arbitration treaties, 106
Argentina, 402
Statute of the River Uruguay, 102
armed conflict
adjudication of, 330–51
cost of, 351
difficulties of fact-finding, 341, 342, 349
effective remedies for the consequences of war, 351
effectiveness of, 350
history of, 330–4
international military tribunals, 335
jurisdiction, 350
mixed claims commissions, 330, 332, 333–4
and power imbalances, 330
rules governing, 330
ASEAN, 158
and the ICJ, 148
ASEAN–Australia–New Zealand Free Trade Agreement, 408
Asian states, 148–65
acceptance of the ICJ's jurisdiction, 151
arbitration between, 160–2, 164
bilateral arbitration agreements, 160–2
bilateral relationships among, 156

cases involving special agreements, 157–60
and ICJ, 149–60
maritime boundary disputes, 164
optional clause declarations, 149–52
and UNCLOS, 162–4
unilateral applications to the ICJ, 152–7
Australia, 30
Aboriginal people, 51
and Antarctica, 53
consent to jurisdiction, 65
David Hicks case, 444
engagement with international law, 47–53
Environment Protection and Biodiversity Conservation Act 1999, 51, 53
executive government, 51, 52
and the ICJ, 43, 61
and international litigation, 61–78
international relations, 51
and ITLOS, 61
lessons from litigation, 53–4
and New Zealand, 421
optional clause declaration, 64
Petroleum (Australia–Indonesia Zone of Co-operation) Act 1990, 49
and public international law, 53
public opinion, 67
Seas and Submerged Lands Act 1973, 49
Trade Policy Statement, 421–2
and the WTO dispute settlement mechanism, 392
Australia–Argentina BIT, 429–30
Australia–New Zealand Closer Economic Relations Trade Agreement, 421
Australia–United States Free Trade Agreement, 421

Bali Nine, 438–9
Ban Ki-moon, 369
Bangladesh, 278, 394
Bárcenas-Esguerra Treaty, 92
Beaumont, Justice, 50

474   INDEX

bilateral arbitration agreements, 149,
150–2
and domestic political pressure, 279
bilateral investment treaties, 401, 402,
433, 466
choice of forums under, 429
definition of 'investment', 409
definition of 'investor', 409
and domestic law, 430
emergence of, 407–9
and inter-state disputes, 415
interpretation and application, 413
and jurisdiction *ratione personae*,
408
and jurisdiction *ratione temporis*,
409
obligation not to expropriate
investments, 411
obligation to accord 'full protection
and security' to investments,
411
obligation to accord 'fair and
equitable treatment' to
investments, 410
obligation to accord MFN
treatment, 412
obligation to accord national
treatment to investors, 411
'observance of undertakings'
obligation (umbrella clause),
413
procedural protection, 417
purposes of, 407
requirement for negotiation, 422
requirement to submit claims to the
courts of the host state, 428
standard structure, 408
substantive standards of protection
in, 409–13
temporal protection, 409
Black, Chief Justice, 49, 52
Bolivia, Peace Agreement with Chile,
89
boundary disputes (land), 98–101, 451
Boutros-Ghali, Boutros, 132
Breard, Angel, 35, 87, 444, 456
Brennan, Justice, 44, 46
Brilmayer, Lea, 193–227, 232

Britain, 29
and the United States, 31
Buergenthal, Judge, 341
Bush, George W., 323

Cambodia, 149
optional clause declaration, 150
and Thailand, 165
Canada–Slovak Republic BIT, 409
Central American Court of Justice, 79
Central America–United States Free
Trade Agreement
(CAFTA-DR), 127
'denial of benefits' provision, 127,
128
Chicago Convention, 152, 153
Chile
Pact of Bogotá, 89
Peace Agreement with Bolivia, 89
China, 165, 465
civil society, 286, 446
Claim of Heirs of Jules Brun, 332
claims commissions, 447–53
factors in which they offer benefits,
452
individual access to, 452
number of, 448
and power imbalances, 448
as victor's justice, 447, 449
climate change, 289
Colombia
objection to the jurisdiction of the
ICJ, 94
and the Pact of Bogotá, 95
security interests, 95
comity, 56, 270
Commission for the Conservation of
Antarctic Marine Living
Resources, 281, 282
Commission on Security and
Co-operation in Europe, 6
Committee Against Torture, 468
conciliation, 425–6
Conference on Security and
Co-operation in Europe, 137
consent, principle of, 8
consular assistance, 440, 444
Contadora process, 21

INDEX

Convention against Torture, 180, 360, 361, 362, 468
Convention for the Conservation of Southern Bluefin Tuna, 267, 268–70
Convention for the Elimination of Discrimination against Women, 360
Convention on Biological Diversity, 273
Convention on Conciliation and Arbitration (Stockholm Convention), 137
Convention on Enforced Disappearance, 361
Convention on Environmental Impact Assessment in a Transboundary Context, 297
Convention on Migrant Workers, 361
Convention on Persons with Disabilities, 361
Convention on the Conservation of Southern Bluefin Tuna, 67
Convention on the Continental Shelf, 49
Convention on the Elimination of All Forms of Racial Discrimination, 66, 172, 309, 318, 360
    Committee on the Elimination of Racial Discrimination, 361–2, 364
    Conciliation Commission, 368
    procedure for dispute resolution between states, 368
    right of individual petition, 364, 365
    state acceptance of its procedures, 364
Convention on the Prevention of Crimes against Internationally Protected Persons, including Diplomatic Agents, 154
Convention on the Rights of the Child, 361, 365
Convention on the Settlement of Investment Disputes between States and Nationals of Other States, 172, 406

ratification, 407
Convention on International Trade in Endangered Species of Wild Fauna and Flora, 273
Convention Relative to the Preservation of Fauna and Flora in their Natural State, 294
Council of Europe
    Committee of Ministers, 135, 136
    European Convention for the Peaceful Settlement of Disputes, 136
    recommendations on nominations of arbitrators, 136
Council of the International Civil Aviation Organization, 152–3
Crawford, James, 271, 281, 282
Crennan, Justice, 50
criminal law, 463
criminal responsibility, 334–40
customary international law, 17
    and environmental impact assessments, 297
    minimum standard of treatment, 410
    rights accorded to foreign citizens under, 355
    rules on the protection of aliens, 404

decisions to enter into litigation
    and attitudes to the ICJ and its jurisdiction, 32–3
    and calculation of risk, 40
    in cases concerning the use of force, 305
    certainty and predictability, 266, 272
    compliance with rulings, 33–4
    cost of preparation and presentation of a case, 36, 250
    damage to relationships or worsening of a dispute, 39
    and domestic political pressure, 36–8, 250, 277, 287
    in environmental disputes, 285–91
    extralegal factors in, 275
    factors in, 24, 28–40, 104, 138, 141, 233, 285–7
    and foreign policy goals, 40, 250, 290

476 INDEX

decisions to enter into litigation (*cont.*)
  and global public opinion, 39–40
  and information asymmetry, 222
  and levelling the playing field, 34–6
  likelihood of success, 30–2
  litigation as a delaying tactic, 38–9
  and the make-up of the bench, 31
  and the nature of the dispute, 34
  and negotiated settlements, 36
  and negotiation, 140
  pragmatic considerations, 40
  publicly declared reasons for, 138
  reputation and national interest
    factors, 279–83
decisions to institute proceedings,
    67–70
  and international lawyers, 68
  and members of the legal academy,
    68
  and public opinion, 67
Declaration on Principles of
    International Law concerning
    Friendly Relations and
    Co-operation among States, 3
democratic peace theory, 286
Democratic Republic of the Congo,
    308
developing countries
  access to markets, 397
  court systems of, 430
  and the DSU consultative process,
    381
  flexibility allowed, 394
  and initiation of litigation, 35, 327
  lack of resources and expertise, 397
  and 'reasonable time' for
    conforming with WTO rules,
    394
  special and differential treatment,
    381, 393
  and the WTO dispute settlement
    mechanism, 378, 393, 395, 396,
    398, 399, 466
diplomatic protection, 356, 431–2,
    434
  challenges to admissibility of claims
    on its basis, 454
  and gunboat diplomacy, 431

politicizing effect of, 432
reasons not to use it as a means of
    settling investment disputes,
    431
right of, 436, 444, 453
scope *ratione materiae*, 438
state of incorporation of companies,
    455
dispute settlement
  acceptance of decisions, 22
  arbitration, 4–7, 261
  assumption that states want disputes
    resolved, 25
  compulsory mechanisms for
    settling, 63
  courts and tribunals, 11–15
  and customary international law, 17
  de-legalization of, 185
  decisions of international courts and
    tribunals, 18
  diplomatic means, 3, 261
  under human rights treaties, 368
  International Court of Justice, 7–11
  judicial decisions and the
    development of international
    law, 15–19
  legal and political dimensions, 34
  legal means, 3, 19, 20
  and negotiation, 140
  and political institutions and
    processes, 24–40
  provisions in conventions, 6
  temporary tribunals, 14
  through bilateral negotiations, 39
Dogger Bank dispute, 333, 351
domestic law
  procedural and substantive
    obligations, 103
  regulatory regimes, 103
DSU (Understanding on the Rules and
    Procedures Governing the
    Settlement of Disputes), 381,
    388
Duke of Brunswick v. *King of Hanover*,
    45
dumping/anti-dumping disputes,
    379
  beneficial effect of dumping, 380

INDEX

Economic Community of West African
States (ECOWAS) Court of
Justice, 180
Ecuador, Pact of Bogotá, 89
Ecuador–United States BIT, 416
Egypt and Israel, Taba strip dispute,
215
Energy Charter Treaty, 408, 418
environmental regulation, 291, 292
compliance procedures, 292
'depth' of, 294–5
and economic development, 298,
299
enforcement of, 295
and environmental impact
assessments, 293, 297
flexible standards, 294
procedural and substantive
obligations, 103, 295
procedural standards, 295–302
specificity and clarity of rules, 295
types of obligations, 295
environmental security, 288
Eritrea and Ethiopia, war between, 440
nature of, 345, 347
treatment of prisoners of war, 348
Eritrea–Ethiopia Claims Commission,
14, 317, 324, 345–50, 450–1
claims involving rape and sexual
abuse, 349
determining the applicable law,
347–50
difficulties of fact-finding, 348
jurisdiction, 346–7, 450
mandate of, 346
testimony of medical personnel, 350
treatment of prisoners of war, 348
Europe
acceptance of the ICJ's jurisdiction,
134
acceptance of the PCIJ, 134
dispute settlement in practice,
137–41
and inter-state litigation, 130–46
international judicial machinery in,
57
and the jurisdiction of international
courts and tribunals, 146

regional dispute settlement
instruments, 136
support for international dispute
settlement, 146
'Western' and 'Eastern', 130
European Convention for the Peaceful
Settlement of Disputes, 136,
138, 373
European Convention on Human
Rights, 353, 360, 367, 373
European Court of Human Rights, 11,
353, 443, 455, 467, 469
compulsory jurisdiction, 360
individual access to, 367
European Court of Justice, 270, 271
expropriation of investments
compensable expropriations, 411
non-compensable regulatory
measures, 411

fair and equitable treatment, 16
Finklestein, Justice, 52
Fischer, Dana D., 40, 245–6
fishing and fisheries, 257
and UNCLOS provisions, 265
forum prorogatum doctrine, 319
Framework Agreement on Trade in
Bananas, 389
France
and the ICJ, 465
optional clause declaration, 65
and Siam, 217, 220, 221
Treaty of Amity and Commerce with
the United States, 403
free choice of means, principle of, 13
Friendship, Commerce and Navigation
Treaties, 403, 404
Fuller, Chief Justice, 44

General Act for the Pacific Settlement
of International Disputes, 65,
66, 70, 142
General Agreement on Tariffs and
Trade, 375
Uruguay Round, 375, 376
General Agreement on Trade in
Services, 389

general principles of law, 17
Geneva Conventions, 335, 336, 347
  rules governing the conduct of
    military operations, 348
  treatment of prisoners of war, 347
genocide, 318
Genocide Convention, 33, 153, 172,
  336
German–American Mixed Claims
  Commission, 333–4
Germany, 29
  Germany–China BIT, 414, 418, 423
  Germany–Pakistan BIT, 417
Gladstone, 112
'global administrative law' project,
  296
global financial crises, 385
Great Britain, inter-state litigation,
  141–6
Guantánamo Bay, 444
Gummow, Justice, 46, 50

Hague Convention, 6, 113, 174, 335
Hague Peace Conference, 107, 108–13
Handbook on the Peaceful Settlement of
  Disputes between States, 131
Harvard Draft Convention on the
  International Responsibility of
  States for Injuries to aliens, 406
Havana Conference, 405
Higgins, Judge, 313
Hill, Justice, 49
Honduras, Maritime Delimitation
  Treaty with Colombia, 86
Huber, Max, 166
Hudson, Manley O., 106, 114, 118
human rights and international
  litigation, 353–73
human rights courts, 353
  and development of international
    law, 27
  regional, 446, 462
human rights, protection of, 437, 438
human rights treaties, 360
  enforcement of, 369
  inter-state complaints under, 368
  monitoring system, 361–3, 368, 371,
    372, 373, 374

reporting obligations in, 363
right of individual petition, 363–7,
  374
state acceptance of their procedures,
  364
states parties to, 373
Human Rights Watch, 363

idealism and realism, 141, 144, 146
implied consent, doctrine of, 319
India, 151, 152–3, 164
  and Bangladesh, 278
  Indus Waters Treaty, 161
Indonesia, 157–8
Indonesia–Netherlands BIT, 417
Indus Waters Treaty, Court of
  Arbitration, 161
Inter-American Commission on
  Human Rights, 467
Inter-American Convention on
  Human Rights, 373
Inter-American Court of Human
  Rights, 11, 354, 455, 457, 467
international arbitration, 461
international arbitration of investment
  disputes, 401, 433, 445, 446
International Bar Association
  Draft Rules on the Mediation of
    Investor–State Disputes, 424
  sub-committee on mediation in
    investor–state disputes, 424–5
International Centre for Settlement of
  Investment Disputes, 172, 406,
  461, 466
  participation in, 466
  success of, 407
International Civil Aviation
  Organization (ICAO), 152–3
international commercial arbitration,
  434
  complexity of issues in, 427
  concession contracts, 426
International Committee of the Red
  Cross, 348, 446
International Convention for the
  Mutual Protection of Private
  Property Rights in Foreign
  Countries, 406

INDEX

International Convention for the
    Regulation of Whaling, 273,
    289
International Convention for the
    Settlement of Investment
    Disputes, 172, 356, 418, 420–2
    'Additional Facility' Rules, 419
    African states and, 172
    provisions to facilitate conciliation,
        425–6
International Court of Human Rights,
    358–61, 373
International Court of Justice (ICJ),
    7–11, 16, 28, 328, 340–3, 461
    acceptance of its decisions, 10
    acceptance of its jurisdiction, 32, 83,
        134, 142, 146, 171, 354
    advisory opinions as a substitute for
        litigation, 327, 328
    advisory opinions on the use of
        force, 325–8
    and African technical boundary
        commissions, 186–7
    approach to evidence, 342
    and ASEAN, 148
    and Asian states, 148, 149–60
    Australia and, 61
    authority of, 8
    binding judgments, 10, 15
    Cambodia, 150
    cases concerning the use of force,
        306, 315, 317–23
    cases involving boundary disputes,
        29
    chambers, 8
    composition of, 8
    compulsory jurisdiction, 114, 133
    and conventions and treaties, 16
    and the *Corfu Channel* case, 314–15
    decisions *ex aequo et bono*, 9, 30
    development of international law,
        15
    difficulties of fact-finding, 341
    docket size, 464–5
    and environmental disputes, 293,
        297
    equitable considerations, 10
    European cases, 139–40

exceptions to the optional clause,
    134, 135
fair and equitable treatment, 16
framing of questions for, 30
function of, 9
incidental jurisdiction, 10
and international human rights law,
    354, 356
jurisdiction, 9, 28, 88–94, 140, 306,
    310, 318, 325
and Latin American states, 79–103
limits of its jurisdiction, 188, 464
maritime boundary disputes, 80, 86,
    139, 234
as a model international court, 26–8
and negotiation, 239
optional clause mechanism, 8, 81,
    134, 143, 212
    basis of jurisdiction, 87, 197, 306
    declarations, 9, 64, 133, 242
    interpretation of, 83, 84
participation in, 9, 32, 464, 465
parties to, 133
political dimension of cases, 139,
    140
and political institutions and
    processes, 20, 21, 22
provisional measures of protection,
    10, 311
reform of, 464
remedies for individuals, 438, 456
as a replacement for other dispute
    settlement mechanisms, 102–4
representatives of the main
    civilizations and legal systems
    of the world, 8
role of, 117, 132, 184, 185, 310,
    454
and the rule of law, 129
significance of, 11
special agreements, 187
state behaviour in relation to, 27
states' reluctance to commit to, 20
territorial disputes, 196
treaty-based jurisdiction, 306
and the UN Security Council, 116
unilateral applications involving
    Asian states, 152–7

480 INDEX

International Court of Justice
(ICJ) (cont.)
and the United States, 128
use of negotiation and litigation,
237
international courts and tribunals,
11–15, 24
acceptance of their jurisdiction, 460
cost of, 471
courts of regional economic and/or
political integration, 27
and domestic law, 57
effectiveness of, 78
and European states, 146
function of, 21
human rights courts, 27
individual access to, 467, 468
influence of state practice on, 240
international criminal courts, 27
jurisdiction of, 196, 241–3, 461
jurisdictional rules of, 196
legal remedies for individuals, 27
non-rivalrous and non-excludable
decisions of, 470
and political institutions and
processes, 19, 73
proliferation of, 131, 235, 461
regional and sub-regional, 462
resolution of inter-state disputes, 27
and the rule of law, 169
and sovereignty, 206
types of, 27
International Covenant on Civil and
Political Rights, 359, 438
inter-state complaints under, 368
monitoring committee, 360, 362
right of individual petition, 364,
365–6, 367
right to life, 439
and state sovereignty, 373
states parties to, 367
International Covenant on Economic,
Social and Cultural Rights, 359
monitoring committee, 360, 362
right of individual petition, 364
and state sovereignty, 373
International Criminal Court, 12, 336,
461, 463

international criminal law, 27, 336
International Criminal Tribunal for
Rwanda, 12, 337
International Criminal Tribunal for the
former Yugoslavia, 12, 337
international criminal tribunals, 463
burden of proof, 339
claims involving rape and sexual
abuse, 349
clarification and expansion of the
law, 338
cost of, 351
difficulties of fact-finding, 339
fairness in, 340
history and jurisprudence of, 337–8
knowledge of complex military
matters, 348, 350
and state co-operation, 340
testimony of medical personnel,
350
international disputes
compulsory mechanisms for
settling, 61
depoliticization of, 22
legal and political dimensions, 21,
139–40, 181
role of national courts, 57
underlying issues, 53
international environmental disputes,
284–304
decisions to enter into litigation,
284–304
and environmental statecraft, 291
factors in decision to litigate, 285–91
first-order and second-order issues,
288–9
and foreign policy goals, 289
growth of litigation on, 291–3, 302,
303
impediments to submission for
independent arbitration or
adjudication, 290
and international relations theory,
291–2
polymorphic nature of, 284
pressure to resolve, 290
strategic and tactical litigation,
290–1

INDEX

uncertainty and, 299
variety of forums available, 285
international environmental law
complexity of, 284
development of, 303
effectiveness of, 292
and environmental impact
assessments, 299
judicial review of decisions, 297
legitimacy of, 284
procedural and substantive
obligations, 296, 298, 300
international human rights
commissions, 446
international human rights courts,
442
individual access to, 443
international human rights law, 42,
439, 463
complaints mechanisms and
techniques, 353
and consular assistance, 455
diversity of international
mechanisms, 354
evolution of, 358–61
right of individual petition, 363–7
state responsibility for acts violating
the rights of foreign citizens,
355–8
international humanitarian law, 452
and criminal prosecutions, 338
individual criminal responsibility for
violations of, 334–40
and institutions to assess criminal
responsibility, 338
institutions to mount and
administer prosecutions,
338
state responsibility for violations of,
340, 351
international investment disputes,
401–34
inter-state disputes, 415–16
and international investment law,
402
investor–state disputes, 414–15
and state responsibility, 414
types of dispute, 414–16

international investment law, 401,
403–16
bilateral investment treaties (BITs),
407–9
development of, 432, 434
efforts to reach multilateral
agreement, 405–7
origins and development of, 403–5
precedent in, 433
and procedures for the settlement of
investment disputes, 402
substantive standards of protection
in BITs, 409–13
withdrawal of states from, 420–2
international judicialization, 460, 462,
463
international law
and armed conflict, 330–51
bias towards more powerful states,
35
collection of data on, 198
common law of international
adjudication, 18
contribution of international
adjudicative bodies, 469
contribution of national courts,
decisions of international courts and
tribunals, 17, 19
development of, 15–19, 109,
469
and diplomatic protection, 357
dispute settlement system, 261
and domestic law, 42, 47–53,
103
fragmentation of, 179, 235
goal of resolving disputes, 25
imposition of public interest rules
on states, 103
and individual rights, 356
individuals as subjects of, 437
liberal theories of, 286
neutral state obligations, 111
place of international litigation in,
3–22
precedent in, 15, 337
principles of, 46
rights of individuals, 54, 357
role of judicial decisions, 16

482 INDEX

international law (*cont.*)
and separate opinions of individual
judges, 18
and state responsibility, 47
on the use of force, 323, 328
International Law Association, Draft
Statutes of the Arbitral Tribunal
for Foreign Investment and the
Foreign Investment Court, 405
International Law Commission
articles on diplomatic protection,
453
Draft Articles on Prevention of
Transboundary Harm from
Hazardous Activities, 296
model rules for arbitration
agreements, 6
international litigation
admissibility phase, 72, 75
appointment of an ad hoc judge, 76
and bilateral agreements, 278
burden of proof, 73
and calculation of risk, 69, 70
cost of preparation and presentation
of a case, 69, 78
diplomatic ramifications, 78
European perspectives on, 130–46
facts and evidence, 73–5
future developments, 460–71
human rights as a subject of, 353–73
impact on bilateral relations, 69
involvement of third states, 77
jurisdictional issues, 63–7
jurisdictional phase, 71, 72, 75
lessons from, 61
the litigation process, 70–3
normative issues, 470
political dimension, 70, 72, 73
procedural and logistical issues,
75–7
public dimension of, 469
and public opinion, 68
reluctance of states to institute, 69
remedies for individuals, 353
scientific evidence, 74
selection of counsel, 76
significance of, 19–22
the substantive case, 73–7

tactical decisions, 70
unpredictability, 69, 70, 78
International Military Tribunal at
Nuremberg, 335
international military tribunals, 335,
351
International Seabed Authority, 302
International Tribunal for the Law of
the Sea (ITLOS), 12, 234, 461
Asian states and, 148
Australia and, 61
European cases, 138
jurisdiction, 13, 301
organization and jurisdiction of, 13
popularity of, 20, 262
Seabed Disputes Chamber, 303
Trust Fund, 36
International Whaling Commission,
68
inter se doctrine, 143
investor–state arbitration, 417–19
consent to, 418
disquiet about, 419–22
host-state consent to, 418
institutions and procedural rules for,
418
structural challenge of, 125–8
United States and, 107, 125–8
investor–state disputes
alternatives to arbitration, 422–32,
433
arbitration, 417–19
causes of action, 430
conciliation, 425–6
consultations, 422
and diplomatic protection, 431–2,
434
hybrid forms of settlement, 433
inter-state dispute settlement,
431–2
international commercial
arbitration, 426–8
jurisdictional issues, 428
legal impediments to submission to
local courts, 430
likelihood of negotiation being
successful, 423
mediation, 424–5

INDEX

methods for settling, 417
and national courts, 428–30, 434
negotiation, 422–4
Iran, 153
and the ICJ, 153
and the United States, 154–5
Iran–US Claims Tribunal, 7, 14, 21,
117, 155, 356, 448–9
Iraq, 344, 345, 449, 450
Israel, 215, 327
Italy–Chad BIT, 418

Japan, 30, 151, 152, 165
Japanese whaling in Antarctic waters,
43
Jay Treaty, 4, 107, 108–13
and the development of
international law, 109
dispute settlement under, 109
maritime commission, 109
Jefferson, Thomas, 109
Jenks, C.W., 189
Jennings, Robert, 42
Johnson, Andrew, 110
Johnson–Clarendon Convention, 110,
111, 115
judicial restraint, 47
jurisdiction
bases of consent, 233
challenges to, 65
ratione temporis, 90
and state consent, 63–7, 196, 209,
222
justiciability, 43, 44, 45, 46, 47, 57

Kabila, Laurent, 308
Khomeini, Ayatollah, 35
Kirby, Justice, 51
Kosovo crisis, 32, 308–9

Latin American states
boundary disputes, 98–101
commitment to peaceful settlement
of disputes, 79, 104
decisions to enter into litigation, 248
Framework Agreement on Trade in
Bananas, 389
and the ICJ, 79–94, 102–3, 104

lack of negotiating capacity, 102
maritime boundary disputes, 80
preference for arbitration, 79, 80,
105
resistance against settlement of
boundary disputes, 99
territorial boundaries, 81
types of disputes, 80
US involvement in, 217
Lauterpacht, Hersch, 143, 146
law of the sea disputes
arbitration, 263–6
complexity of legal issues, 283
decisions to enter into litigation, 283
dispute settlement options, 261–3
domestic political factors in
decisions to litigate, 267
economic issues, 275–9
extralegal factors in decision
making, 275
and national interest, 283
non-binding negotiation, 262
reputation and national interest
factors, 279–83
settlement by litigation, 260–83
League of Arab States, 327
League of Nations, 89, 114, 128, 405
Libya, 184–5
litigation
advantages of, 21
barriers to domestic litigation, 43–7
and binding decisions, 20
capability of resolving a dispute, 34
cost of preparation and presentation
of a case, 36
decisions to enter into, 24, 28–40
function of, 20
international law framework, 24
and legal cultures, 28
'litigation crisis', 29
national and international, 42–57
and negotiation, 237
obstacles for private litigators, 43
parallel international and domestic
litigation, 42, 50, 53
political framework, 25
and political institutions and
processes, 24–40

INDEX

litigation (*cont.*)
  power disparities between the
    parties, 39
  and private rights, 53
  public interest litigation, 57
  service of process on a foreign
    respondent, 51–2
  and sovereignty, 29
Lowe, Vaughan, 37, 281, 290, 303

Malaysia, 157–8
  Group of Experts, 163
  and Singapore, 162, 163–4
  special agreement with Singapore,
    159
Malaysia–Australia Free Trade
  Agreement, 421
Manila Declaration on the Peaceful
  Settlement of International
  Disputes, 3, 7
maritime boundary disputes, 64, 80,
  98–101, 139, 465
  ad hoc tribunals, 234
  by agreement, 242, 254
  arbitration tribunals, 234
  in Asia, 164, 165
  bases of jurisdiction, 235
  cases, 234–7
  and coastal concavities, 249, 256
  consent to jurisdiction, 241, 242,
    252, 258
    ad hoc consent, 254, 255, 258
    ante hoc consent, 236, 242, 243,
      254, 256
  costs and benefits of settlement,
    251
  decisions to enter into litigation,
    230–51, 257, 258
  delimitation in accordance with
    general international law, 94
  and developments in jurisprudence,
    240
  dispute settlement decisions, 251–8
  and domestic political pressure, 247,
    255, 256
  effect of small islands, 247
  efficiency in, 250
  equidistance lines, 244, 257

equitable solutions, 17, 236, 244, 255
and familiarity with international
  procedures and forums, 249
foreign policy factor, 246
implementation problems, 100
issues outstanding after litigation,
  239
jurisdiction to litigate, 241–3
and land boundary disputes, 231,
  232
litigation and, 140
methodology for reaching equitable
  delimitations, 236, 244
at national and international levels,
  233
and negotiation, 245, 251, 254
Nicaragua v. *Colombia*, 94
non-resolution of, 251, 252, 256
party preferences, 251–8
political dimension, 244
possibility of winning factor, 247
and power imbalances, 248, 257
pre-litigation phases of, 245
proportionality, 95–6, 244
and resources on the continental
  shelf, 232, 245, 254, 257, 277,
  279
settlement by negotiation, 230
and sovereignty, 231, 241
special circumstances, 244
temporal urgency in, 245, 250
time and diplomacy factor, 246
use of negotiation and litigation in,
  237, 238
mediation, 424–5
Mexico and the United States, 87, 448,
  457–8
Montreal Protocol, 292
Moore, Justice, 52
Morocco, 166
Most Favoured Nation treatment, 404,
  412
multilateral environmental
  agreements, 291, 294, 463
Multilateral Investment Guarantee
  Agency Convention, success of,
  407
Myanmar, 164

INDEX

national treatment, 405
Nauru case
  appointment of an ad hoc judge, 76
  selection of counsel, 76
negotiation, 140
  and the ICJ, 181
  to identify and define a dispute, 239
  and litigation, 237
  a precondition to litigation, 239
New Zealand, 29, 421
Nicaragua, 21, 97–8, 249
  and Article VI of the Pact of Bogotá, 92
  boundary disputes, 97
  and the ICJ, 97
  lack of negotiating capacity, 97, 98
  and the United States, 97
Nicaragua v. *Colombia*
  Colombia's preliminary objections, 96
  proportionality, 96
Nicaragua v. *Honduras* cases
jurisdictional issues, 306
Nicaragua v. *United States* case
  burden of proof, 316
  importance of, 315–17
  jurisdictional issues, 313, 319
  US participation in proceedings, 320
Nicholls, Lord, 45
Nigeria, 181
Non-Aligned Movement, 326
non-intervention, principle of, 308, 315, 317, 442
non-use of force, principle of, 308, 314
North American Free Trade Agreement (NAFTA), 408, 416
North Atlantic Treaty Organization (NATO), 308–9
Nuclear Non-Proliferation Treaty, 326
Nuclear Tests case
  and domestic political pressure, 287, 290
  and environmental impact assessments, 297
  French perspective on, 69
  involvement of third states, 77
  provisional measures of protection, 71, 72

scientific evidence, 74
selection of counsel, 76
nulla poena sine lege, 336

Oil Platforms case
  jurisdictional issues, 306, 319, 321–3
  US participation in proceedings, 321
Oppenheim's International Law, 146
Organization of African Unity, 182, 346, 451
  Charter, 175
  Commission of Mediation, Conciliation and Arbitration, 175, 176, 177
Organization of American States, 83
  Charter, 82–3
Organization for Economic Cooperation and Development (OECD), Draft Convention on the Protection of Foreign Property, 406, 417

Pact of Bogotá, 82, 83, 84–5, 86, 88, 242
  aims of, 93
  Article VI, 88, 90, 91, 93
  Article XXXIV, 91
  'Belgian clause', 93, 94
  Colombia's withdrawal, 95
  effects of its poor drafting, 94
  and jurisdiction of the ICJ, 80, 306
  ratification, 83
Pakistan
  Indus Waters Treaty, 161
  optional clause declaration, 151
Permanent Court of Arbitration, 6, 112, 138, 333, 461
  ad hoc nature of, 112
  African states and, 174
  lack of permanence, 112–13
  membership of, 133
Permanent Court of International Justice (PCIJ), 8, 134, 262
  and the United Kingdom, 142
  and the United States, 113, 128
Peru, Pact of Bogotá, 89
Philippines, 151, 158
Phillimore, Lord, 143
'political question' doctrine, 46, 56

486 INDEX

private/public goods, 470
Protocol relating to the status of
refugees, 172
Pulp Mills case
breach of procedural and substantive
obligations, 102
and environmental impact
assessments, 299
and procedural environmental rules,
298
sustainable development, 293
Putnam, Robert D., 286

Ramos Horta, José, 48
realism and idealism, 141, 144, 146
Rio de Janeiro Protocol of 1942 on
Peace, Friendship and
Boundaries, 89
Rio Declaration, 294
rule of law, 26, 129, 132–3, 135
Russia, *Volga* case, 282

Sanitary and Phytosanitary Agreement,
392
Santos, Juan Manuel, 95
Schwebel, Judge, 182, 316, 341
Sea-Bed Disputes Chamber, 12, 13
Secretary-General's Trust Fund to
Assist States in the Settlement
of Disputes, 36
self-defence, 315, 316, 322, 323
self-determination, 48, 72, 317
Senegal, 180
Shawcross, Lord Hartley, 406
Siam, 217, 220, 221
Simma, Judge, 300–1, 358
Singapore, 164–5
Group of Experts, 163
and Malaysia, 162, 163–4
special agreement with Malaysia, 159
Society to Advance the Protection of
Foreign Investments, 406
South China Sea, 165
Southern Bluefin Tuna cases
agreement to litigate, 271
involvement of third states, 77
jurisdictional issues, 71, 75, 265, 290
scientific evidence, 74, 75

selection of counsel, 76
and UNCLOS jurisdiction, 273
sovereignty, 44, 157, 206, 442
contested, 193–227
and domestic law, 45
and human rights treaties, 372
and litigation, 29
and the WTO dispute settlement
system, 386
state responsibility, 47, 340, 351, 355–8,
414
Stockholm Chamber of Commerce,
Rules of the Arbitration
Institute, 418
Stockholm Convention on Conciliation
and Arbitration, 6, 137
Sudan, 185–6
Sudan People's Liberation Movement
Army, 185–6
sustainable development, 293
jurisprudence on, 299
procedural approach to, 298
Sutherland Report, 390
Sweden–Bolivia BIT, 415

Taft, William, 323
Tehran hostages dispute
merits phase, 117
provisional measures of protection,
116
significance of, 128, 129
Temple of Preah Vihear case
provisional measures of protection,
151
territorial adjudication, 193–227
agreement to, 194, 226
avoidance of jurisdiction, 196, 213,
222–5
basic assumptions about, 195–6,
213–25
basis for jurisdiction in, 210
cases evaluated, 228–9
collection of data on, 198
common sense about, 195
concept of 'winning' in, 200–1, 218,
220–1
and conflicts that do not reach
adjudication, 212

consent to adjudicate, 198, 226
  ex ante consent to, 194, 208–12,
    213
  ex post consent to, 194, 212, 226
courts, tribunals and jurisdictional
    rules, 196
decisions to enter into litigation, 213
definitional problems, 198–201
as a delaying mechanism, 223–5
and diplomatic negotiations, 216
and domestic political pressure,
    221–2
expectations of, 196, 214, 226
factors affecting, 193
hypotheses about, 201–12, 213
and information asymmetry, 226
initiating parties, 193, 198–9, 202–6,
    207–9, 212
and likelihood of success, 194,
    200–1, 206–8, 209, 222–3
litigation as a maximization strategy,
    195–6, 213, 218–22, 226
methodology for studying, 198–201
and negotiation, 219
and occupation of disputed territory,
    194, 199–200, 202–4, 206, 208
peace dividend scenario, 214–15
side payments scenario, 215–17
by special agreement, 222
symmetry of motivation in, 199, 203
territorial disputes, 195, 197
  and the ICJ, 196
  jurisprudence of, 198
  zero sum nature of, 195, 210, 214,
    219
third-party involvement scenario,
    217
uniqueness of territory, 195, 213–18,
    226
utility of, 226
value attached to territory, 214,
    219–20, 226
Thailand, 150–1, 165
Timor Gap dispute, 43, 48
Timor Gap Treaty, 48, 49
Tokyo Tribunal, 335
Treaty of Amity and Cooperation in
    Southeast Asia, 158

Treaty of Amity, Economic Relations,
    and Consular Rights between
    the United States and Iran, 154,
    155
Treaty of Utrecht, 403
Treaty of Versailles, 89, 335
Treaty of Washington, 31, 110, 111, 115
  dispute settlement provisions, 111
  and neutral state obligations, 111
Trindade, Judge Cancado, 357
Tunisia, 184–5

Uganda, 308
UNCITRAL Rules of Arbitration, 418,
    449
UN Commission on Human Rights,
    358
  expert monitoring committees, 360
  human rights treaties, 360
UN Convention on the Law of the Sea,
    6, 12, 197
  arbitration, 263–6
  Asian parties to, 162
  choice of forums under, 63, 260, 263
  compulsory dispute settlement
    procedures, 236, 240, 264
  exceptions to, 272, 275
  decisions to litigate under, 261
  dispute settlement system, 260–83
  European parties to, 138
  and flags of convenience, 280, 282
  incidental proceedings, 264, 265
  interpretation of, 260, 267–8, 270
  jurisdiction of courts and tribunals,
    264, 301
  limitations of the dispute settlement
    system, 266, 274
  phases of cases, 266
  priority of other tribunals or
    procedures, 268
  prompt release of vessels, 265,
    279–80
  provisional measures of protection,
    265
UNCTAD, 417
Understanding on the Rules and
    Procedures Governing the
    Settlement of Disputes *see* DSU

INDEX

UN General Assembly, 325, 326
  2005 Summit Outcome Document, 132
  Declaration of the High-level Meeting on the Rule of Law at the National and International Levels, 132–3, 135
UN High Commissioner for Human Rights, 365
UN Human Rights Committee, 363, 366–7, 455, 468
  reporting system, 363
UN Human Rights Council
  complaints mechanism, 371–2, 373
  mandate of, 369
  membership of, 370
  Universal Periodic Review, 359, 369–71
    adverse findings, 370
  Working Group on Communications, 372
  Working Group on Situations, 372
United Kingdom (*see also* Britain, Great Britain)
  citizens held in Guantánamo Bay, 444
  commitment to peaceful settlement of disputes, 144
  Commonwealth exception to the ICJ Statute, 143
  contribution to international dispute settlement, 145
  Conventions for the Pacific Settlement of International Disputes, 142
  and the Hague Peace Conference, 142
  and the ICJ, 142, 145, 146, 465
  idealism and realism, 141, 144, 146
  inter-state litigation, 141–6
  and ITLOS, 145
  Oppenheim's International Law, 146
  and the Permanent Court of International Justice, 142, 143
  support for arbitral proceedings, 145
  support for compulsory dispute settlement, 144
  and the United States, 142

United Kingdom–Argentina BIT, 428–9
United Kingdom–Chile BIT, 414
United Kingdom–India BIT, 425
United Kingdom–Singapore BIT, 418
United Nations, 28
  attitudes toward international dispute settlement, 131
  Charter, 24, 25, 131, 305, 337, 380, 422
  Secretary-General's Trust Fund to Assist States in the Settlement of Disputes, 36
  and the United States, 114, 128
United Nations Compensation Commission, 343–5, 449, 450, 452
  criteria defining claimants, 344
  mass claims techniques, 344
United States
  Alien Tort Claims Act, 54, 55
  Andean Trade Preference Act 1991, 389
  Articles of Confederation, 109
  and Britain, 31, 142
  cases concerning consular rights of foreign nationals, 456
  Civil War,
  engagement with international law, 54–7
  and the EU, 125
  and the ICJ, 29, 114, 116, 118, 128, 129, 464, 465
    withdrawal from compulsory jurisdiction, 106, 115, 118, 119, 120
  and international arbitration, 107, 108–13, 129
  as an international litigant, 106–27
  and investor–state arbitration, 125–8
  involvement in Latin America, 217
  and Iran, 154–5
  and the League of Nations, 114, 128
  and Mexico, 448, 457–8
  and the Permanent Court of International Justice, 128
  and a permanent international court, 112, 113–15, 129

INDEX

self-defence, 120, 322, 441
Treaty of Amity and Commerce with
France, 403
Treaty of Peace with Great Britain,
109
treaty protection for US investors,
126, 127, 129
and the United Nations, 114, 128
and the Vienna Convention on
Consular Relations, 106, 120,
440
withdrawal from compulsory ICJ
jurisdiction, 118, 119, 120,
128
and the WTO Appellate Body, 107,
122, 123
and the WTO dispute settlement
mechanism, 121–5, 128
United States–Georgia BIT, 414
Universal Declaration of Human
Rights, 353, 358, 359, 360
UN Security Council, 325, 327
creation of the United Nations
Compensation Commission,
343
and *El Salvador* v. *Honduras*, 100
and the ICJ, 116
legality of its actions, 21
Presidential Statement, 132
responsibility of, 316, 325, 328
tribunals set up by, 12
Uruguay, River, 102
Administrative Commission, 102
Statute of the River Uruguay, 102,
103
Uruguay, Statute of the River Uruguay,
102
use of force
advisory opinions on, 325–8
and arbitration, 323–5
challenges to jurisdiction, 313
decisions on the merits, 313–17
decisions to enter into litigation,
305, 313
implications of losing in litigation
concerning, 305, 328
litigation after the end of a conflict,
312

litigation during ongoing armed
conflict, 307–12
to protect nationals abroad, 441
provisional measures of protection
in cases concerning, 309–12
reasons for resort to the ICJ, 313
special nature of cases concerning,
305–7
uti possidetis principle, 99, 105
ambiguities of, 99

Vienna Convention on Consular
Relations, 154, 356, 444
bilateral treaties and, 445
obligations under, 445
and the US, 106, 120, 440
Vienna Convention on Diplomatic
Relations, 154
Vienna Convention on the Law of
Treaties, 16

Walvis Bay arbitration, 207
Weeramantry, Judge, 298
Whaling case
decision to refer to the ICJ, 273
involvement of third states, 77
scientific evidence, 74
Wilberforce, Lord, 44–5
World Court Project, 326, 462
World Health Organization, 325
World Trade Organization (WTO)
Advisory Centre on WTO Law, 36,
394
Anti-Dumping Agreement, 379
Appellate Body, 13, 121, 122
and civil society actors, 37
Dispute Settlement Body, 14, 121,
385
fairness of trade rules, 14, 22
General Agreement on Trade in
Services, 389
institutional structure, 396
market competition, 379
panels of experts, 13
participation in, 398
policy aims of, 379, 380, 384, 387
political dimension of disputes, 124,
125

490 INDEX

World Trade Organization
(WTO) (cont.)
Sanitary and Phytosanitary
Agreement, 392
structural barriers for developing
countries, 398
Sutherland Report, 390
technical nature of issues, 124, 125
and the United States, 121–5
World Trade Organization dispute
settlement system, 6, 13, 20, 22,
375–400, 461, 465
accessibility of, 382
admissibility of *amicus* briefs, 122,
383, 384
authorized sanctions, 387
balance of rights and obligations,
393
causes of action, 378–80
compensation for delays in
implementation of rulings, 385,
386
compliance with rulings, 391
confidentiality, 382–5
contractual orientation of, 378
cost of retaliation, 388
domestic policy preferences to move
disputes to the panel process,
381
DSU consultative process, 381–2

effectiveness of, 385–91, 393
enforcement mechanism, 377, 466
equal access to justice, 393–8
extralegal factors in, 382, 384
hybrid operation of, 377
ineffectiveness of remedies, 386–7,
391, 399
informal negotiations, 396
institution of proceedings, 378–85
lack of uniform compliance
standards, 399
mandatory consultations, 380
participation in, 30, 393
power imbalances, 377, 378, 387,
390, 399, 400
prospective remedies, 385, 391
punitive measures backed by
enforcement of compliance,
390
remedies and enforcement, 385–93
retaliation for non-compliance with
rulings, 385, 387, 388, 390
states initiating disputes, 395
structural barriers for developing
countries, 394
transparency of, 382, 384, 385
universality of, 461
US participation in, 121–5
use of, 14, 376, 377, 395,
399

For EU product safety concerns, contact us at Calle de José Abascal, 56–1º,
28003 Madrid, Spain or eugpsr@cambridge.org.

www.ingramcontent.com/pod-product-compliance
Ingram Content Group UK Ltd.
Pitfield, Milton Keynes, MK11 3LW, UK
UKHW020348060825
461487UK00008B/576